Return to an Address of the Honourable the House of
dated 29th June 2006
for the

REPORT OF THE
ZAHID MUBAREK INQUIRY

VOLUME 1

Ordered by the House of Commons to be printed 29th June 2006

1082-I London: The Stationery Office £65.00 (inc VAT)

© Parliamentary copyright 2006

The text of this report may be reproduced in whole or in part free of charge in any
format or media without requiring specific permission. This is subject to the material
not being used in a derogatory manner or in a misleading context. Where the
material is being republished or copied to others, the source of the material must be
identified and the copyright status acknowledged.

The full text of this document has been published on the internet and can be
accessed at: www.zahidmubarekinquiry.org.uk

Any enquiries relating to the copyright in this report should be addressed to Her
Majesty's Stationery Office, Licensing Division, St Clements House, 2–16 Colegate,
Norwich, NR3 1BQ. Fax: 01603 723000 or email: licensing@cabinet-office.x.gsi.gov.uk

The Rt Hon Dr John Reid MP
Secretary of State for the Home Department
Home Office
2 Marsham Street
London
SW1P 4DF

5 June 2006

Dear Home Secretary

On 29 April 2004, the then Home Secretary, the Rt Hon David Blunkett MP, asked me to inquire into the death of Zahid Mubarek following the attack upon him by his cellmate at Feltham Young Offender Institution, and to make recommendations to minimise the risk of such attacks in the future. I am pleased to submit my report to you. I am grateful for the assurance your officials have given to the Secretary to the Inquiry that the report will be published soon.

The three people appointed to advise me on areas where my own expertise was limited were Lutfur Ali, Bobby Cummines and Alastair Papps CB. I am glad to report that they have agreed with all the conclusions I have reached and the recommendations I have made, though the responsibility for the report and its contents is mine and mine alone.

I look forward to the Government's response to the recommendations I have made. The six years or so which have elapsed since Zahid's murder have given the Prison Service a real opportunity to address the systemic shortcomings which the attack on him exposed, and everyone recognises that much has been done in the meantime. There will inevitably be a few cases which will slip through the net: no system can ensure that such attacks are eliminated altogether. But there is no room for complacency. There is still much scope for improvement. In Part 5 of the report, I have identified what can still be done to make prisoners less vulnerable to in-cell attacks by their cellmates.

Yours sincerely

Brian Keith

Zahid Mubarek: 1980–2000

Contents

Volume 1

Preface
"A preventable death" — xvii

Part 1
Setting The Scene — 1

Chapter 1:	What led to the Inquiry	3
	The previous investigations into Zahid's death	3
	The impetus for a public inquiry	5
	The establishment of the Inquiry	8
Chapter 2:	How we worked	10
	The advisers to the Inquiry	10
	First steps	11
	The Inquiry progresses	12
	The hearings	14
	The different phases of the Inquiry	17
	The second phase of the Inquiry	18
	Public funding of legal representation	21
	The non-statutory nature of the Inquiry	22
	The CRE interviews	24
	Wrapping things up	26
Chapter 3:	Racism and other topics	28
	Racism	28
	Systemic shortcomings	31
	What kind of attacks?	34
	Sentencing policy	35
	Investigating the investigations	35
	Criticisms of individuals	36
	The Inquiry's second phase	38
Chapter 4:	"A gigantic transit camp"	40
	Feltham's origins	40
	Feltham in 2000	40
	The problems which Feltham faced	43
	The Inspectorate looks at Feltham	44
	Feltham's Board of Visitors	48
Chapter 5:	A life cut short	50
	Zahid's family	50
	Zahid's upbringing	50
	Zahid's offending behaviour	51
	Zahid's time at Feltham	54

Chapter 6:	The night of the attack	57
	Lock up	57
	The night patrol	58
	The alarm goes up	61
	The night patrol sheets	65
	The bigger picture	66
Chapter 7:	The paper trail	68
	The record system	68
	The main prison file	68
	Files within the Inmate Personal Record System	69
	The inmate medical record	72
	Computerised information	72

Part 2
Robert Stewart: "A Very Strange Young Man" — 75

Chapter 8:	Going wrong	77
	Stewart's early life	77
	Stewart's criminal beginnings	77
	How Stewart spent his time	79
	The documents	80
Chapter 9:	Hindley 1997	82
	Mental illness and personality disorder	82
	Stewart's behaviour	83
	Signs of mental illness?	87
	What should have been done?	92
	Signs of personality disorder?	95
	The security information report of 22 November 1997	97
Chapter 10:	Lancaster Farms	100
	The reason for the transfer	100
	Stewart's behaviour	100
	The discharge report	101
Chapter 11:	Back at Hindley	106
	Stewart's return to Hindley	106
	Stewart and Travis set fire to their cell	107
	Stewart's time at Werrington	109
Chapter 12:	Stoke Heath	110
	Information at Stoke Heath	110
	Travis commits murder	110
	The security information reports about the stabbing	111
	The treatment of these security information reports	112

Chapter 13: Onley	115
Stewart's arrival at Onley	115
Stewart's time in the segregation unit	116
The information which Onley had on Stewart	116
The other criticisms of Onley	117

Chapter 14: Back at Hindley again	122
Stewart's transfer to Hindley	122
Stewart's disruptive behaviour	122
Improvements in Stewart's behaviour	124
Stewart's racism	125
Assessing the risk	126

Chapter 15: Hindley sees Stewart yet again	130
Stewart's return to Hindley	130
The intercepted letter	131
The harassment memo of 29 September 1999	135
What would have happened?	137

Chapter 16: Altcourse	139
Stewart's transfer to Altcourse	139
The handling of Stewart's security file	139
Stewart arms himself	140
The request for production	141
The assessment by Chris Kinealy	143

Chapter 17: Stewart's last spell at Hindley	151
Back in Hindley again	151
The recording of security information from Altcourse	152
The security information report of 5 January 2000	153
Monitoring Stewart's correspondence	154
Sending records to Feltham	155
Stewart remains at Feltham	158

Chapter 18: Stewart's healthcare screening	161
What healthcare screening involved	161
Healthcare screening at Hindley	164
Healthcare screening at Hindley after November 1999	166

Chapter 19: The prisoner escort records for Stewart	173
The function of the prisoner escort record	173
Stewart's records	173
Notifying Feltham about Stewart	177

Chapter 20: The missed opportunities	178

Part 3
Feltham: Fate Plays Its Hand — 181

Chapter 21: Stewart goes to Feltham — 183
- The induction process — 183
- Stewart's induction — 184
- The intercepted letter — 185
- The call from Security — 191
- What would have happened? — 195
- How Hindley dealt with the entries on the temporary wing file — 196

Chapter 22: Stewart returns to Feltham — 199
- Why not Lapwing? — 199
- The warning Osprey got about Stewart — 200
- Stewart's cell allocation in Osprey — 202
- The night on Lapwing — 206

Chapter 23: Stewart's last trip to Feltham — 207
- Stewart stays at Feltham — 207
- Stewart's temporary wing file — 208
- Mr Marshall's sighting of Stewart — 208
- Cell allocation in Swallow — 210
- The absence of the temporary wing file — 212
- What would have happened if Stewart's temporary wing file had arrived with him? — 212
- What should have happened? — 214

Chapter 24: Stewart's behaviour on Swallow and his appearance — 215
- An unproblematic prisoner — 215
- Stewart's behaviour on Swallow — 215
- The request for visiting orders — 217
- Stewart's appearance — 218

Chapter 25: Stewart's return from court on 7 and 8 March 2000 — 223
- Stewart's temporary wing file resurfaces — 223
- Stewart's return from court on 8 March 2000 — 228
- Mr Martindale's sighting of Stewart — 232

Chapter 26: Stewart's change of status — 233
- Stewart completes his sentence — 233
- The effect of Stewart's change of status — 233
- Knowledge in Swallow of Stewart's change of status — 234
- Why was nothing done? — 236

Chapter 27: The request to change cells — 239
- Barnes's request to move into cell 38 with Zahid — 239
- Zahid's requests to move out of cell 38 — 240
- Why did Zahid want to move? — 241

	Why was his request not met?	242
	Miss Bigger's memo	243
Chapter 28:	**The incentives and earned privileges scheme**	**244**
	The two sides of Swallow	244
	The workings of the incentives and earned privileges scheme	244
	Stewart's and Zahid's status	245
	The bigger picture	246
Chapter 29:	**The table leg and other possible weapons**	**249**
	The issues	249
	The table	249
	The conversation about weapons	252
	Cell searches	253
	Was what was left of the crossbar found?	254
	The previous fabric checks	257
	The use of wooden furniture in cells	259
	Full cell searches in Swallow	260
	The "KKK" on the notice board	261
Chapter 30:	**The clues in the documents**	**263**
	Stewart's prisoner escort records	263
	Stewart's security file	267
	Stewart's core record	270
	Stewart's warrants	271
	Stewart's main prison file	271
	The flow of information generally	272
Chapter 31:	**The clues in Stewart's correspondence**	**274**
	Notifying the establishment	274
	Checking the warrants and notifying the units	275
	The lack of any system	277
	The response to the findings of the audit	277
	What would have happened?	278
	Monitoring Stewart's telephone calls	280
Chapter 32:	**The personal officers in Swallow**	**282**
	The personal officer scheme at Feltham	282
	Stewart's and Zahid's personal officers	283
	Training, instruction and monitoring	284
	A scheme "in name only"	285
Chapter 33:	**Healthcare screening at Feltham**	**288**
	Stewart's healthcare screening	288
	The review of Stewart's medical record	291
	What would have happened if Stewart's medical record had been reviewed?	293

Chapter 34: *Romper Stomper*	295
Chapter 35: Gladiator aka Coliseum	298
The allegation surfaces	298
The links to the murder of Zahid	298
The existence of the practice	302
Chapter 36: Why did he do it?	315
Motive for murder	315
Transfer	315
Hero worship	317
Racism	318
Jealousy	319
Dislike of Zahid	320
Romper Stomper	321
Remaining on Swallow	321
Remaining in custody	322
Miscellaneous matters	322
Chapter 37: Another series of missed opportunities	324

Part 4
Feltham: The Wider Picture — 327

Chapter 38: Staff morale	329
The significance of staff morale	329
The decline in staff morale	329
Morale during Mr Clifford's time at Feltham	330
The impact of low staff morale	332
Inconsistencies in working practices	333
Chapter 39: Feltham's degeneration into crisis	336
Chapter 40: Where the buck stops	342
"The buck stops here"	342
Mr Welsh	342
Mr Clifford	344
Chapter 41: Staff shortages	347
The significance of staff shortages	347
Absence levels	348
Inefficiencies in deployment	349
Low staffing levels	350
The Personnel Department	355

Chapter 42: Feltham's prisoner population	357
Chapter 43: Financial investment in Feltham	361
Chapter 44: Industrial relations at Feltham	365
The Feltham branch of the POA	365
The profiling exercise	367
Evening association	368
Chapter 45: The separation of Feltham A and Feltham B	372
Chapter 46: The management of the residential units	375
The residential units	375
The senior officer on Swallow	376
The hiking officer for the cluster	381
The principal officer for the cluster	384
The governors	386
Chapter 47: The management of the reception and security functions	390
Reception	390
The Security Department	391
Chapter 48: The management of healthcare screening	394
Chapter 49: The allocation of prisoners to cells	399
The absence of any guidance	399
The Prison Service's objective	399
The need for a national policy	400
The need for local guidance	404
Prisoners' preferences	408
Chapter 50: The management of offenders with personality disorders	410
Chapter 51: Race relations at Feltham	413
The Butt report	413
The CRE's report	416
The Hounslow survey	418
Minimising racial tensions	420
The reporting of racist incidents	421
The managerial shortcomings	423
Lack of external oversight	427
Chapter 52: Monitoring Feltham's performance	432
Feltham's self-auditing procedures	432
The action plans for Feltham	433
Oversight from Prison Service headquarters	434
Chapter 53: An overview of Feltham's underlying problems	438

Part 5
The Way Forward   441

Chapter 54: The scope of the recommendations	443
Chapter 55: Cell-sharing	445
Enforced cell-sharing	445
Prisoners at risk of self-harm	447
Prisoners who prefer to share cells	449
Allocating prisoners to double cells	450
Allocating prisoners to the same wing	458
Chapter 56: Reducing risks in cells	461
Cell furniture	461
Searching for weapons	462
Violence reduction	466
Chapter 57: The flow and use of information	468
NOMIS	468
The applications of NOMIS	470
The limitations of NOMIS	472
Training in and use of NOMIS	474
Data migration	476
Transitional arrangements	477
Other information	489
Monitoring information flow	490
Chapter 58: The prisoner escort record	492
Chapter 59: Assessing risk	497
The cell-sharing risk assessment	497
The OASys assessment	505
MAPPA	508
A risk classification?	509
Chapter 60: Dealing with prisoners	510
The key attributes	510
Training in inter-personal skills	512
Personal officers	514
Whistleblowing	518
Chapter 61: Mentally disordered prisoners	523
The issues the Inquiry addressed	523
The need for change	524
Identifying mentally disordered prisoners	526
Identifying the risk	527
Mental health awareness training	528

	Management on the wings	529
	Sharing information	532
Chapter 62:	Racism and religious intolerance	535
	The Inquiry's focus	535
	Parallel Worlds	536
	Training on BME perspectives	539
	The investigation of complaints	541
	The role of race relations liaison officers	545
	The position of Muslim prisoners	546
	External scrutiny	548
	Race equality schemes	548
Chapter 63:	Final observations	550
	Acknowledgements	550
	Concluding remarks	551

Volume 2 contains the following material

Appendices

Appendix 1: The Inquiry team	553
Appendix 2: List of legal representatives	554
Appendix 3: The Inquiry's terms of reference and procedures	555
Appendix 4: Evidence received by the Inquiry	564
Appendix 5: Delegates at the Inquiry's seminars	569
Appendix 6: Robert Stewart's movements (August 1995 to March 2000)	571
Appendix 7: Systemic shortcomings, and individual failings which were not the consequence of systemic shortcomings	572
Appendix 8: Summary and recommendations	615
Index	**667**

Preface: "A preventable death"

In 2000, Zahid Mubarek, an Asian teenager, was serving a short sentence at Feltham Young Offender Institution. He had not been to prison before. While there, he wrote movingly to his parents, admitting his shortcomings and expressing a determination not to let them down again. He was due to be released on 21 March.

But he was never to get the chance to prove that he had put his past behind him. In the early hours of that morning, he was brutally attacked by another young prisoner, Robert Stewart, with whom he had been sharing a cell for the previous six weeks. According to Stewart, Zahid had been asleep at the time, though some prisoners claimed to have heard screams. What is not in doubt is that Stewart clubbed him several times about the head with a wooden table leg. When help came, Zahid was barely conscious. Such was the ferocity of the attack that his father told the Inquiry that when he saw Zahid in hospital, "his head looked like a huge balloon. He was almost unrecognisable. His face was full of blood with bruising all over it." He died from his injuries a week later. He had been in a coma and never regained consciousness.

Some months before, Stewart had bragged about committing the first murder of the millennium. He was subsequently convicted of Zahid's murder. He was sentenced to life imprisonment. In convicting Stewart of murder, the jury rejected the suggestion that he should be convicted of manslaughter on the ground of diminished responsibility rather than murder.

Shortly after the attack on Zahid, the police discovered that Stewart had strong racist views. They also learned that he had had a violent past while previously in custody, and that his mental health had been questioned. Much of that had been known to some of the prison officers at Feltham at the time. Not surprisingly, questions began to be asked about how he and Zahid had ended up in the same cell. How had Stewart come to share a cell with someone from an ethnic minority? What exactly had been known about Stewart? Had any information about him been passed to the wing? And had any assessment been carried out of the risk Stewart might have posed to any prisoner who shared a cell with him?

To its credit, the Prison Service never sought to deny that it had failed to fulfil its responsibility to look after Zahid while he had been in its care. On the day of Zahid's death, the Director General of the Prison Service, Martin Narey, wrote to Zahid's parents. He frankly stated:

> "You had a right to expect us to look after Zahid safely and we have failed. I am very, very sorry."

And at a public hearing held by the Commission for Racial Equality in the course of its investigation into racial discrimination within the Prison Service, Mr Narey said in terms that Zahid's had been "a preventable death".

After protracted legal proceedings which went on for a number of years, it was decided that there had to be a public inquiry into Zahid's death. This report is the result of that inquiry. It identifies the key stages when, had appropriate action been taken, the tragedy which befell Zahid could have been prevented. It also considers what steps should now be taken to reduce the risk of something like this ever happening again. As I said at the beginning of the Inquiry's hearings:

> "We will do what we can to get at the truth so that Zahid's family will at least have the satisfaction of knowing that such lessons as can be learned from his tragic death may make our prisons a safer place in which to be."

Part 1
Setting The Scene

Chapter 1: What led to the Inquiry

The previous investigations into Zahid's death

1.1 This was no ordinary inquiry. It was initially resisted by the Home Office. It argued that the previous investigations into Zahid's death had been sufficient to identify where the weaknesses in the system lay. But Zahid's family thought otherwise. They took their campaign for a public inquiry all the way to the House of Lords. It was only after the House of Lords had said that a public inquiry was required if the United Kingdom was to comply with its obligations under the European Convention on Human Rights that this inquiry was announced. But since the previous investigations into Zahid's death play an important part in the story, a short summary of them is necessary.

The Butt investigation

1.2 Even before Zahid eventually died from his injuries, the Prison Service had decided to conduct an investigation into the attack on him. The investigation was carried out by Ted Butt, a senior Prison Service investigating officer. His terms of reference were very detailed. In summary, they were to investigate the circumstances surrounding the attack on Zahid, and in particular to consider the risks which arise when prisoners are accommodated in the same cell.

1.3 Feltham is in West London. Mr Butt first visited it within a week of the attack. In the course of his investigation, he interviewed a large number of the staff there. Many of those interviews were recorded, but some were not because it was felt that the interviewees might otherwise be reluctant to talk frankly. His report was in two parts. The first part, which was completed in October 2000, was concerned specifically with the attack on Zahid. It was critical of many aspects of the procedures at Feltham, and it identified a number of shortcomings which had contributed to Stewart continuing to share a cell with Zahid. It contained 22 conclusions and 26 recommendations for change.

1.4 But this part of the Butt report was not a definitive account of the circumstances which led to the tragedy. It did not address in any detail Stewart's history within the prison system before he went to Feltham. Nor did Mr Butt have access to witness statements taken by the police in the course of their investigation into the death of Zahid, since the criminal proceedings against Stewart had not yet been concluded. And although Mr Butt's terms of reference had included a requirement to establish whether any disciplinary action should be taken, he felt unable to make any recommendations in the time available to him. He said:

> "I cannot apportion all the blame to the management team at Feltham at the time of this investigation. Management oversight appears to have been poor for many years, and it would have been impossible for the present team to have dealt with all the deficiencies in such a short time. Therefore I am unable to recommend disciplinary action against any single individual member of staff."

The investigation by the CRE

1.5 On 17 November 2000, the Commission for Racial Equality (the CRE) announced that it would be conducting a formal investigation into racial discrimination within the Prison Service. Its terms of reference included "the circumstances leading to the murder of Zahid Mubarek at Feltham, and any contributing act or omission on the part of the Prison Service".

1.6 The CRE published Part 1 of its report, *The Murder of Zahid Mubarek*, in July 2003. It was, on any view, a comprehensive account of the circumstances which led up to the attack on Zahid, save that, like Part 1 of the Butt report, it did not address in any detail Stewart's history within the prison system before he went to Feltham. It was highly critical of the Prison Service. It identified 16 "action and process areas" in which the Prison Service had "failed to provide an adequate level of custodial care or supervision of prisoners", and four "underlying failure areas which detail the culture and environment [at Feltham] at the time of the murder". But these findings were all made in the context of the overarching function of the CRE's investigation – which was to determine whether, in its dealings with Zahid and Stewart, the Prison Service had been guilty of racial discrimination. The CRE found that it had.

The investigation by the Metropolitan Police

1.7 Apart from investigating the events of 21 March 2000 for the purpose of Stewart's criminal trial, the Metropolitan Police conducted a wide-ranging investigation into whether the Prison Service or any of its employees should be prosecuted for manslaughter on the basis of gross negligence. The senior investigating officer prepared a report on this issue for consideration by the Crown Prosecution Service, but Treasury counsel advised that there was "insufficient evidence to provide a realistic prospect" of securing any conviction for manslaughter – or for that matter for the offences of misconduct in a public office or failing to discharge a duty under section 3 of the Health and Safety at Work etc Act 1974.

The inquest into Zahid's death

1.8 Finally, it is necessary to mention the inquest into Zahid's death, if only to complete the history of the previous investigations into his death. The inquest was formally opened on 31 March 2000, and was then adjourned pending Stewart's trial for the murder of Zahid. Following his conviction, the coroner refused to resume the inquest. She took the view that the constraints to which coroners and inquests were subject made an inquest an unsuitable vehicle for investigating publicly the questions raised by the attack on Zahid. She may have thought that she could not investigate how Zahid came to share a cell with Stewart.

The impetus for a public inquiry

Zahid's family's participation in the Butt and CRE investigations

1.9 Zahid's family did not participate in a meaningful way in either Mr Butt's investigation or that of the CRE. They had been consulted over Mr Butt's terms of reference, but it was questionable whether the way in which his investigation was to be conducted would have enabled them to make a real contribution to it. Mr Narey admittedly informed Zahid's family that the Prison Service wanted to involve them in Mr Butt's inquiry "as far as it is possible and to the extent that you wish", but the House of Lords was eventually to find that "the family were not able to play an effective part in [Mr Butt's] investigation and would not have been able to do so even if they had accepted the limited offer made to them."

1.10 The same was true of the CRE's investigation. Zahid's family were involved in the preparation of the CRE's terms of reference, and they expressed their views on the procedures which the CRE proposed to adopt. But the only public hearing held by the CRE took place on a single day in September 2001 when four high-level witnesses* made

---

* Martin Narey (the Director General of the Prison Service), Sir David Ramsbotham (formerly the Chief Inspector of Prisons), Judy Clements (the Race Equality Adviser to the Prison Service) and Beverley Hughes (the Parliamentary Under-Secretary of State for Community and Custodial Sentences).

statements about issues of policy and were questioned by leading counsel for the CRE. The family admittedly did not take up the CRE's offer to meet counsel and to raise with him the topics they wanted to be covered in his questioning of the witnesses. Nor did they attend the hearing. But apart from that, the investigation was conducted in private without any participation by the family, and without the family being afforded the opportunity to question those people interviewed by officers of the CRE who had dealt with Stewart and Zahid. As the House of Lords was eventually to find, "the family were not able to play any effective part in [the CRE's investigation] and would not have been able to do so even if they had taken advantage of the limited opportunity they were offered."

The requests for a public inquiry

1.11 Within a week of Zahid's death, solicitors representing Zahid's family wrote to the Minister asking for an independent public inquiry into the circumstances of Zahid's death. The Minister's view was that it was then too early to make a decision about a public inquiry until the police investigation and the Prison Service's own internal investigation had been concluded. At a subsequent meeting in November 2000, the Minister was still not prepared to establish a public inquiry – in part because she thought that the CRE's investigation into Zahid's death which was about to be announced would satisfy the need for an independent investigation into it.

1.12 In July 2001, the family's solicitors took the matter up with the Minister again. They pointed out that many questions remained unanswered about how Zahid had come to share a cell with Stewart, a man who "was manifesting extreme racist views in correspondence, and was diagnosed during the criminal proceedings as a psychopath". In the light of the CRE's decision not to allow the family to participate in its investigation in "any meaningful manner" or to allow any part of its investigation to be held in public, the decision of the coroner not to resume the inquest, and the findings of Mr Butt's investigation, they asked the Minister to reconsider her predecessor's decision not to hold a public inquiry. Although the Minister reconsidered that decision, she saw no basis for reversing it.

The claims for judicial review

1.13 In the summer of 2001, three claims for judicial review were brought on behalf of Zahid's family in the name of Zahid's uncle, Imtiaz Amin.

They claimed judicial review of the CRE's decision to refuse to hold its proceedings in public or to allow the family to participate in its investigation, the decision of the coroner not to resume the inquest, and the decision made by the Minister – in the name of the Home Secretary – not to establish a public inquiry. As it turned out, only the claim for judicial review of the decision not to establish a public inquiry was determined. It was heard by Mr Justice Hooper. He thought that the Minister should have concluded that there were features about Zahid's death which required further investigation. So on 5 October 2001, he made the following declaration:

> "On the facts known to the Secretary of State (including the fact that the inquest would not be resumed), an independent public investigation with the family legally represented, provided with the relevant material and able to cross-examine the principal witnesses, must be held to satisfy the obligations imposed by Article 2 of the European Convention on Human Rights."

1.14 The Home Secretary appealed against this decision. On 27 March 2002, the Court of Appeal allowed the appeal and set aside the declaration made by Mr Justice Hooper. But the declaration made by Mr Justice Hooper was restored on 16 October 2003 following a further appeal to the House of Lords. The House of Lords held that in order for the United Kingdom to comply with its obligations under Articles 1 and 2(1) of the European Convention on Human Rights, there had to be an independent investigation into the circumstances of Zahid's death, which had to take place in public and with participation by Zahid's family to an appropriate extent. Neither Mr Butt's investigation nor the CRE's investigation had taken place in public. The family had not been able to play an effective part in either of them. And Mr Butt "did not enjoy institutional or hierarchical independence" so as to give his investigation the necessary degree of impartiality.*

---

* That does not mean that it is now necessary for there to be a public inquiry such as the present one whenever someone dies in custody. Every death in custody is now investigated by the Prisons and Probation Ombudsman. Such an investigation is intended to have the appropriate degree of openness, independent scrutiny and participation by the deceased's family as will satisfy the United Kingdom's obligations under the Convention.

The establishment of the Inquiry

1.15 On 29 April 2004, the Home Secretary announced the establishment of a public inquiry into the death of Zahid. The Inquiry's terms of reference were as follows:

> "In the light of the House of Lords judgment in the case of *Regina v. Secretary of State for the Home Department ex parte Amin*, to investigate and report to the Home Secretary on the death of Zahid Mubarek, and the events leading up to the attack on him, and make recommendations about the prevention of such attacks in the future, taking into account the investigations that have already taken place – in particular, those by the Prison Service and the Commission for Racial Equality."

The Inquiry came to be known as the Zahid Mubarek Inquiry.

1.16 Three comments should be made about these terms of reference. First, the terms of reference make it clear that the Inquiry was established in the light of the judgment of the House of Lords. The purpose of an investigation of the kind contemplated by the Convention was explained by the House of Lords as follows:

> "… to ensure so far as possible that the full facts are brought to light; that culpable and discreditable conduct is exposed and brought to public notice; that suspicion of deliberate wrongdoing (if unjustified) is allayed; that dangerous practices and procedures are rectified; and that those who have lost their relative may at least have the satisfaction of knowing that lessons learned from his death may save the lives of others."

1.17 Secondly, the Inquiry was required by its terms of reference to take into account the investigations which had already taken place, in particular Mr Butt's investigation and that of the CRE. The impact which those investigations should have on the Inquiry was explained by the House of Lords as follows:

> "There are factual areas – for example, the killing itself, and the cause of death – which have already been fully explored and of which little or no further examination is required. Many of the factual findings made by Mr Butt and the CRE can no doubt be taken as read. It will be very important for the investigator to take a firm grip on the Inquiry so as to concentrate the evidence and focus the cross-examination on issues justifying further exploration. Reliance should be placed on written statements and submissions so far as may properly be done

at a hearing required to be held in public. All those professionally engaged, for any party, should bear in mind their professional duty to ensure that the investigation of this tragic and unnecessary death is conducted in a focused and disciplined way."

1.18 Thirdly, the terms of reference focus on two discrete things: the events which led up to the murder of Zahid, and how similar attacks can be prevented in the future. The former looks back at the series of events which culminated in the attack on Zahid. The latter looks forward to such recommendations as can be made to minimise the risk of an attack of this kind happening again. A public inquiry addressing only the former was required by the judgment of the House of Lords. So although the Inquiry's terms of reference made the Inquiry considerably wider than that which the House of Lords said had to take place – and explain why it has taken the time it has – the Inquiry's principal task was to ascertain the facts which led up to Zahid's murder. They would form the basis of a comprehensive case study from which the lessons to be learned from his death could be identified. All of these considerations have inevitably shaped the course taken by the Inquiry.

1.19 Although the Home Office initially resisted a public inquiry into Zahid's death, there has been little hint of any opposition to it since the Inquiry was announced. On the contrary, I was assured by senior Home Office officials that I would receive all the co-operation I needed, and that was repeated to me on the occasions when I met the Minister, Paul Goggins, to keep him abreast of how the Inquiry was going. It is unnecessary to say it, but it should be recorded that although the Inquiry was established by the Home Secretary and was funded from the Home Office budget, it was entirely independent of government.

Chapter 2: How we worked

The advisers to the Inquiry

2.1 Shortly before the Inquiry was announced, I told senior Home Office officials that I wished to have independent advice on a number of areas in which I did not have any special experience or expertise. Those areas were race and diversity, the management and operation of prisons and young offender institutions, and prison life. One of the things I particularly wanted was a view of what life in prison is like from someone at the sharp end: someone who had been to prison himself. Three advisers were eventually appointed. They were Lutfur Ali, Bobby Cummines and Alastair Papps CB.

2.2 Mr Ali is a Muslim. He has wide experience of equality and diversity issues in both the public and private sectors. He was the National Head of Equalities and Diversity for the Department of Health, and he currently works as the UK Director of Equality and Diversity of a major public company which provides support and consultancy services to public and private sector clients. Although Mr Ali advised me on issues of race and diversity, I found his insights into the way prisons are run and what prison life must be like extremely valuable.

2.3 Mr Cummines is a former prisoner. He was sentenced to terms totalling 20 years' imprisonment for various grave offences, and served 13 of them. Following his release from prison in 1988, he obtained a university degree. He was a co-founder of the charity Unlock, The National Association of Ex-Offenders, and he is now its Chief Executive. He gave specialist advice to the Inquiry into the Rehabilitation of Offenders conducted by the Home Affairs Committee of the House of Commons. His irrepressible cheerfulness was refreshing, and his perception of what would have happened on the ground from his particular vantage point has contributed significantly to my findings.

2.4 Mr Papps worked in the Prison Service for the whole of his working life. He has considerable operational experience, having been the Governor of Durham and Frankland Prisons, amongst others, but what I found particularly valuable was his managerial experience. The Inquiry has had to address a number of managerial issues within the Prison Service, and in his time Mr Papps acted as an area manager, a regional director, and an operational director responsible for about half the penal institutions in England and Wales, not including Feltham but including some of those in which Stewart had been. Towards the end of his career, Mr Papps was a member of the Prisons Board, but he did not have personal operational responsibility for any of the matters with which the Inquiry was concerned.

2.5 Unsurprisingly, in the course of his working life, Mr Papps met and got to know individuals of seniority within the Prison Service who were asked to provide the Inquiry with witness statements. Mr Narey, the Director General, is just one example. But once I had decided that I wanted my adviser on the operation of prisons and young offender institutions to have managerial experience in the running of prisons as well, it was inevitable that anyone appointed would have had some professional dealings at some point in their career with senior managers who might be witnesses to the Inquiry. I discussed that at some length with Mr Papps, and I was entirely satisfied that the advice I would get from him would be completely objective and impartial. That remained so throughout the Inquiry. I should add that Mr Papps gave me advice on issues relating to the way some of those prisons for which he had line responsibility had been managed by their Governors. But I thought it right not to seek his advice on any question – such as the allocation of resources to those prisons – which potentially had more direct relevance to senior management at levels above that of the prison itself. The key participants in the Inquiry were told that, and they had no concerns about it.

2.6 The advisers attended virtually every day of the public hearings of the Inquiry. They accompanied me on the many visits I made to prisons and young offender institutions. They also came to the seminars which were held. This report has been immeasurably enhanced by their input throughout the Inquiry. I am glad to say that they have agreed with all the conclusions and recommendations in it, though the responsibility for the report and its contents has been mine and mine alone.

First steps

2.7 To assist me in my task, I was provided with a secretariat and legal team. The secretariat was headed by Bruce Gill, who was seconded to the post by the Home Office. He was responsible for the administrative arrangements for the conduct of the Inquiry and he put the administrative team together. The solicitor to the Inquiry was Duncan Henderson, who came from the Treasury Solicitor's Department. On my behalf, Mr Henderson instructed two members of the independent bar to act as counsel to the Inquiry. They were Nigel Giffin QC and Neil Sheldon. Their primary task was to present the evidence and to question the witnesses, but they also gave me independent advice on matters of law and procedure. Their role was not that of prosecutor or of someone trying to prove a particular case. They were assisting me impartially in my investigation of the facts.

2.8 The Inquiry team established itself at premises in Fleet Street in Central London. That was where I first met Zahid's parents, his uncle, their solicitor and a campaigner on their behalf. I took the opportunity to express to them my condolences for their tragic loss and to assure them of my commitment to get at the truth. It was also where other meetings were held, for example the meetings I had with senior police officers on a strictly confidential basis to keep me up-to-date with their investigation into what came to be called by the media the "Gladiator" allegations. Later on, the Inquiry's offices moved to the International Dispute Resolution Centre, also in Fleet Street. This is where the later hearings of the Inquiry took place.

2.9 In order to provide a measure of focus, a list of the issues which the Inquiry anticipated it would be addressing was prepared. So too was a document setting out the procedures which the Inquiry proposed to adopt. Copies of these documents were made available to the key participants in the Inquiry and to everyone who was asked to provide a statement to the Inquiry. They were also available on the Inquiry's website.

The Inquiry progresses

2.10 The first task of the Inquiry was to gather the information which would be presented as evidence in due course. The Inquiry had very few documents of its own. So very early on the Inquiry team requested organisations which were likely to have material documents to supply them to the Inquiry. The documents produced by the Prison Service, the Metropolitan Police and the CRE constituted the bulk of them, but anyone who had any other relevant documents was requested to supply them. The documents which were considered to be relevant to the Inquiry's work were included in the Inquiry Bundle. By the time the public hearings concluded on 11 March 2005, the Inquiry Bundle consisted of 33 volumes comprising well over 15,000 pages. Copies of the documents selected for inclusion in the Inquiry Bundle were provided to the key participants in the Inquiry, but steps were taken to edit the contents of some documents in order to preserve confidentiality. Examples of such "censorship" included the names of prisoners and the addresses of witnesses.

2.11 The evidence of witnesses was initially to be provided in writing. That enabled me to decide in an informed way who should be asked to give oral evidence at the public hearings. I bore in mind what the House of Lords had said about the need to treat as read many of the factual findings made by Mr Butt and the CRE. Anyone who was known to have relevant information to give to the Inquiry was asked to provide a written statement. They were all informed of the topics with which the Inquiry wanted their statements to deal, and it was left to them to decide how to provide these statements. Mr Henderson, or one of his colleagues, was available to assist them with their preparation. But for the most part the statements were prepared by the solicitors for the key participants in the Inquiry.

2.12 In addition, the Inquiry encouraged anyone who thought they had useful information to give to come forward. We recognised that some people may have wanted to approach the Inquiry in confidence. We respected their wish for privacy, and no documents were disclosed to anyone outside the Inquiry team, nor was any information passed on until any issue of confidentiality which they might have raised had been resolved. However, at the Inquiry's preliminary hearing, I said that we would not rely on any anonymous information unless the circumstances were truly exceptional. As it was, no information was given to the Inquiry anonymously. By the time the public hearings of the Inquiry concluded, the Inquiry had received statements from 116 people.* One of them was Robert Stewart himself. Only two people declined the Inquiry's request for statements,** although both had already given a statement to the police.

2.13 All these statements were included in the Inquiry's Statements Bundle. That bundle also included the statements taken by the police, and transcripts or summaries of the interviews of those people who were interviewed by Mr Butt and in some cases by the CRE. In all, the Inquiry had statements or transcripts or summaries of interviews from 183 people. The Statements Bundle comprised over 2,000 pages.

2.14 I decided that of these potential witnesses, 62 should be requested to give oral evidence. Stewart was not one of them. They were all notified well in advance of the day on which they were scheduled to give evidence, and of the principal topics on which counsel to the

---

* One statement, that of Abdul Qureshi, the Imam at Feltham at the time of the murder, arrived in its final form a few days after the public hearings ended. Another, that of Sir Richard Tilt, the former Director General of the Prison Service, arrived a little later, but that was because the Inquiry sought information from him on one topic only at a relatively late stage.
**Robert Benford and Jim Farrell.

Inquiry anticipated asking them questions. They were also notified of the possible criticisms which counsel to the Inquiry thought I may make about them in due course. The letters telling them about that were confidential between the Inquiry and the witnesses concerned. All witnesses who gave oral evidence were entitled to be separately represented during their evidence, though the overwhelming majority of them were represented by the legal teams representing the key participants in the Inquiry. Only two of the potential witnesses declined to give oral evidence.*

2.15 At an early stage, the Inquiry decided to accord to a limited number of parties the status of Interested Party. They were the parties who were expected by the Inquiry to want to participate actively in its work. Three parties were accorded the status of Interested Party: Zahid's family, the Prison Service and the Prison Officers' Association (the POA). Interested Parties were provided with the relevant documents and took a full part in the hearings. The Independent Monitoring Board for Feltham Young Offender Institution – as the Board of Visitors is now called – was not given the status of an Interested Party, since it was not expected to have a significant input into all the topics to be covered by the Inquiry's hearings. But it did have a particular interest in some aspects of the Inquiry's work, and it was permitted to participate in the Inquiry in a limited way.

The hearings

2.16 The Inquiry held two preliminary hearings. They were on 25 May 2004 and 6 September 2004. The first was held in the video-conferencing suite of the Royal Courts of Justice in Central London, which was where it was then anticipated the hearings of the Inquiry would take place. I outlined the procedures which the Inquiry would be adopting, and gave those present who were thought likely to take an active part in the Inquiry an opportunity to make any preliminary observations. However, that venue was deemed not entirely suitable, and the second preliminary hearing took place at First Avenue House in Holborn in Central London. On that occasion, I gave various directions for the future conduct of the Inquiry. That was where the substantive hearings initially took place. They began on 18 November 2004, and continued until 22 December 2004, when we broke for Christmas. They began again at the International Dispute Resolution Centre on 5 January 2005, and

---

* Anthony Beard and Geoffrey Humphrey.

continued until 11 March 2005. We had been sitting for 67 days. The parties' closing arguments were in writing, and a hearing took place on 28 April 2005 to enable the parties to make closing statements.

2.17 The Christmas break gave us an opportunity to see where we were going. We had set what turned out to be a punishing schedule for ourselves, which had resulted in the Inquiry sitting every day for the five weeks before Christmas without a day's break. It was decided to spread things out a little more after Christmas, and to increase the length of time for which it was anticipated that each of the witnesses would be questioned. Although that meant that the hearings lasted for a few weeks longer than the 10 weeks originally envisaged, we all found that this worked better. It also meant that we were able to keep to our revised timetable.

2.18 The witnesses did not take the oath. The non-statutory nature of the Inquiry – which I comment on later – made that inappropriate. But they were told that the Inquiry expected them to tell the truth as they remembered it. The questioning of the witnesses was principally conducted by counsel to the Inquiry. Their aim was to get from the witnesses everything of relevance to the issues which the Inquiry had to address. Much of it had already been covered in their statements, which were taken as having been read. But there was still considerable scope for many issues to be explored in much greater detail. The thoroughness with which the statements had been prepared by, for the most part, the solicitors representing the Prison Service and the POA meant that their counsel had fewer questions to ask than counsel for Zahid's family. The questioning of a number of the witnesses by counsel for Zahid's family was robust and at times distinctly hostile. Some of the witnesses were understandably discomforted by it. But searching questioning was necessary to ensure that their evidence could be properly evaluated, and that any shortcomings on their part could be properly exposed.

2.19 The Inquiry made full use of such information technology as was available to it: we wanted the hearings to be as paper-free as possible. So all the documents were scanned into an image database using an electronic document management system, and as they were referred to in the course of the hearings, they were displayed in a matter of seconds on monitors to which the lawyers, witnesses, my advisers and I all had access. Large screens sited strategically in the hearing chamber enabled those following and reporting the hearings to see the documents which we were looking at, and enabled them to follow the evidence that much better. Scanning the documents also meant that time was not wasted in searching for them amongst the many hard copy files which would otherwise have been necessary.

2.20 In addition, the oral evidence was transcribed by stenographers providing a live transcription service. This meant that a running transcript of what was being said could be displayed on laptop computers within a few seconds. Corrected transcripts were available within a matter of hours of the conclusion of the day's hearing. These became the primary tool for members of the public wishing to follow the Inquiry's work. A transcript of each day's hearing was posted on the Inquiry's website, as well as the statements of each witness, once they had started to give evidence. Or, if they had not been asked to give oral evidence, the effect of their statements were posted on the website after they had been summarised at the hearing by counsel to the Inquiry. So too were those documents in the Inquiry Bundle which were referred to in the course of the hearing. Other documents were posted on the Inquiry's website as well – for example, rulings made in the course of the hearings which had been circulated to the Interested Parties, written directions which had been given and a timetable showing when particular witnesses were likely to give evidence. The aim was to enable anyone wishing to follow the Inquiry's work to be as able to do so from their home or office as by coming to the Inquiry's hearings.

2.21 All the hearings of the Inquiry were in public, save that for medical reasons two witnesses gave oral evidence in the privacy of my office. However, their evidence was transcribed in the usual way, and a transcript of it was available on the Inquiry's website. They were questioned only by counsel to the Inquiry, but he also dealt with topics which the Interested Parties wanted the witnesses to be questioned about.

2.22 At an early stage, it was recognised that the media had a legitimate interest in reporting what was said at the hearings so that the Inquiry's work would receive the publicity which the media thought it deserved. I wanted reporters to have all the help they needed to fulfil that role. So part of the hearing chamber was given over to the use of journalists, and at both First Avenue House and the International Dispute Resolution Centre they were provided with their own dedicated room with a live feed from the hearing chamber and computer facilities.

2.23 I also gave some thought to whether part of the public hearings could be broadcast. The need to respect the privacy of Zahid's family was an important factor to be taken into account. So too was the need for witnesses to be as relaxed as possible when they gave their evidence and not to feel intimidated by having to give their evidence in the glare of publicity. Subject to one exception, those considerations led me to conclude that the public hearings should not be broadcast, nor should any photographs be taken at them. The one relaxation was for the opening and closing statements. Zahid's family wanted them to be broadcast so that the Inquiry received the publicity appropriate to its importance. And of course witnesses would not be affected by it. None of the other Interested Parties objected to such a course, and I permitted the hearings to be broadcast to that limited extent.

The different phases of the Inquiry

2.24 The original plan was for the hearings to address both elements of the Inquiry's terms of reference: the events which led up to Zahid's murder, and how such attacks could be prevented in the future. But after a while it became clear that something more radical was required if the Inquiry was to fulfil the second element of its terms of reference. So much time had elapsed since Zahid's death, and so much work was said to have been done by the Prison Service to put right the systemic failings which had allowed the attack on Zahid to take place, that it would first be necessary to identify precisely how far the Prison Service had gone to correct those shortcomings. This would mean looking not just at the practices and procedures the Prison Service had put in place, but also at how those practices and procedures were working on the ground. It would then be necessary to look at whether those practices and procedures had eliminated the systemic shortcomings which had contributed to the attack on Zahid taking place. If they had not, thought would have to be given to how those practices and procedures could be improved so as to reduce as far as possible the risk of similar attacks happening again.

2.25 It soon became apparent that hearings in the conventional sense were too blunt an instrument to enable the Inquiry to address these questions. It was decided to divide the Inquiry into two phases, with each phase addressing one element of the Inquiry's terms of reference. Accordingly, the hearings were devoted to investigating the circumstances which led up to Zahid's murder. This obviously involved finding out how Stewart and Zahid came to share a cell, and what had been known about Stewart beforehand. But I regarded my terms of reference as sufficiently wide to require me to investigate not merely whether individual prison officers were culpable, and where systemic shortcomings had existed, but also *where* responsibility for those systemic shortcomings lay. This could have gone well beyond Feltham, all the way up to the higher echelons of the Prison Service, and maybe beyond. That was why the witnesses who were asked to give oral evidence included not merely the front-line officers who dealt with Stewart and Zahid, but also members of junior, middle and senior management at Feltham and the young offender institutions where Stewart had been in the past, and senior management in the Prison Service with area and national responsibilities all the way up to the then Director General of the Prison Service. I believed that the Inquiry's efficiency would be immeasurably enhanced if the second element of its terms of reference was hived off to be considered in a second phase. Counsel to the Inquiry and for the Interested Parties agreed with this approach.

2.26 The division of the Inquiry into two phases made it necessary for me to consider whether I should submit my report to the Home Secretary in two stages. I decided that there would be a single report dealing with both elements of the Inquiry's terms of reference. I appreciated that Zahid's family would have to wait longer for the Inquiry's findings on the events which led up to his murder, and where responsibility lay for the shortcomings which had allowed the attack on him to happen. It also meant that individuals whose conduct was under scrutiny would have to wait that much longer to know whether they would be criticised or not. But the sooner any recommendations for improvements could be made, the sooner they could be considered and – if thought appropriate – implemented. The course of action which enabled the Inquiry's second phase to be completed sooner was by far the more desirable.

2.27 There were some other advantages – less significant but not to be ignored – in proceeding with the second phase of the Inquiry before my findings on the first phase had been published. The publication of a single report would avoid the possibility of any unfairness to the Prison Service of a report identifying shortcomings in the prison system in 2000 without dealing with improvements which had taken place since then. A single report would also avoid any temptation for the second phase to be diverted by disputes about the extent to which any report dealing with issues raised by the first phase had come to the correct conclusions.

The second phase of the Inquiry

2.28 The first step in the second phase of the Inquiry was for me to identify the topics to be addressed in it. I was able to do that by the time I had considered the closing submissions following the conclusion of the Inquiry's hearings. A comprehensive written statement was then commissioned from the Prison Service on its current practices and procedures relating to those topics – to the extent that they had not been identified in the statements which had already been provided to the Inquiry. Similarly, statements were sought from the Courts Service and the Probation Service on the information provided to the Prison Service about prisoners. These statements were published on the Inquiry's website.

2.29 On receipt of these statements, we invited written representations from those representing Zahid's family and the POA, and from a number of individuals and bodies who we thought could make a contribution to the Inquiry's work. Those representations were intended to include any comments on the comprehensive statement from the Prison Service and any recommendations which it was suggested the Inquiry should make. We had earlier in the Inquiry received written representations from some of those bodies. They included a report which the Inquiry had commissioned from the International Centre for Prison Studies at King's College London, on how various issues with which the Inquiry was concerned were handled in developed countries comparable to England and Wales.

2.30 There were in addition certain groups who may well have had useful contributions to make, but who were too diverse to expect written representations from. They were prisoners, and prison staff who were not active members of the POA and who might have had views of their own. The Inquiry therefore commissioned a series of focus groups. Participants were asked to address a series of questions which the Inquiry had identified. We did not want too many people coming to the focus groups, since we might have lost the opportunity to get participants really talking. But too few, and we might have got views which were not necessarily representative of prisoners or staff as a whole. The sessions took place in July and August 2005.

2.31 There were eight focus groups for prisoners – some with serving prisoners, some with former prisoners. Two were exclusively for black prisoners, and two for Asian prisoners. They were organised by Nacro – the National Association for the Care and Resettlement of Offenders – and by the Open Book project at Goldsmiths College in London. There were six focus groups for prison staff. They consisted of officers chosen at random from the Prison Service's payroll, with a mix of long-serving and relatively new officers. They were held in different parts of the country. The participants were uniformed discipline officers only, mostly at prison officer level, with a smattering of senior officers, and a principal officer or two. The sessions were conducted by experienced welfare officers in the Prison Service. The reports of the focus groups have been published on the Inquiry's website.

2.32 After we received the Prison Service's comprehensive statement, I visited a number of prisons with my advisers. The visits took place in July 2005. The purpose of the visits was to help me get a clearer picture of what was supposed to happen, and to see to what extent what was supposed to happen *was* actually happening on the ground. Since the Inquiry would be making recommendations with a view to reducing the risk of attacks similar to the one on Zahid happening in any establishment in the Prison Service estate, and not just in Feltham and the handful of others which were considered in the Inquiry's first phase, those visits covered a range of establishments. I went to Feltham, of course, and to prisons which were said to be performing well – so that an idea of best practice could be obtained. I also went to prisons which were said to be under-performing, so that deficiencies could be identified. The Inquiry sought the advice of the Inspectorate of Prisons – the independent watchdog on the conditions of Prison Service establishments, the treatment of prisoners and the facilities available to them – about which establishments we should visit, and we also took into account the Prison Service's internal performance grading system.

2.33 In total we visited two local prisons, two training prisons and two young offender institutions in addition to Feltham. We also visited Altcourse Prison in Liverpool, a privately managed establishment. We spent up to two days at each establishment we visited. The two local prisons – prisons which serve the courts and tend to hold unconvicted prisoners and prisoners awaiting allocation to training prisons – we visited were Pentonville and Wormwood Scrubs in London. The two training prisons – prisons for convicted prisoners serving their sentences – we visited were Parkhurst on the Isle of Wight and Wayland in Norfolk. The two young offender institutions we visited were Hindley near Wigan and Lancaster Farms in Lancaster. Pentonville, Parkhurst and Hindley were the establishments said to be under-performing. Wormwood Scrubs, Wayland and Lancaster Farms were the ones said to be performing well. I returned to Wormwood Scrubs for an additional day without my advisers to go over the paperwork completed there in detail. We were not accompanied on these visits by representatives of the Interested Parties, though Prison Service personnel obviously showed us around and answered the questions we had for them. We were given access to every part of the establishment we wanted to visit, and our questions were answered with candour and good humour.

2.34 The Inquiry held a series of seminars in September and October 2005. There were six in all. I chaired them, and they were attended by the advisers. I regarded them as an important tool. They were intended to be the forum for brainstorming sessions on a number of the topics the

Inquiry was addressing. I did not want there to be more than eight or so delegates in each session. I feared that greater numbers would inhibit them from contributing to the debate. The intention was to generate a radical discussion on particular areas of practice and policy. We had no formal agenda, but I had circulated a note identifying some of the issues which I wanted the seminars to address. They were held in public. The first three took place at the Strand Palace Hotel in London and the others at the International Dispute Resolution Centre. Many of the delegates were from the Prison Service, because for three of these seminars I asked for presentations on particular aspects of the Prison Service's work. I also wanted the views of Prison Service personnel from the operational, managerial and policy perspectives. The proceedings were recorded, and transcripts of them have been published on the Inquiry's website.

2.35 Finally, I decided that the second phase of the Inquiry would not be enhanced by additional hearings at which further evidence could be given. I did not think that there were issues of such complexity that hearings had to be convened to enable them to be clarified by questioning of particular witnesses.

Public funding of legal representation

2.36 Public funding by the Legal Services Commission is not available for public inquiries, and the Inquiry did not have the power to order the payment of legal costs from public funds. In keeping with established conventions for inquiries of this kind, public bodies and other institutions with substantial resources had to meet their own legal costs, and the legal costs of those whom they supported or represented, unless there were special circumstances which justified a call on public funds. Prison staff who were members of the POA were regarded as a special case, and before the Inquiry was established, the POA had been assured by ministers that the reasonable cost of legal representation of any of its individual members who were called upon to participate in the Inquiry would be met from public funds.

2.37 In addition, the Home Secretary was prepared, on my recommendation, to make awards out of public funds towards the reasonable legal costs of anyone from whom the Inquiry wished to hear, but who would not be able to take part effectively in the Inquiry without legal representation, and who could not afford legal representation at a level appropriate to the extent of their participation in the Inquiry. I made such a recommendation in four cases:

- At the very outset of the Inquiry, I recommended that the legal costs of Zahid's family be met out of public funds.

- Not long after the Inquiry was announced, it became apparent that the Inquiry would be assisted by obtaining evidence from Robert Stewart. I recommended that any legal costs incurred in preparing a statement from him, and in representing him at the Inquiry should he be asked to give oral evidence, should be met from public funds. As it turned out, these costs were minimal, because Stewart decided early on that he did not wish to be legally represented, and he was not asked to give oral evidence.

- Independent Monitoring Boards are resourced by funds from the Prison Service. I feared that their independence might be publicly compromised if the Prison Service funded the legal costs of Feltham's Independent Monitoring Board, and those of its chair at the time of Zahid's murder, Lucy Bogue. I therefore recommended that the cost of their legal representation should be met from public funds.

- Duncan Keys was an important witness in connection with the "Gladiator" allegations. He was an assistant secretary of the POA. But his evidence was disputed by the POA, and the POA could not in the circumstances be expected to fund legal representation for him. I regarded it as important that he was legally represented, and I therefore recommended that his legal costs be met out of public funds.

The Home Secretary accepted these recommendations. The Inquiry did not receive any other applications for public funding.

The non-statutory nature of the Inquiry

2.38 The House of Lords suggested "that the conduct and scope of the inquiry should be as close to the Scottish model as possible". The Scottish model was described as giving the Procurator Fiscal, the investigating officer, the "power to compel witnesses to give him information which is within [their] knowledge regarding any matters relevant to the investigation". And it was described as giving the Sheriff, who conducts the inquiry, the power "to enforce the attendance of witnesses at the inquiry". Until the Inquiries Act 2005 came into force, an inquiry in England and Wales only had those powers if it was a statutory inquiry. The inquiry which bears the closest resemblance to this one – the Stephen Lawrence Inquiry – was such an inquiry. It was set up under section 49 of the Police Act 1996. That gave it the power to summon and examine witnesses. There was no equivalent provision in the Prison Act 1952 or any subsequent statute relating to prisons or young offender institutions. Accordingly, the Inquiry would not have had the necessary power to summon and examine witnesses or to compel the production of documents without further legislation or resort to the rarely used Tribunals of Inquiry (Evidence) Act 1921. Inquiries conducted under that Act are usually confined to situations where a nationwide crisis of confidence has arisen.

2.39 I was concerned about the lack of these powers. So too were Zahid's family's solicitors. Shortly after the House of Lords handed down its judgment in October 2003, the family asked the Minister to put the Inquiry on a statutory footing. However, he decided that the best way to proceed was to establish a non-statutory inquiry, on the express understanding that, if the effectiveness of the Inquiry was put at risk by any lack of co-operation with it, consideration would be given to putting the Inquiry onto a statutory basis. As I said at the Inquiry's first preliminary hearing:

> "There is a respectable school of thought that a less heavy-handed approach is more likely to elicit a willingness to co-operate than one which proceeds on the assumption that the Inquiry may be met by a lack of co-operation."

2.40 Throughout the hearings, I kept the topic under constant review. I was looking to see whether the Inquiry's objectives would be frustrated by the absence of these powers. I was concerned about the four people who declined either to provide the Inquiry with statements or give oral evidence. But in the end I concluded that, regrettable though their lack of co-operation with the Inquiry was, their non-co-operation did not undermine the Inquiry's work. I did not regard any of them as critical witnesses whose evidence the Inquiry could not do without. I therefore did not regard it as necessary or desirable to request the Minister to put the Inquiry on a statutory footing or, when the Inquiries Act 2005 came into force, to request the Minister to convert the Inquiry into an inquiry under the Act.

The CRE interviews

2.41 Informants interviewed by the CRE in the course of an investigation are told that what they say will be kept confidential. The CRE regards that as very important. If informants are not given that assurance, they may well be less candid than might otherwise be the case. And if word gets around that informants run the risk of what they tell the CRE being disclosed subsequently, future investigations may be affected. So when in 2004 the Inquiry requested the CRE to provide it with copies of the statements taken from the CRE's informants, the Inquiry received only the statements of those informants who had consented to that – or to be more accurate, a summary of the interview of one informant, and transcripts of the interviews of the others. The Inquiry did not take the matter further at the time, as it was going to be obtaining statements of its own from all the relevant witnesses, including many who were the CRE's informants. In any event, if they had told the CRE something important which the Inquiry had not unearthed, there would have been a reference to it in the CRE's report.

2.42 However, on 27 April 2005, Zahid's family's solicitors informed the Inquiry, on a strictly confidential basis, that audiotapes of some of the interviews conducted by the CRE had come into their possession. There was little the Inquiry could do with that information. Section 52 of the Race Relations Act 1976 prevented the Inquiry from discovering what was on the tapes without the informants' consent. And the Inquiry could not request the CRE to obtain their consent because the existence of the tapes had been disclosed to the Inquiry in confidence. Nevertheless, I wanted to know what was on the tapes. I speculated that the tapes came from someone within the CRE. If they thought that the tapes contained information which Zahid's family should know about, I began to think that there might after all be material on the tapes which the Inquiry would want to know about.

2.43 It was not until 21 September 2005 that Zahid's family's solicitors permitted the Inquiry to reveal what they had disclosed to us in confidence. That day the Inquiry was provided by Zahid's family's solicitors with the tapes – there were 53 of them in all, relating to interviews with 39 informants – and they were sent to the CRE the following day, once they had been catalogued for the purpose of future identification. The Inquiry was surprised to discover subsequently from the CRE that – with one or two exceptions – transcripts of these tapes did not exist. The Inquiry would have expected them to have been transcribed in the course of the CRE's own investigation. The Inquiry was never told whether the tapes had been transcribed, but the transcripts later mislaid, or whether they had never been transcribed at all. Be that as it may, the Inquiry itself was prepared to arrange for the tapes to be transcribed and to ask the informants for their consent for the transcripts to be used. But in the light of its own legal advice, the CRE insisted on doing that itself, and on its assurance that this would be done quickly so as not to jeopardise the Inquiry's timetable, I agreed.

2.44 Unfortunately, the speed with which the process of transcribing the tapes and seeking the informants' consent to their disclosure to the Inquiry took place fell short of my expectations. On 6 December 2005, the CRE was anticipating that the process of transcribing the tapes and obtaining the informants' responses to the request for disclosure would be completed by Christmas "at the latest". In fact, the majority of the transcripts were only sent to the informants' representatives on 19 January 2006. Moreover, despite the Inquiry having provided the CRE with a contact list, some of the transcripts were sent to the wrong people, thus compromising the very confidentiality which the CRE was so keen to preserve. All of this delayed the ultimate publication of the report by a good few months.

2.45 In four cases, the tapes themselves were inaudible, with the result that the CRE was not able to provide the Inquiry with transcripts at all. But even when transcripts were produced, many of the 35 remaining informants were concerned about their quality. Nevertheless, 27 of them consented to the transcripts being disclosed to the Inquiry – most of them on condition that, for the time being, the disclosure was limited to the Inquiry team – and the last of them was received by the Inquiry on 22 March this year. Of the eight informants whose transcripts the Inquiry was not provided with, five were informants who did not respond to requests for their consent, and three were informants who refused to give their consent. Having said that, though, the transcripts of the interviews of one of those eight informants had already been supplied to the Inquiry in 2004.

2.46 As it turned out, the transcripts provided to the Inquiry added nothing of importance to what I already knew. In a few instances, I asked for and obtained the informants' permission to refer in the report to a passage in the transcripts, but I saw nothing in the transcripts which called for them to be given a wider circulation. Nor was there anything in the transcripts which caused me to suspect that there might be important nuggets of information in those transcripts which I had not been provided with. The only viable option open to the Inquiry to get the latter transcripts would have been to apply to the court for an order requiring the CRE to disclose them to the Inquiry. But that would have taken many months, with no guarantee of an outcome acceptable to the Inquiry at the end of it – in order to obtain transcripts which were likely not to be of assistance anyway. It was against that background that I decided not to press further to be provided with the transcripts of the eight informants who either did not respond to requests for their consent or who declined to give their consent.

2.47 I kept Zahid's family and their solicitors informed of these developments. It was not ideal for them not to see the transcripts and to have to accept my assurance that the transcripts I had read did not add anything of substance to my knowledge of the facts. In addition, it was not ideal for me to sign off the report without having been provided with all the transcripts. But they entirely understood the difficulties the Inquiry faced and were content to trust my judgement about the way forward.

2.48 There is one other point I must make. One of the people interviewed by the CRE was someone who had been a prisoner at Feltham while Zahid and Stewart were there. He was interviewed over 18 months after Zahid's death. The Inquiry was anxious to obtain a statement from him for itself. But he could not be traced, despite the efforts of private investigators engaged by the Inquiry. Since it was impossible to obtain his consent for the disclosure of what he had told the CRE, the Inquiry requested the CRE to exercise its powers under section 52(1)(c) of the Race Relations Act 1976 to provide it with a summary of what he had told the Commission, without identifying him. The Commission agreed to do that, and that summary has been published on the Inquiry's website. He has been referred to in the report as the CRE's informant.

Wrapping things up

The report

2.49 This report is inevitably a long and detailed one. That was unavoidable. But if it had been any longer, I suspect that it would have been simply indigestible. I have therefore attempted to distil my summary and analysis of the evidence wherever I could. For those who are put off by the length of the report, a summary of the report's main conclusions and recommendations is included in an appendix and is also being published as a separate document.

The documents

2.50　The Inquiry received many documents after the public hearings ended in April 2005. For example, the comprehensive statement provided by the Prison Service had 10 lever arch files of documents attached to it. Many documents came from bodies like the Inspectorate of Prisons and the Prison Reform Trust. In addition, I was provided with many locally produced documents as I visited the various establishments in July 2005. All these documents will be stored indefinitely in the Home Office's archives, and on the Inquiry's website, which contains virtually all of the evidence given to the Inquiry and other documents, and will be accessible for at least two years after the publication of this report. The address for the site is: **www.zahidmubarekinquiry.org.uk**.

Zahid's family

2.51　Finally, I must mention Zahid's family. If they did not come into the hearing chamber, they frequently listened to the evidence over the live feed which was relayed to their private room. They were unfailingly courteous to me whenever I met them. They had not wanted to be thrust into the limelight, but their long fight for a public inquiry to find out how Zahid came to share his cell with Stewart – no doubt driven to some extent by campaigners seeking to improve the lot of Asian prisoners – has been a compelling story of hope and disillusion. I saw very little of Mrs Mubarek, who found attending the hearings particularly distressing, but Zahid's father, Mubarek Amin, and his uncle, Imtiaz Amin, maintained a quiet and unassuming dignity throughout, which was an inspiration to everyone. I hope that the Inquiry has proved to be the sufficiently cathartic and informative exercise they wanted.

Chapter 3: Racism and other topics

Racism

3.1 The Inquiry's terms of reference were expressed in wide language. It was therefore necessary for me to decide, in the light of the Inquiry's terms of reference, what the parameters of the Inquiry were to be. In this chapter, I summarise some of the key decisions I made which shaped the course of the Inquiry. I begin with racism.

3.2 The issue of racism has been at the heart of the Inquiry. This was not simply because Zahid's killer was himself a racist, and because his racism may have played an important part in his selection of Zahid as his victim. It was also because of the need to explore whether *explicit* racism on the part of individual prison officers had been the reason either for Zahid sharing a cell with Stewart in the first place or continuing to share a cell with him. There have been lurid allegations about prisoners of different ethnic origins being put in the same cell to see if violence would ensue.

3.3 But apart from that, it has been necessary to explore the extent to which racism might have *unwittingly* played its part in what happened to Zahid. For example, when a particular prison officer was told that a racist letter written by Stewart had been intercepted, he gave instructions for the letter simply to be returned to Stewart, and for Stewart to be told that if he re-wrote it without the offensive material it could be sent out. When Stewart returned to the wing where he and Zahid had been sharing a cell, accompanied by documents showing that he was a racist, he was nevertheless put back in that cell. No thought was given to whether someone who looked like Stewart might have been hostile to Asians. Nor was any thought given to whether Zahid would have been comfortable about sharing a cell with someone who looked like Stewart, or whether he might have felt inhibited about asking for a change of cell. Whether racism unwittingly played a part on any of these occasions could not be answered in a vacuum. These questions could only be answered in their context. That context was the extent to which the vice of racism was endemic at Feltham. Was Feltham, and the Prison Service as a whole for that matter, institutionally racist?

3.4 Institutional racism was considered at length in the Stephen Lawrence Inquiry. That was ground-breaking work. That Inquiry recognised that unwitting or unconscious, and therefore unintentional, racism was more difficult to detect, and therefore all the more insidious, than overt and explicit racism, because those who were infected by it were unaware of the influence it had on them. It also recognised that racism can be systemic, in the sense that the nature and culture of the institution in which it thrives can result in there being a widespread but unappreciated tendency to treat minorities less favourably than the majority. The trouble is that most people genuinely think that they will rise above it. Moreover, individuals who work within an institution which is branded as institutionally racist are not themselves to be treated as racist. It is the failure to appreciate this that makes the presence of institutional racism something which people working within the institution instinctively want to deny. But in the years since February 1999 when the report of the Stephen Lawrence Inquiry was published, institutional racism has become a well-recognised concept, even if it has not been universally understood.

3.5 A detailed analysis of what constitutes institutional racism is not necessary because, as we shall see, the Prison Service in general, and Feltham in particular, are accepted to have been institutionally racist at the time of Zahid's death. For present purposes, all that is needed is the definition of institutional racism formulated by the Stephen Lawrence Inquiry:

> "The collective failure of an organisation to provide an appropriate and professional service to people because of their colour, culture, or ethnic origin. It can be seen or detected in processes, attitudes and behaviour which amount to discrimination through unwitting prejudice, ignorance, thoughtlessness and racist stereotyping which disadvantage minority ethnic people."

This definition was accepted by the Government when the report was published. The then Home Secretary, Jack Straw, emphasised the relevance of the definition for other governmental departments, which naturally included the Prison Service:

> "[The definition formulated by the Stephen Lawrence Inquiry] is the new definition of institutional racism, which I accept… In my view, any long-established, white-dominated organisation is liable to have procedures, practices and culture that tend to exclude or disadvantage non-white people. The Police Service, in that respect, is little different from other parts of the criminal justice system or from government departments, including the Home Office."

In fact, the Home Secretary's stance mirrored one of the key conclusions of the report:

> "We all agree that institutional racism affects the [Metropolitan Police], and police services elsewhere. Furthermore our conclusions as to police services should not lead to complacency in other institutions

and organisations. Collective failure is apparent in many of them, including the criminal justice system. It is incumbent upon every institution to examine their policies and the outcome of their policies and practices to guard against disadvantaging any section of our communities."

3.6 Part 2 of the Butt report dealt with the extent to which racism existed at Feltham. It concluded that Feltham was "institutionally racist". Mr Narey accepted in the course of the CRE's investigation that there was "institutional racism and pockets of malicious and blatant racism" within the Prison Service. Judy Clements, the Race Equality Adviser to the Prison Service, told the CRE's public hearing that the Prison Service was "without a shadow of doubt institutionally racist" when she joined it in 1999. It was never suggested by the Prison Service that, by the time of Zahid's death, it had taken on board the lessons to be learned from the Stephen Lawrence Inquiry, or that it had begun to take such steps as were necessary to put its own house in order.

3.7 These expressions of opinion about racism in the Prison Service in general, and at Feltham in particular, were echoed by the CRE. The CRE published Part 2 of its report, *Racial Equality in Prisons*, in December 2003. I do not think that the CRE made a finding of institutional racism in terms in that part of its report, but its findings – and in particular what it called its two "omnibus findings" – were entirely consistent with the conclusion that institutional racism existed across the Prison Service. Indeed, it is obvious from the Introduction to Part 1 of the CRE report that this was its view, because it spoke of "the institutional racism within the Prison Service".

3.8 I did not believe that I should go behind these conclusions. I acknowledged that I was not bound by the findings of previous investigations, at any rate so far as matters falling within my terms of reference were concerned. However, I had to take the previous investigations into account, and I saw no reason not to accept the conclusion that institutional racism existed within the Prison Service, and therefore at Feltham – particularly when none of the Interested Parties had at any stage invited me to depart from it, and it was not a topic which my terms of reference required me to revisit. I therefore treated it as established that there was institutional racism within the Prison Service and at Feltham. There was no need for anyone to try to prove that fact.

3.9 In these circumstances, one of the key tasks of the Inquiry has been to investigate whether the series of events which resulted in Stewart sharing a cell with Zahid, despite what was known about Stewart, were themselves in any way attributable to a collective organisational failure which was itself informed and shaped by the institutional racism with which Feltham was infected. Many officers played their part, in one way or another, in the series of events which resulted in Stewart sharing a cell with Zahid. To the extent that there were shortcomings on the part of any of them, it is necessary to consider whether they were attributable in any way to the culture of indifference and insensitivity which institutional racism breeds. My approach to the evidence has been informed by that important consideration.

3.10 But it is also necessary to look to the future. The Stephen Lawrence Inquiry said this about institutional racism:

> "It persists because of the failure of the organisation openly and adequately to recognise and address its existence and causes by policy, example and leadership. Without recognition and action to eliminate such racism it can prevail as part of the ethos or culture of the organisation. It is a corrosive disease."

To continue the medical metaphor, a proper diagnosis of the current state of the illness is required if further outbreaks of the condition are to be prevented in the future. So the extent to which the Prison Service continues to be infected needs to be addressed, in order that an informed judgement can be made as to whether the patient has become fit and well, or whether further treatment is required. It is, of course, not possible for the Inquiry to embark on an exercise similar to that carried out by the CRE to determine whether the scourge of institutional racism has been eradicated from the Prison Service. But following the publication of Part 2 of the CRE's report, an action plan was produced by the Prison Service working in partnership with the CRE. It covered the next five years, and was to be actively managed by both the Prison Service and the CRE. This is how the CRE will be monitoring the extent to which race equality is being implemented across the prison estate to see whether the Prison Service can eventually be given a clean bill of health.

Systemic shortcomings

3.11 Feltham has had a chequered history over the last decade. I go into that in a little detail in chapter 4, but for present purposes it needs only to be said that in 1996 Feltham was regarded by the Inspectorate of Prisons as an establishment in deep trouble. The Inspectorate submitted an extremely critical report about Feltham, and another damning report following the visit of its team to Feltham in 1998 when it said that the Prison Service had failed to address the criticisms it had previously made. The response of the Prison Service was to appoint a task force in December 1998, supervised by a steering group chaired by the then Director General. It presented its final report to the steering group in May 1999. So one of the issues which the Inquiry had to address was whether the Prison Service's response to the problems identified at Feltham in 1998 was sufficient for the purposes with which the Inquiry was concerned: had the Prison Service done what it should have done at the time to see that Feltham was in a position to keep prisoners safe from the sort of attack which Zahid sustained?

3.12 But what about the systemic shortcomings which still existed at the time of Zahid's murder? The Inquiry plainly had to investigate where responsibility for those lay. That opened up the Inquiry's work considerably. It meant that the Inquiry would not solely be looking at the actions of the front-line officers at the coalface who had to deal with Stewart and Zahid and make operational decisions about them. The Inquiry would also have to assess the actions of the senior officers who supervised the front-line officers, and the even more senior officers who managed them. Then there were the officers in governor grades who were responsible for ensuring that Prison Service policies were being properly implemented. And there were those at Prison Service headquarters who were responsible for overseeing Feltham and for creating the policies which were to apply across the prison estate.

3.13 If the Inquiry was to investigate responsibility for systemic shortcomings in this way, how far back should the Inquiry have to go? I concluded that the Inquiry's approach had to reflect its terms of reference. The allusions in its terms of reference to Zahid's death, and to the events leading up to the attack on him, suggested that the Inquiry had to focus only on those events which had a sufficiently direct causal connection with what had happened. Subject to one reservation only, I decided that the terms of reference did not require me to provide a comprehensive account of all the reasons for any systemic shortcomings which may have contributed to what happened to Zahid. Those reasons may have been extremely complex, and may have included historical and cultural factors extending back many years or even decades. The Inquiry would not have been the appropriate forum for issues of that kind to be comprehensively addressed. Nor was the Inquiry intended to investigate that sort of thing. It was intended to investigate how and why Zahid met his death so as to ensure that the United Kingdom's obligation under Article 2(1) of the Convention was satisfied, and to make recommendations for the future. An investigation going into the mists of time to discern the genesis for any systemic failings was not required to achieve either of those two goals. The Inquiry had to be effective but, as the House of Lords said, it also had to be focused and disciplined.

3.14 Having said that, there had to be some investigation into the state of affairs at Feltham which allowed the systemic shortcomings to continue. Some starting point for detailed factual investigation was required, and there was ultimately no more logic in the contention made on behalf of Zahid's family that the Inquiry's starting point should be in 1996 rather than when the task force was appointed in 1998. It was a matter of judgement where the line should be drawn, and I decided that an investigation which began, so far as Feltham was concerned, in December 1998 would be effective in establishing the events leading up to Zahid's murder and where the responsibility lay. That was so whether the responsibility lay with individual prison officers, with management at Feltham, or with individuals higher up in the hierarchy who, it might be suggested, made demands on Feltham in the period between December 1998 and March 2000 which it could not be expected to fulfil consistently with providing a safe environment for prisoners like Zahid. I was also confident that a detailed examination of conditions at Feltham between 1996 and 1998 would not have materially enhanced my ability to make recommendations about what changes are needed now to help reduce such attacks in the future.

3.15 My only reservation related to the argument which proceeded on the assumption that those responsible for Feltham at the time would be saying that all reasonable efforts had been made after December 1998 to turn Feltham around, but that things had got so bad by then that it had not been reasonably possible for much progress to have been made by early 2000. If the Inquiry were to accept that explanation, the real responsibility for Zahid's death lay in what had or had not been done before December 1998. If the Inquiry's starting point was December 1998, the Inquiry would have prevented itself, so the argument went, from identifying and investigating that responsibility. In assessing this argument, I was prepared to assume the correctness of the assumption on which it proceeded. For example, Peter Atherton, the Area Manager for London South, which included Feltham, from December 1998 to March 2000, said that "real and visible improvements" at Feltham "could only be completed in years rather than months". But the critical point was that it was unlikely that the Inquiry would have ended up saying that no-one had been to blame. On the contrary, the Inquiry would have been saying that a major cause of any systemic shortcomings in early 2000 had been that the Prison Service had failed to react sufficiently quickly or with sufficient vigour to the concerns about Feltham which had been raised by the Inspectorate of Prisons – and Feltham's Board of Visitors for that matter – in 1996 if not earlier. All that the Inquiry would have debarred itself from doing was identifying the detail of what had gone wrong between 1996 and 1998, and where the individual responsibility for that had lain. Neither the order made by the House of Lords, nor Article 2(1) of the Convention, required the Inquiry to do that, nor did I think that it was contemplated by the Inquiry's terms of reference.

3.16 So much for Feltham. But the way Stewart was dealt with as he went through the prison system was a different matter. The communication of information about him throughout his time in custody, and any assessments which should have been made about the risk he posed to prisoners with whom he shared a cell, went to the heart of the Inquiry's work. I have therefore looked at how Stewart was handled within the prison system from when detailed records of his time in custody survive.

What kind of attacks?

3.17 The terms of reference required me to make recommendations about the prevention of *such attacks* in the future. What sort of attacks were contemplated? All prisoner-on-prisoner attacks, however serious or trivial? Prisoner-on-prisoner attacks in cells, or anywhere in the establishment? And prisoner-on-prisoner attacks in young offender institutions, or anywhere across the prison estate? I decided that the Inquiry would be concerned only with attacks of a serious nature by one prisoner on another, and that the particular focus should be on attacks by one cellmate on another in their cell. Not only is that what happened in the case of Zahid, but prisoners are particularly vulnerable when locked up in a cell together. Apart from anything else, my advisers thought that the Inquiry would be considerably – and in their view unacceptably – opened up if it were to address prisoner-on-prisoner attacks elsewhere in the establishment, since many different considerations applied to attacks of that kind. As it is, many of the recommendations I have made are likely, if implemented, to reduce the risk of prisoner-on-prisoner attacks wherever they take place in the establishment. For example, anything which can be done to improve the flow and use of information, or the identification and management of prisoners with mental disorders, may well have the potential to do that.

3.18 On the other hand, although the attack on Zahid took place in a young offender institution, I decided that the scope of the Inquiry should not be confined to in-cell prisoner-on-prisoner attacks in young offender institutions. The Inquiry should address in-cell prisoner-on-prisoner attacks across the prison estate. It may be that the incidence of these is greater in young offender institutions, reflecting the heightened volatility of young offenders. But I thought that the circumstances which gave rise to such attacks, and the ways in which their incidence might be reduced, were likely to apply equally to young offender institutions and adult prisons. So did the advisers. I think that the evidence showed us to have been correct in that assessment. Indeed, the first significant initiative taken by the Prison Service following the death of Zahid to reduce in-cell prisoner-on-prisoner attacks was to introduce a cell-sharing risk assessment procedure across the whole of the prison estate, and not just in young offender institutions.

Sentencing policy

3.19   It was suggested by groups interested in penal reform that the Inquiry should consider whether it is appropriate for people like Zahid to be sent to prison at all. Were not his offences too minor to justify a custodial sentence? And would he have received a custodial sentence if he had been white? These are important questions, but although it is plainly the case that Zahid would not have been attacked by Stewart if he had not been in custody in the first place, it would, I thought, have taken a far too generous view of the Inquiry's terms of reference if the phrase "the events leading up to the attack on him" had been regarded as covering the appropriateness of the sentence passed on him. An inquiry into prison life would have been opened up to a completely unacceptable degree. Although Patrick O'Connor QC, counsel for Zahid's family, made the point that the sentence on Zahid was wholly inappropriate in the circumstances, in common with the other Interested Parties he did not suggest that that was an issue which the Inquiry should address.

Investigating the investigations

3.20   At one stage, Zahid's family wanted the Inquiry to comment on the adequacy or otherwise of the Butt investigation. They were particularly concerned that the Butt report made no recommendations for disciplinary action. I concluded that this was not within the Inquiry's remit. The adequacy of that investigation had been highly relevant to whether there should be a further investigation, held in public with informed participation by Zahid's family. But although that had been the issue in the judicial review proceedings, it was no longer an issue now that that battle had been won. In short, the Inquiry was not investigating the investigations – whether Mr Butt's or the CRE's. The Inquiry was investigating the events which led up to Zahid's murder, and would be making recommendations about how similar attacks could be prevented in the future.

3.21 Similarly, the Prison Service, the POA and the chair of Feltham's Board of Visitors at the time were concerned about the fairness of some aspects of the CRE's investigation. In particular, they said that some statements had been attributed to witnesses which had never been made, and that in a number of instances their evidence had been summarised inaccurately. I said that I would not investigate those complaints, but that I would bear the allegation in mind if any of the current statements of those witnesses were said to be undermined by anything different in the statements they had made to the CRE.

Criticisms of individuals

3.22 This is a convenient place to comment on the criticisms of individuals which this report contains. The Inquiry was not in the business of finding someone to blame at all costs. Sometimes things go wrong without anyone being to blame. Sometimes it may no longer be possible to establish where blame lies. Sometimes it may look as if someone was to blame, but closer scrutiny shows otherwise. Sometimes it may be apparent that an institution was blameworthy, but the causes and origins of that culpability may be too complex or hazy for blame to be fairly or reliably laid at the door of anyone. But where individuals have been shown to be culpable, I have not hesitated to say so.

3.23 There has been another side to that coin. Of the many thousands of officers in the Prison Service, the few who have been under the spotlight in this Inquiry have been those who chance brought into contact with Stewart or Zahid. It could just as easily have been someone else whose conduct was under scrutiny. That should not be forgotten. Moreover, those who dealt with Stewart or Zahid were having to remember many years later things which may have been inconsequential at the time. They were unlikely to have any recollection of events other than what any contemporaneous documents may have revealed. For the most part, their evidence about what they did was based on what they would normally have done. Again, in some cases, officers did what most other officers would have done at that time in the same situation. That does not make it right, but any criticisms have to be seen in that context. Hindsight should not get in the way of judging officers by the standards of the time. Nor have I ignored the fact that many of the officers were working in the pressure cooker of failing and under-resourced prisons, and that blame should not too readily be attached to them for conduct which could, in part at least, be attributable to underlying systemic shortcomings. And in some cases the very reason why particular officers were asked questions about their conduct was precisely because they did something. There may well have been other officers who did not appear on the radar precisely because they did nothing, despite perhaps having information which called for some action to be taken. That, too, is something which in fairness to them I have borne in mind.

3.24 The benchmark I have used to justify criticism of an individual is whether his or her conduct was contrary to good practice – in other words, the standard of practice to be expected of a reasonably competent holder of the post which the individual held. I have attempted not to apply Elysian standards, or the counsel of perfection, to my assessment of their conduct. A number of refinements to that need to be noted, however. First, if someone could not be expected to know that their conduct was contrary to good practice, I have said so. This would apply, for example, to a failure to comply with an instruction in a Prison Service Order which never came to their attention, for reasons for which they cannot be blamed. It would also apply to a new and inexperienced officer who was just following what more experienced colleagues were doing. Secondly, if conduct on the part of an individual, though culpable, did not actually contribute to the circumstances which gave Stewart the opportunity to attack and kill Zahid, I have said so. Although the Inquiry investigated the events which led up to Zahid's death, I had to concentrate on those events which contributed to it. Thirdly, there may have been reasons in particular cases why an individual strayed into unacceptable behaviour and which mitigate that individual's culpability. If that is the case, I have said so.

3.25 I should add that no criticism has been made of any individual which they have not had a chance to answer. I have already said that individuals who gave oral evidence were informed in advance of the possible criticisms which counsel to the Inquiry thought I might make of them in due course. No adverse comment has been made of such an individual unless they were given an opportunity to deal with the possible criticism when being questioned. Nor has any criticism been made of an individual who did not give oral evidence unless they were given an opportunity to deal with it in correspondence.

The Inquiry's second phase

3.26 This is also a convenient place to mention three important considerations which informed my approach to the second phase of the Inquiry. The first two were formulated by Mr Giffin in his submissions as to what the format for the Inquiry's second phase should be. Since I agreed wholeheartedly with him – as did counsel for all the Interested Parties – I set them out in his words. First, the factual investigation in phase two

> "… is of a radically different nature to the kind of factual investigation which phase one has required. Formal findings of fact as to the current position, still less as to the conduct of individuals, are unnecessary and inappropriate. Praising or blaming the Prison Service for what it has done or not done since 2000 is not an exercise called for by the Inquiry's terms of reference. Ascertaining the current position is simply a means to the end of making the right recommendations for the future, and is something which falls to be done to the extent, but only to the extent, necessary to serve that end."

3.27 Secondly,

> "… it is important to have well in mind the sheer volume of information which might conceivably be relevant at phase two… The aim of phase one has been to be as comprehensive as reasonably possible in investigating the facts which fall within the limited field defined by the words in the terms of reference: 'the events leading up to the attack on Zahid Mubarek'. It is simply not viable to conduct a similar comprehensive investigation into the current functioning of all aspects of information management, personnel management, mental disorder, race relations, prison regime and all of the other matters that might possibly bear upon the prevention of attacks in the future – or at any rate not without committing the Inquiry to a phase two of such extended duration (years rather than months) as to fly in the face of the imperative [of completing phase two as expeditiously as possible so that the Inquiry's recommendations can be considered and, if accepted, implemented]. This is not to dispute that phase two should be thorough and detailed, but it is simply to recognise that the unrestrained pursuit of all avenues of inquiry is not compatible with making potentially life-saving recommendations within a reasonable time…"

3.28 Thirdly, prisoner-on-prisoner in-cell attacks are less likely to occur in a prison which is performing well, where officers are well-motivated and properly managed, and where prisoners enjoy purposeful activity and have generous association. In such a prison, there is less likelihood of individual failings occurring or of systemic shortcomings existing, and it will be less likely that prisoners will take out their frustrations on their cellmates. Conversely, in a prison where the morale of staff is low, where they are being poorly managed, and where prisoners are "banged up" for an unacceptable length of time, such attacks are more likely to occur.

3.29 Many factors can contribute to a prison's poor performance. They include:

- a high and constantly changing prison population

- staff shortages

- low staff morale and difficult industrial relations

- the ineffective management of staff

- racism and religious intolerance

- a lack of adequate training for staff

- a lack of capital investment and financial resources

- a lack of clarity in, or the absence of, local procedures

- the prison's layout

- a lack of support from Prison Service headquarters.

But it would not have been possible for the Inquiry in its second phase to have addressed these factors without becoming an investigation into a root and branch reform of the Prison Service, going far beyond the Inquiry's limited terms of reference. That is not to say that these issues need not be addressed. But they are to be addressed by the Prison Service and others, not the Inquiry. I have simply explored the extent to which these factors contributed to Feltham's degeneration into an establishment in which prisoners were more likely to be exposed to attack by their cellmates.

Chapter 4: "A gigantic transit camp"

Feltham's origins

4.1 The building on the site on which Feltham currently stands in West London was originally a Victorian industrial training school. In 1910 it was taken over by the Prison Commissioners as their second borstal institution. It continued in that role, with wartime interruptions, until the 1970s when plans were made for the demolition of the old Victorian buildings and the construction of a new borstal on the site, designed for offenders needing a special regime.

4.2 Feltham was about a mile away from Ashford Remand Centre. Ashford had started life as a school, and it became a remand centre in 1961. It soon acquired a history of unhappy industrial relations. By the time a new borstal was being contemplated at Feltham, Ashford was regarded as too insecure for holding remand prisoners. So the decision was made to build a new borstal and remand centre at Feltham.

4.3 The borstal was completed first. It had taken many years to build. It opened in August 1983. Its design had taken into account the change of culture which occurred when borstals were replaced that year by youth custody centres, now known as young offender institutions. Instead of dormitories, prisoners were now accommodated in cells. Officers wore uniforms. The atmosphere in the place changed. As for the new remand centre, it was ready by 1986, but industrial action prevented it from opening until March 1988.

Feltham in 2000

4.4 Since then, Feltham has operated as both a young offender institution and a remand centre for young male prisoners. Its convicted prisoners include both those who are at Feltham only until they are allocated to another young offender institution to serve the rest of their sentence, and those who remain at Feltham for the whole of their sentence – or at least until they are 21, when they are transferred to an adult prison. But it also houses many unconvicted prisoners. Indeed, for many years it was the only remand centre for young prisoners for the London area, and pressures on its population were only reduced at the beginning of 2000 when 150 places for young offenders were found at Chelmsford Prison in Essex. It caters for both juveniles, those aged under 18, and young offenders, those aged between 18 and 20. It is part of the Prison Service estate, the Prison Service being an agency of the Home Office. From 1 April 2000, the Youth Justice Board became responsible for obtaining secure accommodation for juveniles, and that meant that the demarcation between juveniles and young offenders then had to be formalised. Work on the physical division of Feltham into two sites began in 1999, and the separation of the two sites was completed on time. The juvenile site was known as Feltham A, and the young offender site as Feltham B, although even before the physical separation of the two sites juveniles and young offenders had been kept apart from each other.

4.5 The construction of Feltham took into account some new design principles pioneered in the United States. It is spread over a relatively large area. The residential wings, known at Feltham as units, consist of two interconnecting sections, each triangular in shape and on two levels. Each section has its own enclosed area for association on the ground floor. Each association area has limited recreational facilities, although they are well used – a pool table, table tennis table and colour television. In March 2000, each of the sections in Feltham A was regarded as a separate unit. When Feltham A was fully operational, it had eight units in all. Each unit in Feltham B, with one exception,* comprised the two interconnecting sections. When Feltham B was fully operational, it had 10 units in all. The units were named after species of birds. In addition to the residential units, there was a healthcare centre, a segregation unit and a unit for prisoners who were regarded as bullies. It was called Waite, so named after a prisoner who died as a result of being bullied. The thrust of much of the evidence was that the physical layout – in particular, the distances staff had to travel to get from one part of Feltham to another – made the establishment a more difficult place to staff and manage effectively. Having seen other establishments with a similar layout, I am sceptical about whether Feltham's geography made a significant contribution to its problems.

4.6 The Inquiry has been concerned with Feltham B, because that is where Stewart and Zahid were serving their sentences. The units in Feltham B served different purposes. Lapwing was the induction unit. Others were for unconvicted prisoners, and the remainder were for prisoners serving sentences or for convicted prisoners awaiting sentence. There was usually at least one unit closed for refurbishment. The nine units which conformed to the regular pattern had an office between the two interconnecting sections and a small office for the senior officer in charge of the unit. They had a mix of single cells, double cells and dormitories which accommodated four prisoners. Cells did not have

---

* The exception was Teal unit. It did not conform to the general pattern. It had only one section, and the type of accommodation was described internally as "hotel" as opposed to "galleried".

their own electricity supply. Prisoners occasionally had the use of battery-operated televisions which were allocated on a rota. Lighting was controlled by the prisoners by a switch inside each cell. There was a light outside each cell which was controlled by a switch outside.

4.7 When all of the cells were occupied up to their intended capacity, the number of inmates in them represented the certified normal accommodation for the unit.* However, there were occasions when population pressures meant that the certified normal accommodation had to be exceeded. If that became necessary, extra beds would be placed in the single cells. This practice, known as "doubling up", was not uncommon at Feltham. Thus, the operational capacity exceeded the certified normal accommodation. In Swallow, which was the unit in which Stewart and Zahid were accommodated and was for convicted prisoners serving sentences, the certified normal accommodation was 60 and the operational capacity 65. In March 2000 Feltham as a whole had a certified normal accommodation of 768 and an operational capacity of 818. The number of prisoners accommodated that month averaged 746.

4.8 Each unit was staffed by prison officers. They were supervised by a senior officer who was in charge of the unit. A cluster of three units was managed by a principal officer – the most senior uniformed rank in the Prison Service. He reported to a residential governor, who was responsible for some of the residential units in Feltham B. He in turn reported to the governor who was the Head of Feltham B, and he reported to the Governing Governor. Throughout this report, the officer in the post of Governing Governor of an establishment is referred to as the Governor. The Governor of Feltham at the time of the attack on Zahid was Niall Clifford.

4.9 There had, of course, to be sufficient staff on duty on the units 24 hours a day, seven days a week. A roster identified which staff would be working on a particular day and which shift they would be working. Unfortunately, Feltham was affected by staff shortages, and in addition there were times when staff were off sick, on leave or on training courses. That meant that there might not be the full complement of staff in place. Sometimes senior officers found themselves in charge of an additional unit as well as their own. Sometimes they would have to do the work of the prison officers to ensure that basic functions were performed. Sometimes staff would have to be "cross-deployed" from other parts of Feltham – frequently from the Security Department – to provide an

---

* So called because section 14(2) of the Prison Act 1952 requires a prisoner's accommodation to be "certified" by an inspector as being suitable as accommodation.

extra pair of hands. In order to check whether the key functions of the unit were being carried out, a senior officer was assigned to act as the "hiking" officer. He would be responsible for the three units in the same cluster, and he would monitor the extent to which functions such as cell-searching and giving prisoners time out of their cells for association were taking place.

The problems which Feltham faced

4.10 Young offender institutions and remand centres have problems of their own within the Prison Service. Conventional wisdom tells us that young offenders are more volatile than adult offenders, and are more prone to misbehave while in custody. They need more time out of their cells in order to relieve the build-up of tension and frustration which being locked up in a cell for much of the day and night produces. Staff shortages at Feltham made that difficult to achieve. In addition, there was less time to work with them to reduce the risk of re-offending or to improve their social skills – partly because their offences, generally speaking, were less serious than those committed by adults, and their sentences would correspondingly be less long, and partly because they were frequently moved out of Feltham after a few weeks to complete their sentences elsewhere and to make room for new remand prisoners. This was why sentence planning – which involves assigning prisoners to behavioural programmes intended to make them less likely to re-offend on their release – was virtually non-existent at Feltham.

4.11 Unconvicted prisoners awaiting trial presented problems of their own. Some of them had to cope with the stress of not knowing whether they would be convicted or what their sentence was going to be. All of them were having to be treated as prisoners who might not be in Feltham for very long. And as a remand centre serving the courts, one of Feltham's key functions was to ensure that prisoners who were due to go to court had been removed from their units and were available to be collected by the escort contractors in the morning without delay. That had a knock-on effect at the end of the day. Large numbers of prisoners would arrive from court in the late afternoon or early evening. They all had to be properly processed and sent to the appropriate units. All of this made Feltham, in common with other combined young offender institutions and remand centres, a difficult place to run.

4.12 In addition, Feltham had problems of its own. As the only remand centre for young prisoners covering the London area, it had an unusually large population, and it was sometimes difficult for family and friends to visit them. But that was not matched by comparable numbers of staff. Because of its location, Feltham has always experienced problems in recruiting and retaining its staff. Levels of pay within the Prison Service compared unfavourably with local employers, including employers at Heathrow airport, with whom Feltham had to compete. Retaining its staff had also been difficult. Staff who were assigned to Feltham after their training tended to stay there for as short a time as possible before they applied for a transfer to an establishment nearer to where they came from – where housing was more affordable. And the pressure of working within an institution which had more prisoners than it could cope with and fewer staff than it needed was itself a disincentive for staff to remain at Feltham. The result was that Feltham had a high proportion of relatively inexperienced staff.

The Inspectorate looks at Feltham

The 1996 inspection

4.13 Against that background, it is not all that surprising that Feltham's recent history before Stewart and Zahid arrived there early in 2000 had been a difficult one. Between 28 October and 5 November 1996, a full inspection was carried out on Feltham by a team from the Inspectorate of Prisons. It was an inspection which had been previously announced. In the preface to his report of that inspection, the Chief Inspector, then Sir David Ramsbotham, drew attention to some of the positive features of Feltham. He thought that there had been a concerted effort to consolidate the different facilities required for sentenced and unsentenced prisoners. He applauded a recent initiative to introduce support for prisoners' families. His impression was that the staff were caring, and he complimented Feltham on the volume and diversity of support by volunteers for a whole range of activities, without which the regime would have been even more impoverished. But he also said that Feltham was bursting at the seams, and was already

> "… a gigantic transit camp, in which day-to-day activities are dominated by the process of finding beds for ever-increasing numbers, particularly of young remand prisoners, and ensuring that they get to court on time."

He thought that it was impossible to run an establishment which catered for both juveniles and young offenders, some of whom were sentenced and others not, not least because the accommodation was not designed for that purpose. The movement of prisoners required to service the courts had a "profoundly unsettling effect" on the establishment. And since Feltham did not have the resources, in terms of education and work places, to satisfy the needs of those prisoners who volunteered for activities which got them out of their cells, far too many prisoners were left locked up and idle with nothing to do. This was not something which had only just been discovered. The Chief Inspector said that these concerns had been brought to the attention of the Prison Service and ministers years before. As the only remand centre for young prisoners covering the London area, it had been set an impossible task. Sir David made a large number of recommendations, 180 in all, not least of which was the acquisition or construction of a remand centre for young offenders to the east of London. Feltham's Governor at the time, Clive Welsh, who arrived at Feltham in February 1997, accepted that the report painted a fairly accurate picture of Feltham as he found it.

The 1998 inspection

4.14 Between 30 November and 4 December 1998, a team from the Inspectorate carried out a further full inspection at Feltham. This time the arrival of the team of inspectors was not announced beforehand. The Chief Inspector was extremely critical of Feltham in his preface to the report of that visit. He noted that nothing had been done by senior management within the Prison Service to address the core problem of overcrowding in an institution which was dominated by the daily need to serve the courts. He said:

> "This report… is, without doubt, the most disturbing that I have had to make during my three years as HM Chief Inspector of Prisons. I have to disclose to the public [that] the conditions and treatment of the 922 children and young prisoners confined at Feltham are, in many instances, totally unacceptable. They are, in many instances, worse than when I reported on them two years ago and reveal a history of neglect of those committed to their charge and a failure to meet the demands of society to tackle the problem of offending behaviour."

Many of the detailed recommendations which he had made two years earlier had not been implemented, and although there were isolated pockets of good practice, designed and delivered by a small number of excellent staff and volunteers against all odds, little had been achieved. In some respects there had been a marked deterioration in the provision of care. He said that there was a shortage of resources, that staff were unable to articulate the role they should perform, and that the current industrial relations procedures were an obstruction to change. He repeated his call for a new remand centre for young offenders to the east of London.

4.15 This report was not published until 26 March 1999, but the Chief Inspector was so concerned about the conditions he had found at Feltham that immediately after his team's visit he telephoned the then Director General of the Prison Service, Sir Richard Tilt, and told him of his intention to raise his concerns with ministers. Sir Richard visited Feltham with the new Area Manager for London South, Peter Atherton. According to Phil Wheatley, the current Director General, they "found conditions were indeed very poor and little had been done to implement the recommendations of the 1996 inspection". Mr Narey does not think that the prefaces to the Inspectorate's reports presented a fair picture. He pointed to some differences between the preface to the report following the 1998 visit and the report itself, and he said that the author of a later report following a visit in October 2000 privately disavowed the preface to that report to him. But whether that is right or not, the reports themselves make grim reading. No-one suggested to the Inquiry that the criticisms they made of Feltham were unjustified. Even if the prefaces were "over the top", and failed to give proper recognition to the good work being done at Feltham alongside the problems, no-one could deny – and Mr Narey did not – that Feltham was an institution which was in trouble on many fronts. As the leader of the task force was to tell the Inquiry, he was unpleasantly surprised by what he found at Feltham. It was one thing to read about Feltham in the Inspectorate's reports: it was quite another thing to see things for oneself.

The creation of the task force

4.16 The Prison Service responded swiftly to the feedback it was getting about the visit of the team from the Inspectorate in 1998. The task force was appointed within a few days of the completion of the visit. It was led by Adrian Smith, who was later to succeed Mr Atherton as Area Manager for London South. The task force's terms of reference cannot now be found, but Mr Smith thought that its purpose was to diagnose Feltham's shortcomings and to identify what had to be done to bring about the improvements the establishment needed. It was for the steering group to decide whether such suggestions for improvement as the task force made were feasible in terms of cost and overall Prison Service strategy.

4.17 The task force ended up working in two phases. By February 1999 it had delivered what it had been commissioned to deliver: it had identified the areas in which improvements needed to be made. The decision was then made that the momentum should not be lost, and the task force remained at Feltham for a while assisting the senior management team in implementing the changes which it had recommended. It moved out of Feltham in March, but it kept in touch with what was going on. In all, it produced five reports between January and May 1999 when it was disbanded. It finished its work by preparing a briefing paper for the new Governor of Feltham, Mr Clifford, who took up his post in April 1999.

The 1999 inspection

4.18 The next visit made to Feltham by a team from the Inspectorate was a short inspection which took place between 28 and 30 September 1999. Again, it had not been announced beforehand. Mr Narey described the report which came out following this visit as "ludicrously over-optimistic", but that does not mean that there was not then light at the end of the tunnel. In his preface to the report, the Chief Inspector said that Feltham was a very different place from the one which his team had left nine months before. He referred to extra money which had been allocated to Feltham as a result of the action plan produced by the task force, to the easing of the overcrowding due to the imminent transfer of a number of prisoners to Chelmsford and the closure of some units for refurbishment, to the arrival of excellent senior members of staff who were transforming physical education and other educational activities, to the move of the healthcare centre to a refurbished unit, and to an improved commitment to change among management and staff. What he described as the "disgraceful warehousing arrangements" for remand prisoners had been eliminated. He referred to the completion of a new staff profiling exercise, intended to bring about a more efficient use of staff, which was due to be introduced, and he confirmed that a subsequent visit had shown that this was working. More staff were available on residential units, which the Chief Inspector said must have had a positive impact on the treatment of young offenders. No doubt he assumed that this would result in them getting more time out of their cells.

4.19 But the Chief Inspector also referred to the continuing concerns he had about Feltham. The one he highlighted was the need to recruit additional staff against the background of the high cost of housing and comparatively low unemployment in the London area. He was concerned that the concentration on recruitment for the juvenile side of Feltham required by the impending handover of responsibility for juveniles to the Youth Justice Board should not be at the expense of recruitment for the young offenders' side of Feltham. He was also concerned that the initiatives which had been put in place as a result of the action plan produced by the task force had not yet produced tangible results. Thus he said:

"A great deal has been achieved as far as creating a platform from which real progress can be made, and recovering what had been lost. I [say] real progress [can be made] because, while plans and resources are there, they have not yet been converted into real and visible improvements in the treatment of and conditions for young prisoners."

The next time the Inspectorate reported on Feltham was some time after Zahid's death.

Feltham's Board of Visitors

4.20 The Inspectorate's concerns about Feltham were shared to some extent by Feltham's Board of Visitors. It was regarded as a model of how a Board of Visitors should behave. It was praised for its high profile within the establishment and for its commitment. Its annual reports tended to be couched in far less dramatic language than those of the Inspectorate, but its anxieties still came through. In its annual report for 1997, it endorsed "most" of the report which the Inspectorate had produced following the 1996 inspection. It too recognised that the expansion in Feltham's population had put considerable pressure on the establishment's ability to provide a decent regime for its prisoners. It was particularly concerned about the problem of "doubling up", stating that "the proximity of lavatories to bedheads in cells designed for single occupancy is entirely unacceptable in a civilised society".

4.21 Its annual report for 1998 was published before the damning report following the Inspectorate's 1998 inspection had been published. The Board's report acknowledged that staff had continued to do their best in an atmosphere of considerable uncertainty about how the new arrangements for juveniles would impact on the institution as a whole, and it praised staff and management for their dedication in looking after some of the most difficult and disadvantaged young men in the country. But it described the staffing problems as severe, and said that this had had a deleterious impact on staff morale. It noted that low staffing levels had resulted in prisoners having little time out of their cells. In some instances, this had gone down to as little as an hour a day. It rightly described that as "unacceptable".

4.22 Its annual report for 1999 was published after the Board had seen a draft of the Inspectorate's report following its 1999 inspection. The Board was pleased that the Inspectorate's very negative report following the 1998 inspection had at last galvanised the Prison Service into taking action to address Feltham's long-standing problems, and it agreed with the Chief Inspector that much had changed for the better over the previous six months. But it returned to its themes of recent years – the use of "doubling up" and the lack of time out of cells. It regarded the introduction of the new profiling exercise as a positive step towards increasing the opportunities for prisoners to engage in purposeful activity and towards getting them out of their cells, as well as enabling meals to be taken at less inappropriate times. But it was concerned that the profiling exercise had caused uncertainty and low morale among some staff. It had been introduced speedily, and some members of staff had found the change unsettling. The Board thought that this was why a large number of officers were applying for transfer out of Feltham. Finally, the Board was concerned that Mr Clifford, who it will be recalled had arrived at Feltham in April 1999, would be leaving Feltham soon following his "well-deserved" promotion to Area Manager. (In fact, Mr Clifford left Feltham in May 2000.) Plainly Mr Clifford had impressed the Board. It said: "He backs his perceptions with active knowledge and understanding." But his departure after only a short time at Feltham meant that there would be a regrettable lack of continuity at the senior end of the management team, which was hardly appropriate when "severe staffing difficulties [continued to] persist".

4.23 This, then, was the institution in which Zahid found himself early in 2000.

Chapter 5: A life cut short

Zahid's family

5.1 Zahid came from a large and close-knit family. They trace their roots back to Pakistan. Zahid's grandfather served in the Engineering Corps in the Pakistani army. With his wife, he came to Walthamstow in East London in about 1960. That is where the family have lived ever since.

5.2 Zahid was the eldest of three children. He was born in October 1980. He was followed by twin boys. His father has worked in the same factory, ultimately as a manager, for 28 years. He has five brothers and sisters. No member of the family, save for a remote cousin, had been in trouble with the police before things began to go wrong for Zahid. The family are Muslims. They are religious but not devout.

Zahid's upbringing

5.3 Zahid went to local primary and secondary schools. He was due to take five GCSEs in the summer of 1997, and was planning to go to a sixth-form college. He was particularly talented at art, he played cricket and football, he represented his school at athletics and went weight training. But Zahid was said by his school not to be making the most of his artistic and athletic skills, and despite support from his family, there was a problem with his attendance at school. Indeed, his father believes that Zahid was struggling academically.

5.4 The first real sign that Zahid was going off the rails came when, out of the blue, he was expelled from school. He was then 15. One pre-sentence report on him subsequently said that this was because he had been seen breaking into a classroom, an allegation which Zahid resolutely denied. Another pre-sentence report on him said that he had been expelled for fighting with another pupil. Whatever the reason for the expulsion, it caused a great deal of friction within the family – particularly as Zahid's parents had wanted him to go on to higher education. Arrangements for him to go to another school did not materialise, and he did not take any of his GCSEs.

5.5 However, Zahid did go on a one-year course with the Prince's Trust at a local college. The course included basic training of the kind which army recruits undergo and techniques in confidence-building. According to his father, Zahid had enjoyed the course so much that he had set his heart on joining the army. He began a course for people interested in public service, but withdrew from it at the end of the first term because he had by then turned to drugs and his use of them was affecting his performance.

5.6 Zahid told the author of one of the pre-sentence reports on him about his use of drugs. He said that he had been using cannabis and heroin since his last year at school. "Friends" had introduced him to drugs, and soon he had become dependent on heroin. He had thought that he could control it. He later realised that he could not. His expenditure on drugs had got to £20 a day. Regrettably, this scenario is not an unfamiliar one.

Zahid's offending behaviour

5.7 Zahid's offending history began when he was 15. On 16 January 1997, he was ordered to attend an attendance centre for 15 hours for possessing an imitation firearm with intent to cause fear of violence. Although he was 16 when he was sentenced, he had been 15 when the offence was committed. According to what Zahid told the author of the pre-sentence report on him, his brothers and his cousin were being subjected to racist abuse by someone who had similarly abused Zahid a couple of days earlier. She wrote that while Zahid's parents' generation might have walked away from prejudice of that kind, boys of Zahid's age found it more difficult. Since the complainant had a claw-hammer, Zahid armed himself with a replica gun and threatened the complainant with it.

5.8 Zahid's subsequent brushes with the law occurred in order to fund his growing dependence on drugs. Over a period of less than 10 months, he committed a total of 11 offences. On 14 April 1999, he was cautioned for two offences of handling stolen goods on 31 March 1999. He was back in court on 15 July 1999, when he pleaded guilty to an offence of theft by shoplifting on 7 July 1999. He had committed this offence while on bail for a similar offence committed on 30 March 1999, and of which he was convicted on 6 August 1999 after pleading not guilty. On 29 July 1999, again while on bail for those offences, he committed an offence of interfering with a motor vehicle in an attempt to remove audio equipment, to which he pleaded guilty on 24 September 1999. Sentencing for all these offences was adjourned to 19 October 1999, partly so that he could be assessed by the community drugs team, and partly to face a further charge of shoplifting, for which no evidence was eventually offered.

5.9 Before then, and while he continued to be on bail for the three offences for which he was awaiting sentence, Zahid committed four further offences. Two were for interfering with a motor vehicle, and the other two were for going equipped for the purposes of theft. Those sets of offences were committed on 25 September 1999 – the day after he appeared in court – and 1 October 1999 respectively. Zahid also failed to keep four appointments which had been made for him to meet members of the community drugs team and other agencies. On 19 October 1999, the court adjourned his case to give him another opportunity to be assessed for his suitability for a community sentence. Again he failed to keep a number of his appointments. On 16 November 1999, the court yet again adjourned his case to give him a final opportunity to be assessed for his suitability for a community sentence. Although he began to keep some of the appointments made for him, albeit turning up two hours late for one of them, he missed several others. He did not go to court at all on 16 December 1999, the day to which the earlier hearing had been adjourned. Not surprisingly, a warrant was issued for his arrest. Zahid was later to say that he had not thought he had to go to court on 16 December 1999. He had thought that he had only been due to go to court on 14 January 2000 for the trial of the charges relating to the offences allegedly committed on 1 October 1999 to which he was pleading not guilty.

5.10 Even then, Zahid did not go to court on 14 January 2000 for his trial. He was convicted of the two charges in his absence. He was later to say that he had gone to court that day, but had arrived after his case had been dealt with. As it was, he was arrested the following day in connection with two further offences which he had committed earlier that day: an offence of attempted theft, and an offence of handling a pair of stolen jeans. He appeared in court on 17 January 2000. The court took the view that the continuing nature of his offending, and his failure to respond to the opportunities he had been offered to show that a community sentence would be appropriate, made custodial sentences inevitable. He was sentenced as follows:

Date of offence	Offence	Sentence
30 March 1999	Theft	21 days' detention in a young offender institution
7 July 1999	Theft	21 days' detention in a young offender institution
29 July 1999	Interfering with a motor vehicle	60 days' detention in a young offender institution
1 October 1999	Interfering with a motor vehicle	60 days' detention in a young offender institution
1 October 1999	Going equipped for theft	90 days' detention in a young offender institution

These terms were to be served concurrently, and therefore amounted to 90 days' detention in a young offender institution in all. He was advised by his solicitors that there were no grounds for appealing against his sentence.

5.11 Over the next few weeks, Zahid went to court on a number of occasions in connection with the offences alleged to have been committed on 25 September 1999 and 15 January 2000. His trial on these charges had been delayed because he was pleading not guilty to some of them. In the end, he was either convicted of, or pleaded guilty to, all of them. Eventually, on 28 February 2000, he was sentenced as follows:

Date of offence	Offence	Sentence
25 September 1999	Going equipped for theft	3 months' detention in a young offender institution
25 September 1999	Interfering with a motor vehicle	3 months' detention in a young offender institution
15 January 2000	Attempted theft	3 months' detention in a young offender institution
15 January 2000	Handling stolen goods	2 months' detention in a young offender institution

All these terms were to be served concurrently, and therefore amounted to 90 days' detention in a young offender institution in all. They were also to be served concurrently with his earlier sentence. Accordingly, Zahid's new sentence of 90 days' detention was to begin immediately, and not after he had served the whole of his earlier sentence. His release date, taking into account the time he had been detained in police custody, was subsequently calculated as 21 March 2000. He was again advised by his solicitors that there were no grounds for appealing against this sentence.

5.12 The only reason why I have set out Zahid's offending history at such length is because of the suggestion made by some that he should not have received a custodial sentence at all. I leave it to others to say whether that is right or not. Maybe his failure to keep his appointments was a symptom of his drug abuse, and an indication that he did not then have the resolve to rid himself of his habit. Maybe he was just hiding his head in the sand and hoping that his problems with the law would simply go away. Some people might say that his unwillingness to co-operate in the search for a suitable community sentence made such a sentence impossible. Others might argue that there was still room for a community sentence in his case. But if the debate is to continue about the appropriateness of his sentence, that debate should be an informed one, with everyone knowing the full picture.

Zahid's time at Feltham

5.13 Zahid served the whole of his sentence at Feltham. Although he was eligible for release on home detention curfew, he was not released early because of the relatively short time he would have been able to benefit from the scheme. He spent his first night on Lapwing, the induction unit. He was then moved to Nightingale. He was there for four nights, and he moved to Swallow on 22 January 2000. Swallow had 38 cells, 19 on each side of the interconnecting office. Zahid was allocated to cell 38, which was on the upper level. It was a double cell. He and Stewart shared the cell together from 8 February 2000 until the night of the attack.

5.14 Zahid shared the cell with another prisoner, G, before Stewart arrived on the unit, but it is not clear for how long that was. The daily record of prisoners' movements on Swallow, known as the roll and movements sheet, shows that G was taken out of cell 38 on the morning of 8 February 2000 and that Stewart was put in there later that day. In a statement which he made to the police, G said that he shared a cell with Zahid "for about two weeks". What is not clear is whether G was already in cell 38 when Zahid was put in there on 22 January, or whether he joined Zahid there a few days later. The former is the more likely, because the roll and movement sheets for Swallow provided to the Inquiry begin on 20 January 2000, and there is no roll and movement sheet which shows G being placed in cell 38.

A computerised print-out based on information supplied to the Control and Information Room is unhelpful because it did not state that Zahid had been sharing cell 38 with G for even part of the time prior to 8 February 2000.

5.15 On one occasion, Zahid was visited by the Imam, Abdul Qureshi. He wanted to encourage Zahid to go to Friday prayers. The impression he got was that Zahid was uncertain about whether to go or not. His recollection is that Zahid said that he had "a problem" with a couple of the inmates who used to go. If these were people Zahid had known before going to Feltham, perhaps he was trying to break his links with those who had introduced him to drugs. In the event, Zahid did not go to Friday prayers while he was at Feltham.

5.16 There has not been the slightest suggestion that Zahid was anything other than a well-behaved prisoner who presented no problems for staff or other inmates. In that respect, he was said to have stood out from other prisoners. He was variously described by the officers on Swallow as a good-natured, polite and very likeable young man, who would go out of his way to chat with officers. The only negative comments about him related to occasions when he had to be asked a number of times to come off the telephone, and when he had to be taken off his pre-release course because he was not doing his work and was distracting other prisoners. His family were supportive. They visited him a number of times, the last time being on the Sunday before he was due to be released.

5.17 Having said that, there was no particular need to treat Zahid with kid gloves. If the one surviving letter which he wrote to another prisoner is anything to go by, Zahid was not a naïve and vulnerable young man. He called himself "Out Lawz" and gave the impression of being able to look after himself. The letters he received suggested that this was not simply bravado. His correspondent thought that Zahid was streetwise – not surprisingly, given his lifestyle over the previous year or so.

5.18 In the six weeks that Zahid and Stewart shared cell 38, they spent almost all of their time there. Stewart would have left their cell only to go to the gym, to collect his meals, to have a shower or for such little association as he was allowed. That would have been the same for Zahid once he had been taken off his pre-release course. Stewart says that he spent 23 hours a day there. That is what he also said at his trial. The hiking officer for Swallow, who was the officer responsible, amongst other things, for monitoring the occasions on which prisoners were allowed out of their cells for association, thought this was a fair assessment, although he added that the amount of time for association would differ from day to day because it was dependent on how many staff were on duty. The more staff there were, the more association prisoners had. Estimates from the officers who worked on Swallow varied, but the thrust of the evidence was that prisoners who were not leaving the unit for classes or other purposeful activity were unlikely to spend much more than two hours a day out of their cells. And they would have had virtually no opportunity for exercise in the open air. Mr Clifford said that Stewart's claim that he had spent 23 hours a day in his cell was an exaggeration, but he accepted that time out of cells at that time was nowhere near the then target of 10 hours a day.

5.19 Stewart had been brought up in the Manchester area. He had come from a young offender institution in the North of England. He had been brought to Feltham because he faced charges in a London court. He was a prolific writer of letters. In one of them, he claimed that he had applied for a number of visiting orders naming Adolf Hitler, Charles Manson and Harold Shipman as his proposed visitors. In fact he received no visits from anyone. Maybe he never asked for visiting orders for members of his family or his friends, as it would have been too difficult and expensive for them to visit him. Nor did he attend any classes, although according to him he had applied to be included in them, and had been placed on a waiting list. He went to court on 7 and 8 March 2000. On each occasion, he returned to cell 38 at the end of the day. He remained in cell 38 with Zahid until the night of the attack.

Chapter 6: The night of the attack

Lock up

6.1 At the time of the attack on Zahid, the hiking officer used to complete a form for each of the units in the cluster for which he was responsible. The form was the checklist and handover sheet. Swallow was in the same cluster of units as Kestrel and Osprey. The sheet for 20 March 2000 shows that four officers were due to be on duty that afternoon in Swallow, three in Osprey and two in Kestrel. But it also shows that two of those nine officers had to be sent elsewhere. One went to supervise visits and another to education. That left seven officers for the three units. That was not a sufficient number for all three units to have association, and the sheet records that no association took place on Swallow that afternoon. Leaving aside those prisoners who were engaged in purposeful activity that afternoon, prisoners would only have been let out of their cells after lunch in order to collect their evening meals and take them back to their cells. That could have been as early as 5.00 pm. They would not be allowed out of their cells again that day.

6.2 A check on the cells, known as a roll check, was carried out at about 5.45 pm. The officer who checked cell 38 was Stephen Skinner. It was one of the last things he did before he went off duty. He looked through the perspex window in the door of the cell. Both Zahid and Stewart were there. Mr Skinner noticed nothing out of the ordinary.

6.3 The checklist and handover sheet shows that three officers were due to be on duty that evening in Swallow, one in Kestrel and one in Osprey, before the night staff came on duty at 9.00 pm. But it also shows that one of those five officers was sent to reception to help out there, and that another had to fulfil a "response" role, which required him to respond to any incident in the establishment. The officer who remained on duty in Swallow was Elizabeth Billimore. One of her functions was to carry out the last roll check of the day before the unit was handed over to the night staff. She did that roll check shortly before going off duty at 8.45 pm. She was required to get some reaction from each prisoner, whether physical or verbal, to ensure that they were in their cells. When she got to cell 38, she saw Stewart and Zahid on their beds, Zahid being in his bed with his blanket up to his shoulders. Zahid asked her for a newspaper. She told him that the newspapers had all been given out. She then proceeded on her way. She had not noticed anything unusual.

6.4 Despite what was shown on the checklist and handover sheet, there was one other officer on duty that evening in Swallow. His evidence is not all that easy to fit in with Miss Billimore's. That is the evidence of

Lee Edmundson. He was due to go off duty at the same time as Miss Billimore that evening. He recalls going to cell 38 to speak to Zahid and Stewart at about 8.30 pm. He knew that Zahid was due to be released the next morning, and he thought that Stewart was due to be moved to another unit. He thinks that Zahid was sitting on his bed, and that Stewart was sitting by the table. He gave them a newspaper and said goodbye, wishing Zahid good luck and telling him to stay out of trouble. They both seemed to be in good spirits.

6.5 At first blush, this does not square with Zahid asking Miss Billimore for a newspaper, and led to it being suggested that Mr Edmundson was trying to distance the officers on the unit from any responsibility for what happened later that night by trying to paint a picture of harmony between Stewart and Zahid that evening. He had read Miss Billimore's statement to the police which had referred to Zahid's request for a newspaper, and he had decided to embellish it. I do not go along with that suggestion. I do not think that Miss Billimore's account is necessarily inconsistent with that of Mr Edmundson. Mr Edmundson could have given them a newspaper, and the request to Miss Billimore could have been for another. Alternatively, it could be that there had not been a newspaper to hand when Miss Billimore did her roll check, but that shortly afterwards Mr Edmundson had found one to give to them. The former is the more likely because the night patrol officer on duty that night in Swallow, Malcolm Nicholson, told the police that Stewart and Zahid had asked him for a newspaper when he had come on duty.

The night patrol

6.6 The night patrol officers came on duty at 9.00 pm. Since nothing was likely to happen at night with all the prisoners locked up in their cells, only one night patrol officer would be on duty in each unit. The unit was said to be on "patrol state". Mr Nicholson was not a trained prison officer, but an operational support grade. He had been in post for only 10 months, and his training for the job had been rudimentary. He was in charge of the 59 prisoners on Swallow that night. He had never encountered anything remotely similar to what was to happen later on.

6.7 The duties of the night patrol officer were covered by Feltham Operational Order No. 11, which came into force on 1 February 2000. The night patrol officer was required to patrol the unit every half-hour. In order to ensure that a unit was properly patrolled, switches were strategically located throughout the unit. They were called pegs. There were six in all in Swallow – three on each side. One switch was on the far side on the ground floor, and the other two were at either end of the first floor landing. Those switches were supposed to be tripped by the night patrol officer as he did his rounds. Each switch was linked to a computerised clock in the administrative section which recorded the fact that the switch had been tripped. The clock did not record the exact time at which the switch was tripped, but rather the half-hour during which it was done. The clock was linked to a printer which could produce a print-out of which switches had been tripped and when.

6.8 The operational order provided:

"Pegging will be done twice per hour between the hours of 22.00 and 6.00. On each occasion two pegs will be made on each side of the unit, one on each level. Pegs may be missed once during the period for the purpose of a meal break…"

The purpose of this provision must have been to allow the night patrol officer to have a one-hour meal break between the hours of 10.00 pm and 6.00 am, but its effect was to enable him to take a longer break if he timed things to his advantage. For example, he could trip the switches at 1.01 am, thus covering the period between 1.00 am and 1.30 am, and trip the switches again at 2.29 am, thus covering the period between 2.00 am and 2.30 am, missing only the period between 1.30 am and 2.00 am. He could thus take a break for almost one-and-a-half hours. Timing things right could also result in the night patrol officer taking breaks of almost an hour at other times in the night.

6.9 Moreover, the requirement to trip only two switches on each side meant that it was possible for a night patrol officer to avoid patrolling the whole of the first floor landings. He could trip the switch on the ground floor and the one at one end of the first floor landing. Since cell 38 was itself at the end of the landing, it was possible for the switch at the other end of the landing to be tripped as well as the one on the ground floor. In that way, the requisite number of switches could be tripped without the night patrol officer going past cell 38 at all.

6.10 It looks as if Mr Nicholson did not follow the operational order to the letter. The print-out for that night shows two periods prior to the attack on Zahid during which the switches were not tripped on Swallow: 12.30–1.00 am and 2.30–3.00 am. Indeed, Mr Nicholson told the police that he thought he was entitled to take two breaks in the course of the night. And if the switches on one side of Swallow were numbers 49–51, and the switches on the other side numbers 52–54, the print-out shows that Mr Nicholson tripped all three switches on one side in each period, and none of the switches on the other side. However, the print-out covers nine residential units, as well as Waite and the segregation unit, and it is plain that Mr Nicholson was not alone in patrolling in a manner which was not entirely in accordance with the operational order. Some of the other night patrol officers took more breaks than Mr Nicholson – for example, the night patrol officer on Mallard – and others followed his practice of visiting each side of the unit in different periods – for example, the night patrol officer on Lapwing. Moreover, when asked by the police to evaluate Mr Nicholson's performance as revealed by the print-out, Peter Taylor, the principal officer responsible for the night pegging system, said that he thought that Mr Nicholson had completed his responsibilities satisfactorily. This suggests that minor departures from the operational order were not regarded as significant. Even that assumes that the terms of the operational order – which had been implemented only seven weeks earlier – had been brought to the attention of the night patrol officers.

6.11 At night, the lights in Swallow were operated by a sensor which turned the lights on if movement was detected. There were a number of CCTV cameras in Swallow. They recorded images only. There was no sound. The videotape from the camera which covered the group of cells including cell 38 was viewed by the police, and it showed a blank screen – apart from about 10 seconds when the lights came on in the unit – until the lights came on shortly after the attack. That appeared to suggest that Mr Nicholson was not doing his rounds. But the sensor could be over-ridden by a switch in the unit's office which would prevent the movement of the night patrol officer doing his rounds from making the lights go on. And in one of the statements which Mr Nicholson gave to the police, he said that his practice was to turn the sensor off so as not to disturb the prisoners when he did his rounds, and to enable him to check the cells without them knowing that he was coming. He was not the only night patrol officer who did that: the CRE reported that several night patrol officers did the same thing. Thus, the fact that the CCTV footage did not show Mr Nicholson patrolling the unit does not mean that he did not do so, especially as the print-out shows when he tripped the switches on his patrols.

6.12 The operational order did not expressly require night patrol officers to check the cells by opening the flap in the door and looking in through the perspex window as they did their rounds. The need to do that was, I think, implicit in the requirement to patrol the unit, since that requirement would otherwise be rendered largely meaningless. But it is worth noting that the operational order expressly required *the dormitories* to be checked "at least six times a night and at irregular intervals by switching on the night light". It would have been better for the operational order to have spelt out an explicit requirement to check *the cells* in some way as well. As it was, Mr Nicholson's practice was to speak to all the prisoners on his first round. If he had a good rapport with them, they were less likely to cause trouble in the night. His practice was also to check the cells occasionally on his later rounds. But he admitted to both Mr Butt and the CRE that he did not check the cells every time he did his rounds. Perhaps he would have done so if the operational order had said in specific terms that night patrol officers should do so.

The alarm goes up

6.13 Each cell had a switch which activated a buzzer in the unit's office and caused the light outside the cell to go on. At about 3.35 am, the buzzer went off. Mr Nicholson was in the office at the time. He could not have known then that it was the buzzer in cell 38 which had been pressed. The equipment in the office would only have told him which side of the unit and what part of that side the cell was in. Thinking that it was the usual request for toilet paper, he picked up a roll and went into the part of the unit in which the buzzer had been pressed. Seeing that the light outside cell 38 was on, that was the cell he went to. It took him less than a minute to get there. According to Stewart, Mr Nicholson arrived almost immediately after he had pressed the buzzer.

6.14 Some prisoners told the police that they had heard screaming during the night. But they disagree as to when they heard it, and some of the prisoners said that it was not unusual anyway. Stewart himself told the Inquiry that Zahid did not scream when he was attacked. According to Mr Nicholson, the office door was ajar. He was listening to the radio – a chat show, not music. It was at a volume which enabled him to hear it without it drowning out those sounds from the unit which should be heard in the office. As it was, the police carried out acoustic tests which showed that someone in the office would have been unlikely to hear anything from cell 38, whether or not the volume of the radio was at the level which might have been expected. In the circumstances, I do not think that Mr Nicholson can be criticised for failing to respond earlier than he did.

6.15 When Mr Nicholson opened the flap in the door, he saw Stewart standing slightly to one side, holding what appeared to be a stick in his hand. Zahid was lying on his bed. Stewart said that Zahid had had an accident. Mr Nicholson looked down at Zahid and saw that he was covered in blood. He realised that Zahid's injuries were serious, but it did not occur to him that they might be life-threatening. He did not go into the cell. It was forbidden for an officer to go into a cell with two prisoners in case the officer was being set up. So he called for help. He did not do so on his personal radio which he had with him. That is what he should have done, because that would have resulted in the call going out for assistance sooner, and would have enabled Mr Nicholson to keep Stewart under observation until reinforcements arrived. And his continued presence there might have discouraged Stewart from attacking Zahid again if that was something he was contemplating. Mr Nicholson told Mr Butt that what he had seen threw him. Plainly his training had not prepared him for an emergency of this kind. Instead, he ran back to the office, turned the lights on in the unit and telephoned the Control and Information Room for assistance. It looks as if he did not say why assistance was needed or how urgent the need for that assistance was. As he told the police, "my mind was racing a bit". That again points to the inadequacy of the training he had received. He says that he had to call the Control and Information Room for assistance a second time before help came, but only one call was recorded on the Control and Information Room's log, and that was timed at 3.40 am.

6.16 Gerard McAlaney was the first officer to arrive. He was the senior officer on night duty that week. He told the police that he was catching up with some paperwork when he was told by the Control and Information Room via his personal radio to contact Swallow. He was in the process of doing that when another message came through on his personal radio for officers whose job it was that night to respond to incidents to go to Swallow immediately. So he went to the unit at once. It took him about 30 seconds to get there. He gave the Inquiry a slightly different version of events. He said that he had already set off for Swallow when the second call came through. Whichever version is correct, though, the thrust of the evidence is that the Control and Information Room first asked Mr McAlaney to go to the unit, and the officers who formed the response team that night were then asked to go.

6.17 When Mr McAlaney got to Swallow, he found Mr Nicholson "in a bit of a flap". Mr Nicholson told him to go to cell 38. While Mr McAlaney was looking into the cell through the window, he was aware of other officers joining them. The light in the cell was on. Stewart was standing there. He told Stewart to move to the back of the cell and drop the table leg he was holding. Stewart did so, and Mr McAlaney then went into the cell. He told Stewart to go outside the cell where other officers held Stewart, and he turned his attention to Zahid. He could see that Zahid was badly injured. He instructed the other officers to get Stewart out of there, and he called for medical assistance from the healthcare centre on his personal radio. Everyone agrees that there was little to be done for Zahid in terms of first aid when medical assistance arrived. He was breathing and not bleeding heavily, but he was obviously seriously injured.

6.18 Stewart was taken to an empty cell in Swallow. Mr McAlaney went to see him there. As he went in he saw Stewart washing himself in the basin, presumably to remove Zahid's blood. He said to Stewart: "It's a bit late for that." Stewart's response was to say that it was obvious that it was him. When Mr McAlaney asked Stewart why he had attacked Zahid, Stewart replied: "I don't even know myself." His clothing was removed for forensic examination, and after he had been given a new set of clothes, he was taken to the segregation unit. While there, he used the heel of his boot to scrawl a swastika on the wall, along with the words "Manchester just killed me padmate". Throughout it all, Stewart was described as quiet and calm. Indeed, within about 30 minutes of the attack, he was apparently asleep in his cell in the segregation unit. When he was woken up and told that the police had come to speak to him, he said: "Why? What have I done?"

6.19 The healthcare officer in the healthcare centre who responded to the call for medical assistance was Sally Berry. She had heard the two calls put out by the Control and Information Room, but she understandably responded only when the call came for medical assistance. It would have been more appropriate for the nurse on duty, Essa Green, to respond, but the call for medical assistance had not used the appropriate code for a serious injury for when a nurse, as opposed to a healthcare officer, was required. Ms Berry assumed that officers were moving a violent prisoner to the segregation unit, it being standard procedure for a healthcare officer to supervise such transfers. By the time Ms Berry got to cell 38, an ambulance had already been called by Graham Davies, a principal officer who, as the night orderly officer, was the most senior member of staff in the prison that night. The ambulance left Feltham at 4.36 am to take Zahid to Ashford General Hospital in Middlesex. He was later transferred to Charing Cross Hospital in Central London, where he died on 28 March 2000.

6.20 There is some uncertainty over how long it took Ms Berry to get to the scene. Mr McAlaney says that he had to call for medical assistance from the healthcare centre two or three times before she arrived. He says that when she arrived, he tackled her on why it had taken her so long, and according to him her answer was simply that it was a long walk. On the other hand, she says that there was nothing in either of the two calls she got which led her to believe that her presence was urgently required, and no-one asked her how long it had taken her to get to the unit. The log recorded the ambulance as having arrived at the prison gates at 3.55 am. Mr Nicholson's request for assistance was recorded as having been made at 3.40 am, and Ms Berry says – and there is other evidence to support it – that she had been on the scene giving Zahid first aid for some time before the paramedics arrived in Swallow at 4.00 am. Bearing in mind the distance between where the healthcare centre then was and Swallow, and the need for Ms Berry to collect her emergency medical kit, Mr Butt's assessment was that Ms Berry arrived on the scene about eight minutes after being called to attend. As it happens, that is also her own estimate of how long it took her to get to Swallow from the healthcare centre, bearing in mind the number of locked gates she had had to pass through. She could not have taken long because she recalls – although the recollection of other officers is different – that when she arrived at cell 38 Stewart had not yet been taken to another cell; he was being held outside it.

6.21 Mr Nicholson and Ms Berry were originally requested to give oral evidence to the Inquiry. However, I subsequently decided that that would not be necessary, and the Interested Parties agreed. There is nothing whatever to suggest that, if Mr Nicholson's patrolling of Swallow that night had been more frequent and had involved checks on what Stewart was doing in cell 38, he would have sensed what Stewart was going to do. Nor is there anything to suggest that if the response of staff had been slightly quicker – for example, if Mr Nicholson had got in touch with the Control and Information Room via his personal radio rather than returning to the office, or if Mr McAlaney had used the appropriate code for a serious injury, or if Ms Berry had got to cell 38 sooner – that could have made any difference to Zahid's chances of survival. Nor is there anything to suggest that Stewart did anything more to Zahid while Mr Nicholson had gone back to the office. In short, there is no reason to think that a different response would have saved Zahid's life. Indeed, it is arguable that the post-attack responses of staff did not come within the Inquiry's terms of reference – which relate to the events *leading up* to the attack on Zahid. In these circumstances, I decided, along with everyone's agreement, that these issues would not be investigated further with a view to anyone being criticised over them.

6.22 The same applies to Feltham's contingency plans for dealing with an incident of this kind. Mr Butt described them as outdated, and he thought that their usefulness was extremely limited. They were in the course of being re-written at the time, but the work had not been completed. It is doubtful whether the effectiveness of Feltham's response to the attack comes within the Inquiry's terms of reference – which focus on events leading up to the attack. In any event, there is nothing to suggest that Zahid's chances of surviving the attack would have been any different.

It was therefore agreed that the Inquiry would not be investigating this topic at all.

The night patrol sheets

6.23 There are a couple of other things about the events of that night which I should mention. Night patrol officers were required to complete a night patrol sheet on which they had to state any period during which they had not tripped the switches, the number of prisoners accounted for and any incidents which had occurred while they had been on duty. Mr Nicholson says that he completed the night patrol sheet that night in the usual way. Although he would normally hand it in when he went off duty, he did not do so that night because he could not find it when he left. He did not think much about it, because he assumed that it had either been seized by the police or got lost in the commotion. Mr Davies's evidence was that the police officer in charge of the investigation into the attack on Zahid took over the office which Mr Nicholson had been using, and the night patrol sheet might have got mixed up with her papers. It has never been found.

6.24 Keith Greenslade, the duty governor on call, was prepared to accept that it had been his responsibility when he arrived at Feltham that night to nominate someone to collate the paperwork. But the fact that he did not do so is hardly a matter for criticism. Mr Greenslade's focus was understandably on Stewart's and Zahid's files, rather than on documents relating to Swallow as a whole. In any event, the procedure to be followed when a prisoner is *seriously injured* said nothing about the collation of relevant documents. The only reference to documents was in the procedure to be followed on the *death* of a prisoner. Even then, there was nothing in that procedure relating to the *collation* of existing documents. It only required the night orderly officer to "ensure that all relevant documentation is *completed*, including incident forms and statements from all staff concerned", and that was what Mr Davies did. As it was, there can have been nothing sinister about the disappearance of the night patrol sheet for Swallow for that night. The key document for ascertaining whether Mr Nicholson had patrolled Swallow properly that night is the print-out recording which switches had been tripped and when, and that has of course survived.

6.25 The second thing to mention is that, although the night patrol sheets for that night for four of the other units have survived, the night patrol sheets for seven other units have not. No definitive explanation for this has been given, but one possibility considered by the CRE was based on the premise that night patrol officers tended not to make entries on the night patrol sheets as the night progressed as they should have done, but instead filled them in at the end of the shift. The suggestion canvassed by the CRE was that they had not even done that on the night in question because of the turmoil which the attack on Zahid had caused, and that they had got rid of the night patrol sheets altogether to conceal that. An equally plausible scenario is that the officer who would normally collect the night patrol sheets was otherwise engaged in dealing with the aftermath of the attack. But whatever happened, it had nothing to do with what led to the attack on Zahid, and I do not propose to consider the matter further.

The bigger picture

6.26 The death of Zahid at the hands of Stewart needs to be seen against the bigger picture. So far as the available information shows, homicides in custody in this country are relatively rare. Recent research published by the Home Office shows that in the 12 years from 1990 to 2001 inclusive there were 26 prisoner-on-prisoner homicides in England and Wales. That was a significant increase in the rate of such homicides when compared with the 16 prisoner-on-prisoner homicides which a previous study found had occurred in the 16 years from 1972 to 1987 inclusive. In effect, the rate of occurrence increased from an average of one a year to an average of just over two a year. It may be that the figures should be slightly larger, because a number of cases in which prisoners were found hanged in their cells were originally believed to be suicides, but were later classified as homicides in the light of further evidence. So it is possible that some other homicides were wrongly identified as suicides. Nevertheless, when one looks at the whole of the prison population, which varied in the 1990s between about 45,000 and 65,000, the number of prisoner-on-prisoner homicides is small. Even smaller are the number of homicides of prisoners by their cellmates. Of the 26 prisoner-on-prisoner homicides between 1990 and 2001, 12 occurred in a shared cell. In all, save possibly for one, the killer was the victim's cellmate. In another case, the victim was killed by his cellmate but outside his cell. There were another two cell-sharing homicides in 2003, and there was a further one in 2004. The 26 homicides between 1990 and 2001 can be contrasted with 759 cases over the same period in which prisoners committed suicide. That is a big number, and involves loss of life on a large scale. That explains why, before the murder of Zahid, the Prison Service's focus was unquestionably directed towards those prisoners at risk of suicide or self-harm rather than towards those prisoners at risk of attack by their cellmate.

6.27 The relative infrequency of prisoner-on-prisoner homicides in the prison system in England and Wales is, of course, no consolation to Zahid's family. Any death in custody is a tragedy for the victim, their family and friends. The Prisons and Probation Ombudsman has said that, given the extent of compulsory cell-sharing, and the profile of the prison population with its growing proportion of dangerous and unpredictable offenders, some risk is inevitable, and that it is perhaps surprising that homicides occur in prison as rarely as they do. But even if it may be impossible to eliminate the risk of fatal attacks altogether, it remains the plain duty of the Prison Service to ensure that it does not expose people to that risk wilfully or carelessly, and to do what it reasonably can to avoid a prisoner being exposed to attack in the way in which Zahid was exposed.

Chapter 7: The paper trail

The record system

7.1 A central issue for the Inquiry has been the extent to which relevant information about Stewart was passed on throughout the prison system. The files which the prison system had on him contained forms of many types, and before we look at how Stewart was dealt with during his time in custody, an understanding of the forms which were used to record and relay useful information and intelligence about him is important.

7.2 The system for keeping records on prisoners which was in operation at the time of Stewart's attack on Zahid had been introduced in 1990. It was known as the Inmate Personal Record System. Stewart's files, and Zahid's for that matter, were supposed to be kept and maintained in accordance with that system. All the files on Stewart which the Inquiry has were provided to us by the police. They had seized them all at Feltham following the attack. So at the time of the attack, all of Stewart's files had got to Feltham. None were still at the other establishments in which Stewart had been. With a couple of exceptions, the files on a prisoner were kept in the establishment's administrative section. Feltham's administrative section was known as Custody Administration. That was where most of Stewart's files were found.

The main prison file

7.3 The largest of the files on Stewart was his main prison file. That contained a number of smaller files and a collection of miscellaneous documents, such as property records, numeracy and literacy tests, court documents, calculations of release dates, print-outs of previous convictions, and documents which were generated when he was on the escape list – a list of prisoners thought to be likely to try and escape – and when he was kept under observation while he was thought to be at risk of self-harm. If Stewart's main prison file is anything to go by, it looks as if it was the repository for paperwork gathered on a prisoner throughout their time in prison, but not the place to keep documents relating to the prisoner's current sentence or their current spell in custody. The main prison file was not, therefore, intended for daily use. It was just too bulky and the documents and files contained within it were filed too haphazardly and non-chronologically for it to have been a useful working tool.

Files within the Inmate Personal Record System

7.4 There were a number of files within the Inmate Personal Record System which contained information about a prisoner. It is unnecessary to refer to them all. Some of them, like records of letters and visits (F2053s) or training records (F2055Cs), do not contain any information about Stewart's behaviour in prison which is useful for our purposes. I shall only mention those which do. What needs to be said is that all the files within the Inmate Personal Record System had to accompany the prisoner when they were transferred to another establishment. When they were released, the files would remain at the establishment at which the prisoner was last detained until they were either destroyed or sent to the Prison Service Records Registry. If the prisoner returned to custody, a request would have to be made for the files to be sent to where the prisoner was then being detained, and married up with any new files which were opened on the prisoner.

The core record (F2050)

7.5 The core record was a folder in which personal information about the prisoner was recorded. It would be opened at reception and then sent to the establishment's administrative section, where details of the current charge faced by the prisoner, any further court appearance, or the prisoner's current offence and sentence, would be recorded. Documents relating to the prisoner which subsequently came to the administrative section were added to the core record using treasury tags, although these might go into the prisoner's main prison file instead.

The custodial documents file (F2051)

7.6 The warrants issued by the court authorising the prisoner's detention were kept in the custodial documents file. The file would be opened in reception when the prisoner was first remanded in custody, and subsequent warrants would be added as and when they were issued.

Record of events (F2052A)

7.7 The F2052A was called a number of different things. The most accurate description of them was wing files, because they were supposed to be kept on the wings where the prisoners were, and had to accompany them whenever they went to another wing. But they were also called history sheets and compacts, and at Feltham they were known as flimsies. They represented a running record about each prisoner, and were supposed to be used to record anything of significance about them. A new wing file was supposed to be opened in reception whenever a prisoner came back to prison for new offences, and there were many wing files opened on Stewart. The wing file which was being used at the time of his attack on Zahid was found in the office in Swallow.

Adjudication record (F2050E)

7.8 The adjudication record contained details of a prisoner's charges and punishments arising from breaches of prison discipline. A new adjudication record was opened whenever a prisoner came back to prison for new offences, and there were many such records opened on Stewart.

Self-harm at risk form (F2052SH)

7.9 A self-harm at risk form was to be opened when it was thought that a prisoner may be suicidal or at risk of self-harm. It enabled a continuous record to be kept about the prisoner's mood and behaviour and about any action taken to help the prisoner. One was opened for Stewart in November 1997.

Information of special importance (F2050A)

7.10 Detailed information about a prisoner in the system which the Inmate Personal Record System replaced was contained in form 1150. Page 24 of that form provided for entries to be made relating to information of special importance. Once the new system was introduced, an information of special importance form was to be used in place of the form 1150. Entries in it were only to be made by, or on the authority of, the manager of the Security Department in a prison, the Senior Medical Officer* or a governor. Surprisingly, it was rarely used for Stewart. An information of special importance form was only completed on him twice.

---

* The Senior Medical Officer was responsible for the management of the healthcare centre. The role is being phased out now that Primary Care Trusts operating within the National Health Service are taking over responsibility for healthcare in prisons.

Security record (F2058)

7.11 The security record was always called the security file. It was to be opened only when a prisoner's background or behaviour made it necessary for the Security Department to maintain a dossier about them. It contained intelligence about the prisoner. It had a red cover to warn staff about the sensitivity of the information it contained. Documents were held in it with treasury tags. It was kept in the establishment's Security Department. Three were opened for Stewart at various times as he went through the prison system. If his security files are anything to go by, they consisted for the most part of security information reports.

7.12 Security information reports were an important means of passing information about a prisoner on to the Security Department. They could be written by any member of staff. Indeed, staff were encouraged to write them, because they were informed that all information was useful, however trivial it might seem to be. The information contained in the record had to be evaluated by a member of the Security Department for its reliability and accuracy. Four options for each were included, ranging from "very reliable" to "untried/very unreliable" and from "true without reservation" to "not known to be true".* The information then had to be assessed. From there it went to the manager of the Security Department for any further comment, and it then had to be signed off by a governor.

7.13 I confess that I was unimpressed by the quality of many entries in the various files relating to Stewart. They contained many inaccuracies, they were often incomplete, and they were frequently expressed in too generalised a way, so that the reader would not know what the writer's view was based on. Another problem was that documents were filed randomly in different files. There was no guarantee that you would find the document you were looking for in the file in which you were expecting it to be. But the most significant problem was that no attempt was apparently made to see whether any files or documents within a prisoner's main prison file might have a bearing on how a prisoner should be managed during their current sentence. That was particularly unfortunate in Stewart's case. Putting to one side the documents about him in his security files, most of the documents which recorded his disruptive and worrying behaviour before he got to Feltham were contained in his old wing files, which were themselves in Stewart's main prison file. So many of the documents which would have told prison officers about the things Stewart had got up to in the past were buried

---

* This was surprising. One might have expected the option which was the least accurate to be characterised as "known to be not true".

in a file which was far too bulky to expect anyone to have the time to go through it.

The inmate medical record

7.14 A medical record was opened for every prisoner when they arrived in prison. It contained all the documents generated by an establishment's healthcare centre on a prisoner while they were there. It could only be reviewed by medical staff, and so its contents were not available to non-medical staff in the establishment who were responsible for managing the prisoner on a daily basis. Documents were held in it with treasury tags. It too moved with prisoners when they were transferred to another establishment. When prisoners were released, it remained where they last were. If they came into the prison system again, it was sent to the establishment where they were being kept, and would be married up with the temporary medical record which would have been opened pending the arrival of the existing one.

Computerised information

7.15 A very surprising feature of the Prison Service's systems is how small a role computerised information was playing – even as late as the early part of 2000 when Stewart and Zahid were at Feltham. The statements given by prison officers to the Inquiry were almost universally consistent in their acceptance that computers played almost no part in their daily lives. That was perhaps a function of the limited amount of information about a prisoner which prison officers on the wings might have had access to. The information to which they might have had access was that on the Local Inmate Database System. This was a network system local to each establishment. It contained some personal data about prisoners, the details of their offences if they were known, information about when they were due to go to court, the cells to which they had been allocated, the sentences they were serving, their release dates, and whether a security file had been opened for them. There was also a single line available for additional text. The Inquiry was told that this usually related to medical or security information, although we saw no examples of that.

7.16 But it is by no means clear that in the early part of 2000 prison officers on wings had access even to the limited information on the Local Inmate Database System. We had no evidence about establishments other than Feltham. The evidence about Feltham was that each unit had a computer terminal, but that at some time previously – certainly before Mr Clifford's arrival at Feltham in April 1999 – it had been moved from the unit's office to the small office for the senior officer in charge of the unit.

7.17 Security Departments at a number of establishments had their own computerised programme. It could only be accessed by members of the Security Department. It was called the Security Intelligence System, but was colloquially known as the 4x4 system, because of the two sets of four options to be ticked in the security information report. It was a "stand-alone" system, in the sense that it was not joined up with Prison Service headquarters or any other establishment. In that respect the recommendation of the Learmont report on prison security in 1995 that there should be a national database for security information had not been implemented.

7.18 The 4x4 system produced a print-out known as an inmate intelligence card, which contained a summary of the information held on prisoners in their security files. For the most part, that information would have come from security information reports. However, the fact that the 4x4 system was not networked meant that there was not a database accessible by all establishments, nor was it possible to transfer the relevant information electronically. So when a prisoner arrived at an establishment, a member of staff in the Security Department would go through the security file which was supposed to arrive with the prisoner. They had to ensure that relevant information about the prisoner in the security file was entered onto the establishment's 4x4 system. What generally happened was that the information on the latest print-out would be treated as a sufficient summary of the contents of the security file at the time it had been printed. That information would then be entered onto the 4x4 system warts and all. Any security information reports or other relevant information which post-dated that information would then be added. A print-out would then be produced incorporating the contents of the previous print-out and the information which post-dated it. That print-out would then be placed at the front of the prisoner's security file, and was treated as the first port of call for anyone wanting to look at a prisoner's security file.

7.19 One of the central issues which the Inquiry has addressed has been the timely and accurate transmission of information about prisoners within the prison system. Did Feltham get the information which it should have got about Stewart? To answer that, it is necessary to look at how Stewart was managed during his many spells in custody. That is what Part 2 of the report addresses.

Part 2

Robert Stewart: "A Very Strange Young Man"

Chapter 8: Going wrong

Stewart's early life

8.1 Robert Stewart was born in August 1980. He lived in the Manchester area all his life, first in Middleton, and then moving to Hattersley when he was 13. His mother has said that he was quiet and reserved as a child. He avoided conflict with other members of his family, and showed little affection for them, though that may have been his response to his mother's admitted inability to be physically affectionate towards him. He would go into his shell and retreat to his bedroom. He had the potential to do well at school. At primary school he was top of his class, and he has himself said that he was good at logical things like problem-solving and maths. But he was unsettled at school. There were instances of anti-social and destructive behaviour, including setting fires and flooding. Indeed, his mother has said that he had been fascinated with fires since childhood. When he was eight, a child psychiatrist noted that he was quick-tempered, easily upset and often disregarded his own safety. For example, his mother had reported that he would scratch himself until he bled. But an improvement in his behaviour was noted a year later after his mother had been counselled about the need to make him feel wanted and secure.

8.2 Stewart's behaviour got worse when he went to secondary school. He got in with a crowd of boys who were as disaffected as he was. He was more a follower than a leader, but his recklessness and lack of concern for his personal safety gave him his own identity within the group. His attendance at school tailed off, and at the beginning of his second year in secondary school he was expelled for setting fire to the sports hall. He remained out of full-time education for the rest of that academic year, and although a placement was found for him at another school for the next academic year, he truanted for most of the time.

Stewart's criminal beginnings

8.3 At the end of that academic year, Stewart was suspended from school, and that was effectively the end of his schooling. He had been getting into trouble all the time at school, being disruptive and offensive to staff. By then his pattern of continual offending had been established. His first recorded brush with the law was when a supervision order for 12 months for an offence of arson was made in December 1993. Stewart was then 13 years old. With some of his friends from Middleton, he had set fire to a shed in a yard in the town centre. He had previously been cautioned by the police for an offence of arson – which may have related to the sports hall which he had set on fire – but that had not got onto his criminal record. This history of arson had led the court to ask for a psychiatric report on him, and the view was expressed that Stewart was showing signs of a personality disorder, but that he was not suffering from any psychiatric illness.

8.4 After that, Stewart was hardly ever out of trouble with the law. In March 1994, he was sentenced to a further supervision order for 12 months for damaging the car of one of his teachers. In December 1994, he was ordered to attend an attendance centre for 24 hours for a total of 17 offences – primarily for stealing from cars and joyriding, but also for two burglaries. In February 1995, a further supervision order for 12 months was made for an offence of joyriding on an excavator, and in May 1995, yet another supervision order for 12 months was made for four offences – shoplifting, breaking a car window, and two of joyriding.

8.5 A few months later in August 1995, just after he had turned 15 and had become eligible for a custodial sentence – or to use the language of today, for a sentence with a custodial element – he received his first custodial sentence: two months' detention in a young offender institution for an offence of burglary. He served his sentence at Werrington Young Offender Institution in Stoke-on-Trent. Apart from some documents in his medical records, no records survive either of that period or of his next two periods in custody – at any rate, the Prison Service has not been able to supply the Inquiry with any such records. However, the records of the Tameside Social Services Department in Manchester show that there were episodes of fighting and solvent abuse, and an occasion when he threw bleach at a prison officer. He was released in October 1995, but a further custodial sentence quickly followed. After a period on remand at Hindley Young Offender Institution near Wigan, he received in January 1996 sentences totalling six months' detention in a young offender institution for seven offences connected with a spree of joyriding, most of which had been committed before he was first sent to detention, but the last of which had not and had involved a high-speed chase by the police. He served his sentence at Werrington before being transferred to Stoke Heath Young Offender Institution in Shropshire.

8.6 Stewart was released in February 1996. He was still subject to the supervision order which did not expire until May 1996. On his release, he told social workers that he had decided that he was not going to get into trouble any more. But he started to offend again. It looks as if the courts did what they could to avoid a continuing cycle of offending and detention. In July 1996, he was ordered to perform 150 hours of community service for offences of joyriding and going equipped for theft. In August 1996, he was ordered to perform a further 150 hours of community service for five offences, again relating to a spree of joyriding. And in October 1996, a supervision order for two years was made for five offences arising from another joyriding spree.

8.7 In February 1997, an offence of violence was added to Stewart's record for the first time. In the course of stealing from a motor vehicle, he was disturbed by the owner and stabbed him with a screwdriver. He was charged with assault occasioning actual bodily harm. That offence was committed in connection with another spree of joyriding and stealing from vehicles. After a period on remand in Hindley, he received sentences totalling eight months' detention in a young offender institution for a total of eight offences, with four others taken into consideration. He served his sentence in Werrington, and was released in August 1997.

How Stewart spent his time

8.8 When not in detention, Stewart lived at home with his parents for much of the time, though he spent a couple of months in a special care unit when he was 15, going home at weekends. His behaviour while in care was recorded as having been unpredictable and disruptive, and it included setting fire to another resident's bedroom. A probation officer was later to write that the family home had been the one stable feature in his life, and though there was little they could do, his parents did their best to support him. He spent the majority of his time with other boys who lived on the same estate. His life, like theirs, was wholly unstructured, with alcohol and drug abuse playing its part in their lifestyle, the hallmarks of which were lack of opportunity and boredom.

8.9 A report prepared on Stewart by the Greater Manchester Probation Service following his conviction for Zahid's murder addressed Stewart's racism. It noted that there was little evidence of racial tension on the Hattersley estate where he had lived, but there was evidence of racial tension in neighbouring Hyde. It recorded Stewart recalling having engaged in what he called "Paki-bashing" when he was between 14 and 16. He and his friends would drive to Hyde, and hold objects out of the window to "bash" Asian victims as they walked down the street. Stewart did not attempt to justify any of that. He said that it was "just something he did" with his friends.

The documents

8.10 This, then, was the sort of young man Stewart was when he was released from Werrington in August 1997. His time back home proved to be very short-lived. On 5 September 1997, when he was just 17, he was remanded in custody following his arrest for a number of offences. He was detained in Hindley. He remained there until 24 November 1997 when he was transferred to Lancaster Farms Young Offender Institution in Lancaster, where he completed the rest of his sentence. His sentence had been a total of four months' detention in a young offender institution for five offences – common assault, criminal damage, going equipped for theft and two of theft.

8.11 Stewart's arrival in Hindley marks the point from which the Inquiry was provided with more or less continuous records of Stewart's time in custody. I say "more or less continuous", because the records were not quite complete. But it is likely that only a few documents are missing, and it may be that they were misplaced when the various files were scrutinised by the police. By the time the Inquiry was provided with them, the documents in many of the files were not in chronological order, and their inclusion in one file and not another was often haphazard. To describe the files as "all over the shop" would not be inaccurate.

8.12 Having said that, much of the information in this chapter has been based on documents provided to the Inquiry by agencies other than the Prison Service, in particular by Tameside Social Services Department. Some of the information in this chapter was based on more recent documents, in particular psychiatric reports which were prepared for Stewart's trial for the murder of Zahid. But the important point is that, apart from a print-out of Stewart's previous convictions, none of the earlier documents got onto the files kept by the Prison Service on Stewart in the years from when their records on him have survived to the death of Zahid. Would they have made any difference if they had? That is a matter of speculation. It has been suggested that they would not have. According to this view they showed that Stewart had been a troubled boy with an interrupted education, a short spell in care and a string of convictions from the age of 13, which were for the most part for run-of-the-mill offences. This history was by no means unusual, and would not have made Stewart stand out as someone who posed a significant risk to either prisoners or staff. But the better view is that these documents contain significant hints of the potentiality for Stewart to develop into someone who could harm himself or others. The prolific nature of his offending, the diagnosis that he had the makings of a personality disorder, the lack of care for his personal safety, the signs of a tendency to harm himself, his fascination with fires and the examples of the times when he had let that fascination get the better of him: taken together, all these were indications of someone extremely troubled who was liable to behave in an unpredictable way. The fact that the materials which documented these features of Stewart's childhood did not get onto his prison files was the first of many missed opportunities to address how Stewart should have been managed while in custody.

8.13 It is also the case that the records on Stewart generated by the Prison Service during his previous spells in custody were not, it seems, sent to Hindley in September 1997. Otherwise, they would have been married up with the documents which were subsequently generated there. We do not know why they did not get to Hindley. They should have been sent there. Maybe they were still at Werrington, from where Stewart had last been released. As it was, it was known on Stewart's arrival in Hindley that he had recently been discharged from Werrington: that fact was recorded on his core record. No-one at Hindley seems to have asked for them. One can only speculate what an inspection of them would have revealed. It has been said that it is unlikely that anything would have been on his records which would have been more significant than the later events which were documented on his files. That may be so, but there is no way of knowing that for sure.

Chapter 9: Hindley 1997

Mental illness and personality disorder

9.1 Stewart's time at Hindley in late 1997 was marked by a series of episodes of increasingly bizarre behaviour. That raises the question whether Stewart's mental state was properly addressed while he was there. The conclusion was reached that Stewart was not suffering from mental illness. That conclusion may well have been correct. After all, the reports prepared on Stewart for his trial for the murder of Zahid all stated that although he was suffering from a personality disorder at the time of the murder, there was no evidence of mental illness.

9.2 This is an important distinction. The term "mental illness" covers a variety of medical conditions. Examples include psychosis, mania and depression. Among other things, they can impair a person's ability to think clearly, communicate effectively and understand reality, and cause significant mood swings. They can be treated with medication which alters the chemical imbalance in the brain which is one of the hallmarks of mental illness. A personality disorder, on the other hand, is not an illness or a disease, but a condition which results in an inflexible and inappropriate response to a broad range of situations – a response significantly different from the way a normal person would respond.

9.3 Whether Stewart was suffering from mental illness was a topic on which the Inquiry had the benefit of expert evidence. Indeed, there were a number of topics on which the Inquiry thought that it would be assisted by the view of a professional in the field of mental illness. It commissioned reports from Professor John Gunn, a distinguished consultant forensic psychiatrist and the Emeritus Professor of Forensic Psychiatry at the Institute of Psychiatry, King's College London. For its part, the Prison Service commissioned reports from Professor Anthony Maden, another distinguished consultant forensic psychiatrist and the Professor of Forensic Psychiatry at Imperial College London. Both Professor Gunn and Professor Maden gave oral evidence to the Inquiry. Since neither of them was instructed to examine Stewart, neither could give a definitive view as to whether he might have been suffering from mental illness, either while he had been at Hindley or at the time of the murder. But subject to that caveat, Professor Maden took the view that Stewart's case was as clear cut a case of a severe personality disorder as one could encounter. He saw no real evidence to suggest mental illness. The disorder was unusual in its severity, but there was no doubt about the diagnosis. The reports on Stewart prepared for his trial were remarkable for the extent of their agreement.

9.4 Professor Gunn agreed with all that, but he would have wanted to enquire about the possibility of mental illness further, since none of the doctors who had examined Stewart for his trial had been able to find out from him why he had behaved as he had. A period of observation in hospital during which he was spoken to by psychiatrists could well have increased the chances of his "inner world" being revealed. A number of the sentiments expressed in Stewart's correspondence discovered after the murder of Zahid – for example, "eating mi padmate Hannible Lecter style [sic]" and notorious murderers passing on their legacy to him – suggested a very unhealthy individual, even if you did not take his language literally. There was a lot more to Stewart than there was to most people with personality disorders. Mental illness could fluctuate, so that even if there were long periods when there were no episodes of bizarre behaviour, the presence of mental illness was still a possibility.

9.5 One thing is clear. The most that can be said now is that when Stewart was at Hindley there was no more than a possibility that he was suffering from mental illness. So the doctors at Hindley cannot be said to have been wrong in concluding that Stewart was not suffering from mental illness. But that is to speak with the inestimable advantage of hindsight. It does not mean that a different conclusion should not have been reached at the time in view of how Stewart was then presenting. It is therefore necessary to explore whether the conclusion that Stewart was not suffering from mental illness was reached at Hindley by luck or by judgement. Everyone agrees that if Stewart had been diagnosed as suffering from mental illness, that would have had serious implications for his management and treatment within the prison system.

Stewart's behaviour

9.6 From the moment of his arrival at Hindley, Stewart proved to be an extremely disruptive prisoner. The things he did were as follows:

- writing graffiti in his cell (11 September)

- attempting to remove a brick from the outer wall of his cell (17 September)*

---

* An information of special importance form was completed following this breach of prison discipline. It inaccurately described Stewart's conduct as an attempt "to dig out of cell". Although Stewart claims that he had removed the brick because he wanted to escape, and was in consequence placed on the escape list, a serious attempt on his part to escape seems unlikely.

- throwing the contents of his cell out of the window and then flooding the cell in the segregation unit to which he had been moved (25 September)

- behaving in a bizarre but unspecified manner, following which he was transferred to the healthcare centre, where he damaged the window frame in his cell (6 October)

- sending out a letter with a map of Hindley drawn on it – a security information report was written, though a reading of the letter suggests that this was nothing more sinister than an attempt to illustrate an anecdote in the letter (10 October)

- flooding his cell in the healthcare centre and causing other damage there, following which he was removed from the healthcare centre and transferred to the segregation unit (11 October)

- flooding his cell in the segregation unit, smearing excrement on the walls and margarine on himself, and placing a noose around his neck (26 October)

- threatening violence to staff and damage to his cell (27 October)

- ripping out the electrics in his cell (28 October)

- burning letters in his cell (29 October)

- pacing up and down in his cell and talking to the walls of his cell after he had incorrectly been told that he was about to be released (5 November)

- eating soap and swallowing a screw, following which he was transferred to the healthcare centre (21 November)

- setting fire to the tracksuit trousers he was wearing after his transfer back to his wing, following which he was transferred again to the healthcare centre, and later with a fellow prisoner, Maurice Travis, who had been a friend of Stewart in Manchester and was to feature in Stewart's life in a dramatic way the following year, inciting each other to harm themselves (22 November)

- placing a ligature around his neck after his transfer back again to his wing, following which he was removed again to the segregation unit, and there banging his head against the wall of his cell and biting his arm (23 November)

- biting his arm and refusing to speak (24 November).

In the light of this litany of bizarre and florid behaviour, Stewart received a number of adjudications, which resulted in him losing his remission to such an extent that he served practically the whole of his sentence. The prison officers who had to look after him could not make him out at all. There were times when he appeared cheerful and settled, but officers also called him "totally unpredictable" and described him as "a very strange young man". He was also said to be unable to control his impulsiveness, and capable of doing anything without warning.

9.7 Some attempts were made to find out if there was anything in Stewart's background which might explain his behaviour. One prison officer, John McKeiver, spoke to Stewart's father a few days before Stewart was transferred to Lancaster Farms. More importantly, Joan Knapman, a probation officer based at Hindley, spoke to Stewart in the segregation unit on the day after he flooded his cell there. Since he was unable to give an explanation for his behaviour other than "he feels like doing it", she spoke to Stephen Green, the probation officer who had supervised Stewart following his release on licence from Werrington, to find out whether there was a history of mental illness or self-harm. He told her that he did not know of any such history.*

9.8 Other attempts were made to find out what lay behind Stewart's behaviour. He was seen by healthcare staff many times. Sometimes he was seen for no more than a minute or two – to see if he was fit to face disciplinary charges or fit to be detained in one of the special cells in the segregation unit for prisoners whose behaviour is so unpredictable that for their own safety or to avoid damage to a cell they need to be confined there. But there were also occasions when staff spoke to Stewart at greater length to try to get at what his problem was. A recurrent theme was his unwillingness to engage in such dialogue, though Dr Andrew Greenwood, the Senior Medical Officer, said that this was not particularly unusual. If Stewart was prepared to talk to staff,

---

* There is no reason to suppose that Mr Green knew that some years earlier Stewart had been showing signs of a personality disorder or had a history of self-harm. The pre-sentence report which had referred to the report about Stewart exhibiting those signs had been prepared by the Tameside Social Services Department, and the Probation Service rarely saw such reports then. Admittedly, in a pre-sentence report which Mr Green wrote about Stewart in April 1998, he referred to an occasion when Stewart had claimed to have swallowed a razor blade. Mr Green cannot recall where he got that information from, but it is unlikely to have come from a report which Mr Green had either forgotten about or never seen, because such a report was not included in the relatively full set of pre-sentence reports with which the Inquiry has been provided. The likeliest explanation is that Mr Green learned about the incident from Stewart himself when he was preparing the report in 1998.

he never offered any explanation for his behaviour. For example, when asked why he had flooded his cell in the segregation unit, and smeared the walls with excrement and himself with margarine, he said that he had done it "for a laugh", though it was noted that Travis had been in the segregation unit at the time, and a possible connection with his presence there was canvassed. Indeed, at one stage, a prison officer referred to Stewart looking like "his hero Travis" after he had had his hair cut. Stewart himself claimed to feel compelled to act in a particular way, though for the most part he denied that he heard voices or had any suicidal intent. However, one particular line of inquiry was not followed up. During his first stay in the healthcare centre, Stewart said that when he was 10 he had been seen by a psychiatrist at Booth Hall, a children's hospital in Manchester. That hospital had been the source of one of the reports referred to in paragraph 8.1, but no attempt was made to get a copy of it.

9.9 Stewart's behaviour at Hindley resulted in him being placed twice on a 15-minute watch, and a self-harm at risk form was opened on him on 5 November. He was, as we have seen, also transferred to the healthcare centre three times. The first time was on 6 October following his bizarre but unspecified behaviour on the wing. An entry in his medical record for that day stated that he had been taking "a cocktail of drugs". While in the healthcare centre, he slept well and appeared settled. So on 11 November, Dr Daya Das, a doctor who worked in the healthcare centre part time, advised that he could be transferred back to the wing. The next entry in his medical record – and therefore suggesting that this happened after he knew that he was about to leave the healthcare centre – referred to him flooding his cell in the healthcare centre and causing damage to a locker and the lino. It was noted that he had not displayed any disruptive behaviour while he had been in the healthcare centre, and the view was expressed that he was behaving as he was in the hope that he would be allowed to stay there. In fact, he was sent to the segregation unit that day.

9.10 Stewart's next stay in the healthcare centre was shorter. He was moved there on 21 November after he had claimed to have eaten soap and swallowed a screw. No-one had actually seen him do any of that. He was sent back to his wing the following day after he had slept well, but was returned to the healthcare centre later that day after he tried to set fire to the clothes he was wearing. When back in the healthcare centre, he seemed to be in a good mood. He was seen chatting and laughing. He was heard bragging to Travis and other prisoners about what he had done. He was also heard inciting Travis to harm himself so that Travis could be moved to the neighbouring cell. On the following day, 23 November, he was transferred out of the healthcare centre, the self-harm at risk form recording the view of Dr Das that Stewart's "behaviour is all an act in order to be on the [healthcare centre] next to Travis".

9.11 There was a good deal of evidence to support the view that Stewart's behaviour was, for the most part, a deliberate attempt to get himself into the healthcare centre. Lindsey Martin, a nurse in the healthcare centre, said that prisoners would try to get transferred to the healthcare centre because it was quieter there, the food was more plentiful and there was more one-to-one attention. While in the healthcare centre, Stewart ceased to behave in an unruly or disruptive way, except when he knew that he was about to be moved back to his wing. His behaviour on the wing on 25 September, which had preceded his spell in the segregation unit, occurred just after he had been accused of stealing another inmate's property. So when he was moved back to the wing, he might well have behaved in a way intended to get himself removed from the wing. That could have accounted for why he wanted to get into the healthcare centre on 6 October. And as for why he may have wanted to get back to the healthcare centre on 21 and 22 November, "his hero Travis" was there then. As he was to tell an officer at Lancaster Farms, "he was 'acting the part' in order to be located in Hindley's hospital with a mate." He told at least two healthcare workers in the healthcare centre at Lancaster Farms the same thing.

Signs of mental illness?

9.12 In these circumstances, the doctors at Hindley who thought that Stewart's conduct was at times manipulative – in the sense that it was designed to engineer his transfer to the healthcare centre – were justified in reaching that conclusion. But that did not necessarily mean that there was no reason to be concerned about Stewart's mental state. After all, manipulative behaviour can itself be indicative of mental disorder, if not mental illness, and there is no doubt that throughout much of his time at Hindley Stewart engaged in prolonged bouts of such abnormal behaviour as might indicate a disturbed mental state. It could not be said that, to the extent that his behaviour was manipulative, it was so proportionate to the end sought to be achieved that it could not be symptomatic of mental illness. Two questions therefore have to be asked. Did there not come a time when his mental state had to be addressed, even if his behaviour was at times manipulative? And if it had to be addressed, could it properly have been addressed without Stewart being referred to a psychiatrist?

9.13 One comment should be made here. Stewart was seen by a number of different doctors, nurses and healthcare officers while he was at Hindley. Most of them only saw him once or twice. It would have been disproportionate for the Inquiry to have sought written statements from all of them, given the lapse of time since his detention there and the fact that for much of the time their entries in Stewart's medical record speak for themselves. The two doctors from whom statements were sought were Dr Greenwood, both in his managerial capacity as responsible for the healthcare centre and as a doctor who saw Stewart a number of times, before going on sick leave from 20 October until the end of the year, and Dr Das who authorised his removal from the healthcare centre on 11 October and 23 November and who was recorded as expressly stating that Stewart's behaviour was "all an act". Dr Greenwood gave oral evidence, but Dr Das was not asked to, since he claimed to have no recollection of Stewart and little, if any, recollection of the events to which his entries in Stewart's medical record related, though he was offered the opportunity to give evidence if he wanted to.

The examination on 18 September 1997

9.14 Apart from the initial screening of Stewart on 6 September, Dr Greenwood saw Stewart twice: on 18 September and 25 September. On 18 September, Dr Greenwood saw Stewart in the segregation unit, where he had been sent on the discovery that he had tried to remove a brick from the outer wall of his cell. The previous day, a deputy governor had instructed staff to watch Stewart carefully over the next few days, and to consider opening a self-harm at risk form if he was behaving strangely. It does not look as if Dr Greenwood knew that. All he had to decide was whether Stewart was "fit for adjudication" – in other words, whether he was fit to face disciplinary charges. In normal circumstances, Dr Greenwood would not know what the prisoner was alleged to have done. All he would have been told would have been the prison rule which the prisoner was alleged to have infringed. There is no reason to suppose that Dr Greenwood was told anything more than that on this occasion. The visit would not have lasted longer than a minute or two. It would have involved little more than Dr Greenwood trying to find out if Stewart knew where he was and why. Stewart had not presented in a way which caused Dr Greenwood concern. Otherwise, he would have probed the matter deeper. Dr Greenwood duly certified Stewart as fit for adjudication. I see no basis to criticise Dr Greenwood for his approach on that occasion.

The examination on 25 September 1997

9.15 The next time Dr Greenwood saw Stewart was rather different. That was on 25 September when Stewart had been placed in a special cell within the segregation unit after he had been sent there following the throwing of the contents of his cell out of the window. Dr Greenwood had to decide whether Stewart was fit to remain there. The notes he made at the time show that he spoke to Stewart through the window in the door of the cell, that Stewart was sullen and would not speak, but that Stewart recognised him. He noted that there was no history of self-harm and no evidence of medical illness. He described Stewart as having engaged in an immature behaviour tantrum. He certified Stewart as fit to remain in the special cell. Nevertheless, he thought that Stewart should be watched every 15 minutes until his behaviour returned to normal. He wanted to be sure that Stewart was eating and toileting himself properly.

9.16 Dr Greenwood readily accepted that talking to Stewart through the window was a wholly inadequate way of examining him. It was only defensible if he could not be examined in some other way. His evidence was that the prison officers would not let him into the cell because Stewart's behaviour was thought to be too unpredictable at the time. But the evidence of Dr Stephen Jefferies, who was the lead GP in the practice which provided medical services to Feltham while Stewart was there, was that if he himself had wanted to see a prisoner, and if that could only be achieved if additional staff were on hand, he would have insisted on such staff being made available. Dr Greenwood did not suggest that he had pressed to be allowed into the cell. In particular, he did not suggest that prison officers had said that Stewart's unpredictability was such that Stewart could not be examined by him even if a number of prison officers were present at the time. The fact of the matter is that Stewart's unpredictability was either so acute as to make a proper examination of him all the more important. Or it was not all that acute, in which case Dr Greenwood might have been deferring a little too readily to the idea that Stewart could not have been examined even with other officers present. Or he may not have considered the possibility of examining him with other officers present at all.

9.17 Moreover, Dr Greenwood did not make arrangements for Stewart to be examined later on, whether by himself or a colleague, even though he accepted that a more adequate examination ought to have followed once it was possible to perform it. It is true that Stewart was certified fit for adjudication by another doctor on the following day, but a brief conversation with a prisoner to see if he is capable of understanding disciplinary proceedings is very different from an examination of the kind necessary to determine whether a prisoner's mental condition is such as to permit him to be confined in circumstances of isolation in a bleak special cell.

9.18 Also troubling is Dr Greenwood's note that there was no evidence of mental illness. For all Dr Greenwood knew, Stewart's previous disruptive behaviour, and the sullenness and non-communication which he had observed, may have been a manifestation of mental illness. Indeed, when commenting in his statement to the Inquiry on what Stewart was like in 1998, Dr Greenwood described him as having previously been "very disturbed". Dr Greenwood accepted that that could only have been a reference to when he had seen Stewart on 25 September 1997. Even if Dr Greenwood had not been referring to Stewart's mental state on 25 September, but to his behaviour which had resulted in him being the subject of adjudication and placed in the segregation unit – which is what Dr Greenwood was rather unconvincingly to say subsequently – his comment that there was no evidence that Stewart was suffering from mental illness begged the question why he had been behaving so disruptively and presenting in such a strange way. Indeed, Dr Greenwood accepted that he had not asked Stewart why he had behaved in the way he had.

9.19 Finally, there is the observation in Dr Greenwood's statement to the Inquiry that Stewart had "full insight into his activities and behaviour" on 25 September. On the face of it, Stewart's non-responsiveness to the questions Dr Greenwood asked of him made it impossible for Dr Greenwood to know what was going through Stewart's mind, let alone whether he had any understanding about what lay behind his disruptive behaviour. Dr Greenwood claimed that what he meant was that Stewart was orientated in space and time and was aware of what was happening around him. I do not find that answer convincing.

9.20 In short, Dr Greenwood did not take the steps which he could and should have taken to make either his examination of Stewart on 25 September, or a subsequent examination later on, an adequate one. Moreover, he was ruling out mental illness, and doing so at a time when on the extremely limited material which he had it could not definitively be ruled out. But I am very far from saying that the stage had by then been reached for consideration to be given to assessing Stewart's mental state, let alone to referring him to a psychiatrist. It just meant that Dr Greenwood should have flagged Stewart up as someone who, if his disruptive behaviour got worse and his non-responsiveness continued, should be looked at again with a view to assessing his mental state.

The telephone call on 26 October 1997

9.21 Dr Greenwood had one other encounter with Stewart, though this was not face to face. He was telephoned at home on 26 October – probably in error because he had been on sick leave for about a week – after Stewart had flooded his cell in the segregation unit, smeared excrement on the walls and margarine on himself, and placed a noose around his neck. This behaviour was the most striking example of his abnormal behaviour up to then, and marked a significant escalation in its intensity. Because of his illness, Dr Greenwood could do little more than give advice about how Stewart should be managed until a more considered decision could be taken about him. His advice was that he should remain in a special cell in the segregation unit overnight if the duty governor agreed. Plainly Dr Greenwood cannot be criticised for the limited advice he gave on this occasion.

The examination on 7 November 1997 and the events leading up to it

9.22 For a while Stewart was prescribed medication which was more appropriate for someone suffering from mental illness. Even then he was not getting his medication regularly. But it was a little time before an assessment of Stewart's mental state was made. He was seen by Dr Das on 27 and 28 October. On each of those occasions Dr Das simply certified him as fit for adjudication. He was seen by a nurse on 30 October. Going on the much fuller entry which was made in his medical record on this occasion, it looks as if it was made by the psychiatric nurse. It included references to recurrent self-injury and overdoses, and to Stewart saying that he heard voices. But no attempt was made to diagnose whether Stewart was suffering from mental illness. Maybe his case was thought too complex for a psychiatric nurse to give an opinion about. Instead, the view was expressed that Stewart should be further reviewed by a doctor – a view shared by another nurse who saw him on 7 November at the request of the Governor who had expressed concern over his physical and mental state. The entry made on that occasion in Stewart's medical record referred to his loss of appetite and sleep, his poor eye contact and his inability to explain what was wrong with him, but also his denial of any auditory hallucinations or instances of self-harm. Eventually, an assessment of Stewart's mental state was made. That was also on 7 November when he was seen by a doctor. It is unclear who the doctor was, but it was not Dr Das or Dr Greenwood. The entry which the doctor made in Stewart's medical record characterised him as having no problems, being neither depressed nor suicidal, and it concluded that he was not mentally ill.

9.23 On the face of it, it is surprising for mental illness to have been definitively ruled out on that occasion. But since my knowledge of the examination of 7 November is limited to the sparse entry in the medical record, it would not be safe to criticise whoever made that entry for prematurely ruling out the possibility that Stewart was mentally ill. However, the fact remains that this doctor and Dr Greenwood ruled out mental illness at a surprisingly early stage of their dealings with Stewart, on the basis of not very much time spent with him. I acknowledge that they worked in an environment in which the behaviour of their "patients" did not match that encountered by doctors in the community. For example, some of the seemingly bizarre things which Stewart did were rational in the context of prison life: smearing oneself with margarine is a recognised way of preventing prison officers from getting a grip on a prisoner, and smearing walls with excrement is a well-known way of registering protest. But the suspicion remains that, because of the prevalence of abnormal behaviour in prison, they developed a tendency to treat that behaviour as the norm, and to attribute it either to the objectives which prisoners wished to achieve or to "behavioural problems" of the kind which brought prisoners into prison in the first place rather than as the signs of mental illness.

The examination on 23 November 1997

9.24 Dr Das examined Stewart on 23 November when he came back to the healthcare centre. The entry he made in Stewart's medical record shows that he thought that Stewart's speech and mood were normal, and that he did not present with any suicidal intent. He questioned whether Stewart's behaviour was manipulative, but Dr Das's view about Stewart was spelt out in the entry in the self-harm at risk form, which referred to his behaviour as having been "all an act". That may have been so, but the fact that his behaviour over the previous few days may have been manipulative did not mean that Stewart was not mentally ill. Maybe that was something which Dr Das was alive to, but decided that there was no reason to go behind the diagnosis of 7 November that Stewart was not mentally ill.

What should have been done?

9.25 Even if the stage had not been reached by Dr Greenwood's examination of Stewart on 25 September for consideration to be given to assessing Stewart's mental state, things had moved on by the time he was examined on 7 November, and certainly by Dr Das's examination of him on 23 November. His disruptive behaviour had not abated. On the contrary, it had got worse and was becoming increasingly concerning. Dr Greenwood himself recognised that, had he been in charge of Stewart's case on 23 November, Stewart's increasingly extreme behaviour would have justified serious thought being given to the holding of a case conference. That was not so much because of concerns about Stewart's mental state – partly because Stewart's behaviour had been regarded as manipulative at times, and partly no doubt because of the diagnosis on 7 November that Stewart was not mentally ill – but rather as a multi-disciplinary approach to try to get to the bottom of his behaviour and to explore ways of managing him in a more pro-active way. The critical question is whether that would have been enough, or whether Stewart should have been referred to a psychiatrist for a second opinion about his mental state.

9.26 Although the healthcare centre had a psychiatric nurse at the time, none of the doctors at Hindley had psychiatric skills. That was regrettable. One of the recommendations which the Inspectorate had made about Hindley following its inspection of Hindley in 1995 had been that "a consultant psychiatrist should have oversight of psychiatric care in the healthcare centre". It had not been implemented by the end of 1997. So if the time had arrived for a second opinion to be sought about Stewart's mental state, the only option was for him to be referred to an outside psychiatrist.

9.27 That was not as easy as it sounds. At the time, the healthcare centre had a budget of only £4,000 a year to spend on mental health issues. That was hardly satisfactory. It meant that only a limited number of prisoners could be referred to a psychiatrist for assessment. So one of a number of things must have happened. Perhaps Dr Greenwood did not press his case for more resources to be made available for psychiatric assessment with sufficient vigour. Maybe Hindley's Governor at the time, Christopher Sheffield, failed to appreciate the need for further resources to be diverted to the healthcare centre for that purpose. Or perhaps Mr Sheffield recognised the need, but there were greater calls on the resources he had, and he could not persuade his area manager to allocate more resources to him. I cannot say which of these possibilities is correct.

9.28 That was not the only problem. Local psychiatrists were unwilling to make prison visits, and it could take as long as four to five months to get an appointment. And if a diagnosis was made which required treatment, that treatment would often be long-term treatment of the kind which would not be available for remand prisoners or prisoners serving short sentences. Such prisoners constituted the overwhelming majority of Hindley's population. Having said that, Dr Greenwood did not regard these problems as a disincentive to making a psychiatric referral in an appropriate case. He used his psychiatric nurse "at the lesser edges", but if he thought that a prisoner needed psychiatric assessment, he would try to get it, however hard that might be. If necessary, he would telephone local hospitals to get an available consultant.

9.29 So should Stewart have been referred for assessment to an outside psychiatrist? That was one of the topics on which the Inquiry thought that it would be assisted by the view of a professional in the field. In the first of his reports, Professor Gunn said that a reliable conclusion about Stewart's abnormal behaviour called for a second opinion from a professional with psychiatric training, and that there was "a very strong case" for such a referral once there had been a series of non-isolated incidents. He remained of that view when he gave evidence, adding that the incident which would have been the real trigger for such a referral was that of 26 October. But he made the point that this was what should have happened in an ideal world outside prison, and he was reluctant to criticise any of the healthcare staff for not doing that, in view of the difficult environment with limited resources in which they had to work. Since only a small number of prisoners could have been referred to a psychiatrist, he said that a number of factors would have dictated whether that should have been done. They were:

- the extent to which the prisoner's disruptive behaviour stood out from that of other prisoners

- his past history

- the ability of staff to identify whether his behaviour may have been due to mental disorder or whether he was trying to achieve a particular result

- whether the facilities existed for psychiatric assessment in the prison he was in

- how long he was due to be imprisoned for.

Bearing these factors in mind, Professor Gunn thought that the healthcare staff were probably acting in accordance with the practice of prison medical staff at the time. His conclusion was that the failure to refer Stewart for psychiatric assessment was not unreasonable in the prison environment of the late 1990s. He felt that an opportunity had been lost, but that was something which would have been happening throughout the prison system at the time.

9.30 In the second of his reports, Professor Maden said that the ideal management of Stewart's case would have been a referral to a psychiatrist following the incident of 26 October, but that not doing so fell within the range of acceptable options where resources were limited. It would have been a safer approach, in the sense that the doctors would have been less vulnerable to criticism had things gone wrong, but it would have been a waste of valuable resources in a case in which the evidence of manipulative behaviour was so apparent.

9.31 I do not detect any significant differences in the conclusions which Professor Gunn and Professor Maden reached. As it is, their views chime with the lay view which I had come to. I do not underestimate the episodes of strange behaviour on Stewart's part. But it is impossible to ignore the practical realities of the situation. Stewart was serving a short sentence for run-of-the-mill offences. Even if he lost all his remission, he was likely to be discharged before an appointment could be made for him to see a psychiatrist. Much of his behaviour was attributable to his aim to achieve particular ends. On a limited budget, I can well understand why referring Stewart to an outside psychiatrist would in these circumstances have been low on the list of priorities. In any event, Dr Greenwood had been off the scene since before the incident that would have been the real trigger for such a referral. Although it should not have happened, it may be that a decision as to whether a prisoner should be referred to an outside psychiatrist was left for Dr Greenwood's return. In short, I do not criticise the medical staff at Hindley for not referring Stewart to a psychiatrist before he left Hindley on 24 November 1997. But serious thought should have been given to holding a case conference about him. And I cannot help commenting that, had the healthcare centre received visits in 1997 from a doctor with psychiatric skills, as it did later on, he or she could have examined Stewart, and the picture which might then have emerged could have been very different.

Signs of personality disorder?

9.32 Although the possibility that Stewart was suffering from mental illness was rejected, no consideration was given to whether he suffered from some other form of mental disorder which did not amount to mental illness, such as a personality disorder. After all, we know, although the doctors at Hindley did not, that Stewart was thought when he was 13 to be showing signs of a personality disorder. And he was diagnosed as having a personality disorder by all the doctors who prepared reports on him for his trial for the murder of Zahid. There is no entry in Stewart's medical record which suggests that the possibility of personality disorder was ever considered during his time at Hindley. Indeed, Dr Greenwood accepted that he did not give any thought to that possibility.

9.33 The reason Dr Greenwood gave for that is understandable. He had only had limited contact with Stewart, and that had been well before his behaviour had degenerated into episodes which were particularly concerning. But a more general point which Dr Greenwood made is more significant. He said that he "did not think of any patient in those terms particularly… because a GP does not usually think in those terms". Writing "personality disorder" in a prisoner's medical record would have served no useful purpose, as it would have meant little to anyone reading it about how the prisoner should be managed. If, say, a prisoner's behaviour suggested that he should not share a cell, it added nothing to his management to consider whether a personality disorder lay at the core of his behaviour. And since Dr Greenwood thought that about 80% of prisoners suffered from some form of personality disorder, describing a prisoner as suffering from a personality disorder brought little to the exercise. If anything, this was an under-estimate: a survey carried out by the Office for National Statistics in 1997 showed that 84% of young offenders on remand suffered from a personality disorder, and that 88% of sentenced young offenders did.

9.34 There is much force in Dr Greenwood's position. Both Professor Gunn and Professor Maden agreed that a diagnosis of personality disorder is of little value in the prison setting. Such a diagnosis on its own catches too high a proportion of the prison population, and as Professor Gunn said, the behaviour which causes a prisoner to be in prison in the first place is usually the same behaviour which causes the prisoner to be classified as having the kind of personality disorder which Stewart was subsequently diagnosed as having.* It therefore means that most prisoners will be diagnosed as having that personality disorder. Moreover, the application of the label of personality disorder could be counter-productive. If too many prisoners are identified as having a personality disorder, prisoners with a severe personality disorder might not be identified. In any event, the diagnosis of personality disorder can tend to shut down further consideration of the prisoner's case. That is because it is sometimes perceived either as a condition which is not treatable or as one which excludes mental illness. The former may be true, but the latter is not. Professor Maden agreed. The additional point

---

* Anti-social personality disorder (which is the term used in the *American Diagnostic and Statistical Manual*, version IV) or dissocial personality disorder (which is the term used in the *International Classification of Diseases*, version 10).

he made was that Stewart was only 17 when he was at Hindley. At that age, one's personality is still evolving, so that diagnosing personality disorder in someone of that age is itself a questionable exercise.

9.35 But what would a diagnosis of personality disorder have meant in terms of the risk which a prisoner posed, whether to other inmates or staff? Professor Gunn's view was that a diagnosis of personality disorder alone is no indication of a prisoner's dangerousness. You can have a serious personality disorder without being dangerous at all. To conduct an assessment of the risks posed by a prisoner to staff or other inmates, what have to be addressed are a variety of factors, including his criminal history and his behavioural traits.

9.36 As it was, there was little in Stewart's criminal history which suggested that he was a real danger to others. The offences of arson were concerning, as was the occasional offence of violence, but for the most part his offences were run-of-the-mill property offences. And apart from the threat of violence to staff on 27 October and the contents of the security information report dealt with in paragraphs 9.37–9.39, Stewart's behaviour in Hindley in 1997, though unquestionably worse than most prisoners, did not suggest that he was a risk to others – certainly no more of a risk than the majority of other youngsters in Hindley. In these circumstances, any criticism of the medical staff at Hindley in general, and Dr Greenwood in particular, for not addressing whether Stewart had a personality disorder is misplaced.

The security information report of 22 November 1997

The contents of the security information report

9.37 It will be recalled that Stewart's third stay in the healthcare centre was overnight on 22 November. Ms Martin was the nurse on duty at the time. She overheard Stewart and Travis talking to each other. What she heard them say caused her to complete a security information report. After saying that they were inciting each other to harm themselves, she wrote:

> "I believe they will go to great lengths to be kept together and could endanger their lives and possibly others. I believe they manipulate the system to their own ends and [are] quite determined to get their own way."

She was unable to identify precisely what it was which had made her think that they might be a danger to others, not just themselves, but whatever it was it had made her "blood run cold". It may have been because she thought that one of them had been talking of setting fire to himself, which could have put others at risk as well. Maybe it was just her impression of them – which was that they wanted to be "the two baddest boys on the block", that they did not care what they did so long as they got what they wanted, and that they were intent on inciting each other to see who would go the further. Whichever it was, her instincts about them proved uncannily accurate: they were both to end up murdering other prisoners.

9.38 In a statement which she gave to the police, Ms Martin said that when she completed the security information report she felt that "they were both capable of stabbing someone". But she did not want them to be stigmatised for the rest of their time in prison for something which she merely thought they were capable of. It was not something which she had actually heard them threaten to do, and so she thought that it would be going "over the top" to mention that. Although she regretted not having put that in the security information report, and regarded that as an unfortunate oversight, I think that she was being too hard on herself. If she had been asked why she had thought them capable of this, she would have had to resort to her overall impression of them – which was, in effect, that she would not have put anything past them. That would have been a reason for thinking that others were at risk of harm from them, but not at risk of harm *by stabbing*. And I am very sceptical about whether she had actually given thought at the time to whether they were capable of stabbing someone. Not only had they not said anything about that, but it is significant that it was only when she was questioned by the police – at a time when she knew that previously Travis had fatally stabbed a prisoner at another young offender institution – that she referred to her belief that they were capable of stabbing someone.

9.39 It might have been better if she had written in the security information report anything which they had actually said which had made her think that they were a danger to others – for example, the comment made by one of them about setting fire to himself. It might also have been better if she had made it clear that her view of them was that, not only were they determined to get their own way on anything they wanted, but that they would do whatever was necessary to achieve it. But if this is to be regarded as criticism of Ms Martin, it is criticism of the most refined kind. In any event, it is extremely unlikely that, had the security information report been fuller, it would have made any difference at all to Stewart's subsequent management within the prison system or would have represented a significant addition to the information which

Feltham should have got about Stewart. As we shall see, the security information report did not get into Stewart's security file. And after Travis had fatally stabbed another prisoner in circumstances in which Stewart was suspected of being involved in some way, any "gut feeling" which anyone might have had about their capacity to harm others would have been overtaken by events.

Where did the security information report go?

9.40 The security information report was included in the papers which the Prison Service provided to the Inquiry about the murder which Travis was to commit. But it was not in Stewart's security file. And we do not know whether its contents were entered onto the 4x4 system at the time, since a print-out of its contents on an inmate intelligence card from this time has not survived either. All of that suggests that although the security information report got into Travis's security file, it did not get into Stewart's. Maybe the original went into Travis's security file, but the Security Department at Hindley either forgot to put a copy of it into Stewart's or found that it was too late to do so because his security file had already gone to Lancaster Farms where Stewart went two days later.

9.41 There was another problem with the security information report. Ms Martin thought that the one provided to the Inquiry was incomplete. She believed that a page was missing. I cannot say whether that is right, though there is nothing on the one page that the Inquiry has which suggests that it might be incomplete. But incomplete or not, the section at the bottom of the page which was supposed to be removed and returned to Ms Martin with a response had not been removed, let alone completed. That could not have been attributable to a copy of the security information report not going into Stewart's file. That had not been done to the original which presumably got into Travis's file.

9.42 There is no doubt that the Security Department was not properly functioning at Hindley at the time. At the beginning of 1997, an audit of the department had rated it as "deficient". By April 1999, the overall rating had become "acceptable", the Security Intelligence System was said to be very well operated, and the procedures relating to security information reports were being followed. It is not possible to say whether the failure of this security information report to get into Stewart's security file or to be processed properly is symptomatic of any systemic shortcomings in the Security Department at the time. But this was the first in a relatively long list of problems about the treatment of security information at Hindley, extending beyond the time when a better performance might have been expected.

Chapter 10: Lancaster Farms

The reason for the transfer

10.1 Stewart was transferred to Lancaster Farms on 24 November 1997. It was a "governor to governor swap", which meant that it had been agreed at the level of residential governor, and had involved a prisoner being transferred from Lancaster Farms to Hindley as well. There is no record spelling out why Stewart was transferred. Nor can one tell whether the move was initiated by Hindley, or whether Hindley settled on Stewart as a suitable candidate for transfer to meet Lancaster Farms' wish to transfer a difficult prisoner to Hindley. The absence of such a record is regrettable. The reason for the transfer was something which those who had to manage Stewart for the rest of his sentence should have known about. So too should those who had to manage him when he was serving any subsequent sentences. If the reason for the transfer had been to separate him from Travis, the message never got through, because as we shall see they were back together in Hindley a few months later sharing a cell. Indeed, there is some evidence that Travis was at Lancaster Farms himself while Stewart was there. That is what the author of the Prison Service's internal inquiry into the murder which Travis was to commit thought.

10.2 On the face of it, transferring a prisoner who had only five weeks of his sentence to serve is surprising. It gave Lancaster Farms hardly any time to get to know Stewart or to begin to address his problems. But one can still see a justification for the transfer. Apart from the need to separate Stewart and Travis in view of Ms Martin's security information report, a fresh start at a different establishment might have given Stewart a chance to settle down. But transfers are not necessarily a good thing. They could be regarded as inimical to the objective of prison officers getting to know the prisoners in their care. And if prisoners know that they might be "shipped out" if they misbehave, a wish to be transferred from an establishment they do not like can make their behaviour all the worse.

Stewart's behaviour

10.3 When Stewart arrived at Lancaster Farms, he went into the healthcare centre. It was thought that he had "self-harm problems", no doubt because of the self-harm at risk form which had been opened on 5 November at Hindley and had never been closed. Within a day or two, Stewart had admitted that his behaviour at Hindley had been an act, and he asked to be moved to ordinary location. That happened on

29 November. He spent six days in the induction unit, and remained on residential wings for the rest of his time at Lancaster Farms until his release on licence on 31 December 1997. He continued to be on the escape list. That appears to have been because he had been on the escape list at Hindley, and little thought seems to have been given to whether his behaviour at Hindley which had resulted in him being regarded as an escape risk was also part of an act.

10.4 Apart from one occasion, Stewart was little trouble while he was at Lancaster Farms. He was initially regarded as rather odd. He was variously described as surly, unco-operative and a "problem child". He kept very quiet and tended to be a loner. His personal officer on the first residential wing he went to described him as follows:

> "A very strange young man. I have tried on numerous occasions to get through to him but to no avail, although he has caused no problems on the wing. I feel he may suffer from some sort of psychological illness."

His personal officer on the residential wing he went to on 18 December has no recollection of him, which may suggest that by then Stewart did not stick out.

10.5 The only specific incident in Stewart's files was an entry in his medical record on 27 December. Stewart had flooded his cell, and when wing staff questioned him, they felt that he was "spaced out and talking gibberish". But he appeared lucid and coherent when spoken to by the medical staff. Without any more information about this incident, it is impossible to tell how significant it was.

The discharge report

10.6 Although Stewart was thought to be odd, there was nothing which suggested that he might be a risk to himself or others, with the exception of comments made in his discharge report. That is a report sent by the establishment in which the prisoner is detained to the probation officer who is to supervise the prisoner on their release on licence. The relevant part of the discharge report on Stewart was written by Peter Rae, a prison officer in the induction unit at Lancaster Farms which Stewart went to when he left the healthcare centre on 29 November. It is dated 2 December. It is addressed to Mr Green, the probation officer from whom Ms Knapman had tried to get information about Stewart, and who had supervised Stewart following his release from Werrington and was to supervise him following his release from Lancaster Farms. By then, Mr Green had seen Stewart quite a few times – once when he had visited Stewart at Werrington, about three or four times when he was supervising Stewart following his release from Werrington, and he had probably visited Stewart once while Stewart had been at Hindley. Interestingly, Mr Green told the Inquiry that he had not seen many reports of this kind. It happens to be the only discharge report for Stewart which the Inquiry has been provided with, whether for earlier or subsequent sentences. Maybe it was a report which was not completed all that often.

10.7 The discharge report was one of the rare occasions when information about Stewart was sent to the Probation Service. The thrust of the evidence was that it was unusual for the Prison Service to provide the Probation Service with information about current prisoners, and that applied just as much to probation officers who were to supervise prisoners on their release as it did to probation officers who prepared a pre-sentence report on them. And although it was said that probation officers seconded to particular prisons gave information about prisoners to external probation officers, there is little evidence of that having happened in Stewart's case.

10.8 In commenting on Stewart's social skills in the discharge report, Mr Rae wrote that Stewart had "no conscience whatsoever". And in the section of the report devoted to other issues of which the supervising officer should be aware, Mr Rae wrote:

> "Has had various psychiatric reports on him whilst at Hindley. I am unaware of the contents. It would appear from his demeanour that he will re-offend in the near future after his release. He does not think ahead and seems incapable of any cohesive thought. A very disturbed, and in my opinion, dangerous young man."

10.9 Mr Rae is now unable to recall Stewart or what prompted him to write what he did. The language he used suggests that he did not simply rely on what officers had said about Stewart in records which Mr Rae had read – though the extent to which he read any records which had been generated at Hindley is questionable, because he mistakenly believed that psychiatric reports had been written on Stewart while he had been at Hindley. It looks as if Mr Rae relied as well on his own impression of Stewart from talking to him. But the question is not so much whether Mr Rae's views about Stewart were justified, but what Mr Green's response to the report was.

10.10 The first question is whether Mr Green ever saw the report. He initially could not say whether he had or not. I think he did. It was date-stamped as having been received by the Probation Service at their office in Hyde in Manchester on 10 December, and Mr Green accepted that it was likely that it would have reached him. Indeed, his evidence proceeded on the assumption that he had seen it because he gave evidence about what he recollected of his reaction to it.

10.11 That reaction was one of surprise. That was because Mr Green's own assessment of Stewart did not match Mr Rae's description of him. So Mr Green's options included asking to see the psychiatric reports which he believed had been prepared on Stewart at Hindley, speaking to Mr Rae to find out why Mr Rae thought that Stewart was disturbed and dangerous, and speaking to Ms Knapman to find out her view about him. He could also have asked for permission from Stewart or his parents to refer him to a psychiatrist and then got in touch with his GP with a request that he be referred to a psychiatrist. But Mr Green decided to do none of these things, even though he claimed to attach great weight to reports on prisoners such as Mr Rae's, because of the time prison officers spend with their charges. Instead, he decided to see what Stewart was like for himself before doing anything else. As it was, when he saw Stewart following his release from Lancaster Farms, Stewart's demeanour was pretty much the same as before, and he showed no signs of disturbed behaviour. Mr Green saw no need for a psychiatric assessment or for any other action.

10.12 I understand entirely Mr Green's wish to form his own view about Stewart, especially as he had worked for some years as a psychiatric nurse. But the difficulty was that Stewart gave him little opportunity to do that. Mr Green's recollection of Stewart was that of a guarded and uncommunicative young man. It is highly questionable whether Mr Green could reasonably have thought that by talking to Stewart he would have got a sufficient account of his life at Hindley and at Lancaster Farms to dispel the concerns raised by the discharge report. After all, it was not as if Mr Green could have asked Stewart about any particular incidents which might have been the ones which gave rise to Mr Rae's concerns: the discharge report had been general in its terms. Moreover, Mr Green had to complete a risk assessment on Stewart. It has not survived, but to complete that assessment solely on the basis of conversations with a young man who was so reluctant to reveal himself when other information about him was readily available is not a stance which can easily be defended.

10.13 I have not overlooked Mr Green's evidence that he made some attempt to discuss Mr Rae's report with Stewart. But although he thought that

Stewart had attributed some of the incidents which Mr Rae must have had in mind to boredom, he could not recall what Stewart's response was. So any suggestion that Stewart had given an account of his conduct which was plausible because it fitted in with what Mr Green already knew about his character is no more than speculation.

10.14 At one point in his evidence, Mr Green advanced another justification for his stance. He contrasted Stewart's disturbed behaviour while in custody with the absence of disturbed behaviour when out of prison. The suggestion was that his behaviour in custody did not call for a reassessment of the risk he posed on the outside. I do not agree. I doubt whether Mr Green's conversations with Stewart in the probation office enabled him properly to form a view about how Stewart was behaving for the rest of the time. And I am sceptical about the proposition that the behaviour of a prisoner in custody has little bearing on his behaviour on the outside.

10.15 In short, Mr Green should at least have spoken to Mr Rae to find out what Stewart had done to make Mr Rae so concerned about him – especially as it was uncommon for a report on a prisoner to be so different from Mr Green's own assessment. And in view of Mr Rae's report, Mr Green should, I think, have spoken to Ms Knapman, his counterpart at Hindley, who had been in touch with him about Stewart on 26 September, bearing in mind that it was at Hindley that Stewart had served the bulk of his sentence. As it was, the discharge report disappeared from view. It was not seen by subsequent probation officers who either supervised or reported on Stewart: the Probation Service maintained separate files for every sentence a prisoner served, and documents held in earlier files would not routinely be looked at. Nor was a copy of it seen by subsequent prison officers who had to manage Stewart. Such evidence as there was suggested that, if a copy of a discharge report was made at all, it simply remained at the establishment from which the prisoner was discharged. It was not added to his main prison file.

10.16 Is it possible that things would have turned out differently if Mr Green had got in touch with Mr Rae or Ms Knapman? With Mr Rae, it is impossible to know since he cannot now say what prompted him to write the report. From Ms Knapman, Mr Green might well have got to hear about the series of increasingly worrying episodes of aberrant behaviour by Stewart at Hindley. But Mr Green is likely to have been told as well that it had all been an act. If he had asked to see the psychiatric reports which he believed had been prepared on Stewart while he had been at Hindley, he would have been told that they did not exist. And in view of what Ms Knapman is likely to have told him, he would understandably not have thought it appropriate to pursue the possibility of Stewart being psychiatrically assessed. In all the circumstances, it is highly unlikely that any further action on Mr Green's part would have resulted in things turning out differently. However, such information as Mr Green could have got about Stewart's behaviour at Hindley and Lancaster Farms for the purpose of informing his supervision of Stewart would have been available for future probation officers to use if the past files were ever married up with current files.

10.17 The evidence about the discharge report illustrates a number of themes which occur time and again throughout Stewart's spells in custody. Mr Giffin described them as follows:

> "(i) a marked tendency for those dealing with Stewart to concentrate upon his immediate, visible presentation, which was only occasionally or intermittently a cause for concern, and to see this as making it unnecessary to look into his past behaviour, or as allaying any concerns about that past behaviour;
>
> (ii) a lack of the will or the opportunity, when dealing with Stewart on particular occasions, to review the whole of his history; and
>
> (iii) a tendency for assessments to be written in a very generalised manner which made the document in which they were contained of little use to the reader unless further information was sought."

I could not have put it better.

Chapter 11: Back at Hindley

Stewart's return to Hindley

11.1 Following his release from Lancaster Farms on 31 December 1997, Stewart remained at liberty for almost three months. Never again was he going to enjoy a period of freedom that long. Within three weeks of his release, he was committing offences again. He tried to break into a car, and while on bail following his arrest, he committed two offences of obtaining property by deception. On 24 March 1998, he was remanded in custody. He was held at Hindley until he appeared at court on 14 April, when he was given a combination order for the three offences: he was placed on probation for 12 months, and ordered to perform a total of 80 hours' community service.

11.2 By the time of his arrival at Hindley, his appearance had undergone a dramatic transformation. Prominent on his forehead were two tattoos: a cross and the letters RIP. What sort of statement Stewart was making about himself is discussed later. Stewart was subsequently to tell a fellow prisoner that he had done it to himself using a mirror when he was drunk.

11.3 Stewart's three weeks in Hindley brought little change in his behaviour. He was on the escape list for much of the time because a map of Hindley which he had drawn was found on him within a couple of days of his arrival there. An information of special importance form was completed about that. So too was a security information report, but it has not survived. According to an entry made by his personal officer in the information of special importance form, Stewart kept to himself and stayed clear of trouble. But his wing manager thought otherwise. When commenting on whether Stewart should remain on the escape list, he described Stewart as "still very unstable and volatile".

11.4 Moreover, when he was screened on his arrival, Stewart told the healthcare officer who questioned him that a week previously he had swallowed a razor blade and taken an overdose, but that he was not then feeling suicidal. He repeated to the doctor the following day that he had recently swallowed a razor blade. He was not thought to be at risk of self-harm, though both the healthcare officer and the doctor said that he should be allocated to a double cell. As we shall see, both then and now, prisoners who are thought to be suicidal or at risk of self-harm are placed in cells which they share with another prisoner. The theory is that the presence of a "buddy" will make them less likely to harm themselves. But it may be that Stewart was not being truthful about what he had done. Swallowing a razor blade was something which at the time he was telling other people he had done. When Mr Green saw him in Hindley to prepare an up-to-date pre-sentence report for the court hearing on 14 April, Stewart told him that he had been in hospital for four days after swallowing a razor blade. The report does not say whether Stewart had said when he had done that. But if he had done it recently, as he was to claim to the medical staff at Hindley, it is likely that he would have told Mr Green that, and that Mr Green would have referred to it in his report.

Stewart and Travis set fire to their cell

11.5 Stewart's liberty following the making of the combination order was short-lived. He did not keep appointments with the Probation Service, and did not start his community service when he was supposed to have done. Moreover, on 7 May he was arrested for robbery, and on 9 May he was remanded in custody. He was kept at Hindley until 19 May when he returned to court. On that occasion, the combination order made on 14 April was revoked, and he was sentenced to terms totalling three months' detention in a young offender institution for each of the offences for which the combination order had been imposed, to be served concurrently, and to a further term of three months' detention in a young offender institution for an offence of handling stolen goods, which had been substituted for the charge of robbery. He was ordered to serve that sentence consecutively to the terms for the offences for which the combination order had been imposed, making six months' detention in a young offender institution in all. He did not serve that sentence at Hindley. Instead, he went to Werrington. We do not know why. It is unlikely to have been simply because his status changed from that of remand prisoner to sentenced prisoner, since that had not resulted in his move from Hindley when that had occurred in 1997. The fact remains that he was at Hindley only for 10 days – from 9 to 19 May.

11.6 His short time there did not prevent him from getting into serious trouble. On his second night, he and his cellmate set fire to the mattresses and bedding in their cell. The fire got out of control, and they called for staff to come to their aid. Stewart's cellmate was Travis, who had been his co-defendant on the robbery charge. Stewart was initially to say – maybe after some pressure from Travis – that he had started the fire alone and had done it for fun, though later on he said that they had thought of it at the same time. Travis was initially to blame it all on Stewart, though later on he said that they had decided to do it together. As it was, Stewart was eventually charged with arson. Despite his involvement, Travis was not – possibly because, by the time consideration was given to whether Stewart and Travis should be charged with arson, Travis had fatally stabbed another prisoner, and it was thought that charging him with murder was enough at that stage. A security information report was completed in connection with this incident, but it has not survived either. The only thing which staff are likely to have read about the arson would have been the entries in subsequent inmate intelligence cards. The only thing they said was that Stewart and Travis had set fire to the mattresses and bedding in their cell.

11.7 How did Stewart come to be sharing a cell with Travis in Hindley? After all, he had only just become eligible to share a cell at all, because while a prisoner is on the escape list, he has to be in a cell on his own. Moreover, it was only six months earlier that it had been thought in some quarters at Hindley that Stewart's disruptive behaviour had been designed to get him close to Travis. And how come Ms Martin's security information report was completely ignored? It is astonishing that despite her warnings Stewart and Travis ended up sharing a cell. No explanation has been offered. The fact that they had both been remanded to Hindley in custody for the offence of robbery as recently as 9 May could have meant that no-one at Hindley who had known about their previous history knew that they were both back in Hindley. But that does not absolve Hindley's Security Department from fault. One of its functions was to vet the security files of new prisoners on the day following their arrival. Had that been done on 10 May, Ms Martin's security information report would have been seen in Travis's security file, even if it had not got into Stewart's – assuming, of course, that the officer who vetted Travis's security file knew that Stewart had returned to Hindley as well. In that event, the message should have gone out that they were not to share a cell with each other. Whether it would have gone out is questionable in view of how the Security Department was then functioning. But if it had gone out, the arson would probably not then have occurred, because it is unlikely that Stewart or Travis would have set fire to their mattress and bedding without the other being there.

Stewart's time at Werrington

11.8 Stewart was not at Werrington for long. He was transferred to Stoke Heath on 30 May. The only contemporaneous document which recorded the reason for his transfer was an entry in a file maintained by the Probation Service. His transfer was said to have been because of his "unruly behaviour". Two incidents may have been behind it. First, on what was probably 25 May, an officer was attacked by a number of prisoners in the segregation unit. After wrecking the unit, five of them managed to escape. It is unclear what Stewart's involvement was, though he was not recorded as having tried to escape. He was simply recorded as having smashed the observation glass in the door of his cell. A security information report was completed, but it too has not survived. References in subsequent inmate intelligence cards based on that security information report are the only surviving source for what happened in this incident. Apart from the incident having been given the wrong date, Stewart's own role in the incident was not recorded completely, which made the references of less use than they might have been. Secondly, on 29 May, Stewart and another prisoner tried to remove the bars from a window in the weights room, and to put one of the weights through the window. That was regarded as an attempt to escape. The security information report relating to this incident has not survived either, and subsequent references to it in inmate intelligence cards gave the wrong date for that as well.

11.9 The worrying feature of all this is that the prisoner with whom Stewart was regarded as having tried to escape was Travis. It is certainly surprising that Travis and Stewart had both been transferred to Werrington. It is all the more surprising that they had apparently been allowed to spend time with each other insufficiently supervised in the weights room. After all, it was known at Werrington that Stewart and Travis had been involved in a fire in their cell at Hindley – an entry to that effect had been made on Stewart's wing file on the day he got to Werrington, and it said they had to be kept apart. What is even more surprising is that, given their background and what was thought to have been an attempt to escape from Werrington, when they came to be transferred again, they were again moved to the same establishment. They were *both* transferred to Stoke Heath, which is where Travis became the first of the two of them to commit murder. They were even allocated to the same wing.

Chapter 12: Stoke Heath

Information at Stoke Heath

12.1 We can make an educated guess at the information which Stoke Heath had about the connection between Stewart and Travis. It is overwhelmingly likely that the security information report completed by Ms Martin would have been in Travis's security file. And it is very likely that the security information reports relating to the arson which they had committed together at Hindley on 10 May and their attempted escape from Werrington on 29 May were on Stewart's security file, because both those reports were referred to in inmate intelligence cards subsequently generated on Stewart. We do not know how effective Stoke Heath's Security Department was at the time. But one of its functions was to vet the security files of incoming prisoners who were transferred from other establishments on the day following their arrival. So the connection between Stewart and Travis which their security files revealed should have been picked up – unless, of course, their security files were vetted by different officers, neither of whom realised that Stewart *and* Travis had both been transferred to Stoke Heath. If that had been appreciated by someone who knew the connection between the two of them, it would hardly have been appropriate for them to have been allocated to the same wing, which resulted in them attending classes together.

Travis commits murder

12.2 On 23 June, Travis fatally stabbed another prisoner, Alan Averill, during a cooking class. It was Averill's 18th birthday. Stewart and Travis had been at Stoke Heath for just over three weeks. Those who attended the class had been split into pairs, and Travis was working with Stewart. Each pair had been provided with a knife, and it was the one which Stewart and Travis had been provided with which Travis used on Averill. He was subsequently convicted of Averill's murder. Stewart was arrested and questioned in connection with the stabbing. Although he was suspected of having been involved in it, no charges were ever brought against him.

12.3 There was an internal Prison Service investigation into the murder. Naturally enough, that focused on how Travis had got hold of a knife and had been able to use it to stab Averill. For our purposes, a number of different questions arise. Was the information which the Prison Service had about Stewart's possible involvement in the stabbing sufficiently recorded in the security information reports which were completed? Did they get into Stewart's security file? And was the information in them sufficiently summarised in the inmate intelligence cards on Stewart when they were subsequently generated?

The security information reports about the stabbing

12.4 Four security information reports were completed about the stabbing and Stewart's suspected involvement in it. The first was written on 23 June by a prison officer who reported some information given to him by a prisoner, W. W had claimed to have overheard Travis and Stewart plotting to take hostages at the cooking class and to "cut the teacher". The security information report did not say whether W had heard what their ultimate aim was – for example, to effect an escape – but he did say that Averill had been in the wrong place at the wrong time, and that Averill had not been the intended victim.

12.5 The next security information report was also written on 23 June. It was completed by another officer who reported some information given to him by another prisoner, G. G had claimed that Travis and Stewart had been "planning to take the whole of the home economics class as hostages… as a means of escape from Stoke Heath". Travis and Stewart were said to be "big buddies". G claimed that it was very likely that Stewart would do anything, even something serious, to "follow Travis wherever he goes". In a statement which he subsequently made to the police, G said that Stewart had told him that once the hostages had been taken he was going to demand that all the prisoners who had been transferred to Stoke Heath from Werrington be brought to the class. G did not say that Stewart had told him that the reason why hostages were going to be taken was to secure his escape, and it may be that the officer to whom G made these claims may have misunderstood that part of what G was telling him.

12.6 The officer who wrote that security information report also made an entry on the same day in Stewart's wing file. It read:

> "An inmate was stabbed today and died. Although Stewart did not do it, he was involved with other inmates who were planning to take the cookery teacher hostage and 'carve him up'. Stewart may come across as a weakling, but he is an exceptionally dangerous individual and all wing staff should read his security file. He was big buddies with the murderer."

12.7 The third security information report was completed on 27 June. It reported information which had come from the police, who had confirmed that "some sort of hostage situation" had been planned to take place in the home economics class on the day in question, and that a demand would be made for transferees from Werrington to be brought to the class. The report concluded:

> "It would also appear that the stabbing was unconnected with and pre-empted this possibility."

Whether that was the opinion of the officer making the report or the police is unclear.

12.8 These three security information reports were all written at Stoke Heath. The final one was written at Onley Young Offender Institution in Rugby. That was where Stewart had been transferred on 26 June. It was completed on 29 June. It reported further information which had come from the police. Stewart had been described by prisoners as "mad". He was referred to as having been "heavily involved" in what had led to the stabbing, and it stated that it had been alleged that he had handed the knife to Travis.

12.9 The documents supplied by the police to the Inquiry show that there was evidence that the stabbing had been planned, and that Stewart had either put Travis up to it or had helped him to plan it or had actually helped him to carry it out. One prisoner made a statement to the police in which he claimed that, on the night before the stabbing, he had heard Travis tell Stewart that he would stab Averill if Averill said anything to him in the cooking lesson. Another prisoner made a statement to the police that after the stabbing he had heard Stewart say to Travis, when the three of them were in the segregation unit, that Travis should say that he, Stewart, had told him to do it. Travis himself told the police that Stewart had passed him the knife by the blade. And the transcript of Stewart's own interview by the police on 25 June shows that he knew that Travis was intending to stab Averill, and he let slip things which suggested that he may have helped Travis to plan it.

The treatment of these security information reports

12.10 Did these security information reports contain sufficient information about Stewart's suspected involvement in the stabbing? We do not know how much of the evidence unearthed by the police in the course of their investigation into the possible involvement of Stewart in the stabbing was revealed to the Prison Service at the time. If the reports contained the full extent of what the Prison Service had been told, nothing more could have been put in them, even if there had been more that the Prison Service could have been told. But if the Prison Service had more information, that should have been recorded in a comprehensive security information report containing the key elements of Stewart's suspected involvement in the stabbing once it was known that Stewart was not going to face charges.

12.11 It was while Stewart was at Onley that it became known that he was not going to face charges over the stabbing. So if the Prison Service then knew more about Stewart's suspected involvement in the stabbing than the existing security information reports contained, one of two things should have happened. The Security Department at Onley should have prepared an up-to-date and comprehensive report which could then have gone into Stewart's security file. Or the Security Department at Onley should have let the Security Department at Stoke Heath know that Stewart was not going to face charges over the stabbing, so that the Security Department at Stoke Heath could produce an up-to-date and comprehensive report, which could then be returned to Onley for inclusion in Stewart's security file. No such report was ever written. But even if the Prison Service knew nothing more of Stewart's possible involvement in the stabbing, it cannot escape criticism here. The police liaison officer at Stoke Heath should have done more to ensure that the Security Department at Stoke Heath received sufficient information about Stewart's possible involvement in the stabbing. And a security information report should have been written to the effect that Stewart was still believed to have been strongly implicated in it, even if the evidence to charge him was not there.

12.12 Did the four security information reports get into Stewart's security file? Here again there is room for criticism of the Security Department at Stoke Heath, since it looks as if not all of them did. Subsequent inmate intelligence cards on Stewart refer to only two of the four reports. That means that they were the only two entered onto the 4x4 system, and that suggests that they were the only two to have got into Stewart's security file. Indeed, by the time that the Inquiry got Stewart's security file, only the last of the four reports was in it. There was a fax in the security file from Stoke Heath to Onley enclosing the third of the four reports, but only a small part of that enclosure remained in the security file, and it would not then have made sense to anyone reading it.

12.13 Were the reports sufficiently summarised in the inmate intelligence cards which were subsequently generated? The summary of the first report was as follows:

> "Strongly suspected of being involved in a stabbing and attempting to take hostages with… Travis."

The summary of the last report was as follows:

> "Info from Dav[entry] Police indicates that Stewart was heavily involved in the pre-planning of the incident which led to the fatal stabbing at [Stoke Heath]. It is alleged that he handed the murder weapon to Travis who carried out the murder."

These summaries give the reader of the cards the basic facts contained in the two reports, and although these entries do not refer to the relationship between Travis and Stewart which the second report and the entry in Stewart's wing file specifically mentioned, their relationship was evident from earlier entries in the cards which covered the arson they had committed together at Hindley on 10 May and the attempt to escape together from Werrington on 29 May. So although it would have been better for all four reports to have been in Stewart's security file, to have been entered onto the 4x4 system, and to have been summarised in the inmate intelligence cards, Stewart's possible involvement in the stabbing (though not the extent of it), his association with Travis, and the things which they had got up to together in the recent past were there. Whether anyone reading these entries would have got a real sense of how dangerous Stewart would be on his own is questionable. The extent to which attempts should have been made at Onley to find out more about Stewart is one of the next topics to be addressed.

Chapter 13: Onley

Stewart's arrival at Onley

13.1 When Stewart arrived at Onley on 26 June 1998, the duty governor, Don Shaw, wanted to know why Stewart was being transferred. The escort staff who had brought Stewart told him that all the prisoners who had witnessed the stabbing at Stoke Heath or had been "on the periphery of it" were being transferred. He was told that Stewart had not been directly involved in the stabbing, and would not be facing any charges arising out of it. So Mr Shaw decided that Stewart could be placed on ordinary location, but he asked an officer in the Security Department at Onley to find out about the stabbing. He did not ask to see Stewart's security file, which should have arrived with Stewart.

13.2 The duty governor on the following day was Susan Schilling. She has since re-married, and is now Susan Chapman. Although she now has no recollection of Stewart's arrival at Onley, what happened is apparent from entries she made on 27 June in Stewart's wing file and in the governors' journal. She spoke to the officer in the Security Department at Onley who had been trying to find out about the stabbing and to the duty governor at Stoke Heath. From the officer in the Security Department at Onley, she learned "some fairly alarming things about Stewart's past both at Stoke Heath and Werrington". From the duty governor at Stoke Heath, she learned that Stewart was "strongly implicated" in the stabbing, and that he was on police bail – which meant that the police were continuing their investigation into the extent of his involvement in it. She decided that, in the absence of fuller information, Stewart should be somewhere more secure than on ordinary location. In an establishment like Onley, which was the equivalent of a category C prison, that meant holding him in the segregation unit. That was where Stewart remained until 30 July, which was when he was informed that he would not face charges in connection with the stabbing.

13.3 Why was the information which Mrs Chapman had on 27 June not available to Mr Shaw on 26 June? For one reason or another, Stewart's security file did not accompany him on his transfer from Stoke Heath to Onley. It should have done. Had it done so, and had it contained the two security information reports of 23 June, Mr Shaw may well have decided that Stewart should not go to ordinary location at all for the time being. And if a prisoner was being transferred from an establishment at which a fatal stabbing had taken place because he was believed to have been implicated in it, the receiving establishment should have been informed of that. That did not happen either. For both those shortcomings, the Security Department at Stoke Heath must be held to be culpable. Fortunately, nothing untoward happened over the next

24 hours while Stewart was on ordinary location, so these shortcomings had no adverse impact, but they still should not have occurred.

Stewart's time in the segregation unit

13.4 The wing file for Stewart's time in the segregation unit does not disclose any incidents of significance. His only breach of prison discipline was changing his appearance by shaving his head. But the entries for two periods are missing: for the period 3–7 July, and for the period from 11 July. It looks as if what happened was that the entries for the period 3–7 July were on one sheet. That was temporarily mislaid on 8 July, and so another sheet was used for the period 8–10 July. The sheet for 3–7 July was then found, and was used to make entries for the period 11–30 July. That sheet then went missing again and has never been found. That does not say much for the record-keeping in the segregation unit. But the significance of the missing sheets is that we do not know which governor on 30 July directed that Stewart should be returned to ordinary location.

The information which Onley had on Stewart

13.5 It is clear that the Security Department at Onley got some information about Stewart while he was there. The security information report which had been written at Stoke Heath on 27 June was faxed to Onley. And on 29 June, Onley itself completed the security information report based on the further information which had come from the police, and included the allegation that Stewart had handed the knife to Travis. But whether Stewart's security file ever got to Onley is unclear. On 28 June, a prisoner security information sheet was printed out from the 4x4 system. It referred to Stewart's transfer having been because he had been involved with Travis in the fatal stabbing on 23 June. It described him as violent, as having the potential to escape and as being an exceptional risk, though the nature of the risk he posed was not stated. That assessment must have been based on information in Stewart's security file. It is possible that this print-out was generated at Stoke Heath, even though Stewart had been transferred to Onley, and was based on information which had already been entered onto the 4x4 system at Stoke Heath. If that is right, the prisoner security information sheet tells us nothing about whether Stewart's security file ever got to Onley. It is equally possible, though, that the print-out was generated at

Onley. Since the information it contained would in those circumstances have to have been entered onto the 4x4 system at Onley, that would have meant that Stewart's security file had reached Onley by then. I note that an inmate intelligence card which had to have been printed before 20 August was placed in Stewart's security file at some stage. But since that card was not necessarily generated at Onley – it could have been generated at Hindley when Stewart was transferred back there on 19 August* – it does not assist on whether Stewart's security file ever got to Onley.

13.6 If Stewart's security file never got to Onley, that was the fault of the Security Department at Stoke Heath. If it had not accompanied Stewart on his transfer to Onley, Stoke Heath should have ensured that it was subsequently sent there. But the Security Department at Onley cannot escape criticism. Once the department realised that it did not have it, staff there should have pressed Stoke Heath for it. But even if Onley never got Stewart's security file, so that the prisoner security information sheet would have been generated at Stoke Heath and found its way into Stewart's security file after he had left Onley, the information Onley still had about Stewart meant that he should have been regarded as a real cause for concern. He was known by the Security Department at Onley to have been up to no good at Werrington and Stoke Heath, and Mrs Chapman knew that he was "strongly implicated" in the stabbing. She may not have known any more than that, but it is not possible to tell now whether she brought that to the attention of the Security Department at Onley. But if she did, all the more reason for the department to have got hold of Stewart's security file. If that had been done, the Security Department at Onley would have got some details about the "fairly alarming" things which it had been told about, presumably covering the arson at Hindley on 10 May and the incidents at Werrington on 25 and 29 May, as well as finding out more about the stabbing from the security information reports of 23 June.

The other criticisms of Onley

13.7 Plainly Stewart could not have remained in the segregation unit indefinitely. His anticipated release date was 20 August 1998. That was still some way off, and soon Onley's Board of Visitors would have been

---

* The fact that one of the entries in it referred to Stewart *currently* being on police bail did not mean that it had to have been printed before he ceased on 30 July to be on police bail: the reference to him being currently on police bail could have been because he was on police bail when the security information report on which the entry was based was written.

pressing for him to be returned to ordinary location, unless there were strong security reasons why he should not have been. Keeping him in the segregation unit may have been justified while it was being decided whether he should face charges arising out of the stabbing, but if the decision was made not to press any charges against him, were there any other security reasons which would have justified keeping a particularly careful watch on him? Considering such security reasons would have involved making an assessment of the risk he posed to other prisoners. The information which Mrs Chapman had received about him, and the additional information about him in his security file which Onley should have obtained, should have been a sufficient prompt for that assessment being made.

13.8 What actually happened was that no assessment was made of the risk Stewart posed to other prisoners. It has been suggested that Onley's police liaison officer attempted to get some more information about the stabbing from the police, but even if he did, no note of what he learned has survived. The fact is that Stewart was simply returned to ordinary location, without any consideration being given to the risks he posed, simply because the decision had been made that he would not be facing charges in connection with the stabbing.

13.9 This approach was flawed. There are any number of reasons why a decision may be made not to prosecute a suspect for their possible involvement in a crime, many of which would not justify the conclusion that the suspect did not pose a risk to others. The most obvious reason is the lack of sufficient admissible and reliable evidence to place before a court, even though the suspicion of involvement in the crime is strong. It was not appropriate to remove Stewart to ordinary location, simply because he was not going to be prosecuted over his involvement with the stabbing, as if nothing had happened.

13.10 In short, although Stewart had to be returned at some time to ordinary location – where he would have been in a single cell because Onley only had single cells – some thought should have been given to the risk Stewart might have posed. I have not overlooked the evidence that Onley did not have anyone with psychiatric experience in its healthcare centre. Nor have I ignored the fact that formal risk assessments were not part of the culture within the Prison Service at the time, and that there was no recognised assessment tool in place at Onley. But there is no reason why Onley was not capable of carrying out some sort of informal *ad hoc* multi-disciplinary assessment of the risks which potentially dangerous prisoners might pose, with contributions from wing staff, the Security Department, the healthcare centre, probation officers and the police liaison officer. It was true that in the month before his return to ordinary location, Stewart had caused no trouble in the segregation unit. But this was, after all, a prisoner who, in the space of a few weeks before coming to Onley, had

- set fire to his cell in a manner sufficiently serious for him to be prosecuted – he had been charged with arson by 17 July, which was when he went to court, which was itself almost two weeks before he was returned to ordinary location

- attempted to escape

- been involved in some way in a riot

- been strongly implicated in the planning and execution of a fatal stabbing, along with a possible plan to take hostages.

If an event as rare as a homicide in prison, coupled with Stewart's suspected involvement in it and his recent behaviour in custody, was not sufficient to warrant some thought being given to the risk he might pose, it is difficult to imagine what would.

13.11 It is no excuse to say that there was not enough time for that to be done before he was transferred back to Hindley on 19 August. It was known that he would be remaining in custody after 20 August – the date when he would otherwise have been released – pending his trial on the charge of arson, and it has not been suggested that he would have to have been transferred out of Onley simply because his status on 20 August would have changed from a convicted to a remand prisoner. In any event, there was no reason why an unfinished assessment at Onley could not have been completed elsewhere.

13.12 What would have happened if some thought *had* been given at Onley to the risk which Stewart might pose? According to Professor Maden, not a lot. Although Stewart would have qualified for his personality disorder to have been classified as severe, along with about 10% of the prison population, Professor Maden thought that in terms of the risk which Stewart posed to other prisoners, he would not have stood out as being particularly out of the ordinary. It was true that he would commit offences for no reason other than for a laugh or because he was bored. But his offences were run-of-the-mill offences: what was missing was an offence of the kind which would have drawn attention to his dangerousness. He was willing to get involved in trouble if someone else started it, but his record showed that he was rarely the prime mover. And his violence was not predatory. He did not seem to go out of his way to look for people to assault. His violence was often a response to the situation he found himself in – for example, when he was confronted in the course of stealing a car. As for the arson, Professor Maden was under the impression that Stewart had been egged on to set fire to the cell. And Professor Maden did not think that the stabbing at Stoke Heath would have made much of a difference to the assessment, even if Stewart had been involved in the planning of it and had handed the knife to Travis. There was nothing to suggest that Averill had been targeted because of any faction of prisoners to which he belonged.

13.13 The factual assumptions made by Professor Maden which caused him to think that Stewart would not have stood out from the crowd were, I think, incorrect. Stewart could have been just as much to blame for the arson as Travis. And if Stewart had been involved in the planning of the stabbing at Stoke Heath, he was participating in a very predatory crime. In that event, the fact that Averill had not belonged to any identifiable faction would have been irrelevant. And if one moves away from his offending history to his behaviour in prison aside from the arson and the stabbing, we see many examples of Stewart deciding himself to act in a very predatory way.

13.14 Professor Gunn was more circumspect. In his view, Stewart had demonstrated that he was capable of violence and needed careful management. A policy judgement always has to be made, taking into account the management of prisons and the availability of resources, about how far it is appropriate to seek to avoid the statistically very low risk of an attack of the kind to which Zahid was subjected. And if thought had been given to the risk Stewart might pose to other prisoners, he would have been regarded as the kind of prisoner who should not share a cell with anyone. Professor Gunn did not say in terms that Stewart would have stood out as being out of the ordinary if thought had been given to the risk he might pose to other prisoners. But the real possibility remains that he would have done.

13.15 In the end, we can only speculate about the view which would have been taken at Onley if thought had been given to the risk which Stewart might have posed to other prisoners. But it is not unlikely that a multi-disciplinary team armed with the information which it should have had about Stewart would have identified him as potentially dangerous to other prisoners. If that had happened, a suitable warning about him could have been placed on his records, which could be seen by anyone who dealt with him as he moved around the prison system. It is also possible that he would then have been regarded as a suitable candidate for a psychiatric referral. But even if he would not have been, a multi-disciplinary assessment would have been an opportunity for the Prison

Service to consider whether any link between his behaviour and his mental state should be investigated.

13.16 The responsibility for ensuring that Stewart was assessed for the risks he posed lay with the governor who directed that Stewart be returned to ordinary location. That may have been Mrs Chapman, but it could have been anyone else. The relevant entry would have been made in the wing file covering Stewart's time in the segregation unit, but the sheet with that entry has gone missing. I have no reason to suppose that it has been deliberately mislaid, but the consequence is that the governor who may have been susceptible to criticism cannot be identified.

Chapter 14: Back at Hindley again

Stewart's transfer to Hindley

14.1 Stewart's transfer back to Hindley on 19 August 1998 was his fourth transfer in less than four months. As I said earlier, transfers are not necessarily a good thing. But although we do not know for sure the reason for Stewart's transfer back to Hindley – since the reason for it was not recorded anywhere – we can make an educated guess. From 20 August he was to be held on remand awaiting trial for the arson committed at Hindley in May. Onley is in Rugby, and his transfer back to Hindley meant that he would be closer to the court in which he would be tried, as well as being closer to his home, making visits by his family and friends that much easier.

14.2 On 12 October, Stewart was sentenced to 12 months' detention in a young offender institution for the arson. Some weeks later he was sentenced to 21 days' detention in a young offender institution, to be served with the 12 months' detention, for an offence of shoplifting committed on the day the previous April when the combination order had been made. He served the whole of his sentence at Hindley – apart from a failed attempt to transfer him to Deerbolt Young Offender Institution in County Durham – until he was released on licence on 2 July 1999.

Stewart's disruptive behaviour

14.3 Stewart's release on licence was delayed considerably as a result of the trouble he got into while he was serving this sentence. He had continued to behave disruptively, though his conduct was nothing to compare with his seemingly bizarre – but in reality manipulative – behaviour in the autumn of 1997 or with the dramatic events of May and June 1998. There were instances of fighting, bullying and assaults on other prisoners. There were occasions when Stewart damaged his cell and his bedding. There were times when he was found in possession of makeshift blades and screws. There were times when he was abusive to staff. On one occasion, he threw his meal at his cell door. And during this period a letter was intercepted in which Stewart said that if he got his "L plates", he would go sick and take hostages. He was referring to a sentence of life imprisonment, which he would be liable for if he committed two offences for which such a sentence was automatic. A security information report was completed about this letter in January 1999, but the letter itself has not survived.

14.4 Also in January 1999 there was an incident which was serious enough to be reported to the police, when another prisoner had to be treated for an injury. Stewart's wing file referred to him having stabbed the other prisoner with a sharp piece of wood below the eye. However, the incident may well have been less serious than it sounds. Police records show that the prisoner's injuries were described as very minor, and that it was more a case of him being hit in the face with a piece of wood taken from a window frame rather than being stabbed near the eye. And the prisoner refused to press a complaint against Stewart. A security information report was written about this incident. It has not survived, but if the summary of the incident in an inmate intelligence card which was subsequently printed out is anything to go by, the seriousness of the incident may have been exaggerated.

14.5 One other thing happened in January 1999. Stewart swallowed a battery. At any rate, that was what he claimed. He said that he had done it for a laugh. Dr Greenwood was informed of that by telephone. He did not see Stewart, but gave advice about what should be done. However, he looked at what Stewart claimed to have done only in terms of its possible physical implications. He did not give any thought to whether, if Stewart had indeed swallowed a battery, it said something about his mental state. Dr Greenwood should have done that, if only to flag Stewart up as someone whose mental state may have to be considered if odd behaviour like this was repeated. As we shall see, though, it was not.

14.6 Stewart's violent and disruptive behaviour over the period caused a number of comments to be recorded in his files by prison officers about him. Many are chilling in their prescience. In October 1998, Stewart's personal officer wrote that Stewart could not "be trusted for even a minute". In December 1998, in the context of an allegation of bullying, Stewart was called "a disaster waiting to happen", and described as "constantly a threat to the security of the establishment". These words were picked up by his personal officer again in March 1999:

> "This lad is a disaster waiting to happen. He *cannot* be trusted and I feel as if we are just waiting for our next problem with him."

Similar views were expressed by other officers later that month. One officer described Stewart's history in prison as "appalling" in the context of an assessment of his suitability for early release on home detention curfew, and assessed the risk that he would commit violent offences as high. And a few days later, another officer also described him as "a disaster waiting to happen", and wrote that he had to be closely supervised at all times.

14.7 I do not suppose that one officer's colourful description of Stewart, probably regarded by other officers as a convenient way to describe him, reflected an actual expectation that he would commit a violent offence of the utmost seriousness. The comments probably reflected an instinctive feeling that Stewart was highly unpredictable, and that his offending could well escalate to physical violence.

14.8 Concerns were also being expressed about Stewart by non-prison staff at Hindley. Mrs Joyce O'Mara, a probation officer attached to Hindley, wrote an assessment of Stewart on 16 November 1998. She was focusing on his offending behaviour outside prison rather than on his disruptive behaviour within it, but she referred to the "buzz" which he was still experiencing when offending. He had no sense of the seriousness of the arson, and no empathy for the victims of his offences. She regarded him as "in the high risk of offending category with the risk of harm [to] the public increasing". She did not know about Stewart's involvement in the stabbing at Stoke Heath. That rather suggests that information held in a prisoner's security file which would be relevant to an assessment of the risks which the prisoner posed was not being relayed to internal probation officers. Had she known that Stewart had been strongly implicated in the stabbing, her concern about the risk he posed would have been even greater. She told the Inquiry that in her view Stewart was not ready to change.

Improvements in Stewart's behaviour

14.9 But change he did – outwardly at any rate. Towards the end of his sentence, everyone who dealt with Stewart noticed a marked improvement in his behaviour. Apart from an occasion in March 1999 when he refused to obey an order, and an occasion in May 1999 when he threw paint at another prisoner, the files no longer record instances of violent or disruptive behaviour on his part – at any rate, none which were proved to have happened. On the contrary, the change in him was noted. It seems to have started from his return to ordinary location following a spell in the segregation unit in the aftermath of the "stabbing" of the other prisoner. A governor had recorded Stewart as saying that he wanted to return to ordinary location and that he would do his best to stay out of trouble.

14.10 Within six weeks of the move, Stewart's personal officer was writing that he was conforming at the moment, and a month later another prison officer wrote the same thing, though he did not want to tempt fate by being too positive about Stewart. By May 1999, his personal officer was writing that Stewart seemed to want to keep out of trouble, and in June 1999 she wrote:

> "The improvement in this young man's attitude and behaviour is quite remarkable. He has only four weeks left and in my opinion deserves some kind of recognition for the way he has turned himself around."

It was no doubt in response to these comments that Stewart was granted enhanced status in Hindley's incentives and earned privileges scheme. And a few days before his release, his sentence plan review recorded that there had been a big improvement in his attendance and behaviour, and that he had worked well in education. By then, his risk of violent re-offending was assessed as low.

14.11 Mrs O'Mara said that she would not have reduced her assessment of that risk. That difference of opinion probably reflects a difference of approach to the assessment of risk between prison officers and probation officers. Prison officers are prone to look at the here and now. They tend to think that if a person is behaving at the moment, there is no cause for concern. A probation officer with more experience of the assessment of risk is probably less likely to take such a short-term view.

14.12 Although these entries in Stewart's files referred to an improvement in his attitude as well as his behaviour, there is no suggestion that he ceased to be what he had always been – quiet and a loner. Even during his period of improved behaviour, he was described as "one of the quieter inmates" on an alcohol awareness programme he was attending. His personal officer described him before his behaviour changed as being very hard to have a conversation with, which is how he had presented in the past. As we shall see, that was how he was to present when he went to Feltham.

Stewart's racism

14.13 Mrs O'Mara's evidence to the Inquiry was that it had been known in Hindley that Stewart was racist. I fear that her memory is at fault. She was unable to recall what made her think that, or when she might have been told about it. If her opinion had been based on what she had been told by a member of staff or a prisoner, she would have written a security information report about it. Indeed, it is difficult to think of any circumstances in which she would have found out that Stewart was a racist without thinking that a security information report should be completed. As it is, there is no evidence whatever of a security information report having been written, nor of Hindley's Race Relations Liaison Officer having been alerted. And none of the other Hindley witnesses who were asked about it – Harold Dunne, who was a principal officer at Hindley in charge of operations, and who was temporarily promoted to Head of Operations in May 1999, and Ms Martin – had heard about it. What has happened, I think, is that Mrs O'Mara now thinks what she does as a result of her subsequently hearing of Stewart's murder of Zahid. She herself accepted that this may be the case. I do not say that Stewart was not a racist when he was at Hindley. All I am saying is that Stewart's racism was not generally known about while he was there.

Assessing the risk

14.14 Unlike Onley, Hindley had a number of double cells. I recognise, of course, that Stewart returned to Hindley in the days before a formal cell-sharing risk assessment scheme was introduced. And to the extent that thought was ever given to the topic of cell-sharing, Mrs O'Mara's opinion was that it focused on which prisoners needed to share cells in order to minimise the risk of self-harm. But common sense tells us that, in an establishment where prisoners share cells, some thought should be given to a prisoner's unsuitability to share a cell because of the risk they might pose to other prisoners. Indeed, Mr Dunne told the Inquiry that it would have been surprising if Stewart had been thought suitable to share a cell in the light of his possible involvement in the stabbing at Stoke Heath. Mr Sheffield said much the same thing.

14.15 But it does not look as if any thought was given to whether Stewart was suitable to share a cell. A decision that he should not share a cell could be expected to have been documented – Mr Dunne said as much – but he had not seen any record of such a decision. And we know that in November 1998 Stewart was moved from a single to a double cell. One hopes that this would not have happened if Stewart had been regarded as unsuitable to share a cell – especially as his behaviour was so poor at the time. But there was no system in place for identifying those prisoners who should not share a cell. There should have been. The principal officer temporarily responsible for security at the time must bear the primary responsibility for that.

14.16 Stewart's trial and sentence for the arson at Hindley in May 1998 was the catalyst for some risk assessments to be carried out on him. A risk assessment was carried out by a probation officer, Patrick Dawson, for the purpose of a pre-sentence report he was preparing for the court. The tool he used – form RM1 – was not particularly sophisticated, but by using it Mr Dawson identified Stewart as someone who was highly likely to cause a high level of harm to prison staff and other prisoners. But that was only because the arson had been committed in prison, and considerable harm could have been caused if the fire had got out of hand. I do not suppose that even Mr Dawson would say that this assessment purported to be an assessment of the risk Stewart might have posed while in custody to other prisoners. Having said that, the assessment should have triggered the completion of a more sophisticated form, form RM2. Mr Dawson does not recall if he completed one. If he did, it has not survived.

14.17 These forms are not sent to the prison at which the offender is detained. What Hindley did receive was the pre-sentence report Mr Dawson prepared. That was to be expected. The evidence to the Inquiry was that a pre-sentence report should go with the prisoner to the prison as a matter of course. The parts of the report which were relevant to the risk Stewart continued to pose read as follows:

> "With hindsight he could see the risk this behaviour [the arson] posed to himself and his cellmate. But I did not feel he could see the wider implications of the fire affecting other inmates or staff… who might well have been put directly at risk by behaviour that had no purpose or intent beyond possibly alleviating boredom… The intent seems to be not against any individual or the institution but involves an element of fun that perhaps reflects an immaturity that cannot see the consequences of behaviour. Such attitudes are apparent in all his offending and therefore at this level the arson charge is no different from other offending. This suggests that the risk of re-offending and the risk of harm remain significant."

A few weeks later, in response to a standard request from Hindley for information which would be used in planning Stewart's sentence, Mr Dawson wrote:

> "Whilst offending in the community is a problem, more serious behaviour appears to have occurred when he has been in custody and in the company of a young man by the name of Travis. They are unlikely to meet up during this present sentence. It would be interesting to note whether a change in behaviour takes place."

14.18 These assessments are useful as far as they go. They told Hindley that Stewart was prone to misbehave in prison out of boredom or fun, and that he did not think of the consequences of what he was doing. They told Hindley that his arson was not an isolated act, and that there had been other instances of misconduct in prison. But they did not refer to the stabbing at Stoke Heath, and although Professor Maden thought that the pre-sentence report was a good risk assessment, I fear that it told Hindley very little about whether Stewart posed a real risk to the safety of staff or other prisoners.

14.19 A risk assessment was carried out in Hindley as part of the process for planning Stewart's sentence. It was in the context of that that Mrs O'Mara had written her assessment of Stewart. The form which was used for that purpose and which the Inquiry was provided with – form ACR1 – may be incomplete. It referred to Stewart's lack of concern for his victims or for his own safety, but it said nothing about whether he should be regarded as a risk to other prisoners. That is not surprising. There was little or no input into the process by officers on the wing who were dealing with Stewart on a daily basis. And although that part of the form which dealt with risk assessment was to be completed by the prisoner's personal officer, that was not what happened in practice. It certainly was not what happened in Stewart's case. The risk assessment was therefore based on little more than Stewart's offending history – and but for the fact that the arson had been committed while he had been in custody, it did not focus on his behaviour in custody at all.

14.20 The closest one gets at Hindley to a real warning about what Stewart might get up to in custody was an entry in his wing file on 20 November 1998:

> "Due to this inmate being involved in an incident at Stoke Heath where an inmate was stabbed (fatal) and a possible hostage incident in the education where Stewart was heavily involved he should not be re-allocated to Stoke Heath. See security file for further information!!"

We do not know what prompted this entry. It may have had something to do with the Security Department's contribution to the risk assessment carried out in connection with the planning of Stewart's sentence. But nothing came of it. No thought, it seems, was ever given to whether Stewart posed a particular risk to other prisoners, and his management in the prison was therefore not informed by any such assessment. In the same way that such an assessment should have taken place at Onley, so too should such an assessment have taken place at Hindley. Even though formal risk assessments were not part of the culture within the Prison Service at the time, Stewart's manipulative behaviour at Hindley in 1997 and the dramatic events in May and June 1998 called for nothing less. It may be that the need for such an assessment would have been less obvious while Stewart was on remand awaiting his trial for the arson. That may distinguish Hindley from Onley, where he was at all times a convicted prisoner. But that cannot be said after his sentence for the arson – especially as his behaviour was then so poor.

14.21 Later on, Hindley introduced a formal scheme for determining how potentially dangerous offenders should be managed. That scheme had not been introduced when Stewart was sentenced for the arson. But as I said in relation to Onley, there is no reason why there could not have been some sort of informal *ad hoc* multi-disciplinary assessment of the risk Stewart posed, with contributions from wing staff, the Security Department, the healthcare centre, probation officers and the police liaison officer. There should have been a system in place for the Security Department to have initiated an exercise of that kind. There was not, and for that the principal officer temporarily in charge of the Security Department at the time must bear the primary responsibility as well. Again, it is not unlikely that such an assessment would have resulted in Stewart being identified as potentially dangerous to other prisoners and as unsuitable to share a cell. It may be that he would have been considered as a suitable candidate for psychiatric referral. But even if he would not have been, a multi-disciplinary assessment would have been a further opportunity for the Prison Service to consider whether any link between his behaviour and his mental state should be investigated.

Chapter 15: Hindley sees Stewart yet again

Stewart's return to Hindley

15.1 Following Stewart's release from Hindley on 2 July 1999, he remained on licence for a while. The probation officer who supervised him was Amy Poulson. She completed forms RM1 and RM2 on him. She did not think that Stewart was as much of a risk as Mr Dawson had thought. Although she identified police and prison officers as at risk from him, she thought that there was only a "medium" likelihood that he would cause them harm, though if he did the level of harm would be high. No doubt she was influenced, understandably, by what she described as his "positive moves to behave in a more responsible manner while in custody". She summed up her opinion of him as follows:

> "Limited insight into behaviour. Impulsive and immature young man. Not showing signs of any motivation to change lifestyle. Is reporting regularly which is positive sign and shows no concerns re expression of anger."

15.2 Stewart was not free for long. On 28 July, he was remanded in custody and returned to Hindley following his arrest for two joyriding offences and an offence of robbery. He was subsequently sentenced to three months' detention in a young offender institution for the joyriding offences, but since he was pleading not guilty to the robbery, he was committed to the Crown Court for trial on that charge. That was why he remained in custody after he had served his sentence. There is no record of what happened to the robbery charge, though Stewart wrote in a letter that it was to be "thrown out". There is a document which shows that Stewart was due to appear at the Crown Court on 9 December 1999. Since he was released on that day, it looks as if no evidence was offered on the charge. He remained at Hindley until 5 November, when he was transferred to Altcourse Young Offender Institution in Liverpool.

15.3 Stewart's wing file for this spell at Hindley has not survived. There is no evidence of a recurrence of the disruptive and violent behaviour which had characterised much of his previous time in custody. But a couple of significant events occurred during this period, which suggest that, while Stewart was keeping his head down in prison, he was causing trouble outside it, or at least making plans to.

The intercepted letter

15.4 Some time in August, a letter Stewart had written to a prisoner at a women's prison was intercepted. We do not know why that was, but presumably it was in the course of the random monitoring of prisoners' correspondence. Nor do we know when it was, though the letter was referred to in a prisoner security information sheet which was printed on 13 August. In the letter, Stewart admitted that he had carried out a robbery at gunpoint. He was referring to the robbery charge he was facing, and was confident that it – and an associated firearms charge – would be dropped. He said that he would not be committing any robberies again, unless it was of a lottery winner. But he referred to a friend of his having hidden his gun, and to his plan to rob someone who he knew carried a large amount of cash on him. He also said that he had got someone to get him the address of the Governor and a few others off the "voting register", and that if he was "stitched up", presumably by prison staff, he would arrange for them to be subjected to sinister deliveries, such as a wreath, or unsolicited visits, such as from the gas man.

15.5 A security information report was written about the letter on 16 August. The summary it contained of the letter was incomplete. It did not refer to the confession to the robbery – which may well have interested the police – or to Stewart's plan to rob the man with the cash or to what he would do if he was "stitched up". And it referred to Stewart having got only the Governor's address, not the addresses of some others. Since the letter obviously came from Stewart, the officer who completed the security information report understandably evaluated the information which the letter contained as being very reliable and true. But he did not tick the appropriate consequence code, which in effect required him to identify how likely he thought it was that Stewart would carry out what he had said. And although he ticked a box which suggested that the contents of the security information report had been entered onto the 4x4 system, there was no reference to the entry in any of the inmate intelligence cards which were subsequently printed out. That suggests that the security information report was not entered onto the system after all. One should not blame the officer concerned too much for these errors. He had been off work on long-term sickness leave, and in order to ease him back into work he was assigned to the Security Department where the work was unfamiliar to him. It is questionable whether it was right for the Security Department to be used in that way, and the errors may say something about the extent to which the officer was being supervised by the principal officer who was temporarily in charge of the Security Department, and about the extent to which she was being supervised by Mr Dunne.

15.6 When Mr Dunne came to sign off the security information report, he commented on how names can be added to, or removed from, the electoral roll. He wrote that Hindley's police liaison officer should be informed about the gun, and added that Stewart was "a dangerous individual". He accepted that when he signed it off, he should have noticed that the appropriate consequence code had not been ticked.

Should Stewart's correspondence have been monitored?

15.7 No other action was taken over the letter. That is surprising. The monitoring of a prisoner's correspondence is permitted – albeit for no longer than is strictly necessary – if it will assist in preventing or detecting criminal activities or in countering a threat to the security or good order of the establishment. Indeed, if the random monitoring of a prisoner's correspondence reveals information which it is thought the police should have, and results in that prisoner being described as dangerous, common sense tells us that, for a while at least, all that prisoner's correspondence should be monitored. Not just because it may contain more information of use to the police, but also because it may reveal what the prisoner is getting up to in prison. And Stewart's letter was not just about possible criminal activity in the community. It was also about his behaviour in prison.

15.8 Mr Dunne's reason for not giving instructions for Stewart's correspondence to be monitored was that he thought that Stewart was simply showing off in the letter. He did not think that Stewart would actually do what he had threatened to do. Indeed, he did not think that Stewart had got the Governor's address, or that he intended to harass staff in the way he had said. What made Mr Dunne think that? I understood his answer to have been that it was because of Stewart's reasonably good behaviour in the immediate past. In my opinion, that was not a sufficient reason not to take Stewart's threats seriously. On the contrary, the fact that Stewart had been behaving reasonably well was a reason for thinking that if he now threatened to do something, he meant it. I can understand a degree of scepticism about Stewart's ability actually to put his threats into effect. But the fact that Stewart had made these threats was sufficient to set alarm bells ringing. Indeed, to be fair to Mr Dunne, he himself acknowledged that monitoring Stewart's correspondence might have been an appropriate precaution to have taken.

Should Stewart have been referred to the Potentially Dangerous Offenders' Panel?

15.9 By this time, Hindley had introduced a formal scheme for determining how potentially dangerous offenders should be managed in prison. The question therefore arises whether the interception of the letter should have triggered the invocation of that scheme in Stewart's case. But first I should say something about the scheme, because it was a model which could have been replicated to some advantage across the prison estate.

15.10 The scheme involved the establishment of a Potentially Dangerous Offenders' Register. It had been set up by a Governor's Order issued by Mr Sheffield in March 1999. Its purpose was to identify prisoners who may be "dangerous" and who posed "a serious risk to others… inside or outside of prison". The scheme would be operated by a multi-disciplinary team known as the Potentially Dangerous Offenders' Panel chaired by a governor. Any member of staff could refer a prisoner to the Panel for possible inclusion on the Register, and the Panel would decide whether to place him on the Register. If he was placed on the Register, the Panel would decide how he should be managed in prison, and would review his case periodically. One of the topics the team was expressly required to consider in respect of a prisoner on the Register was the type of cell in which he should be accommodated: single, double, furnished or unfurnished. The initiative for its establishment was attributed to the recently appointed Senior Probation Officer at Hindley, who had drawn on her experience of chairing risk assessment panels for potentially dangerous offenders in the community.

15.11 Mr Giffin's comments on the scheme were as follows:

> "It may be thought that the Potentially Dangerous Offenders' system as established at Hindley in March 1999 had much potential to address cases such as that with which the Inquiry is concerned. Potentially, it represented a means of: picking out from the crowd those prisoners who required particular attention because of the potential risks which they posed; reviewing and sharing the information held about those prisoners; thinking systematically about how to manage such prisoners; and reaching conclusions and decisions capable of being prominently recorded and if necessary passed on between establishments. It could be argued that such a system is precisely what was lacking at Onley (and indeed at Hindley itself) in the summer of 1998."

This precisely reflects my own view.

15.12 I do not think that anyone at Hindley can be criticised for not referring Stewart to the Panel when it was set up. Its establishment happened to coincide with his improved behaviour. If he was to be referred to the Panel, there needed to be something to trigger the referral. Should the letter which was intercepted in August 1999 have been regarded as such a trigger? Mr Dunne thought not. He cited Stewart's improved behaviour as justification for that view. He said that young prisoners had to be given a chance to change, and to have given Stewart no credit for the improvement in his behaviour would have been counter-productive in the long run. He also said that in the context of the population of Hindley at the time, Stewart was not a prisoner who caused particular concern. Gang-related violence was a real problem at Hindley, and it was the prisoners who were members of those gangs who posed a greater risk than Stewart. He was regarded as a loner. Jim Heavens, who succeeded Mr Sheffield as Hindley's Governor at the end of August 1999, thought otherwise. His view was that Stewart should have been referred to the Panel for possible inclusion on the Register, though he said that this would have been on the "far edge" of those cases for which such a step would have been appropriate.

15.13 It is very difficult now for the Inquiry to second guess Mr Dunne's judgement at the time – especially as the Inquiry has the priceless advantage of knowing what Stewart went on to do. It could be said that Mr Dunne should have referred Stewart to the Panel, leaving it to the Panel to decide whether he should be included on the Register, rather than to pre-empt consideration of his case by the Panel by not referring him to the Panel at all. But there was, of course, a limit to the number of prisoners who could have been referred to the Panel, and Mr Dunne was in the best position to say whether there were many other prisoners who were more deserving of the Panel's attention. That is borne out by such information as the Inquiry has about those prisoners who were referred to the Panel in 1999. Many of them, though admittedly not all, were facing charges or serving long sentences for really serious crimes, such as rape and kidnapping. Of those who had been sentenced, their sentences could for the most part be counted in years rather than months. I appreciate that Stewart was facing a charge of robbery, and possibly a firearms charge as well, but he was actually serving sentences totalling three months' detention for joyriding offences. In the circumstances, and not without some hesitation, it cannot definitively be said that Mr Dunne should be criticised for not referring Stewart to the Panel then.

15.14 But that is by no means the end of the story. Even if there were other prisoners who had greater claims than Stewart on the Panel's limited time and resources, Stewart's past behaviour should still have been regarded as making him a potentially dangerous prisoner, despite his recently improved behaviour. The intercepted letter showed that Stewart had not in truth changed, even if he was keeping his head down in prison. So even if Stewart had not come within that limited number of really dangerous prisoners who were on the Register, it would have been wrong to say that his improved behaviour meant that he was no longer a matter of concern. He may not have been as obviously dangerous as some, but he still stood out from the majority of the prison population as someone who posed a risk to those whom he chose to target.

The harassment memo of 29 September 1999

15.15 During Stewart's time in Hindley, he sent a number of letters to a woman who worked as a chatline operator. The woman was white, but her children were of mixed race. The letters were threatening and abusive. In one of the letters he enclosed his pubic hair. In another he referred to her "nigger kids". The letters gave Stewart's name and his prison number.

15.16 The woman complained to the police about these letters – and about a campaign of harassment of which the letters were part – on 29 September 1999. That same day a memo was sent by the Security Department at Hindley to the correspondence officers on all of Hindley's wings instructing them to forward to the Security Department any correspondence being sent to the woman. Her name and address were given. What is likely to have happened is that the police that day notified Hindley – maybe the police liaison officer, maybe the Discipline Office (as Hindley's administration section was called) – that letters were being sent to the woman by someone at Hindley. The memo did not refer to Stewart, but it is inconceivable that whoever within Hindley then got in touch with the Security Department did not inform the Security Department that the letters had been written by Stewart. It would, of course, have been better if the memo had named him. Even though Stewart could have got other prisoners to write to the woman for him, at least the correspondence officers on his wing would have paid particular attention to whether any letters written by him were addressed to the woman. Maybe they were told that the memo was about Stewart.

15.17 We do not know exactly what Hindley was told about the letters. They may have been told what the letters said and about the pubic hair. They may simply have been told that the letters were harassing and unwelcome. If they were told what the letters said and about the pubic hair, they would have been alive to how objectionable Stewart's conduct had been. But if they had not been told about it, they should have asked the police for details. So what Hindley should *then* have done is to be judged not merely in the light of what they actually knew about the letters, but also in the light of what they would have known about the letters had they made the obvious enquiries about them to the police. In fact, nothing was done – not even completing a security information report or making an entry on Stewart's wing file.

15.18 What should have been done? All the outgoing letters of prisoners who are charged with offences under the Protection from Harassment Act 1997 had to be monitored. That was provided for by Chapter 2 of PSO 4400, an instruction issued by Prison Service headquarters. Of course, at this stage Stewart had not been charged with any offences in connection with the letters – whether under the 1997 Act or otherwise. So Chapter 2 of PSO 4400 had not been strictly engaged and it therefore did not require any action to be taken. But one of the Standing Orders issued by the Prison Service permitted the reading of a prisoner's correspondence when there was reason to believe that it might contain indecent or grossly offensive material which was intended to cause distress and anxiety. That, no doubt, was why Mr Dunne told the Inquiry that he thought that once the police had told Hindley about the letters, all Stewart's outgoing letters should have been monitored. Indeed, he went further. Stewart should have been warned about his conduct, and he should have been referred to the Potentially Dangerous Offenders' Panel for it to consider whether he should be placed on the Register. And the Race Relations Liaison Officer should have been informed if Hindley had known about the racist element in the letters or would have been told about it by the police had they asked what the letters said.

15.19 Mr Dunne was right to go that far. If there had been any doubt about referring Stewart to the Panel over the intercepted letter to his friend in prison, there could have been little doubt now about the need for the Panel to consider his case. That was because the Panel's remit had recently been widened to include prisoners who were subject to the 1997 Act. It was true that Stewart had not yet been charged with any offence under that Act. But since the letters bore his name and number, the fact that they had been sent by him could hardly have been disputed. So even if the letter of the Panel's extended remit did not mandate his referral to the Panel, its spirit certainly did. And it is unarguable that from then on his correspondence should have been monitored – if only to check that he was not harassing anyone else. Why were neither of these steps taken? The answer is we do not know, because we do not know who dealt with the matter in the Security Department when the police got in touch with it on 29 September. We therefore do not have their explanation for why they did nothing. But the fact that these events did not trigger the monitoring of Stewart's correspondence or his referral to the Panel speaks volumes about the efficiency of the Security Department at the time.

What would have happened?

15.20 We can only speculate what the Panel would have done if Stewart had been referred to it by the Security Department following the information received from the police. It may be that it would have done no more than require his correspondence to be monitored. But if the Panel knew about the racist element in the letters, it might well have wanted to ensure that Stewart's management in prison was such that his racism could not be taken out on other prisoners. That could well have resulted in the Panel saying that Stewart should not share a cell with someone from an ethnic minority unless they were demonstrably good friends.

15.21 Likewise, we can only speculate about what would have happened if the Security Department had given instructions for Stewart's correspondence to be monitored following the interception of his letter to his friend in prison in August in which he had admitted committing a robbery at gunpoint, and the information received from the police towards the end of September about the harassing letters to the chatline operator. It may be that a person is not told that a decision has been made to read *all* their correspondence as opposed to some of their correspondence at random. But it is likely that they would get to learn about it if, for one reason or another, a letter was not sent out, and that might well result in them modifying what they say in future letters. We therefore do not know whether Stewart would have written the letters in the terms which we now know he did had he known that his correspondence was being read – though he would have expected after he had attacked Zahid that his letters would be read, and that did not stop him from making racist references in them.

15.22 As it was, letters retrieved by the police in the course of their investigation into Zahid's murder from the people they were sent to show that Stewart had strong racist views. Undated letters – but from their context probably written in August and September 1999 respectively – refer to "niggers" and a "Paki bastard". Another undated letter – but probably written in September 1999 – refers to Salman Rushdie, and contains a drawing of a hanged man with the words "Ijah Tullah [sic] (dead)" pointing at him with an arrow. In a letter from Altcourse (where Stewart was between 5 November and 2 December), in which Stewart referred to the possibility that he might have to go to Feltham, he described it as a "tru niggaz jail [sic]", where he could not let his depositions be seen because they had "got nigger this nigger that". He concluded an undated letter – but which he wrote from Hindley some time after 23 December 1999 – with a swastika and the letters KKK. Particularly chilling, though not in the context of his racism, was a comment he made in a letter to Travis from Altcourse dated 9 November. He was talking about the murders committed by Travis and another prisoner, and he then added:

> "Everyone thinks am next. Let's wait + see. If I get out in 4 wks (trial date 9.12.99) it could be the 1st murder of the millennium! Ha ha."

It has to be said that one wonders whether anyone reading that at the time would have taken Stewart seriously.

15.23 But the point is a simple one. Had these letters still been written after Stewart knew that his correspondence was being monitored, and had they been read as they should have been, his racism would have been apparent for all to see. However else he was to be managed while in prison, he should not thereafter have shared a cell with someone from an ethnic minority unless they were plainly good friends.

Chapter 16: Altcourse

Stewart's transfer to Altcourse

16.1   Stewart was transferred to Altcourse on 5 November 1999, the only time he was detained in a privately managed establishment. The reason for the transfer was again not documented. But in the letter he wrote to Travis in which he had joked about committing the first murder of the millennium, he said that it had been because of an incident involving a member of the Education Department, whose address he had obtained. Indeed, in a security information report written two months later when Stewart had returned to Hindley awaiting sentence for another series of offences, it was said that he had been removed from Hindley because he was passing the addresses of members of the Education Department to other prisoners. And in the prisoner escort record – which was the form to be completed when a prisoner was taken somewhere – covering his transfer from Hindley to Altcourse, there was a reference to "threats to Gov" without any further explanation. This is another example of inefficiency within Hindley's Security Department. If these incidents – assuming that they were two separate incidents – were sufficiently serious to warrant Stewart's transfer from a prison where he was well known to one where he had never been before, one might have expected a security information report to have been completed about them, or for information about them to have been entered onto the 4x4 system. If there was a security information report, it has not survived, and the information was never printed out on any inmate intelligence cards.

The handling of Stewart's security file

16.2   When Stewart arrived at Altcourse, relevant information about him in his security file had to be entered onto the 4x4 system. But instead of entering the details of each incident which had resulted in a security information report being completed, a very brief summary of the security information reports which had been written prior to 1999 – in no more than a few words and ending mid-sentence – was entered onto the system. And the consequence code which was collectively applied to all the information about Stewart's behaviour in prison before 1999 was such that it did not give rise to any security implications of significance. The consequence code was defended on the basis that the information was old, that it did not relate to his behaviour on his current sentence, and that a year is a long time in a young offender's life. But the consequence code was settled on when Stewart arrived at Altcourse, before his behaviour there could be assessed. Moreover, it did not take into account at least three worrying security information reports all written in 1999: the attack on the other prisoner in January 1999 and the two letters in January and August 1999. All those security information reports were in Stewart's security file at the time.

16.3 Had this summary been relied on at Feltham, and had Stewart in consequence been regarded at Feltham as less dangerous than he was, the impact of the shortcomings in the summary may have been significant. But Feltham did not rely on the summary. The inmate intelligence card at the front of Stewart's security file when he got to Feltham was one which was subsequently generated at Hindley, and that included a far fuller summary of the security information reports written in 1998, as well as a summary of the two reports completed in January 1999. In any event, as we shall see, Stewart's dangerousness as revealed by his security file was picked up by Feltham's Security Department.

Stewart arms himself

16.4 Stewart remained at Altcourse until 2 December 1999 when he was transferred back to Hindley. He was regarded by the manager of the residential unit on which he was held as very quiet, but he caused no trouble and achieved the highest level on Altcourse's incentives and earned privileges scheme until a few days before he left. That was when he and his cellmate, who was also from the Manchester area, armed themselves with metal tubes and a confrontation took place on two occasions with local prisoners from Liverpool who had been threatening them. The tubes had come from a chair in their cell. The need to remove Stewart from a prison where prisoners from Liverpool were in the overwhelming majority was almost certainly the reason for his return to Hindley, but the actual reason for his transfer was again not documented.

16.5 One of these incidents resulted in a security information report being completed. The other did not, though details of it were contained in Stewart's wing file and in an incident report which was put into Stewart's security file. Sketchy details about both incidents were entered onto the 4x4 system at Altcourse, though no reference was made in them to a significant feature about the incident for which the security information report was written – that the tubes had come from a chair in Stewart's cell. So when the Security Department at Altcourse came to print out an inmate intelligence card on Stewart before he returned to Hindley, the card did not mention Stewart's use of a weapon made from cell furniture.

That could potentially have been a highly significant omission in the light of how Stewart was subsequently to attack Zahid. But again that oversight did not affect Stewart's management at Feltham. Feltham did not rely on the inmate intelligence card generated at Altcourse. It relied on the inmate intelligence card subsequently generated at Hindley. As we shall see, the problem was that this card did not refer to this security information report at all.

The request for production

16.6 On 15 November, the Metropolitan Police faxed to Altcourse a request for the production of Stewart at a police station in Liverpool on 25 November. The fax gave the reason for the request as follows:

> "Stewart is a named suspect in an allegation of racially motivated Malicious Communication and Harassment Act offences."

Stewart was duly taken to a police station in Liverpool – though not the one named in the fax – and he was interviewed by the police in connection with the letters he had written from Hindley. He was not charged on that occasion, and it looks as if nothing further happened until well after Stewart had left Altcourse. But there is no evidence of any action having been taken at Altcourse in the light of this information while Stewart was still there. The way he was managed at Altcourse did not change. In particular, the police were not asked for further information about what Stewart was supposed to have done. So no-one at Altcourse knew what form the harassment had taken, who the victim was, or the strength of the evidence against Stewart.

16.7 Walter MacGowan was the Director of Altcourse at the time. That is the equivalent title in the private sector of the Governor of a public sector prison. He mounted a vigorous defence of Altcourse's stance. At that stage, the allegation was just that – an allegation. No charges had been brought. There had been nothing in the way Stewart had behaved at Altcourse to suggest that he might be a racist. He was sharing a cell with a prisoner of mixed race, who had known Stewart at Hindley and who had asked to share a cell with him. That may have been because he wanted to be with a fellow Mancunian, though he told the police that he did not think that Stewart was a racist. But the overarching point Mr MacGowan made was that a request by the police to produce a prisoner had never in his experience resulted in thought being given to whether the management of the prisoner should be changed. He could envisage circumstances in which a request by the police to produce a prisoner might contain information about a direct threat posed by the prisoner which would require some action on the part of prison staff. But he would have expected such a threat to be specifically referred to in other documents.

16.8 These points are not without force, though Mr Dunne did not deploy any of them in connection with Hindley's lack of response to the memo of 29 September. I take the point that if the police had thought that what Stewart was supposed to have done might affect his management in prison, prison staff might well have thought that the police would have told them that. But the police have their own things to do, and thinking about how prison staff should look after a serving prisoner they want to interview is not necessarily one of them. As it is, I do not accept that what Stewart was supposed to have done might not have had some implications for his management in prison. Stewart may have been prepared to share a cell with a prisoner of mixed race who had wanted to share a cell with him. But that may simply have been because he felt safer sharing a cell with someone from Manchester. The fact was that the communication which he was supposed to have sent was described in the request for production as "racially motivated". That should have caused Altcourse at least to think about whether they should continue to share a cell.

16.9 But the real point is that the offences for which Altcourse knew Stewart was to be questioned were offences of the kind which could be carried out by a prisoner. After all, he could pursue any campaign of malicious communication or harassment from prison by writing letters or making telephone calls. So even if there was no reason to suppose that what Stewart had done had implications for his management in prison, the very minimum which should have been done was what was necessary to protect the chatline operator from further harassment from him while he was still in prison. If he had been writing to her, his correspondence should have been monitored to ensure that no letters with her name and address were sent. If he had been telephoning her, his telephone calls should have been monitored. But not even that was done. No attempt was made to find out what form the harassment had taken, or what the woman's name, address and telephone number were. For all the staff at Altcourse knew, Stewart could have been continuing with his campaign of harassment, and unless the woman complained again, no-one would have been any the wiser.

16.10 But it goes further than that. If Stewart was capable of subjecting one person to a campaign of harassment, for all staff at Altcourse knew he could be doing it to others. The decision should have been made to monitor all his correspondence. That is what Mr Dunne accepted should have happened at Hindley when they had been told by the police that Stewart had been sending harassing letters to a woman. If his correspondence at Altcourse had been monitored from 15 November, the undated letter he wrote from Altcourse in which he described Feltham as a "tru niggaz jail" would have been picked up. That is because his reference in it to having to go next to a police station in London on 6 January 2000 meant that it must have been written after 25 November. But the letter in which he had bragged about committing the first murder of the millennium would not have been picked up because it had been written before 15 November. Whether the letter he had written after 15 November would on its own have resulted in any change to the way in which he was managed at Altcourse is questionable, but there may well have been other letters which were not retrieved.

16.11 But again the real point is that Stewart's correspondence should have been monitored the whole time he was at Altcourse. The monitoring of his correspondence which should have begun at Hindley should have been carried on there. It was not. As it turned out, that was down to shortcomings at Hindley, not Altcourse. The reason it was not carried out at Altcourse initially was because it had never been started at Hindley, and Hindley had never told Altcourse about the information it had got from the police at the end of September. One specific opportunity for Hindley to inform Altcourse of that was completely missed. The prisoner escort record had a section in it to be completed by the Security Department of the sending establishment. There was a box in that section marked "Stalker/harasser" to be ticked if appropriate. That box in the prisoner escort record which accompanied Stewart to Altcourse was not ticked when it should have been. The box marked "Security information attached" *was* ticked, and therefore Stewart's security file would have got to Altcourse. The vetting of the file would have revealed the memo of 29 September. But since there was nothing in the memo which showed that it related specifically to Stewart, Altcourse's Security Department cannot be blamed for not picking that up.

The assessment by Chris Kinealy

16.12 For part of his time at Altcourse, Stewart was held on Melling unit. The manager of the unit was Jim Farrell. He has not co-operated with the Inquiry. He did not provide the Inquiry with a witness statement, and did not come to the Inquiry's hearings. All we have to go on is his statement to the police. But there is no reason to doubt what he said in that statement. That was that he had either read Stewart's security file or been briefed on Stewart by staff in the Security Department. He had therefore been surprised how quiet Stewart was. That had "seemed to be at variance" with the behaviour Mr Farrell would have expected from someone whose security file suggested that he was a "problem prisoner". So one day he had mentioned Stewart "in passing" to Chris Kinealy, a registered mental nurse in Altcourse's healthcare centre who was visiting the unit to see another prisoner. He had asked Mr Kinealy to have a chat with Stewart so that Mr Farrell could have a further insight into him. Since his talk with Stewart was prompted by an informal request of that kind, Mr Kinealy did not read Stewart's medical record beforehand.

The entry in Stewart's medical record

16.13 Mr Kinealy saw Stewart for between half an hour and an hour on 16 November. The relevant parts of the entry he subsequently made in Stewart's medical record were as follows:

> "In my opinion he has a long-standing, deep seated personality disorder. He shows a glaring lack of remorse, feeling, insight, foresight or any other emotion... He has an untreatable mental condition and I recommend no further action. Only time will have any influence on his personality and behaviour."

Mr Kinealy has no recollection of any of this now. He does not know whether he looked through Stewart's medical record when he made the entry. He thinks that he would have skimmed through it. What Mr Farrell recalls is Mr Kinealy telling him afterwards that Stewart was a psychopath, which he told Mr Farrell meant that Stewart had no conscience or remorse for what he did.

16.14 There is no criticism of Mr Kinealy's diagnosis of personality disorder. The cold, affectless, unempathic presentation Mr Kinealy noted was described by Professor Maden as at the heart of psychopathy. Stewart's grossly abnormal "inner world" did not begin to mean that he was suffering from mental illness. Professor Gunn did not disagree. Outside the constraints of prison life, he would have been cautious about diagnosing Stewart after one conversation only, and he had some reservations about what he understood Mr Kinealy's methodology to have been. He would have been reluctant to exclude mental illness so quickly, but did not disagree with the diagnosis Mr Kinealy had reached. The debate over Mr Kinealy's entry in Stewart's medical record related to the absence of any reference to Stewart's possible dangerousness, the absence of any reference to Stewart's personality disorder being psychopathic, and the comment that his disorder was untreatable.

Stewart's dangerousness

16.15 Mr Kinealy's evidence was that when he interviews a prisoner, in addition to trying to make a diagnosis of their condition, he tries to assess whether the prisoner is a threat to others. It looks as if the conclusion Mr Kinealy reached was that Stewart was not a threat to others. He told the police in June 2000 that he had not considered that, Stewart "presented an immediate high risk of danger". His evidence to the Inquiry was that, if he had thought that Stewart was a risk to others, he would have said so in Stewart's medical record, completed a security information report to that effect, and referred Stewart to a psychiatrist. Since he had done none of those things, he assumed that he had not come to that view. But he accepted that it would have been preferable to have spelt out in the entry he made in Stewart's medical record his view that Stewart was not a risk to others.

16.16 Mr Kinealy did not read Stewart's security file. He said that he would not have been allowed to look at it. I do not understand why it would have been off-limits to Mr Kinealy, but if it was, he could have asked Mr Farrell to tell him what the file revealed. It looks as if Mr Kinealy did not do that. Mr Farrell did not mention in the statement he made to the police that Mr Kinealy had done that. If Mr Kinealy had done that, it is likely that Mr Farrell would have told him about Stewart's possible involvement in the stabbing at Stoke Heath, which Mr Farrell told the police he knew about. Mr Kinealy told the Inquiry that if he had been told that, it is likely that he would have remembered it. Since he does not remember it, it follows that it is likely that he was not told about it. Moreover, Mr Kinealy said that if he had been told what the security file on Stewart revealed, it is unlikely that he would have concluded that Stewart was not a risk to others – especially as his own view of Stewart was that he was devoid of remorse, feeling, insight or foresight. It may be, as Professor Maden was to say, that Mr Kinealy could not have known how dangerous Stewart was. But the thrust of Mr Kinealy's own evidence was that, in the light of what he has since discovered the security file on Stewart revealed, he would have concluded that Stewart posed a risk to himself and to others.

16.17 Mr Kinealy was therefore at fault in concluding that Stewart was not a risk to others, without having asked Mr Farrell to tell him what Stewart's security file revealed. Admittedly, Mr Farrell's request for him to see Stewart was made "in passing", and Mr Farrell might not have had the time then to tell Mr Kinealy more about Stewart. In addition, there were many calls on Mr Kinealy's time and he was working under some pressure. Nevertheless, to conclude that Stewart did not pose a threat to the safety of others, without knowing what was in Stewart's security file, was ill advised.

16.18 Mr Farrell must also bear some of the brunt of this criticism. For sure, he has to be commended for looking at or being briefed on Stewart's security file, for noting the contrast between Stewart's past and current behaviour, and for wondering whether Stewart's mental state needed to be assessed. In all of Stewart's time in prison, he was the one person who took any steps to obtain psychiatric advice about Stewart. Although he had known Stewart for a comparatively short time, he had seen enough to want Stewart investigated further. But Mr Farrell should still have told Mr Kinealy what he knew about Stewart's past so that it could have informed Mr Kinealy's own assessment of Stewart. And once Mr Kinealy had told him that Stewart was a psychopath, he should have asked Mr Kinealy specifically whether Stewart posed a risk to others. If Mr Kinealy's response had been that Stewart would not, Mr Farrell should have checked whether that response had taken into account Stewart's past behaviour.

16.19 Would the course of events have been any different if Mr Kinealy had known about Stewart's past behaviour? As I have said, he himself accepted that he would have concluded that Stewart posed a risk to himself and others. His evidence was that in those circumstances he would have asked for Stewart to be assessed by a psychiatrist. I doubt whether that would have been feasible. Although Mr Kinealy did not know it then, Stewart was to be released in just over three weeks. If Hindley's experience was anything to go by, it took some time to get an appointment with a psychiatrist. So even if one had been made, it is likely that it would have had to be cancelled on Stewart's release.*

16.20 There is little doubt that psychiatrists have much to offer over and above diagnosis. As Professor Gunn said, clinical risk assessment is not new, even though the focus until recently was on the risk of self-harm rather than on the risk of harm to others. An understanding of someone's "inner world" helps in the evaluation of risk. A registered mental nurse such as Mr Kinealy may be quite good at doing that, but in a complicated case someone with a lot more experience should take on that assessment. Professor Maden did not dispute the important role psychiatrists have in the assessment of risk. But he limited that

---

* This assumes that the healthcare centre at Altcourse, like Hindley in 1997, did not have a psychiatrist attached to it.

to people suffering from mental illness. He thought that psychiatrists had little to offer in the assessment of risk of people suffering from a personality disorder.

16.21 It is unnecessary for me to reach a conclusion on whether Stewart should have been referred to a psychiatrist for a risk assessment. That is because not even Professor Gunn would have criticised Mr Kinealy for not suggesting such a referral in Stewart's case. Such an assessment would have been useful "in an ideal world", but the practical constraints of prison life militated against such a referral. In any event, he was doubtful whether a psychiatrist could have got much out of Stewart. Stewart may have been "a bit of an enigma", but if he was not prepared to open up, the referral would not have achieved anything. From what Professor Gunn had read about Stewart, he thought that the chances of a psychiatrist getting Stewart to talk were not high.

16.22 Returning, then, to what would have happened if Mr Kinealy had concluded that Stewart posed a risk to himself or others, and had made a note of that in his medical record and had completed a security information report to that effect. If he had followed this course of action, would that assessment have been acted on? It *should* have been, of course, but *would* it have been? We cannot say for sure one way or the other, but I think it very unlikely. It is very doubtful whether such an assessment would have had any impact at Hindley when Stewart went back there. If he had not been regarded as a candidate for referral to the Potentially Dangerous Offenders' Panel while he had been at Hindley, it is unlikely that a security information report to the effect that Stewart was dangerous, following his stay at another establishment for less than four weeks, would have cut much ice with Hindley's Security Department. They would have thought they knew him best. And Mr Kinealy's entry in the medical record was not picked up at all at Hindley's healthcare centre when Stewart returned there. It is very unlikely that any comment about Stewart's dangerousness in his medical record would have been picked up at Feltham. As we shall see, no-one read his medical record while he was there – although whether it would have been read if Mr Kinealy had marked the front cover of the medical record in a prominent way to highlight his entry, as he admitted he sometimes did, is another matter. And although a warning about Stewart's dangerousness as revealed by his security file was written on a temporary wing file opened at Feltham, as well as in the wing observation book of the unit he was in on his first visit to Feltham, that warning was either lost sight of or ignored. That suggests that if Mr Kinealy had written a security information report about Stewart's dangerousness, and if its contents had been conveyed to the staff on the units where Stewart was held at Feltham, it would have met the same fate.

Stewart's psychopathy

16.23 Although Mr Kinealy described Stewart to Mr Farrell as a psychopath, there is no reference to psychopathy in Mr Kinealy's entry in Stewart's medical record. His personality disorder was not described as psychopathic. How important that omission was depends on whether it would have added anything of value to what Mr Kinealy had meant to convey by the language he used in his entry. That itself turns on what "psychopathic" means. The term "psychopathic disorder" is more of a statutory concept in the Mental Health Act 1983 than a clinical one. But in its clinical context it denotes the severity of a personality disorder, such as that measured on a recently developed tool known as the PCL-R scale. But the term does not refer to a particular type of personality disorder. And Mr Kinealy did not have either the statutory or the clinical use of the term in mind when he spoke to Mr Farrell, because he thought that the terms "psychopathic disorder" and "personality disorder" were synonymous. That did not quite square with Mr Farrell's evidence that Mr Kinealy told him that a psychopath was someone with no conscience or remorse. But all that means is that Mr Kinealy believed that the personality disorder from which Stewart suffered was one in which the patient lacked any kind of empathy for those who were adversely affected by his behaviour. That was what he spelt out in his entry in Stewart's medical record. Accordingly, no criticism can fairly be made of the absence of a reference to psychopathy there.

The treatability of Stewart's disorder

16.24 Mr Kinealy described Stewart's mental condition as untreatable, and recommended no further action. If Mr Kinealy had only been referring to *medical* treatment, his note could not have been criticised. There is no known medical treatment for personality disorders. But whether Stewart's mental condition was treatable *in some other way* depends on what you mean by treatable. Professor Maden spoke eloquently about the deficiency in empathy or emotion which is part of the personality disorder syndrome. People with such a deficiency are not able to see how their behaviour affects others. Because they cannot identify with other people's pain or suffering, they are not inhibited from causing them harm. If they feel like stabbing someone, they will go ahead and do it. This deficiency is untreatable in that you cannot give empathy to people who do not have it. But it may be regarded as treatable if by that you mean that you can work around the deficiency, using cognitive behavioural programmes delivered by forensic psychologists to reduce the risk of offending. Such programmes would not be available for prisoners like Stewart, because they are only available for prisoners who have committed particular types of offences or whose sentences are very long.

16.25 I did not regard Professor Gunn as saying anything significantly different from that. Although a personality disorder may be incurable, you can work on the personality defects which are the manifestation of the disorder. Professor Gunn added psychotherapy – whether milieu, group or individual – to cognitive behavioural programmes as another available tool. But he accepted that the availability of such facilities for a 17-year-old with the behavioural problems Stewart was showing in 1997 was then, and is now, "almost unheard of in the UK", and the view that personality disorders were "untreatable" was a commonly held belief in the healthcare field at the time. If that was the position in 1997, it would also be true of 1999.

16.26 Mr Kinealy was alive to these issues in 1999. A paper which he had written about psychopathic personalities shows that he was sceptical about the benefits of therapy and cognitive behavioural programmes. Its thesis was that the treatment of psychopaths – whether by therapy or otherwise – had failed, and that the realities of prison life could have a positive effect on their behaviour. However, he was prepared to recognise in his evidence that there was a school of thought which held that work could be done with patients suffering from a personality disorder – perhaps in a therapeutic setting. Such a facility was not available at Altcourse. It may have been available in a secure hospital or at Grendon Prison near Aylesbury which is run as a therapeutic community, but to get Stewart referred to the psychiatric unit of a secure hospital or to Grendon would have been virtually impossible given his age and the absence of really serious offences on his record. Mr Kinealy said that there were only 1,200–1,500 places nationally in psychiatric units in secure hospitals. And Professor Gunn said that getting a prisoner into Grendon was harder than getting a boy into Eton.

16.27 But what Mr Kinealy really had in mind in his note was that prisoners suffering from a psychopathic disorder can be admitted to secure hospitals only if treatment is likely to alleviate, or prevent a deterioration of, their condition. That has been regarded as excluding prisoners who have a condition which is untreatable, even if there are ways of treating the manifestations of the condition by working around them. Since prisoners with personality disorders were for that reason not being referred to secure hospitals at the time, it was not surprising that their disorders were called untreatable. That, I think, is what Mr Kinealy had in mind when he wrote his note.

16.28 In the end, Mr Kinealy accepted that it would have been more accurate for him to have written that whether Stewart's mental condition was treatable or not, he could not recommend any further action because of the limited resources available for helping prisoners with such a condition, and because of his belief that Stewart would not have been acceptable for any of the available programmes for such prisoners. In an ideal world, and applying a counsel of perfection, that is what he should have written – if not in so many words. Though the fact that Stewart would not have been treated – whether by his inclusion in behavioural programmes or by psychotherapy – meant that Mr Kinealy's note did not have the effect of shutting out *available* treatment for him.

Stewart's wing file

16.29 We have so far addressed the entry made by Mr Kinealy in Stewart's medical record. There is no entry by Mr Kinealy about Stewart in his wing file which was maintained at Altcourse. Mr Farrell would have expected Mr Kinealy to have made such an entry, and Mr Kinealy's own evidence was that he would have made a short entry himself. But the wing file maintained on Stewart at Altcourse was not opened until 25 November – that is, about three weeks after he moved there. Stapled to it was a wing card – which is the same as a wing file but on a single card – whose first entry is dated 17 November. It is therefore possible that there was no wing file being maintained at Altcourse on 16 November when Mr Kinealy spoke to Stewart. So although it is possible that Mr Kinealy omitted to make an entry in a wing file because he could not lay his hands on Stewart's current one, it is equally possible that Mr Kinealy made an entry in another wing file which has not survived. In these circumstances, it would be wrong to criticise Mr Kinealy for not making an entry in Stewart's wing file.

16.30 As it was, the only entry which Mr Kinealy could have been expected to have made in a wing file was that he had spoken to Stewart. He could, in theory, have added that in his view Stewart posed a risk to the safety of other prisoners. But since he was known to be a registered mental nurse, anyone reading such an entry would have readily grasped that this was an opinion expressed after a discussion about Stewart's mental state. In view of the importance attached to the confidentiality of such discussions, it would not have been appropriate for Mr Kinealy even to have mentioned that.

Chapter 17: Stewart's last spell at Hindley

Back in Hindley again

17.1 Stewart was transferred back to Hindley on 2 December 1999. He was there for one week only before being released on licence on 9 December. That week was uneventful apart from an allegation that he was bullying another prisoner. He was free for just two weeks. On 23 December, he was back at Hindley, having been remanded in custody following his pleas of guilty to charges of aggravated vehicle taking, dangerous driving and driving whilst disqualified. He had "hot-wired" a car and been chased by the police at high speed. On 13 January 2000, he was sentenced to 25 weeks' detention in a young offender institution on each of the three charges, to be served concurrently.

17.2 When Stewart arrived at Hindley on 23 December, he was seen by Mrs O'Mara as part of the induction process. She recalled him from her previous dealings with him. Based on what he told her, she recorded that he did not have a history of self-harm and was not a suicide risk. She did not get the previous files on him, because when she had come across him in the past she had not been worried that he might harm himself.

17.3 While Stewart was at Hindley, the police were continuing their investigation into the harassing letters he had sent from there. On 6 January, he was charged with four offences under the Malicious Communications Act 1988 and the Protection from Harassment Act 1997. Since at least one of the letters contained racist abuse, one wonders why he was not charged with racially aggravated harassment under section 32(1) of the Crime and Disorder Act 1998. Maybe it was because the front sheet of the file which the police submitted to the Crown Prosecution Service had not been completed properly: the box marked "Racially aggravated?" had been left blank. Be that as it may, Hindley was informed by fax on 7 January that Stewart had been charged with various offences over the letters. The charges were due to be heard at South Western Magistrates' Court in South West London. Hearings relating to those charges took place on 11 January, 25 January and 8 February. Stewart was brought to London for them. So he was away from Hindley on the nights of 10, 11 and 12 January, 24 and 25 January and 7 February. He spent those nights at Feltham with the exception of 12 January which he spent at a police station. Following his appearance in court on 8 February, he went back to Feltham. That was where he remained until he attacked Zahid. He was never to return to Hindley.

17.4 For the rest of his time at Hindley, Stewart kept his head down. To outward appearances at least, he continued to be well behaved. On 8 January 2000, his personal officer noted on his wing file that he was not a problem on the wing and was generally quiet. On 16 January, another personal officer commented that he was sure that Stewart would progress to enhanced status on the incentives and earned privileges scheme. And on 22 January, another officer said that Stewart seemed to have put his disruptive past behind him.

The recording of security information from Altcourse

17.5 When Stewart returned to Hindley on 2 December 1999, the information on him already on the 4x4 system there had to be updated. That involved entering the details of the two occasions at Altcourse when Stewart had armed himself with weapons. That was not done. Nor was it done on any of the occasions when Stewart returned to Hindley – on 23 December, 13 January and 26 January – though it may be that Stewart's security file did not come back with him the last time he returned to Hindley. The oversight in not entering the details of the two incidents onto the 4x4 system was particularly surprising since the incidents were referred to on the inmate intelligence card generated at Altcourse shortly before Stewart was returned to Hindley. Entering onto the 4x4 system what that inmate intelligence card said about the two incidents should have been the obvious thing for the security staff at Hindley to do. If that had been done, Hindley could not have been criticised for not picking up on the fact that the metal tubes had come from a chair in Stewart's cell. But Hindley did not do even that.

17.6 The result was that the details of these two incidents never got onto the inmate intelligence card generated at Hindley, which was the card at the front of Stewart's security file when he got to Feltham. Might the outcome have been any different if the details of the two incidents had got onto the card generated at Hindley? That depends on whether those details would have referred to the fact that the metal tubes had come from a chair in Stewart's cell. If they had not – and Hindley could not have been criticised for that if they had simply reproduced the details in the inmate intelligence card generated at Altcourse – the outcome would not have been any different. But if the details had referred to how Stewart got the metal tubes, it is possible, though no more than that, that security staff at Feltham – if they had picked up on it – would have alerted the units on which Stewart was being held to the particular need to check his cell furniture. Whether such a warning would have got through to the officers carrying out the daily checks on the cells on Swallow, and whether they would have heeded it, is impossible to say. However, all this was no more than a possibility, because the ingenuity of prisoners in finding new ways to fashion weapons out of such materials as they have knows no bounds. So it may be that the fact that the metal tubes were fashioned by Stewart and his cellmate out of their cell furniture may well not have been regarded as particularly significant by security staff at Feltham.

17.7 The two incidents at Altcourse were not the only incidents which never got onto the crucial inmate intelligence card generated at Hindley on Stewart's return there. It did not refer to the security information report written on 16 August 1999 about the intercepted letter, nor to the incident or incidents which resulted in Stewart's transfer to Altcourse on 5 November 1999. It is not possible to tell whether that was because of a failure to have proper systems in place or because of inefficiency on the part of an individual officer. Nor did it refer to the allegation of bullying, though that was never reported to the Security Department, and in any event the last entry in it, which was dated 25 December 1999, referred to a prisoner escort record which had described him as "vi-dr-we-es", which meant violent, drugs, weapons and escaper. But even if those incidents had got onto the inmate intelligence card generated at Hindley, I do not suppose that they would have affected his management at Feltham. After all, the fact that Stewart was dangerous *was* picked up at Feltham when his security file was vetted on his arrival there. However, it would at least have disabused Feltham of any idea that Stewart had been trouble free since January 1999.

The security information report of 5 January 2000

17.8 On 5 January 2000, the last security information report on Stewart before his attack on Zahid was completed. It related to an occasion when a number of prisoners taunted a member of the Education Department by telling her that they knew where she lived. But she did not know whether Stewart was one of them. She simply associated Stewart with what was happening because it was he who she believed had been passing the addresses of members of the Education Department to other prisoners. The officer in the Security Department who assessed this report suggested, amongst other things, that Stewart was not to have any dealings with the Education Department, and that if he received a custodial sentence for the offences for which he was awaiting sentence, he should be transferred to another establishment. He also recommended that Stewart be placed on the prominent nominal list. That was a classification for security purposes of a high-profile prisoner who presented as a threat.

17.9 It has been suggested that Mr Dunne, who signed off this security information report, should have referred Stewart to the Potentially Dangerous Offenders' Panel at that stage. That is academic, as Stewart should have been referred to the Panel following the information Hindley got from the police at the end of September 1999 about the campaign of harassment on which he was engaged. If he had already been referred to the Panel, it is difficult to think of any additional steps which the Panel might have thought could appropriately be taken. If he had not already been referred to the Panel, I doubt whether it would have been appropriate to refer him to the Panel then when it was not known whether he would get a custodial sentence. And by 13 January when he was sentenced, the security information report had been closed. That was because the section of the report which had to be completed before the report could be closed and required that the action to be taken be identified said: "Feltham 10-1-00". So it looks as if the officer who completed that section thought that Stewart's transfer to Feltham was to be permanent. Where they got that erroneous idea from, we do not know.

Monitoring Stewart's correspondence

17.10 Once Hindley knew on 7 January that Stewart had been charged with offences under the Protection from Harassment Act 1997, all of his outgoing letters should have been monitored.* Chapter 2 of PSO 4400 itself spelt out the reason for that: "to prevent prisoners… charged with offences [under the Act] from continuing to harass their victims from within prison." Mr Heavens accepted that the fact that Stewart's correspondence should have been monitored should have been recorded on his wing file, no doubt because it was on the wings that the

---

* There is an internal inconsistency within Chapter 2 of PSO 4400 about when the obligation to monitor a prisoner's correspondence is triggered. Paragraph 20(b) said that it applied to prisoners "charged with" offences under the 1997 Act. In Stewart's case, that would have been on 7 January. But paragraph 6 said that it applied to prisoners "remanded in custody for, or convicted of, offences" under the 1997 Act. In Stewart's case, that would have been on 11 January. The correct approach would have been to take the earlier of the two dates.

monitoring would take place. Chapter 2 of PSO 4400 also required that fact to be recorded on the Local Inmate Database System and on the prisoner's core record. None of that happened. That was because there was no system in place at Hindley for routinely informing wings when a prisoner's correspondence had to be monitored under Chapter 2 of PSO 4400. It was the Security Department's responsibility to inform wings of that, but it either failed to do so or had not been told by the Discipline Office, which would have got the fax about Stewart being charged, that the charges were ones which triggered the application of Chapter 2 of PSO 4400. Either way, the failure to monitor Stewart's correspondence at Hindley was a serious matter.

17.11 As before, we can only speculate about what would have happened if Stewart's correspondence had been monitored. Maybe Stewart would not have subsequently expressed himself as we now know he did had he known that his correspondence was going to be read. The letter which he concluded with a swastika and the letters KKK may have been sent out before 7 January. But if it was sent after that, it would have been picked up, as would any other letters Stewart sent which have not been retrieved. Obviously we cannot say whether his racism would have been exposed in letters he sent from Hindley after 7 January. But if it had been, he should not thereafter have shared a cell with someone from an ethnic minority unless they were plainly good friends.

17.12 But all this is by the way. As we have seen, Stewart's correspondence should have been monitored at Hindley after the interception of his letter to his friend in prison in August 1999, and certainly after the information which Hindley got from the police at the end of September 1999 about the campaign of harassment on which Stewart was then engaged. All that happened on 7 January was that the obligation to monitor his correspondence *under Chapter 2 of PSO 4400* was triggered.

Sending records to Feltham

Stewart's security file

17.13 Prisoners' security files had to accompany them when they were moved to another establishment. At any rate, that was what the Security Manual provided. But in April 1999, a different instruction was circulated by the Prison Service's Security Group. It said that under no circumstances should prisoners' security files accompany prisoners. The reason was to ensure that if anything unexpected happened during the transfer, prisoners could not see their security files. Instead, they had to be sent by first class or registered post – if possible, within 24 hours of the prisoners' departure.

17.14 That change in the process was not a good idea. It meant that the receiving establishment would be without the information which the security file contained for at least a day or two. And for prisoners who were only going to be away from the sending establishment for a day or two, their security files would arrive at the receiving establishment just as they were leaving. These problems were subsequently appreciated – but only after Zahid's death. In July 2000, establishments were informed that the earlier instruction had been wrong, and they were reminded what the Security Manual provided for. Either way, though, it was obviously important for the movement of security files to be properly documented.

17.15 What happened to Stewart's security file? Hindley's recorded posting receipt book shows that on 11 January 2000 a package was sent to Feltham by recorded delivery. Since Stewart's security file was seen by a security officer in Feltham's Security Department on 12 January, we can infer that this package contained Stewart's security file – so it only arrived at Feltham on the day Stewart left. Moreover, the sending of the security file should have been shown in a book maintained by Hindley for that purpose – the security file booking-out book. But the police were never referred to an entry in that book for 11 January relating to the sending of Stewart's security file to Feltham, and we can infer from that that, although the security file was sent to Feltham that day by recorded delivery, that was not entered in the security file booking-out book.

17.16 The security file had come back to Hindley by the time Stewart returned to Feltham on 24 January, but only just. It was not posted back to Hindley until 20 January – a week later than it should have been. Hindley's security file booking-out book shows that Stewart's security file was sent out by post to Feltham on 25 January. It could not have arrived at Feltham in time to be seen before Stewart left Feltham on 26 January, since he was recorded as leaving the unit he had been on at 6.45 am. But that is where the trail goes cold. We know it was back in Feltham by the time of the attack on Zahid: it was found that night in the Security Department by Mr Greenslade. But we do not know whether it had gone back to Hindley and been sent to Feltham for a third and last time when Stewart went there on 7 February. Feltham's Security Department did not operate a system for recording the movement of security files. But according to a messenger at Feltham, a package was sent by recorded delivery from Feltham to Hindley on 28 January. And Hindley's post-received book recorded a package arriving there on 30 January, though the book did not identify where incoming packages came from or what they contained. The probability is that this was Stewart's security file, but there is no way of knowing that for certain. It is therefore possible that the security file did not come back to Hindley. But it is more likely that it did, though for a second time its despatch back to Feltham was not recorded in the security file booking-out book.

Stewart's wing files

17.17 A new wing file for Stewart was opened when he went to Hindley on 23 December. Although it should have been sent to Feltham when he first went there on 10 January, it was not. So when entries were to be made at Feltham on 12 January in Stewart's wing file, a temporary one had to be opened. The temporary one went back to Hindley with Stewart on 13 January: we know that because an entry was made in it at Hindley on 14 January. Indeed, both the temporary wing file and the new one were used interchangeably at Hindley: entries were made at Hindley in the new one on 16 and 22 January and in the temporary one on 14 and 27 January. Both wing files eventually ended up at Feltham, though when they arrived we cannot tell. Nor can we tell whether the temporary wing file went back to Feltham with Stewart on 24 January and came back to Hindley with him on 26 January, so that the entry could be written in it on 27 January. All we can say is that the temporary one had got back to Feltham by 7 March, because an entry was made in it that day at Feltham. It should have accompanied Stewart when he returned to Feltham on 7 February. It may have done, in which case it was mislaid at Feltham for a while. Or it may have been sent to Feltham later. Mr Dunne accepted that it sometimes happened that Hindley sent a prisoner's wing file to another establishment after the prisoner had left Hindley.

17.18 As we shall see, the entries made in the temporary wing file opened on Stewart on 12 January at Feltham were at the very heart of the issues which the Inquiry addressed. So how the temporary wing file was handled when it got back to Hindley is of some importance. I shall deal with the entries in the temporary wing file in Part 3 where I explore how Stewart was dealt with at Feltham. Although strictly out of order – because I have been dealing in Part 2 with how Stewart was dealt with elsewhere – I shall deal with how Hindley handled the temporary wing file when it got back to Hindley after I have looked at the circumstances in which it was opened at Feltham.

Stewart's medical record

17.19 Stewart's medical record should have accompanied him on his three journeys to Feltham on 10 January, 24 January and 7 February. It is clear that it did not: the box marked "Medical record attached" in the prisoner escort records for each of those journeys was not ticked, and Feltham's medical reception register for 7 February actually noted that Stewart had arrived without his medical record. It had arrived by 7 March: an entry was made in it at Feltham that day. But when it arrived at Feltham is impossible to say.

17.20 On the face of it, this was a serious flaw in Hindley's processes. There might have been a special reason for Stewart's medical record not having arrived at Feltham on 7 February: Feltham's medical reception register shows that prisoners from a number of other establishments arrived that day without their medical records. That led Dr Greenwood to think that a bundle of medical records might have been left at court or in the prison van. But that does not explain why Stewart's medical record was not sent with him on 10 or 24 January. Maybe it was thought that Stewart would only be at Feltham for a couple of days, and that it was not worthwhile sending his medical record with him for such a short time. But if that was what was thought at Hindley, it was wrong. A prisoner's medical record should have accompanied him at all times.

17.21 All this meant that Stewart's medical record would not have been available for consideration by Feltham's healthcare staff when they came to check his health on the three occasions he went there from Hindley. In particular, they would not have seen Mr Kinealy's note diagnosing Stewart as suffering from a deep-seated personality disorder which deprived him of any conscience or emotion. But as we shall see, it looks as if Stewart was not examined on any of these three occasions by any member of the healthcare staff at Feltham anyway. So no-one would have looked at Stewart's medical record then if it had been there. As it turned out, therefore, the non-arrival of Stewart's medical record until later on made no difference to how Stewart was managed at Feltham. Whether it would or should have done if Stewart had been examined by healthcare staff at Feltham is considered later on.

Stewart remains at Feltham

17.22 How did it come about that after Stewart's appearance at court in London on 8 February, he was not returned to Hindley, but stayed at

Feltham? The question is potentially an important one, because if he had returned to Hindley, he may have stayed there – apart from other temporary visits to Feltham for further court appearances – until 19 March when he was due to complete his current sentence. He would then have been kept in custody awaiting his trial on the harassment charges, but he may not have been transferred to Feltham then, or at least not immediately. In that case, he would not have shared a cell with Zahid, apart from perhaps the odd night, before Zahid was due to be released on 21 March.

17.23 We do not know who made the decision that Stewart should stay at Feltham following his appearance at court on 8 February. Nor do we know when that decision was taken. If the decision was documented anywhere, no note of it has survived. But the normal operational practice at the time was for prisoners who were due to appear in court to be held at the establishment which served that court. That was because courts often required prisoners to be produced at short notice. The decision to apply that practice to a particular case would be made administratively in the establishment which served that court. Since it was a purely administrative decision implementing a well-established practice, it would not need to be approved by a governor.

17.24 There had been no question of Stewart remaining at Feltham following his appearance at court in London on 11 January, because he was due to be sentenced at Tameside Magistrates' Court in Manchester on 13 January for the offences to which he had pleaded guilty on 23 December. So the likelihood is that the decision to keep Stewart at Feltham was made in the Observation, Classification and Allocations Department at Feltham, following his return there from court on 8 February, when his case had been adjourned for four weeks to 7 March. A similar decision could equally have been made, of course, when Stewart returned to Feltham from court on 25 January, which had been when his case had been adjourned to 8 February. If it was thought appropriate for him to remain at Feltham on 8 February, why was it not thought appropriate for him to remain at Feltham on 25 January? There is no answer to that question, but the seeming inconsistency does not undermine the likelihood that Stewart remained at Feltham on 8 February simply because he was due to appear at court in London again on 7 March. Certainly, there is no reason to suppose that Mr Dunne's recommendation, when he signed off the security information report of 5 January, that Stewart should be transferred out of Hindley if he received a custodial sentence had any part to play in the decision. His recommendation had been overtaken by the need for Stewart to be close to the court in London where he was due to appear.

17.25 In the circumstances, the decision that Stewart should remain at Feltham was in accordance with the prevailing practice and was not one for which anyone could be criticised. It is true that, but for that decision, Stewart would not have had the opportunity to attack Zahid. And the paucity of the regime at Feltham, and the alienation which Stewart undoubtedly felt as a result of being in an unfamiliar part of the country with prisoners he did not feel comfortable with, may have resulted in him posing more of a threat to other prisoners at Feltham than would have been the case at Hindley. But it cannot seriously be suggested that whoever made the decision that Stewart should remain at Feltham should have foreseen that at the time.

17.26 It is questionable, though, whether the need to serve the courts should have been the only, or even the paramount, consideration in that decision. I can see how transfers from one part of the country can be both expensive for the Prison Service and uncomfortable for the prisoner, and can provide opportunities for escape. But it is not a good idea for prisoners, especially young ones, to serve their sentences some distance from their home, where visits by members of their family or friends are difficult and where they may find themselves mixing with prisoners from very different backgrounds. The practice at the time was for matters of this kind not to be taken into account when deciding whether prisoners should be transferred to a prison closer to the court where they are awaiting trial. The Prison Service has not suggested that there has been any change of practice since then. This is not a topic which comes within the Inquiry's terms of reference, but it is one which the Prison Service should look at again.

Chapter 18: Stewart's healthcare screening

What healthcare screening involved

18.1 There are two topics which straddle many of Stewart's spells in custody. They relate to how his healthcare screening was conducted, and the contents of the prisoner escort records when he was moved somewhere. I deal with those topics in this chapter and the next.

When screening took place

18.2 In Prison Service jargon, a "new number" is a prisoner who has never been to prison before, or a prisoner who has been to prison before but is back in prison either on a new charge if unconvicted, or for a new offence if convicted but not sentenced, or serving a new sentence. "New numbers" had to be seen by a healthcare worker in reception at the time of their arrival in prison, and by a doctor within 24 hours. The same applied to prisoners who were transferred from one establishment to another. We called them transferees in the Inquiry. There is another group of prisoners, who we called returnees. They are prisoners who had left the establishment for one reason or another – for example, to go to court or hospital – and returned later that day. They did not need to be seen by a doctor within 24 hours of their arrival, provided that they had been under prison escort while they had been away. However, if their status had changed while they had been away – in other words, if they had been committed to the Crown Court for trial, or if they had changed from being an unconvicted to a convicted prisoner or from an unsentenced to a sentenced prisoner – they had to be seen by the doctor within 24 hours of their return as well as by a healthcare worker in reception.

The nature of the screening

18.3 The nature of the screening by the healthcare worker in reception depended on whether the prisoner was a "new number" or not. If they were, a first reception health screen would be carried out. That involved the completion of the first reception health screen questionnaire. The answers the prisoner gave under various headings, such as physical health, drug/alcohol history and mental health, were recorded on the form. An average of 10 minutes per screening was to be allowed, which reflected the time it would take to complete the form. There were only two questions in the form which required the healthcare worker to form a judgement about prisoners. They were whether they seemed excessively withdrawn or depressed, and whether they seemed excessively anxious. If the healthcare worker thought that the prisoner was at risk of suicide or self-harm, a self-harm at risk form had to be opened. But this screening was not a preliminary mental health assessment. If doing that was the function of anyone, it was the function of the doctor who saw the prisoner within 24 hours of his arrival. Accordingly, training in mental health awareness, though plainly of use if someone had had it, was not necessary for this aspect of the healthcare worker's job.

18.4 A first reception health screen was not required for transferees or returnees. Apart from looking at their medical records to see if they revealed anything of concern, the healthcare worker only had to ask prisoners if there was anything which was causing them worry or anxiety. If the prisoner was presenting with symptoms of anxiety or concern, the healthcare worker had to assess whether the prisoner was at risk of suicide or self-harm.

18.5 The nature of the screening by the doctor also depended on whether the prisoner was a "new number" or not. If they were, the doctor was required to perform "a physical and mental state examination" of the prisoner, to take "a full medical and psychiatric history and make a systematic enquiry for any significant signs or symptoms, especially those pertaining to suicide, self-harm, infectious disease and substance abuse". The relevant healthcare standard issued by the Prison Service also said this:

> "Physical examination will consist of a full clinical examination of the cardio-vascular, respiratory, abdominal, locomotor, genito-urinary and central nervous systems… Examination of the patient's mental health should take account of any known psychiatric history, with particular regard to in-patient admissions, alcohol and substance abuse, and any attempt at self-harm. A present mental state examination should be performed, including assessment of the patient's general appearance and behaviour, thought processes, affect, memory, concentration, orientation, cognitive function, insight *and, where applicable, an assessment of the level of dangerousness.*"

18.6 This kind of examination was not required for transferees and those returnees who had to be seen by the doctor. What was required for them was merely an assessment of their physical and psychiatric health, with particular regard to indications of recent substance abuse and the potential for self-harm.

The status of these requirements

18.7 Dr Greenwood's evidence was that the healthcare standard which incorporated these requirements was not actually laying down hard and fast rules which had to be met. He described it as "aspirational" and designed to encourage better performance. That was because, as we shall see, he simply could not deliver examinations of the kind contemplated by the standard. That may be what Dr Greenwood thought, but he was wrong. The letter from the Director of Health Care Services for Prisons in August 1994 which brought a new set of healthcare standards to the attention of Governors said nothing of the kind. Local practice had to be brought into conformity with these standards within three years. Compliance with them was to be monitored through the Prison Service's normal auditing processes.

The availability of medical records on screening

18.8 Doctors were supposed to have the prisoner's medical record when they saw prisoners within 24 hours of their arrival. So too – in theory at least – were the healthcare workers when they saw prisoners at the first reception health screen, though the nature of their screening of the prisoners did not naturally lend itself to an examination of the prisoner's medical record. That should not have been a problem with transferees, because they were supposed to arrive with their medical records. Nor should it have been a problem for returnees, since the establishment already had their records. And it would not, of course, have been a problem for "new numbers" who had not been to prison before. There were no existing medical records for them, and one had to be opened for them. But it could have been a problem for "new numbers" who had been to prison before. When prisoners were released, their medical records were kept at the establishment where they had last been. So if a "new number" who had been to prison before arrived at an establishment which was not the one they had left at the end of their previous sentence, their medical record would have to be retrieved from it. And even if a "new number" arrived at the establishment from which they had last been released, it could take a little time to retrieve their medical record from wherever it was being kept. A well-run healthcare centre should have had a system in place to enable the records to be retrieved so that they were available when prisoners were seen by the doctor. And if the records had not been available then, there should have been a system in place to enable them, when they became available, to be reviewed by the doctor to see whether it affected the assessment they had made of the prisoner.

Healthcare screening at Hindley

18.9 Stewart was seen by a healthcare worker when he arrived at Hindley as a "new number" on 5 September 1997. The answers which he gave about himself gave no cause for concern. He was seen the next day by Dr Greenwood. Dr Greenwood did not, of course, know about the previous psychiatric assessments of Stewart, and nothing of significance emerged when Dr Greenwood spoke to him, save that he noted that Stewart told him that at the age of 12 he had been seen by a "psych (school)". That may have been a reference to the consultant psychiatrist who had seen him when he was 13, but Dr Greenwood understandably thought that it was more probable that he would have thought that Stewart had been referring to an educational psychologist. He would not have followed up such a reference unless there were other causes for concern at the time, which there were not. There is no realistic basis for criticising Dr Greenwood for this approach.

18.10 But that does not mean that healthcare screening at Hindley was satisfactory. The evidence revealed a number of problems. A written statement of the screening procedures was not made available to all doctors and healthcare workers, as it should have been. The existing medical records of "new numbers" who had been in prison before were often not married up with their newly opened records. When they eventually were, they were rarely, if ever, reviewed to see whether the assessment of the prisoner should be changed. Even if the records were there when a doctor saw the prisoner, they would only be looked at if justified by the prisoner's presentation. At any rate, that was Dr Greenwood's practice, and there is no reason to suppose that the doctors who worked in the healthcare centre part time would have done anything different from the Senior Medical Officer.* The first reception health screen for "new numbers" often lasted less than the 10 minutes thought necessary. "New numbers" rarely, if ever, got the full mental health examination the health standard envisaged, and they only got the physical examination contemplated by the standard when it was regarded as clinically necessary. And there were occasions when returnees who should have been seen by the doctor, and maybe many transferees as well, were not.

18.11 These problems were not new. Reception screening had been criticised by the Inspectorate following a visit to Hindley in 1995. It had said:

---

* So, for example, no-one picked up the fact that Stewart's first reception health screen questionnaires showed that he had given different answers at different times to the same questions relating to whether he had ever harmed himself or attempted suicide.

> "Reception interviews carried out by healthcare staff should be in accordance with the correct procedures. A physical examination should be included in the reception process."

A later report following a short inspection in December 1998, which had not been announced beforehand, said that this recommendation had not been implemented. It acknowledged that during the inspection Dr Greenwood had said that he could not deliver the kind of physical examination contemplated by the standard. Indeed, Dr Greenwood told the Inquiry that such an examination would last about 20 minutes, let alone the time on top of that which would have been needed to carry out the examination of the prisoner's mental state as required by the standard. On that topic, his evidence was that general practitioners could not be expected to carry out examinations of that kind. Apart from anything else, most prisoners at Hindley just wanted to get in and out as quickly as possible.

18.12 I can see where Dr Greenwood was coming from – at any rate to some extent. I rather doubt whether an assessment of the level of dangerousness required by the standard could be a properly informed one. And such examinations would have been much more difficult to carry out in establishments with a high turnover of prisoners, such as young offender institutions where prisoners tend to be serving shorter sentences and remand centres which were serving the courts. With the number of prisoners who had to be seen, the pressure on the time of healthcare workers and doctors would have been considerable. But an assessment of whether a prisoner was at risk of self-harm was a critical aspect of health screening. It was a topic which could not be overlooked. Moreover, the Inspectorate concluded that the recommendation it had made in 1995 should still stand. If implementing that recommendation on current resources was not possible, further resources should have been made available. Dr Greenwood's evidence was that he raised the need for further resources to comply with the standard with Hindley's Governor at the time, Mr Sheffield, and with the Area Health Adviser. More money was not forthcoming. So either the standard asked for too much in terms of healthcare screening. Or Dr Greenwood did not press his case with sufficient vigour. Or Mr Sheffield failed to appreciate the need for further resources to be diverted to healthcare screening. Or Mr Sheffield did recognise the need, but there were greater calls on his resources, and he could not persuade his Area Manager to allocate more to him. Those are the various possibilities. Fault lies somewhere. It is not possible to say where.

18.13 Having said that, these flaws in the system at Hindley are unlikely to have had any significant impact on Stewart's management. We do not know whether he was seen by a doctor at Hindley when he returned there as a transferee from Onley on 19 August 1998.* Nor do we know whether the existing medical record for him was looked at on the three occasions he returned to Hindley as a "new number" on 24 March 1998, 9 May 1998 and 28 July 1999, prior to his last spell there. But even if it was not looked at, it is unlikely that it would have told Hindley's medical staff much they did not already know about him. Dr Sushil Suri, who worked at the healthcare centre part time, was the doctor who saw Stewart on each of those occasions. He had been around in 1997, and would no doubt have recalled Stewart's seemingly bizarre behaviour and that it had been characterised as an act. We do not know how long he spent with Stewart on those occasions. But his note of each examination does not unequivocally show that Stewart's mental state was ignored. What can be said is that if the considered opinion had been reached in 1997 not to refer Stewart for an assessment by a psychiatrist then, it is unlikely in the extreme that any of these examinations, even if they had been conducted in the way the standard contemplated, would have resulted in such a referral.

Healthcare screening at Hindley after November 1999

18.14 Healthcare screening at Hindley should have taken on a new meaning when Stewart returned there on 2 December 1999. That was because there was now in Stewart's medical record Mr Kinealy's note diagnosing Stewart as suffering from a deep-seated personality disorder which deprived him of all "remorse, feeling, insight, foresight or any other emotion". By then, Stewart's medical record was quite bulky, but Mr Kinealy's note was towards the top of it. At that stage there would have been only three documents above it, and it should have stuck out to someone glancing through the record because Mr Kinealy's note was a longish piece of continuous text. It therefore should have been

---

* Dr Greenwood assumed that Stewart had not been seen by a doctor on this occasion since there was no reference to that in Stewart's medical record. He tried to justify what he thought was an omission on the erroneous basis that transferees did not have to be seen by the doctor. But the practice at Hindley was for the doctors to record on the back of the first reception health screen questionnaire any notes they made when they saw "*new numbers*". That would be in the prisoner's medical record. Any comments they made on *a transferee or returnee* were noted in the medical reception register for transferees and returnees, which would not be in the prisoner's record. Since we do not have the medical reception register for Hindley at the time, we do not know whether Stewart was seen by a doctor on this occasion.

read when Stewart was, or should have been, screened whenever he returned to Hindley again.

Stewart's return to Hindley on 2 December 1999 as a transferee

18.15 Stewart was accompanied by his medical record when he arrived back at Hindley. We know that from the prisoner escort record for the journey which recorded that his medical record was attached. He was seen on his return by a healthcare worker who noted that he was fit and well. But he was not seen by a doctor. That is apparent from the medical reception register. That was another example of what had been happening at Hindley for some time: not just returnees, but sometimes transferees, were not being screened.

18.16 How was that allowed to happen? The healthcare centre maintained two medical reception registers: one for "new numbers", the other for transferees and returnees. One of the healthcare workers on duty wrote the names of all new arrivals in the registers. All the "new numbers" and transferees had to be seen by the doctor. But since not all the returnees had to be seen by the doctor, an asterisk was supposed to be placed against the name of every person in the second register who had to be seen by the doctor. Sometimes, maybe often, an asterisk was mistakenly omitted. Maybe the healthcare worker confused a transferee with a returnee who did not have to be seen by the doctor. Maybe they thought that the status of a returnee had not changed – thereby making it unnecessary for the returnee to see a doctor – when in fact it had changed. On this occasion, none of these things happened. We know that because the register actually said that Stewart was a transferee. The fact is that for various reasons too many prisoners slipped through the net. Dr Greenwood was to admit that this was an area they had struggled unsuccessfully to get right. Indeed, it was a long time before he realised it had been happening.

18.17 We can only speculate what would have happened if Stewart had been screened and Mr Kinealy's note had been read. Although Hindley's medical staff did not know it then, Stewart was to be released in a week's time. So if, for example, it had been decided to refer him to the Potentially Dangerous Offenders' Panel, his referral would have been overtaken by his release. It may be that Mr Kinealy's note would have prompted a note to be made on the front cover of the medical record referring any future reader to Mr Kinealy's diagnosis. That is especially so if Mr Kinealy's note had said that Stewart posed a risk to others – which is the conclusion he would have reached had he known about

Stewart's past history. But it is difficult to think of anything else which might have been done which would not have been regarded as violating medical confidentiality.

Stewart's arrival at Hindley on 23 December 1999 as a "new number"

18.18 The healthcare worker who saw Stewart in reception when he returned to Hindley on 23 December 1999 was Ms Martin, the nurse who had written the security information report about him and Travis in November 1997. She did not associate Stewart with that incident, and did not realise that she had dealt with him before. All she knew from what Stewart told her was that the last establishment he had been in was Hindley. Since the Discipline Office was where the medical records of prisoners who had been released from Hindley were kept, she would have known that this was where Stewart's medical record was.

18.19 Ms Martin did not have Stewart's existing medical record with her at the time. She therefore did not know about Mr Kinealy's diagnosis. So she opened a new one. She cannot be criticised for that. There was no system in place at Hindley for the existing medical records of returning "new numbers" such as Stewart to be retrieved from the Discipline Office for the first reception health screen. Should there have been? One of the problems was that the Discipline Office closed at 4.00 pm, and prisoners invariably arrived after that. If it really was necessary for the existing medical records of returning "new numbers" to be available to healthcare workers in reception, the solution would have been for the records to have been kept in the healthcare centre, even if additional storage space had to be created – or at least kept somewhere where they could be retrieved at all hours. Having said that, it would be unreasonable to expect a healthcare worker to disappear from reception when such a prisoner arrived to retrieve his medical record, especially when the healthcare worker was only required to complete a first reception health screen questionnaire based on the answers the prisoner was then giving. In the circumstances, I do not criticise Hindley for not having a system in place for the medical records of returning "new numbers" to be available for the first reception health screen. As it was, the answers Stewart gave about himself gave no cause for concern.

18.20 I have not overlooked what the relevant healthcare standard – the one for "new numbers" – said on the topic at the time:

> "The [healthcare worker] will ensure that in each case all available documentation which may assist the screening and subsequent medical examination, including documents or information received with the prisoner from external sources (e.g. the police), are assembled and noted before screening takes place."

But that rather begs the question of what documentation was "available" at the time of the screening by the healthcare worker in reception. I do not believe that it can fairly be said that a medical record held in a cabinet in the Discipline Office – which was locked for reasons of confidentiality and security – was "available" to healthcare workers in reception if they had to leave reception to get it. And it would not have been a sensible use of limited resources to have the healthcare centre's administrative officer on duty after normal working hours to retrieve the medical record on the few occasions when the need to retrieve it arose.

18.21 Stewart was seen by Dr Suri the following day. He did not have Stewart's existing medical record either. All he had was the new one opened by Ms Martin and the completed questionnaire. So he too did not know about Mr Kinealy's diagnosis. Again, he cannot be blamed for that. There was no system in place at Hindley for the existing medical records of returning "new numbers" such as Stewart to be retrieved for the examination by the doctor which had to take place within 24 hours of the prisoner's arrival. But unquestionably there should have been. New arrivals who had to be seen by the doctor were seen on the day following their arrival. It would not have been difficult to identify the "new numbers" whose records were in store at Hindley. The healthcare worker in reception the previous day could have made a list of them. In any event, a list of the "new numbers" who had arrived the previous day but who had been released from Hindley following their previous sentence could have been retrieved from the Local Inmate Database System, which was updated overnight. And it would not have been difficult for the medical records of those "new numbers" to have been retrieved that morning by the administrative officer attached to the healthcare centre. Dr Greenwood said that this was not practicable. He claimed that the new record and the existing one could only have been married up later. I do not understand why. Nor do I understand why the existing one could not have been reviewed by the doctor later on, once it had been retrieved, to see whether it affected the assessment which had been made of the prisoner on examination.

18.22 It may be that practical considerations were not the only reason why they were not married up in time for the doctor's examination. Dr Greenwood's practice, as I have said, was not to look at the prisoner's existing medical record, even if he had it, unless something triggered the need for him to do so. That rarely happened, and it was very unusual, he said, for the contents of such a record to alter the management of a prisoner. I doubt whether Dr Greenwood's practice is defensible. The pressure on him in having to see so many prisoners may have made a prolonged study of a prisoner's medical record impracticable. But if it was there, he should have looked through it quickly to see if there was anything of importance.

18.23 What would have happened if Dr Suri had had Stewart's existing medical record and read Mr Kinealy's diagnosis? We do not know what Dr Suri would have done, but both Ms Martin and Dr Greenwood told the Inquiry what they would have done. Ms Martin would have asked the registered mental nurse at Hindley whether Stewart should be referred to Hindley's visiting psychiatrist. Dr Greenwood said that he would have agreed with Mr Kinealy's view that no further action was appropriate, and that some particular event was needed to trigger an assessment of the risk Stewart posed. Dr Greenwood's approach would not, I think, have been an unreasonable one, and it is more likely than not that Dr Suri would have done the same thing. But what would have happened if Mr Kinealy's note had said that Stewart posed a risk to others? That is a matter of complete speculation. It may be that Dr Suri would have discussed his case with Dr Greenwood. That may have caused them to look at Stewart's history. And that may have resulted in Stewart being referred to the Potentially Dangerous Offenders' Panel. That, I think, is what should have happened. But whether it would have happened is just guesswork. We cannot take it further.

Stewart's arrival at Hindley on 6 January 2000 as a returnee

18.24 Stewart was taken to a police station in Liverpool on 6 January 2000. That was when he was charged with the four offences relating to the letters he had sent. He went back to Hindley the same day. The healthcare worker who saw him in reception described him as fit and well. As a returnee whose status had not changed, he did not have to be seen by a doctor within 24 hours of his arrival. That was why there was no asterisk against his name in the medical reception register. Ironically, though, he was seen by Dr Greenwood. By then, the new medical record opened on him by Ms Martin on 23 December would have been married up with his existing one. But it is unlikely that Dr Greenwood would have had it with him on that occasion, since it was never intended that he should see Stewart.

Stewart's arrival at Hindley on 13 January 2000 as a transferee

18.25 Stewart had been away from Hindley for three nights. He had been taken to Feltham on 10 January for his first appearance in court on 11 January in connection with the charges over the letters. He had stayed at Feltham on the nights of 10 and 11 January, he had stayed at a police station on the night of 12 January, and he had been sentenced at Tameside Magistrates' Court in Manchester for the driving offences on 13 January. Although his absence from Hindley had been short, he had to be treated as both a transferee, having been transferred from Feltham to Hindley, and as a returnee, returning from court after a change in his status. So for both those reasons, in addition to being seen by a healthcare worker in reception, he had to be seen by a doctor within 24 hours of his arrival.

18.26 Stewart was seen by a healthcare worker in reception on 13 January. It was noted that he was fit and well. And he was seen by Dr Suri – presumably on 14 January – who recorded in the medical reception register that Stewart had no medical problems. Unlike the last time when Dr Suri had examined Stewart – on 24 December 1999 – he would have had Stewart's medical record on this occasion. If Dr Suri's practice was the same as Dr Greenwood's – as it is likely to have been – he would not have looked at Stewart's record, as there was nothing in Stewart's presentation on that occasion to warrant such a course of action. So the fact that Mr Kinealy's note was not picked up was down to Dr Greenwood's practice of not looking at the record as a matter of routine – a practice which the doctors who worked at the healthcare centre part time could be expected to have followed.

18.27 I do not think that it would be right to criticise Dr Suri for that omission. He has not had an opportunity to explain why he did not look at Stewart's medical record then, since it was only known towards the end of the Inquiry's hearings that it was he who had seen Stewart on this occasion, because the medical reception register was only produced to the Inquiry late in the day. But he would, no doubt, have said that he had been following Dr Greenwood's practice. Had he done what he was supposed to have done and glanced through the record, he would have seen Mr Kinealy's note. There would have been only five documents on top of it then. What would Dr Suri have done then? There is no reason to think that he would have acted any differently from how he would have acted if he had read Mr Kinealy's note when he examined Stewart on 24 December.

Stewart's arrival at Hindley on 26 January 2000 as a transferee

18.28 Stewart had been away from Hindley for two nights. He had spent them at Feltham. The healthcare worker who saw him in reception on his return noted that he was fit and well. But he was not seen by a doctor as he should have been – whether within 24 hours of his arrival or at all. The likeliest reason for that is that, although the medical reception register recorded him as a transferee from Feltham, there was no asterisk against his name. If he had been seen, it is unlikely that Mr Kinealy's note would have been picked up, because it is unlikely that the doctor who saw him would have looked at his medical record in view of his current presentation. Again, that omission would have been down to Dr Greenwood's own practice which others could be expected to have followed.

18.29 So a combination of problems – transferees not always being seen by the doctor, and even if they were, not having their medical records reviewed by the doctor – resulted in Mr Kinealy's diagnosis of Stewart as suffering from a long-standing deep-seated personality disorder which deprived him of any emotion or conscience not being picked up at Hindley. The view could responsibly be taken that, if it had been, no immediate action would have been required. But it should have been very different if Mr Kinealy's note had said that Stewart posed a risk to other prisoners.

Chapter 19: The prisoner escort records for Stewart

The function of the prisoner escort record

19.1 The prisoner escort record was introduced in January 1999 in response to a number of high-profile deaths of people in the custody of the police and the Prison Service. One of those deaths was that of Christopher Edwards, who was killed by his cellmate in Chelmsford Prison in November 1994. His killer was acutely mentally ill, and Mr Edwards suffered from mental health problems too. The attack had occurred during their first night together after they had both arrived at the prison from court. An inquiry was established jointly by the local health authority, the local social services authority and the Prison Service. It was chaired by Kieran Coonan QC. By the time its report was published in 1998, an internal Prison Service inquiry had already recommended that the means by which information was transmitted from the police to the Prison Service should be considered at national level. That recommendation had fed into a Home Office review on the topic, and the report of the Coonan Inquiry recorded that it had been decided by then that the existing forms were to be replaced by the prisoner escort record.

19.2 As its name suggests, the prisoner escort record was designed to travel with the prisoner whenever the prisoner was moved somewhere. But its name is a bit of a misnomer. It suggests that its principal function was to provide an auditable record of a prisoner's movements. That was *one* of its functions, but it was by no means its only one – or even its most important one. Its most significant function was to give relevant information about prisoners to enable them to be appropriately managed at the receiving establishment. That is borne out by one of the things which the Prison Service Instruction which introduced it required Governors to do, namely to ensure that "reception, security and healthcare staff knew about the form and the need to pass on information from it to appropriate staff within the prison". As Mr Wheatley said in his statement to the Inquiry, the prisoner escort record was to be the primary means by which important information about the risks posed by or to a prisoner was to be communicated.

Stewart's records

19.3 A total of nine prisoner escort records were completed at Hindley for Stewart. They related to the following movements:

- 4 August 1999 to court

- 25 August 1999 to court
- 8 September 1999 to court
- 1 October 1999 to court
- 5 November 1999 to Altcourse
- 6 January 2000 to police station
- 10 January 2000 to Feltham
- 24 January 2000 to Feltham
- 7 February 2000 to Feltham.

They covered the return journey back to Hindley, with the exception of the one to Altcourse, no doubt because the journey back to Hindley took place four weeks later. In addition, two prisoner escort records were completed at Altcourse for Stewart:

- 25 November 1999 to police station
- 2 December 1999 to Hindley.

19.4 The records completed at Altcourse were properly completed, but none of the ones completed at Hindley were. They contained a variety of omissions and inconsistencies:

- One of the sections was to be completed by a member of the Security Department. Boxes had to be ticked if the prisoner was violent, an escape risk, a stalker/harasser or a drug user. If he was none of those, a box marked "No known risk" had to be ticked. The section then had to be signed by a member of the Security Department. There was no consistency whatsoever as to which boxes were ticked. On two occasions, none of the boxes were ticked – not even the "No known risk" box. On two occasions, the only box ticked was the violent box, and on all the other occasions, the violent, escape risk and drug user boxes were all ticked. On no occasion was the stalker/harasser box ticked, even though the Security Department at Hindley knew from 29 September 1999 that Stewart was alleged to have been harassing someone. On one occasion, a member of the Security Department signed the section which had to be signed by a member of the healthcare centre. And on the last occasion, the section to be completed by a member of the Security Department was not signed at all.

- Another of the sections could be completed by any member of staff. Boxes had to be ticked if the prisoner was, for example, suicidal or at risk of self-harm. If there were no entries in the warning boxes in that section, a box marked "No known risk" had to be ticked. That section was never completed at all.

- If any of the warning boxes had been ticked, information about the reasons for that had to be included in another section headed "Further information", unless an additional report was attached. In fact, on those occasions when an entry was made in that section, it was too abbreviated to be of any real help.

As Head of Operations at Hindley at the time, Mr Dunne must bear the responsibility for there not having been a suitable system for ensuring that prisoner escort records were properly completed.

19.5 For the Inquiry's purposes, the important records were the last three – the three which accompanied Stewart on his trips to Feltham. The violent and escape risk boxes were ticked in each of them. Hindley was right to have ticked them. The violent box had to be ticked if the prisoner had a history of violent behaviour or had recently committed an assault on a member of staff or another prisoner. Stewart's two previous convictions for assault, his suspected involvement in the fatal stabbing at Stoke Heath, his threats to take hostages and his bullying, taken together, justified the violent box being ticked. The escape risk box had to be ticked if the prisoner was on the escape list or if a risk assessment or recent intelligence on him suggested that he required a higher level of security than normal. Stewart could legitimately be treated as coming within the latter rubric in view of the letter which had been intercepted in August 1999 and his alleged harassment of the chatline operator. The message that Stewart was violent and required a higher level of security than normal was therefore brought to Feltham's attention, despite the fact that in the three records which went to Feltham, the stalker/harasser box was not ticked, the section which could have been completed by any member of staff had not been completed at all, and on the last record the section to be completed by the Security Department had not been signed.

19.6 The section headed "Further information" in the three reports which accompanied Stewart to Feltham all referred to weapons, though twice using the abbreviation "WE" in the hope that this would be understood. Staff working in Feltham's Security Department would probably have known what it meant. It was an abbreviation for "weapons" used on the 4x4 system. But the prisoner escort record was not intended to be seen by staff in the Security Department. It was to be looked at on reception and then sent to the establishment's administrative section. Staff working there would not have been familiar with the 4x4 system and might not have known what the letters "WE" referred to. In any event, without an explanation about why Stewart was associated with weapons, it would have meant very little. It could have meant that he had convictions for using them, or simply for carrying them, or that he had been caught with them in prison, or that they had been found concealed in his cell. As it was, his involvement in the fatal stabbing and the recent charge he had faced of armed robbery – but which had not been proceeded with – probably justified it. But staff in reception at Feltham reading it would have been none the wiser.

19.7 Two of the three prisoner escort records which accompanied Stewart when he went to Feltham – the first and the last – specifically said that security information on Stewart was attached. That would not have been Stewart's security file, because that went to Feltham by post. The evidence was that this information consisted of the latest print-out of an inmate intelligence card on Stewart. But I regard that as unlikely. Information on an inmate intelligence card is regarded by most security officers as too sensitive for all and sundry to be able to read it. It is much more likely that the information consisted of the latest print-out of a prisoner security information sheet on Stewart. There are examples of such sheets in Stewart's security files. They contained brief details about a prisoner – such as whether he had a security file, whether he was violent, suicidal or mentally unstable, whether he had the potential to escape, and whether he was an exceptional risk.

19.8 I do not doubt that prisoner security information sheets on Stewart were attached to the three prisoner escort records which accompanied him when he went to Feltham. In the case of prisoners who had a security file, the practice at Hindley at the time was to staple it to the front of the prisoner escort record. The one record which did not state that security information was attached to it was the one covering Stewart's journey to Feltham on 24 January. But the corner of it is torn in such a way as to suggest that something was once stapled to it. That was likely to have been the latest print-out of the prisoner security information sheet.

19.9 But attaching the sheet to the prisoner escort record was not an acceptable substitute for completing the further information box correctly. Apart from anything else, it might become detached from the record: the one attached to the record for the journey on 24 January did. And the information which it contained was sketchy to say the least. There is in Stewart's security file a prisoner security information sheet generated just before he went to Altcourse. That almost certainly contained the same information which the sheets attached to the prisoner escort records contained. It said little more than that Stewart was violent, had the potential to escape, and was an exceptional risk, though what he was at risk of was not stated.

Notifying Feltham about Stewart

19.10 It would, of course, have been open to the Security Department at Hindley to telephone Feltham to warn them in advance of the arrival of a prisoner with a bad security record. There is nothing to suggest that Hindley ever did that or that there was a system in place for ensuring that this be done. Again, Mr Dunne must bear the responsibility for that. Hindley certainly did not warn Feltham in advance about Stewart when he was transferred to Feltham on 10 January. Indeed, as we shall see, the reaction of Feltham's Security Department on 12 January when his security file was first seen there suggests that it was the security file which resulted in warnings being written in the temporary wing file which was opened, rather than any special message from Hindley about him. In any event, the evidence was that if the Security Department at Hindley had telephoned Feltham about him, they would only have done that prior to his visit there on 10 January. It would have assumed that after that Feltham would have made its own assessment of him from the security file.

19.11 Hindley, should, I think, have notified Feltham in advance of Stewart's arrival there on 10 January about the sort of prisoner they were getting. So it was no thanks to Hindley that Feltham's Security Department picked up on Stewart's dangerousness when it vetted his security file. Whether his dangerousness was brought to the attention of the people who needed to know it at Feltham is another matter altogether.

Chapter 20: The missed opportunities

20.1 The history of Stewart's management within the prison system before he went to Feltham for the last time reveals a number of missed opportunities. It is easy to be wise after the event, but by the summer of 1998, Stewart should have stood out from the crowd. In the space of six weeks, he had set fire to his cell, attempted to escape, been involved in some way in a riot, and been strongly implicated in the planning and execution of the fatal stabbing of another prisoner, along with a possible plan to take hostages. All of that against the background in the previous year of a series of bizarre behavioural episodes which, though understandably regarded as manipulative, could nevertheless have been the product of mental disorder of one kind or another. Put together, this called for some assessment to be made of the risk he might pose to other prisoners. And when he returned to Hindley in August 1998 – an establishment which had double cells – his history within the prison system should have resulted in some thought being given to his suitability to share a cell.

20.2 We can only speculate about what would have happened if Stewart's potential dangerousness had been properly addressed. I have already said that it is likely that he would have been assessed as posing a risk to the safety of other prisoners and as someone who was unsuitable to share a cell. So the opportunity at that stage to manage him in a way which might have resulted in him not eventually sharing a cell with Zahid was missed. That opportunity was not lost simply because those who were responsible for his management misjudged him. It was lost because the signs that Stewart was a troubled young man – which came from both the warnings about him from officers who had come across him and the documents which described the many instances of his bad behaviour – were not picked up. Why were they not picked up? The answer is that procedures which should have caused questions about the risks a prisoner posed were just not there. Those procedures – such as the Potentially Dangerous Offenders' Panel at Hindley which came in after Stewart's behaviour had settled down, and the cell-sharing risk assessment procedure which came in after Zahid's death – were introduced subsequently. But by then it was too late.

20.3 Eventually, Stewart's behaviour improved. But we know from what he got up to when he went back to Hindley in the summer of 1999 that he was keeping his head down and avoiding trouble. He may have realised that you do not get very far if you behave badly in prison. But the letters he was sending out showed that he was not simply a pest. He was a menace who had to be watched. His correspondence should have been monitored, and he should have been referred to the Potentially Dangerous Offenders' Panel. Again, we can only speculate about what would have happened if that had been done. But it is likely that his racism would have been revealed, and at the very least that would – or at any rate should – have resulted in an instruction going out that if Stewart was to share a cell it should not be with someone from an ethnic minority unless they were demonstrably good friends. Had that been done, the chances of him ending up in a cell with Zahid at Feltham would have been much slimmer. It was another missed opportunity to manage Stewart properly. And it happened because of the shortcomings in the Security Department at Hindley – individual shortcomings on the part of

- Mr Dunne for not suggesting that Stewart's correspondence be monitored when he signed off the security information report of 16 August, and

- the officer in the Security Department who was told about Stewart's harassment of the chatline operator for not bringing that to the attention of the principal officer who was temporarily in charge of the Security Department, who could then have given instructions for Stewart's correspondence to be monitored and considered whether to refer him to the Panel,

as well as systemic failures that allowed inefficiencies of that kind to flourish.

20.4 As it was, Stewart's possible racism became known at Altcourse when they were told that he was suspected of engaging in racially motivated harassment. Even though Hindley had been to blame for not monitoring his correspondence up to then, his correspondence should have been monitored at Altcourse from then on. And if that had started then, it might have continued when Stewart returned to Hindley. If the letters he wrote while at Feltham are anything to go by, the letters he wrote at Altcourse and Hindley after staff at Altcourse should have begun to read them would have revealed his racism for all to see. It was another missed opportunity to pick up on the sort of young man Stewart was.

20.5 The final missed opportunity of real significance was the failure to take on board Mr Kinealy's diagnosis of Stewart as suffering from a deep-seated personality disorder which deprived him of any conscience or emotion. It would have been infinitely better if Mr Kinealy had been made aware of the contents of Stewart's security file. His note would then have said that Stewart posed a risk to the safety of other prisoners – which would have been Mr Kinealy's view if he had informed himself about Stewart's past behaviour – at least anyone having to manage Stewart should have known what sort of young man he was. As we shall see, this note was never read by healthcare staff at Feltham. Whether it would have resulted in Stewart being treated differently in Feltham if it had been is something which I consider in Part 3.

Part 3

Feltham: Fate Plays Its Hand

Chapter 21: Stewart goes to Feltham

The induction process

21.1 Stewart was due to appear at court in London on 11 January 2000 in connection with the four charges he faced over his campaign of harassment of the chatline operator. So he was taken to Feltham the day before. He spent the nights of 10 and 11 January there. Both those nights were spent in a single cell in the induction unit, Lapwing.

21.2 The induction of a new arrival into the life of a prison has, in theory at least, two elements to it. First, it prepares prisoners for prison life. If the process is working properly, it lets them know how the prison works, and what they can expect from it. In Feltham, that involved prisoners on the day following their arrival in Lapwing having the establishment's rules explained to them, and getting visits from the chaplaincy, physical education and CARATS (Counselling, Assessment, Referral, Advice and Throughcare Scheme), a service for prisoners with drug or alcohol problems. The reports of the Inspectorate following its visits to Feltham in 1996 and 1998 pointed to serious inadequacies in that process.

21.3 But from the Inquiry's point of view, the second element is the more important of the two. That is the receipt and analysis of information about prisoners to inform the way they should be managed while in the establishment. That was not happening at Feltham at all, beyond deciding the unit on which they should be located. This element of the induction process consisted only of an officer on Lapwing talking to prisoners briefly on the day of their arrival or the following morning, and completing a rudimentary form based on answers given by prisoners – covering things like their religion, whether they had learning difficulties, whether a self-harm at risk form had been opened on them before, and whether they were willing to work. And apart from any current wing file which might exist, prisoners' files did not go to Lapwing at all.

21.4 Should the induction process at Feltham have included some consideration of how the incoming prisoner should be managed for the duration of his stay – perhaps on the lines of a traditional reception board? Mr Clifford thought that Feltham's high turnover of inmates made such a process impossible to achieve. You could not have seen all the incoming prisoners unless the complement of governors was increased, and that was not an option.

21.5 Whether it was feasible to have a traditional reception board depended on how many inmates would have to go through it. We can take out of the equation incoming prisoners who were only going to be at Feltham for a short time – in Feltham jargon, the "in and outs" – people like

Stewart, who were sent to Feltham temporarily, invariably because they were due to appear in a court in the London area. And prisoners who had gone through a proper induction process at Feltham recently and who had been away from Feltham only for a short time could also be ignored. But there would be no basis for taking, say, unconvicted prisoners out of the equation, so that a reception board considered the cases only of convicted prisoners. Many convicted prisoners did not stay at Feltham for long, and many unconvicted prisoners could be on remand at Feltham for quite a time. So it was said that there would still be far too many inmates having to go through the induction process to make a traditional reception board feasible.

21.6 I am sceptical about that. The evidence was that although there was an average of 62 receptions into Feltham a day in the 12 months up to 29 February 2000, fewer than 10 were "new numbers" and transferees. The rest were returnees, who could have gone through a traditional reception board when they first arrived at Feltham as a "new number" or transferee if one had existed. So I am not convinced that a reception board for the few "new numbers" and transferees who arrived at Feltham every day would have been anything like as impracticable as was suggested.

21.7 But the absence of a traditional reception board would not have mattered too much if there had been other procedures operating sufficiently well to ensure that proper consideration was given to an incoming prisoner's own safety, the risks he posed to staff or other inmates, and the productive use of his time to make him better equipped to lead a crime-free life on his release. How a prisoner spent his time could have been catered for by proper sentence planning. And the risks he posed to himself and others could have been met, in part at least, by the proper vetting of an incoming prisoner's security file by the Security Department, and the relaying of any relevant information to those who had to deal with the prisoner – officers on the unit to which he was allocated, and those responsible for supervising any of his activities. I shall come a little later to whether that was happening properly, but sentence planning was not taking place at Feltham at all.

Stewart's induction

21.8 The prison officer who completed the induction processing form for Stewart was Deborah Hogg. She had been working in Lapwing since early 1999, having joined the Prison Service in 1997. She did not complete the form until 12 January – two days after Stewart's arrival. It is not possible to say why it was not completed earlier. It was not as if there had not been time to complete it on 10 January, since the daily record of prisoners' movements on Lapwing, known as the roll book, shows him as having arrived there at 1.45 pm. The roll book for 11 January does not give the time when he arrived back in Lapwing from court, but it was unlikely to have been too late for the induction processing form to have been completed then. Since Stewart was an "in and out", there would have been no need for him to see anyone from chaplaincy, physical education or CARATS.

21.9 The danger of relying only on the answers a prisoner gives when completing the induction processing form is apparent from what Stewart said. The box to indicate whether, in the past, a self-harm at risk form had been opened on him had the "No" option circled. As we have seen, a self-harm at risk form had been opened on Stewart at Hindley in November 1997. It does not look as if this inaccuracy in the form was ever picked up. It could have been important, because if the "Yes" option had been circled, the need to check any history of self-harm on his part would have been triggered. Checking that would have shown that Stewart had a history of disruptive and concerning behaviour in prison which could have affected his management at Feltham. As it was, Stewart's previous history was discovered by another route.

The intercepted letter

21.10 The completion of the induction processing form was not Miss Hogg's first contact with Stewart on 12 January. When she had come on duty that day, someone had advised her to watch out for him. She was warned that he might be violent to staff, and she thinks there might have been a reference to racism in the context of something having happened the previous day at the servery involving some African prisoners. I have no reason to doubt any of that. It was the reason why, when she collected the outgoing post a little later, and saw a letter from Stewart there, she decided to look at it. But her recollection about the possibility of him being violent *to staff* is interesting. Stewart had no history of violence to staff, and in any event this was before any information about Stewart had come to Lapwing. Miss Hogg did not recall what made her think that she might have been warned about that. But as we shall see, another officer recalls a similar warning being given to her a couple of weeks later. It rather suggests that if prison officers get a sense that a prisoner may be violent, they think in terms of violence to members of staff rather than violence to other prisoners.

21.11 The source of Miss Hogg's belief about the possible risk which Stewart posed to staff may have been Steven Martindale, the senior officer in charge of Lapwing at the time. He had been on Lapwing for 18 months, having joined the Prison Service in 1986. He had a gut feeling that Stewart needed to be watched. He thought Stewart was strange and that his manner was "quietly intimidating". When interviewed by Mr Butt, Mr Martindale spoke of "several occurrences", but he was never to say what they had been when he gave evidence. Maybe he was just using loose language. Maybe there were things which had happened involving Stewart, but Mr Martindale did not want to admit them because he thought that he could then be criticised for not recording them at the time. Whatever it was, he gave instructions for Stewart to be put in a single cell. That was a precaution they took on the unit with a prisoner who they thought was an unknown quantity and who might therefore be a threat to a cellmate. He was fairly sure that he had mentioned to his staff what he thought about Stewart. The probability is, therefore, that what Miss Hogg heard about Stewart when she came on duty was what Mr Martindale had already told other officers about him.

21.12 When Miss Hogg looked at Stewart's letter, she saw that it was to a friend of his. She recalls that it referred to there being a lot of "niggers" on the unit. She has wavered about whether the letter also referred to "Pakis". She told the police that the letter probably had, but that was not what she said to Mr Butt. By the time she gave evidence to the Inquiry, she thought that it *had* referred to "Pakis". She could recall that what Stewart had written was that he knew what he would like to do. She thought that this might have been a reference to what he would like to do to "niggers" or "Pakis", but that was not what the letter had actually said. As we shall see, she showed the letter to Mr Martindale. He did not read it all the way through as he should have done, but he recalls that it compared the number of black people at Feltham with the number at prisons in Manchester. The letter was racist, but he did not regard it as threatening. In view of the subsequent note which Miss Hogg made about the letter, which referred to it as being "threatening", and what we now know about Stewart's attitude to "Pakis" – from what he did in Hyde when he was growing up and from other letters he wrote which were subsequently retrieved from their recipients and referred to "Pakis", including one written on the day before and another written on the day after his attack on Zahid – I have no difficulty in accepting that the letter referred to "Pakis" as well, and that it was threatening in its tone, even if no direct threats were made. But we do not know precisely what the letter said because it was never retained.

21.13 The effect of Miss Hogg's evidence was that if the letter had contained direct threats, she would have stopped the letter and written a security information report about it, presumably attaching the letter to the report. I have no reason to doubt that. But since the letter did not contain direct threats, she decided to ask Mr Martindale what she should do with it. He told her that she should return it to Stewart, telling him that if he wanted the letter sent out he would have to use different language. So Miss Hogg returned the letter to Stewart, and gave him the advice which Mr Martindale had suggested. We do not know what became of the letter. Maybe Stewart kept it and wrote another letter in less offensive terms. Maybe he took it with him when he left Feltham and sent it again later. For what it is worth, that is what Stewart says he did.

21.14 Miss Hogg told the Inquiry that she did not think that writing about "niggers" and "Pakis" necessarily made Stewart a racist. She was pressed on that. Her response was that she knew that accusing someone of racism was a serious matter, but when push came to shove, she accepted that "he may have had issues" over race. I think that her reluctance to admit that she had realised at the time that Stewart was a racist was because she feared that she could be criticised for not doing more than she did. What she did realise was that she had to record the incident. She looked for Stewart's wing file. When she realised that there was not one, she opened a temporary one, and on the front inside cover she wrote the following:

> "On vetting this inmate's mail, a letter I considered to be racist and threatening was returned to him and told that it would not be posted out. There was reference to 'a lot of niggers' on the wing plus other similar references."

21.15 It was later that morning that Miss Hogg completed the induction processing form. There is a box on the form for the prisoner's offences. One of the offences which she recorded for Stewart was "abusive mat". Stewart must have told her that he had been charged with sending abusive material. After all, that was why he was at Feltham. She had not known that before. It is unclear whether she knew that this meant that his correspondence had to be monitored, or whether she simply thought that it should be monitored. But she took the precaution of adding the following note in his wing file immediately after her first entry:

> "One of his offences is for sending abusive material so monitor his post."

This was the only time anyone noted the need to monitor Stewart's correspondence. Miss Hogg should be given credit for that.

21.16 The advice Mr Martindale gave Miss Hogg took no account of what he thought was supposed to happen under the local and national rules. As Mr Martindale himself accepted, he believed they required the letter not to have been returned to Stewart. Instead, it should have been retained in his file,* and a note made in both his temporary wing file and the "letters withheld book" that the letter had been stopped. Stewart should have been told that this was what had happened.**

21.17 Mr Martindale sought to justify his non-compliance with what he understood the rules to require on the basis that the function of the induction unit was to introduce prisoners, who could well be in prison for the first time, to the ways of prison life. He therefore adopted a policy of give and take. It was often not appropriate to come down too hard on such inmates the first time they did something wrong, whatever the rules might strictly require. And when it came to the use of inappropriate language, many young prisoners did not have much of an idea about what language was acceptable and what was not.

21.18 Mr Martindale's approach found some support in the evidence of Mr MacGowan, the Director of Altcourse. If a racist letter was intercepted at Altcourse, he would have done what Mr Martindale did, provided that the prisoner was someone who had been behaving reasonably. The important thing was, if possible, to give a young inmate the chance to put things right. However, the letter would not be returned to the prisoner if it was sufficiently beyond the pale to justify its retention, or if the inmate was a problem prisoner. Unlike Mr Martindale, Mr MacGowan was aware that the relevant Standing Order said that the letter was only

---

* The relevant Standing Order said that it had to be placed on the prisoner's F1150. Since that form had been replaced by the Inmate Personal Record System, it is unclear in what file it should have been placed. The prisoner's security file would seem to be the most natural place for it.

**It is arguable that none of this had to be done. Letters which contained prohibited material were only "liable to be stopped", suggesting that there was an element of flexibility in the matter. I do not believe that those who drafted the relevant Standing Order intended to leave the stopping of such letters to the discretion of individual officers. Rather, I suspect that this was just sloppy language. Moreover, it is questionable whether the letter contained prohibited material within the relevant rule – which was paragraph 34 of section B of Standing Order 5. Material which is "grossly offensive" as this was was only prohibited if the writer's intention was to cause distress or anxiety to the recipient or any other person. It is doubtful whether Stewart had that intention when he wrote the letter. And it is questionable whether the letter came within the only other possible classes of prohibited material, namely material which was "indecent and offensive under the Post Office Act 1953", or "which would create a clear threat or present danger of violence or physical harm to any person, including incitement to racial hatred". But since Mr Martindale accepted that at the time he thought that the rules *required* the letter to be withheld and that fact to be recorded, it is unnecessary to consider the matter further.

"liable to be stopped", and it ultimately depended on the circumstances of each case.

21.19 Mr MacGowan's evidence mitigates the course which Mr Martindale took to the extent only that it shows that Mr Martindale was not alone in taking the approach he did. But the difficulty with this stance – and the reason why it cannot be condoned – is that on this approach the matter is not going to be reported. No-one else is going to be any the wiser about the fact that an inmate has written a letter of an inappropriate kind. And if the letter contains racist language, no-one is going to be any the wiser about the racist attitudes which the language may show the prisoner to have. As it happened, in Stewart's case, a note was made by Miss Hogg in Stewart's temporary wing file which she wrote for that purpose. But that was no thanks to Mr Martindale. He never suggested to her that she do that.

21.20 In any event, the wrong judgement call was made in Stewart's case. Not only did the letter use racist language, but it was threatening as well. That was what Miss Hogg had written in Stewart's temporary wing file. If Mr Martindale had not picked that up, that could only have meant that he had not read the letter sufficiently before telling Miss Hogg to return it to Stewart. Moreover, Stewart was not a newcomer to prison, and he was a prisoner about whom Mr Martindale had had concerns before Miss Hogg showed him the letter.

21.21 There is another dimension to all this. Racist incidents had to be reported to Feltham's Race Relations Liaison Officer. That had been spelt out in a recent Governor's Order, which Mr Clifford had issued in July 1999 and which purported to "remind" staff "again" of the need to report racist incidents. Mr Martindale knew that. What he said was that he had not thought at the time that Stewart's letter constituted a racist incident. And why was that? It may be that the answers he gave when questioned in the Inquiry did not do justice to the point he was trying to get across. What he told the Inquiry was that verbal and physical abuse, if racist, could amount to a racist incident. However, written abuse, even if racist, could not. If one concentrates on what constitutes an incident, one sees, I think, what Mr Martindale was trying to say – which was that the references in the Governor's Order to "witnessing the incident" and "the course of the incident" made him think that racist *incidents* involved some sort of victimisation or confrontation or dispute or overt display of racism, as opposed to the "victimless" expression of racist views in private correspondence.

21.22 I do not for one moment think that the use of racist language in a private letter cannot amount to a racist "incident". But that is beside the point.

It was not because Mr Martindale did not think that the letter amounted to a racist incident that he did not report it to the Race Relations Liaison Officer. He did not report it to the Race Relations Liaison Officer because he did not think that any action should be taken over the letter at all. Everything which he failed to advise Miss Hogg to do – such as withholding the letter or completing a security information report about it or telling the Race Relations Liaison Officer about it – stemmed from his view that no action needed to be taken over it. Those were the steps which should have been taken – as well, of course, as telling Stewart why the letter was being withheld.

21.23 Mr Martindale was pressed about why he did not think that any action needed to be taken over the letter. Could it be that he was indifferent to expressions of racism on the part of prisoners? His answer was that he was not prepared at the time to label Stewart as a racist despite what Stewart had written. He said that you have to get to know someone before branding them a racist. Presumably he thought that many young prisoners who are not consciously hostile to particular ethnic groups use racist language as a form of abuse. But Stewart's letter was not an example of mere racist abuse – even assuming that the distinction which Mr Martindale implicitly made was an acceptable one. Stewart's letter revealed a deep-seated hostility towards black and Asian prisoners. The problem was that the prevalence of racist abuse on the part of prisoners – which had gone unchecked at Feltham for so long – had shaped Mr Martindale's attitude towards racist language in prisoners' letters. He thought that it was not worth bothering to do anything more than he did. His response to the letter was an example of the unacceptably relaxed view taken of racist language which the culture at Feltham had bred.

21.24 In the course of the Inquiry, the rhetorical question was asked whether Mr Martindale's approach to the letter would have been any different if it had been written, not by a white racist, but by a Muslim fundamentalist who was railing against Christian infidels on the wing or by a black prisoner who spoke of large numbers of, say, "white trash" there? These scenarios were not put to Mr Martindale when he gave evidence, so it would be unfair to make unfavourable assumptions about what he would have done. If Mr Martindale was confronted *now* with such a letter from a Muslim fundamentalist, he might well take the action which he should have taken over Stewart's letter. But that might be due to the heightened awareness in the UK of young radicalised Muslims. What he would have done in January 2000 if a letter revealing hostility to Christian or white prisoners had been intercepted is something we can only speculate about.

21.25 These criticisms of Mr Martindale do not apply to Miss Hogg. She did not know about the requirements of the local and national rules. That is not as surprising as it sounds. The evidence was that what was done with Stewart's letter represented Mr Martindale's normal practice on Lapwing. There was in addition some evidence that the "letters withheld book" was not being used in other units anything like as consistently as it should have been. Miss Hogg may well not have known what was supposed to happen, and I am not inclined to disbelieve her. In those circumstances, she did what might have been expected of her: to take advice from a more senior colleague and follow that advice when it was given. It would be too harsh to criticise her for not questioning that advice. The advice she received from a far more experienced officer in charge of the unit would not have struck her as being so glaringly wrong that no junior officer in her position could be expected to have gone along with it.

The call from Security

21.26 While this was going on in Lapwing, something else of importance was happening in Feltham's Security Department. It will be recalled that Hindley sent Stewart's security file to Feltham by recorded delivery on 11 January. It must have arrived by 12 January because that was when Robert Benford, a senior officer in Feltham's Security Department, opened the envelope in which it came and looked at it. By then Stewart's security file consisted of three separate folders. Mr Benford did not provide the Inquiry with a statement, so we can only go on his statement to the police. He saw the inmate intelligence card at the front of the latest folder. Although the card was incomplete, Mr Benford realised immediately that Stewart was a danger to staff and other prisoners. Having scanned the whole file, he decided to warn the staff on Lapwing about him. There were some hints in the evidence about the Security Department being sensitive about information on a prisoner going round the establishment. But if there was a reluctance to share such information, that did not prevent Mr Benford from wanting to let people outside the Security Department know about Stewart. That was perhaps an indication of how much Mr Benford thought Stewart stood out from the crowd.

21.27 There is some uncertainty about what Mr Benford did next. He told the police that he had mentioned to a governor that he had read Stewart's security file and that he intended to let the unit know what was in it. He thinks, but is not sure, that the governor he spoke to was Helen

Clayton-Hoar, who was acting as Head of Operations at Feltham at the time. He does not say that he showed her Stewart's security file, and the impression his statement gives is that he was not looking for advice about what he should do. He was merely informing her what he was proposing to do. Mrs Clayton-Hoar has no recollection of this conversation. She does not doubt that Mr Benford told a governor about what he was proposing to do. It would not have been a surprising thing for him to do. She merely queries whether it was her. But I think that it is very likely that it was her. She was the governor responsible for the Security Department at the time, and although Mr Benford could have mentioned it to John Byrd, the governor responsible for the units which included Lapwing, she would, as Mr Benford's line manager, have been the more natural governor for Mr Benford to have mentioned the matter to. And it is not surprising for her not to have any recall of it now – or even when Mr Benford asked her four months or so later whether she remembered the conversation. There was no reason for it to have stuck in her mind.

21.28 The officer who Mr Benford spoke to about Stewart's security file was Mr Martindale. He asked Mr Martindale to come to his office and look at it. Mr Martindale said that this was unusual. To be asked by the Security Department to look at a prisoner's security file only happened occasionally. But when Mr Martindale got there, he understood why Mr Benford had called him. Stewart's was the largest security file he had seen on a prisoner. He read through it. As he was to say to the police:

> "I formed the impression he was very dangerous and a threat to both staff and other inmates. His file seemed to encompass violence, weapons, he was implicated in a previous prison murder and there were references to his outgoing prison mail which included potential escape. In short he was everything you don't want to find with a prisoner."

So when he got back to Lapwing, he warned his staff about Stewart, telling them to be careful with him.[*]

21.29 Mr Martindale also made two entries about Stewart. The first was in Stewart's temporary wing file which Miss Hogg had opened that

---

[*] Miss Hogg told the CRE that it was through Mr Martindale that she discovered that Stewart was facing charges for sending "abusive material". That cannot be correct. There was nothing in Stewart's security file about the charge he was facing under the Protection from Harassment Act 1997. She can only have got that information from Stewart during his induction.

morning. Immediately under the two entries made by her, he wrote in red and in capitals:

> "Staff are advised to see the security file on this inmate (held in Security). Very dangerous individual. *Be careful*."

In order to highlight the importance of this entry and to make sure that staff saw it, Mr Martindale marked it with a large asterisk in red, he put another large asterisk in red on the front cover, and wrote next to it: "See inner page." The second entry he made was in the wing observation book. As its name suggests, that is a book kept in the unit in which events of significance are recorded, so that members of staff who are not on duty at the time can read later about anything of importance which has happened. The entry which Mr Martindale made in capitals against Stewart's name and cell number was:

> "Staff are advised to read the security file (in Security) on this individual. He is a very dangerous character. Please be careful."

21.30 Both Mr Benford and Mr Martindale must be complimented on how they acted over Stewart's security file. It was one of the rare occasions on which steps were actively taken to bring concerns about Stewart to the attention of others. Mr Martindale's two entries told staff about Stewart's dangerousness clearly and unequivocally. After all, Stewart was due to leave Feltham that day, and others might have thought that in those circumstances it was unnecessary to do anything. But Mr Martindale plainly thought it was necessary to do something, even if he did not know that Stewart was due to return to Feltham a fortnight later when he was next in court.

21.31 In these circumstances it might be thought a little churlish to criticise Mr Martindale further, but there are a number of points which need to be made nevertheless. It may be that Mr Martindale's advice to staff to read the security file for themselves was a little impractical. You could hardly expect large numbers of staff to descend on the Security Department to read Stewart's security file. Since Mr Martindale had read it, it would have been better if he had informed them what Stewart had got up to in the past. Maybe he told the officers who were there what he had read about Stewart – Miss Hogg thought that he had told them a bit of what was in Stewart's security file. But there were officers who were not there, and they could only have gone on the entries Mr Martindale had made. They would not have been any the wiser about what Stewart had actually done in the past. Neither of the entries spelt out what had happened to make Mr Martindale think that Stewart was dangerous. As Mr Clifford told the Inquiry, Feltham was full of dangerous prisoners, and it could be argued that to say someone was dangerous without explaining why was "meaningless". Nor did the entries say whether Stewart was a danger to staff, or to other inmates, or to both – though, despite what he told the police, the language Mr Martindale used in the entries he made rather suggests that it was the risk of harm to staff which he had in mind, which reinforces the point that this was the way in which prison officers tended to view the possibility of harm. Nor did they suggest any particular way Stewart should be managed, for example that he should be accommodated in a single cell. It may have been very unusual for an entry to be made that a prisoner should not share a cell, but Mr Martindale had taken the precaution of putting Stewart in a cell on his own even before he knew anything about Stewart's security file. In fact, as we shall see, when Stewart next returned to Lapwing, he shared a cell with another prisoner.

21.32 The next point is an even more important one. Mr Martindale did not tell Mr Benford about Stewart's intercepted letter. That oversight was particularly misjudged. Once Mr Martindale had seen Stewart's security file, the very least he should have done was to tell Mr Benford about the letter. Otherwise the Security Department would not know that the hostility of this dangerous young man was currently focused on black and Asian prisoners. This was a serious omission. To be fair, Mr Martindale did not seek to excuse it, beyond saying that he had been very busy at the time.

21.33 That feeds into another point. Entries in Stewart's temporary wing file about the letter were not enough. It was well known that at Feltham prisoners' wing files sometimes did not accompany them as they should have. Stewart's case was a paradigm example of that. He arrived on Lapwing without his current wing file. Wider dissemination of the fact that Stewart had written a racist letter was required. That could only have been achieved if the Security Department had been told about it.

21.34 The last point is that when Mr Martindale made his entry in Stewart's temporary wing file, he would have seen Miss Hogg's earlier entries in it. The first one should have told him that she had thought that Stewart's letter was racist *and* threatening. In view of all that Mr Martindale had discovered about Stewart from his security file, what he should have done was to try to get the letter back from Stewart, to check what it said, and to tell Mr Benford about it. When it was put to Mr Martindale that this is what he should have done, he did not disagree.

21.35 What about Miss Hogg? When Mr Martindale came back from the Security Department and told staff to be careful about Stewart, should she have asked him whether he had told the security staff about the letter? And should she have asked him whether they ought to try to get the letter back from Stewart? I do not think Miss Hogg should be criticised for not doing either of these things. She could reasonably be expected to have assumed that Mr Martindale would have told security staff about the letter. And she could reasonably be expected to have thought that what Mr Martindale reported about Stewart was insufficient to undermine the correctness of the advice he had given her about the letter.

21.36 Nor is there any room for criticism of Mr Benford or Mrs Clayton-Hoar. Mr Benford was not told about the letter, so he cannot be expected to have taken any action over it. Had he followed up what Mr Martindale had done, he would have discovered that the entries Mr Martindale had made in the wing observation book* did not give any details about Stewart and placed the onus on the officers who read it to find out about him. But it would be far too much to expect Mr Benford to have checked up on the action Mr Martindale had taken, or for that matter to ask him about the way in which he was intending to give his staff information about Stewart. A more difficult question is whether Mr Benford should himself have considered whether it was appropriate for Stewart to share a cell. His statement to the police does not say that he did. But I do not think that he can be criticised for that either. Stewart was due to leave Feltham that day, and in any event that was a decision for the unit to make. And no criticism can be attached to Mrs Clayton-Hoar either. She never saw Stewart's security file, and was entitled to leave any decisions about what should be done about it to Mr Benford.

What would have happened?

21.37 Would the outcome have been any different if Stewart's letter had been dealt with as it should have been – in other words if, in addition to it being withheld, the Security Department had been informed about it through a security information report and the Race Relations Liaison Officer had been told about it? That depends on what they would have done about it, but I suspect they would have done very little. Mr Byrd was the Race Relations Liaison Officer at the time, and Stewart would have left Feltham by the time he would have been told about the letter. In any event, it is extremely unlikely that if Stewart had still been at

---

* Mr Benford is unlikely to have discovered anything about the entry in Stewart's temporary wing file because that left Feltham with Stewart that day.

Feltham it would have occurred to Mr Byrd that the letter might have implications for Stewart's management there.

21.38 Nor do I think that the Security Department would have done much with a security information report about the letter. It would, no doubt, have gone into Stewart's security file, but the contents of his security file were not brought to the attention of the units which Stewart was on when he returned to Feltham again. There is no reason whatever to suppose that the Security Department would have acted any differently if his security file then had a security information report about the letter. Maybe the completion of such a report at Feltham might have been picked up when Stewart returned to Hindley. But even if it had changed his management at Hindley – which itself is extremely doubtful – there is no reason to suppose that any change in the management of Stewart at Hindley would have affected his management at Feltham.

21.39 Would the outcome have been any different if Mr Martindale had been more specific in the entries he had made in the temporary wing file or the wing observation book, or if he had written that Stewart should not be allowed to share a cell? That depends on whether those entries would ever have been read on Swallow where Stewart ended up with Zahid. The entry in the wing observation book would not, because that remained on Lapwing. But as we shall see, the entries in the temporary wing file were read on Swallow. In an establishment which is performing well, they should have been enough to prompt anyone reading them to realise that Stewart should not share a cell with anyone, let alone with someone from an ethnic minority. Again, as we shall see, they were not a sufficient prompt at Feltham for that to have been appreciated. So something very specific had to be written about the need for Stewart not to share a cell if that was not to happen. Mr Martindale should have realised that. He therefore should have spelt it out, and that could well have resulted in Stewart either not sharing a cell with anyone, or at least not with a black or Asian prisoner.

How Hindley dealt with the entries on the temporary wing file

21.40 The temporary wing file with Miss Hogg's two entries and Mr Martindale's entry went back with Stewart to Hindley on 13 January. We know that because an entry was made in it at Hindley on 14 January. That entry was made by Elvis Thompson, a probation officer at Hindley. He made another entry about Stewart in the temporary wing file on 27 January after Stewart had returned to Hindley from Feltham for the second time. The entries consisted merely of stamps showing that Stewart was interviewed by a probation officer on those days. But the entries were made immediately below those made by Miss Hogg and Mr Martindale.

21.41 Stewart was seen by Mr Thompson because he had returned to Hindley after spending time elsewhere. A couple of nights away does not readily strike one as requiring a long meeting with a probation officer, and there is therefore no reason to doubt Mr Thompson's recollection that his interviews with Stewart lasted no longer than a few minutes. But what about the entries made by Miss Hogg and Mr Martindale? Mr Thompson was not asked to provide the Inquiry with a statement, but in his statement to the police he said that he had not read them. That is surprising. It is likely that the highlighting of Mr Martindale's entry – the asterisks and the fact that it was written in red – would have caused him to read it. And it was not as if Mr Thompson thought that the entries had been made at Hindley, so that Hindley already knew what they said. The entries were both dated 12 January, which should have caused Mr Thompson to realise that they had been made at the establishment from which Stewart had just come. But Mr Thompson may well have thought that the entries would have been seen by the officers on Stewart's wing, and that they would have taken such steps as were appropriate in the circumstances. So it was not thought likely that Mr Thompson might be susceptible to criticism.

21.42 It would, of course, have been very different if the temporary wing file had been seen by officers on Stewart's wing. If they had read the entries made at Feltham, a number of steps would have been appropriate: the completion of a security information report, a referral to the Race Relations Liaison Officer and the monitoring of Stewart's post. But it does not look as if the temporary wing file ever got to Stewart's wing. The wing file which was being used on his wing was his existing one which had never been sent to Feltham. Entries were made in that on 16 and 22 January. Why the temporary wing file did not get to Stewart's wing is not something which the Inquiry was able to establish. But it was a serious failing. It meant that action which undoubtedly should have been taken was not. Having said that, we do not know what the monitoring of Stewart's correspondence would have revealed: none of the letters he sent from Hindley between then and 7 February when he left Hindley for the last time were retrieved by the police.

21.43 Should the entries have been picked up anywhere else at Hindley? Mr Dunne thought that if they were to be picked up anywhere, it ought to have been in reception on 13 January. I disagree. The Inquiry had very little evidence of reception procedures at Hindley, but I would have thought it would have been asking far too much for reception staff to have gone through a temporary wing file on a returning prisoner. That was precisely the exercise which should have been carried out when he got to his wing. That made the fact that it appears not to have got to his wing all the more serious.

Chapter 22: Stewart returns to Feltham

Why not Lapwing?

22.1 Stewart was next due in court in London on 25 January 2000. So he went back to Feltham on 24 January. He spent the nights of 24 and 25 January there. He spent the first night on Osprey, and the second night on Lapwing. As an incoming prisoner, he should have spent his first night on Lapwing, but that did not matter much in his case. He was an "in and out" prisoner, and he had had on his previous visit the sort of induction regarded at Feltham as appropriate for such an inmate.

22.2 Why did he not spend his first night on Lapwing? We do not know, but not infrequently incoming prisoners went straight to a residential unit. In some cases there might have been a particular reason for that. But more often than not it was because Lapwing was full, and incoming prisoners had to be accommodated elsewhere. "New numbers" were given priority over transferees for the available spaces in Lapwing. That may well account for why Stewart did not spend his first night in Lapwing, especially as he was not only a transferee but a transferee who had spent time on Lapwing recently, as well as being an "in and out".

22.3 There was still, of course, a need for incoming prisoners who did not spend any time on Lapwing to go through the induction process. The evidence suggests that this was very much a hit-and-miss affair. No system was in place to ensure that inmates who went straight to a residential unit did not slip through the net. For example, as we shall see, when Stewart returned to Feltham for the third and last time, he did not spend any time on Lapwing, and did not go through an induction process at all.

22.4 The decision as to which unit prisoners should go to was made by staff on reception. If they were not going to Lapwing, their allocation would depend in part on whether they had been convicted or not. But for that, it depended on where there were spaces. That, no doubt, was how Stewart ended up on Osprey. At the time, Osprey was used for unconvicted prisoners, but it had a sprinkling of convicted ones.* It was perceived by Keith Denman, the principal officer responsible for the cluster of units which included Osprey, as a unit for more difficult prisoners. Maybe that was why it was described 18 months later, at a meeting of the race relations management team, as "the bad boys unit".

---

* Stewart was both. He was a convicted prisoner serving a sentence for the offences for which he had been sentenced on 13 January. He was an unconvicted prisoner awaiting trial on the charges relating to the letters to the chatline operator.

The warning Osprey got about Stewart

22.5 There was no question of Stewart's security file being vetted in the Security Department before he left Feltham on 26 January. As we have seen, Stewart left Lapwing at 6.45 am, and his security file would not have arrived back from Hindley before 26 January, since it had only been posted to Feltham the previous day. Nor is there any documentary evidence, one way or the other, which tells us whether Stewart arrived on Osprey with the temporary wing file which contained the entries made by Miss Hogg and Mr Martindale. All we know for sure is that it was back in Hindley on 27 January. The officer who was on duty on Osprey when Stewart arrived, Julie Goodman, who had become a prison officer in November 1997, told the police five months or so later that as far as she could remember he had not come with his wing file. Osprey's roll and movements sheet did not have a column for recording whether a prisoner arrived with his wing file. But Lapwing's did, and that did not show Stewart arriving the following day with his wing file. The strong probability, therefore, is that he did not arrive on Osprey with it either. But that did not mean that Miss Goodman knew nothing about Stewart. The officer who had brought Stewart to Osprey from reception was Robert Marshall. When he did an evening shift, he worked in reception. When he did a day shift, he was based on Lapwing. He told her something about Stewart which struck her as sufficiently important to make a note about him in the wing observation book.

22.6 There is a measure of disagreement about what she was told. Mr Marshall's evidence was that he told Miss Goodman that Stewart was "extremely dangerous", that he had a history of assaulting staff, that he had been involved in an attempt to take hostages, and that he had a particular problem with female staff. Miss Goodman claims to have no recollection of the events of 24 January, but the note she made in the wing observation book against Stewart's name was:

> "Be aware when unlocking this inmate – has a tendency to assault staff. Been informed by Officer Marshall."

That, no doubt, was the basis of what she later told the police:

> "He said words to the effect 'Julie be aware this inmate I know of old and so watch yourself when you unlock him because he likes to assault staff'."

She says that Mr Marshall could not have said anything to her about Stewart being extremely dangerous, or that he had been involved in an attempt to take hostages, or that he had a particular problem with female staff. If he had told her any of those things, she would have mentioned them in the entry she made in the wing observation book.

22.7 I think it unlikely that Mr Marshall told her everything that he claims to have done. First, his evidence to the Inquiry was itself an embellishment of what he had told the police when they had interviewed him five months or so later. Although he had said that he had told her that Stewart was extremely dangerous and had a history of assaulting staff, he had not said that he had also told her that Stewart had been involved in an attempt to take hostages or that he had a particular problem with female staff. Secondly, the effect of his evidence to the Inquiry was that he did not really think that Stewart had a particular problem with female staff. He told Miss Goodman that only because he had understood the target of the attempt to take hostages to have been a woman prison officer. That would not have been a sufficient basis to tell her that Stewart had a particular problem with female staff. Thirdly, he shifted his position about the source of his information about Stewart. He told the police that he had read about Stewart's attempt to take hostages and "acts of extreme violence against other inmates and staff" in the files. However, he told the Inquiry that it was unlikely that he had read Stewart's files, but had got that information either from Mr Martindale or from reading Mr Martindale's entry in the temporary wing file. The former is the likelier of the two: Mr Marshall is likely to have been one of the officers to whom Mr Martindale spoke about Stewart on 12 January. The strong probability is that Mr Marshall told Miss Goodman that Stewart was very dangerous – since that is undoubtedly how Mr Martindale saw Stewart – and that he had a history of assaulting staff, but no more than that.

22.8 Three comments can be made about all this. First, Miss Goodman should have mentioned in the entry she made in the wing observation book that Stewart was said to be very dangerous. As it turned out, that did not matter, because Stewart was never to be on Osprey again. But Miss Goodman was not to know that. And she should have made a similar entry in Stewart's wing file, so that the warning she was recording could be seen by staff on any other units Stewart was subsequently on. If, as is likely, the temporary wing file opened by Miss Hogg on 12 January had not come with him to Osprey on 24 January, she should have opened another temporary wing file and made the entry in that.

22.9 Secondly, Miss Goodman and Mr Marshall agree that whatever else he may or may not have told her, he told her that Stewart had a history of assaulting *staff*. In fact, Stewart did not – apart from the one occasion in 1995 when he threw bleach at a prison officer. He had a history of assaulting or bullying *other prisoners*. Indeed, Mr Marshall said that the warning he got from Mr Martindale about Stewart did not relate solely to assaults on staff. Why then did he not tell Miss Goodman that Stewart also posed a risk to other prisoners? His evidence to the Inquiry was that implicit in his warning that Stewart had a tendency to assault staff was also a warning that he posed a risk to other prisoners. I regard that explanation as unconvincing. The fact that some prisoners may have a tendency to assault staff says nothing about the risks they pose to other prisoners. They could well regard prison staff as the enemy and other prisoners as their friends: the "them and us" attitude in prison is a prevalent one. The real reason, I believe, why Mr Marshall limited his warning to Stewart having a history of assaulting *staff* is because of the tendency of prison officers to think in terms of the risks which prisoners pose to them.

22.10 Thirdly, this whole episode demonstrates the problems which can arise about the recording and flow of information about prisoners. The fact that any warning at all about Stewart was given to an officer on Osprey hinged on the chance fact that the officer who happened to escort Stewart from reception recognised him because he also worked on Lapwing where he had got to hear about him. Had Mr Martindale's entry in Stewart's temporary wing file on 12 January been more detailed, anyone reading it would have got a clearer picture of the risks Stewart posed. And had his temporary wing file accompanied him when he arrived at Osprey on 24 January, Miss Goodman would have been able to see for herself that, in addition to being a danger to staff, Stewart was a racist as well. She says that had she known that, she would not have put Stewart in a cell with an Asian prisoner that night.

Stewart's cell allocation in Osprey

22.11 Stewart spent his one night on Osprey in a double cell, cell 4. His cellmate that night was A. A was an Asian prisoner. Like Stewart, this was A's first night on Osprey. He had come from reception as well. It may be that they arrived from reception at about the same time. One of the documents shows that the Control and Information Room was informed at 6.36 pm that Stewart was to be accommodated in cell 4, and that the Control and Information Room was informed at 6.38 pm that A was to be accommodated there as well. But that does not reflect the times they arrived on the unit, or the order in which they arrived. Indeed, when Miss Goodman made the relevant entries in the roll and movements sheet for Osprey for that day, she entered A's name before Stewart's. And although Miss Goodman told the police that Stewart and A had arrived together, she does not now know why she said that.

22.12 There was a third prisoner who arrived that evening from reception. That was M. M was an Asian prisoner as well. The documents do not tell us when he arrived, although Miss Goodman entered M's name in the roll and movements sheet after A's and Stewart's. Whether he arrived with Stewart and A, or after them, Miss Goodman cannot recall. M was put in cell 38 that night. He had been in that cell the previous night. He had shared that cell with another Asian prisoner, Y, but before Stewart, A and M arrived in Osprey from reception, Y had been moved to the segregation unit in connection with an assault which he was supposed to have committed that day. When Y would return to Osprey depended on when his adjudication took place, and that would not have happened until the following day.

22.13 Osprey, like Swallow, had a certified normal accommodation of 60 and an operational capacity of 65. Immediately before the arrival of Stewart, A and M, there were 59 prisoners there already. The arrival of the three of them meant that there would be 62 prisoners in Osprey that night, so that doubling up had to take place in at least two of the single cells – more if any of those cells had been out of commission that night.

22.14 If it was known that a prisoner who left in the morning would be returning in the evening, his kit would usually be left in the cell, and he would go back to that cell when he returned. It is likely that this is what happened to M. So whether he arrived with Stewart and A, or whether he arrived after them, Miss Goodman can be assumed to have realised that he would be returning to cell 38. And she knew that cell 4 was empty. The roll and movements sheet shows that one of the prisoners who had been in that cell the night before had left Osprey and the other had gone to another cell. All of that meant that, leaving aside any risks which Stewart might have posed, there were three options* open to Miss Goodman for allocating Stewart and A when they arrived. She could have put

- Stewart with M in cell 38 and A alone in cell 4

- A with M in cell 38 and Stewart alone in cell 4

- Stewart and A in cell 4, leaving M on his own in cell 38.

22.15 There was no local procedure in place at the time to assist officers on how to make cell allocation decisions. Nor was there any national

---

* This presupposes that A had not arrived before Stewart and had not already been put in cell 4. If A had been put in cell 4 before Stewart arrived, Miss Goodman's only two options would have been to put Stewart in cell 38 with M or in cell 4 with A.

procedure either. As it was, Miss Goodman went for the third option. The questioning of her by Mr O'Connor related to why she did not go for the second option, which would have resulted in Stewart not sharing a cell. After all, she knew from what I have found Mr Marshall had told her that Stewart was a very dangerous prisoner.* Was something else at play here? Mr O'Connor never spelt it out, but the unspoken presence of the "Gladiator" allegations – in which prison officers were alleged to have put incompatible prisoners in the same cell and placed bets on the outcome – must have been in everyone's mind.

22.16 In fact, there was a relatively plausible reason why the third option may have been the least inconvenient option of the three. That was because it was likely that Y's kit would still have been in cell 38 pending his adjudication. A prisoner is never moved into a cell while its former occupant's kit is still there because of the opportunity for theft. Yet that is what would have happened if Miss Goodman had gone for either of the first two options. In theory, of course, Y's kit could have been stolen by M, but that could be discounted because prison officers knew that stealing from your cellmate is regarded by prisoners as conduct of the most despicable kind. I accept that it would not have taken long to bag up Y's kit, especially to release another bed at times of pressure on space, but another member of staff would still have been needed to do it. Moreover, Miss Goodman thought that Stewart and A were both "in and outs" – certainly the roll and movements sheet for the following day showed them both leaving Osprey and not returning. If they were sharing a cell together, they could have been moved out the next morning without disrupting the routines of other prisoners.

22.17 But that is not a complete answer to the point. If Miss Goodman had been worried about the suitability of Stewart sharing a cell, whether with A or with anyone, there were steps she could have taken to separate them. She could have put A in one of the single cells which were used for doubling up with another prisoner and put Stewart in cell 4 on his own. Or she could have investigated the possibility of Stewart being accommodated in another unit. She did not take either of those courses despite the warning she had got from Mr Marshall. The question is why. Was it because she never really considered whether a particular prisoner was suitable to share a cell, her practice being simply to fill the available spaces in the most convenient manner at the time? Or was it because she did consider the suitability of prisoners sharing cells, but saw no reason why Stewart and A should not share a cell? Or did

---

* This presupposes that Mr Marshall had told Miss Goodman about Stewart *before* she had decided which cells he and A should be put in. Miss Goodman assumes that he did. Her first statement to the Inquiry proceeded on that assumption.

it cross her mind that they might be unsuitable cellmates, but she put them in the same cell anyway – perhaps because she was indifferent to what might happen or out of a deliberate wish to cause trouble?

22.18 Even taking into account the "Gladiator" allegations, a finding that Miss Goodman placed Stewart and A together with the positive wish to see whether sparks might fly would be a very strong finding indeed, and I am not prepared to make it. There is no evidence that she knew anything of what had been discovered about Stewart's racism on his previous visit to Feltham. And she had not been with Stewart long enough for his appearance alone to have registered with her to such an extent that it should have alerted her to the possibility that he might be a racist. It was not uncommon at Feltham for white prisoners to share cells with prisoners from ethnic minorities. I have already said that her evidence was that had she known that Stewart was a racist, she would not have put him in a cell with an Asian prisoner. I have no reason to disbelieve her.

22.19 Nor do I think she deliberately ignored the question of whether a particular prisoner was unsuitable to share a cell with other prisoners. But that was not a question she would have addressed consciously. It was only if a prisoner really struck her as being unsuitable to share a cell, whether with all prisoners or particular kinds of prisoners, that she would try to give effect to what she thought was the most appropriate way of dealing with the situation. As it was, it did not strike her that Stewart and A should not share a cell, and that was why she took no steps to separate them. But she should have done. With the advantage of hindsight, putting Stewart in a cell with another prisoner was not the right course to take in view of what Mr Marshall had told her about Stewart being very dangerous. Although she had been told that Stewart posed a risk to staff, she did not know whether the risk Stewart posed was *only* to staff, or whether it was to other prisoners as well. So while Stewart remained an unknown quantity, Miss Goodman should have taken steps to ensure that, for the time being at least, Stewart was in a cell on his own.

22.20 But it is easy to say that now. One should not ignore the practical realities facing Miss Goodman at the time – which were that she had two "in and out" prisoners, who had come to the unit relatively late in the evening, at a time when she had a cell for two prisoners which was empty. Without any procedure for making cell allocation decisions, and with cell-sharing risk assessments not being part of the culture within the Prison Service at the time, it is not all that surprising that she made the decision which would have struck her then as being the obvious one but which can now be seen to have been incorrect. It was the wrong decision, but she should not be pilloried for that.

22.21 Moreover, what she did that night did not affect the ultimate course of events. Had she found some way to put Stewart in a cell on his own, and had she opened a temporary wing file and noted Mr Marshall's warning in it, it is unlikely that Stewart would have been dealt with any differently when he returned to Feltham again on 7 February. Any new temporary wing file she opened is likely to have been married up with the one opened by Miss Hogg on 12 January. As we shall see, that did not get to the unit where, apart from two nights, Stewart was to spend the rest of his time at Feltham until he had been there for four weeks. So any warning about Stewart in a temporary wing file opened by Miss Goodman would likewise not have been seen until Stewart had spent a number of weeks sharing a cell with Zahid.

The night on Lapwing

22.22 On his return from court on 25 January, Stewart went to Lapwing. He arrived there at 6.20 pm with another prisoner, W. They were put in the same cell. We do not know W's ethnicity. He and Stewart were the only new arrivals at that time – the previous arrival having been 25 minutes earlier, and the next arrival being 30 minutes later. Stewart and W were both listed in Lapwing's roll book as "in and outs". So it would have been perfectly natural for them to have been put in the same cell – but for the fact that Mr Martindale had had sufficient concerns about Stewart two weeks earlier to put him in a cell on his own, and that had been before the racist letter had been intercepted and before he had read Stewart's security file.

22.23 The Inquiry was unable to get to the bottom of all this. We did not find out which officer had processed Stewart and W when they got to Lapwing on 25 January. Mr Martindale did not know whether he had been on duty then. But if it had been thought inappropriate for Stewart to share a cell when he was an unknown quantity, it was all the more inappropriate for him to share a cell when so much worrying information about him had been discovered. But one of the reasons why the Inquiry did not pursue the matter further was because the events relating to Stewart's second visit to Feltham were not causatively linked to what he was eventually to do. It was how he was dealt with when he came back to Feltham for the third time, coupled with what had been discovered and recorded about him when he had first gone there, which contributed to what was ultimately to happen.

Chapter 23: Stewart's last trip to Feltham

Stewart stays at Feltham

23.1 Stewart was next due in court in London on 8 February 2000. So he went back to Feltham on 7 February. He spent the first night on Kestrel, and the second night on Swallow. As we have seen, the decision that he should stay at Feltham until he was next in court on 7 March, and not return to Hindley in the meantime, was probably made at Feltham on 8 February by the Observation, Classification and Allocations Department. That decision may have contributed to the problems which Feltham experienced in dealing with Stewart. It must have been relatively rare for a prisoner who had arrived at Feltham as an "in and out" – and who might have been expected to stay there for no more than a couple of nights – to have remained there for much longer. Perhaps the comparative rarity of that happening had a part to play in the problems in processing Stewart which, as we shall see, occurred on reception, in the Security Department and in the healthcare centre.

23.2 We do not know why Stewart did not spend either of those two nights on Lapwing. Presumably Lapwing was full. But being an "in and out" prisoner, who had previously gone through what passed for induction at Feltham, that would not have mattered too much if the induction process had been working properly. Kestrel, like Osprey, held mostly unconvicted prisoners, with a sprinkling of convicted ones. Swallow was the other way round. Most of the inmates held there were convicted prisoners.* We do not know why Stewart spent his first night on Kestrel, and why he then went to Swallow. It may be that Kestrel was the most convenient unit that night for putting an "in and out" prisoner, and that once it had been decided on 8 February that Stewart was going to remain at Feltham, it was thought better for him to go to a unit for convicted prisoners.

---

* Kestrel had previously been re-roled – Prison Service jargon for a unit whose function had recently changed. It had been used to hold prisoners who were about to be discharged or were due to appear in court the following day. If Feltham was a transit camp, Kestrel was a goods siding within it. There had always been problems there. Swallow was for prisoners who were considered to be "quite settled and looking for employment". It had recently been refurbished and had re-opened in January 2000 with the staff who had previously been working on Raven and the prisoners who had been accommodated there. Different dates were given for its re-opening. One witness said it re-opened on 14 January, another said 18 January.

Stewart's temporary wing file

23.3 Stewart arrived on Kestrel without a wing file. Kestrel's roll book, unlike Osprey's roll and movements sheet, had a column for recording whether a prisoner arrived with his wing file. So did Swallow's roll and movements sheet. They show that Stewart did not arrive with his wing file. So the crucial wing file – the temporary one with Miss Hogg's and Mr Martindale's entries in it – had either stayed at Hindley, or had been sent to Feltham but had not got to Kestrel or Swallow. That meant that no-one on Kestrel on 7 February – or on Swallow on 8 February – knew about the warnings in the temporary wing file.

Mr Marshall's sighting of Stewart

23.4 But it is possible that there was an opportunity for Kestrel or Swallow to have been warned about Stewart. He was recognised one evening by Mr Marshall, who was working a shift on reception as one of the officers responsible for searching incoming prisoners. Mr Marshall recalls telling the senior officer on duty in reception that evening, Colin Diaper, about Stewart. His best recollection of what he said was that Mr Diaper should keep an eye on Stewart because he was "raving bloody mad". What he had in mind was that Stewart was unpredictable and there was something not quite right about him. For his part, Mr Diaper did not recall Mr Marshall warning him about Stewart, but since such warnings were not uncommon, he did not doubt what Mr Marshall had said. I have no reason to doubt Mr Marshall's evidence, and whatever his precise words to Mr Diaper were, the strong probability is that he said something to Mr Diaper along the lines that Stewart needed to be watched.

23.5 There is no certainty that this happened either when Stewart arrived from Hindley on 7 February or when he returned from court on 8 February. Mr Marshall told the police that it happened "a month or so after" the time he had escorted Stewart to Osprey. That had been on 24 January. He could not be more precise when he gave evidence to the Inquiry. So what he was describing could just as easily have happened on later occasions when Stewart returned to Feltham after going to court. As we shall see, those occasions were on 7 and 8 March. But whenever it happened, the unit Stewart was going to should have been warned about him.

23.6 One way of doing that would have been to tell the officer who was to escort Stewart to the unit to pass on a suitable warning about him. Mr Marshall expected Mr Diaper to do that, and Mr Diaper accepted that it would not have been unreasonable for Mr Marshall to have expected him to do that. But it is unlikely that Mr Diaper did that, because if he had, one might have expected there to have been a note in Kestrel's wing observation book on 7 February or a note in Swallow's on 8 February. There was no such note in either.

23.7 But that would not have been the best way of passing on a warning about Stewart to the unit he was going to. If he later went to another unit, the warning would have to be passed on again. Since the wing observation book remained on the unit where it was kept, the warning would have to be relayed in some other way, and there was no guarantee the new unit would get it unless it was in one or other of Stewart's wing files – either the new one opened in Hindley on 23 December or the temporary one opened on 12 January with Miss Hogg's and Mr Martindale's entries in it – if either of them were to hand. As we have seen, they did not go with Stewart when he went to Kestrel on 7 February or to Swallow on 8 February.

23.8 But that did not mean that the wing files were not in reception when Stewart returned to Feltham on those days. As it is, we do not know where they were. We are completely in the dark about the one opened on 23 December. The last entry in it was made at Hindley on 22 January. We do not know whether it was ever married up with the temporary one. All we know is that it had arrived at Feltham by the time of the attack. As for the temporary wing file, there are two possibilities. One is that it came with Stewart when he arrived at Feltham on 7 February, but that instead of accompanying him to Kestrel where he spent that night and then going with him to Swallow the next night, it got misfiled – perhaps with his core record – and was only discovered when his core record was retrieved from Custody Administration for his visit to court on 7 March. At least one officer who had worked in reception thought that was a possible explanation. The other possibility is that it did not come with Stewart to Feltham on 7 February, but was sent to Feltham later. On that scenario, it got filed away in Custody Administration on its arrival, rather than being sent to Swallow.

23.9 Although a note about Stewart's dangerousness *could* have been made in one or other of his wing files if either of them had arrived with him from Hindley on 7 February, *should* such a note have been made? Not if the temporary wing file had arrived with him, because the entry made in it by Mr Martindale would have been sufficient to draw Stewart's dangerousness to the attention of the staff on the unit he was going to.

But if the temporary wing file had not arrived with Stewart from Hindley, but the original one had, a note about Stewart's dangerousness should have been made in that. If that had not arrived with Stewart either, another temporary wing file should have been opened at reception, and a note about Stewart's dangerousness should have been made. But it was not. It should have been, and Mr Diaper as the senior officer on reception that day should have done it rather than Mr Marshall. Mr Marshall may have told Mr Diaper about Stewart so that a watch could be kept on him while he was *in reception*. But once Mr Diaper had information that Stewart was dangerous, he should have passed that on to the unit Stewart was going to.

23.10 All of this applies only if Mr Marshall saw Stewart in reception on either 7 or 8 February. If this happened on 7 or 8 March, the need to record anything in Stewart's wing file would not have arisen. As we shall see, on each of those days he arrived in Swallow from reception with his temporary wing file containing Miss Hogg's and Mr Martindale's warnings about him, so Swallow should then have known the sort of young man they were dealing with.

Cell allocation in Swallow

23.11 We do not know whether Stewart shared a cell on the night he spent in Kestrel, but what happened in Swallow is well documented. Stewart arrived there relatively late on 8 February. The Control and Information Room was informed of the cell to which he had been allocated at 7.59 pm, and an entry was made about his arrival in Swallow's roll and movements sheet at 8.00 pm. At that time, the unit was on patrol state, with all prisoners locked in their cells and only a night patrol officer on duty. The officer on duty was Simon Diaper, Colin Diaper's nephew. He was relatively inexperienced. He had only joined the Prison Service in June 1999, and had yet to complete his probation period. He had had no training about how to allocate prisoners to particular cells when they arrived on a unit. Nor had anyone told him what to do, or what he was supposed to look at. And as we have seen, there were no local or national procedures to guide him.

23.12 It is here that fate played its hand. Swallow's roll and movements sheet shows that when Stewart arrived there were 59 prisoners on the unit. So his arrival brought the number up to the certified normal accommodation of 60. On the assumption that none of the cells were out of commission and that there had been no doubling up prior to Stewart's arrival, that meant there was only one space available for him on the unit. That space was in cell 38. That was a double cell. Zahid was already in it. As we have seen, he had been sharing it until that day with G. G had left the cell that morning. Simon Diaper says he placed Stewart in cell 38 because that was the only cell in which there was space. He was to remain there until the night he attacked Zahid.

23.13 There is no reason to disbelieve him. Whether there was a practice at Feltham to put unsuitable prisoners with each other to see what would happen, there is nothing to suggest that this might have happened in this case. Zahid's family do not suggest that it did – at any rate, Mr O'Connor did not. The fact that cell 38 was the only cell with space in it – assuming there had been no doubling up and there were no cells out of commission – is the obvious reason why Stewart was put into cell 38. The fact that the unit was on patrol state at the time suggests that Mr Diaper would not have had a malign motive to put Stewart in with Zahid. There would not have been anyone else around to see whether any trouble arose between them. And since Stewart arrived without his temporary wing file, Mr Diaper would not have known that he might be a danger to his cellmate.

23.14 The fact that cell 38 was the only cell available did not mean that Mr Diaper had no other options. If he had thought, for one reason or another, that Stewart should not share a cell with anyone, he could have put him temporarily in one of the classrooms, or asked the officer who escorted him to Swallow to look after him for the time being, while he sought guidance from a more senior officer about what to do or asked reception whether he could be sent to another unit. Alternatively, he could have asked a more senior officer to send other officers to the unit, so that he could move a prisoner out of a single cell and put that prisoner in cell 38 with Zahid, and put Stewart in the single cell. And if he had thought that Stewart could have shared a cell but not with Zahid, he could have put Stewart in one of the cells which could be doubled up – assuming that there was already a second bed in there.

23.15 But it did not cross Mr Diaper's mind to do any of that. That was not so much because it did not occur to him that Stewart should not share a cell – or at least not with Zahid. It was rather because he was not aware of any occasion when a decision about cell allocation had been made other than on the basis of what was convenient. He had never known a decision to be affected by what was in a prisoner's wing file. So the question of Stewart's suitability to share a cell with Zahid – or anyone else for that matter – did not cross his mind.

The absence of the temporary wing file

23.16 Mr Diaper knew that Stewart's wing file had not accompanied him because it was he who made the entry about that in Swallow's roll and movements sheet. What should he have done about that? Should he have refused to accept Stewart onto the unit at all? Should he have asked the officer who brought him to the unit where his wing file was? If he accepted him onto the unit, should he have let reception know that he had arrived without his wing file? And should he have opened a temporary wing file to be used until the current one turned up? As it was, Mr Diaper did none of these things. He said that if he should have taken any of these steps, he had not known that. He had seen experienced officers accept new prisoners into Swallow without a wing file, and he had thought that this was acceptable.

23.17 The trouble was that there was no written guidance – whether national or local – about what should be done when a prisoner arrived on a wing without his wing file. Nor had anyone told Mr Diaper what to do. So there is no reason for me not to accept Mr Diaper's explanation for his inaction as truthful, even though other more experienced officers might have acted differently. The evidence suggests that there was a local practice at Feltham at the time that if a prisoner came from another unit without his wing file, the receiving unit should refuse to accept him. But that was impractical for prisoners who arrived from another establishment. The unit had little choice but to accept such a prisoner, while raising a temporary wing file on him, and asking reception or Custody Administration where his current wing file was. But it may well be that this practice was not always followed to the letter. The practice of turning away prisoners who arrived from another unit without their wing files was described only as an "informal agreement", and there was nothing laid down in black and white as to what was supposed to happen. So Mr Diaper may well have seen other officers, more experienced than himself, doing what he was later to do – accepting prisoners onto the unit without a wing file and doing nothing about it.

What would have happened if Stewart's temporary wing file had arrived with him?

23.18 There is little doubt about what Mr Diaper *should* have done if the temporary wing file had arrived with Stewart and he had read the warnings about Stewart in it. Even though the suitability of a prisoner to share a cell with another prisoner had never really crossed his mind, the suitability of Stewart to share a cell with anyone, let alone Zahid, was something which he should have considered. If Stewart was very dangerous, he should not have shared a cell at all until it was known that his dangerousness did not put other prisoners at risk. To that extent, he was an unknown quantity until his security file could be looked at. So for the time being, at any rate, he should have been accommodated in a single cell. But if he had to share a cell, the one thing which should not have happened – in the light of his racism which the warnings about him revealed – was for him to share a cell with a black or Asian prisoner. So if Stewart's temporary wing file had arrived with him, Mr Diaper should have taken one of the various options discussed in paragraph 23.14. The same is true if his uncle had opened another temporary wing file about Stewart in view of the warning he had got about Stewart from Mr Marshall. That is so even though his uncle would have limited his entry to a comment about Stewart's dangerousness, since he did not know about Stewart's racism.

23.19 But *would* he have done that if Stewart's temporary wing file had arrived with him? That presupposes that he would have read the warnings in it. He could hardly have failed to see what Mr Martindale had written in red on the front cover, and that, I assume, would have led him to read the entries. But I am sceptical whether Mr Diaper would have taken any action that night. He said he would: at the very least, he would have asked a more senior officer for advice. That is understandably what Mr Diaper wants to think he would have done, but his evidence on this topic does not lie easily with his own experience that he had not come across a time when cell allocation had been affected by a prisoner's wing file or anything other than convenience. I believe that what is likely to have happened is that Mr Diaper would have been reluctant to ask for advice, fearing that he might be thought indecisive, and that he would still have put Stewart in cell 38 with Zahid. But I also think that if he had been on duty the next day he would have asked the officer in charge of Swallow whether Stewart should stay in cell 38, and that if he was not going to be on duty the next day he would have left a note for the officer in charge of Swallow to that effect. However, even if Mr Diaper would have done what he claims he would have done, and had sought advice from a more senior officer, we can only guess what that advice would have been.

What should have happened?

23.20 Stewart's temporary wing file did not come with him. So the question is: what should Mr Diaper have done, assuming there was no other reason to cause him to think that Stewart might be dangerous? At one stage, it looked as if that assumption could not be made. In Part 1 of its report, the CRE referred to an officer who it did not identify but who remembered "giving a warning about Stewart to the officer on Swallow unit responsible for assigning prisoners to their cells". This must have been Mr Diaper because the reference was in the context of what happened on 8 February and referred to the fact that the officer on Swallow was a recent recruit still on probation. Mr Diaper told the Inquiry that he did not recall ever receiving such a warning, and the CRE did not raise the matter in the course of its interview with him. Mr Marshall was asked by the Inquiry whether he might have warned Mr Diaper about Stewart, in view of the warning he had given to Miss Goodman. He said that he had not. In the circumstances, we cannot take the matter further. It looks as if the CRE may well have confused what they thought had happened on Swallow with the warning Mr Marshall gave to Miss Goodman on Osprey.

23.21 So the question remains: what should Mr Diaper have done, assuming there was no other reason to cause him to think that Stewart might be dangerous? The answer is: not much. He could have got in touch with reception to find out where Stewart's wing file was. If it had not been returned to Feltham by Hindley, they would have told him that Stewart had arrived without it. If it had come to Feltham with him, it had been misplaced, and the likelihood is that reception would not have been able to lay their hands on it. In these circumstances, even if Mr Diaper had applied his mind to the consequences of Stewart arriving without his wing file, he would have had little option but to proceed as he did. He could have opened a temporary wing file on him, but that would not have enhanced his knowledge of Stewart. So the only thing he should have done, but did not do, was to let the officer in charge of Swallow know the following day that Stewart had arrived without a wing file – either by telling him that or by leaving a note for him. As we shall see, the officer in charge of Swallow at the time was Mr McAlaney. His supervision of staff on Swallow left much to be desired. What he would have done if he had been told that Stewart had arrived without his wing file is a matter of complete speculation. But I suspect that he would have done nothing except to say that a temporary wing file should be opened.

Chapter 24: Stewart's behaviour on Swallow and his appearance

An unproblematic prisoner

24.1 Stewart remained on Swallow for the next six weeks. If the records are anything to go by, his behaviour gave no cause for concern. He was never sent to the segregation unit. He was never made the subject of any adjudications. No security information report was completed on him. No entry was made on him in the wing observation book. And no-one wanted to make an entry in his wing file about him. If they had, they would have discovered during his first few weeks there that it was missing, and no-one was apparently aware of that. At any rate, no steps were ever taken to look for it, or to open a temporary one. But although no-one could possibly have predicted what Stewart was going to do, the question still has to be asked whether his behaviour or appearance were such as to give officers on Swallow any concerns about the suitability of him continuing to share a cell with Zahid.

Stewart's behaviour on Swallow

24.2 Stewart's behaviour on Swallow has to be put into its proper context. Prisons and young offender institutions have a disproportionate number of people who may present in a threatening or unusual manner in the context of society at large. Your behaviour in prison will have to be particularly threatening or unusual if it is to stand out. And there was nothing in Stewart's relationship with Zahid which might have made him stand out. There was no evidence that he and Zahid gave the impression of not getting on – apart from one prisoner who told the police that he recalled them arguing once. So Stewart's behaviour has to be judged in the context of apparent harmony between them. And it must also be remembered that there was not all that much time for Stewart to have been observed. Six weeks may sound like a long time, but the time out of cells for prisoners on Swallow in the early part of 2000 was very limited. Prison officers had few opportunities to interact with inmates, or to observe their interaction with each other. And since prison officers might be expected to spend more time with difficult and disruptive prisoners, the fact that Stewart and Zahid did not cause any trouble while they were on Swallow meant that less attention would have been paid to them.

24.3 The impression created by the records was confirmed by the evidence of the staff on Swallow. No-one recalls anything which suggested that Stewart might have been unusually aggressive. The same picture emerges from the many statements the police took from other prisoners on Swallow. The only incidents of aggressive behaviour on the part of Stewart which they spoke of were his tendency to bang his table-tennis bat on the table when he lost a match, and an occasion in the showers when he squared up to another prisoner before backing down – an incident which prison officers apparently did not see. Admittedly, the CRE's informant – whose evidence we received in summarised form – said that many inmates believed Stewart to be dangerous, but he did not say what had led them to think that.

24.4 Stewart was careful to express his racism only when he was around prisoners he thought were white. Jamie Barnes, the only prisoner on Swallow to give oral evidence to the Inquiry, and whose mixed race origins were not immediately apparent, said that he had heard Stewart refer to black prisoners as "niggers" and black people as "them". On the rare occasions when Stewart mixed with other prisoners, it was mainly with members of white gangs, and according to Barnes, Stewart would say that although the black prisoners thought they were "hard" they were not as "hard" as him. There is nothing to suggest that either prison officers or black prisoners heard him say any of that, and it is plain that Stewart tended to keep his racism to himself while he was on Swallow. If he let it slip at times, that would only have been when he did not think there would be any repercussions. As Barnes said, with so many black and Asian prisoners on Swallow, you would have had to be suicidal to be openly racist. Even with the benefit of the informant's evidence, the CRE concluded that there was no evidence to indicate any "demonstrative and open" expression of racism by Stewart while he was on Swallow. Presumably they meant that he only allowed his racism to emerge with prisoners he thought would not mind it.

24.5 While Stewart was on Swallow, he continued to be what he had always been – quiet and a loner. Apart from his appearance, that was what staff remembered most about him. His fellow prisoners got the same impression. But that was not likely to be regarded as particularly surprising. Stewart was not from the London area, and he did not know anyone else on Swallow. And often young prisoners kept themselves to themselves. That was their defence mechanism. So there was no particular reason why Stewart's withdrawn and uncommunicative demeanour alone would have alerted staff to the possibility that he posed a risk to the safety of other prisoners in general or to his cellmate in particular. It would have been different if they had known what was in his security file. Then, just as Mr Farrell at Altcourse had done, they would have seen a mismatch between his current behaviour and his previous record. But staff on Swallow did not have the temporary wing file which told them of the need to look at his security file – at any rate not until he had been on Swallow for a month, and by then staff had got used to him.

24.6 Having said all that, had their antennae been sufficiently attuned, staff should have picked up that there was something not quite right about Stewart. Mr Martindale picked it up. As we have seen, when Stewart arrived on Lapwing, Mr Martindale had a gut feeling about him. Maybe that had as much to do with Stewart's appearance as anything else. But he picked up on something about Stewart immediately. To be fair, so too did some of the officers on Swallow. One of them, Ross Farmer, told Mr Butt about a "general feeling" in the unit that Stewart needed to be watched. Lee Edmundson, the officer who gave Stewart and Zahid the newspaper on the night of the murder, thought that Stewart might be trouble. They may not have been able to put their finger on it, but what they were articulating was the sense that Stewart was an unknown quantity. He was so taciturn and reserved that no-one really knew what was going on in there, and he was not going to let anyone in. But not all staff on Swallow picked that up, and one is left with the sense that the "jailcraft"* of which prison staff speak so proudly, and which might have enabled them to spot the problem prisoner, may have let some of them down.

24.7 Zahid himself thought that Stewart was odd. He told his family that Stewart was "a bit weird". He also told them that Stewart kept staring at him, which anyone would have found disconcerting. We do not know whether he told prison officers that, but as we shall see, he asked prison officers – albeit just the once – whether he could move out of cell 38. That may have been because he wanted to be with Barnes, but there was almost certainly a strong element of wanting to get away from Stewart as well.

The request for visiting orders

24.8 In a letter Stewart sent to a friend while on Swallow and retrieved by the police after the murder of Zahid, Stewart wrote that he had sent his friend a visiting order for Adolf Hitler, Charles Manson, Harold Shipman and the children of two well-known celebrities. The practice was for requests for visiting orders to be made on the appropriate form, which was then handed to an officer on Swallow to be forwarded to the Visits Department. The request would invariably be sticking out of an unsealed

---

* The word prison officers give to the skills they develop in the course of managing the prisoners in their care.

envelope, so that the officer to whom it was handed knew what it was. It would not have been usual for officers to look at who the request was for, but they might look at it if it also contained a letter they had decided to read.

24.9 I am not prepared to accept that Stewart was telling his friend the truth. He referred to *a* visiting order whereas separate requests had to be made for each proposed visitor. He spoke of the visiting order having been sent to *his friend*, whereas visiting orders were only sent to those who had been named as the proposed visitor. And it was exactly the sort of claim Stewart would have made up for effect. But if Stewart had requested visiting orders for the people he claimed, and if the requests had been seen by an officer on Swallow – both very big "ifs" indeed – I doubt whether the fact that Hitler's name was included in so disparate a list of people should have prompted anyone to think that Stewart was racist. It would just have made them think how puerile Stewart was. And it might have reinforced their view that Stewart was a bit of an oddball. But it cannot fairly be said that they should have thought anything more about him than that.

Stewart's appearance

24.10 Stewart wore his hair very short. Not so long ago he would have been called a skinhead, although by the beginning of 2000 the style was very fashionable. The overwhelming majority of prisoners had shaved heads. But the feature of Stewart's appearance which was unmistakable were the two tattoos prominent on his forehead: a cross and the letters "RIP". All the officers on Swallow who were questioned about those tattoos knew the letters stood for "rest in peace". None of them thought that the tattoos, even when coupled with his virtually shaven head, suggested that Stewart may have been making a particular statement about himself.

24.11 Both the CRE and the Metropolitan Police informed the Inquiry that they did not regard Stewart's tattoos as racist symbols. Taken separately I agree. But put them together and something different emerges. The association of the cross and death brings to mind the Ku Klux Klan.* And on a wider front, the juxtaposition of symbols for the Church and death

---

* I have assumed that the cross represented the symbol for the Church rather than the Cross of St George, which might have associated Stewart with an extreme form of nationalism. And as we shall see, he was to admit writing the letters "KKK" on the noticeboard in his cell.

suggests something along the lines that the taking of life for a worthy cause may be justified. That is redolent of the views of the extreme right. When you couple that with a hairstyle which not so long ago was associated with the foot soldiers of the National Front, you would be forgiven for thinking that Stewart might have been trying to articulate a statement of support for its views. Although the National Front might deny it, its immigration policies are seen as hardly indistinguishable from unbridled racism. By that route, it would be possible to link Stewart's appearance with a hostility towards black people and people from ethnic minorities.

24.12 The possibility that the tattoos revealed Stewart as racist was something which never crossed the minds of the officers on Swallow – that, at any rate, was their evidence, although the CRE's informant said that they knew he was. But it crossed the minds of the other prisoners on Swallow if Barnes's evidence is to be believed. He told Mr Butt that "everyone" on the unit thought that Stewart was "NF" because of the tattoos, and that "lots of people" interpreted the tattoos as a "sign for [a] racist group". He said much the same thing to the police. And the CRE's informant said that some days before Zahid's murder, prisoners had formed a crowd around Stewart in the showers. They wanted to know if he was racist. Stewart was said to have stuttered "not really" but added that he "sometimes hates what people do". That the prisoners on Swallow thought that Stewart was racist was not borne out by the statements the police took from the CRE's informant and other prisoners on Swallow, although one of them said that he had asked Stewart whether he was racist, which rather suggests that he thought Stewart might be. As it was, Stewart had replied that he was not.

24.13 The CRE's informant offered an explanation for why none of the prisoners who gave a statement to the police apart from Barnes talked about Stewart's racism. He claimed that he had told the police that officers on Swallow had told inmates: "You were in your cells. You never saw or heard nothing. Remember, you've got jobs on the wing." He said that he could not recall the names of the officers who had said that, but that he would have given their names to the police. I am very sceptical about all of this for a number of reasons. If he told the police what he claims he told them, it never got into his police statement. Moreover, there were things he told the CRE which he could not possibly have known about, at any rate not at first hand. For instance, he claimed that when the Governor had visited Stewart, Stewart had told him that he was going to kill himself. The Governor was supposed to have said: "Go on then." So far as the Inquiry can tell, not even Stewart alleged that. In addition, much of his speculation about what had happened could not have been right. For example, he told the CRE that it was "bullshit" that staff could not remember who had put Zahid and Stewart into a cell together. In fact, there was never any doubt that it had been Simon Diaper. And he told the CRE inconsistent things. For instance, at one stage he claimed that Stewart should have been in another unit because he was dangerous. But later on he said that Stewart should not have remained on Swallow because he was at risk from other prisoners, citing the incident in the showers as an example of an occasion when staff did not intervene because they wanted him beaten up. All in all, I do not believe that I should give much credence to what the CRE's informant has said.

24.14 Did Zahid associate the tattoos with racism on Stewart's part? Barnes says that Zahid did. He told the police that Zahid had said of Stewart: "I don't like him. Those things on his head, he's NF." Did Zahid tell his family that? Zahid's father told the Inquiry that Zahid *had* said that his cellmate was racist. But when it was pointed out to him that he had not said that in his statement to the Inquiry, he accepted that Zahid might not have told him that. I do not think that Zahid did say that. If he did, his father would have remembered it when he made the statement. All the talk about racism in the Inquiry had understandably made Zahid's father think that he had spoken about racism as well. But Zahid may not have wanted his family to know that his cellmate was racist because he did not want them to worry about him. For example, his cousin, Tanzeel Ahmed, recalls Zahid mentioning that his cellmate had "RIP" on his forehead. He said that they had laughed it off, Zahid giving "that impression perhaps to cover his own feelings about it". The strong likelihood is that Zahid, along with a few of the other prisoners on Swallow, had a real inkling that Stewart might be racist.

24.15 Did the tattoos make the officers on Swallow think that Stewart might be racist? I can see how *intellectually* the link between the particular tattoos which Stewart had and racism might be regarded as tenuous. I recognise as well that prison officers have far less time than the prisoners themselves to think about what particular inmates are like. And as many of the officers on Swallow told the Inquiry, lots of prisoners have tattoos – including facial tattoos, some strange ones and in odd places – and in that respect Stewart did not stand out. Indeed, they would have to guard against making snap judgements on the basis of prejudicial or stereotypical assumptions about someone's appearance. So I am not inclined to disbelieve their assertions that it did not occur to them that Stewart might be racist.

24.16 But *should* that have occurred to them? I have to say that their instincts should have told them that there was something very worrying about someone whose tattoos, when analysed, could be seen to be making a statement about death – and in such a dramatic way. These tattoos were on any view extremely unusual. Maybe that was why he was twice recognised when he passed through reception. Given the kind of tattoos they were and their prominent position on the shaven head of a guarded and uncommunicative young man, it should have occurred to the officers on Swallow at the very least that there was something particularly menacing about Stewart. And it should also have occurred to them that there was at any rate a real possibility that Stewart was a racist who might be hostile to prisoners from ethnic minorities and who for that reason should not have remained in a cell with Zahid.

24.17 Why did this possibility not occur to them? I think it had much to do with the lack of awareness about racial issues which was so commonplace at Feltham and was one of the hallmarks of its institutional racism. Staff often failed to pick up on any undercurrents of racism which may have been bubbling below the surface, unless its manifestation was so overt that it would have been obvious to anyone. The prevalence of racist abuse, which no-one had done anything to stamp out, gave the impression that racism would be tolerated, and that had desensitised staff to such an extent that the signs that Stewart might be racist did not register with them.

24.18 But in any event the staff on Swallow should have realised that Stewart was sufficiently strange and looked sufficiently menacing to make most people uncomfortable about sharing a cell with him. Some prisoners called him "madman" or "sicko" because of his tattoos. And it goes further than that. Most people who have to live in confined conditions of great intimacy with someone else would prefer to do that with someone from their own background. The ethnic differences between Stewart and Zahid should have made staff realise that Zahid was likely to have been even less comfortable about sharing a cell with him than other prisoners would have been. And because Stewart was such an unknown quantity, some thought should have been given to whether *anyone* should be required to share a cell with him. Leaving aside any question about his dangerousness, he was such an oddball that staff should have considered whether it was *fair* to require another prisoner to have to put up with him – let alone one whose ethnic background made him so different from Stewart anyway.

24.19 Curiously enough, there were some officers who claimed that Stewart was himself vulnerable as a result of his appearance. He was not a big lad, and they said that his tattoos might attract "unwanted attention". They feared he might be picked on. I am very sceptical about whether that was what they really thought, although there is some support for their view in the statement of the CRE's informant. It looks to me as if they realised that they could be criticised for not appreciating that Stewart might be a racist who should not have been put in a cell with Zahid. They wanted to deflect that criticism by showing that they *had* given thought to the sort of young man Stewart was. What may not have occurred to them was that his supposed vulnerability would itself have been a reason for Stewart to have been put in a cell on his own for his own protection. Perhaps that was why this view of Stewart was very much a minority one.

Chapter 25: Stewart's return from court on 7 and 8 March 2000

Stewart's temporary wing file resurfaces

25.1 Stewart was next due in court on 7 March. Swallow's roll and movements sheet for the day shows him leaving the unit for reception in the morning without a wing file. It shows him returning to the unit that evening, but this time with his wing file. We know that this was the temporary wing file with the entries of Miss Hogg and Mr Martindale as an entry was made in it when he arrived in Swallow that evening.

25.2 No-one on the unit appears to have known that it did not have Stewart's wing file between 8 February and 7 March – whether the temporary one or the one opened at Hindley on 23 December – apart from Simon Diaper, and he did not mention it to anyone else. Certainly none of the officers on Swallow felt the need to read his wing file or to make any entry in it during that time. If they had, they would have discovered that it was missing, and that would – or at least should – have led to the discovery that it had never arrived on the unit. The fact that no-one discovered for a period of four weeks that it was missing tells us a number of things about Stewart and life on Swallow. First, Stewart was keeping his head down at the time: no-one had sought to make an entry in his wing file about him. Secondly, very little interest was being paid to him: no-one had sought to read anything about him. Thirdly, no-one was monitoring his progress on the unit: his personal officers had not thought it necessary to record how he was getting on in his wing file.

25.3 The officer who recorded Stewart's return to Swallow that evening in the roll and movements sheet was Ian Morse. He noted the time of Stewart's return as 6.25 pm, although it was not until 7.19 pm that the Control and Information Room was informed of Stewart's allocation once again to cell 38. It was Mr Morse who made an entry in Stewart's temporary wing file. The entry read: "7/3/00. Received Swallow from CRT." CRT presumably meant court. But it is not the entry itself which is important. It is where the entry was made – on the same page as the entries made by Miss Hogg and Mr Martindale, with only the two stamps showing that Stewart had been interviewed by a probation officer at Hindley in between. There were no other entries on that page. Mr Morse accepted that he must have read them. And there is no doubt that he took no action about them. So the crucial question is why he did nothing.

25.4 Mr Morse says that he cannot now recall whether he read these entries. But a glance at the front inside cover of the temporary wing file shows how prominent Mr Martindale's entry in red is. It jumps out at you.

Anyone writing anything on that page could not fail to see it. A prison officer seeing such an entry would undoubtedly have read it, and having read it would almost certainly have read Miss Hogg's entries above it. Mr Morse was prepared to accept all that. That was why he accepted that, although he claimed not to recall reading the entries, he must have read them.

The inside cover of Stewart's temporary wing file

25.5 I am sceptical about Mr Morse's claim that he cannot recall whether he read the entries. It was suggested there was no particular reason for Mr Morse to have remembered Stewart returning to the unit that evening. There was nothing out of the ordinary about it. But the entries were too stark and dramatic for Mr Morse to have forgotten them so quickly, especially as he would have cast his mind back after the murder of Zahid only two weeks later to what he could remember about Stewart. He would have realised that the entries placed him in a quandary. If he claimed he had not read them, no-one would believe him. If he admitted he had read them, he would be criticised for not acting on them. The best solution to the problem was to say he could not remember reading them. In that way, he could avoid being questioned about why he took no action while at the same time avoid being accused of falsely denying that he had read them. But in telling the police that he had no recollection of reading the entries, what he in fact said was that he did not recall "being fully aware of seeing" Mr Martindale's entry. That rather strained language, I suspect, was the result of Mr Morse realising that people might be sceptical about a bald assertion that he could not remember seeing the entries. Indeed, when it was put to him that in expressing himself in that way he was hedging his bets in order to avoid criticism for either failing to read the entries or not acting on them, he said he could not disagree with that suggestion. As it was, he also told the police that he "never equated [Stewart] with that… entry after that", which suggests that he had read the entry when Stewart first came to Swallow.

25.6 When Mr Morse was asked by the police about the entries, he had another strategy for deflecting any criticism for not having acted on them. He attempted to distance himself from Stewart and the entries about him. For example, he told the police that he had "no personal recollection" of Stewart. He subsequently accepted that this was not accurate, but explained that he had been trying to get across to the police that although he could remember Stewart, he could not remember anything particular about him. Even that was inaccurate. He remembered Stewart's tattoos. Again, he told the police that he would not have time to read entries in prisoners' wing files, in view of the many inmates coming into the unit a day – on average 25–30 of them. He subsequently conceded that nothing like that number of prisoners came into the unit every day. Indeed, the roll and movements sheet for Swallow for the day in question shows six prisoners arriving that day – between 2.40 pm and 6.25 pm. When Stewart arrived at 6.25 pm, there was only one other prisoner with him. That prisoner arrived with his wing file, but he had left Swallow with it that morning, so unlike Stewart's his wing file was not being looked at for the first time.

25.7 The fact remains that, although Mr Morse claims to have no recollection of having read the entries, he accepted that he must have read them. And we know that he did nothing about them. The question is why. Mr Morse was naturally unable to answer that. To attempt to answer that would have been inconsistent with his claim that he could not recall having read the entries. But what could Mr Morse have said in his own defence if he had not committed himself to a line which prevented him from doing that?

25.8 There are two possible stances he could have taken. The first is based on the criticism I have already made about the lack of detail in Mr Martindale's warning. Could Mr Morse have legitimately said that it was too vague – in the sense that it did not identify whether other prisoners were at risk from Stewart – to take any action about it? I do not think so. Mr Morse did not know what was in Stewart's security file. Until he read Stewart's security file, Stewart was an unknown quantity. Not as much of an unknown quantity as Stewart would have been if he was coming to Swallow for the first time. Mr Morse had seen how he had been behaving for the previous four weeks. But an unknown quantity nevertheless because Mr Morse knew from Mr Martindale's warning that Stewart was capable of getting up to something, even if he did not know what. So Mr Martindale's warning called for *some* action on Mr Morse's part – if only to defer making any decision about Stewart until he had found out what was in Stewart's security file. Since the Security Department was closed by then, that would have involved looking at the file the next day. That is what other officers on Swallow would have done – at any rate those who were questioned on what they would have done if they had read what Mr Morse had. None of them said they would have done nothing. Mr Morse would say, no doubt, that it is easy for them to say that now. What they would actually have done on the night in question could well have been different.

25.9 But Mr Martindale's warning was not the only warning about Stewart. There were Miss Hogg's entries as well. They told Mr Morse that Stewart was a racist who wrote racist and threatening letters. Two things should have struck Mr Morse then. First, if Stewart went back to the same cell, he would be sharing it with Zahid to whom Stewart might be hostile. Secondly, Zahid might himself have picked up on Stewart's hostility towards prisoners from ethnic minorities, and might be extremely uncomfortable about sharing a cell with him. It may be that Zahid never mentioned that during the four weeks they had been sharing a cell, but maybe he was reluctant to do that in case it got back to Stewart. The combination of Mr Martindale's warning about Stewart's dangerousness, Miss Hogg's entries about Stewart's racism and the threatening way he expressed his hostility towards prisoners from ethnic minorities should have caused Mr Morse to conclude that he could not wait until he had seen Stewart's security file the next day before doing something. He should have realised that they ought not continue to share a cell even for one more night. His recollection now is that there was another officer on duty in Swallow at the time – Martin Ashworth – and so with his help moving Stewart to another cell could have been achieved. The unit was admittedly already up to its certified normal accommodation of 60. So either Stewart would have had to be moved to a single cell, and its occupant required to double up elsewhere. Or Mr Morse should have got in touch with reception and asked for Stewart to be moved to another unit. Whether Mr Morse would have been readier to protect a white prisoner from a black prisoner who was hostile to white prisoners or from a Muslim prisoner whose fundamentalism made him hostile to Christian prisoners is again something we can only speculate about.

25.10 Secondly, could Mr Morse have legitimately said that action did not need to be taken because Stewart had, by all accounts, been behaving himself during the four weeks he had been on Swallow? For all Mr Morse knew, this might not have been the first time that Stewart's temporary wing file had been on the unit. If other officers had seen the warnings about Stewart and had done nothing about them, maybe Stewart's current behaviour belied the warnings about him. Again I do not think so. As I have said elsewhere, there was a tendency for prison officers to concentrate on the here and now. If prisoners were behaving themselves, the fact that they had misbehaved in the past could be put to one side when considering how they should be managed. That would be a blinkered view, but it was a prevalent one, and it may well have explained Mr Morse's inaction. But I do not think that it justified it. Mr Martindale's warning was just too strong to have been overridden by Stewart's unproblematic recent behaviour. The language he used, the highlighting in red, and the emphasis on the need for staff to be careful all pointed to the need to treat Stewart with the greatest possible caution. The fact that he had not been causing any problems could well have meant that he was simply keeping his head down, maybe biding his time before he did something serious. That was what Mr Morse should have been thinking. If he had, then he would have realised that inaction was not an option.

25.11 One cannot exclude the possibility that something more damning lay behind Mr Morse's inaction. It could conceivably be that he did nothing because it simply did not occur to him to do anything: he was either too lazy, or too incompetent, or both, to do anything about Stewart. It could even conceivably be the case that he did nothing because he was indifferent to the welfare or safety of prisoners in general, or of prisoners from ethnic minorities in particular, and did not care if he left Zahid with a dangerous and racist cellmate. But although these possibilities cannot be entirely discounted, I rather think that the explanation for Mr Morse's inaction was simply that although Stewart was a pretty odd character, he had not been presenting as a problem prisoner. He may have been a problem prisoner in the past, but prisoners – especially young ones – change. Perhaps Stewart had seen the best way to get on in prison was to behave. Whatever the reason, Stewart was now behaving in an acceptable way, and there was no need to let his past catch up with him. But although that would explain Mr Morse's inaction, I do not think it goes anywhere near justifying it. It should have occurred to him that, whatever Stewart's behaviour had been like over the previous few weeks, he should not have been sharing a cell with Zahid. It is at least possible that this did not occur to him because the culture of allowing racism to go unchecked at Feltham had made him insensitive to the danger which a white racist prisoner – even one who was not behaving disruptively – might pose to his Asian cellmate, and to the discomfort which an Asian prisoner might have about sharing a cell with someone who looked and behaved like Stewart.

Stewart's return from court on 8 March 2000

25.12 When Stewart went to court on 7 March, his case was adjourned to the following day. So he had to return to court on 8 March. Swallow's roll and movements sheet for that day shows Stewart leaving the unit for reception in the morning with his wing file, and returning to the unit with it that evening. Throughout the Inquiry, we assumed that the wing file he returned with was at least his temporary one. That was, I am sure, a fair assumption. After all, the wing file he had left the unit with that morning had been the temporary one. It may be that the temporary wing file had by then been married up with the one opened at Hindley on 23 December. If it had, both came back with him. If it had not, only the temporary one did.

25.13 The officer who recorded Stewart's return to Swallow that evening in the roll and movements sheet was Stephen Skinner, the officer who conducted the roll check on cell 38 on the night of the murder. He had been a prison officer for two years. Unlike Mr Morse the previous evening, he did not make an entry in Stewart's temporary wing file. So there was not in his case the natural opportunity which Mr Morse had had to read the warnings about Stewart which were in it. But that did not necessarily mean that Mr Skinner did not read them. He might have done. If he had, he would have been in the same position as Mr Morse, because like Mr Morse he did nothing about them. But Mr Skinner said that he did not read them. If he had, he would have taken some action over them. Since he did nothing, he is as sure as he can be that he did not read them. But if he did not read them, the question to be asked is: why not?

25.14 The entries which Mr Skinner made in the roll and movements sheet for that evening show that Stewart was one of only three prisoners who arrived after 6.00 pm. One arrived at 6.50 pm, and two including Stewart arrived at 6.55 pm. Mr Skinner informed the Control and Information Room of Stewart's allocation to cell 38 once again at 6.57 pm. Like Stewart, the other two prisoners had been in Swallow before. But only one of them had left the unit that morning with his wing file and returned with it. That was the prisoner who arrived at 6.50 pm. The other prisoner had neither left the unit that morning with it nor returned with it.

25.15 It was after these three prisoners had been put in their cells that Mr Skinner would have had reason to look at their wing files. He had to record the details about them in the roll and movements sheet, and to inform the Control and Information Room of their arrival. For both of those purposes he needed their prison numbers. The most obvious place to get them was from the front cover of their wing files. But that did not necessarily mean that Mr Skinner looked at the front cover of their wing files. Their prison numbers would have been apparent from the entries made in the roll and movements sheet that morning. But even if Mr Skinner did not look at the front cover of their wing files at that stage, he is very likely to have looked at them subsequently – if only to see whose files he had when he was filing them away with the wing files of the other prisoners in the unit. The strong probability, and Mr Skinner did not suggest otherwise, is that at some stage – maybe before making the entries in the roll and movements sheet, maybe after – he looked at the front cover of their wing files.

25.16 A glance at the front cover of Stewart's temporary wing file shows how prominent Mr Martindale's instruction – "* See inner page" – both in red ink and in capitals really is. It certainly stands out. That is not surprising. It was intended to. Mr Skinner could not have missed it. He said as much when giving evidence. So why did he not follow the instruction Mr Martindale had left for anyone who looked at it and read the entries inside it? Mr Skinner said it was because Stewart had been in the unit for a month or so and had not drawn any attention to himself. That answer was unconvincing. The fact that Stewart had caused no problems on the unit might have explained why Mr Skinner did not look inside his temporary wing file if Mr Skinner had thought that the entries inside said that Stewart had caused problems in the past. The culture was that anything which did not accord with an officer's own experience of a prisoner could be ignored. But Mr Skinner was not to know that the entries showed Stewart to have been a problem prisoner. He did not know what was in the wing file at all. It could have been anything. All he knew was that there was an instruction to look inside it.

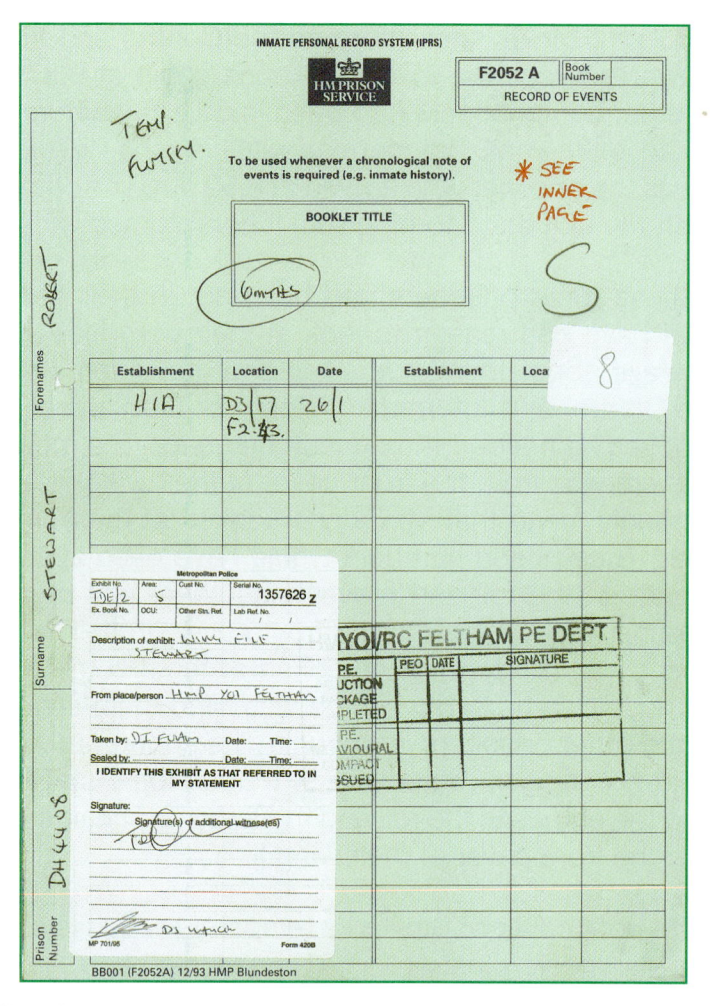

The front cover of Stewart's temporary wing file

25.17 There is another reason why I am less than convinced that Mr Skinner did not look inside Stewart's temporary wing file. Once he had put the three prisoners in their cells, there was little for Mr Skinner to do. If his recollection that the unit was on patrol state is right, he would have been alone in the office. He would have had to file the wing files of Stewart and the other prisoners. With time on his hands, and human nature being what it is, it would have been surprising if Mr Skinner had not looked inside Stewart's temporary wing file – if only out of curiosity – especially as Stewart was such an oddball. But there may well have been other distractions – perhaps a cup of tea and a newspaper – and in the end I am not able to say that the probabilities are that Mr Skinner looked inside it. He may well have done, but I am not sufficiently convinced that he did to disbelieve his denial that he looked inside it.

25.18 But he should have looked inside it. He said more than once in his evidence that he wished he had. I can understand that. It was a serious error not to. He did not know whether before that night he had seen an instruction of the kind which Mr Martindale had written on the front cover. So if he had seen such an instruction before, it would have been relatively unusual. All the more reason to look inside the temporary wing file on this occasion, even if the prisoner to whom it related had not given any cause for trouble. It should have struck him that an instruction of that kind would not be there without good reason.

25.19 I have not forgotten the evidence which suggested that the importance of a prisoner's wing file was not readily appreciated at Feltham at the time. Mr Morse, for example, regarded it simply as a place to record the prisoner's movements within the establishment and to list the courses he had taken or the classes he had attended which might affect his ultimate release date. And Claire Bigger, another officer on Swallow – who has since married, and is now Claire Hodson – was surprised at how much weight other prisons gave to wing files when she moved to another establishment. But that was no excuse for ignoring the clear instruction which Mr Martindale had left.

25.20 What would Mr Skinner have done if he had read Miss Hogg's and Mr Martindale's entries? He said that he would have asked for a "wing meeting" to discuss Stewart to which the principal officer in charge of the cluster of units which included Swallow would have been invited. He also said that he would have put Stewart in a single cell if one had been available. Mr Skinner undoubtedly now likes to think that he would have taken decisive action of that kind, but I am sceptical about that. The lack of curiosity which resulted in him not looking inside the temporary wing file is likely to have been matched by a lack of drive to do anything if he had looked inside it. If he had not bothered to look inside it in the first instance, he is unlikely to have bothered to take any action if he had. It is not as if there was no precedent for inaction in the face of these entries. Look at what happened the previous evening.

25.21 What Mr Skinner should have done was to read what was inside Stewart's temporary wing file. And once he had done that, he should have done what Mr Morse should have done the previous evening – which was to do what was needed to make sure that Stewart did not share a cell that night with anyone, let alone share one with a prisoner from an ethnic minority.

25.22 There is one final point I should make. This analysis of what Mr Skinner did and should have done may be affected if, by then, the temporary wing file had been married up with the wing file opened at Hindley. If it had been, the two of them would have arrived on the unit attached to each other. In that case, and if the existing file had been on top of the temporary one, Mr Martindale's note on the front cover of the temporary one would not have been seen by Mr Skinner. But there are two reasons why, if they arrived on the unit attached to each other, the existing wing file is likely to have been below the temporary one. First, Mr Morse had made his entry on the previous evening in the temporary one. Secondly, although they were separated when they were received by the Inquiry, it is likely that they were attached when seized by the police, because the police used one exhibit label for both of them. That exhibit label was stuck to the temporary one, which suggests that it was on top. So the strong probability remains that Mr Skinner saw what Mr Martindale had written on the front cover of the temporary wing file.

Mr Martindale's sighting of Stewart

25.23 One other thing happened when Stewart returned from court on either 7 or 8 March. As Mr Martindale was passing through reception on his way to other duties, he saw Stewart coming in through reception. That must have been when Stewart returned from court on one of those two dates, because Mr Martindale recalled it happening "sometime after" he moved from Lapwing to reception – a move which took place on 6 February. He remembers telling another officer working on reception, Gordon Meek, "what a nasty bit of work Stewart was". He took no further action because he assumed Stewart was accompanied by the temporary wing file on which he had written the warning about Stewart on 12 January. For his part, Mr Meek recalled Stewart because of his distinctive tattoos. He had a vague recollection that on one occasion he was told that Stewart had a bad reputation, perhaps to do with making threats to staff. But he could not recall who it was who had told him that or when.

25.24 I do not think that Mr Martindale can be criticised for not taking any further action at the time – for example, finding out which unit Stewart was on and warning the unit about him. Since he was not on duty in reception at the time, it was sufficient for him to have simply mentioned what he knew about Stewart to a member of staff who was then on duty. In any event, the assumption Mr Martindale made about Stewart's temporary wing file was entirely justified. There was nothing to cause him to think that it was not with Stewart at the time. And as we have seen, it was in fact with Stewart on both 7 and 8 March. Subject to the reservations I have expressed about the adequacy of Mr Martindale's entry in the temporary wing file, he was perfectly entitled to assume that it would be, or had been, read by officers on the unit Stewart was on, making a further warning from him about Stewart unnecessary.

Chapter 26: Stewart's change of status

Stewart completes his sentence

26.1 Stewart shared cell 38 with Zahid in Swallow for six weeks. During that time, there was one specific occasion when Stewart ought to have been moved out of the cell, and a number of occasions when Zahid might have been. The occasion when Stewart should have been moved out of the cell was when he ceased to be a convicted prisoner serving a sentence, and became an unconvicted prisoner on remand awaiting trial.

26.2 It will be recalled that Stewart was serving a sentence of 25 weeks' detention in a young offender institution. Taking into account the time he had spent in custody on remand awaiting sentence, he was due to be released on 19 March 2000. But that was a Sunday. Prisoners are not released on Sundays. A prisoner due to be released on a Sunday is in fact released the previous Friday. However, Stewart was awaiting trial on the charges arising out of his harassment of the chatline operator. He had not been granted bail in respect of those offences. So he remained in custody after Friday 17 March, although it was only on 19 March that his status actually changed from that of a convicted prisoner to an unconvicted prisoner on remand.

The effect of Stewart's change of status

26.3 Rule 7(2)(b) of the Prison Rules 1999 provides that under no circumstances shall an unconvicted prisoner be "required" to share a cell with a convicted prisoner. The use of the word "required" suggests that an unconvicted prisoner cannot be forced to share a cell with a convicted prisoner. If prisoners do not want to, they can say so. But it is not a blanket prohibition on convicted prisoners sharing a cell with an unconvicted one. If unconvicted prisoners are content to share a cell with a convicted one, they can. However, it cannot simply be assumed that unconvicted prisoners are content to share a cell with a convicted one. They have to be asked, and their consent has to be obtained. That is the effect of rule 7(2)(a) which requires unconvicted prisoners to be kept out of contact with convicted prisoners "unless and to the extent that they have consented to share residential accommodation".

26.4 There has been no suggestion that Stewart was asked whether he was happy to continue to share cell 38 with Zahid after 19 March, let alone that he ever said he was content to do so. So Stewart and Zahid should not have been sharing a cell after that. Indeed, Stewart should have been moved out of Swallow altogether in view of the need to keep unconvicted prisoners out of contact with convicted prisoners. He should have gone to a unit for unconvicted prisoners. In one sense, of course, the failure to move Stewart out of cell 38 was a significant contributory factor to what was to happen. If he had not been there, he could not have attacked Zahid. But it may well be that if Stewart had been asked whether he was content to stay with Zahid in cell 38, he would have said "yes". In that case they could legitimately have continued to be in the same cell. I know that Stewart claims to have asked an officer – whom he cannot identify – for a move "to the remand unit" on 19 or 20 March, but I am not prepared to take his word for that. The reason he wanted to move, he says, was because he would have been able to wear his own clothes and would have been entitled to a more generous canteen allowance. But there was evidence which I have no reason not to accept that Stewart would have got the privileges which unconvicted prisoners got if he had remained on Swallow. I might have been more inclined to believe him if he had said he did not want to remain in Swallow because other prisoners might have put pressure on him to share whatever he got as an unconvicted prisoner. But he did not say that.

26.5 The fact remains, though, that there is the possibility that Stewart – if only for a change of scenery or to be away from Zahid for the few days that Zahid was still due to be there – would have said, if asked, that he did not want to share a cell with a convicted prisoner. It is therefore necessary to investigate why Stewart's change of status did not result in a change of cell. It was not as if the establishment was bursting at the seams on 19 March so that there was no other unit he could have gone to. There were 715 prisoners at Feltham that night, way below the certified normal accommodation at the time of 768. And even if Stewart could not have been moved out of Swallow, he could have been moved out of cell 38. On the night of the attack, cell 23 in Swallow was empty. That was a single cell which could be used for doubling up. We know it was empty because that was where Stewart was put before being taken to the segregation unit.

Knowledge in Swallow of Stewart's change of status

26.6 When prisoners are due to be released, there are a number of documents they have to sign. The most important is the form setting out the conditions of their licence and when their licence expires. Another one is for prisoners whose sentence is three months or more. They have to sign a document in which they acknowledge that they must not have anything to do with firearms or ammunition for the period set out in the document. These forms were sent to the unit which the prisoner was on by the discharge clerk in Custody Administration. An officer on the unit would then get the prisoner to sign the documents, and they would be returned to Custody Administration.

26.7 These documents were sent to Swallow by the discharge clerk on 1 March for Stewart to sign. She sent out similar documents – at any rate the document about firearms – for Zahid to sign on the same day. The officer who got them to sign the documents was Martin Ashworth, the officer who Mr Skinner thought had been on duty with him on 8 March. He had been a prison officer since 1995. In his statement to the Inquiry, he said that he did not think he knew that Stewart was not going to be released on his release date, but was to remain in custody as an unconvicted prisoner instead. But to be fair to him, he did not have the documents in front of him when he made his statement. They were shown to him when he gave evidence. They showed that there was an important difference between the documents signed by Stewart and the ones which Zahid had to sign. The document setting out the conditions of Stewart's licence, which said that his supervision was due to commence on 17 March, was stamped in capitals: "Not for release. Held on other cases". So too was the memorandum under whose cover it was sent. When Mr Ashworth saw those stamps, he accepted that he must have known at the time that Stewart's status was about to change – although the document setting out the conditions of Stewart's licence would have led him to think that Stewart's status was going to change on 17 March.

26.8 Three small points remain unexplained. First, Mr Ashworth was supposed to countersign the document relating to firearms. He did that in Zahid's case, but not in Stewart's. Secondly, Mr Ashworth got Stewart to sign his documents on 6 March, and Zahid signed his document relating to firearms then as well. But the document setting out the conditions of Zahid's licence, which he might have been expected also to sign that day, was not signed by him at all. The document had to be countersigned by a prison officer. In Zahid's case, it was countersigned by a governor on 21 March. This was after the attack. So it looks as if someone discovered that the document had not been issued to Zahid at all, and then issued it belatedly. Thirdly, a document about Stewart was sent to the senior officer of the segregation unit asking for confirmation of Stewart's discharge address and the name and address of the probation officer who would be supervising him on licence. Someone has written on it in red ink "NFR", presumably meaning "not for release". Why it was sent to the segregation unit is a mystery because, except in the immediate aftermath of the attack, Stewart was never there.

26.9 But this is to digress. Mr Ashworth knew on 6 March about Stewart's impending change of status, as did at least one other officer on Swallow. That was Lee Edmundson. He recalls something about Stewart being due to move to another unit because his status had changed, or was about to.

26.10 Finally, there is some evidence that Mr Morse knew about Stewart's change of status. That evidence came from Jamie Barnes. He told the police two days after the attack that in the course of a conversation which he and Zahid had had with Mr Morse on the Friday before the attack – 17 March – Zahid had told Mr Morse that Stewart "was on remand so he should be on a remand wing". In his evidence to the Inquiry, Barnes said that he did not know whether Mr Morse had known about Stewart's change of status at the time, but that he had heard Mr Morse ask other officers whether Stewart should still be on the unit. Mr Morse has no recollection of this conversation, but he was at pains to say that this did not mean that it did not happen. I think it did. There were parts of Barnes's evidence which I was sceptical about, but this was not one of them.

26.11 Barnes claimed that when he told Mr Morse that Stewart should be on a remand wing, Mr Morse said that while there was no room on the remand wing then, Stewart was supposed to be moving on the Monday. I am very sceptical about that. There was more than one unit for unconvicted prisoners, and the population of Feltham at the time suggests that there would have been room on such a unit for Stewart. And it is unlikely that Mr Morse would have been able to find out on the Friday whether there would be an additional space for an unconvicted prisoner on the Monday. Apart from anything else, that would depend in part on how many young prisoners the courts in London remanded in custody on the Monday.

Why was nothing done?

26.12 So if three officers on Swallow knew about Stewart's change of status, why was nothing done about it? The answer is that they were not expected to have done anything about it themselves. That is because information about a prisoner's change of status came to the unit from Custody Administration, and officers on Swallow assumed that this information would trigger the move of a convicted prisoner whose status had changed to a unit for unconvicted prisoners. That information was in the form of a discharge sheet printed out from the Local Inmate Database System which units received from Custody Administration. Mr Ashworth initially told the Inquiry that it arrived weekly, but later he said that it arrived daily. The sheet listed all those prisoners at Feltham whose sentences were due to expire that day. That list included prisoners like Stewart who were not going to be released after their sentences expired.

26.13 However, it was wrong for officers on Swallow to assume that, just because the discharge sheet included information about such prisoners, staff would automatically move them. There was no guidance at all about what units should do with that information when it arrived. Mr Ashworth accepted that it was for the desk officer on a unit which housed convicted prisoners to get in touch with the units for unconvicted prisoners to find out where there was space for prisoners whose status was about to change. Once that had been done the prisoner would be moved. But that presupposed that it was for the desk officer on a unit which housed convicted prisoners, not just to note the arrival of the discharge sheet when it came from Custody Administration, but also to look at it to see if there were any prisoners whose sentences were expiring that day but who were not to be released because they were going to remain in custody on remand. Mr Ashworth in effect said this did not happen. The discharge sheet was sent "for information only".

26.14 I should say something here about the function of desk officers. They were based in the unit's office. They recorded the movements of prisoners in and out of the unit. They dealt with applications by and complaints from prisoners. They handled queries or requests for information from Custody Administration. Since the desk officer had to be relatively familiar with the establishment's procedures, the post was usually given to the most senior of the prison officers on duty.

26.15 Since information about a prisoner's change of status came to the unit from Custody Administration, Mr Edmundson and Mr Morse can be excused for not having done anything about it themselves. In any event, they may have known something about Stewart's change of status, but not whether it had changed or whether it was due to change. The responsibility for ensuring that Stewart was moved, if it was down to anyone, rested with the desk officer on duty in Swallow on 17 March when the discharge sheet which should have included Stewart's name was meant to come from Custody Administration, or with the desk officer in Swallow on 19 March when Stewart's status actually changed.

26.16 We do not know who the desk officer was on 17 March, but Mr Ashworth was the desk officer on 19 March. He does not say he tried to find out on which unit for unconvicted prisoners there was space for another one. He cannot really be blamed for not remembering from 6 March when Stewart's status was going to change. Nor can he be blamed for not looking at the discharge sheet for 19 March to see whether there were any convicted prisoners on the unit whose status was changing that day. No such instruction had been given for desk officers to do that. But since he had known on 6 March that Stewart's change of status might not be picked up from the discharge sheet, he should have made a note about it on 6 March, and left a message in the office to remind the desk officer who was to be on duty on the day Stewart's status changed that he should be found accommodation in a unit for unconvicted prisoners that day. Mr Ashworth accepted that he should have done that, but said that there was nowhere to record that information. I think there was. Although the wing observation book was intended to record things which happened in the unit, I see no reason why it could not have been used to record information of this kind.

26.17 Although Mr Ashworth can be criticised for not making a note on 6 March about Stewart's impending change of status, the real problem was that there was no effective system in place for ensuring that convicted prisoners whose status changed were properly identified, and for ensuring that they were moved to a unit for unconvicted prisoners. It may be that that was because it was not going to happen all that often that a prisoner was not going to be released at the end of his sentence. But it was bound to happen occasionally, and there should have been a procedure in place for staff to follow when it did.

26.18 Two final points should be made. First, Mr Byrd, the governor responsible for a number of units which included Swallow, appears to have thought that the rule requiring unconvicted prisoners not to share a cell with a convicted prisoner did not have to be complied with immediately. It could be left for a few days if they were getting on with each other. That was not the right approach. Compliance with rule 7(2) was mandatory. Unless an unconvicted prisoner agreed to continue to share a cell with a convicted prisoner – in which case they could continue to do so for much longer than a few days – they should have been separated immediately. Secondly, it would be wrong to leave this topic without recording the irony which is at the heart of it. The rule that unconvicted prisoners should not share a cell with convicted ones was plainly intended to protect unconvicted prisoners from convicted ones, not the other way round. It was Stewart with his new status as an unconvicted prisoner who the rule actually protected, not Zahid. The irony is that it was Zahid who needed protection from Stewart.

Chapter 27: The request to change cells

Barnes's request to move into cell 38 with Zahid

27.1 I have said that there were a number of occasions when Zahid might have been moved out of cell 38. I deal in chapter 28 with one of them. In this chapter, I deal with those times when Zahid is said to have asked for a move. If he did, questions arise about why he might have wanted to move out of cell 38 and why that did not happen. But first I must deal with an earlier occasion, before Stewart arrived in Swallow, when Jamie Barnes claims to have asked to move *into* cell 38 to be with Zahid.

27.2 Barnes says that when Zahid's previous cellmate left, he asked Mr Skinner if he could move into cell 38 with Zahid. Zahid was with him at the time. Barnes cannot now recall what Mr Skinner's response was, but since nothing came of the request, he made the same request to Mr Morse a few days later. Mr Morse said that he could move in with Zahid, provided that he signed an agreement to behave properly. Barnes frankly accepts that his behaviour at the time was bad. Nothing came of that request, so Barnes mentioned it to Mr Skinner again a couple of days later. This time Mr Skinner told him he was busy, and there could not be any cell moves that day. A day or so later Stewart was put into Zahid's cell, so the opportunity for Barnes to move in with Zahid was lost.

27.3 Neither Mr Skinner nor Mr Morse has any recollection of Barnes asking to move into cell 38 with Zahid, although Mr Morse was prepared to accept that he may well have wanted to share a cell with Zahid. He recalls that they got on well together. Mr Ashworth remembers Barnes asking more than once if he could change cells, and he could not exclude the possibility that one of those occasions involved sharing with Zahid. But Barnes's version of events cannot be correct – at any rate not in its entirety. If he is right, Zahid was alone in his cell for getting on for a week after his cellmate left and before Stewart joined him. That is wrong. As we have seen, G moved out of cell 38 on 8 February which was the day Stewart moved in. Barnes could have been asking in advance to move into cell 38 with Zahid when G was to move out, perhaps at the end of G's sentence. But that was not Barnes's evidence. Moreover, Mr Butt had the opportunity to look at Barnes's wing file. It was not available to the Inquiry. Mr Butt noted four entries in it referring to times when Barnes had wanted to move to other cells to be with other prisoners who were named. Zahid was not one of them.

27.4 In the circumstances, I doubt whether Barnes asked to move into cell 38 to be with Zahid. But even if he did, he would have asked to do so just the once, and that would have been on 8 February when G moved out. At that time Barnes was in a single cell. *If*, and it is a big if, Barnes asked on 8 February to move into cell 38 to be with Zahid, the likeliest reason he was not allowed to was that it would not happen until he had shown that he could behave properly.

Zahid's requests to move out of cell 38

27.5 Barnes is one of the sources for the suggestion that Zahid asked to move out of cell 38. Barnes had been in a double cell since 23 February. He says that on the Friday before the attack – which would have been 17 March – he and Zahid spoke to Mr Morse about Zahid moving into his cell. He claims that Mr Morse said that Zahid could not. When it was pointed out to Mr Morse that Stewart was a remand prisoner and should be on a remand wing, he said that Barnes could move into cell 38 with Zahid when Stewart was moved out of the wing the following Monday. Barnes claims it was because of Zahid's imminent release that he did not mention it again on the Monday when Stewart was not moved out. He also claims he asked Mr Ashworth if Zahid could move into his cell.

27.6 There are many reasons to be sceptical about Barnes's claim that he asked for Zahid to move into his cell. First, in his statement to the Inquiry, Stewart confirmed that Zahid and Barnes asked to share a cell, but he did not say that the request was for Zahid to move into Barnes's cell. Moreover, he did not think they asked for that on the Friday. He thought it was on the Sunday or the Monday. And Barnes never said that Stewart had been present when the request was made. Secondly, I have already said that I doubt whether Mr Morse said anything about there being no room then on a remand wing for Stewart or that Stewart was supposed to move out of Swallow on the Monday. Indeed, if the request was for Zahid to move into Barnes's cell, Stewart's change of status was irrelevant. Thirdly, Barnes told the Inquiry that after Stewart had arrived on Swallow, he asked to share a cell with Zahid on occasions other than the Friday before the attack. He did not say anything about those occasions to the police. Fourthly, since Barnes's requests to move to other cells were apparently recorded in his wing file, one might have expected a request for Zahid to be moved into his cell to be similarly recorded. It apparently was not. Fifthly, Barnes did not tell the police that he had asked Mr Ashworth whether Zahid could move into his cell. And finally, although this is by no means decisive, no prison officer has any recollection of a request for Zahid to move into Barnes's cell.

27.7 For these reasons, I am not prepared to accept that Barnes asked for Zahid to move into his cell. But that does not mean that Zahid never himself asked to move out of cell 38. There is evidence that he did. It came from his cousin and his father. They both say that when they visited Zahid, he told them that he had asked to be moved from his cell. Zahid's cousin, Tanzeel Ahmed, recalls Zahid telling them that on 20 February and 5 March. Zahid's father recalls Zahid telling them that on 5 March. When I initially read their witness statements, I bore in mind that they might have been inclined to think that this was what Zahid had said in order to cast the Prison Service in a bad light. But I decided that this would not be a sufficient reason not to accept their evidence on the topic, and that I should not ask them to go through the ordeal of giving oral evidence. As it was, Zahid's father wanted to, and I was glad that he did.

27.8 They were not to know, of course, whether Zahid asked more than once to move out of cell 38. But if they got the impression from what Zahid had told them that he had made such a request more than once, they would have said so in their statements. They did not, and I can therefore be relatively confident that they did not get the impression that Zahid had asked to be moved more than once. I can think of no sensible reason why Zahid would have claimed to them that he had asked to be moved if he had not made such a request. Telling them that he had asked to be moved could only cause them to be concerned about him. Why move if you are content where you are? So the probabilities are that Zahid did indeed ask for a move out of cell 38, and going on when he first mentioned to his family that he had done that, it must have been quite soon after Stewart had moved into cell 38 with him.

Why did Zahid want to move?

27.9 It is possible that Zahid wanted to move out of cell 38, not so much because he did not like Stewart or felt uncomfortable about sharing a cell with him, but because he wanted to share with Barnes. After all, Barnes told Mr Butt that he had known Zahid on the outside, and he told the police that he and Zahid were friends, spending all their time on association together. I have already discussed in chapter 24 the reasons why I think Zahid would have been uncomfortable about continuing to share cell 38 with Stewart, and I said then that it was more likely than not that a strong element in Zahid's wish to move was to get away from Stewart. But I doubt whether Zahid gave that as his reason for wanting to move. He would not have wanted that to get back to Stewart. Since he got on so well with Barnes, and could well have wanted to share a cell with him, it is far more likely that he gave that as the reason for wanting to move.

27.10 Should Zahid's request for a move in order to share with Barnes have prompted the officer to whom it was made to consider whether there may have been something else behind it? The officer would – or at any rate should – have appreciated that there was something not quite right, something menacing, about Stewart. And the officer should have realised that it was possible that Stewart might have been hostile towards Zahid because Zahid was Asian. Any failure on the part of the officer to recognise that possibility would have been another example of the indifference to the safety of prisoners from ethnic minorities which individual and institutional racism breeds. In an institution running well, I would have expected the officer to ask Zahid whether the fact that he was sharing with Stewart might be one of the reasons for his request, or to tell Zahid's personal officers about his request so that they could find out if there was anything behind the request which they ought to know about. We cannot take it further, since for all we know the officer to whom Zahid spoke may have questioned him about Stewart, and Zahid may not have mentioned his concerns about Stewart even then.

Why was his request not met?

27.11 Elizabeth Billimore, the officer who did the last roll check on Swallow on the night of the murder, said that as a general rule prisoners would not be allowed to change cells simply to share a cell with a friend. But that was not because of a wish to discourage friendships between cellmates. It was because a change of cells involved time and trouble for staff, and they should not be burdened with supervising cell changes simply to accommodate prisoners' cell-sharing requests. She was not saying that there was a policy in place to refuse such requests. It was just that the practical obstacles were such that invariably such requests had to be refused. Miss Bigger said much the same thing. You would be spending all day moving prisoners, she said, if every request by a prisoner to share a cell with a friend was accommodated. Other officers did not think that the practical obstacles were all that great, although they acknowledged that practical, as well as security, considerations might result in the request being refused. So whether a request was granted could depend on how inconvenient a move was at the time, whether it had any security implications, and which officer was approached. It would also depend on how the request was made. Two officers said that their practice was to encourage prisoners to put requests of this type in writing. Otherwise, the request might be overlooked if the officer to whom it was made was not on the unit again for some time.

27.12 The upshot of all this is that it is impossible now to say why Zahid's request was not met. So we do not know whether the reason was a justifiable or unjustifiable one. And if it was an unjustifiable one, we do not know whether it was for a racially neutral reason, such as indifference, incompetence or overwork, or whether race, such as Zahid's ethnic origin, was a factor in it. Nor do we know whether the request was made at a convenient time, or whether it was put in writing. If it was not put in writing, it could have been overlooked if the officer to whom it was made was not on duty for a while. And if it was put in writing, it may be that we would not have been any the wiser anyway, since there does not appear to have been any system in place for recording written requests of this kind.

Miss Bigger's memo

27.13 In her statement to the Inquiry, Miss Bigger recalled writing a memo after Zahid's murder to Peter Windsor, the Head of Feltham B, in which she had said that she thought that Stewart and Zahid had asked to share a cell. Dave Comber, the manager of the Security Department, and Andy Darken, the chairman of the Feltham branch of the POA, told the CRE that they had heard much the same thing, though they cannot now recall where they got that from. Miss Bigger was vigorously questioned about that by Mr O'Connor. It was put to her that she may have known that Zahid had said that he did not want to share a cell with Stewart, but that she had written what she did because she wanted to show that there had been no hint of disharmony between Stewart and Zahid. Miss Bigger rejected that suggestion. She said that her mistake had been to confuse Stewart and Zahid with two other prisoners. I might have been sceptical of that explanation but for the subsequent discovery of her memo to Mr Windsor about Stewart and Zahid. It said nothing about Stewart and Zahid having asked to share a cell. So she could not have written it to create the misleading impression that Stewart and Zahid had got on.

Chapter 28: The incentives and earned privileges scheme on Swallow

The two sides of Swallow

28.1 It will be recalled that each of the residential units at Feltham consisted of two interconnecting sections. The two sections of Swallow were known as the red side and the blue side. The red side mostly housed prisoners who were taking part in purposeful activity such as employment or education. The blue side mostly housed prisoners who were not. Inmates who had reached the enhanced level of the incentives and earned privileges scheme operated on Swallow tended to be on the red side.

28.2 Cell 38 was on the blue side. So Zahid and Stewart were unlikely to have advanced to the enhanced level of the scheme, because if they had, they would probably have been moved to the red side. Moreover, if Zahid had proceeded to the enhanced level, but Stewart had not, there was a good chance that they would not have continued to be accommodated on the same side, let alone in the same cell. That is another way in which Zahid might have been moved out of cell 38 and away from Stewart.

The workings of the incentives and earned privileges scheme

28.3 The incentives and earned privileges scheme on Swallow consisted of three levels: basic, standard and enhanced. The higher the level, the greater the privileges which the prisoner enjoyed. Those privileges included getting more money to spend in the canteen, and having more association with other prisoners. All prisoners started on standard, and they either progressed to enhanced, or remained on standard, or were demoted to basic.

28.4 But beyond those basic facts, there is little by way of accurate information about how the scheme worked. If there was a document which set out the scheme – at any rate how it was intended to operate on Swallow – that document no longer exists. All we can go on is the recollection of staff, and their evidence differed considerably. For example, one officer said that if a prisoner got nine or more crosses for poor behaviour on his points and levels sheet in the relevant period – he did not say what that period was – the prisoner would go down to basic. If he got between five and eight crosses, he would remain on standard. If he got four crosses or less, he would be considered for enhanced. But another officer thought that a prisoner had to go for two weeks without getting any crosses at all if he was to be promoted to enhanced.

28.5 Another area of lack of clarity was whether there was a cap on the number of prisoners who could be made up to enhanced. There was some evidence that no more than 20 prisoners could be made up to enhanced, so that if a prisoner met the requirements for promotion to enhanced – whatever they may have been – he might have to wait until there were less than 20 others on enhanced. The effect was that only prisoners on the red side would have reached the enhanced level. But the weight of the evidence was otherwise. If there was a cap at all, it was on the number of prisoners who could go on evening association – evening association being one of the privileges of being on the enhanced level, and being enjoyed only by those on the red side. If that is right, a prisoner could be made up to enhanced, but stay on the blue side because there were no spaces on the red side, although enjoying the privileges of the enhanced level, save for evening association.

Stewart's and Zahid's status

28.6 Equally unclear is what level Stewart and Zahid were actually on. If a prisoner could proceed to enhanced, but could nevertheless remain on the blue side pending space on the red side, the fact that Stewart and Zahid remained on the blue side did not mean they had not proceeded to enhanced. Neither Zahid's wing file nor either of Stewart's wing files mentioned what level they were on. And the points and level sheets on which any ticks or crosses would have been recorded against them have not survived.

28.7 Mr Clifford told the police that his understanding was that Stewart and Zahid had both been on the standard level at the time. When he gave evidence, he could not recall what had given rise to that understanding, and it may be that he was simply making an assumption based on the fact that they remained on the blue side. The absence of any reference in their wing files to a change in their status suggests that their status did not change. There was evidence that changes of status would normally be recorded there, although the making of entries in prisoners' wing files was by no means routine on Swallow. On the other hand, the roll and movements sheet for Swallow for 18 March 2000 shows that cell 38 was allocated a television set that day. The evidence was that only enhanced prisoners were entitled to televisions in their cells. That suggests that either Stewart or Zahid, or both of them, had proceeded to enhanced. In the circumstances, it is not possible to say, one way or the other, whether either of them had progressed to enhanced, but the possibility that one or other or both of them had progressed to enhanced cannot be excluded.

28.8 But even if Zahid had progressed to enhanced, he could well have remained in a cell with Stewart. There may have been no room for him on the red side. Moreover, like Zahid, Stewart did not cause any trouble while on Swallow, and he would appear to have been just as eligible to proceed to enhanced as Zahid. They might both have proceeded to enhanced and yet had to stay on the blue side if there was no room on the red side, in which case it would have been natural for them to continue to share cell 38. On the other hand, if there had been room for them on the red side, that might only have been in a double cell, and it would have been natural for them to share that. In short, there is no guarantee whatever that if Zahid had progressed to the enhanced level, he would no longer have been sharing a cell with Stewart.

The bigger picture

28.9 But the bigger picture still needs to be looked at. An effective scheme which encourages and rewards good behaviour can transform a prison. But it can only really work if the rewards are tangible. If prisoners are denied even one of those rewards, such as evening association, simply because there is no room in the part of the unit for those entitled to it, they are likely to get embittered. That is especially so if different schemes operate on other units and if there is no written statement of how your scheme is supposed to work. The former produces resentment if the schemes on some units are more favourable to prisoners than yours. The latter produces frustration if, because of a lack of clarity, you do not know where you stand.

28.10 It took Feltham a long time to learn these rather obvious lessons – if indeed it ever learned them. As long ago as July 1995, the Prison Service issued an Instruction to Governors setting out a national framework for incentives and earned privileges schemes. The instruction recognised that no single scheme would be suitable for all establishments, but it required every establishment to operate a scheme which was consistent with the national framework. In particular, the criteria for assessing prisoners' behaviour and for determining when they should move to a higher or lower level had to be clear, well-publicised and easy to administer. And boards or panels had to be established for making decisions as to status and for handling appeals. Establishments had to introduce schemes complying with the national framework by the end of 1995.

28.11 When the Inspectorate visited Feltham in 1996, it found that each unit operated its own scheme. Prisoners would get to hear how the scheme on their unit worked from other prisoners. There were examples of prisoners not knowing what was required of them to get to the next level, and of some prisoners being denied the opportunity to advance to the next level at all by conditions for advancement with which they could not comply. The Inspectorate's report said that the operative scheme should be explained by members of staff, and that every prisoner should be given a written document explaining it as well. Some of these concerns were echoed by the Board of Visitors in its annual report for 1996.

28.12 Little, if anything, was done to put a proper scheme in place during the stewardship of Clive Welsh, Mr Clifford's predecessor as Governor of Feltham who took over in February 1997. He frankly admitted that it was not high on his list of priorities. He was aware of the need for a standardised scheme, but was advised by his residential governors that if he tried to get rid of the existing though disparate schemes across the establishment, he would be met with resistance from staff. He did not think the issue was one on which he should flex his muscles and confront the local branch of the POA. As a result, when the Inspectorate returned to Feltham in 1998, it found that little had changed. The system was open to abuse because officers could move prisoners within the levels without any management checks. The schemes which some of the units operated were very complicated. There did not appear to be much of a difference in the privileges which were available on the various levels. And the number of different schemes meant that prisoners were confused. The Inspectorate concluded that "a simple, standardised system of genuine incentives to good behaviour was needed with… management controls on the movement between levels".

28.13 Eventually the baton was taken up. In July 1999, Mr Clifford issued a Governor's Notice asking for volunteers to help Peter Windsor, the Head of Feltham B, and John Byrd, the governor responsible for some of the residential units in Feltham B including Swallow, who had been tasked to lead a team which would "review, update and standardise" the incentives and earned privileges scheme. Mr Byrd does not now recall being involved, but Mr Windsor does. The Inquiry has not seen the fruit of his team's labours, but it looks as if a new standardised scheme had been *published* by the end of the year. It was referred to in the minutes of a meeting of the Board of Visitors on 8 December 1999 and in the action plan produced by the team from the Prison Service's Standards Audit Unit which carried out a combined standards and security audit at Feltham between 22 November and 10 December 1999.

28.14 When it was *introduced*, though, is unclear. The minutes of the Board of Visitors' meeting suggest that it had been introduced in four of the units in Feltham A in December 1999, and Mr Denman, the principal officer responsible for three units in Feltham B including Swallow, said that it had been introduced in each of his units by the time he returned to work from sick leave in January 2000. But that is not borne out by officers who were working on Swallow at the time. Not one of them recalls a new scheme being in place in Swallow by the time Zahid was murdered. I am sure they are right. If the new scheme had been introduced by then, and was operating in Swallow at the time, there would surely have been some documents to show that.

28.15 Overall, the picture which emerges is a pretty dismal one. More than four years after each establishment was required to have an incentives and earned privileges scheme which applied across the establishment, that had not happened at Feltham – at any rate not so that it had any impact on Swallow. To this day, we do not know how prisoners' behaviour there was assessed or what they had to do to justify advancement to a higher level or demotion to a lower one. It does not look as if there was a board or panel making decisions about the level a prisoner should be on, though we do not know that for sure. If there had been one, that would have been another opportunity for the warnings about Stewart in his temporary wing file to have been picked up. For the Inquiry to be in the dark even about the level which Stewart and Zahid were on at the time is a serious indictment of how the operation of the scheme was recorded.

Chapter 29: The table leg and other possible weapons

The issues

29.1 Stewart used a table leg to club Zahid to death with. It came from Stewart's table in the cell. We only have Stewart's word for when he took it off the table – and he has said different things at different times. But it plainly was not taken off that night. The table had lots of things on it, and they had to be removed before the leg could be taken off. It is inconceivable that Stewart took everything off the table that night, then removed the leg, and then put everything back on the table before battering Zahid with it. So the question has to be asked: should the fact that it was no longer attached to the table have been noticed by officers when they had previously searched the cell? But there is an even more important issue to be addressed. There is some evidence that officers may have actually discovered another possible weapon in the cell, but did nothing about it.

The table

29.2 There were two tables in cell 38 – one for each prisoner. Some prison furniture is made of metal and is in a fixed position so that it cannot be moved. These two tables were not like that. They were made of wood and were free-standing – as were the tables in all the cells in Swallow. They each had four legs. Each of the legs was attached to the frame at the top of the table by a metal bracket, which was held in place by a large hexagonal screw going through the bracket into the leg. The shorter sides of the table each had two bars stabilising the legs – one higher up, the other lower down. And the two lower stabilising bars were joined by a crossbar.

29.3 Photographs were taken of the cell shortly after the murder. They show one of the table legs from Stewart's table lying on the floor. That was what Stewart used to club Zahid with. The bracket was still fixed to the frame but the screw was missing – another reason why the table leg could not have been taken off that night. They also show that one of the two lower stabilisers was missing from Stewart's table – and so was the crossbar. In addition, they show a handkerchief draped over the other lower stabiliser from Stewart's table. When that handkerchief was removed, a large piece of the stabiliser in the shape of a splinter was seen to be missing.

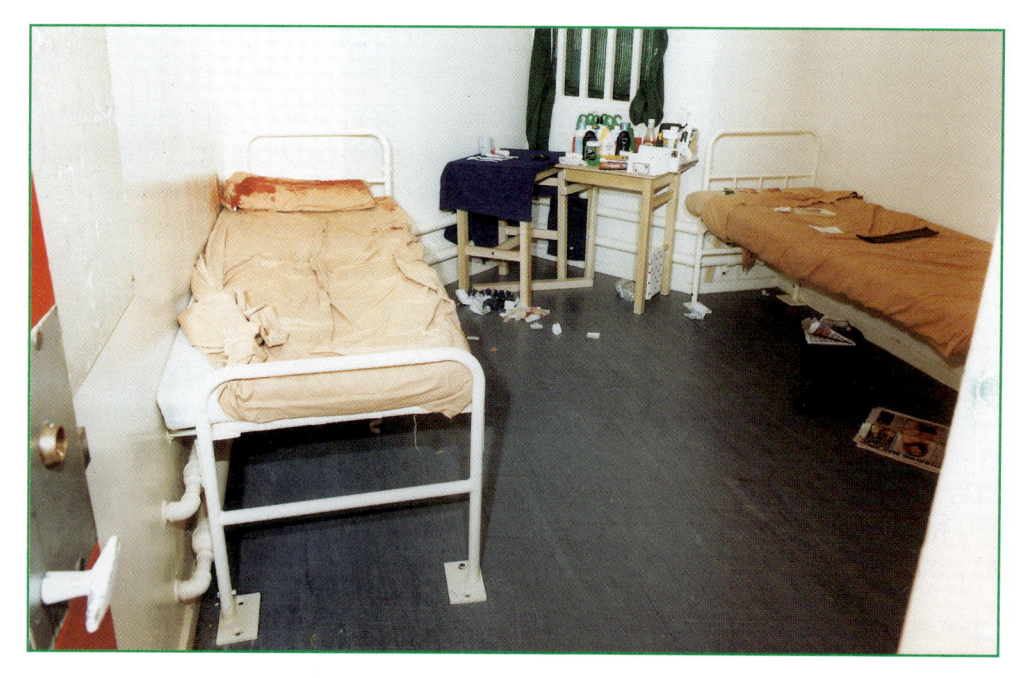

Cell 38 shortly after the murder with Zahid's bed on the left

Stewart's table in Cell 38

CHAPTER 29: THE TABLE LEG AND OTHER POSSIBLE WEAPONS

The photograph of Stewart's table used at his trial

Stewart's makeshift dagger made from the stabiliser

29.4   The missing stabiliser was found wedged between some pipes close to the floor behind the head of Stewart's bed. As for the splinter, it had been used by Stewart to create a makeshift dagger with a sharp point. He had used thread from his blanket to fashion a handle so that he could get some grip on it. It was found with a pornographic magazine under a pillow on Stewart's bed in the aftermath of the attack when one of the officers picked the pillow up in order to prop Zahid's head up. Two prisoners on Swallow – Jamie Barnes and Michael Hampton – had seen Stewart with the dagger in his cell on the Saturday before he attacked Zahid. Hampton had seen Stewart winding the thread round the handle, and Barnes had seen him produce it from under his tracksuit top.

29.5 The missing crossbar was never found. But in his statement to the Inquiry Stewart revealed what had happened to it. It could not be re-attached to the table, so he tried to dispose of it by snapping it into pieces by putting it between the pipes by his bed and the wall and then flushing the parts down the toilet. If any part was left – and he could not recall whether any was – he would have left it behind the toilet. As for when he removed the table leg, he has said different things at different times. When he was interviewed by the police shortly after the murder, he said he had broken the table a week or 10 days before the murder in a flash of temper. He later told the CRE that about three weeks before the murder the table leg had fallen off when he took the crossbar off to make the dagger. He was to tell the Inquiry that he had made the dagger no more than a week after he had moved into cell 38. But once he had removed the table leg, he would prop it in place so that it would look as if it was still attached to the table.

The conversation about weapons

29.6 In the course of their investigation, the police tried to interview all the prisoners who had been on Swallow at the time. They took statements from the majority of them. Three of them – Barnes, Hampton and Sunil Bhartti – referred to a conversation involving Stewart and Zahid which took place one morning during association. Barnes said that the conversation had taken place on Monday 20 March, the last full day before the attack, with the murder happening in the small hours of the Tuesday. But Bhartti was unsure. He initially told the police on the day after the murder that the conversation had been on the Sunday. In a later statement, he changed that to the Monday. But in an even later statement, he said he could not be sure what day it had taken place. The likelihood is that it was on the Monday.

29.7 There are some minor differences in their recollection of the conversation, but they agree on the general thrust of it. They were by the table football at the time, and Stewart was with them. Zahid came over to them from the direction of the unit's office, and said that a prison officer had found something of Stewart's. They disagreed as to the words Zahid had actually used from "your stuff" to "your thing" to "the tool". But two of them – Hampton and Bhartti – claimed that Zahid had said it had been found "in" or "down" the toilet. Barnes was asked by the Inquiry about that. He said that nothing had been said about where it had been found. Even so, all three agreed that Stewart had replied to the effect that they had not found everything, and he either patted his stomach to indicate that he had something there – that is what Barnes and Bhartti said – or lifted his tracksuit top and showed a piece of wood sticking up from his waistband – which is what Hampton said. Hampton added that it did not have the green thread around it.

29.8 There is no reason to suppose that a conversation on these lines did not take place. Neither Hampton nor Bhartti gave evidence because the Inquiry was unable to make contact with them. But no-one challenged Barnes's account of it when he gave evidence. And the account of the three of them is sufficiently similar to suggest that they were not making it up, and sufficiently different to indicate that they did not agree on a story to tell. It is also borne out by Stewart himself, because when the gist of what Barnes, Hampton and Bhartti had said was put to him by the Inquiry, he did not deny it. Indeed, he agreed that Zahid had referred to something having been found. He claimed it was the dagger he had had on him at the time.

29.9 The effect of this evidence – if what Zahid was telling the others was true – was that something had been found in cell 38. If so, it had to have been what was left of the crossbar which Stewart had left behind the toilet. It could not have been the dagger – assuming that Stewart had not had it on him – or the table leg, because they would unquestionably have been removed from the cell if they had been found. And the same applies to the stabiliser found wedged between the pipes. So who found what was left of the crossbar and when? That is where the trail ends. No officer has admitted to finding anything in cell 38 at about this time. And the two officers who searched cell 38 on the Sunday and Monday say that nothing was found.

Cell searches

29.10 Before resolving this conflict in the evidence, it is necessary to say something about the rules for the searching of cells. There were two kinds of searches. One was a full and comprehensive search, but that took place relatively infrequently. The other was an accommodation fabric check, commonly referred to as an LBB check, which stood for "locks, bolts and bars".

Full searches

29.11 Each cell had to be fully and comprehensively searched every three months. These searches had to be on randomly selected days so that they could not be predicted. The relevant quarter for our purposes was from 1 January to 31 March 2000. Since there were 38 cells in Swallow, an average of about three cells a week – or 13 cells a month – had to be searched. Because each search was quite a substantial exercise, the searching of the cells had to be staggered: they could not all be left to the last couple of weeks in the quarter. There is an issue as to whether any of the cells in Swallow were being searched in this way at the time. I return to that topic later, but assuming that cell 38 was not searched before Stewart went there on 8 February, it did not have to be searched between then and the night of the murder, provided that it was to be searched before the end of March. So the absence of such a search cannot be said to have contributed to the murder of Zahid.

Fabric checks

29.12 The function of fabric checks was to detect any evidence of an attempt to break out of the cell. They had to be carried out on each cell every day, and that was intended to deter any prisoners from trying to escape. They had to take place at unpredictable times. Staff were required to pay particular attention to things like window frames and bars, and all walls, floors and ceilings. Furniture and other fittings were of secondary importance. They needed only to be checked when they were fitted to the wall or floor. It was anticipated that problems relating to furniture and fittings would be picked up by staff "detailed for that purpose". The Inquiry was not told what that meant, but I have assumed that it was a reference to the quarterly search. That was when the non-fixed furniture would be checked. However, when checking walls and floors, staff had to move any furniture which obstructed their access to surfaces which had to be checked. It was a limited check. The thrust of the evidence was that it would not last more than a minute or so.

Was what was left of the crossbar found?

29.13 There are really only two possibilities. Either what was left of the crossbar *was* found, but the officer who found it has kept quiet about it. Or it was *not* found, and what Zahid told Stewart in the presence of Barnes, Hampton and Bhartti was not true. This latter possibility is by no means a fanciful one. It was initially suggested by Mr Cummines who regarded it as perfectly tenable in view of his experience of prison life. It proceeds on the twin premises that Zahid knew about Stewart's weapons and felt uncomfortable about him having them. The first of those hypotheses is entirely plausible since Stewart was not concealing the dagger from fellow prisoners, and he told the CRE that Zahid knew that he had removed the table leg. And it is just as likely that Zahid was uncomfortable about Stewart having weapons. How could Zahid get Stewart to offload them without breaking the first rule that prisoners learn – that if you value your welfare, you do not "grass" on fellow prisoners? The possibility is that by pretending that staff were onto Stewart's cache of weapons, Zahid reckoned that Stewart would get rid of them by disposing of them elsewhere in the unit and thereby not run the risk of getting into serious trouble if they were found.

29.14 I see the force of this, but in the end I do not regard it as likely. Apart from having himself to get rid of what was left of the crossbar, Zahid would have had to explain to Stewart why Stewart had not been questioned over the find. After all, Zahid would have realised that Stewart would think that prison officers would have been much more likely to assume that it belonged to him rather than Zahid, and they would have wanted to question Stewart about it. It is possible that if Stewart had raised that with Zahid, Zahid could have pretended that he had told the officers that what they had found had been his, but he ran a real risk that Stewart would see through him. He would have known that if Stewart asked any of the officers whether he was going to get into trouble over his confession that what had been found had been his, the officer would have said that nothing had been found. If Zahid was manipulative enough to think that this was a way of getting Stewart to get rid of his weapons – which Barnes doubted – he would have been clever enough to work out the downside of the strategy for himself. And anyway, why would he run the risk of crossing Stewart the day before he was due to be released?

29.15 That means that what was left of the crossbar must have been found by one of the officers. The obvious candidates are the officers who carried out the fabric checks in cell 38 shortly before Zahid told Stewart what had been found. They were Mr Skinner, who carried out the fabric checks on the blue side of Swallow on Sunday 19 March, and Sundeep Chahal, who was a relatively recent recruit to the Prison Service, having joined in March 1998, and had been at Feltham for about four months, and who carried out the fabric checks on the blue side of Swallow on Monday 20 March. It is theoretically possible, I suppose, that some other officer could have gone into cell 38 and found what was left of the crossbar, but that is very unlikely. Zahid was probably told about the find just before he told Stewart about it. And Mr Chahal confirmed that the fabric checks took place on the blue side during morning association, despite the need for them to be done at unpredictable times. So since Stewart would have been told about the find during morning association, and since that was when the fabric checks took place, it is likely that what was left of the crossbar was found during the fabric checks.

29.16 But which fabric check? The one on the Sunday or the one on the Monday? Since the likelihood is that Zahid told Stewart about the find on the Monday, and since Zahid is likely to have been told about the find just before that, it is overwhelmingly likely that what was left of the crossbar was found during the fabric check on the Monday – the fabric check carried out by Mr Chahal. For his part, Mr Chahal denied that he found anything in cell 38 when he did his fabric check that morning. Mr Skinner said the same thing for the Sunday. The weekly fabric security check form which they signed is of no help on this issue. By signing that form, they were only certifying that they had carried out the fabric check. The form was not intended to be used to identify anything which may have been found in a particular cell during the search. If something suspicious was found, that would have to be reported in some other way – either verbally to the officer in charge of the unit or by a security information report.

29.17 The fact is that once the possibility of Zahid lying to Stewart has been rejected, the Inquiry is compelled to find that what was left of the crossbar must have been found by a prison officer. Despite his denial, that must have been Mr Chahal. Why did he do nothing about it? He could not tell us, of course, because to do so would have been inconsistent with his claim that nothing had been found. But we can make an educated guess. What was left of the crossbar did not look like a weapon. And if it had been behind the toilet, it had not been particularly well hidden. So Mr Chahal may have thought that there was nothing particularly sinister about it. He spoke to Zahid about it – not necessarily because he thought it was Zahid's, and was making stereotypical assumptions that Asian prisoners were more likely to have weapons in their cells than white prisoners, but perhaps because Zahid was in cell 38 when what was left of the crossbar was found or because he was the first of the occupants of cell 38 who Mr Chahal saw. Not wanting to put the blame on Stewart, Zahid offered some explanation – perhaps that the table leg got broken accidentally – which appeared to Mr Chahal to be acceptable. Since Zahid was a pleasant lad who was due to be released the next day, Mr Chahal decided to leave it at that.

29.18 Mr Chahal was not necessarily at fault in not reporting what he had found. Some officers said that if they found furniture which had been broken accidentally, they would remove the broken piece, but allow the rest of the furniture to remain in the cell if it was still functioning properly and safely, and not take the matter further from a disciplinary standpoint. Other officers would have acted differently. But whatever else Mr Chahal did or did not do, his find should have prompted him to check the tables in the cell since he would – or at any rate should – have realised that one of them was where what was left of the crossbar could have come from. Had he done that, he would have discovered that one of the legs was no longer attached to Stewart's table, and that the crossbar and one of the stabilisers were missing, as was a large splinter from the other stabiliser. The table leg would have been removed from the cell when it was discovered, and Stewart would not have been able to use it to club Zahid with. Indeed, the discovery that the table leg had been detached should have prompted a thorough search of the cell, and of Stewart and Zahid as well, and that would presumably have resulted in both the missing stabiliser and the dagger being found. It is likely that in that event Stewart would have been sent to the segregation unit. Zahid may have been sent there as well, pending a determination of who the weapons belonged to. But two things are clear. There is a real possibility that they would not have been sharing a cell that night. And even if they had, the weapons which Stewart could have used were likely to have been removed.

The previous fabric checks

29.19 There is still the question whether earlier fabric checks should have resulted in the discovery of the detachment of the table leg and the removal of the missing parts of the table. Here it is not just Mr Skinner and Mr Chahal who are under the spotlight. Even if one takes the latest when Stewart says the table leg was detached, it had been removed for a good few days before the murder. So the officers who did the fabric checks for the blue side of Swallow in the previous week are under scrutiny here as well. We do not know who those officers were, because the Inquiry was not provided with the weekly fabric security check form for the previous week. It is not necessarily the case that all the damage had been done to the table at the same time, but it probably was.

29.20 As we have seen, Stewart said that the table leg was propped in place so that it would look as if it was still attached to the table. There is no reason to disbelieve that. So staff carrying out the fabric checks would only have discovered that the table leg had been removed if they had to lift or move the table. There would have been no need for them to do that in order to check the wall behind the table or the part of the floor it was on. The CRE thought otherwise, but I disagree. The wall behind the table and the part of the floor it was on were sufficiently visible without the table having to be moved or lifted. And since the procedures for conducting fabric checks said that furniture needed to be checked only when it was fixed to the wall or floor, the table itself did not have to be checked. Some officers said that their practice was to do that – whether by giving the table a quick shake or inspecting it visually. But whatever some officers did, neither the letter nor the spirit of the procedures for fabric checks required that to be done. Indeed, coming from Raven, where the furniture had been fixed metal furniture, the natural inclination for some officers would have been not to check the furniture at all.

29.21 But in order to check the wall behind the table and the part of the floor it was on, staff would have had to look underneath the table. Views might differ on this topic, but I think that when doing that they should have noticed that one of the lower stabilisers and the crossbar were missing. And in order to check the wall at the head of Stewart's bed, staff would have had to look at the pipes behind it. I think that they should have noticed the missing stabiliser wedged in there. What should all that have led them to do? Although the discovery that they were missing or hidden may not have been relevant to checking *the fabric* of the cell for escape attempts, and although any action was therefore not strictly required by the letter of the procedures for fabric checks, nevertheless their jailcraft should have told them that the missing parts of the table could have been used for all sorts of improper purposes, including use as a weapon or to facilitate an escape in some way. That should have caused them to check the cell more thoroughly – nothing like the quarterly search, but nevertheless for a few minutes. Not merely to find the missing crossbar, but also to look for anything else, because if the occupants of the cell were using the missing parts for some improper purpose, you would want to find out what else they were up to. Such a search would – or at any rate should – have resulted in a number of things: the discovery that the table leg had been detached, the finding of the missing stabiliser and what was left of the missing crossbar, and the discovery that the handkerchief draped over the lower stabiliser was concealing the removal of a large splinter from it.

29.22 None of the previous fabric checks had resulted in any of that being done. The likelihood is that the officers who conducted those checks did not notice that the stabiliser or the crossbar were missing. It is unlikely that if they had noticed their disappearance, they would have done nothing about it. And why did they not notice that these parts of the table were missing? The likelihood is that they did not look under the table at all. As I have said, they should have done – not only to comply with the spirit of the procedures for the fabric checks, but also with its letter. Had they done what they should have done, the process would inexorably have led to the discovery of what had been done to the table. Stewart could well have ended up in the segregation unit. At the very least, the table and its parts would have been taken away – and the potentiality for them to be used as weapons removed.

29.23 The fact is that for at least a week things which should have been noticed if the walls and floors were being checked properly were not noticed. That says much about the quality of the fabric checks being carried out. The senior officer in charge of the unit should occasionally have checked whether staff were doing the fabric checks properly. But as we shall see, there was no senior officer in charge of Swallow in the five weeks or so before Zahid's murder.

The use of wooden furniture in cells

29.24 Whether cells should have free-standing wooden furniture or bolted-down metal furniture is an important and difficult question. Wooden furniture can be used as weapons and can be broken down to make weapons, whereas metal furniture cannot be dismantled to make weapons, and if fixed cannot be used as weapons either. The use of wooden furniture to make weapons was, and had been, a frequent occurrence. Indeed, a prisoner was killed by his cellmate with a table leg at Cardiff Prison in 1992. On the other hand, metal furniture is regarded as clinical and austere, and for that reason unsuitable for young offenders confined to their cells for long periods. And the ingenuity of prisoners to fashion weapons out of very limited materials means that it is almost impossible to eliminate in-cell weapons in their entirety. Maybe it is better to recognise that, while at the same time attempting to achieve a measure of normality and decency for prisoners in their cells.

29.25 Later in this report, I address what the way forward should be. But in the context of what happened to Zahid, Mr Giffin was surely right when he argued that "it is difficult to suppose that the absence of a wooden table would have stopped Stewart from killing Zahid, had he been absolutely determined to do so. But it is also conceivable that Stewart might not have chosen to carry out the attack had a heavy weapon not been readily and silently to hand."

Full cell searches in Swallow

29.26 Before 2000, returns setting out the result of the full quarterly searches had to be submitted to the Security Department every month. The Inquiry has only seen one such return. It covered a three-month period for Raven for the months of October, November and December 1999. It was a running document, in the sense that, when a cell was searched, an entry was made in the return. From the beginning of 2000, the returns had to be submitted by the senior officer in charge of the unit every quarter, the quarter being the calendar quarter. The Inquiry has not been provided with the return for Swallow for the first three months of 2000. That gave rise to the suspicion that the quarterly searches were not taking place on Swallow at all in the period between Swallow re-opening following its refurbishment – on 14 or 18 January – and the night of the murder.

29.27 The recollection of staff on Swallow was mixed. Two members of staff claimed to recall cell-searching taking place during that period, but they were in the minority. Two members of staff said that they could remember that no cell-searching took place during that period. And four members of staff said that they could not recall any cell-searching taking place during that period. Mr Windsor and Mr Byrd found it hard to believe that it was not happening, but Mr Windsor accepted that a system which required a signed return to be submitted once every three months would mean that any shortcomings in this area could go unnoticed for some time.

29.28 But the most compelling evidence was that of Douglas Weir, a senior officer who joined the Prison Service in 1992. He was the hiking officer for the cluster of three units which included Swallow up to 15 March 2000 when he became the senior officer in charge of Swallow – though ironically he was on leave then, and did not actually take up his new post until after Zahid's murder. He told the police when they interviewed him on 30 March that there had not been any cell-searching on Swallow since it had re-opened – which he thought was 18 January. In his evidence to the Inquiry, he explained that either when he was being interviewed by the police, or shortly before, he was looking or had looked at Swallow's return for the quarter ending 31 March 2000. It was because of what that document told him that he could be so sure that there had not been any cell-searching during the period. He had no idea what happened to the document, but maybe it went missing because it was not retained by the police since it was a live document – in the sense that it would continue to be used, in theory at least, for the day or so until the end of the quarter.

CHAPTER 29: THE TABLE LEG AND OTHER POSSIBLE WEAPONS

29.29 Mr Weir's evidence convinced me that full cell searches were not taking place on Swallow as they should have been. That was the fault of Mr McAlaney who, as we shall see, was the senior officer in charge of Swallow until 15 February when he moved to the Detail Office. But should the hiking officer not have picked that up? Mr Weir said that he did. The checklist and handover sheet – which the hiking officer had to complete every day – had a box in which he had to record whether any cells on each of the three units for which he was responsible had been searched. True, he had to rely on the staff on the unit for that information unless he happened to be on the unit when a cell was being searched. But Mr Weir knew from the entries he had made in the checklist and handover sheets that the cells on Swallow were not being searched. Perhaps those who read those entries may not have been aware of that: if an average of 13 cells had to be searched every month, the fact that cells were not being searched for a few days, or even longer, would not be inconsistent with that requirement. But Mr Weir claims that he mentioned at the operational meetings for senior staff which took place every morning that cell searches were not being done on Swallow, leaving it to managers to decide whether staff should be deployed from elsewhere in the establishment to do the cell searches if there were not enough staff on Swallow to do them. I have no reason to disbelieve him. The principal responsibility for cell-searching not having been done lies, of course, with Mr McAlaney, but it also lies with Mr Denman, the principal officer responsible for the three units including Swallow, and Mr Byrd for not ensuring that additional staff were temporarily deployed to carry out this work.

The "KKK" on the notice board

29.30 When cell 38 was inspected after the attack on Zahid, the letters "KKK" were found written on the noticeboard in the cell. They were very small, measuring about 1.5 cms in length. Stewart admitted in his statement to the Inquiry that he had written them, but he was unable to say when. Could this be said to have been "the writing on the wall"? One cannot expect them to have been noticed on any of the fabric checks, but a full search of the cell should have revealed them. As it was, graffiti was common in the cells at Feltham, and even if what Stewart had written had been discovered earlier than it was, we do not know whether he would have admitted responsibility for it then. So had it been noticed, for all the staff knew, it could have been put there by a previous occupant of the cell. I have already said that the lack of any full search while Stewart was in cell 38 could not be said to have contributed to the murder of Zahid. But the fact remains that if the writing had been discovered while Stewart was still there, there was the possibility that he had been responsible for it. That should have prompted some thought being given to whether he should continue to share a cell with someone from an ethnic minority.

Chapter 30: The clues in the documents

Stewart's prisoner escort records

30.1 It is easy to be wise after the event, but looking back on Stewart's time at Feltham, it is plain that, despite his unproblematic behaviour while he was there, there were a number of opportunities for the risks which he posed to have been picked up. In this chapter, I deal with the documents which could have told staff in reception and in the Security Department that Stewart was a troubled young man with a worrying past who needed to be watched, and I comment on the flow of information more generally. But first I look at Stewart's prisoner escort records.

Incoming prisoner escort records

30.2 It will be recalled that prisoner escort records were prepared at Hindley for each of Stewart's three visits to Feltham. The violent and escape risk boxes were ticked in all of them, and they each said that Stewart was associated with weapons. Prisoner security information sheets were attached to them. They confirmed that Stewart was violent, had the potential to escape, and was an exceptional risk – without stating what of – but they did not say what those assessments were based on. They nevertheless flagged Stewart up as a possible source of trouble.

30.3 Should these documents have been read by staff on reception at Feltham? I would not have been all that surprised if their evidence had been that scrutinising the prisoner escort records was not their job. Their constant refrain was that they had much to do just to make sure that the flow of prisoners through a busy reception went smoothly. And Feltham's was a very busy reception indeed. At the time there was a single reception for both Feltham A and Feltham B. As we have seen, there was an average of 62 prisoners a day coming into the establishment in the 12 months up to 29 February 2000. And they all tended to come in towards the end of the day – sometimes very late. All this on top of reception regularly being understaffed. So if reception staff had said that checking the prisoner escort records was the responsibility of staff in Custody Administration – which was where the records went the following day – that would not have been surprising.

30.4 But that was not their evidence. For the most part, reception staff acknowledged the need to pass on relevant information on the prisoner escort record of an incoming prisoner. Maybe that was because they recognised that it would be easy to accuse them of exaggerating the work which had to be done when a prisoner came through reception, bearing in mind that there would not be so much to do with returnees, who represented the overwhelming majority of the prisoners passing through reception. If there was any disagreement, it was about who in reception had to read the record: the senior officer in charge of reception at the time, or the documentation officer who allocated the prisoner to the unit and who collated the paperwork which accompanied him. So if the record showed him to be an escape risk, that information should be passed to the Security Department. And if the record contained a warning about a prisoner, that should be relayed to the unit on which he was to be accommodated. That was in line with the instructions issued by Prison Service headquarters when the prisoner escort record was introduced. Staff on reception were required to alert "appropriate staff" to information in the record. Examples of who the appropriate staff were included healthcare, security staff and the duty governor, but not, interestingly enough, the wing on which the prisoner was being housed. The instructions presumably envisaged that staff on the wing would be informed by, say, staff in the Security Department if the record contained information they needed to know. And although the instructions did not require any warnings in the prisoner escort record to be entered in the Local Inmate Database System, using the single line of text available for that purpose would have been the obvious thing to do.

30.5 But I do not believe that any of that was happening in reception at Feltham. One officer who worked in reception said that he had never seen a prisoner escort record which he thought contained a warning he needed to pass on. Another said that they were not looked at in reception as a matter of course. That is much more likely to have been the practice – especially with returnees who formed by far the largest number of prisoners coming through reception and who would have been known within Feltham, and with "in and outs" who were not going to be there for long. Processing incoming prisoners through reception within a limited timeframe often late at night was laborious enough without having to go through the prisoner escort records as well. It would not have been the first time that instructions from Prison Service headquarters had been ignored.

30.6 Would Stewart's management at Feltham have been any different if the warnings contained in his prisoner escort records *had* been relayed, via the Security Department, to the residential units on each of his visits to Feltham? Certainly not on the first two. The need for Stewart to be watched had been picked up by Mr Martindale on Lapwing even before he was asked to look at Stewart's security file. It was for that reason that he had been put in a single cell. So if the warnings on the first prisoner escort record had been relayed to Lapwing, it is extremely doubtful that he would have been treated any differently. Nor is he likely to have been managed any differently on Osprey if the warnings on the second prisoner escort record had been relayed to it. Miss Goodman knew from Mr Marshall that Stewart was very dangerous. If she did not regard that as a sufficient reason for putting him in a cell on his own, I do not suppose that there was anything in Stewart's prisoner escort record to have caused her to act differently.

30.7 But what about Stewart's last visit to Feltham? Although reception staff would still have thought of him as an "in and out" on 7 February, and as a returnee on 8 February, the fact remains that meaningful warnings in the prisoner escort record generated at Hindley for this visit should have been relayed to the appropriate staff. The question which arises is whether the warnings in the record were sufficiently meaningful for that to be done.

30.8 The violent box is a good example of boxes losing their value as a result of over-use. As I said earlier, the violent box was correctly ticked on Stewart's prisoner escort record. But it was a box which was invariably ticked. One witness said that 60–70% of the prisoner escort records accompanying prisoners arriving at Feltham had the violent box ticked. Another put it as high as 90%. With the violent box being ticked with such frequency, its value as an indicator of risk was significantly diminished. The trouble was that without further information on the record – and invariably there was none – staff in reception would not know why the box had been ticked. The correct approach would still have been for them to pass the risk on to the Security Department, leaving it to the staff there to assess, in the light of any other information about the prisoner, what information needed to be relayed to the unit on which the prisoner was located. But at the same time one can understand why staff in reception might be questioning whether it was right to notify the Security Department every time the violent box was ticked.

30.9 The tick in the escape risk box was another matter. No-one suggested that this box was devalued as a result of over-use. The same is true of the reference to Stewart's association with weapons. There was not a dedicated box in the record for a prisoner's connection with weapons, and Hindley's practice had been to refer to it in the section headed "Further information". The evidence from those who worked at Feltham was that a tick in the escape risk box or a reference to weapons should have prompted some action on the part of staff in reception. Since there was nothing on the record to explain why Stewart was regarded as an escape risk or what his connection with weapons was, the most appropriate action would have been to pass on the information to the Security Department, leaving it to the staff there to look at any other information on Stewart and decide what information about him should be given to Swallow.

30.10 There is nothing to suggest that the warnings on Stewart's last prisoner escort record were passed on to the Security Department by staff in reception. But what would staff in the Security Department have done if they had been? Dave Comber, the manager of the Security Department, said that by themselves the warnings would not have prompted anyone in the Security Department to get in touch with Swallow. That reflected Mr Comber's view – which I share – that the prisoner escort record is of limited value. I return to that point in chapter 58, but for the moment it is sufficient for me to say that I agree entirely that the fact that some boxes in the prisoner escort record were ticked was of far less use to staff in the Security Department than the other documents they saw which contained information about a prisoner – the security file if there was one, the core record and the warrants. If information on the prisoner escort record had any use, it was simply to highlight for staff in the Security Department the things which those documents had to be looked at for. So in relation to Stewart's last visit to Feltham, the question is not so much whether his management on Swallow would have been any different if the warnings contained in the last prisoner escort record had been relayed, via the Security Department, to Swallow, but rather whether his management on Swallow would have been any different if Swallow had been told what the other documents about him revealed.

Outgoing prisoner escort records

30.11 There is one curious feature about Stewart's trips to court on 7 and 8 March. Prisoner escort records should have been created for each trip. The Inquiry was not provided with them. Did they go missing or were they never created? The latter is unlikely. Stewart would not have been allowed out of Feltham without one. Nor would the escort contractor have taken him to court without one. And the proper completion of prisoner escort records was one area where the team from the Prison Service's Standard Audits Unit – which carried out the combined standards and security audit at Feltham between 22 November and 10 December 1999 – found performance to be acceptable. So what happened to them? Paul Clark, the principal officer in charge of reception at the time, said that when prisoners returned from court he kept back some of the prisoner escort records because he wanted to check how long the escort contractors were keeping prisoners locked up at court. Although he did not say so in so many words, the effect of what he was saying was that the prisoner escort records for Stewart on 7 and 8 March must have been among those which he held back. Mr Clark said that this happened with only a few prisoner escort records, although Mr Comber told Mr Butt that he had not been seeing the prisoner escort records "of late", implying that the Security Department was not getting any of them. Either way,

Mr Clark should have sent them to the Security Department when he had finished with them, and he should have filed them properly in the meantime so that they would not get lost.

Stewart's security file

30.12 The majority of prisoners arrived at Feltham without a security file. That was not surprising. "New numbers" would not have had a current security file, and even if a security file had been opened during an earlier sentence, the Security Department at Feltham – as at other establishments – never asked for the security files which had been opened on earlier sentences, and which were languishing either in the Security Department or in the dead records store of the establishment from which the prisoner had been released or in the Prison Service Records Registry. And as for transferees, a security file would not have been opened at the previous establishment unless there was a need for one to be opened – for example, if the prisoner was the subject of a security information report.

30.13 But Stewart's security file had been at Feltham for some time before he murdered Zahid. It was looked at during Stewart's first visit to Feltham by Mr Benford, and he spoke to Mr Martindale about its contents. It could not have been looked at during Stewart's second visit to Feltham in time to alert the units he was on about him, because it only arrived at Feltham after he had left. But the disappearance of Stewart's temporary wing file made it all the more important for his security file to be looked at again when he returned to Feltham for the last time on 7 February. If it had been looked at, the warning Mr Martindale had got from Mr Benford could well have been repeated, and the staff on Swallow would have been alerted to what Stewart had got up to in the past. A direct warning of this kind might have had an even greater impact than the entries in Stewart's temporary wing file should have had. Moreover, as we have seen, Stewart's behaviour when he was on Swallow gave no cause for concern. Perhaps the staff on Swallow would have looked at him more warily had they known about his previous disruptive behaviour. After all, it was the mismatch between Stewart's current and past behaviour which had caused Mr Farrell at Altcourse to ask Mr Kinealy to see him.

30.14 Was any information about what Stewart's security file revealed about him relayed to the staff on Swallow? In the absence of any wing file on Stewart, the obvious place to record any information received about him from the Security Department was in the wing observation book. But there was nothing in there about Stewart. It is extremely unlikely that if information was given to staff on Swallow about Stewart by the Security Department, an entry to that effect would not have been made in the wing observation book – especially as it was not that usual for a warning that a prisoner was particularly dangerous to be given by the Security Department. So the strong likelihood is that no information about what Stewart's security file revealed was relayed to the staff on Swallow.

30.15 Why was that? One possibility has already been mentioned. That was that Stewart's security file did not go back to Hindley when Stewart left Feltham on 26 January. If it remained at Feltham, the likelihood is that it would simply have sat in the filing cabinet in the Security Department where it had been put after Stewart arrived at Feltham for the second time on 24 January, and would not have been looked at again. But the probability is that it did go back to Hindley, returning finally to Feltham on a date which cannot now be identified, but some time after Stewart returned to Feltham for the last time on 7 February.

30.16 So if Stewart's security file came back from Hindley some time after 7 February and arrived at Feltham by the time he had gone to Swallow, why were the staff on Swallow not told what it revealed about him? There are only two possibilities. One is that the security file was not looked at again in the Security Department. The other is that it was looked at, but for one reason or another the officer who looked at it decided not to pass on the information it contained about Stewart. Some of the witnesses suggested that the officer in question might have decided not to do that because it was known that Mr Benford had already warned the unit Stewart had originally been on about him. But that is a very unlikely explanation. There was no system in place for recording on the security file whether it had already been vetted or whether any concerns which it revealed about a prisoner had been passed on. So the officer looking at the security file would not have been able to tell whether any action had been taken on it. It is just possible that he had heard from Mr Benford, or someone else in the Security Department, that when Stewart had first come to Feltham his unit had been told what was in his security file. But that is unlikely, and anyway it would not have justified the officer doing nothing. If it had been thought appropriate for the staff on Lapwing to have been told about Stewart earlier, it would have been appropriate for the staff on Swallow to have been told about him then.

30.17 Nor is it likely that Stewart's security file had been looked at, but that it was not thought to contain anything which required a warning about him to be sent to his unit. Anyone picking up the file would have realised that it was unusually bulky. Anyone opening it would have seen the inmate intelligence card at the front of it. And anyone reading the card would have appreciated that the file contained information of real significance.

30.18 That last point needs some refining. As we have seen, the inmate intelligence card at the front of the file when it arrived at Feltham suggested that Stewart had been trouble-free since January 1999. That had not, of course, been the case. But a number of witnesses made the point that young offenders can change far quicker than adults, and for that reason the focus tends to be on their current behaviour, not on how they have behaved in the past. So it is possible that anyone looking at Stewart's security file could have concluded that he posed no immediate risk to others because it was assumed – incorrectly – that he had not been in trouble for over a year.

30.19 One of the problems facing those responsible for vetting security files was that there were no guidelines about when a warning about a prisoner should be passed on to his unit. So different officers might have had different views about whether a prisoner posed such a risk that a warning about him should be passed on. Moreover, Mr Comber made the point that at that time there was no system in place in the Security Department for identifying which prisoners posed a threat to staff or other inmates. It was geared to checking what charges prisoners were facing and which prisoners should receive category A status. But Mr Benford had been able to identify Stewart as a source of potential danger. All things considered, it is much more likely that, despite Stewart's apparent unproblematic behaviour for some time, any officer in the Security Department reading his file after 7 February should have done what Mr Benford did on 12 January – and warned Stewart's unit that he was someone who needed to be watched.

30.20 Why was that not done? The conclusion must be that no-one looked at Stewart's security file when he came back from Hindley some time after 7 February. That may have been because of the staffing pressures within Feltham's Security Department at the time. There was no security collator in post until James Ferguson arrived on 14 February, and the lack of staff elsewhere in the establishment meant that staff were often cross-deployed from the Security Department to help out. It was so bad that one day in early February the department had to close down altogether. There was no system in place to ensure that all incoming security files were vetted. And the absence of any system for monitoring whether they were being vetted, as they should have been, meant that management did not pick up on the fact that there must have been some security files which were just not being read. Regrettably Stewart's was one of them. That would explain why Stewart's name was not on the list of dangerous prisoners kept on a board in the Security Department.

30.21 But it would not have taken a member of staff long to vet the security files of those incoming prisoners who had them. "New numbers" did not have security files at all. The security files of "in and outs" did not normally get to the Security Department if they had arrived with the prisoners. They would remain in reception until the prisoners left. The security files of returnees did not have to be vetted carefully, because they should have been vetted when they had first arrived at Feltham, and so they only had to be checked to see whether anything significant had happened in the few hours they had been away from Feltham. So really the only security files which had to be vetted with care were those of transferees and prisoners who had had security files opened on them since the last time they came to Feltham.

30.22 What would have happened if Stewart's security file had been looked at when he came back to Feltham for the last time? That is not difficult to answer. On Stewart's first visit to Feltham, Mr Benford had thought it appropriate to ask the senior officer on Lapwing to read the file for himself. It is reasonable to assume that the officer in charge of Swallow would have been told what was in his security file. That would – or at any rate should – have resulted in a close watch being kept on him while he was on Swallow. It might even have resulted in him being put in a single cell.

Stewart's core record

30.23 The security file was not the only file relating to an incoming prisoner which staff in the Security Department were supposed to look at. They also had to go to Custody Administration to look at the prisoner's core record. They had to "flick through" it to see if anything caught the eye. To show that they had looked at it, they had to mark it with the letters "SV" – meaning "security vetted" – and put the date on it with their initials. That, at any rate, was Mr Comber's evidence.

30.24 Stewart's current core record was opened at Hindley on 23 December 1999. It would have come with him when he returned to Feltham for the last time. But it does not look as if it was looked at by staff from the Security Department then. It did not bear any of the markings which it should have had if it had been vetted. Someone wrote "9/3" inside the back cover of the folder containing Stewart's *main prison file*, but that could not have meant that Stewart's *core record* had been vetted, which was something Mr Comber thought was possible. Apart from the fact that the annotation was on the cover of a different folder, it did not include the letters "SV" nor was it initialled. And "9/3" could have meant anything: it certainly does not necessarily refer to 9 March, let alone 9 March 2000, although that was the day after one of Stewart's court appearances.

30.25 What would have happened if Stewart's core record had been looked at? There is no reason to suppose that it did not contain then what it contains now. It was not particularly bulky, and anyone "flicking through" it would have seen two recent prisoner security information sheets on Stewart which had been printed out at Hindley from its 4x4 system on 7 January and 22 January – no doubt in anticipation of Stewart's visits to Feltham on 10 January and 24 January. They said that he was violent, that he had the potential to escape, and that he was an exceptional risk – even though what he was at risk of was not stated. Moreover, it contained the three prisoner escort records relating to his three journeys to Feltham. I do not say that anyone looking at these documents should necessarily have thought that the staff on Swallow should have been warned about him. But the documents contained enough to make anyone looking at them realise that looking at Stewart's security file was particularly important. So if his core record had been looked at, it is unlikely that his security file would have slipped through the net.

Stewart's warrants

30.26 The warrants authorising Stewart's detention on the charges he was facing in London were in his custodial documents file. They showed that his charges were for offences under the Malicious Communications Act 1988 and the Protection from Harassment Act 1997. The file was kept in Custody Administration, and when staff from the Security Department went there to look at a prisoner's core record, they were supposed to look at the warrants as well. That was also Mr Comber's evidence. Had that been done in Stewart's case, it would have been known that his correspondence had to be monitored under Chapter 2 of PSO 4400. That message did not get through to staff on Swallow who would have been responsible for reading all Stewart's letters. It should have done.

Stewart's main prison file

30.27 No-one suggested that the staff in the Security Department at Feltham would look at prisoners' main prison files. I can understand why. Stewart's was extremely bulky, and the documents and files within it were not in any particular order. If his was not out of the ordinary, they would have taken far too long to check. But Stewart's contained many useful nuggets of information which were not in his security file. The wing files which had been opened during his previous sentences and his adjudication records were in it. Anyone reading them would have had a much fuller picture of how he had played up in the past. One can only speculate about whether Stewart's management on Swallow would have been any different if it had been looked at, but it would undoubtedly have complemented his security file.

The flow of information generally

30.28 The failure of the Security Department to pass the warnings about Stewart in the prisoner escort records and his security file on to Swallow is just one of a series of problems with the flow of information within Feltham. Another related to the movement of prisoners' wing files, and the misfiling of Stewart's temporary wing file in Custody Administration. And in the next chapter we look at the failure to tell staff on Swallow about the charges which Stewart was facing. But problems relating to the flow of information at Feltham had been around for some time. In July 1997, a prisoner had hanged himself in his cell after the unit he had been on had not been told of his history of self-harm. And in July 1998, a prisoner had taken his cellmate hostage after the unit he had been on had not been told of his history of mental illness and that he had always been placed in a cell on his own in the past. I refer to that incident in greater detail in chapter 49 since it has implications for cell-sharing. But these incidents show that the need to iron out deficiencies in the flow of information at Feltham had been apparent for a good few years.

30.29 The problems with the flow of information had been picked up by the Inspectorate. The report following its inspection of Feltham in 1996 recommended that "a strategy should be developed to enable previous convictions, pre-sentence reports and other information to be made available to staff". And the report following its visit to Feltham in 1999 noted that there were still "no clear protocols to enable information to be cascaded to staff". The reason for that may have been that Feltham was not pressed by Prison Service headquarters to do anything about it. One of the recommendations made in the report of the Coonan Inquiry following the death of Christopher Edwards was that "the Governor, the Senior Medical Officer and the Senior Probation Officer should review periodically the arrangements which govern the receipt and transfer of information which has been received from outside the prison". That applied to information received from other Prison Service establishments just as much as it did to information received from outside agencies, and it covered the internal transfer of information once it had been received within the establishment. But this recommendation had not been implemented by the time of Zahid's murder – primarily because it was thought that if an establishment had shortcomings in this area, they would be picked up by the Prison Service's Standards Audit Unit when it audited an establishment's compliance with the Prison Service's operating standards.

30.30 I am not convinced about that. Certainly the team from the Standards Audit Unit which carried out the audit at Feltham in November and December 1999 identified some issues relating to the transfer of information. For example, they noted that no attempts were being made to identify those prisoners who had been convicted of offences to which the requirements of PSO 4400 applied, and so relevant information on that issue was not being passed on to the units. But they did not pick up on any problems with the flow of information from the Security Department or with prisoners' wing files not accompanying prisoners as they went from one unit to another. There was, and is, little substitute for an establishment having its own protocols for the transfer of information and carrying out its own review of whether they are working.

30.31 What would have happened if this recommendation had been implemented? We can only speculate. There is no certainty that Feltham would have carried out such a review, or that the review would have identified the problems which existed, or that any instructions given to staff as a result of the review would have been followed. But if Feltham's response to an instruction from Prison Service headquarters to review its practices relating to the flow of information had been an adequate one, it is certainly possible that systems would have been in place to ensure that:

- the Security Department would have told Swallow about Stewart, rather than Swallow having to rely on the contents of his temporary wing file

- his temporary wing file would have been with Swallow when he first arrived there, rather than arriving on Swallow much later when officers would be less likely to read it because they had seen how he behaved

- Swallow would have been informed that he had been charged with offences to which Chapter 2 of PSO 4400 applied, with the result that his correspondence would have been monitored.

Chapter 31: The clues in Stewart's correspondence

Notifying the establishment

31.1 By the time Stewart arrived at Feltham for the first time, he had already been charged with offences under the Protection from Harassment Act 1997. That triggered the application of Chapter 2 of PSO 4400, which meant that all his outgoing letters had to be monitored. As we have seen, that did not happen at Hindley while he was there. It did not happen at Feltham either. It is necessary to find out why, and what would have happened if it had been done.

31.2 PSO 4400 envisaged that establishments would be notified by the police when a prisoner had been charged with an offence under the 1997 Act by form POL1 – a police form used to notify prisons or prisoner escorts of prisoners who posed an exceptional risk of some kind. But the POL1 was about to be phased out, and in 1999 it was replaced by the prisoner escort record. PSO 4400 contemplated that from then on the prisoner escort record would be the means by which establishments were notified that Chapter 2 of PSO 4400 had been triggered in the case of a particular prisoner.

31.3 So when Stewart first came to Feltham on 10 January 2000, the prisoner escort record which had been generated at Hindley for that visit should have referred to the fact that Stewart had been charged with an offence under the 1997 Act and that the provisions of Chapter 2 of PSO 4400 applied. It did not do that. That may have been an accident of timing. It will be recalled that Hindley's Discipline Office only heard on 7 January that Stewart had been charged with offences under the 1997 Act, and it was on the same day that the relevant section in the prisoner escort record was completed in Hindley's Security Department. Maybe Hindley's Security Department had not by then been informed by the Discipline Office that Chapter 2 of PSO 4400 had been triggered in Stewart's case. But that does not explain why no reference was made to that in either of the subsequent prisoner escort records generated at Hindley for Stewart's visits to Feltham on 24 January and 7 February. Either Hindley's Discipline Office did not tell the Security Department that Chapter 2 of PSO 4400 had been triggered in Stewart's case, or Hindley's Security Department did not act on the information. Either way, Feltham was not informed that Stewart was subject to Chapter 2 of PSO 4400 in the way which PSO 4400 envisaged.

31.4 But PSO 4400 had foreseen that this might happen. It recognised that the POL1 might not arrive with the prisoner – and by implication after the POL1 had been phased out, that the prisoner escort record might not refer to the prisoner's status under Chapter 2 of PSO 4400.

It acknowledged that the warrants which arrived at the establishment with prisoners would, or at least should, identify whether they had been charged with an offence under the 1997 Act, and it required the establishment to get further information from the police – no doubt, the names and addresses of the persons who prisoners were supposed to have harassed, so that any letters which they wrote to them could be stopped. The warrants which would have accompanied Stewart when he arrived at Feltham from court on 11 January, 25 January, 8 February, 7 March and 8 March, and those which accompanied him when he arrived at Feltham from Hindley on 24 January and 7 February, all stated that he had been charged with offences under the 1997 Act.

Checking the warrants and notifying the units

31.5   PSO 4400 did not identify where in the establishment the outgoing letters of someone subject to Chapter 2 of PSO 4400 should be monitored. That was left to individual establishments to decide. A Governor's Order issued by Feltham's then governor, Clive Welsh, on 14 January 1999 shows that responsibility for monitoring the correspondence was down to staff in the unit where the prisoner was.* But who was supposed to notify the unit that a particular prisoner's outgoing letters had to be monitored? That depended – in part at least – on who was actually supposed to check the warrants for charges under the 1997 Act when they arrived.

31.6   It was the responsibility of the senior officer on duty in reception to check the warrants of an incoming prisoner. They had to do that to ensure that the prisoner could be lawfully detained. But if they came across warrants which showed that the prisoner had been charged with offences under the 1997 Act, were they supposed to notify the unit about that? Or was that down to Custody Administration, who would be using the warrants the next day to note on the prisoner's core record the charges he faced and when he was next due in court? Or was it down to staff in the Security Department, who would be looking at

---

* Some of the text is missing from the bottom of one page – or perhaps the top of the next page – in the copy of the Order provided to the Inquiry. Mr Welsh believes that a complete page is missing, but the pagination of the Order and the numbering of the paragraphs suggest otherwise. It looks as if the text was not missing from the original, but rather that it was copied in such a way as to erase a couple of lines. But what remains in the text makes it clear where responsibility for monitoring a prisoner's correspondence lay.

the warrants when they went to Custody Administration to look at the prisoner's core record?

31.7 Mr Welsh's Order of 14 January 1999 is not as clear as it might have been on the topic. It referred to the staff on reception being informed by the police or the courts if a prisoner was subject to Chapter 2 of PSO 4400, but it did not say that they had to check the warrants for information of that kind, or what they were to do with the information once they got it. It referred to Custody Administration ensuring that the information was recorded on the Local Inmate Database System and on the prisoner's core record, and notifying the Chief Probation Officer in the area where the prisoner was to be discharged about it. But it did not say that it was down to Custody Administration to notify the prisoner's unit that his correspondence had to be monitored. And it did not refer to what staff in the Security Department had to do at all.

31.8 One thing is clear. No-one suggested that the senior officer on duty in reception had to look out for warrants which showed that the prisoner had been charged with offences under the 1997 Act, despite a passage in the instructions relating to prisoner escort records which implied that this was one of the roles of reception staff. After all, they would have had enough to contend with going through the reception processes with the many prisoners who came through reception. Indeed, the witnesses who had worked in reception asserted that they knew nothing then of Chapter 2 of PSO 4400 or its requirements. I am not inclined to disbelieve them.

31.9 But if reception staff did not have a role to play in checking the warrants for this purpose, who did? Staff in Custody Administration or staff in the Security Department? Mr Welsh and Mr Byrd said it was down to staff in the Security Department, and that was what the principal officer in charge of reception thought. Others thought differently. Some said staff in the Security Department had no role to play in the identification of those prisoners who were charged with offences under the 1997 Act or in the notification of them to the units. One witness thought that responsibility for identifying such prisoners lay with Custody Administration. The fact of the matter is that confusion reigned. It is not possible now to tell whose job it was to identify those prisoners who were subject to Chapter 2 of PSO 4400 or whose job it was to notify the units of the prisoners whose correspondence had to be monitored.

The lack of any system

31.10 The lack of clarity arose because the initiative outlined in Mr Welsh's Order of 14 January 1999 was never taken forward. Chapter 2 of PSO 4400 was described by Helen Clayton-Hoar, the Acting Head of Operations, as a "dead letter", and Mick Cowan, the new Head of Operations, said that its implementation in 2000 had to start "from scratch". Most senior managers had a sense that a system for monitoring correspondence under Chapter 2 of PSO 4400 was operating – or at least were unaware that such a system was not operating – but they had little idea of what was happening on the ground. That was because nothing was. Indeed, that was the conclusion reached by the team from the Prison Service's Standards Audit Unit who visited Feltham between 22 November and 10 December 1999. Its report – which was accompanied by an action plan calling for the implementation of a proper system for identifying those prisoners who were subject to Chapter 2 of PSO 4400 and notifying those responsible for monitoring their correspondence – was received by Feltham on 17 January 2000, though senior managers had been told of the team's findings early in December 1999.

The response to the findings of the audit

31.11 The action plan had to be approved by the Area Manager. His approval did not come through until February 2000, and the deadline which the action plan laid down for the implementation of a new system was 31 March 2000. Mr Cowan, who had returned to Feltham at the end of January 2000 after a year or so at another establishment, was responsible for its implementation. Some preliminary work had already been done on Mr Comber's initiative prior to Mr Cowan's arrival.

31.12 It was on 6 April 2000 that a proper system for implementing Chapter 2 of PSO 4400 came on stream. That was when Mr Clifford issued a Governor's Order identifying where responsibility lay for ensuring that Chapter 2 of PSO 4400 was complied with. In short, it was for staff in reception to identify from the warrants the prisoners to whom Chapter 2 of PSO 4400 applied, and to stamp their wing files to that effect. It was for staff in the Security Department to notify the units which prisoners had to have their correspondence monitored – presumably they got that information from the warrants they looked at in Custody Administration – and to give them the name and address of the person who the prisoner should not contact, which they had got from the police. And it was for staff in Custody Administration to enter on the Local Inmate Database

System and on the prisoner's core record the fact that they were subject to Chapter 2 of PSO 4400. If this Order had been in place a few weeks earlier, and if it had been complied with, the letters which Stewart wanted posted would have been read by staff on Swallow.

31.13 I acknowledge that this Order was issued only six days after the deadline set out in the action plan. But we still need to ask why it took getting on for four months for Feltham to implement a proper system to ensure that the correspondence of prisoners who were charged with offences under the 1997 Act was monitored. It is no excuse to say that those responsible for its implementation were working to the deadline set out in the action plan. The audit team's finding that there was no system in place was one of the findings described in the report as "significant". Temporary measures of a basic kind could have been put in place almost immediately until something more sophisticated was devised. Nor was this as complex an exercise as both Mr Comber and Mr Cowan said it was. It was not rocket science. At its most basic level, all that had to be decided was who should check the warrants for charges under the 1997 Act, and who should tell the units which prisoners' correspondence had to be monitored. Even Mr Clifford acknowledged that things took too long. With characteristic understatement, he said that "there [was] a longer period of inaction there than [he] would have preferred".

31.14 But it would be wrong to criticise Mr Comber or Mr Cowan here. So far as Mr Comber was concerned, the issue was one for the Security Department only when a management decision had been made that staff in the department had a role to play in the system. In any event, Mr Comber himself was relatively new to the department, having become its manager in November 1999, and he had accumulated a good deal of time off in the first few months of 2000. As for Mr Cowan, he was having to get to grips with his new job and the very many issues which came across the desk of the Head of Operations. The real problem was not so much the delay in implementing a proper system once its absence had been identified, but rather the fact that nothing had previously been done to carry Mr Welsh's initiative forward and that the absence of a proper system had not thereafter been picked up.

What would have happened?

31.15 Some of the letters Stewart wrote while on Swallow were retrieved by the police from the people to whom they were sent. But Stewart probably wrote many others, and in any event there is no way of knowing whether any of them would have been expressed in the same way had he known they were going to be read. Under the system introduced in April 2000, Stewart would have known that they were going to be read, since it said that prisoners had to be told their correspondence would be monitored. But as I said when commenting on his letters from Hindley, Stewart continued to make racist references in the letters he sent after he had murdered Zahid, even though he was likely to have expected that these letters would be read. Perhaps the benevolent attitude adopted to the letter which had been intercepted on 12 January made him think that even if his letters were read some of them would not be stopped.

31.16 I put to one side a flurry of letters dated 20 March 2000 – the day before the murder – found in cell 38 afterwards. Since they had not been handed in, there would not have been an opportunity for staff to read them. But if they had read the letters written while he was on Swallow which the police subsequently retrieved from the people he had sent them to, they would have seen a plethora of racist comments and on occasions threats to use violence in order to secure his transfer to another prison. I acknowledge that what had triggered the need to read Stewart's letters was the allegation that he had been harassing the chatline operator, and that the purpose of reading them would have been to see whether he was continuing to harass her. But they could hardly have ignored what else they would have read. I summarise the letters in the order in which they appeared in the Inquiry Bundle with the Bundle page number – but they were not necessarily sent in that order because many of them were undated:

- B1924. Stewart wrote of his dislike of Feltham. He said that he would do "whatever it takes" to get "shipped out" including "damaging cells, people, screws, hunger strikes, hostages". He added that he "may go as far as Travis did but I doubt it". He signed the letter off with a drawing of a cross which resembled a Nazi medal with a swastika in the centre.

- B1936. Stewart wrote: "There's too many nigger's in ere, fuckin 3 quarters of the jail, it's like Planet of the Apes (Ha ha) 'Congo'." He signed the letter: "Love Hitler (ha)".

- B1938. Stewart wrote that he was "padded up wid Hitler and Salman Rushdie" and was "thinking up a way to rid these egg & spoons".* He also commented on the "funny nicknames… nigger's ad".

---

* Presumably rhyming slang for "coons".

- B1948. Stewart again likened Feltham to "Planet of the Apes", and he spoke of going sick to get a "shipout".

- B1952. Stewart wrote: "It's all nig nog down ere", and he referred to "Ainsley Harriot" on the servery.

- B2005. This was the letter in which Stewart spoke of having sent visiting orders for Adolf Hitler and others. He spoke of his liking for films renowned for violence. Most important of all, he expressly referred to killing his cellmate in order to get transferred to another establishment. His actual words were: "If I don't get bail on the 7th, I will take xtreme measures to get shipped out, kill me fuckin padmate if I have to, bleach me sheets & pillowcase white & make a Ku Klux Klan outfit & walk out me pad wiv a flaming crucifix & change the [cross] on me ed to… [a swastika]…" He added the name Stephen Lawrence just before his signature.

- B2017. Stewart again referred to Feltham as "Planet of the Apes" and referred to his cellmate as "a Packi".

31.17 Again, the point should not need to be spelt out. Had the letters still been written if Stewart thought that they were going to be read by prison staff, and had they been read as they should have been, the threat he posed to his cellmate, especially one he regarded as "a Packi", could not have been plainer. Not only should he not have shared a cell with someone from an ethnic minority. He should not have shared a cell at all.

Monitoring Stewart's telephone calls

31.18 PSO 4400 required prisoners facing charges under the 1997 Act to have their outgoing telephone calls monitored as well as their correspondence. Although Mr Welsh's Order required units to do that, the missing part of the Order means that we do not know whether he said how that was to be done. Presumably what was contemplated was the recording of all such telephone calls so that they could be listened to subsequently.

31.19 As it was, the state of Feltham's monitoring equipment at the time meant that this could not be done. The acquisition of new equipment was discussed at a meeting of the Security Committee at the end of January 2000. What was contemplated was equipment which could be moved to the unit of any person whose telephone calls had to be monitored. We do not know whether that was done, but no-one suggested that

Stewart's outgoing telephone calls were ever monitored while he was on Swallow. Of course, we do not know whether Stewart said anything in his outgoing telephone calls which might have caused concern if they had been listened to. But Feltham was not alone in having defective equipment at the time. The problem was a common one across the prison estate. So this is not an area in which Feltham's management should be singled out for criticism.

Chapter 32: The personal officers in Swallow

The personal officer scheme at Feltham

32.1 Prisoners have many concerns. They need to be able to raise them with someone – preferably someone who they have confidence in. After all, you tend to open up more with people you have a rapport with. If Zahid had felt able to talk candidly to staff, maybe he would have told them of his concern about continuing to share a cell with Stewart. The scheme which could be said to foster closer relationships of the kind which might encourage prisoners to be more forthcoming about their concerns is the personal officer scheme.

32.2 Personal officer schemes were introduced in young offender institutions in 1988. According to a new set of Prison Service operating standards issued in 1994, the idea behind such schemes was for prisoners to have ready access to a specified officer for advice, guidance and help with personal problems. We know from the Inspectorate's report following its visit to Feltham in 1996 that a personal officer scheme had been introduced at Feltham by then. But the role of the personal officer at Feltham was not spelt out until the then Governor, Mr Welsh, issued a Governor's Order on the topic in January 1999.

32.3 Mr Welsh noted that it was not easy to carry out personal officer work in some parts of the establishment. He was referring to prisoners who would not be remaining for very long at Feltham, either because they were unconvicted and might be released imminently or because they were likely to be allocated to another young offender institution to serve the rest of their sentence. But he wrote that the personal officer scheme had a number of elements as a minimum. Apart from acting as role models, the "basics" which personal officers should do included learning about a prisoner's personal history, engaging him in conversation, and providing him with support. Mr Welsh stressed that personal officers had to ensure that prisoners could approach them in confidence and be confident that their problems would be handled discreetly. Personal officers had to make comments in the prisoners' wing files, recording positive as well as negative behaviour.

32.4 The Order said that a guide/handbook for personal officers was being prepared. If it was, it did not get to Swallow, and the Inquiry has never seen it. And although the minutes of a meeting of Feltham's senior management team in October 1999 referred to job descriptions for personal officers being in production, they did not get to Swallow either and the Inquiry has likewise never seen them. So officers would only have known what personal work involved if they had been trained on how to carry it out, or been told by senior officers on the unit what to do, or if they had watched what more experienced officers did.

32.5 At Feltham, personal officers looked after a number of specified cells. They were the personal officers for the prisoners who happened to be in those cells at the time. That had two disadvantages. First, if an inmate moved out of his cell into one which was not in the group of cells covered by his personal officer, he would have to have another personal officer. The confidence which a prisoner may have had in his personal officer would have to be built up again. Secondly, cellmates would have the same personal officer. That was unlikely to result in any conflict of interest on the part of the personal officer – though that possibility cannot be excluded – but it could result in an inmate being less candid with his personal officer about any concerns he had about his cellmate. However, there was one feature about Feltham's scheme which was a good idea. Each cell had two personal officers to cater for the absence of one of them if off duty or on leave. In that way, there was likely to be at least one of them on duty to whom the prisoner could turn. But even that was not guaranteed. There was nothing to suggest that their shift patterns and leave were co-ordinated to ensure that at least one of them was there every day.

Stewart's and Zahid's personal officers

32.6 The two personal officers responsible for the prisoners in cell 38 on Swallow were Claire Bigger and Lee Edmundson. They claimed to have had a narrow view of their role. They said they had never seen Mr Welsh's Order. They thought that personal officers were no more than a prisoner's first point of contact if he wanted to raise something. They did not think that they needed to familiarise themselves with the prisoners they were responsible for, or to see how they were getting on. So they did not try to get to know Stewart or Zahid better. And they never looked at their wing files or made entries in them, any more than they would have done for any other prisoner. That was why there were no entries by them in either Stewart's or Zahid's wing files. It was also why the absence of Stewart's temporary wing file for four weeks was not noticed.

32.7 Other personal officers on Swallow professed to have a different view of their responsibilities. Between them, they said that they would read the wing files of the prisoners for whom they were responsible to find out about their backgrounds and what had happened to them while they had been in prison. They would try to speak to them regularly, and look out for them when they were on association. And they would make entries in their wing files – usually once a week – even if nothing noteworthy had happened. But it has to be said it was easy for them to say that. The way they monitored the prisoners for whom they were responsible was not under scrutiny.

32.8 It is too much of a coincidence that the two officers who were the personal officers for Stewart and Zahid took one view of their role, and that most of the other officers on Swallow who were asked about the role of personal officers took another. Either Miss Bigger and Mr Edmundson have minimised the role of the personal officer in order to explain away their failure to get to know Stewart and Zahid, or read their wing files, or make entries about them in them. Or they genuinely did not know what personal officer work involved – perhaps in common with other officers on Swallow, who are now saying they took steps to familiarise themselves with the prisoners they were responsible for because they fear they will be criticised if they admit to thinking that the scheme was as narrow as Miss Bigger and Mr Edmundson claim to have thought it was.

Training, instruction and monitoring

Training

32.9 No local training for personal officer work took place at Feltham. The Inspectorate's report following its visit to Feltham in 1999 said that it was "unclear… as to how it was intended to provide training and support" for personal officers. And the action plan produced by the team from the Prison Service's Standards Audit Unit early in 2000 called for *all* residential officers to be trained in personal officer work. Some of the more recent recruits, such as Miss Bigger who joined the Prison Service in 1998, would have had a session on personal officer work in their initial training, but that would have been linked to sentence planning, which was not happening at Feltham. Special courses on personal officer work were available for more experienced officers, such as Mr Edmundson who joined the Prison Service in 1995, but those who tended to go on them were officers who worked in prisons where a personal officer scheme was regarded as essential, such as a prison with a unit for prisoners serving life sentences. A local prison with a high turnover of prisoners like Feltham, where the population of the prison could change within a few weeks, was far less likely to send their officers on such courses. The upshot was that neither Miss Bigger nor Mr Edmundson ever had any dedicated training on personal officer work. That is what they told the Inquiry, and it was borne out by the evidence on what training was available.

Instruction

32.10 Whether officers were told by the senior officers in charge of their units how they were to carry out their duties as personal officers was very much a hit-and-miss affair. It was up to the senior officers to decide what they should tell their staff. But such evidence as there was suggested that if a new officer was not told what to do initially, they would not be told later. That is because it was assumed that once an officer had worked on a unit, they would know what to do.

Monitoring

32.11 It was for the senior officer in charge of the unit to check that personal officer work was being carried out. The only evidence of how that was to be done was for the senior officer to check whether personal officers were making entries in the wing files for the prisoners for whom they were responsible. But that could not have been taking place on Swallow, because otherwise the lack of entries in Stewart's and Zahid's wing files would have been picked up. Indeed, one senior officer accepted that if a wing file was looked at, the presence of some entries in it might lead to the conclusion that personal officer work was being carried out, even though the entries may have been made by other officers. The principal officers in charge of clusters of three units did not apparently pick up on the deficiencies in the monitoring by senior officers of the work of personal officers. So it looks as if little attention had been paid to what the Inspectorate had said following its visit to Feltham in 1996:

> "Managers should monitor and supervise to ensure staff make regular contact with inmates, complete the work that should be done, make accurate notes, and keep up to date with assessing the risks, needs, and progress of the young men."

A scheme "in name only"

32.12 All of this suggests that making the personal officer scheme work was very low on Feltham's list of priorities. Indeed, most people were candid enough to accept that. The Head of Feltham B thought that Feltham was not working to best practice in the area. Others were more forthright. One senior officer said that personal officer work was not being done at all. One of the principal officers agreed, and said that the scheme existed "in name only". Even Mr Byrd, the governor responsible for a group of units including Swallow, who tended on many topics to minimise the problems which Feltham faced, acknowledged that work was needed to ensure that the scheme operated to a better standard. Nothing was done to improve things prior to Zahid's murder, except to allocate personal officers to specified cells rather than particular prisoners, and we have seen the disadvantages of that.

32.13 So I do not think Miss Bigger and Mr Edmundson were exceptional in not carrying out properly the duties of personal officer. What they were doing was probably no less than what many other officers were doing at Feltham. But I am sceptical about their assertion that they did not know what personal officer work was supposed to involve – at least at its most basic level. They may not have known about the need to make regular entries in prisoners' wing files, but they should have realised that personal officer work was an example of the "jailcraft" which prison officers speak so proudly of. You should not need to be told that if you are the personal officer for prisoners in a particular cell, you should try to get to know them so that there is a familiar face if they want to raise something which is troubling them.

32.14 I have not overlooked the many hours prisoners spent in their cells which gave personal officers less time to spend with the people they were responsible for. The only time personal officers could talk to them was during association, and personal officers had to supervise the other prisoners as well then. Nor have I ignored the fact that there was no profiled time for personal officer work. It had to be fitted in with other duties. But I do not believe that Swallow was so understaffed, and the work of prison officers so arduous, that time could not have been found for the few minutes a day it would have taken to speak to the handful of prisoners for whom Miss Bigger and Mr Edmundson were responsible. It seems they were affected by the general malaise at Feltham – that personal officer work was not seen as something which needed to be done.

32.15 The fact of the matter is that if personal officer work was going to be effective at Feltham at all, Swallow was one of the units where it ought to have been working properly. Swallow was, after all, a unit for convicted prisoners, who were settled and looking for employment. It was not like a remand unit with a high turnover of unconvicted prisoners, where staff were constantly having to deal with getting prisoners to and from

CHAPTER 32: THE PERSONAL OFFICERS IN SWALLOW

reception for appearances in court. If the scheme was not working on Swallow, it was not going to work anywhere at Feltham.

32.16 Two final points should be made. I said at the beginning of this chapter that effective personal officer work might have resulted in Zahid confiding in a member of staff about why he was uncomfortable about continuing to share a cell with Stewart. But it looks as if one of the officers on Swallow, Ross Farmer, did get to know Zahid reasonably well. In his statement to the Inquiry, he said that Zahid would come and talk to him "openly and honestly" during association. He believes that if Zahid had a problem, Zahid would have raised it with him. Mr Skinner told the CRE much the same thing. But Zahid never told them about any problem he had with Stewart. So it may be that even if Miss Bigger and Mr Edmundson had worked at getting to know Zahid, he would not have confided in them about Stewart.

32.17 The second point is that whether or not Zahid would have confided in them, effective personal officer work might have had another highly significant result. It should have been the prompt for Mr Edmundson to look at Stewart's temporary wing file.* If he had done that, he would have seen Mr Martindale's warnings about Stewart's dangerousness and Miss Hogg's comments about his racism. His racism should have resulted in him not sharing a cell with a prisoner from an ethnic minority unless they were demonstrably good friends. His dangerousness should have prompted thought being given to whether he should share a cell at all.

---

* But not Miss Bigger. The last time she was on duty on Swallow before the attack on Zahid was on 8 March. It was only on the previous evening that Stewart's temporary wing file had arrived in the unit, and it had gone with Stewart to court by the time Miss Bigger came on duty the next day.

Chapter 33: Healthcare screening at Feltham

Stewart's healthcare screening

33.1 Stewart should have been seen by a healthcare worker whenever he went to Feltham. And he should have been seen by a doctor when he went to Feltham as a transferee from Hindley. Those occasions would have been an opportunity for his medical record to be reviewed. But it does not look as if anyone looked at his medical record. So no-one at Feltham knew about Stewart's troubling behaviour at Hindley in the latter part of 1997, or his claims in April 1998 and January 1999 to have swallowed a razor blade and a battery, or Mr Kinealy's diagnosis of him at Altcourse. Why was that? And if his medical record had been reviewed, what action would have been taken?

Screening by a healthcare worker

33.2 As we saw in chapter 18, both transferees and returnees had to be seen by a healthcare worker in reception when they arrived in prison. The completion of the first reception health screen questionnaire was not required. They only had to be asked if there was anything which was causing them anxiety or concern. If prisoners were presenting with symptoms of anxiety or concern, the healthcare worker had to assess whether they were at risk of suicide or self-harm. Those national requirements were incorporated into a local protocol at Feltham. The protocol in force when Stewart came to Feltham was dated 23 June 1999 and had, like its two predecessors, been introduced by Dick Cronk, the Head of Healthcare at Feltham at the time. It said that a note had to be made on form F2169A that this more streamlined screening had taken place.

33.3 Stewart was undoubtedly seen by a healthcare worker on reception when he returned to Feltham from court on 7 March. He was recorded on his F2169A to have been "fit and well". The form was stapled to the front cover of his medical record and was therefore apparent whenever the record was opened. However, that was the only entry in Stewart's F2169A for any of the three occasions when he arrived at Feltham from Hindley as a transferee – 10 and 24 January, and 7 February – or for any of the five occasions when he went back to Feltham from court as a returnee – 11 and 25 January, 8 February, and 7 and 8 March. At first blush, that suggests that the only occasion on which he was seen by a healthcare worker was on 7 March.

33.4 But appearances can be deceptive. The evidence of one of the healthcare workers was that she would not necessarily make a note on a prisoner's F2169A if she saw him in reception. In the case of a returnee, she would only make a note if there was something which was causing the prisoner concern. On the other hand, neither transferees nor returnees were seen by a healthcare worker at Feltham as a matter of course, even though they should have been. A principal officer who worked on reception said that returnees would not be seen by a healthcare worker on reception unless something untoward had happened during the day, and another healthcare worker said that she would only see returnees if specifically requested to do so.

33.5 The fact that Stewart was seen, and a note made in his F2169A, when he came into reception on 7 March as a returnee, when nothing untoward appeared to have happened that day and he was apparently fit and well, does not fit into the general picture at all. But if Stewart's F2169A was representative of other prisoners' forms, transferees and returnees were sometimes being seen by healthcare workers without a record being made of that in their F2169A. And sometimes they were not being seen at all. That was because there was a shortage of healthcare staff, and "new numbers" were being given priority when it came to screening by a healthcare worker. This problem was picked up – to some extent at any rate – in the course of the standards and security audit at Feltham in November and December 1999. The team noted that "prisoners who have had a change in status are sometimes located on the wings without being assessed by a healthcare worker". The action plan which came out of the audit imposed a deadline of June 2000 for ensuring that all prisoners were seen by a healthcare worker.

Assessment by a doctor

33.6 Transferees also had to be seen by a doctor within 24 hours of their arrival. But as we saw in chapter 18, returnees did not have to be seen by one, provided that they had been under prison escort while they had been away. However, if their circumstances had changed – in other words, if they had been committed to the Crown Court for trial, or if they had changed from being an unconvicted to a convicted prisoner or from an unsentenced to a sentenced one – they too had to be seen by the doctor within 24 hours of their return. But a full examination of their physical and mental state was not required. What was required was an assessment of their physical and psychiatric health, with particular regard to indications of recent substance abuse and the potential for self-harm. These national requirements were also incorporated into Feltham's local protocol, save that another category of prisoners who had to be seen by the doctor within 24 hours – apart from "new numbers" and transferees – was described as "off bails". The Inquiry assumed that this referred to prisoners who had arrived at Feltham as "new numbers" or transferees, who had subsequently been released on bail, but who returned to Feltham after their bail had been revoked.

33.7 Stewart did not have to be assessed by a doctor on any of the occasions he went back to Feltham from court as a returnee as his circumstances had not changed. But he should have been assessed by a doctor within 24 hours of his arrival on the three occasions he came to Feltham from Hindley as a transferee. Had he been assessed, the doctor would have made an entry about him in his medical record, and put his initials against Stewart's name in the medical reception register in which the names of all incoming prisoners were recorded. But there is no entry in Stewart's medical record showing that he was seen by a doctor on any of the three occasions he came to Feltham as a transferee. Nor do any doctor's initials appear against his name in the medical reception register for those dates. We can therefore be pretty sure that he was not seen by a doctor at all.

33.8 That may not have been a practical possibility on his first two visits to Feltham. The practice was for the doctor to see an incoming prisoner in the morning following his arrival, but on 11 January Stewart was taken to reception from Lapwing at 7.30 am, and although we do not know the time he was taken to reception from Osprey on 25 January, it was likely to have been relatively early. So he could not have been seen by a doctor at a time when the system was ready for him to be seen. As it was, a practice had grown up at Feltham that "in and outs" were simply not seen by the doctor – or by a healthcare worker for that matter. It is noteworthy that on two of the three occasions Stewart was an "in and out", that fact was recorded in the medical reception register. Those occasions were his first two visits to Feltham. Neither the national healthcare standard nor the local protocol exempted "in and outs" from healthcare screening. But why should an entry have been made in the medical reception register if it was not to have some effect? It is instructive to note that a new protocol introduced at Feltham after Zahid's murder required all transferees and returnees to be seen by a doctor within 24 hours of their arrival "without exception".

33.9 This partly explains why Stewart was not seen by a doctor on his third visit to Feltham. He was likely to have been regarded as an "in and out" when he arrived, because it was not known then that the Observation, Classification and Allocations Department at Feltham would decide the next day that he would be staying at Feltham. And on 8 February he was taken to reception from Kestrel at 7.00 am. So again he would not have been seen at the time when the system was geared up for him to be seen. But if Feltham's practice was for "in and outs" not to be seen by a doctor – which itself was not a practice sanctioned by the national healthcare standard – the additional problem was that there was no system for ensuring that prisoners who ceased to be "in and outs" and were to remain at Feltham would then be seen by the doctor. That may have been how Stewart slipped through the net. Alternatively, he may have slipped through because the medical reception register for 7 February did not describe him as an "in and out", even though that is how he would have been regarded at the time.

33.10 As it was, Stewart was by no means exceptional in not being seen by a doctor. Very few, if any, transferees or returnees were being seen by a doctor. Dr Stephen Jefferies, the lead GP in the practice providing medical services to Feltham, said he only saw limited numbers of them, and even then that was sporadic. Geoffrey Humphrey, who succeeded Mr Cronk as Head of Healthcare in September 1999, attributed that to the need to give priority to "new numbers" and the limited hours which doctors worked. I return to this issue in chapter 48, but the fact remains that Stewart was not the only transferee not to be seen by a doctor within 24 hours of his arrival at Feltham.

The review of Stewart's medical record

Review by a healthcare worker

33.11 The relevant healthcare standard – the one for prisoners other than "new numbers" – stated:

> "The [healthcare worker] will assemble and check the prisoner's healthcare record, court warrants (where applicable) and other available documentation which may assist in the screening and subsequent medical examination…"

So the healthcare worker had to "check" the medical records of transferees and returnees when they arrived at reception and assemble them for when the prisoners were to be seen by the doctor. "Checking" the medical records did not simply mean checking that they were there. Since the records to be assembled were those thought likely to "assist in the screening", they had to be looked at to see if there was anything relevant in them. But the local protocol at Feltham did not mention the requirement to review a prisoner's medical record as part of the screening process. We cannot tell whether that omission was deliberate. As we have seen, the local protocol required healthcare workers to make an entry in the prisoner's F2169A, which the protocol acknowledged was in his medical record. So the local protocol at least contemplated that the medical record would be opened. But whether Mr Cronk had actually intended healthcare workers to review the medical record is another matter.

33.12 Whatever Mr Cronk may have had in mind, Dr Jefferies thought that healthcare workers ought to review the medical records. Mr Humphrey thought otherwise. In the circumstances it is unsurprising that practice was haphazard. The healthcare worker who gave evidence on the topic, Wendy Prior, said that she only sometimes reviewed the medical record. And if she did, it would only be a cursory review to see whether the prisoner had had any recent problems. Such a review might not have involved going any further than the first reception health screen questionnaire. Having said that, there would have been only five documents on top of Mr Kinealy's note about Stewart at the time, and Mrs Prior said that if a healthcare worker had had time to review the record, it should not have been missed. As it is, the Inquiry was not able to identify the healthcare worker who saw Stewart on 7 March. We do not know whether they looked at his medical record, and if they did, whether they saw Mr Kinealy's note.

Review by a doctor

33.13 Neither the relevant healthcare standard nor the local protocol said that the doctor *had* to review the medical records of transferees and those returnees whose circumstances had changed. But good medical practice suggests that it should have been done. Indeed, Dr Jefferies said that he regarded a consideration of a prisoner's medical record as critical to a proper assessment of the prisoner, and if an inmate was brought to him without one, he would insist that efforts be made to get it. If he did not have sufficient time to read it in detail for his assessment of the prisoner, he would put it to one side and complete his review of it later. So one way or another, if Stewart had been seen and assessed by a doctor on any of the three occasions when he arrived there as a transferee from Hindley, Mr Kinealy's note would have been read. The trouble was that he was never seen by a doctor.

33.14 All this presupposes, of course, that his medical record accompanied him when he came from Hindley. Mrs Prior thought that as many as half the transferees arrived without their medical records. When that happened, the practice at Feltham was for an entry to be made in the medical reception register to that effect. The following day the healthcare centre at the establishment from which the prisoner had come would be asked to post or fax the prisoner's medical record – depending on its size – and in the meantime a "dummy" medical record would be opened, presumably to be replaced by the real one when it came. But this did not happen with Stewart. As we have seen, his medical record did not accompany him on any of his three visits from Hindley. Despite that, it was only on his last visit on 7 February that the medical reception register recorded that his medical record did not arrive with him. We know that it had come by 7 March, because that was when an entry was made in his F2169A which was stapled to it. So not only was he not seen by a doctor on any of the three occasions he came to Feltham as a transferee. If he had been seen by one, his medical record would not have been available for the doctor to review.

What would have happened if Stewart's medical record had been reviewed?

33.15 By the time Stewart arrived at Feltham, his medical record was a relatively bulky file. It is too much to have expected anyone reading it at the screening stage to have picked up on his troubling behaviour in the latter part of 1997 or his claims to have swallowed a razor blade and a battery. But Mr Kinealy's note would – or at any rate should – have been noticed by anyone looking at the file, and the question then arises what they should have done about it.

33.16 We do not know what the healthcare officer who saw Stewart on 7 March would have done if they had reviewed Stewart's medical record and therefore read Mr Kinealy's note. But both Mrs Prior and Dr Jefferies were questioned about what they would have done. Mrs Prior said that she would have asked the outreach team – which comprised a group of psychiatric nurses – whether Stewart should be referred to a psychiatrist. She would have done that because she would have been alarmed that he had been described in such stark terms as lacking remorse or any other emotion. She had never seen anything like that before. She would have thought that Stewart could remain on ordinary location while he was waiting to be seen by the outreach team. She added that she would also have thought that he should not share a cell in the meantime, but there was, I believe, a strong element of hindsight about that. She could not recall whether she had ever expressed such a view to a unit before, and I doubt very much whether the question whether Stewart could share a cell would have occurred to her at the time.

33.17 For his part, Dr Jefferies said that he would have regarded Stewart's lack of insight and remorse as worrying. He would have interviewed

Stewart in order to get a better picture of him for himself. What he would have done then would have depended on what emerged from the interview. It might have resulted in him referring Stewart to a psychiatrist for assessment. That was something he did once or twice every few months. It was quite feasible because specialist psychiatric services were provided by two registrars who worked five days a week and by a consultant who came to Feltham part-time.

33.18 I have no reason to doubt Mrs Prior's evidence about seeking the views of the outreach team. That was very much in line with what Ms Martin at Hindley would have done if she had seen Mr Kinealy's note when Stewart arrived at Hindley as a "new number" on 23 December. Nor have I reason to doubt what Dr Jefferies says he would have done. Indeed, he would have been even more likely to want to see Stewart for himself if Mr Kinealy's note had said that he posed a risk to others – which is what Mr Kinealy would have written if he had known what was in Stewart's security file. It will be recalled that Dr Greenwood said that no further action was appropriate unless something happened later on which triggered the need to assess the risk Stewart posed. Dr Jefferies went further and said that he would have interviewed Stewart to make up his own mind whether a psychiatric referral should be made. Many different courses of action may be reasonable, but although Dr Jefferies's approach would have been the wiser of the two, that does not mean that Dr Greenwood's approach was unreasonable.

33.19 It is questionable whether, even if Dr Jefferies had interviewed Stewart, he would have referred him to a psychiatrist. After all, Stewart was just one of very many prisoners who had personality disorders of one kind or another. But the real question is not so much whether Stewart would ultimately have been referred for a psychiatric assessment of his mental state, but whether at some time before 21 March the message would have gone out to Swallow from anyone in Feltham's healthcare centre that Stewart was not to share a cell, and whether it would have been acted upon. I doubt very much whether Swallow would have been told anything of the kind. There was very little communication between the healthcare centre and the residential units at Feltham, and the prevailing culture relating to medical confidentiality would have inhibited the healthcare centre from telling the units how a particular prisoner should be managed. In any event, the need to address in a rigorous and focused way the question whether a prisoner posed a risk to his cellmate was barely recognised at the time – not just at Feltham, but across the prison estate as a whole. So all in all, I think it very unlikely that the undoubted shortcomings in the procedures within the healthcare centre could be said to have contributed to what eventually happened to Zahid.

Chapter 34: *Romper Stomper*

34.1 There was no in-cell electricity in Swallow when Stewart and Zahid were there. So none of the cells had television sets which could be powered from the mains. But Swallow had six black and white, battery-powered portable television sets. They were allocated to cells by rotation between 5.00 pm and 8.30 pm and were collected at breakfast the next day. They were tuned in to the five terrestrial channels and could be watched until the batteries gave out.

34.2 It will be recalled that cell 38 was allocated one of those television sets on the evening of Saturday 18 March. That night, at 00.40 am, Channel 4 broadcast *Romper Stomper*, a film with an 18 certificate. No terrestrial channel in the UK is permitted to broadcast films other than those approved by the statutory regulators, and so *Romper Stomper* had to have been regarded as suitable for showing on terrestrial television by the Independent Television Commission.

34.3 Professor Gunn described the film as follows:

> "[The] film was made in 1992 and portrays racial violence in Melbourne. Some of the scenes are horrific. There is a vivid portrayal of neo-Nazi culture, which in this case is struggling against the relative success of Asian immigrants. A gang of violent boys is portrayed as brave, brutal, and self-destructive. The leader of the gang (portrayed by Russell Crowe) is vividly tattooed, including with swastikas. The gang ultimately loses because of the superior forces of the Asian men, and because of the treacherous behaviour of a highly disturbed middle-class girl suffering from epilepsy who joins the gang. The film ends with the murder of the leader of the gang by the second-in-command, the two men having fallen out over how to manage the girl. The film does not portray racist violence as either ideal or successful. Perhaps its most chilling moment is when the leader reads out passages from *Mein Kampf*, Hitler's book, describing the superiority of the white race… [The film] is ultimately *not* a glorification of racial violence… [It] could be taken as a tragic drama portraying the ultimate destructiveness of racial violence, especially to the perpetrators. However it may require some level of sophistication to follow this."

I have seen the film myself, and I agree with that assessment of it. Whatever Stewart may have got out of it, it is a serious film, whose message is one of anti-racism and the futility of violence. It was made by a reputable director, and when it was released it was nominated for a number of Australian Film Institute awards.

34.4 Stewart referred to the film in six of the seven letters he wrote on 20 March and which were found in his cell after the attack. But the impression he gave was that he had not seen it on the Saturday night when it had been on. In three of the letters, he said he had seen it at Altcourse, and in one of them he said that he would have "loved to have [seen] it" when it had been on "the other night". Nevertheless, I think it likely that Stewart did see it on the Saturday night. He told the Inquiry that he had, and Zahid was to tell his cousin, Tanzeel Ahmed, during his family's last visit to Feltham that he had seen it. It is unlikely that Zahid would have watched it alone. Stewart would have watched it with him.

34.5 I deal in chapter 36 with whether the film may have played its part in prompting Stewart to attack Zahid, but I have a strong sense of unease about Stewart being able to watch it at all. So did Professor Gunn. The film had a profound influence on Stewart. He identified with the gang leader to such an extent that in two of the seven letters he wrote on 20 March he said that he had been in the film, and in one of them he said that he had been the star. Those letters were full of lurid racist comments and visions of racist violence. That, no doubt, was what prompted the CRE to criticise Feltham for failing to have a procedure for vetting the suitability of certain television programmes for prisoners with in-cell television sets. The CRE based its view in part on the discretion given to Governors, in a Circular Instruction issued by Prison Service headquarters on the showing of films *on video*, "to prohibit the showing of any material they consider unsuitable taking account of the… characteristics of the inmates".

34.6 It may be relatively easy to prevent prisoners from watching a film on video, but to prevent them from watching a film on terrestrial television is another matter altogether. It would have been possible to arrange for officers to monitor the television schedules to look out for programmes which might be unsuitable for viewing by prisoners. But except for films on video, I am sceptical about how practicable it would have been for them to get hold of copies of such programmes in advance, and then to have had the time to watch them to form their own judgement as to their suitability. Even assuming that such a programme could have been identified, nothing could have been done about it, apart from removing all television sets from all prisoners on all the units where they had only battery-operated sets before the units went on patrol state for the night. The trouble with that was that in-cell television is universally recognised as a very significant factor in reducing the tensions which arise from the boredom experienced by prisoners when confined to their cells for long periods with little or nothing to do. This consideration was not addressed by the CRE. So it never addressed the question whether it was better to let one unsuitable programme be watched rather than forgo the benefits which come from prisoners having television sets in their cells at all. Although I can see where the CRE was coming from, I do not share its view that Feltham deserved criticism in this area.

34.7 Even though many people would be uneasy about Stewart getting so excitable on watching *Romper Stomper*, any attempt to censor programmes on terrestrial television would have been fraught with difficulties. If prisoners can see particular programmes before coming into prison, and after leaving prison, it is questionable whether stopping them watching those programmes during their limited stay in prison would have any effect. And how do you decide which programmes should not be shown? You can lay down the criteria to be taken into account, but the application of those criteria will be a very subjective judgement, and two censoring officers may quite reasonably have diametrically opposed views about a particular programme. What do you do with news items – for example, those which show Muslim prisoners being mistreated in military prisons in Iraq – which could cause much resentment on the part of radicalised young Muslims in prison? And should you not treat unconvicted prisoners differently from convicted prisoners?

34.8 The position is no different today now that in-cell electrically powered televisions are the norm across the prison estate. The technology does not exist for there to be an override mechanism which prevents a particular channel from being broadcast. If prisoners are to be stopped from watching a particular programme, either their television sets have to be removed, or their electricity supply has to be cut off, for the duration of the programme. It is not desirable to deny prisoners the use of their televisions for that time.

Chapter 35: Gladiator aka Coliseum

The allegation surfaces

35.1 On 6 May 2004, the CRE received a telephone call from someone claiming to be a prison officer at Feltham. He would not give his name. The caller alleged that officers at Feltham were playing a "game" called "Coliseum". It involved putting unsuitable prisoners in a cell together. He named Nigel Herring, who had been the chairman of the Feltham branch of the POA since July 2001, as one of the instigators of the practice. The CRE recorded the call.

35.2 The caller was subsequently identified as Duncan Keys. He was not a prison officer at Feltham. He was an assistant secretary of the POA, though he had worked at Feltham as a prison officer between 1982 and 1988. When he was subsequently interviewed by the police, he told them that the game involved putting together those prisoners who might come to blows, and betting on the possible outcome. He said he had heard about the practice from one of his colleagues, Tom Robson, a member of the National Executive Committee of the POA and within whose remit Feltham came, who had told him that he had heard about it from Mr Herring. Mr Keys was to tell the Inquiry that Mr Robson had told him about the practice when they were in a pub near Feltham in early December 2003 – soon after the House of Lords had ruled that there had to be a public inquiry into Zahid's death, but before any inquiry had formally been announced by the Home Secretary.

35.3 Mr Robson and Mr Herring were also interviewed by the police. Mr Robson remembered Mr Herring using the word "Coliseum" but he was very hazy about the details. What he could remember was that he thought at the time that whatever he was being told was nonsense. For his part, Mr Herring told the police that he had known nothing of the practice, that he had not spoken to Mr Robson about it, and that he had heard about it for the first time at a meeting with members of the National Executive Committee of the POA on 18 May 2004.

The links to the murder of Zahid

Mr Keys's suggestion

35.4 In his telephone call to the CRE, Mr Keys suggested that the practice was linked to the murder of Zahid. He claimed that the practice was the reason why Stewart and Zahid had ended up in the same cell: Zahid, he said, "was killed because people thought it would be funny to see what would happen when they put a young Asian lad in with someone who wanted to kill Asians". But there had been no basis for him to make that link. He had initially assumed that Mr Robson had raised the matter with him in view of the forthcoming public inquiry – not because Mr Robson was linking the attack on Zahid with the practice, but because Mr Robson did not believe there was any truth in what Mr Herring had told him and therefore thought that this kind of talk was inappropriate in the run-up to the Inquiry. Indeed, Mr Keys told the Inquiry that his reaction to what Mr Robson had told him was one of disbelief. If there had been such a practice, it would have come out in Mr Butt's investigation or in the investigation by the CRE or in the police investigation which resulted in Stewart's trial for murder, even if the practice had had nothing to do with Zahid's death. So his original view was that there was nothing in the story which Mr Robson was passing on to him – let alone that the practice had had anything to do with how Stewart and Zahid had come to share a cell.

35.5 Mr Keys's evidence to the Inquiry was that by the time he had telephoned the CRE, he had begun to link Zahid's death to the practice. But his reason for doing so was only because the practice had by then seemed less implausible than when he had first heard about it. He remained of the view that if the practice was widespread, it could not have been kept under wraps. But the existence of the practice was less implausible if it was a small discrete operation limited to a few malevolent prison officers. And he had heard that something about prison officers putting prisoners in cells with a view to trouble arising between them had been mentioned at disciplinary proceedings involving a member of the POA at Feltham.* The flaw in Mr Keys's process of reasoning was to assume that if the practice was going on, it must have had something to do with Zahid's death. Nevertheless, despite that flaw, Mr Keys began to link Zahid's murder with the practice, and that accounted for what he told the CRE.

35.6 By the time he was interviewed by the police on 20 July 2004, Mr Keys had realised the flaw in his reasoning. He attributed what he had told the CRE to the "amateur detective" in him. He accepted that perhaps he had put two and two together and made five. Indeed, in his witness

---

* This turned out to be incorrect. The practice had not been mentioned at the disciplinary proceedings which Mr Keys had had in mind. Since the Inquiry's hearings, Mr Herring has provided the Inquiry with documents which appear to relate to a police investigation arising from the allegations in those disciplinary proceedings. Although the documents referred to some allegedly inappropriate behaviour on the part of one officer, that behaviour did not relate to a practice of the kind which Mr Keys was talking about.

statement to the police dated 27 July 2004, he recognised that he had jumped to his conclusion too readily. And by the time he provided the Inquiry with a statement dated 12 January 2005, he was acknowledging that there had been "no direct evidence that [Zahid] being placed in [a cell with Stewart] was anything to do with the practice". He publicly apologised for the very considerable distress which must have been caused to Zahid's family by what he had told the CRE and the subsequent publicity it had received.

The programme on Channel 4

35.7 Mr Keys was not the only person to suggest that something malevolent may have been behind Stewart and Zahid sharing a cell. On 4 October 2002, Channel 4 broadcast a programme about Zahid's murder. It was suggested that there may have been "a more sinister explanation" for them being in a cell together, and there was talk of "a practice inmates knew as 'wind-up'". A former prisoner at Feltham said:

> "They'll put you in a cell [with] someone, you know you don't like the person, or the person is like a bully or stronger than you… the screws know that gets to you, so they put [you] in a cell just to get on your nerves. Then when you come out they expect you to do something to them like going mad, that's why it's called a wind-up… And when you do that they think 'yeah, yeah, we've got him'."

But there is a big difference between putting someone in with another prisoner so that it gets "on your nerves" and you do something you should not when you come out of your cell, and putting a young Asian teenager in with a racist to see whether they come to blows. As it was, the prisoner did not link the practice to Zahid's case, and there was nothing else in the programme which did.

35.8 The solicitor for Zahid's family, Imran Khan, and one of the family's campaigners, Suresh Grover, the director of the Monitoring Group which assists victims of racism and religious intolerance, appeared in the broadcast. They did not comment on this part of the programme, although they may not have been told about it before they were interviewed. Nor did they bring it up in the legal proceedings as an additional reason for a public inquiry, nor did they mention it to the police investigating Mr Keys's allegations. It only came up when a video of the programme was viewed by counsel to the Inquiry some months after Mr Keys's allegation had got into the press. But all that is by the way. The point is that the programme did not unearth any direct evidence to support the suggestion that Stewart was deliberately placed in the same cell as Zahid to see if they would come to blows.

The allocation of Stewart to Zahid's cell

35.9 The absence of any direct evidence to support the suggestion does not, of course, mean the suggestion cannot be true. But it can only be given credence if there were something about how Stewart and Zahid came to share a cell which supports the suggestion. As we saw in chapter 23, the only space in Swallow when Stewart went there for the first time on 8 February was in cell 38 where Zahid already was – and Mr Diaper did not know about the warnings in Stewart's temporary wing file, because it had not arrived with him when he got to Swallow. So the circumstances in which Stewart came to be placed in cell 38 suggest the very opposite of a malign motive on Mr Diaper's part. Putting him in cell 38 was the obvious thing to do.

35.10 The fact remains, though, that Stewart was left in cell 38 with Zahid for another six weeks or so. Even if there had been nothing sinister in his original allocation to cell 38, could he have been left there when staff on Swallow realised what Stewart was like, in the hope or expectation that sparks would fly between them? I discount for this purpose the possibility that the warnings in Stewart's temporary wing file played a part in Stewart continuing to share cell 38 with Zahid. First, his temporary wing file arrived in Swallow on 7 March – four weeks after Stewart first got there. There had not been any trouble between them up to then, and so whatever the temporary wing file said about Stewart, he and Zahid would not have been seen as obvious combatants so as to attract the betting which the practice was said to involve. Secondly, it is unlikely that anyone – apart, of course, from Mr Morse – read the warnings in the temporary wing file. I have already found that Mr Skinner did not, and as for the other officers on Swallow the culture throughout Feltham at the time was that entries in prisoners' wing files were only occasionally made, and when made rarely read. Thirdly, although Mr Morse read the warnings in the temporary wing file, he is unlikely to have made his entry in it on 7 March – thereby drawing attention to the fact that he had read it – if the warnings in it had prompted him to keep Stewart and Zahid together to see if they came to blows.

35.11 But leaving aside the temporary wing file, could Stewart have been left in cell 38 simply because he was seen as an oddball, and had an air of menace about him? Could he have been regarded as such an unknown quantity that he became a prime candidate for an "evens" bet in a "game" which called for punters to weigh up the odds? This possibility cannot be excluded, but there is no evidence for it whatsoever. There is nothing to contradict the obvious reason why Stewart remained with Zahid in cell 38: there did not appear to be any problems between them. Admittedly, Zahid asked to be moved out of cell 38. But as I have said, it is far more likely that he gave as his reason for the move the fact that he wanted to share a cell with Jamie Barnes rather than that he felt uncomfortable about continuing to share a cell with Stewart. All in all, a practice along the lines of what Mr Herring is said to have told Mr Robson had nothing to do with Zahid's murder.

The existence of the practice

35.12 Even though the practice had no part to play in how Stewart and Zahid ended up sharing a cell, it is still necessary to consider whether the practice existed at Feltham – whether then or later. The practice received wide publicity during the Inquiry's public hearings and caused understandable concern. If the practice existed, it would have had obvious implications for phase two of the Inquiry since it would have been necessary to address how the practice can be detected and rooted out. Apart from anything else, the character and conduct of Mr Keys, Mr Robson and Mr Herring have been called into question, and the Inquiry owed it to them to find out where the truth lies.

35.13 Apart from Mr Keys's evidence of what Mr Herring told Mr Robson, there is no evidence whatever of the practice. Putting a prisoner in a cell with someone unsuitable so that he might "go mad" when the cell was unlocked – which was the suggestion made by the inmate in the television programme – is very different from putting unsuitable prisoners in the same cell to see whether they would come to blows, and betting on the outcome. So a careful examination of the evidence of the three principal protagonists is called for.

Mr Keys's evidence

35.14 Mr Keys lives near Feltham. Mr Robson was a good friend of his, and they used to meet after work for a drink when Mr Robson's responsibilities as a member of the National Executive Committee took him to Feltham. On the evening in question, as Mr Robson stood up to go to the bar, he told Mr Keys that it was "very very important" that Mr Keys should remind him to tell Mr Keys about something which had happened at Feltham that day. Mr Keys attributed that request to Mr Robson's tendency to forget things. When he returned from the bar, Mr Robson said: "You are not going to… believe what I am going to tell you." He went on to tell Mr Keys that, when he and Mr Herring were in the office of the POA at Feltham that day, Mr Herring had told him about a "game" played by prison officers at Feltham known as "Gladiator" or "Coliseum". It consisted of putting unsuitable prisoners together in the same cell. The pairing could be one black and one white, one big and one small, or a bully paired with another bully or someone who was particularly weak. The officers would bet on the outcome. If the prisoners were of equal strength, the bet would be on who would win. If they were of unequal strength, the bet would be on how long it would take for an assault to happen.

35.15 Mr Keys said that Mr Robson did not think that any of this was actually going on. But there were two things which really annoyed Mr Robson. The first was that Mr Herring was peddling this rubbish when there was a public inquiry in the offing. No doubt that was why Mr Robson was so anxious to tell Mr Keys about it. The second was that although Mr Herring gave Mr Robson the impression that he thought there was something in it – because Mr Herring was not discounting it out of hand – Mr Herring found the whole thing very amusing and was joking about it. For his part, Mr Keys thought that it was very unlikely that such a practice was going on. If it had been, it would have come out before then. But he did not completely reject the possibility out of hand that the practice was going on. He knew of previous instances of inappropriate behaviour at Feltham – the case of the "Raven Three", referred to later on, was an example – and he wanted to think about it more. After mulling it over, he decided not to do anything about it. He reasoned that the allegation was so likely to be spurious that it would not be right to give wider publicity to something which wrongly put prison officers in a bad light.

35.16 Later on, Mr Keys changed his mind. What sparked it off was the erroneous impression he had that a practice of the kind Mr Herring had spoken about may have been mentioned in disciplinary proceedings, and his belief that the practice might not have come to light if only a few people had been involved. So he raised the matter informally with some of the full-time officers of the POA at a meeting at the POA's regional office in Leeds on 19 March 2004. To cut a long story short, rightly or wrongly he got the impression that either the POA was not taking the matter seriously or was trying to cover it up. He thought it was something which needed to be investigated properly. So he got in touch with the CRE about it because he knew that it had investigated Zahid's murder. He did not want it to get out that he was the CRE's informant because of the way people in the POA might have reacted.

Mr Robson's evidence

35.17 Mr Robson professed to have a very imperfect recollection of his conversations with Mr Herring and Mr Keys. He attributed that to his poor memory, which he had been worried about for some time. He had sought advice about it, but he tended to forget things which he did not need to retain. If his memory was as poor as he said it was, it is important to distinguish between, on the one hand, what he can remember about his conversation with Mr Herring and, on the other, what he assumes Mr Herring told him as a result of what Mr Keys says Mr Robson told him about it.

35.18 Mr Robson gave evidence to the Inquiry on 3 and 4 March 2005. He claimed then that all he could remember of his conversation with Mr Herring was Mr Herring using the word "Coliseum". He could not remember the context in which the word had cropped up. But when he had been interviewed by the police on 22 July 2004, his memory had been significantly better. He then had "a feeling" that Mr Herring had told him that "prison officers played a game at Feltham of matching two prisoners in a game of what was described as Coliseum or Gladiators… And that the two prisoners would be put together to see what reaction was got." He thought that there had been some mention of betting going on, but he could not be certain of that. He recalled that he had had a strong reaction at the time. His actual words to the police were: "I was amazed that some idiot could talk like this… in [the] light of the publicity that was about to descend upon Feltham… [over] a nasty racist murder there." He remembered thinking that what he was being told was "complete fiction".

35.19 Mr Robson claimed to have equally little memory of his conversation with Mr Keys later that day. He recalled mentioning something about "Coliseum" to Mr Keys, but he could not remember whether it had had anything to do with prisoners being put into cells for unacceptable reasons. However, he knows he would have given Mr Keys a reasonably accurate account of what Mr Herring had said, because he would have been using Mr Keys as a "sounding board" to see what Mr Keys thought about whatever it was that he was telling him.

Mr Herring's evidence

35.20 Mr Herring has always said that he knew nothing about the practice until 18 May 2004 when, with other members of the Feltham branch committee, he went to a meeting with the union's National Executive Committee at the POA's head office. The meeting had ostensibly been arranged to discuss the relationship between the branch and the national committee. During the meeting, Steve Gillan, one of the vice-chairmen of the national committee, asked the Feltham representatives whether they could shed any light on an allegation that prisoners had been put in cells in order to encourage violence in "Gladiator/Coliseum" style contests. The only committee member who knew anything about it was Mr Morse, the officer who had been on duty on 7 March when Stewart arrived on Swallow with his temporary wing file. According to Mr Herring, Mr Morse, who by then had moved to the Security Department, had heard about the allegation from the police liaison officer at Feltham. Mr Herring's evidence to the Inquiry was that until then he had never heard about the allegation himself, that this was what he had said at the meeting on 18 May and that he had never talked about it to Mr Robson.

The POA is informed

35.21 There is no strong reason to doubt Mr Keys's evidence that he raised the existence of the practice with some of the full-time officers of the POA at the meeting at the POA's regional office in Leeds on 19 March 2004. Only a week or so later, Colin Moses, the national chairman of the POA, was asking Andy Darken, Mr Herring's predecessor as chairman of the Feltham branch of the POA, whether he knew anything about the practice. That was on 25 March following a meeting at the POA's headquarters. That is what Mr Darken told the police. True, Mr Moses told the police that he thought that he might have heard about the practice from Stephen Cox, a full-time official of the POA who had represented the POA member who was the subject of the disciplinary proceedings which Mr Keys had had in mind. But Glyn Travis, another full-time official of the POA, told the police that he thought that he had heard it from Mr Keys at a meeting of full-time officers of the POA. He told them that the meeting had been at Lynden House in Wakefield, but there is no reason to suppose that he was not talking about the same occasion as Mr Keys. Wakefield is just outside Leeds, and Lynden House was the hotel they were all staying at.

A cover up?

35.22 Although Mr Keys was not to know it, he was being a little too harsh on the POA in thinking that it was not taking the matter seriously or was trying to cover it up. It was not just a case of Mr Moses asking Mr Darken about the practice a week or so after he had heard about it. One of the people Mr Keys says he reported the practice to on 19

March was Mark Freeman, the deputy general secretary of the POA. Mr Freeman was to tell the police that he thought that he had first heard about the practice from Mr Gillan, who told the Inquiry that he had first heard about it from Mr Travis on 25 March at the POA's headquarters. But whoever Mr Freeman had first heard it from, he told Paul Carroll, the Prison Service's Head of Employee Relations, about it on 26 April when they met at a POA branch officials' training course. Mr Carroll was to tell the police that, although Mr Freeman had spoken to him in confidence, he told Mr Freeman that it was his duty to report what he had been told. That is what Mr Carroll did. Phil Wheatley was told about it, and on 28 April Commander Gary Copson, the police adviser to the Prison Service, began an investigation into the allegation – over a week before Mr Keys spoke anonymously to the CRE.*

35.23 Commander Copson concluded his investigation on 15 May 2004. He found that there were no grounds to support the allegation, and that there were some grounds for supposing that it was false. There undoubtedly was some delay in bringing Mr Keys's allegations to the attention of the Prison Service. This was presumably because of the POA's natural reluctance to give wider currency to an allegation which their full-time officers thought was too far-fetched to be true and would only result in unwarranted damage to the reputation of the nation's prison officers, the vast majority of whom were dedicated and conscientious members of staff. Even so, enquiries were already being made about the practice by the POA, and the Prison Service was eventually told of Mr Keys's allegations. Not immediately, and perhaps only when it was realised that the allegations would not go away, but nevertheless some time before Mr Keys took his concerns to the CRE.

The conversation between Mr Robson and Mr Keys

35.24 The point was forcefully made that Mr Keys must have realised that if he disclosed to a public body like the CRE what he claims Mr Robson had told him, he would have exposed himself to considerable hostility from those who thought that he was being disloyal to his colleagues. So it was argued that what he claimed Mr Robson had told him must be true. He would not have risked being the target of the animosity to which he has apparently been subjected since then if it was not. I see the force in that, but I cannot go along with it. Mr Keys would only have been worried about the possibility of antipathy towards him if he had known his identity as the source of the allegation would come out. He

---

* This was, no doubt, the investigation which got back to Mr Morse via the police liaison officer at Feltham.

had no reason to suppose it would. He did not give the CRE his name. He pretended he was a prison officer working at Feltham. He did not know at the time the call was being recorded. Although he used his own telephone at the office of the POA to make the call, it did not occur to him that the call could be traced back to him. And I doubt whether he would have gone as "over the top" as he did had he thought that he would be identified as the caller.

35.25 On the other hand, there was always going to be a strong attack on Mr Keys's credibility. It took him a good three months to tell anyone what he claims Mr Robson told him. And in his telephone call to the CRE he said many things which were either untrue – for example, that he was a serving officer at Feltham – or things which he had no basis for claiming – for example, that Zahid had been a victim of the practice, that "lots of other inmates" had been similarly treated, that "the usual wall of silence had gone up", that the practice was "common knowledge" at Feltham and that Mr Herring was one of the instigators – whereas all he had been told was that Mr Herring had known about what was going on. But ultimately the untruths and exaggerations on Mr Keys's part can be attributed to a variety of factors. He was very worked up about what he was doing. He wanted to make sure that the allegation he was making would not be ignored. He was angry at how Mr Herring had been treating it as a bit of a joke. And he had not rehearsed precisely what he was going to say to the CRE, with the result that much of what he said was "off the cuff". So all in all, I do not think that what he told the CRE seriously undermines the credibility of what he told the Inquiry.

35.26 There are two points I regard as critical. First, did Mr Keys have any convincing reason for embellishing some flippant remarks which Mr Robson had attributed to Mr Herring, let alone making up in its entirety a conversation with Mr Robson about Mr Herring which never took place? On Mr Keys's account of the conversation, it was not Mr Robson who was going to get into trouble if he revealed what Mr Robson had told him: it was Mr Herring who would have. Was there any reason to suppose that Mr Keys had it in for Mr Herring? Mr Keys accepted that there was some friction between the Feltham branch and the national committee at the time of his call to the CRE. The national committee had wanted to discuss the Inquiry with the Feltham branch committee. No doubt the national committee wanted to discuss the strength of Mr Keys's allegation. So they asked the members of the Feltham branch committee to go to a meeting at the POA's head office on 4 May. Mr Herring responded by saying that if the meeting was to take place, Mr Darken should be invited and an agenda should be prepared. Having got what he thought was an unhelpful reply from the national committee,

Mr Herring responded that the branch committee was "occupied with local affairs on that day and [would] be unable to attend".

35.27 I do not believe for one moment that this stand-off between the branch committee and the national committee would have been a sufficient reason for Mr Keys to lie about Mr Herring. But the real reason why it was suggested that Mr Keys might have attributed to Mr Herring things which he never said was to bolster Mr Robson's position on the national committee, at a time when the branch was beginning to have less confidence about how Mr Robson did his work and no longer wanted him to represent it, and when he was facing substantial criticism from Mr Herring for having criticised Mr Darken for destabilising industrial relations at Feltham. I do not doubt that both Mr Robson and Mr Herring were lobbying for support from the national committee for their respective views about Mr Darken. Indeed, the Inquiry has seen memoranda which they sent to the national committee on 29 March and 14 April respectively. But this is far too Machiavellian for my taste. Having observed Mr Keys carefully during his evidence, he simply did not strike me as so conniving and manipulative as to have embarked on a strategy of that kind. I acknowledge that he had to press on with his allegation once he was revealed to have been the mystery caller. But it is, in my opinion, too far-fetched that a misplaced sense of loyalty to Mr Robson in his dispute with Mr Herring over Mr Darken caused him to tell lies about Mr Herring to the CRE. So all in all, I have not discerned any sufficiently plausible motive for Mr Keys to have attributed to Mr Herring via Mr Robson things which Mr Herring never said.

35.28 The second point is this. Although Mr Robson's evidence to the Inquiry was that he had only a very hazy recollection of what Mr Herring had told him, what he told the police Mr Herring had told him was really quite detailed. When it comes down to it, there is not much of a difference between that account of what Mr Herring told Mr Robson and what Mr Keys says Mr Robson told him Mr Herring had said. In other words, Mr Robson's account *to the police* of what Mr Herring had said was very much the same as what Mr Keys says was Mr Robson's account *to him* of what Mr Herring had said. Mr Robson did not suggest that what he told the police did not represent his best recollection at the time of his interview of his conversation with Mr Herring. Mr Keys's account to the Inquiry of what Mr Robson told him is itself not very different from what he told the police when he was interviewed by them two days before Mr Robson's interview, and therefore before he would have known what Mr Robson was to tell them. In these circumstances, the similarity between Mr Robson's account to the police of his conversation with Mr Herring and Mr Keys's evidence of Mr Robson's account of that conversation to him suggests that Mr Keys's account of what Mr Robson told him is broadly accurate.

35.29 All of this disposes of two possibilities which have been canvassed. The first is that Mr Keys made the whole thing up. On this scenario, there was no conversation between Mr Keys and Mr Robson at all, and Mr Robson went along with Mr Keys's version of events once Mr Keys had been identified as the caller to the CRE. Maybe Mr Robson went along with it enthusiastically, because he saw it as a way of getting back at Mr Herring for trying to undermine his opinion of Mr Darken. Maybe he went along with it reluctantly, because he knew that if he did not support Mr Keys's version of the conversation – at least to a limited extent – Mr Keys would be disbelieved, and he did not want to see a good friend of his pilloried for making false claims against Mr Herring.

35.30 The second possibility is that Mr Herring made an impolitic and ill-judged "off the cuff" remark to Mr Robson about the way prisoners were treated, that Mr Robson relayed that to Mr Keys, but that Mr Keys embellished it – possibly because he did not like Mr Herring, or because he wanted Mr Herring's flippant comment to be taken seriously and he let his imagination over what Mr Herring had said run riot. That would explain why Mr Robson had only a vague recollection of what Mr Herring had said. It demonstrated merely an unseemly attitude on Mr Herring's part towards prisoners but not much more than that. In my view, neither of these scenarios can stand with Mr Robson's relatively detailed account to the police of what Mr Herring had told him. So the issue then becomes not so much what Mr Robson told Mr Keys, but what Mr Herring told Mr Robson.

The conversation between Mr Herring and Mr Robson

35.31 On the face of it, Mr Robson was not the obvious person to whom Mr Herring might have divulged such a practice as gladiatorial-style contests between prisoners. Mr Robson himself conceded that if Mr Herring was being serious he did not think that Mr Herring would have said anything *to him* about such a practice. He also acknowledged that Mr Herring would not have regarded him as a person to share a laugh with about a subject as worrying as that. But that does not mean that Mr Herring would not have told Mr Robson about such a practice. Mr Herring is someone who says what he wants to say – to whoever he thinks ought to hear it. But the critical point is: why would Mr Robson tell Mr Keys about a conversation with Mr Herring about the Gladiator allegations if Mr Herring had not told him anything of the kind? There is no convincing answer to that question. Mr Robson had no reason in

December 2003 to make things up about Mr Herring. The differences which arose between them came much later.

35.32 I did not find Mr Robson's professed loss of memory convincing. It may be that he tends to remember things he needs to, and to forget things he does not. But if Mr Herring had spoken to him about a subject as serious as this, he is likely to have remembered it. All the more so if he had thought that Mr Herring was being serious about it. But also if he had thought that Mr Herring was joking. Even if your memory is poor, you are likely to remember a joke in such bad taste. And whether Mr Robson thought Mr Herring was joking or not, what Mr Keys says about how Mr Robson raised the subject with him also tends to show that it must have stuck in Mr Robson's mind. After all, the account he gave to the police of his conversation with Mr Herring was sufficiently detailed to show that it had remained with him for a good few months.

35.33 So why would Mr Robson claim a greater loss of memory than he really has? I suspect that he realised, like Mr Morse over the entries in Stewart's temporary wing file, that what Mr Herring had told him placed him in a quandary. If he told the Inquiry what Mr Herring had said to him, he could be exposing himself to the hostility which Mr Keys has apparently faced, and to criticism for not having brought it to the attention of the national committee at the time, so that they could decide what should be done. And he could hardly say that he had no recollection of the conversation, because he had given a relatively detailed account of it to the police. The best solution to the problem was to say that he had only a very hazy recollection of what was said.

35.34 Turning to Mr Herring, there are two things which could be said to affect his credibility. The first relates to an article he wrote which appeared in the May 2004 issue of *Gatelodge*, a magazine for members of the POA. In it, he referred to a recent disturbance at Feltham in the course of which an officer had found himself under attack. Mr Herring described him as grabbing "two bin-lids" and defending himself "in gladiatorial style". The suggestion was that although the incident itself had had nothing to do with prisoners engaged in gladiatorial-style contests, the language Mr Herring used was too much of a coincidence. But there are a number of possible explanations for Mr Herring's language. Mr Giffin persuasively summarised them as follows:

"Did some enemy of Mr Herring at POA headquarters read the text of his column and pick up the innocent reference to use against him? Was Mr Herring's use of the term a subtle message or joke aimed at those 'in the know' about something else that was going on at Feltham? Or had Mr Herring, contrary to what he now says, already got wind of the allegations by the time he wrote his column, leading him to use the term either as a two-fingered salute to those making the allegations, or as a means of starting to construct some explanation for how such allegations might have surfaced. Or was the use of Roman language in the column genuinely coincidental, but perhaps the cause of the name 'Gladiator' being attached to the practice when previously it was only the name 'Coliseum' that had been used?"

I agree with Mr Giffin's comments: without any obvious reason for preferring one of these explanations to another, the point does not take the matter further.

35.35 The second point relating to Mr Herring's credibility was his claim that he did not know about the allegation until 18 May 2004, although when he was interviewed by the police he left open the possibility that he might have been told about it when he had been "half pissed somewhere" and had forgotten about it – an acknowledgement that if he had been told about it when he was sober, he would have remembered it. As it is, I do not believe his claim that he did not hear about it until 18 May. He was close to Mr Darken, and if Mr Darken had been told about the allegation by Mr Moses – as Mr Darken was to tell the police – it is inconceivable that Mr Darken would not have asked Mr Herring about it, even if Mr Darken thought there was nothing in the allegation. That is especially so after 10 May, which was when members of the national committee went to Feltham to discuss the allegation with Feltham's new Governor, Andrew Cross, cutting out the members of the branch committee. At the very least, Mr Herring would have asked Mr Darken what was going on. Similarly with Mr Morse. Mr Morse knew about the allegation well before the meeting on 18 May. He is bound to have told Mr Herring about it, even if he thought that it was nonsense.* Moreover, the correspondence between Mr Herring and the national committee over the meeting of 4 May suggests there was some unspoken reason why Mr Herring did not want the meeting to go ahead. It does not take much imagination to conclude that Mr Herring knew that the national committee wanted to discuss Mr Keys's allegation and that he did not want to until he knew what was going to be said.

35.36 Ultimately, I am as sure as I can be that Mr Herring did indeed tell Mr Robson about a practice called "Gladiator" or "Coliseum" – broadly speaking in the terms that Mr Keys says Mr Robson described to him.

---

* These two points are significantly diminished by the fact that Mr Darken and Mr Morse were not asked whether they told Mr Herring about the allegation, and their relationship with Mr Herring was not explored in detail. But the points are still worth making.

Going back to Mr Robson's evidence, the fact of the matter is that, even if one puts aside what Mr Robson told the police, what little he claimed to recollect at the Inquiry's hearings was highly significant. He still recalls Mr Herring having used the word "Coliseum". I have no reason to doubt that. If Mr Herring had used the word "Coliseum", what could Mr Herring have been talking about if it was not a practice to do with gladiatorial-style contests between prisoners?

Why did Mr Herring tell Mr Robson what he did?

35.37 This is the $64,000 question. Was Mr Herring telling Mr Robson what he really knew about the practice? Or was he passing on some gossip he had picked up at Feltham – gossip he thought was groundless, which was why he was joking and laughing about it? Or was he just making it up – because he thought it was funny to make flippant remarks in bad taste about the treatment of prisoners? The issue is by no means easy because the person who can really say what he meant denies making the remarks at all.

35.38 I do not think that a practice of the kind Mr Herring told Mr Robson about can be dismissed as "complete fiction". The Prison Service is bound to have its fair share of officers who treat prisoners inappropriately. Any organisation of its size will. Instances of brutality and serious mistreatment of prisoners on the part of prison officers surface from time to time. They may be few and far between, but they still exist. The Inquiry itself unearthed a few examples. These included the case of the "Raven Three" – in which three white members of staff handcuffed an ethnic minority prisoner on Raven to the bars of his cell, removed his trousers and smeared his bottom with black shoe polish – and two white trainee prison officers urinating on a black trainee during a training course.* And there are precedents for abusive practices flourishing undetected for some time, even though they are sufficiently commonplace to have acquired a name: the practice known as "Reflections" at Brixton Prison – in which prisoners were held in the segregation unit as a means of controlling them so that they could "reflect" on their disruptive behaviour – was an example of that. So the "Gladiator" allegations cannot be dismissed simply on the basis that it is inconceivable that any prison officer could resort to such behaviour. On the other hand, Mr Keys was surely right when he said that the practice, if it existed, could not have been widespread. The idea that large numbers of prison officers could be involved in so obvious an abuse of prisoners without it getting out

---

* The two trainee prison officers were dismissed, but the "Raven Three" were merely issued with warnings.

is fanciful. So if it existed, it did so on a small scale – maybe limited to Feltham only.

35.39 It was suggested that the introduction of cell-sharing risk assessments across the prison estate would have made it difficult for a practice of this kind to survive. I rather doubt that. The cell-sharing risk assessments would have identified those prisoners who could not share a cell. But that left huge numbers of prisoners who could share a cell. The practice was still perfectly viable if unscrupulous officers wanted to engage in it.

35.40 But I am doubtful whether the practice existed even on a small scale. Mr Keys's allegations were leaked to the Sun, which published an article about them on 28 May 2004. The story was picked up by the Guardian which reported it as well. The allegations were widely reported both on television and in the press when Mr Giffin referred to them in his opening statement at the Inquiry's hearing on 18 November 2004. And the same thing happened in March 2005 when Mr Keys, Mr Robson and Mr Herring gave evidence. Indeed, Mr Khan made a public appeal for anyone who knew anything about the allegations to come forward. So too did the Sun. No-one has, and so Mr Herring remains the only source for the existence of the practice. Even if it existed on a small scale, it must have come to the attention of at least some officers who would have been sufficiently shocked by it to come forward. I do not believe that not one of them would have come forward to confirm its existence if it really was going on. That was especially so after most of the reports in the media failed to refer to the retraction by Mr Keys of his claim that the practice had been the reason why Stewart and Zahid had ended up in the same cell. And it has to be said that the statement made by Mr Khan gave the same impression. If the public was still being told that the practice had had something to do with how they came to share a cell, all the more reason for someone to have come forward and confirmed the existence of the practice if it had still been going on.

35.41 So if the practice as described to Mr Keys was not going on, why did Mr Herring tell Mr Robson that it was? I doubt whether Mr Herring would have made up a story out of nothing. He must have heard something which he decided to pass on to Mr Robson. But what was that? The answer, I think, was the practice known as "wind-up". The programme on Channel 4 was not the only source for it. Some of the prisoners and prison staff who participated in the Inquiry's focus groups cited instances of incompatible prisoners being paired with each other to oppress or control them. And Chris Myant, who was head of the CRE's press office in 2000, and was involved in the CRE's formal investigation into the Prison Service, told the police when they were looking into Mr Keys's allegations that during the CRE's investigation he had been told at "various times" by prison officers and others of a practice called "wind-up" in which prisoners who might argue with each other were put in the same cell. He was never told of any specific occasion when that happened, nor was he given any evidence to confirm it. But the combination of the programme on Channel 4, the anecdotal evidence which emerged from the focus groups and what Mr Myant heard suggests that there could have been rumours going around about a practice of putting unsuitable prisoners in cells together. I am not able to say for sure whether the rumours were true or not, but what I think probably happened was that Mr Herring had heard of the rumours, and that was what he told Mr Robson about. Mr Herring's contributions to *Gatelodge* show that he has a fertile imagination and at times an offensive turn of phrase. On one occasion he talked of vulnerable young offenders "dribbling for attention, affection and help". I can well imagine him embellishing the rumours by surmising how the practice worked and speculating on the betting which could take place on the side – not so much telling Mr Robson that that was actually going on, but rather joking about how far the practice could be taken. But Mr Robson had not realised that Mr Herring's talk of betting on the outcome was his own embellishment of the rumours, and he passed what Mr Herring told him on to Mr Keys as if what Mr Herring had said was actually going on.

35.42 In short, I can put the public's mind at rest about the existence of a practice where unsuitable prisoners were deliberately put in the same cell *with officers betting on the outcome*. But the real possibility that unsuitable prisoners have at times been put into the same cell – either to wind them up so that they would misbehave when they were let out or to see whether they would argue with each other – is certainly one which cannot be excluded, even though no hard and fast examples of such a practice have been given otherwise than in the anonymous setting of the Inquiry's focus groups with prisoners and prison staff.

Chapter 36: Why did he do it?

Motive for murder

36.1 The primary focus of the Inquiry's investigation was not on why Stewart attacked Zahid, but how he came to be in a position to carry out the attack. So the Inquiry explored – in considerable detail – what was known about Stewart, the extent to which that information was passed on, and how he and Zahid ended up sharing a cell. But a narrative of the events which led up to the attack on Zahid would be incomplete without some discussion of what might have motivated Stewart to behave as he did.

36.2 This is not a topic on which any definitive findings can be made. Stewart would have had to give oral evidence if that was to be done, and I wanted to avoid that if it was possible because I feared it might cause Zahid's family too much distress. Even if he had, the reliance which could have been placed on his evidence is highly questionable. Moreover, Stewart would have had to be examined by Professor Gunn and Professor Maden, and their reports suggested that even then there was likely to remain uncertainty about Stewart's true motivation. In the circumstances, I decided that I would not attempt to make any firm findings about what lay behind the attack in Stewart's mind, or even to come to any view as to the likely reason for the attack. I decided that I would simply identify those reasons which I regarded as plausible possibilities for it. When the Interested Parties were informed of what I had in mind, none of them suggested otherwise. In this chapter, I discuss the various possibilities in turn, beginning with what Stewart told the Inquiry was the reason for his attack on Zahid.

Transfer

36.3 Stewart did not like being at Feltham. He loathed the place. For him, it was the worst prison he had been in. The intensity of his dislike for Feltham came out most graphically in the letters he wrote while he was there, which were subsequently retrieved by the police. Stewart was not adept at articulating the reasons for his sense of alienation and isolation. The limited time he had out of his cell was something he mentioned more than once. But the large number of London gangs, many of whose members were black, was what really got to him. Maybe his racism would have made him uncomfortable about them in any event. But the real problem for him was that he felt threatened and intimidated by them. Being white and from the north, he saw himself as different from them. He felt that he was on their territory. It was that sense of being a stranger in what he saw as a hostile place which resulted in him making the dagger which was discovered under his pillow. He thought he needed to have something to defend himself with from possible attack.

36.4 There was not much Stewart could have done to get himself transferred out of Feltham. Any application for a transfer was likely to fail while he was still awaiting trial on the harassment charges. But there is some evidence that he had been thinking hard about what he could do. He told the CRE that he had been thinking of confessing to crimes he had committed in the north so as to get himself transferred there. He even claimed to have used that strategy to get out of Onley. So if he was so anxious to be transferred out of Feltham that he was prepared to own up to crimes which he had not been charged with, it may be that he would take what he described in one of his letters as "xtreme measures to get shipped out". In one letter, he doubted whether he would go so far as to kill someone, but in another he actually talked of killing his cellmate if that was what was needed to get him transferred. He was to claim that actually killing Zahid was not what he had intended. He told the CRE that "a few hits to the head" would have been enough to get him transferred. He told the Inquiry that a "fairly serious" assault on Zahid would have achieved his objective, and although he now realises that "one blow to his head using a table leg would have been enough", he wanted the result to be seen as sufficiently serious to warrant more than simply time in the segregation unit. It is difficult to assess the significance of his use of the table leg rather than the dagger. Each could have been used to inflict lethal injuries, just as much as non-fatal ones.

36.5 To an outsider, the idea of clubbing one's cellmate a number of times about the head in order to get a move to another prison is hardly a rational thing to do. No sensible person would regard it as a proportionate means of achieving that objective. And even if Stewart had only intended to give Zahid a sufficient beating to get himself moved, there was no guarantee that he would in fact be moved while he was still awaiting trial in London on the harassment charges. But that could equally be said about all the other reasons why he might have attacked Zahid: the disparity between the triviality or irrationality of those reasons and the gravity of what he did is immense however one looks at it. As it is, the desire to get away from the increasing sense of isolation and stress which Stewart felt at Feltham was regarded by Amy Poulson, who had been Stewart's probation officer from 1999 and who wrote the report on him following his conviction for Zahid's murder referred to in paragraph 8.9, as one of the three main factors pertinent to any consideration of his motivation. The fact is that Stewart's warped thinking was such that one cannot exclude this as at least a plausible explanation for why he attacked Zahid.

Hero worship

36.6 Stewart had always looked up to Travis. It will be recalled that one officer referred to Travis as Stewart's "hero". The influence Travis had on Stewart was something which had been noted by Stephen Green, Stewart's probation officer in 1998, who supervised Travis as well. Could Stewart have attacked and killed Zahid to show Travis that he was capable of committing murder as well? That was also regarded by Ms Poulson as one of the three main possibilities.

36.7 Stewart has always denied that anything of this kind had any part to play, but I do not think the suggestion can readily be rejected. It was, after all, in the context of murders committed by Travis and another prisoner that Stewart joked about committing the first murder of the millennium. The fact that he wrote that everyone thought that he would be next suggests that he was acknowledging that it was almost expected of him. When in one of his letters from Feltham he speculated whether he would go so far as to murder someone in order to get transferred, it is noteworthy that he spoke of Travis in the same breath. And there was one particular similarity between Stewart's attack on Zahid and the murders committed by Travis and the other prisoner. Travis's victim, Alan Averill, was killed on his birthday, the other prisoner's victim was killed on the day of his grandmother's funeral – although there is some doubt whether the killer knew that – and Zahid was attacked on the morning he was due to be released. Stewart referred to the choice of those dates in one of the letters he wrote after the attack. He linked his attack with theirs by saying "we're all evil", and was to admit during cross-examination at his trial that he had that linkage in mind at the time – although whether he had it in mind when he wrote the letter or when he attacked Zahid is unclear. All of this suggests that he could well have decided to attack Zahid as his ultimate attempt to get on equal terms with Travis. It is at least a plausible possibility for what happened.

36.8 But there is one linked possibility which I do not regard as plausible. During the investigation into Zahid's murder, Travis told the police that he and Stewart had planned Averill's murder together, and that both of them were going to stab him. However, when it came down to it, Stewart did not join in. Not only that, complained Travis: Stewart put *all* the blame for the murder on him. According to Travis, Stewart later apologised for "grassing" Travis up, and said that he would do anything to put things right. Travis claimed that when he discovered that Stewart had an Asian cellmate at Feltham, he told Stewart to kill him, and told him this was the only way Stewart could pay him back for what he had done to him. Travis was subsequently to retract all that. For his part,

Stewart has always denied that he attacked Zahid so that the slate between him and Travis would be wiped clean. Indeed, he claims that Travis told him in a letter that he had only made the claim initially so that he could attend Stewart's trial. The Inquiry never saw that letter – Stewart claims it was written in code, and was intercepted anyway. But what is certainly the case is that no letter of the kind which Travis must have written to Stewart if Travis's original claim had been true was ever found in Stewart's cell.

Racism

36.9 Stewart was not consistent in his racism. He had a Bob Marley tattoo on his arm. And while at Altcourse he had teamed up with a fellow Mancunian who was of mixed race. The bond which they had was a geographical one. That had the effect of subliminating any hostility Stewart might have felt towards him on racial grounds. But Stewart revealed his true colours in his correspondence. Because he was such a prolific writer of letters, there is plenty of material to go on. So far we have looked for the most part only at those letters which should have been read if his correspondence had been monitored. But the letters he wrote both on the day before the attack on Zahid and in the weeks and months afterwards also show him to have been harbouring violent fantasies about blacks and other people from ethnic minorities. Indeed, in letters found in his cell written on the day before the attack, he talked of nail-bombing various Asian communities. Violence towards Asians was on his mind, as it had been when he went "Paki-bashing" when he was younger. And there was a strong element of triumphalism when he daubed a swastika on the wall of the cell he was put in after the attack.

36.10 Despite that, Stewart denied, both before and during his trial, that racism played any part in his attack on Zahid. It could have happened to anyone, he said, whatever their colour or ethnicity. But he was to change his stance later on, implicitly accepting, I think, that his earlier position had had much to do with maintaining his defence of diminished responsibility at his trial. He was, according to Ms Poulson, "beginning to acknowledge that racist thoughts may have been used by him to fuel his anger" about Zahid's imminent release. He told the CRE that the attack was, in part at least, a reflection of how he felt about black and Asian prisoners on the unit. And he admitted to the Inquiry that "racial prejudice played some part" in his attack on Zahid, that prejudice being fuelled by his time at Feltham.

36.11 Professor Maden was able to articulate a persuasive defence of Stewart's original position. He pointed out that there were some very unusual features about Stewart's attack on Zahid. There had been no chance of Stewart escaping, and he was unusually calm afterwards. His lack of emotion or remorse were "remarkable". That led Professor Maden to think that Stewart was so alienated from the rest of the human race that any problems he might have had about people of another ethnic origin were minor compared to the degree of alienation from people in general. But he was not questioning the fact that Stewart's racism may have been a contributing factor. Professor Gunn's view wavered over time, but he was finally to accept that Stewart's virulent racism was a plausible explanation for the attack. I am sure that was the correct view to take.

Jealousy

36.12 Ms Poulson picked up on Stewart's anger about Zahid's imminent release. Could Stewart have been so jealous of Zahid's discharge from Feltham that it contributed to his decision to attack Zahid? After all, given Stewart's intense dislike of Feltham, he might have felt particularly envious of someone who was about to leave – especially someone who was happy to be leaving and was talking about it, as at least one officer said Zahid was. But ultimately the only thing which points to jealousy over Zahid's imminent release as being a factor in Stewart's thinking was the timing of the attack. There was no other obvious reason why Stewart should have chosen that night to attack him.

36.13 It is entirely plausible that Stewart chose that night to attack Zahid because Zahid was leaving the next day. But that only explains why he attacked Zahid *then*. It does not begin to explain why he attacked Zahid at all. He told Ms Poulson that he had been brooding over whether to attack Zahid for a couple of days, and the obvious reason why he attacked Zahid *when* he did was because it would have been his last opportunity to do so, rather than because he resented the fact that Zahid was soon to leave. Stewart himself denied the suggestion that he was jealous of Zahid's imminent release. He had seen too many prisoners leave prison, including ones with whom he had shared a cell, for it to have bothered him. There is a remote possibility that he was so distressed by Zahid's imminent release that he took his anger about it out on Zahid, but it is too fanciful to suppose that this alone might have caused him to attack Zahid. Something else would have had to be in play for distress over Zahid's imminent release to have concerned him so much.

36.14 There is another linked possibility which I also do not accept. In his first report, Professor Gunn included in his list of eight possible contributory factors the possibility that Stewart was giving Zahid "a traditional pre-release beating". But the only evidence about the extent of such a practice came from a prisoner, who spoke of a prison tradition called "banging": it involved an inmate being "rushed", which meant being beaten by other prisoners. That suggests a communal beating rather than one in the dead of night by just one prisoner on another in the privacy of their cell. And both the ferocity and nature of the attack are completely inconsistent with the kind of rite of passage which "banging" exemplifies.

Dislike of Zahid

36.15 In his statement to the Inquiry, Stewart said that he and Zahid had had a few arguments during their time together. But he added that they had not been about anything serious, and that they had been the sort of arguments people who are locked up together for long periods of time sometimes have. They centred on things like who was responsible for cleaning the cell and which radio station they should listen to. That was consistent with what Stewart told the police and what was in his proof of evidence prepared for his trial. It is also consistent with what staff and other prisoners said. None of them noticed any particular problem between them. Even Jamie Barnes said "they seemed to get on OK".

36.16 But there is evidence of a deterioration in their relationship, at least from Stewart's perspective, in the days leading up to the attack. Stewart told the CRE that Zahid started using his things without permission, and when added to their disagreements about cell-cleaning and the radio, they were not speaking to each other by the Saturday before the attack. They got over that, but on the Monday Stewart discovered that a couple of his shower gels were missing. When he saw someone using the same kind of gel in the shower that day, Stewart asked him where he had got it. He was told enough to make him think that Zahid had given it to him. The deterioration in their relationship was picked up by Ms Poulson. Stewart told her that things of his had started to go missing from the cell, and that he had begun to think that Zahid was undermining his standing on the unit by "taking advantage" of him and "thinking that he could tell me what to do". From talking at length to

Stewart, her judgement was that his thoughts of taking action to secure his transfer from Feltham then became focused on Zahid. This is quite plausible, and it is a possibility which cannot be excluded.

Romper Stomper

36.17 Stewart told the Inquiry that although he watched the film *Romper Stomper* on the Saturday night before he attacked Zahid, the film had had nothing to do with it. Professor Gunn was initially inclined to go along with that: he would have expected a more immediate reaction on Stewart's part if the film had prompted him to attack Zahid. But *Romper Stomper* continued to play on Stewart's mind. Look at the references he made to it in the letters he wrote on the day before the attack. Professor Gunn had not initially realised that the letters with those references had been written so soon before the attack. The possibility that it played a part in what was to happen is not wholly implausible, and is one which cannot be discounted. Professor Gunn ultimately went along with that. As he said, you could not rule out the possibility that Stewart was re-enacting a scene from the film – especially as the film depicted white skinhead racists attacking Vietnamese refugees with wooden clubs.

Remaining on Swallow

36.18 Professor Gunn identified disappointment at not being moved to a unit for unconvicted prisoners after Stewart's status had changed as being a possible contributory factor in his decision to attack Zahid. But that possibility proceeded, in part at any rate, on the assumptions that Stewart had asked to be moved and that if he remained on Swallow he would be denied the privileges unconvicted prisoners enjoyed. As we have seen, I do not think that either of these assumptions were justified. Stewart told the CRE that he was not disappointed when he was not moved straightaway. And when he was cross-examined on the topic at his trial, he said that he was not angry about not being moved because he thought that it would probably happen on the Tuesday. All in all, I do not believe that any disappointment about not being moved out of Swallow played a part in his thinking when he decided to attack Zahid.

Remaining in custody

36.19 It will be recalled that Stewart threatened to take extreme measures to get transferred, including killing his cellmate, if he did not get bail when he was next in court on 7 March. He did not get bail either then or on the following day. His attack on Zahid was the realisation of that threat, but was it prompted by anger over the rejection of his application for bail? Professor Maden thought it might have been, even though Stewart expressed himself as not "bothered" by the refusal of bail, and said that he did not usually get bail. Bail was not something which he was expecting to get.

36.20 I do not regard the passage of two weeks between the refusal of bail and the attack on Zahid as significant. Stewart would have had to remain in custody until he had completed his current sentence, so the impact on him of the refusal of bail would only have been felt on 17 March, when he would otherwise have been released. And as I have already said, he told Ms Poulson that he was brooding over attacking Zahid for a couple of days.

36.21 One view is that all this is subsumed in the reason Stewart himself gave for attacking Zahid. The fact that Stewart did not get bail was the reason he had to explore other ways to get out of Feltham. So rather than attacking Zahid simply because he was disappointed that he continued to be in custody, which I do not regard as plausible, the far more likely possibility is that he attacked Zahid in the light of the consequence of the refusal of bail. That was that he would have to remain at Feltham until his trial on the harassment charges, and attacking Zahid was, in his view, the best way of bringing his time at Feltham to a quicker end. But another view, which I regard as just as plausible, is that since he had not got bail, he was not going to allow a "Paki" like Zahid to enjoy his freedom.

Miscellaneous matters

36.22 There are three miscellaneous points I should make. First, Professor Gunn identified a number of other possible explanations for the attack on Zahid which he readily conceded could amount to no more than speculation in the absence of further clinical investigation. Stewart may have been suffering from a fluctuating psychotic condition, or a neurological abnormality, or a sleep disorder of some kind. Since Stewart was not examined with a view to ascertaining whether these conditions might have been present, we cannot take the matter further. For what it is worth, Stewart denied that he had ever had blackouts or that he was unaware at the time of the attack of what he was doing.

36.23 Secondly, a number of things were troubling Stewart while he was at Feltham – not least of which were the number of black and Asian prisoners he encountered there and who he felt intimidated by, the sense of alienation and isolation he felt at being in what he saw as a hostile environment far from home, and the frustration he felt about being "banged up" for so long in his cell. All these factors could have made him particularly fragile, and could have had the effect of magnifying any resentment he may have felt about Zahid, about sharing a cell with him and about being at Feltham. It may be that it was a combination of a whole variety of factors which caused him to attack Zahid when he did. As Professor Maden was to say, there was unlikely to have been one understandable grand motive in Stewart's mind.

36.24 Thirdly, the possibility cannot be eliminated that Stewart may have had no motive at all. At his trial, he said that he simply felt like attacking Zahid, and that he did not have any particular motive for doing so. With a callousness which must have struck everyone who read them as chilling, Stewart wrote in his letters about the murder that Zahid "was a nobody really" and "that cunt's not waking up again". As Professor Maden said, Stewart's lack of concern for other people or for the consequences of his actions meant that he was not constrained by the things which would restrain a normal person. Maybe it was as simple as that.

Chapter 37: Another series of missed opportunities

37.1 Stewart's murderous attack on Zahid could not have been predicted. No-one could have foreseen so vicious an attack by someone who had no chance of escaping detection. Professor Gunn and Professor Maden were agreed about that. But the six weeks Stewart spent at Feltham, coupled with his two earlier visits for a couple of days each, gave staff ample opportunities to recognise that he posed a risk to any person from an ethnic minority with whom he shared a cell – even if an attack of the kind which was to take place could not have been expected. The tragedy was that these opportunities were missed. Had any of them not been, the course of events might have been very different.

37.2 It started with the lack of information Feltham got about Stewart from Hindley. The inmate intelligence card at the front of his security file did not refer to the intercepted letter in which he had talked of committing an armed robbery, or to his use of parts of cell furniture as weapons at Altcourse. It gave the impression that he had been trouble-free since January 1999. And Hindley was never to warn Feltham about the sort of prisoner it was getting. It was left to the Security Department at Feltham to pick that up from Stewart's security file. It is to its credit that it did. But it did so only the first time Stewart went to Feltham. The result was that although Lapwing was warned about Stewart's dangerousness, Swallow never was. That was because no-one in the Security Department looked at Stewart's security file again when he returned to Feltham for the last time. There was no system in place to ensure that the security files of prisoners coming back to Feltham were looked at again with a view to briefing the inmate's current unit about him.

37.3 In any event, the Security Department only knew about Stewart's dangerousness. It knew nothing of his racism. That was because Mr Martindale had not told it about Stewart's racist letter which had been intercepted. So even if the Security Department had told Swallow about the contents of Stewart's security file, it could not have told them about his racism.

37.4 Other important steps were not taken when Stewart came to Feltham. He was never seen by a doctor and his medical record was never reviewed. So Mr Kinnealy's note about Stewart suffering from a personality disorder which robbed him of any feeling for other people was never looked at. And his warrants were not checked to see whether he faced charges which required his correspondence to be monitored. It is difficult to say what would have happened if his medical record had been reviewed, but the monitoring of his correspondence should unquestionably have resulted in Stewart being placed in a cell on his own. At the very least, he should not have continued to share a cell with Zahid for a moment longer.

CHAPTER 37: ANOTHER SERIES OF MISSED OPPORTUNITIES

37.5 To their credit, Mr Martindale and Miss Hogg made entries in the temporary wing file which Miss Hogg opened about Stewart's dangerousness and racism. But the file disappeared for a while. It was misfiled in Custody Administration. Yet when Stewart went to Swallow without it, nothing was done to find out where it was. It did not get to Swallow until Stewart had been there for four weeks. During that time, he had not been in any trouble, and if staff had read that he was dangerous and a racist, they may not have been lulled by his unproblematic behaviour in the meantime into doing nothing about it. As it was, the only member of staff who read Stewart's temporary wing file was Mr Morse, and he did nothing as a result. Stewart's personal officers did not even look at it. Mr Skinner handled it the day after Mr Morse had read it, but he did not even bother to look inside it, even though it was prominently marked with an instruction to do so.

37.6 Other things went wrong while Stewart was on Swallow. Some staff on the unit sensed that there was something odd about him, but it never crossed anyone's mind to question whether Zahid might be uncomfortable about sharing a cell with him. In part, that was down to Zahid's personal officers. They never tried to get to know him, or to build up any kind of rapport with him which might have made him sufficiently trusting of them to tell them why he did not want to continue to share a cell with Stewart. As it was, his request to move out of cell 38 was either overlooked or refused for reasons which are not readily apparent.

37.7 Finally, there were the weapons Stewart had in the cell. Although what was left of the crossbar was discovered by Mr Chahal, he did nothing about it. His find should have prompted him to check the table. If he had done that, he would have discovered that the leg propping up the table was detached from it. Not only would Stewart not have been able to use it on Zahid, but that would have prompted a thorough search of the cell. Both the missing stabiliser and the dagger would have been discovered, and that would have resulted in Stewart – and maybe Zahid as well – being sent to the segregation unit. But one thing is clear: they would not have been sharing a cell on Zahid's last night.

Part 4

Feltham: The Wider Picture

Chapter 38: Staff morale

The significance of staff morale

38.1 Many of the things which led to Zahid's murder were down to the failings of individual officers at Feltham. No-one on Lapwing told the Security Department about Stewart's racist letter which had been intercepted. No-one in the Security Department checked Stewart's security file when he returned to Feltham for the last time. It never occurred to anyone on Swallow that Stewart might be racist and that Zahid might have been uncomfortable about sharing a cell with him. Zahid's personal officers took no particular interest in him. And his request to move cells and the way his cell was searched left much to be desired. On their own, these shortcomings were not directly attributable to the problems Feltham faced, such as the shortage of staff, the large number of prisoners and the demands of getting them to and from the courts. The wider pressures to which Feltham was subject should not be used as an excuse for individual responsibility.

38.2 But staff morale tends to be low in institutions which are not performing well. And a demoralised workforce will find it hard to raise its game. Staff will become entrenched in their existing practices and will be resistant to change. That is why the failings of individual officers have to be seen in the context of Feltham as a whole. They must be judged in the light of what the establishment was really like at the time, and not against an ideal standard based on the wisdom of hindsight. That does not make individuals any the less accountable for their failings. But it may explain why their failings were so widespread. In this part of the report, I consider why things at Feltham went wrong, and where responsibility for that lies – whether within the establishment or beyond. But first I look at staff morale at Feltham – and the attitudes it spawned – as well as the inconsistencies in working practices which affected performance and could be said to have demoralised staff even more.

The decline in staff morale

38.3 The Inspectorate was relatively upbeat about Feltham's workforce when it inspected the establishment in 1996. The "predominant culture" among the staff was "one of wanting to care and develop the regime". It detected "a sense of purpose and unity" across the establishment. But by 1998 things had changed. It found "little to suggest that staff cared what happened to the young prisoners in their charge", and there were "too many examples of distant and disinterested staff". Mr Welsh was inclined to think that the Inspectorate had over-emphasised the positive attitude of staff at the time of the earlier inspection, but he still acknowledged that there had been some decline in attitudes and morale over the intervening years.

38.4 The reason for the downturn is not immediately apparent. It was not as if the number of prisoners Feltham had to take grew over the period – though there had been a relatively big increase in the months leading up to the 1996 inspection. But I am sure that what made staff get dispirited was the fact that they could not see anything which would change Feltham from an establishment where the need to get large numbers of young remand prisoners to court on time dominated the daily life of the prison, preventing anything else from being done. Certainly Mr Welsh thought staff could not see light at the end of the tunnel.

38.5 The effect of the criticisms of Feltham's staff in the Inspectorate's report following its inspection in 1998 only served to increase their despondency. Mr Welsh said that they felt they were just being "kicked again". It led Lucy Bogue, who was the chair of Feltham's Board of Visitors at the time of Zahid's death, to describe morale then as being "at an all time low". But the criticisms of staff in the report could have been handled by Feltham's senior management with greater sensitivity. If staff had become demoralised because they saw no real possibility of the establishment changing in the foreseeable future, they needed to feel that management realised that the downturn in morale and their negative attitude to their work was not something for which they alone should be blamed. They did not get that assurance. Moreover, they needed to be told that Prison Service headquarters was determined to get to grips with Feltham's problems, and to be given some confidence that there was a commitment to change on the part of senior management. Although staff could see members of the task force at the establishment, it has not been suggested that they received the reassurances they needed. Mr Welsh was about to leave Feltham, and he thought it was for the new Governor to brief staff about where the establishment was going. And although Mr Atherton presumed that the task force would engage with the staff on this issue, he did not know whether they did or not. The leader of the task force, Adrian Smith, did not suggest that they did.

Morale during Mr Clifford's time at Feltham

38.6 Mr Clifford sensed the negative staff attitudes when he arrived at Feltham in April 1999. There was "a kind of inertia" throughout the establishment, and he had "never seen as entrenched a bunch of staff".

A potent symbol of the staff's reluctance to change things was the silence which Mr Clifford encountered when he addressed staff shortly after his arrival.

38.7 The weight of the evidence suggests that things did not improve during Mr Clifford's stewardship of the establishment. That does not necessarily reflect badly on him. Things were not going to change in a matter of months. And many particular factors were in play at the time. Staff shortages were particularly acute between October 1999 and April 2000, and that coincided with the introduction of new work profiles in October 1999 which some staff resented because of the impact they would have on their shift patterns. This was also the time of the build-up towards the physical separation of Feltham A and Feltham B, and additional staff and resources were being earmarked for juveniles at the expense of young offenders. With morale at such a low ebb, this was just about the worst time for that initiative to come on stream. But the division of Feltham was dictated by the assumption of responsibility for the funding of the juvenile estate by the Youth Justice Board, and Mr Clifford had little control over the staff shortages. And abandoning the introduction of the new work profiles would have sent out the wrong message. Attitudes had to change, and if that meant challenging entrenched attitudes, that had to be done.

38.8 The news of Mr Clifford's promotion to Area Manager in November 1999 also had an unsettling effect on the establishment. Governors should remain in post for longer than Mr Clifford remained at Feltham, and succession planning should be robust enough to take that into account. It did not make much sense for a man with a reputation for getting things done – which was the reputation Mr Clifford had arrived at Feltham with – to move on just months after he had been brought in to drive through a programme of change. There were many, of course, who were pleased that they would be seeing the back of him. They thought that the agenda for change would not be pushed through, and that they could return to their previous ways. And his personal style did not endear him to everyone. There were others, though, who saw Mr Clifford's imminent departure as potentially a significant reversal of fortune for Feltham. It would be seen as a lack of commitment to effect change. They feared it would make staff feel that the POA represented the real management at the establishment.

38.9 It would be wrong to criticise Mr Clifford for applying for promotion. He could not be expected to put his career advancement on hold while he tried to put Feltham on the road to recovery, especially as he had already passed up one opportunity to apply for promotion, and opportunities for promotion did not come round regularly. There was no suggestion that he misled the Prison Service into thinking that he would not be applying for promotion, though it is questionable whether he should have told Feltham's Board of Visitors that he intended staying at the establishment for three years without at the same time telling them that he wanted to apply for promotion before then if the opportunity arose. Nor can the Prison Service be criticised for promoting him. If he had been sent to Feltham because of his reputation as a man who could get results, it would have been unfair for his strengths to have counted against him. As it turned out, Mr Clifford did not leave Feltham as soon as his promotion was announced. He remained there until May 2000, about six weeks after the murder of Zahid. He was promoted "in post", which meant that he would enjoy the pay and conditions of the grade to which he was promoted, though for the time being he would remain in his present post. But there was a delay in announcing that he would be remaining at the establishment for some time to come. It would have been much better if his promotion and the fact that he was staying put for a while had been announced at the same time.

The impact of low staff morale

38.10 It would also be wrong to think that all staff at Feltham were infected by negative attitudes of the kind which low morale breeds. As with any institution, Feltham had both good members of staff and bad ones. There were those officers who retreated to the office on the unit when they could have got prisoners out of their cells. However, there were also officers who did what they could to improve the regime for the young prisoners in their care, but whose efforts were crippled by staff shortages. Mrs Bogue recognised both of these descriptions. There were some officers, she said, who were "apathetic towards delivering care", but there were also other very good officers who were keen to do their best for the many damaged young men who spent time at Feltham. In her opinion, the trouble was that the minority of staff who were opposed to change may have had a disproportionate effect on the majority of staff who realised that change had to be made.

38.11 Ultimately these things are very much a matter of impression. But Mrs Bogue's view coincided with what I felt as the Inquiry proceeded. The dispiriting conditions in which staff had to work undoubtedly affected them, but I also sensed what Mr Giffin described as "a pervasive culture which actively destroyed staff from working as effectively as they should have done", fostered in part by a powerful local branch of the POA. This resistance to change may well have affected the way in which Stewart and Zahid were dealt with by the staff with whom they both came into contact. It is less easy to suppose that the flow of information in and out of the Security Department, or the handling of Stewart's racist letter, would have been any different if morale had been better. But if staff had not been as disenchanted as many of them were, they might have been more alert to Stewart's possible racism and Zahid's discomfort about sharing a cell with him. They might also have taken a greater interest in Zahid, given more thought to his request to move, and been more careful when they came to search his cell.

Inconsistencies in working practices

38.12 The problems for staff at Feltham were not simply the product of low morale. In many cases, there were no procedures in place to guide them about how they were to do their work. An obvious example was the absence of local procedures for the making of cell allocation decisions. That meant staff were sometimes left to work out for themselves how they did things.

38.13 There was no easy answer to this problem. There were already an enormous number of written guidelines for staff to read and assimilate. That was only to be expected in an institution as complex as a prison where staff have to carry out so many different tasks. Providing staff with yet more written guidance could well have resulted in staff suffering from information overload. After a while written procedures become just too much to digest – especially for front-line officers whose skills are practical rather than literary.

38.14 This state of affairs may explain why staff were often unaware of Governor's Orders. They went to every unit and department in Feltham, copies of them being handed to senior officers at their regular morning meeting. But what happened to them then differed according to what the practice of the senior officer was. In some units, they were simply filed in a folder. In others, they were stuck on a notice board for a while before being filed. There was a staff information room, but staff did not use it often. The consequence was that Governor's Orders often passed staff by.

38.15 Nor was increased training necessarily the answer. Mr Clifford was articulating what many people think when he said that new recruits to the Prison Service should simply emerge from training college with a set of skills in very basic prison work. The best way to learn how to put them into practice and perform more complicated tasks was on the job: being told what to do and watching how it was being done by others, and then by doing it oneself under supervision. "Endlessly sitting people down in front of a tutor talking at them" often fails to take into account the boredom threshold. People who attend training sessions know how easy it is to lose one's concentration and to forget what one is being told. Mr Clifford's view is one which I subscribe to, though it is heresy to many who point out that the length of basic training for new recruits to the Prison Service compares unfavourably with other developed countries comparable to the UK. There may, of course, be room for formal training in more specialised functions, where there are set procedures which have to be followed. Reception and security are examples which spring to mind. And there should have been training about young offenders, whose needs are very different from adult prisoners. But even that could be delivered locally, rather than requiring officers to go on extended courses.

38.16 As it was, staff at Feltham learned how to carry out particular tasks by watching them being done by more experienced officers who they would shadow for a few days. Although that may have been common across the prison estate, it was probably more prevalent at Feltham, because of an impetus to give staff on individual units a high degree of autonomy. The problem arose when the officers being shadowed had picked up bad habits. Their poor practice would have been regarded by the inexperienced officer as the norm. That put a high premium on effective supervision of the more experienced officers by senior officers, and effective management of senior officers by principal officers. Senior officers needed to be alive to how the work was being done on their units by the more experienced officers, so that they could correct bad practice when it was apparent. And they needed to supervise the work of inexperienced officers, so that they could advise them where they were going wrong. For their part, principal officers had to check that the senior officers for whom they were responsible were instilling best practice into basic grade officers. That was where things broke down at Feltham. Mr Clifford admitted as much. In an illuminating passage in his evidence to the Inquiry, he said that "senior officers… had been effectively sidelined. The mechanism whereby any kind of structure of doing the work could be explained to new officers did not exist." That was why work was carried out in so many different ways – and in bad ways at that.

38.17 The absence of a structure for ensuring that new officers were told how to do their work was a serious failing of Feltham's management. But it was also the consequence of a failure to recognise the need for newly promoted senior and principal officers to be trained in the skills and responsibilities of middle management. There was some management training, but at least one senior officer left the Inquiry with the impression that he regarded the training he received as insufficient, and another never went on a management training course because he could not be spared at the time. Mr Wheatley acknowledged that the amount of management training for newly promoted senior and principal officers was nowhere near what was desirable. That perhaps reflected a failure to appreciate what a big step up such promotions were.

Chapter 39: Feltham's degeneration into crisis

39.1 Poor morale may have made Feltham a difficult place for staff to work at. But problems do not arise overnight. They are often the product of a state of affairs which has been in existence for some time. The Inquiry's starting point for detailed scrutiny into the affairs at Feltham was December 1998, when the task force was appointed following the unannounced inspection of the establishment by the Inspectorate in November and December 1998. But it is necessary to go back further than that to put what happened from December 1998 onwards into its proper context.

39.2 Feltham had been a problem for the Prison Service for a long time. The Inspectorate's warnings following its inspection of Feltham in 1996 did not come out of the blue. Mr Narey could not recall a time when he would have considered Feltham an establishment to be proud of. That may have had something to do with the establishment taking over the functions of Ashford Remand Centre, and inheriting the unsettled industrial relations which Ashford had been renowned for. Mr Welsh described the culture there as having been characterised by the belief that prisoners were best managed by locking them up, and that staff, not management, should run the establishment. The Inquiry has not investigated the correctness of that, but certainly there were difficulties on the industrial relations front in the late 1980s when prison officers' terms and conditions of service were overhauled as part of an initiative known as Fresh Start. Other difficulties continued in the years up to and including 1998. The local branch of the POA actively opposed various measures which Mr Welsh wanted to introduce, and there were a number of "failures to agree" under the nationally agreed procedural arrangements, many of which were not resolved. Without straying from its self-imposed starting point, it was not possible for the Inquiry to decide whether the local branch of the POA was behaving unreasonably, or whether Mr Welsh was trying to push through reforms which the POA could legitimately oppose in the interests of its members.* But poor industrial relations tend to have an adverse effect on any institution, and Feltham was no exception in this respect.

39.3 However, the major problem was that the establishment was being asked to do too much with too few resources. There was a dramatic increase throughout the country in the number of juveniles and young offenders being held in custody between 1993 and 1998. The impact of large numbers of young men being remanded in custody and receiving

---

* For example, the branch committee lodged what was acknowledged to be a measured and well-argued failure to agree about the conversion of Albatross into the healthcare centre. But its stance on other failures to agree was thought, by managers at least, to be unreasonable.

custodial sentences was felt particularly keenly at Feltham, since it was the only remand centre for young prisoners covering the London area. But that had not been matched by the investment needed to enable it to keep pace with its increasing population. Feltham simply did not have the staff it required. That had an adverse effect on the regime which it could provide for the young men in its care. I have already referred to the problems it had in recruiting staff because its levels of pay compared unfavourably with other local employers, and in retaining them because so many wanted to move out of London where housing was more affordable. That meant the budget Feltham had for staff salaries was slightly underspent. But it would still not have been able to afford the number of staff it really needed on the budget it had.

39.4 The other problem was that Feltham was neither fish nor fowl. Most prisons are either local prisons, which serve local courts and house unconvicted or unsentenced prisoners, and those convicted prisoners awaiting transfer to other establishments, or training prisons, where prisoners serve their sentences and are provided with training facilities and vocational courses. Feltham operated as both types of prison. The result was that all its inmates got a raw deal. The prisoners who were serving their sentences there did not benefit from sentence planning in that nothing was offered to them by way of behavioural programmes to prepare them for their release. The prisoners who were awaiting trial or sentence had to put up with being housed in overcrowded conditions. And all prisoners had to spend far too much time in their cells.

39.5 The high degree of autonomy which individual units enjoyed was also a problem. The initiative had been introduced by a previous Governor in the early 1990s. It was driven partly by the geographical fragmentation of Feltham. Its rationale was that if you had a competent senior officer in charge of a unit, he would establish working practices suitable for that unit and for the officers who worked on it, and those officers would take their cue from him. It was known as "team working" or "strategic management". But it depended for its success on the calibre of senior officers, and the initiative foundered on the inability of some of them to lead from the front. Many of them did not see the role of senior officer as anything other than being part of the team – albeit the most senior member of the team. Indeed, staff shortages often meant that they had little opportunity to manage their staff. They spent much of their time doing the same jobs as basic grade prison officers under their command – acting, in effect, as an extra pair of hands.

39.6 The "strategic management" initiative had three adverse consequences. First, it resulted in what Mr Clifford described as "delivery by lowest common denominator, i.e. if there was no will collectively on the staff to do things on time or at all, then they would not occur". Secondly, it resulted in a proliferation of working practices – some good and some bad. Mr Welsh said that he "had never come across anything as chaotic as this in the whole time" he had been in the Prison Service. And in a note which Mr Wheatley wrote after visiting Feltham in June 1999, he described the system as "inefficient and a recipe for organisational anarchy". One of the reasons for including the units in clusters was to move towards a measure of consistency in working practices. Thirdly, it added to the disproportionate influence which the local branch of the POA was said to have over the running of the establishment. The regime on each unit would be decided by the unit, where the branch's influence was strong, rather than by Feltham's senior management team.

39.7 There is one other factor which may have contributed to the establishment's problems prior to December 1998. The suggestion has been made that Feltham was poorly served by its senior management. Its governors were ineffective, as were members of the senior management team, and in any event they were not provided with adequate support from their superiors at area manager and operational director level. In view of the Inquiry's starting point for detailed scrutiny of Feltham, these suggestions were not explored in detail – certainly not sufficiently to enable findings of fact to be made about where responsibility lay. But no-one has suggested that the establishment was managed well in the period leading up to the starting point for the Inquiry's detailed factual investigation. Mr Welsh became the Governor of Feltham in February 1997, and undoubtedly things got worse under his stewardship. He himself said that he was not going to argue otherwise. Maybe he did not get the support he needed from his Area Manager. Maybe Prison Service headquarters did not have the political will to address the establishment's problems until the Inspectorate's report following its inspection in 1998 made determined action critical. Maybe Feltham's endemic problems meant that things were inevitably going to get worse. But maybe Mr Welsh concentrated on the minutiae of running a busy prison, and was more concerned with fire-fighting – dealing with problems as they arose – rather than preparing and taking forward a dynamic strategy to respond to the findings of the Inspectorate. After all, the problems Feltham had always faced were no different while Mr Welsh was in charge, so that the deterioration of Feltham may have been attributable to a lack of leadership on Mr Welsh's part. That again was not something which could properly have been explored in detail, and it would be inappropriate for me to express any view on the topic. But by any standards Mr Welsh was passed a poisoned chalice, and he could hardly have been expected to turn Feltham round quickly. As

Mr Narey said, when prisons go off the rails, it takes a long time to get them back on track.

39.8 But a concerted effort to turn a failing prison round is more likely to succeed if individual members of management are held to account for things which go wrong. The one area of its work for which Feltham was consistently praised was its ability to get prisoners to court on time. Might that have been – in part at least – because the courts' timetables would have been affected if prisoners had arrived late, and the presiding judge might have asked for someone from the establishment to attend court to explain the delay? Few things concentrate the mind more effectively than the possibility of being criticised in public. So if there had been greater accountability on the part of senior management at Feltham for the things which went wrong, might that have galvanised them into doing more to put things right?

39.9 Although Feltham had deteriorated between the two visits by the Inspectorate in 1996 and 1998, the report following the inspection in 1996 still made grim reading. I summarised the effect of the report in paragraph 4.13. Since the warning signs were apparent, there should have been some initiative from Prison Service headquarters to ensure that things got no worse. Again, the Inquiry did not explore in detail what the Prison Service did or did not do, but it was never disputed that the Prison Service's response to the report following the 1996 inspection was inadequate. As Mr Clifford said, it should not have taken two critical reports from the Inspectorate to make the Prison Service take the problems at Feltham seriously. Maybe the establishment was lost sight of at a time when the Inspectorate was raising many other concerns about the Prison Service and was highlighting other failing institutions. But one thing can be said with a good deal of confidence. Whether or not the Prison Service had adequate systems in place for identifying those prisons which were failing, it had not yet learned how to turn them round. That was accepted by both Mr Clifford and Mr Wheatley.

39.10 While on the subject of the Prison Service's response to the Inspectorate's report following the inspection in 1996, there was a suggestion that the Prison Service ignored the reports of Feltham's Board of Visitors. That was based on the fact that Sir Richard Tilt had not seen the annual report of the Board for 1998 when he visited Feltham in February 1999 and met members of the Board. It will be recalled that this report was published before the Inspectorate's report following its visit to Feltham in 1998 was published, but it highlighted some of the more significant problems which the establishment faced – in particular, the decline in staff morale, the increasing problem of staff shortages, and the limited time prisoners had out of their cells which that caused. The Director General of the Prison Service could not, of course, be expected to read the annual reports of all Boards of Visitors. He relied on his staff to draw to his attention the ones they thought he had to know about and to summarise them sufficiently for him. That did not happen with the annual report of Feltham's Board of Visitors for 1998 – maybe because it contained much praise for staff and management. As it was, by the time Sir Richard met the Board, he had been told what the Inspectorate's report would say. He had been taken aback by the severity of the criticisms of the establishment. The gravity of the situation had not properly been brought home to him, which was why he immediately established the task force.

39.11 Sir Richard was aware that Feltham was not in good shape, but he did not know just how bad it had become. That only highlights the inability of the Prison Service at the time to identify those prisons which were failing badly. We can see now that Feltham was failing badly, but Prison Service headquarters had no real grasp of that at the time. There could have been a number of reasons for that. The establishment was seen, as I have said, to be performing well in its core task of getting prisoners to court on time, and success on that front may have masked its other shortcomings. And it has been said that the Area Manager and Operational Director at the time never got a grip on Feltham. Certainly Mr Butt's view was that "management oversight appears to have been poor for many years". I do not doubt that Mr Welsh drew Feltham's problems to his Area Manager's attention when they met. But Mr Narey was shocked by how anodyne the Area Manager's reports about Feltham were. And Mr Smith, the head of the task force, said that they did not read as if there was a crisis looming. You would not have thought that the Area Manager and the Inspectorate had been talking about the same establishment. Maybe the supposed blandness of the Area Manager's reports about Feltham led to the Operational Director's failure to appreciate how bad Feltham was becoming – especially as their patch included a number of other prisons in London which had significant problems of their own – though Mr Narey's understanding was that the Operational Director was not the easiest man to work with, and that he was often away, spending much of his time on Council of Europe business. It is easy to say it now, and one can understand why Mr Welsh might have been reluctant to do it at the time, but if the Area Manager and the Operational Director had indeed taken their eye off Feltham, perhaps Mr Welsh should have done what Mr Narey suggested he might have done – which was to bypass the Area Manager and the Operational Director altogether, and go straight to the Director General about Feltham's shortcomings.

39.12 There may have been other reasons for Prison Service headquarters not picking up on Feltham's problems earlier, but again this was not explored in sufficient detail – and the Area Manager and Operational Director in post at the time were not asked to give evidence at the Inquiry in the light of the Inquiry's starting point. Indeed, when given the opportunity to comment on this part of the report when it was in draft, they both explained why any criticism of them was unjustified. So it would not be right to make any definitive findings about the allegations which have been made against them. But the fact that Prison Service headquarters was not sufficiently alive to Feltham's problems is not something which can seriously be contradicted.

Chapter 40: Where the buck stops

"The buck stops here"

40.1 President Truman had a sign on his desk in the Oval Office which read: "The buck stops here." The sign had been made at a reformatory in Oklahoma, where it had been on the desk of the Warden. The Warden was right. In prison, the buck does indeed stop with the Governor. If there are systemic failings in a prison, the Governor is accountable for them. The Governor has to explain how they arose – and if they were already there, the Governor has to explain how they continue to be present. But there is a limit to what can be expected of Governors. They cannot be expected to know everything which is happening in their prison, or be able to put everything right. That is especially so in a prison where systemic failings are widespread. Governors have to rely on their senior management team for many things. The question is whether, in the period between December 1998 and March 2000, Mr Welsh, and after him Mr Clifford, did what could reasonably be expected of them to put Feltham on the road to recovery.

Mr Welsh

40.2 Mr Welsh was in post for only four months or so between the inspection by the Inspectorate in December 1998 and Mr Clifford's arrival in April 1999. But these last few months were marked by two significant events. One was the appointment of the task force whose remit was to diagnose Feltham's shortcomings and identify what had to be done to bring about the improvements which the establishment needed. The appointment of the task force, and the involvement of the Director General in its work, was a very unusual step for the Prison Service to take. It demonstrated its commitment to tackling the problems Feltham faced. The other was the decision made by Mr Atherton towards the end of January 1999 that Mr Welsh was no longer the right choice to stay on and lead the programme of change which Feltham required so urgently and that he would have to be replaced. So not only did Mr Welsh know that Feltham was to benefit from some serious strategic thinking from outside. He also knew that he had very little time left at the establishment. Though not a lame duck during that time, he could hardly have introduced important new initiatives. If he had, he could have been criticised for queering the new Governor's pitch and for not having introduced them earlier.

40.3 Two points should be made about the task force. First, the intention had originally been to provide it with a dedicated support team who would implement the changes which it recommended. But it was later thought that this might be seen as an alternative line management, which could have created problems for the senior management team. So it was decided that such changes as were recommended would be implemented by the new Governor's senior management team. The task force did not want to box the new Governor into a particular way of implementing the recommendations it made. Secondly, the development of a long-term strategy to address the more deep-rooted problems Feltham faced would take some time. Meanwhile, there were some things which Feltham's management could do without much delay to bring about some modest improvements in the short term. These "quick wins" were identified relatively soon after the task force started its work. The most important of them was an improvement in the regime allowing prisoners more time out of their cells.

40.4 Some "quick wins" were achieved during Mr Welsh's last few months at Feltham. The move of the healthcare centre to Albatross which had been refurbished was completed, and some of the outstanding "failures to agree" were resolved. But the thrust of the evidence was that too little had been achieved. The baton had not been taken up by the senior management team in place at the time. That was certainly Mr Atherton's view. Mrs Bogue thought much the same. She did not discern any significant improvement before Mr Clifford's arrival. The regime was just as bad as before. And in a briefing paper for Mr Clifford, which the task force prepared as its work was wound down, it referred to "the torpor" with which the opportunities to achieve and report "quick wins" had been seized by Feltham's management. That indicated, said the task force, "the lack of ownership the establishment had of the task force's work and the benefits that undoubtedly arose from it". There was plainly some resistance to the task force from certain elements within Feltham's management. They resented a team coming in from outside and telling them where improvements needed to be made. That had not been lost on the task force. In its final report to the steering group before it was disbanded, it reported that its role had been "in tension (not always creative) with line management in the establishment".

40.5 It would be wrong to criticise Mr Welsh too much for the unwillingness of his senior management team to implement the quick fixes the task force had identified. With the task force responsible for identifying the direction in which Feltham should go, his position as the Governor was compromised. And with his departure from Feltham so imminent, his effectiveness was unquestionably affected. Moreover, the spectre of being remembered as the man who had presided over a particularly bad time in the establishment's history loomed large. It would be understandable if he had become dispirited at the time. But he should have picked up on the pockets of resistance to its work which the task force was to identify, and he should have been more pro-active in motivating his management team to drive through the immediate measures which the task force wanted introduced.

Mr Clifford

40.6 Mr Clifford arrived at Feltham a few weeks before the task force was disbanded in May 1999. He had acquired the reputation of a man who got things done, and he was determined to repeat at Feltham the successes he had achieved at Cardiff and Durham prisons. He bore the task force's recommendations in mind, though he focused principally on the shortcomings the Inspectorate had identified. Having said that, Mr Clifford was very much his own man. He would form his own judgement on where and why things were going wrong, and what needed to be put right. I do not doubt his drive or his commitment to Feltham. Nor do I believe that the knowledge that he would be leaving Feltham sooner rather than later, following his promotion "in post" in November 1999, lessened his determination to achieve change. He challenged what he found to be unacceptable, and he did what he could to get across his message that standards had to improve.

40.7 Feltham's Board of Visitors noted that Mr Clifford walked the ship, and was regularly seen around the establishment. In that way, the message went out that he was going to be "hands on". But his personal style was not to everyone's taste, and it may not have been right for this critical time in Feltham's history. He was a forthright man, who had a tendency to talk down to staff, and to be long on criticism while short on praise. He gave the impression of not suffering fools gladly. He may well have alienated some members of staff whom he rubbed up the wrong way. In an establishment where staff morale was so low, what was needed was a Governor who was able to get staff on his side. The anecdotal evidence suggested that this was an area in which Mr Clifford did not succeed.

40.8 Mr Windsor described Mr Clifford as "more of a leader than a manager". There is a good deal of truth in this observation. Mr Clifford was a man who led from the front. He left no-one in any doubt about who was in command. That is not to say that he would not listen to others if he thought they had something to say. But his strengths lay more in pursuing his own strategy for improving Feltham, by his example of being so visible and by showing that his reputation for turning round failing prisons was justified.

40.9 It has to be said that Mr Clifford did not have all that much to show in terms of achievement by the time he left Feltham in May 2000. There were, it is true, some noteworthy successes. As we shall see, he paved the way for the separation of Feltham A and Feltham B. He changed the function of Kestrel which housed only prisoners who were due to be discharged. The new profiling exercise which brought about a more efficient use of staff was implemented during his stewardship, even though it took some time for the benefits of the new shift patterns to be seen. And a job rotation scheme was introduced to prevent staff from becoming stale in jobs they had been doing for too long. But what he had rightly regarded as his priority – the improvement of living conditions for prisoners, in particular in the regime, so that they had more time out of their cells for association and purposeful activity – had not been achieved. Progress had been made in some areas: the facilities in the gym had been improved, showers were supervised in the gym so that it ceased to be a no-go area for some prisoners, the outside playing fields were being brought back into use, and the Inspectorate commended the work which had been done in the Education Department following its inspection in September 1999. But these were only small pockets of improvements. That was what the Inspectorate found when it visited Feltham in October 2000, a visit which had not been announced beforehand. While acknowledging that "considerable progress" had been made "in developing sound foundations on which a suitable regime [in Feltham could] be provided and delivered", it found "virtually no change in the way that the majority of young people [in Feltham B] were treated".* Feltham had then had the misfortune of losing another Governor a few months after Mr Clifford's departure when his successor had had to retire through illness. Anecdotal evidence suggests that any overall improvements which Mr Clifford had been able to achieve were lost during this period. But the fact remains that daily life on the units by the time Stewart murdered Zahid was little different from when Mr Clifford had arrived at Feltham almost a year earlier.

40.10 It is not possible to say now how much, if at all, that was due – in part at least – to Feltham's senior management team. Many of those who were already there when Mr Clifford arrived were themselves relatively new to the establishment. As we shall see, there were managerial weaknesses at a number of levels. Mr Clifford would have preferred to pick his own

---

* These quotations come from the preface to the report which was published following the visit – the preface which Mr Narey claimed the author of the report privately disavowed to him.

team, and if he had done so it is possible that improvements might have been achieved more quickly. But it is questionable whether one or two people would have made a practical difference, given the entrenched and endemic nature of Feltham's problems. It was not then the practice of the Prison Service to allow an incoming Governor to have an entirely new management team. Some continuity with the past was regarded as desirable. In any event, it was not as if Mr Clifford was not given some new blood. A new Head of Feltham A, Janine Morris, came with him, and a new Head of Feltham B, Peter Windsor, arrived a few months later, even though Mr Windsor was not Mr Clifford's first choice for the post. And although Mr Clifford expressed concerns about the capacity of some of his managerial team, he never gave Mr Atherton the impression of any weak links.

40.11 However, it would be wrong to judge Mr Clifford's tenure at Feltham simply by results. The core problems – too few staff, too many prisoners, too little investment and a supposedly militant local branch of the POA – were problems which he inherited, and could not be changed overnight. So too was the forthcoming diversion of resources for the successful separation of Feltham A and Feltham B. Whether any blame for Feltham's continuing decline can be attributed to Mr Clifford depends to a great extent on how he coped with these problems. I deal with each of them in the next five chapters.

Chapter 41: Staff shortages

The significance of staff shortages

41.1 Staff shortages were at the heart of Feltham's problems. If an establishment operates with less than its full complement of staff, a heavier burden will fall on the staff who are there. If they are overworked, their performance will be affected. Mistakes are more likely to occur, and staff will probably approach their work with less enthusiasm. So staff shortages will have a significant effect on morale. And operating with a reduced workforce increases the levels of absence through sickness, because staff who are overworked need more time off to cope with the stress which overworking creates.

41.2 But staff shortages on the residential units also had more tangible consequences. At times staff were not released to go on training courses. They were sometimes cross-deployed from elsewhere in the establishment to ensure that core functions, such as supervising at meal times and escorting prisoners engaged on purposeful activity, could take place. The Security Department was the principal casualty of that. There were times when it had no prison officers working in it. Again, staff shortages on the residential units meant that staff there would have to focus on the core functions of the unit to the detriment of other tasks, such as personal officer work or the routine searching of cells or attendance at meetings of the race relations management team. Officers were sometimes brought in from other residential units, which had a knock-on effect on those units. Senior officers would be forced to spend much of their time acting as an extra pair of hands instead of concentrating on their supervisory role. And most important of all, staff shortages on the residential units had a direct impact on the time prisoners spent out of their cells. The fewer officers there were available to supervise association, the less association prisoners got. This was the ultimate cause of the shocking fact that many prisoners were locked up in their cells for as much as 23 hours a day.*

---

* The Inquiry never received accurate figures for the time prisoners had out of their cells. Prisoners not engaged in purposeful activity could be in their cells for 22–23 hours a day. The Inspectorate's report following its visit to Feltham in 1999 referred to "the recorded level of 15 hours purposeful activity per week" as unacceptable. The Prison Service's own figures show that in the four months up to 31 March 2000, prisoners in the cluster of units which included Swallow had an average of 9.18 hours a week of purposeful activity, but since the documents on which these figures were based have not survived, their accuracy could not be tested.

Absence levels

41.3 One of the causes of the staff shortages at Feltham was its high absence levels. Staff are often absent from work, and not just because they are sick. They have to go on training courses, and they are, of course, entitled to annual leave. The Prison Service factors staff absences into its calculations of the staffing levels establishments need. It proceeds on the assumption that 20% of an establishment's staff will be non-effective. Feltham's non-effective rate was 26%, and a disproportionate amount of that was attributable to staff sickness.

41.4 That was something which Feltham had to sort out for itself. It would not have been right for Mr Clifford to approach Prison Service headquarters cap in hand and ask for more staff because Feltham's workforce were unusually prone to sickness. If members of staff were too ill to return to work in the foreseeable future, they should have been removed from the payroll. If they were not returning to work as soon as they were able to, steps should have been taken to get them back to work.

41.5 I have little doubt that the pressure cooker environment in which staff were working at Feltham increased the levels of stress for staff. A greater emphasis on the importance of occupational health may have been helpful. But anecdotal evidence suggests that not all short-term sickness absence was genuine, and long-term sickness absence was hardly addressed at all. Things were just allowed to drift. I do not think that the problem was addressed by Mr Clifford. He may have wanted a robust approach to be taken, not only with those he thought were throwing "sickies" or were malingering, but also with those with little prospect of ever returning to work. To do that, he had to change the culture of line managers who had got into the habit of not reviewing the frequency of the absence through sickness of members of staff, not monitoring whether they returned to work as soon as possible, and not challenging them when their absence went on for a long time.

41.6 What was needed was a protocol to force line managers to take the problem seriously. Mr Clifford did not initiate one. I acknowledge that since a change of approach was required from line managers, immediate improvements were not possible. Indeed, Nick Pascoe, who was Feltham's Governor from October 2000 to November 2003, said that it took him two-and-a-half years to get to grips with the problem. Moreover, this was an area in which the co-operation of the Personnel Department was needed, and according to Mr Clifford it was not performing well at the time. But Mr Clifford could have made a start at dealing with the problem, and it does not look as if he did.

Inefficiencies in deployment

41.7 It had been acknowledged for some time that staff at Feltham were not deployed efficiently. Mr Welsh had tried to introduce new profiles for staff to make better use of their time, but without success because his attempts to do so had been opposed by the local branch of the POA. During its time, the task force recommended that another profiling exercise should be carried out with a view to the introduction of new profiles. It thought the exercise should start from scratch, rather than building on the work done by Mr Welsh.

41.8 Staff profiling is not a straightforward task. Its aim is to match the staff you have with the work which needs to be done. You do that by identifying the number of man-hours needed for that work, and then working out the most efficient way of deploying your staff, so that no more than the number of staff needed to carry out the work are assigned to it, that staff are not left with time on their hands, and that staff are engaged on work which matches their abilities. Quite sophisticated management skills are needed to realise what you want to achieve. It is to Mr Clifford's credit that he was able to introduce new profiles for all members of staff in Feltham B. They were developed in-house by a team of non-professionals in the field, though they had the help of Management Consultancy Services, a division within the Prison Service which acted as management consultants to establishments which needed advice and assistance. Apart from deploying staff more efficiently, the new profiles were intended to extend the core day by 45 minutes. One effect of that would be to enable prisoners to have their evening meal later. The new profiles came on stream on 3 October 1999, though it took some time for their benefits to be recognised, and they did not have an immediate impact on the regime.

41.9 A new profiling exercise was undertaken after Mr Clifford left Feltham. It was introduced by Mr Pascoe. Unlike Mr Clifford, he got Management Consultancy Services to draw up the new profiles themselves. He asked them to come up with profiles which would allow prisoners to be out of their cells from some time in the morning until the evening with the exception of mealtimes, with a senior officer and four other officers on duty. He left it to Management Consultancy Services to devise a way of achieving that over a seven-day period. They came up with staff profiles which enabled that to be achieved. Their report came out in March 2001, and the new profiles were introduced the following July. Indeed, not only was the exercise achieved within existing resources. It also generated a number of savings which Feltham was permitted to retain and reinvest in other ventures.

41.10 If Mr Pascoe's profiling exercise could improve the regime so dramatically by the summer of 2001, why could that not have been achieved by the profiling exercise which Mr Clifford initiated? The evidence on the topic of Mr Atherton and Mr Wheatley, who was the Deputy Director General at the time, differed in its emphasis, but the thrust of it was that Management Consultancy Services could only give Mr Clifford limited assistance in his profiling exercise. That was partly because the advice and assistance they gave to establishments was just that – advice and assistance. Profiling was done across the prison estate in-house at the time, albeit with Management Consultancy Services on hand to help out. It was also partly because the advice and assistance they gave involved discussions with the local branch of the POA. Management Consultancy Services had lost credibility with the local branch of the POA at Feltham in the course of Mr Welsh's profiling exercise, which was why he had been unable to introduce new profiles. Greater involvement by Management Consultancy Services in Mr Clifford's profiling exercise could have prevented the new profiles from being agreed with the local branch of the POA. By the time of Mr Pascoe's profiling exercise, the role of Management Consultancy Services had changed. They did not have to get agreement with the local branch of the POA for the new profiles they had devised. Moreover, Mr Wheatley had introduced a three-year programme to drive out inefficiencies, and Management Consultancy Services were resourced to spearhead that initiative. Their function was to review an establishment's existing working arrangements to see whether things could be done for less money. And 40 establishments a year were selected for this scrutiny. Feltham was one of those chosen in the first year of the initiative. I have no reason to doubt the evidence of Mr Atherton and Mr Wheatley on this topic, and although it is at first sight surprising that two profiling exercises produced such different results, I can see how the professional involvement of Management Consultancy Services in a significant way rather than from the sidelines could well have made all the difference. Moreover, Mr Pascoe had many staff who worked longer hours – the equivalent of 30 additional members of staff in all.

Low staffing levels

41.11 Although high absence levels and inefficiencies in deployment played their part in contributing to staff shortages, the overarching problem was that there were times when the number of staff in post fell well below the number which Feltham was said to need. Mr Welsh had managed to get the number of staff back up to the Prison Service's target figure by the time he left, but there was no significant increase in the number of staff in post following the increase in the target figure in July 1999 from 363 to 432 staff.* That figure was increased to reflect the requirements of the Youth Justice Board for staffing levels in Feltham A, but since the funding for that was not going to be available for a while, there could have been no expectation that the new target figures would be achieved quickly. What the figures show, however, is that by 31 March 2000, the target figure was for there to be 430 staff in post, including 361 discipline officers, whereas there were actually 400 staff, including 344 discipline officers. That shortfall mirrored what had been identified in September 1999 following the completion of the new profiles. There had then been a shortfall of 29 officers, once the "predictable non-effectives" had been factored into the equation.

41.12 The POA told the Inquiry that even if the targets for the number of staff in post had been achieved, Feltham would still not have been able to deliver the regime which ought to have been available for its inmates. They said that the problem was essentially one of resources. If the establishment had been given a more realistic target figure for the number of staff in post, and if its budget had been increased to fund the recruitment of additional members of staff, the regime which everyone wanted could have been delivered. The evidence on the topic was impressionistic, and I cannot come to a conclusive view on it. I note, for example, that Mr Welsh said that with the staff he had, he could only have got about three hours' association for unconvicted prisoners. But whether that would have been so at the end of his time at Feltham when he hit the target number for staff in post I cannot say. Similarly, Mr Pascoe was able to provide the regime he wanted, but whether he was only able to do that because some of the staff were then working longer hours, I do not know.

Recruitment of staff

41.13 I referred earlier to the particular pressures which Feltham faced in recruiting and retaining staff. In the old days, prison officers had been provided with quarters in which to live. These were phased out in the 1980s, and for many years London Weighting had been the only mechanism used to offset the unfavourable levels of pay within the Prison Service when compared with local employers with whom Feltham had to compete. But in October 1999, Mr Atherton and Mr Clifford were able to secure the agreement of the Personnel Policy Group at Prison Service headquarters for a scheme, known as Headstart, which enabled new recruits to receive the rate of pay normally attained, as a result of periodic

---

* Staff in post included those in governor grades, principal officers, senior officers and basic grade officers.

increments, in the third year of employment. It took some time before this scheme began to pay dividends, but when it did Feltham became a less unattractive place at which to work. Prison Service headquarters must bear the responsibility for the scheme not having been introduced earlier. Ever since the early 1990s when the Prison Service acquired agency status, it had been free to set its own rates of pay. I know the POA was, in Mr Welsh's words, "not mad keen on anything that smacked of local pay". Despite that, Headstart was implemented, and had serious thought been given in Prison Service headquarters to improving the package which new recruits to Feltham would enjoy, a scheme on the lines of Headstart could have been introduced earlier.

41.14 Recruitment procedures did not help either. Staff were recruited and trained centrally. Delays in recruiting suitable staff occurred because candidates had to be assessed for suitability to work in the Prison Service at job simulation assessment centres, and it took time for such assessments to be set up. And delays occurred in training new recruits, because it took time for places on the Prison Service's basic training course to become available. The task force had suggested that assessments at job simulation assessment centres local to Feltham be arranged, but that only happened once, and it produced just nine suitable candidates for the 24 posts it had to fill. Nor was it accompanied by a system allowing places to be reserved on training courses for those recruited at such assessments. The answer to the first of those problems was to arrange for more assessments to take place locally. And the answer to the second was for training to be devolved to individual establishments. Both those initiatives were introduced for London establishments in 2002, after Bill Duff had become the Area Manager for London South. There is no good reason why these initiatives could not have been introduced earlier. It was not as if the Prison Service had been unaware of the staffing problems at Feltham. Feltham's Board of Visitors had drawn attention to it in its annual report for 1998, which had elicited a response from the Minister to the effect that the Prison Service was undertaking a review of its recruitment processes. There is nothing to suggest that the review was completed, or that anything came out of it.

41.15 But this was an area in which the management at Feltham has to take some of the criticism as well. The task force had required Mr Welsh to draw up and implement a staff recruitment plan for 1999/2000. It identified the cost of the exercise as £12,000. Mr Welsh interpreted that as requiring him to identify simply what form of recruitment advertising campaign would produce the best results for that kind of expenditure. He did not draw up a plan as such, but he discussed with Feltham's Head of Personnel the possibility of advertising for recruits on local radio and in the local press. It may be that the £12,000 which the task force had budgeted for related to the costs of a recruitment campaign, but I do not believe that this was the only thing the task force had in mind. It wanted Mr Welsh to draw up an improved recruitment strategy. That he did not do. Maybe that was because a request he had made in 1998 for approval for the introduction of local pay flexibility at Feltham to encourage the recruitment and retention of staff had been rejected by Prison Service headquarters. Maybe it was because the Personnel Department was not set up to give him the help he needed to produce it. But the fact remains that he drew up nothing.

41.16 Nor did Mr Clifford. The briefing paper he received from the task force had a section in it devoted to recruitment and retention of staff. It suggested that a more imaginative and methodical approach to recruitment would yield benefits. It identified the features which an improved recruitment strategy should include. Mr Clifford's initial stance in his evidence was that there was not much he could do until he had a clear idea of how many vacancies there were at Feltham. Over-recruiting, he said, was almost as bad as under-recruiting. He added that it was not until September 1999 that the Personnel Department was geared up to giving him the management information he needed about current and projected staffing levels, and what effect wastage would have on the number of staff in post, and that it was not until the end of October 1999 that it was functioning properly. But he went on to acknowledge that this would not have justified putting off such recruitment as was needed. Save for Headstart, I am not aware of what he did, apart from having a recruitment open day, and linking into a national initiative to recruit staff from ethnic minorities. Maybe he thought that the combination of Headstart and the new profiles would result in Feltham having the staff it needed.

Retention of staff

41.17 On top of the difficulty of persuading staff to remain at Feltham, rather than going to live in another part of the country where housing was more affordable, the establishment faced an additional problem of retaining its staff in the build-up to the assumption by the Youth Justice Board of responsibility for the funding of the juvenile estate. When new prisons were opened, procedures agreed with the POA nationally required the Prison Service to trawl among its existing workforce for officers prepared to transfer to them. An establishment was permitted to delay the transfer of a member of staff to another establishment for only six months, and the POA at Feltham refused to agree to an extension of that period. In any event, you would not want to keep for too long a member of staff who wanted to transfer to another establishment: their frustration in having to stay might affect their work. Many staff left Feltham for other establishments during Mr Clifford's time there. The flow of staff was staunched later on, when the national agreement was terminated and staff no longer had the right to transfer to new establishments. It is unfortunate that the nationally agreed procedures were not terminated earlier. That may reflect the grip which the POA had on the Prison Service nationally. But it may also reflect the absence of strategic thinking at Prison Service headquarters at the time. One significant consequence of the difficulties which Feltham had in retaining its staff was that it had a high number of inexperienced staff who had been in the Prison Service for less than two years. Indeed, of the 344 discipline staff in post on 31 March 2000, 58 were undergoing basic training.

Overtime

41.18 If it was proving difficult to recruit new staff in sufficient numbers, and if some staff were leaving to work at new establishments and establishments for which the Youth Justice Board was to be responsible, what else could have been done to improve staffing levels at Feltham? Detached duty – the name the Prison Service gave to the secondment of staff from other establishments – was a possibility, but it may have been difficult identifying establishments where staff were surplus to requirements. In any event, Mr Clifford thought that detached duty brought with it its own inefficiencies. One can understand why. It might take a few weeks for seconded staff to get the hang of how things worked at Feltham, and before they could put their newly found knowledge of the way things were done at Feltham to the test, they might be called back to the establishment they had come from.

41.19 The other possibility was to encourage staff to work longer hours by paying them the equivalent of overtime. This was a contentious issue in the Prison Service. Overtime had been abolished in the late 1980s as part of the Fresh Start initiative. To re-introduce overtime – albeit calling it something else – would have been regarded as diluting the doctrinal purity of its abolition. But overtime by another name already existed – in the form of what the Prison Service referred to as *"ex gratia* payments", which were payments made to members of staff who volunteered to work for longer hours on an *ad hoc* basis. *Ex gratia* payments were only made in limited circumstances – for example, to officers who escorted prisoners to hospital and guarded them while they were there. Mr Atherton was unwilling to countenance the extension of the use of *ex gratia* payments to improve staffing levels at Feltham. That would have been a step too far towards a return to the bad old days of overtime. Instead, he pinned his hopes on reducing the staffing levels needed at Feltham, and he planned to do that by reducing the number of prisoners who went there. As we shall see, some success was achieved on that front.

41.20 I understand, of course, the desire to hold the line against overtime payments. It would have been wrong for the long-term interests of the Prison Service to be sacrificed on the altar of short-term gains at Feltham. Extending *ex gratia* payments could have been seen as the thin end of the wedge. But the dire plight Feltham was in called for radical initiatives. Some *ex gratia* payments were already being made in specific areas, and it would have been appropriate to extend their application if that could have brought about an improvement in the regime. However, I acknowledge that it would have been an extremely difficult decision to take at the time, and it is easy now – looking back many years later – to say that the wrong judgement was made.

41.21 But a scheme which could have been regarded as overtime under another name *was* introduced nationally later on. It was known as "contract hours", and it permitted staff to apply to work for a set number of additional hours a week over a specified period. They had to commit themselves to do that in advance. That was how Mr Wheatley, whose brainchild it was, rationalised it as being different from overtime. The scheme was only to be used for those establishments with staff shortages. Approval for its use had to be given by area managers, and the cost of the scheme had to come out of the establishment's own budget. It was introduced at Feltham in the spring of 2001. It had the beneficial side effect of reducing staff sickness. On one of his subsequent visits to Feltham, Mr Wheatley noted that the take up had been the equivalent of about 30 additional members of staff. It is a pity the idea was not thought of earlier. Maybe minds were instinctively closed to anything which might smack of overtime. But maybe it reflected the absence of innovative thinking at Prison Service headquarters at the time.

The Personnel Department

41.22 As we have seen, some of the problems associated with staff shortages were attributed by Mr Clifford to shortcomings in the Personnel Department. For his part, Mr Welsh thought that the department was functioning adequately when he left Feltham, but Mr Clifford was not alone in being critical of it. A principal officer who had come to Feltham in September 1998 found the place in a mess. It was astonishing, he said, that the department did not even know how many people were actually employed at the establishment. The problems may have had something to do with the absence through sickness of the Head of Personnel since shortly before Mr Clifford's arrival, and Mr Welsh may have underestimated the impact this would inevitably have had on the running of the department. The starting point for the Inquiry's detailed examination of Feltham meant that it would have been inappropriate to explore whether the department had been under-performing in the past, and where responsibility for that lay. But the task force found that Feltham struggled to organise a recruitment campaign, and that had to be due, at least in part, to shortcomings within the Personnel Department.

41.23 The task force identified the appointment of a new Head of Personnel – if the then post holder was to be absent for a prolonged period – as the first item on its list of what needed to be done to improve Feltham's recruitment strategy. That did not happen until the summer of 1999, although in the meantime a senior executive officer responsible for finance was doubling up and covering the personnel function as well. But within a relatively short time after that, the department began to function effectively again with a proper complement of administrative staff.

41.24 Mr Clifford agreed that this had been a rather tardy response to a problem which had required a speedy resolution. So why did it take so long to put the department on the road to recovery? Mr Clifford attributed it to the uncompetitive salaries being offered and the recruitment procedures of the Civil Service, which required posts to be filled only after open competition and which prevented him from recruiting a new Head of Personnel while the incumbent was still in post, albeit absent on long-term sick leave. He assumed that he would have discussed the problem with Mr Atherton. But Mr Atherton said that it was for the Governor to find solutions to problems of this kind. If there was a policy getting in the way of a speedy and sensible solution to the problem, something could be done about that. He did not recall being made aware of any such problems – or indeed any problems in the Personnel Department – until he visited Feltham in September 1999.

41.25 It is not now possible to say where fault lies for the undoubted delay in getting the Personnel Department back on its feet. Maybe Mr Clifford did not identify sufficiently quickly the problem as one which needed to be prioritised. Maybe he should have asked Prison Service headquarters to help by permitting exceptional short-term measures to be taken, such as waiving normal recruitment procedures, or allowing an enhanced salary to be paid in order to find a suitable Head of Personnel speedily, or seconding suitable administrative officers from another establishment. Or maybe Mr Clifford did everything he reasonably could within the constraints imposed on him, and it was Mr Atherton who should have suggested a way through the procedural thicket to get the Personnel Department the staff it needed.

Chapter 42: Feltham's prisoner population

42.1 If staff shortages were at the heart of Feltham's problems, the size and nature of its prisoner population came a close second. It was not simply a matter of the establishment having to accommodate too many inmates. Its throughput of prisoners – or "churn" to use the Prison Service's term for it – caused problems too. Many inmates did not have the benefit of what passed for an induction process at Feltham. An ever-changing population had significant implications for the flow and use of information about prisoners, and the opportunities for staff to get to know them – as well as creating pressures for convicted and unconvicted prisoners to be kept in the same unit. And the large number of inmates who had to be held at any one time meant that there were enormous pressures on the facilities in the way of work, education and the gym which Feltham offered. The result was that if prisoners were not engaged in purposeful activity of some kind, and there were insufficient officers to supervise association, they had to remain in their cells. All of this on top of the psychological impact on some inmates of having to share a cell designed for one occupant, and staff being less sensitive to the needs of individual prisoners when there were so many of them.

42.2 The core recommendation made by the task force to overcome the problem of overcrowding was that the number of unconvicted and unsentenced prisoners coming to Feltham should be reduced by about 150. That would cut down the "churn" factor, and it was proposed to achieve that by reducing the number of courts within Feltham's catchment area. That would allow doubling-up in cells to be eliminated, and the number of beds in dormitories to be reduced from four to two. And it would mean that the extreme measures of temporarily housing prisoners in the healthcare centre, the segregation unit and the anti-bullying unit could be avoided. In order to ensure that a cap on Feltham's population remained in place, the task force also recommended that its certified normal accommodation should not be exceeded. Its certified normal accommodation would therefore be equated with its operational capacity. That was recognised to be an exceptional measure, but was thought to be justified by Feltham's large number of residential units.

42.3 The recommendation to reduce the number of convicted and unconvicted prisoners was made in the middle of January 1999 in the first report the task force submitted to the steering group. It was one of the "quick wins" which the report identified. The steering group adopted this recommendation at its meeting a few days later. The recommendation that the certified normal accommodation should not be exceeded was made in the next report submitted by the task force to the steering group at the end of January 1999. The task force believed that the reduction of Feltham's population by diverting 150 unconvicted and unsentenced prisoners to other establishments could be achieved by April or May 1999.*

42.4 The Population Management Unit at Prison Service headquarters was asked to come up with ideas for how this could be achieved. Thought was given to Rochester Prison in Kent and Chelmsford Prison in Essex taking young offenders from courts in South and East London, but the unit's preferred option in March 1999 was for a wing at Pentonville Prison in North London to be reclassified as a wing for young offenders, and for the adult prisoners it currently held to be transferred to the Mount in Hemel Hempstead, Hertfordshire. By April or May 1999, the idea of creating places for young offenders at Chelmsford had become the preferred option, and this is what happened. Eventually, 150 places for young offenders were found there, but this did not materialise until February 2000.

42.5 If this was one of the quick fixes the task force had identified, why did it take a year or so for the plan to see the light of day? Since Chelmsford Prison was in a residential area, the public had to be won over to the introduction of young offenders there, the staff there had to be made ready to deal with them and the POA had to be consulted. In addition, a suitable regime had to be organised for the new intake and arrangements for purposeful activity had to be made, escorting arrangements needed to be changed, and arrangements for the transfer out of Chelmsford of some of the adult prisoners already there had to be made. These things take time, although Mr Atherton accepted that the places for young offenders at Chelmsford could have been found a little earlier.

42.6 However, a reduction in Feltham's population could have been achieved relatively quickly without the Chelmsford option. That can be seen from what actually happened at Feltham during 1999 and the early part of 2000. Admittedly, it was not until October 2001 that Feltham's certified normal accommodation and its operational capacity were equated. However, Feltham was able to bring both its certified normal accommodation and its operational capacity down significantly in the 12 months following the task force's work. The operational capacity was reduced from 922 to 865 in June 1999, and to 818 in March 2000, though an unofficial operational capacity of 818 had been in place since October 1999. The certified normal accommodation was reduced from

---

* Indeed, it was subsequently proposed that Feltham's certified normal accommodation and operational capacity would temporarily be reduced even further to enable the refurbishment of the units to proceed on a staggered basis.

849 to 802 in July 1999, and to 768 in March 2000.* And both the operational capacity and the certified normal accommodation came down further in November 2000 following a riot in Quail which resulted in the unit having to be closed down. The reduction in operational capacity and certified normal accommodation in March 2000 no doubt reflected the availability of places for the 150 young offenders at Chelmsford, but the earlier reductions had taken place despite these places not having been available.

42.7 These reductions were mirrored in the reduction in Feltham's actual prisoner population. It had an average of 898 prisoners in January 1999, but from then on the number reduced, so that between May and November 1999 the average monthly population ranged between 795 and 828, and between December 1999 and March 2000 it ranged between 746 and 788. Between November 1999 and March 2000, its population never exceeded its certified normal accommodation.** In theory, that should have resulted in doubling-up being eliminated. But that did not happen, presumably because it would have involved inmates constantly having to be moved from units which were bursting at the seams to units where there were places. Doubling-up only ended following a visit to Feltham by Mr Narey during Mr Pascoe's time as Governor – as did the reduction in the numbers of prisoners held in dormitories from four to two.

42.8 In short, Feltham's chronic overcrowding had been reduced to some extent by the time of Zahid's murder, but not enough and not for long enough for it to have had an impact on the problems which overcrowding had created. As it was, much of the reduction in numbers had occurred before the 150 places for young offenders became available at Chelmsford. That had been achieved by the adoption of a number of short-term measures including the device of delaying the re-opening of units which had been closed for refurbishment. If that could have been achieved in 1999 and during the early part of 2000, you wonder whether it could have been achieved earlier if the real problems facing Feltham had been realised by area management and Prison Service headquarters before 1999, as they should have been.

---

* There is one document which suggests that at some stage Feltham's operational capacity was 732 and its certified normal accommodation 769. But it is unclear when the document was produced, and the figures did not include places for prisoners who were properly on the anti-bullying unit or in the segregation unit, nor places for prisoners on those residential units which were closed.
**These figures are based on the Prison Service's statistics, although since Feltham's own figures show that an average of 724 prisoners were held there between 21 February and 21 March 2000, it looks as if there has been an error somewhere.

42.9 Having said that, it would be wrong to ignore the population pressures facing the Prison Service as a whole at the time. The overall prison population grew very sharply between 1993 and 1998, and latterly at a much faster rate than the Home Office had predicted. But it then plateaued, and did not grow much between 1998 and 2001, probably because of the introduction of home detention curfew, which allowed prisoners to be released early. And to the extent that the population grew, increasing numbers of prisoners could be absorbed as more places to hold them became available. But the population pressures which the Prison Service faced were still considerable, and Feltham was not the only establishment to have been affected by them.

Chapter 43: Financial investment in Feltham

43.1 Feltham was under-resourced in the years leading up to Mr Clifford becoming the Governor. However, such was the paucity of funding that the Inspectorate noted in 1997 that Feltham actually had the largest annual cost per prisoner of any young offender institution in the country. According to Mr Narey, the establishment's budget increased in the five years up to 1999 by only 9.5%, far less than wage inflation of about 16%. The Prison Service was concentrating on improving security at the time following a series of high profile escapes, and although Feltham benefited from that, there was no funding available for improvements on other fronts. The absence of capital investment, when coupled with the establishment's budget not keeping pace with inflation, meant that it did not have the funding it needed to provide a decent regime for its prisoners.

43.2 In this respect, Feltham was not alone. Like other establishments, the funding it received depended on the resources made available to the Prison Service by central government. But these were limited, and in the late 1990s establishments were having to make efficiency savings. Their annual budgets were marginally lower in real terms in the financial year before Mr Clifford arrived at Feltham than in previous years. If the budget of an establishment was to be increased, that would have to be at the expense of other ones. It was difficult to identify establishments which could absorb a decrease in their budget without compromising standards. Moreover, the bulk of an establishment's expenditure goes on wages. Mr Atherton put it at about 75%. Since staff are employed for the most part on terms which prohibit enforced transfers, much of an establishment's budget cannot be moved. And there was no easy way to reduce an establishment's expenditure which did not relate to staffing costs. Much of the expenditure was contractually committed, and although budgets could be shaved here and there, not much more than that could be done.

43.3 So the only real leeway the Prison Service had was to distribute funds which had been earmarked for specific capital projects unevenly between establishments, and to divert them to the establishment in greatest need. But that would not have solved the problem of under-resourced establishments. Funds which had been ring-fenced for use on particular projects – such as the funds provided by the Youth Justice Board to fund the juvenile estate, and a sum in excess of £200m to be distributed to the Prison Service's 140 or so establishments for the expansion of cognitive skills and education programmes and the treatment of drug abuse – could only be spent on those projects.

43.4 After Zahid's murder, there was a considerable increase in investment in Feltham. The Prison Service's annual expenditure on the establishment increased from £19.2m in the financial year covering Mr Clifford's time there to £24.4m in the financial year covering Mr Pascoe's first full year as Governor. Since the average number of inmates held at Feltham decreased during that time from 798 to 650, the annual cost per prisoner increased from £24,030 to £37,507.* This was made possible by additional funds being made available for the young offender estate for the 2000/2001 financial year. This increased level of investment, coupled with the decline in Feltham's prison population, resulted in the significant improvements which everyone acknowledges were made at the establishment following Zahid's death. The critical questions are whether any extra money was earmarked for Feltham in the 1999/2000 financial year which broadly speaking covered Mr Clifford's period as Governor, and if so, whether it was enough.

43.5 The first of these questions is not difficult to answer. Feltham received an injection of funds for the 1999/2000 financial year to its "baseline funding", which was Prison Service jargon for an establishment's annual budget to meet its annual running costs. These funds came from two sources. First, it was thought that in the preceding financial year, Feltham's expenditure would turn out to be less than its budget by about £300,000. The task force recommended that this underspend be used by the establishment itself rather than be clawed back by Prison Service headquarters as would normally happen. The steering group approved that recommendation. However, it is not clear whether the whole of that underspend was ploughed back into Feltham. There was some evidence that only about £250,000 was retained by the establishment. But either way it was a sizeable amount. Secondly, instead of Feltham's budget being cut by £275,000 as had previously been planned, the steering group approved an additional injection of £500,000 for the 1999/2000 financial year for Feltham. So all in all, the establishment's baseline funding increased by £750–800,000 for 1999/2000. In addition, it received "project funding" from the Youth Justice Board for Feltham A, and £700,000 for "extra education, drug strategy and a bail information scheme". Since Feltham was a "red light" establishment – one which was failing – it jumped the queue for this funding.

43.6 The second question is not so straightforward. The quality of financial information which Feltham had produced was said to have been so poor that it was difficult to know how much was being spent at any given time. It was therefore difficult to predict whether at the end of the financial year it would have underspent or overspent on its budget,

---

* These figures differ from the calculations originally provided to the Inquiry which wrongly used Feltham's certified normal accommodation rather than the average number of prisoners held at Feltham.

and by how much. The steering group had to make an educated guess at what the establishment needed for the 1999/2000 financial year. So the £750–800,000 represented the sum which it was thought would enable Mr Clifford to run Feltham at its existing staffing levels, and have something left over to allow him to take such modest initiatives as he thought appropriate – at any rate until a more accurate picture of the establishment's needs, and the cost of meeting them, emerged. That is not to say that this injection of funds was regarded as sufficient to put Feltham back on the road to recovery. More resources would undoubtedly be needed if the establishment was to provide a decent regime once again. But it was thought to be enough for it to be getting on with for the time being so that it would not decline any further. And since the task force had concluded that Feltham had not been using its existing resources efficiently, there was a danger that throwing too much money at it would result in it being squandered.

43.7 That explains an apparent inconsistency in what Mr Clifford was saying at the time. In May 1999, he is recorded as having told Feltham's Board of Visitors that the establishment was "well resourced", whereas in June 1999, Mr Wheatley recorded him as saying that "more resources were needed in order to ensure that the establishment delivered the quality of regime required". What he told the Board of Visitors represented his opinion, formed within a few weeks of arriving at Feltham, that Feltham had the money for the work which *needed* to be done. What he told Mr Wheatley after he had been in post for longer was that more funds were required if he was to do at Feltham what he *wanted* to do.

43.8 It is not possible to say now whether the injection of funds which Feltham got for the 1999/2000 financial year was sufficient to arrest Feltham's decline. It looks as if the Inspectorate may have thought it was. Following its inspection of Feltham at the end of September 1999, it spoke of the changes at Feltham since its last report and of the improvements in the offing, though it will be recalled that Mr Narey thought that the report was "ludicrously over-optimistic". Indeed, the reduction in the numbers of prisoners at the establishment in the 1999/2000 financial year meant that the annual cost per prisoner increased to £24,030 for that year from £18,992 for the 1998/1999 financial year. But whether or not Feltham's budget for the 1999/2000 financial year was sufficient to arrest its decline, it was not set at an amount which was sufficient for the regime to be improved to a level which would be regarded as acceptable. Feltham's actual expenditure in the 1999/2000 financial year was about £2.5m greater than in the previous year. The increase in expenditure was about three times the new money which had been earmarked for it. So even if the establishment's baseline funding had gone up, it looks as if Mr Clifford still exceeded its budget by a considerable margin – and even then he had little to show for it in terms of an improved regime.

43.9 Mr Clifford did not regard Feltham's budget as a constraint on the incurring of such expenditure as he thought was necessary. He regarded keeping within the budget as a secondary consideration. His policy was to spend what was needed to improve the regime. He did not think his job was at stake if he exceeded his budget. Mr Pascoe said much the same thing. But the Prison Service did not see it quite that way. A further increase in baseline funding would not be available while the establishment had no idea of what its expenditure was and until a suitable source of funds could be identified. And after Zahid's death, Mr Clifford was told to suspend further recruitment while the current budget was being overspent – though to be fair it was thought that a reprofiling exercise at Brixton Prison in South London might have resulted in officers who were found to be surplus to requirements there being transferred to Feltham. In the end, the projected overspend was reduced by the closure of a unit for refurbishment.

43.10 The distribution of finite resources is, of course, a complex matter. Difficult decisions had to be made by the Prison Service about where its priorities lay. Although it knew that more funds had to be made available to Feltham, the lack of a proper management information system which Mr Clifford was to inherit and a perception that resources had not been spent efficiently in the past made it difficult for the task force to present a case for substantially increased investment in a specific sum. In the circumstances, it would be unfair to criticise the Prison Service for refusing to sanction an approach which committed it to open-ended expenditure for Feltham during the 1999/2000 financial year.

Chapter 44: Industrial relations at Feltham

The Feltham branch of the POA

44.1 The Feltham branch of the POA was criticised by a number of witnesses for its confrontational stance with management. Mrs Bogue was one. Mr Clifford was another. They said the branch was opposed to change, regardless of whether it was in the interests of its members or the needs of the establishment. It put an undue premium, so it was said, on staffing levels, relying on the spurious pretext of safety to justify its position. It insisted on staffing levels being strictly adhered to, so that prisoners would only be allowed out of their cells if the agreed number of staff were on duty.

44.2 Andy Darken, the chairman of the branch at the time, rejected these criticisms. To the extent that they came from Mr Clifford, Mr Darken regarded Mr Clifford as being the type of manager to whom the branch was a hindrance. He accused Mr Clifford of not sharing information with the branch or engaging with it in a constructive way. And to the extent that the branch raised issues relating to health, safety and staffing levels, the branch was doing no more than properly representing the interests of its members. At least one member of Feltham's middle management rejected the suggestion that the branch was a bar to progress. Keith Greenslade, a principal officer at Feltham who was temporarily promoted to a governor grade, did not believe the branch was opposed to change *per se*. And he thought that in most cases the concerns the branch had were raised in a reasonable manner.

44.3 But there is little doubt that the perception at Prison Service headquarters was that the Feltham branch of the POA was a bar to good industrial relations. In May 2001, Mr Wheatley spoke of the branch committee as "continuing to be a substantial drag on progress", and Mr Narey described the branch as "traditionally difficult, almost priding themselves on being unco-operative with management". He did not think that Mr Darken was committed to the changes which had to be made. Indeed, Mr Narey threatened the branch with the privatisation of Feltham B if things did not improve. This perception was shared by the Inspectorate at the time. It was a recurring theme in its report following its visit to Feltham in October 2000. It saw the branch committee as determined to present itself as an alternative management, and it regarded it as the main obstacle to putting Feltham on the road to recovery. Mr Pascoe thought much the same thing. He said staff would speak to their POA representative before they spoke to their managers. All these comments were expressed in terms which suggested that relations with the branch committee had been poor for a long time. Mr Welsh believed that the branch committee had been allowed to become too powerful as a result of staff disillusionment which made the rank and file unwilling to stand up to the more militant local officials, and the failure of Feltham's management in the past to tackle them. The result, according to Mr Atherton, was that Feltham was an establishment "where everything was organised for the convenience of the staff".

44.4 It is plain that Mr Welsh had had his own problems with the branch committee. I touched upon them earlier. His attempt to introduce new profiles foundered on its opposition to his proposals. Like Mr Pascoe, he thought that the more junior levels of Feltham's management felt inhibited about taking some decisions for fear of being criticised by the branch committee. But there is little to suggest that industrial relations at the establishment were going through a particularly bad patch during Mr Clifford's time as Governor. In a debate on Feltham in the House of Lords on 23 June 1999, the Minister then responsible for prisons told the House that the Area Manager had reported that currently industrial relations there were good. In a presentation to the Prison Service Strategy Board, Mr Wheatley did not mention industrial relations as a particular problem facing Feltham, unlike other establishments he referred to. And although the Inspectorate was extremely forthright in its report following its visit to Feltham in October 2000 about what it saw as the pernicious influence of the branch committee,* its report following its inspection in September 1999 had not referred to the branch committee at all. Maybe that inspection had not addressed the issue of industrial relations: it had, after all, been a short visit, and an unannounced one at that. But maybe the devastating tone of the Inspectorate's report following its inspection of Feltham in November and December 1998, and the recognition by the Prison Service that the establishment needed to change as shown by the creation of the task force, persuaded the branch committee to adopt a less confrontational approach – for the time being at any rate.

44.5 Of the various issues which arose between Mr Clifford and the branch committee during his time as Governor, two in particular were explored in some detail by the Inquiry: the branch's attitude to the profiling exercise initiated by Mr Clifford, and its stance on the amount of

---

* It was the criticism of Mr Darken in this report which caused the Prison Service to transfer him from Feltham. Mr Darken claimed that he was unfairly being made a scapegoat for the establishment's problems. He commenced legal proceedings against the Prison Service, which were settled on the basis that there had been procedural shortcomings in effecting his transfer, and on terms that neither the Prison Service nor Mr Darken would publicise the settlement of the action as a victory.

association prisoners on enhanced status in Feltham B were to enjoy in the evenings.*

The profiling exercise

44.6 The new work profiles were due to be implemented on 3 October 1999. The branch committee was not invited to participate in drawing them up, but it was to be consulted over them and its agreement to their introduction was to be sought. On 23 July 1999, Mr Darken informed Mr Clifford of the branch committee's opposition to the extension of the core day which the new profiles would have brought about. He said that it would have an adverse effect on the health of its members. That objection was resolved by a compromise which resulted in the core day being extended by 30 minutes, and the branch committee agreed to the new profiles in July 1999 following a vote of the branch's membership. Indeed, when Mr Clifford wrote to Mr Darken on 27 July 1999, he acknowledged that their recent meeting over the new profiles had been positive. He added that their meeting had shown "a desire and willingness on both sides" to progress the exercise positively. It made sense, of course, for Mr Clifford to stress the positive side of the negotiations, even if he feared that consultation with the staff over the new profiles would not run smoothly.

44.7 On 22 September 1999, Mr Atherton wrote a memo to Mr Narey. He reported that the branch committee had been "throwing in last minute challenges to the whole package", despite the co-operation it had previously given to management. He thought that the branch committee was "seriously split" over the new profiles, and that one branch official was "determined to wreck" the whole exercise. On the same day, the branch committee wrote to Mr Clifford identifying eight points of dispute. With the exception of one of them, we do not know whether these points were resolved, or whether the branch committee or management capitulated on all or any of them. But the dispute did not prevent the new profiles from being introduced on 3 October 1999 as planned.

44.8 On 18 November 1999, over six weeks into the new profiles, Mr Atherton was reporting to Mr Wheatley that there were clear signs of industrial unrest. He informed Mr Wheatley that a group of disaffected staff

---

* Another one looked at was the re-use of exercise yards and the use of an area outside Swallow for football and basketball, which had been opposed by the branch committee on the basis of the risks to the health and safety of its members.

wanted the branch to withdraw from the new profiles, and the branch committee had only just managed to survive a vote of no confidence in it. Mr Darken claimed to know nothing about a vote of no confidence, and he denied that the dispute within the branch had had anything to do with the new profiles. But he acknowledged that there had been a good deal of dissatisfaction with the new profiles on the part of staff. Indeed, "failures to agree" were subsequently lodged in respect of particular aspects of the new profiles, though they were all later to be withdrawn.

44.9 Two things emerge from this account of what the documents show. First, although the later opposition to the new profiles may have come from a faction within the branch committee, it could just as easily have come from a disenchanted group within the membership. Without investigating the matter in detail, which the Inquiry did not want to do as it was relatively tangential to what the Inquiry had to address, it cannot be assumed that it was the branch committee which was opposing the new profiles. Secondly, whether the later opposition came from the branch committee or the membership, it may be that this opposition to aspects of the new profiles was justified. Again, the Inquiry did not wish to spend time investigating the merits of the eight points of dispute or the topics on which "failures to agree" were lodged. But without doing so, it could not be assumed that the objection to these aspects of the profiles was unjustified. It may be that root and branch opposition to the whole of the profiling exercise could properly have been regarded as irresponsible. But the new profiles would have an impact on working practices and arrangements, and that was, of course, a legitimate area for the branch committee to be concerned about. So the criticism that the branch committee was resistant to change on this topic at least is one I cannot reach a conclusion about.

Evening association

44.10 One of the eight points of dispute in the branch committee's letter to Mr Clifford of 22 September 1999 related to Mr Clifford's intention to phase out the role of the hiking officer. The letter informed Mr Clifford that the branch committee was prepared to agree to the abolition of the hiking officer provided that evening association only took place in the cluster of three units if at least nine officers were on duty. So if there were less than nine officers on duty, each of the three units would be on patrol state, and none of the prisoners would get evening association. The letter said that this proposal would "maintain the safety and security of the area".

44.11 On the face of it, the proposal – and the justification for it – made little sense. If evening association could take place on each of the three units when nine officers were on duty, the proposal assumed that three officers were sufficient on one unit to enable evening association to be supervised safely and securely. Yet the effect of the proposal would have been that even if there were three officers on duty on one or two of the units, not even the prisoners on those units would get evening association.

44.12 When Mr Darken gave evidence to the Inquiry, he did not seek to justify the branch committee's proposal on the basis of safety or security. Instead, he advanced two other benefits which he claimed the proposal would produce. First, a system which provided for all three units to be on patrol state unless there were at least nine officers on duty would give "greater certainty to the detailing",* so that the Detail Office could "convert shifts in order that the regime could be maintained through the core day". Secondly, the increased "certainty of regime" which the proposal would create would enable prisoners to know where they stood.

44.13 I do not follow either of these arguments. It was, of course, extremely important for the regime to be delivered during the core day. If staff absences meant that the regime could only be delivered by deploying staff from a later shift to an earlier shift, then that is what had to be done even if it left the later shift with less than its full complement of staff. But the branch committee's proposal did not make delivery of the regime during the core day any more likely. It concentrated on what staff on the late shift would be required to do once the detailing for the day had already taken effect. No wonder Mr Wheatley received no satisfactory answer when, on a visit to Feltham in October 2000, he asked staff in the Detail Office what the rationale for the branch committee's proposal was.

44.14 Nor would the branch committee's proposal have resulted in prisoners knowing whether they would enjoy evening association on a particular day. Whether all or any of the units in a particular cluster would get evening association would depend on the number of officers in that cluster on duty. The most that could be said was that evening association would be less frequent under the branch committee's proposal than if a unit could have evening association if three officers were on duty in it. In that limited sense, I suppose it could be said that the branch

---

* "Detailing" is the term used within the Prison Service to describe the deployment of staff within an establishment.

committee's proposal would put an end to any false hopes that evening association would be the norm.

44.15 There is an issue whether Mr Clifford ever agreed to the branch committee's proposal. By the time of Mr Wheatley's visit in October 2000, the proposal had been custom and practice at Feltham for some time. But whether it had been agreed by Mr Clifford or not, Mr Pascoe was able to unscramble it within a couple of months of his arrival. The agreement he reached with the branch committee acknowledged that there had to be at least three officers on duty in a unit before evening association could take place on that unit. But its effect was to permit evening association on one or two units in the cluster, even if the other unit or units in the cluster could not have evening association. That was achieved by all three units in the cluster having evening association if nine officers were on duty, two of the units having evening association if eight officers were on duty, and one of the units having evening association if seven officers were on duty. It also provided for staff to be cross-deployed between clusters to ensure the best use of staff, and thereby to make evening association more likely.

44.16 But did Mr Clifford ever agree to the proposal? He did not recall ever doing so, but he could not be categorical on the topic, and he had "a horrible feeling" that he might have let it "slip through". Mr Darken said that Mr Clifford not only agreed to the proposal, but actually signed a written agreement which gave effect to the branch committee's proposal, doing so "eagerly". He was sure that the branch committee would have provided Mr Clifford with a copy of it, although he had no recollection of having done so himself. Mr Herring, who succeeded Mr Darken as chairman of the branch, said that he was there when Mr Clifford signed it.

44.17 I do not believe Mr Clifford consciously agreed to the proposal or signed any agreement for its implementation. He is a highly intelligent man, and would have seen immediately that there was no rational basis for it. It undermined the incentives and earned privileges scheme because it meant that one of the key elements of enhanced status – evening association – would only occasionally be enjoyed, and it ran counter to his desire to improve the regime for prisoners as much as possible. The idea that he would have embraced the proposal "eagerly" is absurd, even if it would have made negotiations over the new profiles easier. And if he had signed an agreement giving effect to the branch committee's proposal, at least one copy of it is likely to have survived. As it was, Mr Darken said that the branch committee's copy of it was disposed of once the new agreement with Mr Pascoe had been concluded. But that does not explain why Mr Pascoe was unable to find Mr Clifford's copy of it when he arrived at Feltham. What is likely to have happened is that Mr Clifford simply did not appreciate the significance of the proposal at the time, and the branch committee opportunistically treated his silence on the issue as acquiescence to it. It is an example of the branch committee trying to get an easier life for its members – by reducing the unsocial hours they would otherwise have had to work – on the spurious pretext of safety and security considerations, to the detriment of prisoners on enhanced status.

44.18 That was the hallmark of Mr Darken's chairmanship of the branch committee. There may have been an uneasy truce while Mr Clifford was Governor, during which time the establishment's other problems made industrial relations at Feltham appear better than they were. But overall the branch committee opposed management initiatives whenever it could – whether it was the removal of mugs and kettles from unit offices to remove the temptation for officers to retreat there instead of getting prisoners out of their cells, or the listener scheme under which inmates who were at risk of self-harm received support from other prisoners, and which did not impact on the staff's working conditions at all. And in 2001 Mr Herring was to praise Mr Darken in *Gatelodge* for having "unsaddled" more Governors at Feltham than at any other establishment. It is not a coincidence that the weight of the evidence was that industrial relations at Feltham improved after Mr Darken's unhealthy influence had been removed following his transfer elsewhere.

Chapter 45: The separation of Feltham A and Feltham B

45.1 The physical separation of Feltham A and Feltham B in advance of the assumption of responsibility for the funding of the juvenile estate by the Youth Justice Board was completed by 17 January 2000. The work had included creating a new education department, a new reception area and new visiting facilities for Feltham A. These measures were funded by a significant injection of funds by the Youth Justice Board. But this building programme was not the only consequence of the new funding arrangements. Feltham A was to be run with its own management team, and its own complement of staff, in order to provide an enhanced regime for the juveniles who would be coming to it.

45.2 All of this resulted in a marked improvement in the care of juveniles at Feltham. That was particularly apparent in staffing levels. For example, the review of the establishment's working arrangements conducted by Management Consultancy Services in the course of Mr Pascoe's profiling exercise revealed that 26 officers were detailed for a unit of 60 juveniles in Feltham A, compared with an average of 36 officers being detailed for a cluster of three units of 180 young offenders in Feltham B.

45.3 There is little doubt that Feltham A's relatively generous ratio of staff to prisoners was achieved at the expense of Feltham B.* The former's recruitment programme had resulted in many members of staff at the latter transferring to it. It was not simply a matter of Feltham B losing staff to Feltham A permanently. In view of the need to give Feltham A the fillip it needed, staff would be cross-deployed from Feltham B to make up any shortfall. And very often the staff Feltham B lost – on both a permanent and temporary basis – were those who were keen to play a more fulfilling role with prisoners. Indeed, staff were not permitted to transfer to Feltham A if they had a history of long-term absence through sickness. The consequence was that some of the staff who were left in Feltham B were the less experienced or less motivated members of the establishment's workforce. The exodus to Feltham A may not have been encouraged by management, but there was no suggestion that it was discouraged either. Maybe it was thought that the replacement of departing officers by new members of staff would have a positive effect on the culture of Feltham B. Either way, Mrs Bogue described what she called "the parasitic loss of staff" as "crippling Feltham B".

45.4 None of this should have come as much of a surprise. In its briefing paper to Mr Clifford, the task force described the way in which Feltham would cope with the new arrangements as one of the "change management

---

* Mr Narey was in a minority of one in expressing the view that Feltham B got no worse as a result of the recruitment of staff from Feltham B to Feltham A.

challenges", and acknowledged that "invidious comparisons" might be made between the two sides of the establishment. In its report following its inspection of Feltham in September 1999, the Inspectorate was concerned that the spotlight on the juvenile estate under the new funding arrangements "should not result in less attention being paid to the far larger number of older young prisoners". In its annual report for 1998 and at its meeting with Sir Richard Tilt in February 1999, Feltham's Board of Visitors expressed its concern about what it perceived to be the likely disparity of funding provided to the two sides of the establishment. The Board was looking for reassurance that steps were going to be taken to ensure that the already impoverished regime for young offenders would not suffer any further.

45.5 To be fair, I do not think the impact on Feltham B of the new arrangements for Feltham A caught anyone unawares. Everyone could see what could happen, and no-one was surprised when it did. Nor was there all that much anyone could have done to prevent it from happening. It would hardly have been sensible for Feltham to forgo the additional funds which the Youth Justice Board was planning to provide to improve Feltham A for fear that there might be adverse consequences for Feltham B. These funds came to about £11m in terms of capital investment. And it was not as if Feltham B gained nothing from the investment in Feltham A. It had some of the old facilities to itself, namely the old education department, reception area and visiting facilities. In due course, it was hoped that an improvement in Feltham B would be a "spin-off" from the improvements to Feltham A. Nor would it have been sensible to discourage staff from transferring to Feltham A. That might have put the success of Feltham A in jeopardy, with potentially serious consequences for the establishment as a whole.

45.6 At one time, it looked as if something specific might have been done to lessen the impact on Feltham B of the new arrangements for funding Feltham A. According to Mr Welsh, the funding to enable Feltham A to have an appropriate regime for juveniles was initially calculated on the basis of the cost of the limited regime for *un*convicted and *un*sentenced young offenders. That would have had a knock-on effect on the regime in Feltham B for sentenced young offenders. That could have been avoided if the funding had been calculated on the basis of the more generous regime for sentenced young offenders. Mr Welsh requested that the original basis of the calculation be reviewed. He did not know what the result of his request was since he had left Feltham by then. But documents provided to the Inquiry by the Prison Service after the Inquiry's hearings ended show that the funding was subsequently increased. It is not possible to identify what the reason for that was, but its timing suggests that it was in response to Mr Welsh's request.

Whether the increase in funding was sufficient is not something the Inquiry was able to investigate.

45.7 That is not to say that other things could not have been done to lessen the impact on Feltham B of the new arrangements for funding Feltham A. The earlier introduction of "contract hours", the earlier termination of the national agreement giving staff the right to transfer to other establishments, and earlier thought to recruitment issues might have reduced the staffing problems in Feltham B. And speedier initiatives might have reduced the size of Feltham B's prison population earlier.

Chapter 46: The management of the residential units

The residential units

46.1 Up to now in this part of the report, I have been addressing the problems experienced throughout Feltham. In this chapter, and the next two, I look in more detail at the problems facing particular parts of Feltham. I start with the residential units.

46.2 The evidence the Inquiry heard naturally concentrated on Swallow, and it is through the prism of life on Swallow that the management of the residential units in Feltham B has to be seen. But it should not be assumed that Swallow was necessarily any worse than any of the other residential units in Feltham – or any better for that matter. The fact that many things went wrong on Swallow may have been representative of the generality of the residential units at Feltham at the time. Indeed, there was little evidence about how Swallow – or Raven before it – compared with other units, and such evidence as there was tended to be impressionistic. Perhaps the best overview came from Mrs Bogue. She thought that some units performed better than others – partly because of the role the unit had and partly because of the quality of the staff. She recalled Swallow as not functioning particularly well, but it had not struck her as standing out as worse than other units at the time.

46.3 A slightly different view was expressed by Mr Weir. He thought that he had been appointed to be the senior officer in charge of Swallow at least in part because standards were thought to have slipped there. He thought Mr Windsor had mentioned that to him, but Mr Windsor had no recollection of such a conversation. Mr Windsor believed that Swallow had a number of fairly experienced staff, and would not therefore have been performing too badly.

46.4 When looking at the management of the residential units in Feltham B, it is important to bear in mind the chain of command. Mr Windsor was the Head of Feltham B. Two residential governors reported to him, one of whom was Mr Byrd, who was responsible for two clusters of three residential units. One of the clusters included Kestrel, Osprey and Swallow. The principal officers responsible for each of the two clusters reported to Mr Byrd. Keith Denman was the principal officer responsible for the cluster which included Swallow. Reporting to Mr Denman were the senior officers in charge of each of the units in the cluster.

The senior officer on Swallow

The role of Mr McAlaney

46.5 It will be recalled that sometime in January 2000 – the evidence varied from 14 to 18 January – staff who had worked on Raven and the prisoners accommodated there moved to Swallow following its refurbishment. Mr McAlaney had been the senior officer on Raven. However, he told the Inquiry that following the move from Raven, he went to work in the Detail Office. He claimed he did not accompany the staff when they moved to Swallow, though he still helped out on Swallow occasionally. He did not know how frequently that was, and he did not know who became the senior officer in charge of Swallow.

46.6 The recollections of other members of staff about Mr McAlaney's role differed. Some of them thought that he had been the senior officer in charge of Swallow for a while. Indeed, Mr Denman was sure that Mr McAlaney had moved to Swallow from Raven. Others thought that he had not moved to Swallow with the rest of the staff on Raven, but had gone straight to the Detail Office. Mr Weir's recollection was consistent with that, since he had no recall of working with Mr McAlaney while he had been the hiking officer for the cluster of three units which included Swallow. Others could not recall Mr McAlaney's role at the time one way or the other.

46.7 Mr McAlaney's claim never to have been the senior officer in charge of Swallow was his oral evidence to the Inquiry. It was not what he had said in the written statement he had provided the Inquiry with. That said that he had been on Raven until early 2000, and that by March 2000 he was working in the Detail Office. It said nothing about what he had been doing in the meantime. As it was, one of the statements he gave to the police filled this surprising gap. That statement was made on 13 June 2000. It said that he had been the senior officer on Swallow between early January and late February 2000. He told the Inquiry that this was incorrect. It was not what he had actually told the police, and he did not know how the error had got into his statement. But he acknowledged that this statement was about the regime on Swallow, and the police officer who took the statement from him could only have been asking him about that because the police officer had thought that he had been responsible for Swallow. If Mr McAlaney's evidence to the Inquiry was right, the police officer had completely misunderstood what he had been saying about his role at the time.

CHAPTER 46: THE MANAGEMENT OF THE RESIDENTIAL UNITS

46.8 There were other things in his statement to the police which suggest that at some time he had been the senior officer on Swallow. One part of his statement related to his knowledge of Stewart and Zahid. In that part of his statement, he said that most of his duties related to the supervision of prison staff. If he had been in the Detail Office at the time, his duties would have related to the deployment of staff, not their supervision. And he acknowledged that he knew both Stewart and Zahid. He later claimed that he knew Stewart from when Stewart had been on Osprey, even though Stewart had been there for only one night – on 24 January 2000. And as for Zahid, he was to claim that he had not meant to say that he actually knew Zahid. What he had meant to say was that he vaguely recollected his name.

46.9 All things considered, I was extremely sceptical of Mr McAlaney's claim not to have been the senior officer in charge of Swallow at any time. That scepticism increased when the daily staff planning and reporting forms for the relevant period – known as the SPAR Bs – were produced to the Inquiry. The SPAR Bs were the forms used by the Detail Office to record the daily deployment of staff. An analysis of the SPAR Bs shows three things:

- Between 14 January – the earliest date given for the move to Swallow – and 15 February, Mr McAlaney did not work in the Detail Office at all.

- Mr McAlaney did not work at all during much of this period. He had a mixture of rest days, annual leave and time off in lieu. But when he was working he did 12 shifts as the hiking officer for the cluster of three units which included Kestrel, Osprey and Swallow, and he did nine shifts as the officer in charge of one of those units. Since Kestrel and Osprey had senior officers in charge of them – Robert Shewan and Gary Fanthorpe respectively – it is likely that the unit Mr McAlaney was in charge of for those nine shifts was Swallow.

- Between 15 February and 21 March, Mr McAlaney did 17 shifts in the Detail Office and 20 shifts as the hiking officer for the cluster of units which included Kestrel, Osprey and Swallow.

Many of these shifts were half shifts, but the only conclusion to be drawn from this analysis is that for much of the time from when Swallow reopened until the night of the murder, Mr McAlaney was the hiking officer for the three units. But he only went to the Detail Office on 15 February. Prior to that, he had been the officer in charge of Swallow. That is the finding I make.

377

46.10 I appreciate that Mr McAlaney only worked nine shifts as the officer in charge of Swallow, but he would not have forgotten that by the time he made his statement to the police. I do not believe that in his evidence to the Inquiry he was simply trying to distance himself from a unit on which a murder had taken place. There must have been more to it. He must have wanted to distance himself from Swallow because he knew that things had not been done properly on his watch. I doubt whether he thought that his officers should have picked up on Stewart's strangeness or Zahid's concern about sharing a cell with him, or that he would be criticised in some way for their lack of jailcraft. After all, Stewart had only been on Swallow for a week or so before Mr McAlaney ceased to be the officer in charge of it. It is more likely that Mr McAlaney knew that cell-searching had not been taking place properly, and he feared that this would come out when questions were asked about how no-one had noticed that the table leg had become detached from the table and why the dagger had not been found.

Mr McAlaney's management style

46.11 Since Mr McAlaney was the senior officer in charge of Swallow for a while, it is necessary to look at his managerial style. He was, I think, uncomfortable with his managerial role. He preferred working with prisoners rather than supervising staff. That was why he was happy during times of staff shortages to do the work of basic grade officers while he was the senior officer in charge of Raven. And he avoided the role of desk officer – which would have given him a greater overview of what was happening on the unit – because he did not like office work. He was "hands on", but only in the sense that he was prepared – indeed, happy – to involve himself in the day to day tasks of the unit as an extra pair of hands. Admittedly, the frequent staff shortages made it inevitable that there would be times when it would be necessary for him to make up the numbers.

46.12 But I fear that all this was at the expense of his supervisory role. He acknowledged that governors at Feltham were continually pressing principal officers and senior officers to get to grips with their units and manage their staff properly. But he thought he was already doing that. He did not think there was anything else he could have done. I cannot go along with that if his handling of those of his staff who acted as personal officers is anything to go by. If Miss Bigger and Mr Edmundson did not know that they had to make entries in the wing files of the prisoners they were responsible for, that was down to Mr McAlaney not having told them. After all, had he been checking prisoners' wing files regularly to see whether entries had been made in them by personal officers – as he claimed he did – he would have discovered that they were not doing that. That is just an example – but a telling one – of Mr McAlaney's approach to his managerial function. In his defence, it should be said that he had, in Mr Denman, a principal officer who, as we shall see, was struggling with his own managerial responsibilities for Swallow. That is an important consideration, but it did not justify Mr McAlaney's abdication of his supervisory role.

The break in the chain of command

46.13 If Mr McAlaney had not been the senior officer on Swallow at any time, it would have been without a senior officer for about two months. As it was, it was without one for a month until 15 March, when Mr Weir was appointed to the post. That would have been bad enough, but it was compounded by the fact that Mr Weir did not take up the post until after the attack on Zahid because he was then on leave. And it was not as if no-one knew about the lack of a senior officer in charge of Swallow. Someone must have decided to put Mr McAlaney in the Detail Office, just as someone must have decided to appoint Mr Weir to the vacancy in Swallow. And the absence of a senior officer from Swallow would have been noticed at the daily operational meetings, just as the officer in the Detail Office who completed the SPAR Bs would have seen that there was one less senior officer in charge of the units in the cluster which included Swallow. So although Mr Byrd and Mr Windsor expressed surprise that Swallow was without a senior officer in charge of it for so long, we have to proceed on the assumption that they – and Mr Denman for that matter – knew that there was this break in the chain of command for some time.

46.14 Was anything done about it? Two pieces of evidence suggested that something was. The first suggestion was that one of the basic grade officers in Swallow was asked to take on the role temporarily. That suggestion came from Mr Weir. In his statement to the Inquiry, he said that Mr Morse "was fulfilling the role of senior officer" on Swallow after Mr McAlaney left for the Detail Office. But no-one else confirmed that, and Mr Morse himself denied it, saying that it was not part of his function – even if he had been the basic grade officer with the most experience – to give instructions to his colleagues or to ensure that particular tasks were carried out. Responsibility for doing that, said Mr Morse, lay with the hiking officer or the principal officer. To be fair, when Mr Weir came to give oral evidence, he accepted that the role he had ascribed to Mr Morse was based on his "impression" that Mr Morse was in charge – and he acknowledged that he may have got that impression from the fact that Mr Morse was the officer with the greatest experience. So it looks as if Mr Morse was not asked to take on the role of senior officer in charge of Swallow. Indeed, no-one was.

46.15 The second suggestion was that one of the senior officers in charge of another unit in the cluster of units which included Swallow had covered for Swallow in addition to his other duties. That suggestion came from Mr Shewan. In his statement to the Inquiry, he said that he had "additional duties covering for the absence of the residential senior officer on Swallow" over and above his own substantive role as the senior officer in charge of Kestrel. But in his oral evidence he explained that the only time he would have been on Swallow in any managerial capacity was when he was there as the hiking officer. He did not regard his role as senior officer in charge of Kestrel as including any function for covering as senior officer in charge of any other unit. Mr Fanthorpe, the senior officer in charge of Osprey, said much the same thing.

46.16 So if no-one on Swallow was temporarily promoted to the rank of senior officer to be in charge of it, and if a senior officer in charge of another unit in the cluster did not cover for Swallow, what should have been done to fill the gap? Two possibilities were mentioned. One was that Mr Clifford and Mr Windsor would have expected the principal officer responsible for the cluster to exercise greater managerial oversight of a unit without a senior officer in charge of it. But Mr Denman disagreed. Some might say: "He would, wouldn't he?" He was the source for the second suggestion, which was that it was for the hiking officer to fill the managerial gap created by an absent senior officer. I shall come to the roles of the principal officer and the hiking officer later in this chapter, but no-one ever said that either of these suggestions saw the light of day. The fact is that nothing was done to fill the gap in the management of Swallow. The staff there were left to get on with their work after Mr McAlaney left without any managerial supervision, and that represented all the time that Stewart was on Swallow except for his first week there.

46.17 That is not to say that standards would necessarily have been any different if someone had been put in to cover as the senior officer in charge of Swallow between Mr McAlaney's departure for the Detail Office and Mr Weir's return from leave. You could argue that if someone had been put in to cover for Mr McAlaney, some of the basic functions such as cell-searching, record-keeping and personal officer work would have been performed, and that the fabric checks might have been done better. You would also have had someone there to whom the staff could turn for advice. But the officers who were there had been managed by Mr McAlaney for some time – on Raven before they all went to Swallow. If they had got into bad ways, things were not likely to have improved quickly. Maybe cell-searching would have restarted, and an improvement made to the quality of the fabric checks. But it is too much to expect that in the space of a few weeks a culture which put effective personal officer work and the proper maintenance of records in abeyance would change.

The hiking officer for the cluster

46.18 The hiking officer was always a senior officer. The hiking officer for the cluster of units which included Swallow was Mr Weir. That was his job from early January to 12 March 2000. He was succeeded by Dave Gargan. On the shifts the hiking officer did not work, the role would be assigned to one of the senior officers in charge of each of the units in the cluster or to another senior officer. That was how Mr McAlaney, Mr Shewan and Mr Fanthorpe all took turns in being the hiking officer when Mr Weir or later Mr Gargan were not there.

46.19 No written job description of the role of hiking officer was produced to the Inquiry. In the event, there were two different views of the role. The two hiking officers themselves thought that their job was simply to check whether functions such as cell-searching and giving prisoners time out of their cells for association were taking place. The purpose of doing so was to monitor the extent to which the core day was being delivered on each of the units in the cluster. They would do that by looking at the records the unit maintained, by talking to staff on the unit and by observing for themselves what was going on. The checklist and handover sheet was the form on which they recorded the things they had to check. They would not stray beyond the ambit of the form, and look at other aspects of life on the unit. So they did not check whether personal officer work was being carried out, or how the incentives and earned privileges scheme was operating, or whether the monitoring of prisoners' correspondence was taking place.* Nor did they assess the quality of the work being done.** In respect of those aspects of the core day which they had to monitor, their function was simply to check that the work had been done. If the senior officer in charge of the unit was

---

* That is not to say that they did not have functions relating to particular prisoners. Mr Weir said that the hiking officer had to deal with allegations of assault and bullying, and to check that case conferences took place for prisoners at risk of self-harm.
**The only apparent exception to this related to the wing observation book. According to Mr Gargan, the hiking officer had to check the quality of the entries in it.

not there, it was not for the hiking officer to assume his responsibilities. The hiking officer might only be expected to visit the unit more often.*

46.20 Mr Denman took a different view. He said that the *raison d'etre* for the hiking officer was to fill in for the senior officer in charge of the unit when he was not there. That was why his function was not limited to checking whether or not certain tasks had been completed. He had to check if they had been completed properly, and to look at the rest of the unit's functions, including personal officer work, the incentives and earned privileges scheme and the monitoring of correspondence.

46.21 Mr Denman had had a vested interest, of course, in expressing that view. It got him off the hook if he was supposed to have taken over responsibility for supervising Swallow once Mr McAlaney had gone to the Detail Office. As it was, Mr Denman's view did not sit easily with the checklist and handover sheet itself. That showed that the hiking officer had to complete the form *for each of the three units* while the units were not on patrol state. One wonders why the form contemplated an audit *for all three units* if the hiking officer's role was just to stand in on any unit when the senior officer in charge of it was not there.

46.22 As with most things, the answer lies somewhere between the two. The senior officer in charge of the unit would very often not be there. He could not be there for every shift on those days he worked, and there were many days he did not work – what with rest days and annual leave. So as Mr Windsor – who was one of the architects of the role of hiking officer – said, someone was needed to fill in for the senior officer in charge of the unit when he was not there. That was all the more important after the number of senior officers on each residential unit had been reduced from two to one, and the creation of the role of hiking officer in their place. But the hiking officer would also check the other units in the cluster, and respond to any operational emergencies which arose. What it comes down to was that if the senior officer in charge of the unit was not there, the hiking officer was supposed to assume managerial responsibility in his place. But if the senior officer in charge of the unit was there, the hiking officer would do what Mr Weir described as a "mini-audit of the regime", and simply record whether certain tasks were being performed. The problem was that Mr Weir and Mr Gargan were aware of the latter function of the hiking officer, but not the former. That could have been avoided if Mr Windsor had put something in writing about the nature of the hiking officer's role, and if

---

* This description of the role of the hiking officer was shared by Mr Shewan. He was the only one of the three senior officers in charge of units in the cluster to be asked about it.

Mr Denman had checked what the hiking officers were actually doing. Neither of those things happened.

46.23 If the hiking officers' unawareness of the true nature of their role was one problem, what happened to the checklist and handover sheets which they completed and how useful they really were was another. The hiking officers said that the sheets were looked at and discussed at the daily operational meetings. But Mr Shewan thought otherwise. His recollection was that once the sheet had been completed, it was placed in a folder, which would be given to the next hiking officer. If it was not known who that would be, the folder would be left in the Detail Office. The following day, the hiking officer would remove the sheet from the folder and pass it on to the principal officer or the residential governor, whoever he happened to see first. He assumed that the principal officer would analyse its contents in due course. In short, there is uncertainty about who actually read the sheets and whether anything was done about the information they contained.

46.24 In any event, it is questionable whether the sheets were particularly useful. Some of the information they contained was based on what the hiking officers were told. They had no way of verifying the accuracy of the information for themselves. For example, to ascertain whether fabric checks had taken place they would look at the appropriate form – known as the weekly tool and LBB security check – but they would not investigate whether the form had been completed accurately. Moreover, some of the information was insufficient. The form required the hiking officers to state whether any association had taken place. But it did not require them to specify how long the association had been. All they had to find out was whether prisoners had had at least one hour's association a day – irrespective of what Feltham's target for association was. Indeed, Mr Gargan did not know what the target was.

46.25 But most important of all, if the information which the sheets contained was to be properly assessed, other documents were needed. One example of that related to the number of officers on duty. Although the sheets identified the number of officers who had been detailed to be on duty on a particular shift, there was no requirement to record any late changes to the detail on the sheets. Mr Shewan happened to do that on the only sheet which the Inquiry was provided with,* but Mr Gargan said that his practice was to record late changes on the SPAR Bs. So anyone wanting to check how many officers were on duty on a particular shift

---

* This was the checklist and handover sheet for 20 March 2000 for the cluster of units which included Swallow. The Inquiry asked the Prison Service for the ones for January to March 2000, but they were never provided. Presumably they have not survived.

needed the SPAR B for that day as well. Another example related to cell-searching. Since an average of 13 cells had to be searched every month, the fact that the sheet for one day showed that no cell-searching had taken place that day would not be worrying. It would become a matter of concern if cells were being searched infrequently over a period of time, but you would need to have the sheets for a lengthy period to see whether a pattern of that kind emerged. That is what anyone wanting to check whether cell-searching was taking place would need. It does not look as if anyone was aware of any of these problems. I would have expected Mr Windsor, Mr Byrd and the principal officers to have been.

46.26 Mr Pascoe abolished the role of the hiking officer while he was Governor. But that did not necessarily mean that there had been no need for the role before then. Apart from the greater resources Mr Pascoe had, his evidence about the system he introduced to replace the hiking officer was inconclusive. He said that in his time each unit had been run by a senior officer and four other officers, but he was not asked what had been done to cover for the many hours when the senior officer would have been off duty.

The principal officer for the cluster

46.27 The principal officer for the cluster of units which included Swallow was Mr Denman. He was relatively new to Feltham, having gone there on promotion from the rank of senior officer in September 1998. He had a number of specific tasks which he had to do when they cropped up, but he would try to visit the three units in his cluster at least once every day. After all, his principal function was to ensure that they were running smoothly.

46.28 Mr Denman's office was next to Kestrel, about five minutes walk from Swallow. But his visits to the units were little more than perfunctory. The amount of time he would spend on a unit depended on what staff wanted to talk to him about. If there was nothing specific for him to do, he would move to the next unit. He would look at any recent entries in the wing observation book, but for the most part he relied on staff to bring things to his attention. He did not check up on the less visible areas of the unit's work, such as personal officer work, even though one of the objectives in his performance appraisal had been the implementation of a personal officer scheme. He also accepted that he might not have been checking the returns for cell-searching. Staff in Swallow did not recall him ever expressing any dissatisfaction with the way things were done there. And Mr Fanthorpe, the senior officer in charge of Osprey, felt that he never got a clear steer from Mr Denman.

46.29 It is plain that Mr Denman's approach to his job left much to be desired. But he was refreshingly candid about his shortcomings. He did not try to say that he was unaware of what he had to do. He acknowledged he should have done more to check up on things on his units. And he acknowledged that a measure of complacency had crept into his work. He attributed his lack of pro-active management to the malaise which had infected Feltham. The establishment had come as a shock to him, and he just fell in with its ways. He had initially tried to lead his staff from the front, but found himself increasingly swimming against the tide of an establishment with many problems, not least of which was that it was so under-resourced in terms of staff. All of that should not be underestimated, but I am sure that Mr Denman would himself acknowledge that he should not have allowed himself to get sucked into so defeatist a frame of mind.

46.30 Part of the problem lay with the role of the principal officer at Feltham. Principal officers are at the cusp of management. They are uniformed officers – indeed, they are the most senior uniformed grade in the Prison Service – and as such can relatively easily be identified with by the rank and file. But they have the level of seniority and experience to exercise real control over the direction in which the establishment is going. Mr Clifford had a slightly schizophrenic view about them. He wanted them to act as if they were managers, and yet from shortly after his arrival they ceased to attend the daily governors' meetings. Mr Pascoe found when he arrived at Feltham that their decisions were constantly being questioned. That could not have done much for their self-esteem.

46.31 Mr Denman's failure to get to grips with the units he was responsible for was a significant component in the problems which continued to plague Swallow, even though his responsibility for the staff on Swallow in the few months leading up to the attack on Zahid only began when they moved there from Raven. But he may have been no worse than other principal officers responsible for a cluster of units. For example, Ken Penwright, the principal officer responsible for the cluster of units which included Lapwing, Mallard and Nightingale, was said by Mr Byrd to have been even less pro-active than Mr Denman. And like Mr McAlaney, Mr Denman could have been better served, as we shall see, by his own line manager, Mr Byrd. Mr Byrd never told him to adopt a more pro-active management style, or that he was dissatisfied with Mr Denman's performance. Indeed, in his annual appraisal, Mr Byrd praised his management skills and commented on how hard he had worked.

46.32 I should say a little more about Mr Penwright here, because of his responsibility for Lapwing where Stewart's racist letter was inappropriately dealt with. Mr Penwright had only been the principal officer for his cluster of units since November 1999. He had also become the Staff Resource Manager in charge of detailing, and he viewed that as his main job. He regarded his responsibility for the cluster as very much a temporary assignment until someone else took over the role from him. He would say that this was why, on his visits to the units for which he was responsible, he did little more than ask whether things were running smoothly and have a general chat with staff. He did not check whether the procedures – such as the monitoring of prisoners' correspondence – were being carried out, let alone whether they were being carried out well.

46.33 Mr Penwright was getting close to retirement, and was uncomfortable about the changes which had taken place in the Prison Service in recent years. He had begun to become idle, and I fear that this affected his attitude to his work. His role as Staff Resource Manager was one of overview, with two senior officers actually producing the detail. Although I accept that Mr Penwright wanted to get the detailing right, I do not think that the combination of his two functions made his job particularly arduous. He could have put more effort into his responsibilities for the three units. But having said that, it is extremely questionable whether anything he might have done during the two months or so before Stewart's racist letter was intercepted would have made any difference to how it was handled.

The governors

Mr Byrd

46.34 Mr Byrd was the governor for two clusters of three units in Feltham B. They included the cluster which had Swallow in it. He was also Feltham's Race Relations Liaison Officer, and may have had responsibility for reception. I come to those two roles later on. For the moment, I am concentrating on his role as a residential governor. Like Mr Denman, he was relatively new to Feltham, having gone there on promotion from the rank of principal officer in September 1998, though he had spent 10 years at Feltham from 1981 to 1991 as a senior officer.

46.35 Mr Clifford wanted his senior managers to be far more pro-active than they had been in the past. He did not want them simply to be firefighters, responding to problems as they arose, and assuming that everything was alright unless they were told otherwise. He wanted them to be on the lookout for bad practice, and to challenge it when they came across it. He wanted them, to use one of his favourite words, to be "directive". That was not simply because Mr Clifford was instinctively more comfortable with senior managers who made their presence known. It was because Mr Clifford regarded forceful and decisive management as essential to arrest Feltham's decline. He did not see Mr Byrd as fitting into this mould. Decent and honourable though Mr Byrd was, Mr Clifford did not think that Mr Byrd had "a directive bone in his body".

46.36 Having seen Mr Byrd give evidence over a sustained period, I can see where Mr Clifford was coming from. Mr Byrd came across as a mild-mannered man, who lacked the vision to do anything imaginative or to set about changing the *status quo*. For example, when he visited the units for which he was responsible, he said that he would check that everything was happening as it should. But the examples he gave of the things he did were to look at the relevant entries in the wing observation book, to inspect any open self-harm at risk forms, to check on the prisoners who were on the escape list, and to see whether appropriate standards of cleanliness were being maintained. Important though all these functions were, they were the easy things to check up on. What did not feature in his scheme of things were the less tangible functions which required pro-active management – for example, how the incentives and earned privileges scheme was being run, whether personal officer work was being carried out properly, and whether staff were aware of what should be recorded on prisoners' wing files.

46.37 Sometimes things did not get done because they were low on Mr Byrd's list of priorities. The standardisation of the incentives and earned privileges scheme was an example of that. But more often things did not get done because Mr Byrd did not realise that things were going wrong. For example, although he now accepts that there were large parts of Feltham B where the personal officer scheme was not functioning except at the level of prisoners knowing who their personal officers were, he thought at the time that the scheme was working reasonably well. And it was only with the advantage of hindsight that he could see that the procedures for dealing with staff sickness were not as robust as they might have been, and that staff could build up a lot of sickness leave before being challenged about it. The same applied to the monitoring of prisoners' correspondence. Mr Byrd accepted that he should occasionally have checked that processes relating to that function were being complied with. His excuse for not doing so was that it was difficult to check everything. But he accepted that this was another symptom of his general approach – if something was not visibly and obviously wrong, the assumption was that it was working reasonably well. And to the extent that he was checking on whether things were being done, he accepted that his focus was on seeing whether they were being done, rather than whether they were being done well.

46.38 Did Mr Byrd get wind of what Mr Clifford thought about him? Mr Byrd said that he did not. He had no sense of any dissatisfaction with his work. But if that is the case, he must have been pretty thick-skinned. It is possible that Mr Clifford may have toned down what he said to Mr Byrd because he would not have wanted to offend his sensibilities. But I am sure that he would have left Mr Byrd in no doubt about what he wanted from him, and his sense of frustration about Mr Byrd would have come across.

46.39 This, then, was the man who was Mr Denman's line manager. Mr Denman needed a much more pro-active residential governor to galvanise him out of the sense of defeatism which overwhelmed him. He did not find that in Mr Byrd. That was not so much because Mr Byrd was uninterested in carrying out his job to the best of his ability. It was more a case of Mr Byrd not having that forceful streak in his character and the breadth of vision which Mr Clifford wanted and Mr Denman needed.

Mr Windsor

46.40 Mr Windsor was the Head of Feltham B. As such, he was one of the two deputy governors of Feltham. He was responsible for all the residential units in Feltham B, as well as the segregation and anti-bullying units. He was also relatively new to the establishment, having gone there on promotion from a more junior governor grade in July 1999.

46.41 Mr Windsor was not as "directive" as Mr Clifford would have liked either, but there was much to be said for Mr Windsor's view that he had to complement Mr Clifford's robustness. Being "directive" was not his style, though he was far more capable of being forceful and decisive than Mr Byrd. The care of young offenders had been his abiding interest throughout his career in the Prison Service, and he came across as a man who cared deeply for their welfare. Mr Clifford thought that Mr Windsor would have been better suited to working in a training prison where the demands on him would have been less and where his undoubted talents could have been better deployed. Although Mr Windsor did not entirely agree with that, Mr Clifford's assessment of Mr Windsor struck me as being right. He was not suited to working in an establishment which gave its inmates so little time out of their cells, where purposeful activity was so limited, and which had no sentence planning to speak of. It is not surprising that rightly or wrongly the view was taken later on that Mr Windsor was getting burned out. Mr Windsor did not accept that. He acknowledged that he was getting tired, but he said that everyone who worked at Feltham felt like that. Although he would have liked to stay on at the establishment to complete the job, he was moved on within a year of Zahid's murder.

46.42 For these reasons, Mr Windsor was less effective at an establishment like Feltham than he would have been elsewhere. That is not necessarily a criticism of him. The Prison Service should have seen that Feltham would not bring out the best in him. Without in any way minimising Mr Windsor's undoubted attributes, what was needed for the role which Mr Windsor was asked to perform at that particular time in Feltham's history was someone whose flair was in introducing systems and getting them to work. That was not one of Mr Windsor's particular strengths.

Chapter 47: The management of the reception and security functions

Reception

47.1 Two significant criticisms have been made in Part 3 of Feltham's reception in its handling of documents relating to Stewart. The first was its failure to read the warnings about Stewart in his last prisoner escort record and to pass those warnings on to the Security Department. The second – which proceeds on the assumption that Stewart's temporary wing file returned with him when he came back to Feltham for the last time – was reception's failure to send the file with him when he went to Kestrel that night. Other criticisms could be made of Feltham's reception – for example, its failure to follow up the non-arrival of Stewart's current wing file. But they did not have any bearing on what was subsequently to happen. His current wing file would only have told reception that Stewart appeared to be settling down.

47.2 Line responsibility for reception normally lay with the Head of Operations. That was Mick Cowan, but he had only returned to Feltham a couple of weeks earlier after a year or so at another establishment, and he could not have been expected to have identified shortcomings in the system which might have resulted in these failings, let alone to have taken any steps to put them right. The responsibility for that would have been with those who had had line management responsibility for reception before then.

47.3 Helen Clayton-Hoar acted as Head of Operations from August 1999 until Mr Cowan's return to Feltham. But she claimed not to have had any responsibility for reception. She had strategic responsibilities – for example, she prepared Feltham's Strategic Development Plan following the recommendations of the task force – and was the governor responsible for the Security Department. Indeed, when she drafted the job description for the post of Acting Head of Operations – which she says she agreed with Mr Clifford – she recorded the fact that the post did not then include responsibility for reception.

47.4 So if Mrs Clayton-Hoar was not responsible for reception, who was? The Inquiry initially assumed that it was Mr Byrd. That had been what Paul Clark, the principal officer in charge of reception at the time, had said in his statement to the Inquiry. And Mr Byrd was named as responsible for reception in an undated organigram provided to the Inquiry by the Prison Service. But Mr Byrd's evidence was that he did not take over responsibility for reception until April 2000.

47.5 This issue was not explored with Mr Clark or Mrs Clayton-Hoar since the uncertainty only arose when Mr Byrd gave evidence, and that was after Mr Clark and Mrs Clayton-Hoar had given theirs. I would be very reluctant to go behind the only document which can properly be regarded as contemporaneous – the job description drafted by Mrs Clayton-Hoar – which excluded reception from the responsibilities of the post. I would equally be reluctant to go behind Mr Byrd's own evidence, which was entirely consistent with Mr Windsor's evidence that he acquired line management responsibility for reception in April 2000 following the separation of Feltham A from Feltham B.

47.6 What is likely to have happened is that Mr Clifford assumed that reception would be the responsibility of the Acting Head of Operations after Stuart Eley, the deputy governor who had been responsible for reception, left Feltham in June 1999. Mr Windsor made the same assumption. But at the same time Mr Clifford did not notice that the job description Mrs Clayton-Hoar had drafted excluded responsibility for some areas. There was, therefore, an unintended interregnum in line management responsibility for reception for several months until Mr Cowan returned to Feltham at the end of January 2000. Mr Cowan noticed within a short time of his arrival that staff on reception were not examining the prisoner escort records sufficiently carefully. That is something a governor responsible for reception in 1999 should have been able to pick up as well. He or she may also have picked up – if indeed it was the case – that wing files which arrived with prisoners were not accompanying them when they went to their units but were being sent to Custody Administration by mistake.

47.7 Moreover, he or she may have noticed the absence of training for reception staff, despite the recommendation in the report of the Coonan Inquiry that staff who were going to work on reception should receive dedicated training on reception work. The system in operation at Feltham – that someone new to the work would shadow someone experienced in it for a few days – was unsatisfactory if it was not accompanied by anything else. If bad practices had crept in, they would simply be copied and in that way perpetuated.

The Security Department

47.8 Two significant criticisms have been made in Part 3 about the Security Department's handling of information about Stewart. The first was the failure of anyone in the department to look at Stewart's security file when he came back to Feltham for the last time, and to pass on relevant information it contained to the staff on Kestrel or Swallow. The second – which proceeds on the assumption that the department had a role to play in identifying the prisoners whose correspondence had to be monitored under Chapter 2 of PSO 4400 – was that no-one from the department checked Stewart's warrants to see whether he had been charged with offences under the Protection from Harassment Act 1997.

47.9 But these failures were only the tip of the iceberg. The Security Department was in a poor shape. Dave Comber, who took over as manager of the department from Mr Penwright in November 1999, after Mr Clifford had found Mr Penwright doing a crossword in the office,* said that the team from the Prison Service's Standards Audit Unit which visited Feltham between 22 November and 10 December 1999 had found almost every part of the department's activities to be either deficient or unacceptable. Mrs Clayton-Hoar agreed. It is not possible to say for sure whether the department had been in gradual decline for some time, or whether it had deteriorated sharply in the course of 1999. That is because surprisingly the department had not featured at all in the Inspectorate's reports on Feltham. But I suspect that the decline had happened relatively recently, because Mr Clifford had told Mrs Clayton-Hoar when he gave her responsibility for the department that it was "broadly running OK". This dislocation between appearance and reality only makes sense if its decline had occurred over a short period. But Mr Comber and Mr Cowan could not have been expected to turn the department around in the few months that they were responsible for it. As I have said earlier, Mr Comber had accumulated a good deal of time off in the first few months in 2000, and Mr Cowan was having to get to grips with the very many issues which came across the desk of the Head of Operations.

47.10 One of the problems was that Mr Penwright resented Mrs Clayton-Hoar as his line manager. They were like chalk and cheese. He was from the old school of prison officers, used to working with prisoners and enjoying the traditional camaraderie of male officers. She was a relatively new recruit to the Prison Service, having made it to a governor grade through the accelerated promotion scheme, and having spent most of her time – though not all – in Prison Service headquarters and addressing managerial functions. Mr Penwright felt uncomfortable both about reporting to a woman and about someone he did not think had a feel for the job. With retirement beckoning, he had become complacent, especially as he reckoned that after five years performing the role of the manager of the Security Department, he had been in the job for too long. As it was, Mr Penwright was left to his own devices for a long time, though he made the point that it was only his final appraisal as manager of the Security Department which had contained a poor evaluation of him.

---

* Mr Clifford thought that Mr Penwright should have been working at the time, but Mr Penwright said that he was on his lunch break.

47.11 From Mrs Clayton-Hoar's point of view, she needed someone to show her the ropes. She had no experience of security work apart from the security-related tasks required of prison officers on the wings. She had had little training for the role, and no handover to speak of when taking it on. She was going to use the forthcoming visit by the team from the Standards Audit Unit to help her understand the job. She needed a principal officer in the Security Department who was willing to devote time to explain to her how things worked there. She did not get that from Mr Penwright. The consequence of all that was that she tried to concentrate on those areas of her wide role as Acting Head of Operations where she felt more confident.

47.12 The other problem with the Security Department was that its functions were regarded as less important than some of the other functions within the establishment. Feltham was not unique in this respect. Hindley's Security Department was thought of in the same way. Any department from which staff are regularly cross-deployed to such an extent that sometimes the department had no prison officers working in it at all would be perceived in that light. All the more so if its staff were either less experienced or were returning to work after long-term absence through sickness, as happened at Hindley. Bearing in mind that Mr Clifford's priority related to life in the units, it was understandable that a department which did not have direct dealings with prisoners would be viewed within the establishment as a bit of an "add-on".

47.13 Mr Clifford has to take some responsibility here. He should have realised that Mrs Clayton-Hoar needed someone other than Mr Penwright as manager of the Security Department, and he should have appointed Mr Comber – or someone else – to the post sooner than he did. He knew that Mr Penwright was coasting. He should not have waited until the incident with the crossword to bring a new manager in. But in addition, Mr Clifford thought of Mrs Clayton-Hoar as playing a caretaker role until a new Head of Operations could be appointed. He sought to justify her appointment as Acting Head of Operations on the basis that at that stage in her career it was better to give her responsibility for functional departments rather than to expose her to the difficulties of managing residential units. But ultimately, he knew that giving her the job was a gamble, and he only gave it to her because there was no-one else available. If she only got the job by default, Mr Clifford should instead have raised the problem of having no-one suitable to appoint as Head of Operations or Acting Head of Operations with Mr Atherton. He did not do so. It might have been possible for Mr Atherton to have done something about it.

Chapter 48: The management of healthcare screening

48.1 We saw in chapter 33 that Stewart should have been seen by a healthcare worker on the five occasions he came through Feltham's reception as a returnee, and on the three occasions he came to Feltham as a transferee. On the occasions he arrived as a transferee he should have been seen by a doctor as well. We cannot tell how many times he was seen by a healthcare worker. We know that he was seen by one on 7 March 2000, and he may or may not have been seen on other occasions as well. But it is tolerably clear that he was never seen by a doctor, and that means that a doctor would never have reviewed his medical record. So he remained at Feltham from 7 February until 21 March 2000 without anyone seeing Mr Kinealy's note. If what happened to Stewart was representative of what was happening to other transferees and returnees arriving at Feltham, neither the national requirements for healthcare screening nor the local protocols produced at Feltham to incorporate them were being complied with.

48.2 Who had responsibility for ensuring that these requirements were complied with? The relevant Prison Service standard on healthcare placed the responsibility on the establishment's Managing Medical Officer. But no-one had been appointed to that post at Feltham. Instead, Feltham had a Head of Healthcare, Geoffrey Humphrey, and the lead GP in the practice which provided medical services to Feltham, Dr Stephen Jefferies. Dr Jefferies had been engaged in that capacity since 1995, and Mr Humphrey had taken over from Dick Cronk in September 1999. So which of them had responsibility for ensuring that the national requirements were complied with?

48.3 Mr Humphrey did not co-operate with the Inquiry as fully as the Inquiry wished. He provided the Inquiry with two statements, and the Inquiry also had a transcript of his interview with Mr Butt. But he refused the Inquiry's requests to give oral evidence for reasons which were not persuasive. It is regrettable that someone who was a member of the senior management team at Feltham at the time has chosen not to co-operate fully with the Inquiry's work, and at one stage I considered whether Mr Humphrey's refusal to make himself available to be questioned was itself evidence of an awareness on his part that his conduct was susceptible to criticism in some respects. As it has turned out, I have found Mr Humphrey to be at fault in a number of respects without having to draw that inference.

48.4 Despite that, the evidence of where responsibility lay for ensuring that the national requirements were complied with was clear. Dr Jefferies, it is true, had some quasi-managerial responsibilities. He was, for example, the point of contact between his practice and the establishment, for which he was allocated an additional, non-clinical session of time. And he participated in discussions about how the provision of healthcare at Feltham could be improved. But his input into those discussions was from the clinical point of view. He had no control over the budget for healthcare. He had no responsibility for the deployment of staff. And his authority to give instructions to healthcare staff was limited to clinical issues. His primary role was as a clinician looking after the medical needs of prisoners.

48.5 There was nothing in Mr Humphrey's witness statements which contradicted any of this. The only comment he made about Dr Jefferies's role was that Dr Jefferies trained and managed the GPs from his practice. As for his own role, Mr Humphrey did not have a job description, but the way he described his job in his witness statements showed that his brief was to manage the delivery of healthcare at Feltham. That included both the production of protocols which were intended to incorporate the national requirements *and their implementation*. That was tantamount to an acceptance by Mr Humphrey that he was responsible for ensuring that the national requirements for the healthcare screening of prisoners on their arrival at Feltham were met. In the circumstances, there was no compelling reason for Mr Clifford to have appointed a Managing Medical Officer – at any rate to oversee that function: Mr Humphrey was fulfilling that part of the Managing Medical Officer's responsibilities.

48.6 But that does not necessarily mean that Dr Jefferies bore no responsibility for the national requirements for healthcare screening not being complied with. He knew what the national requirements were. He therefore knew that transferees had to be seen by a doctor within 24 hours – as had returnees if they had not been under prison escort while they had been away from Feltham or if their circumstances had changed. But he knew that very few transferees and returnees were being brought to him. He was aware of that because the medical reception register of transferees and returnees was brought to him when he saw a prisoner, and he only saw that register infrequently. There were particular circumstances when he saw transferees – when the prisoner was convicted of murder or had been transferred to Feltham for medical reasons. But apart from that, the times when he would be asked to see transferees – and returnees for that matter – seemed to him to be random. And he could not recall ever seeing any "in and outs". So it must have crossed his mind – or at least it should have done – that many transferees and returnees, and all the transferees who were "in and outs", were not being seen by a doctor within 24 hours. Did he do what was sufficient to bring that to Mr Cronk's, and later to Mr Humphrey's, attention?

48.7 To answer that, it is necessary to go through Dr Jefferies's correspondence with Mr Cronk and Mr Humphrey. As far back as July 1998, Dr Jefferies drew Mr Cronk's attention to the risk of "in and outs" not being seen by healthcare staff on reception or by a doctor the next day, and the difficulty which the doctors had in seeing all the returnees and "off-bails" in addition to the transferees. As a result, Mr Cronk agreed that the returnees did not have to be seen by a doctor, even though that would be contrary to the national requirements. In March 1999, Dr Jefferies drew Mr Welsh's attention to the fact that arriving prisoners were not always being seen by healthcare staff in reception. And in August 1999, after Mr Cronk had issued a new instruction requiring returnees to be seen by the doctor after all, Dr Jefferies wrote back saying that returnees and "off-bails" were actually being brought to the doctors "on a very hit and miss basis", even though on at least one occasion they had been referred to as returnees in the appropriate medical reception register.

48.8 Dr Jefferies brought these concerns to Mr Humphrey's attention after Mr Humphrey took over from Mr Cronk in September 1999. In October 1999 he wrote to Mr Humphrey about an occasion when returnees had not been seen because of "the burden of work and the lack of supporting staff". The context of the letter – a complaint about the conditions in which Dr Jefferies had to work when he saw prisoners on Lapwing – shows that he was referring to returnees not having been seen by the doctor, rather than by healthcare staff on reception. His memo could have been read as saying that, although the returnees had been brought to the doctor to be seen, they were not in fact seen by him, but Dr Jefferies told the Inquiry that he had meant that they had not been brought to the doctor at all. We do not know how Mr Humphrey read the letter, but there was no response to it, even though it had said that these areas of concern had been the subject of correspondence before, and had complained of there having been little willingness to rectify them.

48.9 Finally, on 6 December 1999, Dr Jefferies wrote two letters to Mr Humphrey. One dealt with Dr Jefferies's assessment of healthcare needs at Feltham. The other dealt specifically with his concerns over healthcare screening. It did not systematically address the particular groups of prisoners, but it referred to "new numbers" not being seen by the doctor. It also criticised the facilities available to the doctors, and questioned the veracity of some records which purported to show that prisoners had been interviewed by healthcare staff on reception. The letter stressed the importance of reception healthcare screening, and asked for an opportunity to discuss with Mr Humphrey what Dr Jefferies described as "a significant deterioration in the service that is being provided". Dr Jefferies may not have spelt out what was going wrong, in terms of reception healthcare screening, with "new numbers", transferees, returnees, "off-bails" and "in and outs" respectively, but the whole of the correspondence shows that he had done what could reasonably have been expected of him to bring to Mr Cronk's, and later to Mr Humphrey's, attention the concerns he had and wanted to discuss.

48.10 What was Mr Humphrey's response to these expressions of concern? His reply to both letters of 6 December 1999 was contained in one memo. It acknowledged the need for Dr Jefferies to have an opportunity to discuss his concerns about reception healthcare screening, but Mr Humphrey said that he was too busy "to dedicate his time" to those concerns, and he suggested that Dr Jefferies discuss them with the shift manager. This was a dismissive and wholly inappropriate response to concerns legitimately raised by Dr Jefferies. It probably reflected the differences which had arisen between them over the contractual arrangements between the establishment and Dr Jefferies's practice. But any tension in their working relationship was no excuse for Mr Humphrey's failure to respond appropriately to Dr Jefferies's concerns.

48.11 Indeed, a couple of weeks after Zahid's murder, Mr Humphrey sent a memo to the healthcare manager – a principal officer – which rather disingenuously implied that it had only just been brought to his attention that reception healthcare screening was not "always consistent" with national requirements. Was it a coincidence that the same day Mr Humphrey received a memo from the primary care shift manager – a senior officer – which had been written after a recent conversation between them and which informed Mr Humphrey that "returns and change of circumstances" had not been seen in the past by a doctor? "Change of circumstances" must be a reference to returnees whose circumstances had changed, and "returns" is therefore likely to be a reference to transferees. Mr Humphrey said in one of his witness statements that this memo was the first time he had been made aware of "the problem". He could have been referring to another problem alluded to in the memo – that staff in reception were having prisoners escorted to their units without telling healthcare staff, who had, therefore, not had an opportunity to see them. But if the problem Mr Humphrey was referring to was the problem of some prisoners not being seen by the doctor, that was not true – not merely because of the letters he had received from Dr Jefferies, but also because the problem had been highlighted by the audit team from the Prison Service's Standards Audit Unit following its visit to Feltham in November and December 1999. The team had referred not only to returnees sometimes not being assessed by healthcare workers on reception, but also to occasions when "new numbers" were not being seen by a doctor within 24 hours.

48.12 What could Mr Humphrey have done to improve things? There may not have been much that he could have done without more healthcare staff and doctors. The problem with healthcare screening on reception was that there were not enough healthcare workers to see all the incoming prisoners when they arrived, and they were under considerable pressure from reception staff to visit them in their units later on so that reception could be cleared. The problem with the need for the doctor to see all the arriving prisoners – apart from the returnees whose circumstances had not changed – was that it took time to conduct a proper examination of a prisoner. We have seen Dr Greenwood's view on the topic from his experience at Hindley. The doctors could not have seen more prisoners in the morning sessions without jeopardising the quality of their examinations. And there was a limited amount of healthcare screening that the doctors could do in the afternoon session, bearing in mind the surgeries they held for prisoners already at Feltham.

48.13 But this does not mean that nothing could have been done. Obviously the "new numbers" had to be given priority. So too had the "off-bails" as they had been out of prison for a while. But returnees whose circumstances had changed and transferees who were "in and outs" were the least likely to need screening. If something was wrong with returnees, they could have been seen in a normal surgery before going out of Feltham for the day. And transferees who were due to return in a day or two to the establishment they had come from could be seen by that establishment on their return. After "new numbers" and "off-bails", priority could have been given to transferees – especially as there were likely to have been very few of them. Nothing appears to have been done by Mr Humphrey prior to Zahid's murder to prioritise things in that way. He should, at the very least, have given thought to resurrecting the protocol which permitted returnees not to be seen by a doctor. Maybe he did, but his refusal to co-operate fully with the Inquiry means that he never took the opportunity afforded to him to say so.

48.14 I do not criticise Mr Clifford over the shortcomings of healthcare screening at Feltham. In terms of line management responsibility, Mr Humphrey reported to him. But Mr Clifford was not aware of incoming prisoners not being seen by healthcare workers on reception. And although he suspected that some prisoners missed out on being seen by a doctor within 24 hours, he hoped that they would be seen the next day. As it was, no-one – whether Mr Humphrey or anyone else – raised with him any problems about healthcare screening for his intervention or decision. It may be that Dr Jefferies did not do so because he had found that when he had wanted to discuss other healthcare issues with Mr Clifford, Mr Clifford had referred him back to Mr Humphrey. But the fact remains that no-one brought the problems with healthcare screening to Mr Clifford's notice.

Chapter 49: The allocation of prisoners to cells

The absence of any guidance

49.1 When Stewart was first on Lapwing, he was put in a cell on his own because Mr Martindale had a gut feeling about him. For the night he was on Osprey, he was put in a cell with an Asian prisoner because Miss Goodman had no concerns about him. When he returned to Lapwing, he shared a cell with another prisoner, but we do not know anything about who he was. Nor do we know whether he shared a cell with anyone on his one night in Kestrel. But when he came to Swallow, he was put in the cell with Zahid because that was where the only available space was.

49.2 The decisions about which cell Stewart should be put in were made by individual officers exercising their own judgement at the time. There was the conventional wisdom that prisoners at risk of self-harm or suicide should not be put in a cell on their own. There were a few basic rules about which prisoners should not share cells: those charged with murder, those at stage 1 of the anti-bullying procedure and those on the escape list. And there were rules prohibiting certain kinds of prisoners sharing cells with each other, such as convicted and unconvicted prisoners. Apart from these rules – which were either contained in different sets of instructions or just taken for granted without being written anywhere – staff had no guidance, whether national or local, to help them decide how to allocate prisoners when they arrived on the unit.

The Prison Service's objective

49.3 For many years, Government policy has had as its objective the end of enforced sharing of cells. The White Paper, *Custody, Care and Justice: The Way Ahead for the Prison Service in England and Wales*, which was presented to Parliament in September 1991, said this about cell-sharing:

> "Wherever possible, prisoners should not be required to share cells. But some cell-sharing will still be appropriate, to meet prisoners' preferences, and where it is necessary in a prisoner's own interest to require that prisoner to share a cell – for example to protect him or her from what appears to be the risk of suicide…"

This was precisely what Lord Woolf had recommended in his report on the prison disturbances in 1990, and it echoed one of the recommendations contained in the May Report into prison services in 1979. This objective has remained official government policy, but as Beverley Hughes, the Minister then responsible for prisons, told the CRE at the public hearing it held in September 2001, other calls on the resources available to the Prison Service were being given higher priority.

49.4 Mr Narey's view is that, despite the Government's commitment to that objective in the long term, there is no real likelihood of it being realised in the foreseeable future. The principal reason for that is that successive changes in sentencing policy have caused the prison population to grow very substantially over the last decade. Despite the present programme for building new prisons, the prison population is increasing at a faster rate than the growth in available places. So even if prisons are being built with far more cells intended for occupation by one prisoner than before, the demand for single cells far exceeds the supply.

49.5 When it became apparent that the Government's objective could not be realised in the foreseeable future, and that many prisoners who should otherwise have been accommodated in a single cell would have to share a cell after all, what should the Prison Service have done? The answer is relatively plain. In those establishments where there were some single cells, the valuable resource of the single cell should have been reserved for those who really needed them and not squandered on those who did not. Such cells should therefore have been used for those prisoners who would have posed a risk to their cellmate if they shared a cell. And they should not have been allocated to prisoners – of whom there would admittedly have been very few – who would have preferred to share a cell.

The need for a national policy

49.6 There is a respectable argument for saying that if the UK is to comply with the European Prison Rules, which were adopted by the Commonwealth of Ministers of the Council of Europe in 1987, there has to be a national framework which gives guidance to staff about which prisoners should be allowed to share a cell. The rules are not legally enforceable under domestic law, but rule 14 states, so far as is material:

> "1. Prisoners shall normally be lodged during the night in individual cells except in cases where it is considered that there are advantages in sharing accommodation with other prisoners.
>
> 2. Where accommodation is shared it shall be occupied by prisoners suitable to associate with others in those conditions…"

49.7 Paragraph 1 is tolerably clear. Accommodating a prisoner in a single cell should be regarded as the norm. Requiring prisoners to share a cell should be treated as exceptional. The explanatory memorandum to the rules gives examples of situations which might be regarded as exceptionally justifying putting more than one prisoner in the same cell – where they have expressed a preference to share a cell, or where they might benefit from having company, for example when they are suffering from stress or have been identified as potential suicide risks. This is a requirement which the Prison Service has plainly honoured more in the breach than in the observance. That is almost certainly the reason rule 14 has played virtually no part in its overall thinking about cell-sharing. But the Prison Service is not alone in that respect. One of the findings of the research commissioned by the Inquiry from the International Centre for Prison Studies at King's College London, is:

> "In practice there has been a rapid growth in the number of prisoners in many jurisdictions, a growth which has outstripped the measures taken to increase the number of prison places. The effect of this is that few if any of the countries in Western Europe which make legislative provision for individual confinement appear able to honour that principle."

49.8 But for present purposes our focus is primarily on paragraph 2. That does much more than require staff to ensure that prisoners in particular categories should not share a cell. Plainly, men and women should not be placed in cells together. Nor should adults and young offenders, or convicted and unconvicted prisoners. Indeed, the need to keep them all separate save for organisational activities as part of an established programme of treatment is dealt with in rule 11. What paragraph 2 contemplates is some assessment by staff about the suitability of individual prisoners to share a cell.

49.9 One view is that such an assessment involves no more than ensuring that a prisoner who is *known* to pose a risk to other prisoners should not be allowed to share a cell. But the better view, I think, is that a prisoner's suitability to share a cell should be assessed whenever it is proposed to put him or her in a cell with others. That is not just consistent with the principle in paragraph 1 that the sharing of cells should only be allowed in exceptional circumstances. It also reflects the reference in the explanatory memorandum to the need for adequate information to be made available "to those concerned". It is possible that this is a reference only to those responsible for supervising prisoners when they are in their cells, but the better view is that it applies to those who make the managerial decision that a particular prisoner should be put in a cell with another prisoner. Again, prior to Zahid's murder, no system for considering the suitability of a prisoner to share a cell existed.

49.10 Leaving aside the requirements of the European Prison Rules, the need for a national framework to give guidance to staff about the allocation of prisoners to cells is obvious. Prisons contain large numbers of inmates with a propensity for violence – and not just those who have committed violent offences. And the frustration which being in prison produces can sometimes manifest itself in violent behaviour. That could well lead to prisoners with a readiness for violence being aggressive towards their cellmate. As I have already said, common sense tells us that, in an establishment where prisoners share cells, some thought should be given to a prisoner's unsuitability to share a cell because of the risk they might pose to other prisoners. It also tells us that to ensure that systematic thought is given to this issue, a policy needs to be formulated nationally giving officers guidance about which prisoners should be allowed to be in a double cell, and whether there are any kinds of prisoners they should not be allowed to share a cell with.

49.11 I acknowledge that a formalised system of assessing the risks which a prisoner poses to a potential cellmate would make further demands on the valuable time of officers and healthcare staff working on reception. Likewise, I acknowledge that assessing risk is not an exact science, and calls for a decision to be made on sometimes very skimpy information. But no-one has suggested that, with the introduction of a national policy since Zahid's death, the exercise has not been a worthwhile one. There is no compelling reason why it needed Zahid's death to bring about its introduction – especially as previous homicides of prisoners by their cellmates had not done that. I also acknowledge that the number of prisoner-on-prisoner homicides generally – and the number of homicides of prisoners by their cellmates in particular – is relatively small, when compared with the number of prisoners committing suicide. In these circumstances, the Prison Service naturally focused its attention on those prisoners who were at risk of harm from themselves. But if you are having to consider whether prisoners are a risk to themselves so that they are made to share a cell, you might as well consider at the same time whether prisoners are a risk to others so that they should be accommodated on their own, or should share only with certain types of prisoner. The tools you should be using for both exercises are the same. The need to have established procedures to meet the far more widespread incidence of suicide did not absolve the Prison Service from its responsibility to separate prisoners who posed a risk to others.

CHAPTER 49: THE ALLOCATION OF PRISONERS TO CELLS

49.12 One gets the strong impression that the relative rarity of homicides of prisoners by their cellmates meant that the Prison Service never really learned the lessons from those few occasions when it happened. The Inquiry was provided with a few of the reports of the internal investigations into those homicides. They are surprisingly brief, and contain little discussion, if any, about wider issues such as cell allocation and the sharing of information. A handful of cases in which the prisoner appeared to have committed suicide by hanging himself were later reclassified as homicides when it had become apparent that their cellmates had either hanged the victims themselves or forced or pressurised them into doing so. If the investigations had been more thorough, it is questionable whether any of these cases would initially have been classified as a suicide at all.

49.13 The Prison Service's response to the report of the Coonan Inquiry into the killing of Christopher Edwards at Chelmsford Prison in 1994 was an example of lessons not being learned. In fairness to the Prison Service, it has to be acknowledged that the report did not include any recommendations for the introduction of cell-sharing risk assessments. But on the night Christopher Edwards was killed, both he and his killer were spending their first night in prison, having been remanded in custody by the magistrates' court. So the recommendations which the Coonan Inquiry made related more to the passing on of information about new prisoners to the Prison Service by outside agencies. The introduction of the prisoner escort record was a response to the report. But the Prison Service did not provide us with any evidence that it had systematically gone through the recommendations made by the Coonan Inquiry, and Mr Wheatley accepted that it looked as if the report was not subject to the detailed scrutiny which a similar report would receive today. Indeed, Mr Narey made a very telling remark about the inquiry into Christopher Edwards's killing. He regarded the way in which Christopher Edwards's family had subsequently been treated and misled by the Prison Service as providing a more important lesson to be learned from the inquiry than how he came to be sharing a cell with his killer. Mr Narey may not have intended his words to come out in that way. But while it is imperative for relatives to be treated with respect, civility and above all honesty after a tragedy of that kind, and to be given all the appropriate information about it, it is perhaps surprising that Mr Narey gave greater prominence to that than to the circumstances which exposed Christopher Edwards to attack in the first place.

The need for local guidance

49.14 The need for a local policy to be formulated at Feltham had been identified following a serious incident in July 1998 when a prisoner took his cellmate hostage, held a shard of plastic from the toilet seat he had broken to his cellmate's throat, and threatened to kill him if staff did not leave the cell. The stand-off continued for almost three hours before the hostage was eventually released. During this ordeal, his arm had been burned with a cigarette and a noose had been placed around his neck.

49.15 A report about the incident was prepared by Katy Millard, who had been the duty governor at the time. The facts her report unearthed were disturbing. The assailant had been at Feltham twice before. He was regarded as aggressive and stroppy. At the time of the incident he had been there for five months. While there, he had begun to display psychotic symptoms, complaining that "he heard voices telling him to do things and that he felt generally people everywhere were against him". Although he remained on ordinary location, he was prescribed medication, and appeared to settle down. After a while, though, he stopped taking his medication, and was admitted to the healthcare centre on the advice of Dr Jefferies. While there, he was aggressive and abusive. He was placed on report, and eventually spent three days confined to his cell in the segregation unit. But instead of being returned to the healthcare centre, he was returned to ordinary location without Dr Jefferies or the visiting psychiatrist being consulted. The latter subsequently agreed that he could remain on ordinary location.

49.16 The staff on this unit – Partridge – knew him well, and had always put him in a single cell. But he got on the wrong side of prisoners there, and was moved – again without the doctors being consulted – to Raven where the staff did not know him. The officers there thought of him as a disciplinary rather than a psychiatric problem, and after five weeks he went first to the segregation unit and then to Quail, which was where the incident occurred the following night. He was placed in a double cell with his eventual victim. On the night of the incident, his victim had told staff that he wanted to change cells. Neither Mrs Millard's report, nor a report on the incident prepared by Robert Rowland, the then chair of the Board of Visitors, spelt out why the victim wanted to move cells, whether he gave his reasons at the time, or why his request was not met. But it was known that he was a vulnerable prisoner – his elder brother had committed suicide six months previously and he himself was suffering from depression. That was in Mr Rowland's report but not in Mrs Millard's – at least not in the surviving parts of her report provided to the Inquiry.

49.17 Unlike Stewart, the assailant had been identified as being mentally ill and as someone who should have been in a cell on his own. Nevertheless the similarities with what happened to Zahid are obvious. An inmate was allowed to share a cell with a vulnerable prisoner – when he should not have been sharing a cell with anyone – because information on his unsuitability to share a cell had not got through to the unit. And a vulnerable prisoner was subjected to a shocking attack from his cellmate despite having requested a change of cell.

49.18 Mrs Millard's report made a number of recommendations relating to prisoners who spend time in the healthcare centre and who are not taking their medication. But the recommendation which is relevant for present purposes reads as follows:

> "*A clear policy needs to be formulated over locating inmates in double cells*. Partridge unit said that they never put [the assailant] in a double cell. This information was not passed on. Where the [healthcare centre] decides that an inmate is fit for normal location but should not share a cell, this must be clearly recorded. As the reverse happens at present (i.e. inmates are fitted for normal location but only multi-cell, generally where there are fears over self-harm) this should not be impossible. It is likely of course that staff will have some concerns over accepting such inmates."

The body of this recommendation was about the need to pass on information, but the need for a policy about when prisoners should not be allowed to share a cell was spelt out in the first sentence.

49.19 Whether that recommendation should have been taken forward depended, in part, on how prevalent prisoner-on-prisoner in-cell assaults were. The anecdotal evidence was that they were very rare. Fighting was common, but not between prisoners in their cells. Prisoners preferred to fight when they knew that officers would be around to intervene, and inmates confined to cells for long periods were much more likely to emerge full of anger and ready for a fight rather than take out their frustrations on a cellmate. But I do not believe that assaults by one cellmate on another were all that infrequent. Prisoners may well be reluctant to report such attacks for fear of reprisals. The physical evidence of serious violence would be apparent, but that did not lessen the extent of under-reporting less serious incidents. Moreover, requests to change cells were very common. Many of them may have had nothing to do with the fear of attack by a cellmate, but even if only a small proportion of such requests did, the problem was a sizeable one. And the only research done at Feltham on the topic suggests a more than minimal level of in-cell assaults. Statistics prepared for Mr Butt's investigation showed that of the 189 prisoner-on-prisoner assaults reported for the 14 months from 1 March 1999 to 30 April 2000, 30 were assaults by one cellmate on another. That represented about 15% of all such reported assaults. We do not know how many of them were serious, and although Mr Clifford thought that one every two weeks or so was not a particularly high number, Mr Butt said that this was "a high proportion and should have alerted the management team to the need to investigate" them further.

49.20 So what was done about Mrs Millard's recommendation that a policy about cell-sharing be formulated? The answer is very little. Mr Welsh issued a Governor's Order which required prisoners to be certified by a doctor as fit for adjudication if they were transferred to the segregation unit. It also required prisoners who left the segregation unit to be returned to the healthcare centre if they had previously been patients there rather than be placed on ordinary location, and only to be transferred then to ordinary location if a doctor certified them as fit for that. Finally, it required the relevant records about a prisoner to accompany him when he was discharged from the healthcare centre. But it did not deal at all with the question of cell-sharing. That is to be contrasted with Mr Cronk's original draft for the Governor's Order, which was sent to Mr Welsh, and which specifically concerned the location of prisoners in double cells. His proposed form of words was ambiguous. It stated that a prisoner's suitability to share a cell should be "confirmed" before he was put in a double cell. That could have meant that consideration should always be given to whether a particular prisoner was suitable to share a cell with another inmate. But from the context of the rest of the draft, it looks as if what Mr Cronk had in mind was that a prisoner should not be placed in a double cell until the Local Inmate Database System had been consulted to see whether there was any indication that he should not share a cell.

49.21 Mr Welsh's explanation for not formulating a policy about when prisoners should not be put in a double cell was that he had read the first sentence of the recommendation in the context of the recommendation as a whole – which in his view was about those cases in which healthcare staff had said that the prisoner should be located in a single cell if he was to go back to ordinary location. In any event, he saw the incident which had given rise to the recommendation as a one-off, and it was not appropriate to issue formal instructions whenever someone made a mistake. Finally, he made the point that deciding whether a particular prisoner should not be permitted to share a cell was part of a prison officer's jailcraft, for which he did not need the guidance of a formal set of instructions.

49.22 For my part, I would not have read Mrs Millard's recommendation in the way Mr Welsh did. True, one situation where a prisoner should be put in a single cell is where that is the medical advice. But that is just one example, and Mrs Millard was suggesting a policy initiative to legislate for other situations as well. Nor do I agree with Mr Welsh's other reasons for inaction. The murder of Zahid was itself a one-off, and yet it triggered the decision to implement the cell-sharing risk assessment scheme. And there is little point in relying on prison officers' jailcraft if they do not use it.

49.23 In that connection, the evidence of the officers who were asked about prevailing practice was instructive. Not one of them suggested that they considered whether it was safe to put a prisoner in a double cell. To the extent that they addressed the question of cell-sharing at all, they looked at the suitability of particular kinds of cellmates. One of them said that he was aware of a practice of not mixing prisoners from different races in order to avoid manifestations of racism, though he may have been saying that only really happened when a prisoner expressed a preference not to share a cell with a prisoner from another race. Another said that he tried not to put prisoners who spoke different languages in the same cell. Miss Goodman claimed that staff on Osprey talked to prisoners to assess whether they were compatible before requiring them to share a cell. I am sceptical about that – even though her senior officer, Gary Fanthorpe, said much the same thing. It will be recalled that Miss Goodman did not consciously address the question of whether or not Stewart was suitable to share a cell with other prisoners.

49.24 The failure to implement Mrs Millard's recommendation and to formulate a policy that gave officers guidance about which prisoners should be allowed to be in a double cell and whether there were any kinds of prisoner they should not share a cell with was an important missed opportunity at Feltham. It might have led to useful guidance being given to prison officers which – if it had been followed, in itself questionable – would have led to Stewart being put in a cell on his own.

49.25 Two final points should be made. First, in defence of Mr Welsh, one should not forget that assessing the risks which a prisoner posed to his cellmate was not part of the culture within the Prison Service at the time. And the need to formulate a policy at Feltham for deciding which prisoners should not be allowed to share a cell was not identified by the Board of Visitors either. It only arose because of Mrs Millard's recommendation. Secondly, once her recommendation was not taken forward, the opportunity to do something about it was effectively lost, because the need to have a policy on cell-sharing was no longer on the radar. You could argue that the fact that prisoners spent so much time in their cells at Feltham meant that the issue was always going to be there. But Feltham was not alone in locking up prisoners for long periods, and there is nothing to suggest that other establishments had a policy about cell-sharing either. In the circumstances, it would be unfair to criticise Mr Clifford for not running with this particular baton. It had been dropped some time before he arrived on the scene.

Prisoners' preferences

49.26 Although the majority of prisoners would prefer to be on their own given the choice, a few – those who enjoy the company of others – are happier sharing a cell. Having a cellmate helps to pass the time. You have someone to talk to and play cards with. And common sense tells us, in theory at least, that if prisoners have to share cells, officers would try to accommodate any requests they might make, for example to share with a friend, or not to share with a smoker.

49.27 The desirability of taking into account a prisoner's wish to share a cell, and with whom, was recognised by the national operating standards issued by the Prison Service in 1994. They provided that the "allocation of cells and other living accommodation should take into account… the preferences of individual prisoners". And the commentary on that requirement made it clear that it did not relate solely to a prisoner's preference for the type of cellmate or the particular prisoner with whom the inmate wanted to share the cell, but whether the prisoner wanted to share a cell at all. It said that "individual preferences may relate to *cell-sharing* and smoking".

49.28 Mr Narey said that having a say in the identity of your cellmate was something which happened across the prison estate. Once prisoners got to their wings, staff would do their best to shuffle them around so that prisoners who wanted to share together could do so. But requests to have a particular cellmate would often be refused. A variety of reasons were given for that, including the need to control gang activity and to prevent undue pressure being placed on, say, a co-defendant to adopt a particular stance at his trial. But it was operationally impossible to give effect to every prisoner's preference to have a cell of their own. There were simply too few to go round. They were reserved for those who earned them through good behaviour or who were assessed as being in need of being on their own. That was certainly true in the days of Mr Narey's predecessor, Sir Richard Tilt, who would breathe a sigh of relief at the end of each day knowing that he had actually found a place somewhere for everyone. It was different for Mr Narey. Population pressures, though still acute, had eased, and by then the emphasis had shifted from the security issues which had dominated the Prison Service in the mid-1990s to the "decency agenda" for which Mr Narey had the backing of Jack Straw, the Home Secretary at the time.

49.29 At Feltham Mr Welsh incorporated the requirement in the national operating standards into Feltham's Business Plan for 1998/1999. It said that requests by prisoners for single, shared or non-smoking cells were to be met as far as possible. He was not suggesting that at reception a prisoner should be asked what his preference was, but that when a prisoner got to his unit, any reasonable request he had would be met if possible. Mr Welsh accepted that staff were unlikely to have read this passage in the Business Plan, but like Mr Narey he had no reason to think they were not responding to prisoners' requests if they could.

49.30 But if what happened on Swallow was anything to go by, this assumption was not justified. As we have seen, when it came to requests to change cells in order to share with a friend, officers on Swallow had differing views on how significant the practical obstacles to meeting that request were. For some, the practical obstacles were so great that such requests would as a general rule not be met. Others had a more relaxed view about them. I understand Mr Welsh's point that this was an area in which detailed guidance was undesirable – it would not be possible to address all possible situations in one policy document. But it was even more undesirable for the success of a request to change a cell to be dependent, in part at least, on which officer was approached.

49.31 Neither Mr Welsh nor Mr Clifford knew that personal preferences were routinely being ignored by some officers. I do not blame them for that. The problem should have been picked up by the senior officer in charge of the unit. He should have ensured that the practical obstacles which some officers saw as standing in the way of a request for a change of cell were not exaggerated.

Chapter 50: The management of offenders with personality disorders

50.1 No-one on Swallow knew that Stewart had been diagnosed by Mr Kinealy as suffering from a long-standing, deep-seated personality disorder. He was regarded as odd and a bit of a loner. And there was an air of menace about him. But he never behaved in a disruptive way which made him stand out from other prisoners. What would have happened if officers on Swallow had known what Mr Kinealy's note had said? Would Stewart have been managed in the same way?

50.2 The prevalence of personality disorders among prisoners means that the overwhelming majority of them have to be managed within the prison setting. The chances of them being transferred to a secure hospital are remote. The reason for that, as we have seen, is that a diagnosis of personality disorder is regarded as a diagnosis of exclusion from NHS services. That has been recognised by the Department of Health and the Home Office, on whose initiative a number of dedicated units – some in secure hospitals and some in prisons – have been opened since Zahid's death, for prisoners whose personality disorder is severe and who are regarded as dangerous. This programme – known as the Dangerous and Severe Personality Disorder Programme – has places, at the time of writing, for about 300 prisoners. Stewart would not have qualified for the programme even if it had existed then, and the untreatability of his condition meant that he could not have been transferred to a secure hospital.

50.3 Nor would there have been much which could have been done to assess the extent to which Stewart's personality disorder would have made him a risk to other prisoners. The tool which is used, the PCL-R scale, was at the time confined to prisoners in the adult high security estate. It would not have been used to measure the severity of Stewart's personality disorder. He would not have been regarded as old enough or dangerous enough – or as having committed offences of sufficient gravity – for it to have been used on him. And there were – and still are – differences of view among forensic psychiatrists about the extent to which it is an accurate predictor of risk.

50.4 So it is quite certain that if Mr Kinealy's diagnosis of Stewart's personality disorder had been discovered while Stewart was at Feltham, he would have remained within the normal prison setting, just as had happened at Altcourse where Mr Kinealy made his original diagnosis. That would have been so if Mr Kinealy had said in his note that Stewart was a risk to others, which is what he would have thought if he had read Stewart's security file. The question then is: could he have been better managed while on ordinary location so as to reduce the risk he posed?

50.5 The management of such prisoners while on ordinary location was not something about which the Prison Service had many creative ideas. If a prisoner's personality disorder manifested itself in disruptive behaviour, the prisoner would be moved to the healthcare centre or sent to the segregation unit. If it was prolonged, you would try to ring the changes by shuffling them between the two, interspersed with spells on ordinary location. As a last resort, the prisoner might be transferred to another prison in the hope that a change of surroundings would cause them to settle down. Initiatives commenced before Zahid's murder, but which did not come to fruition until well after it, are said to have ameliorated the problem, but the Inquiry did not hear of any strategy for the management of such offenders while they were on ordinary location.

50.6 Mr Giffin identified a number of measures which might have been taken for the management on ordinary location of a prisoner like Stewart, whose personality disorder Professor Maden thought would have been shown on the PCL-R scale to have been severe enough to put him in the 10% of prisoners who suffered from severe personality disorders. They were:

- not placing such a prisoner in a shared cell

- if the prisoner is to share a cell, carefully selecting their cellmate

- ensuring that, whatever difficulties there were generally in operating a proper personal officer scheme, such a prisoner had a personal officer who was fully aware of their background and who made a particular effort to get to know the prisoner and to keep an eye on their state of mind

- checking the correspondence and searching the cell of such a prisoner more frequently and carefully than would otherwise have been the case

- ensuring, again regardless of the difficulties which might be faced in providing a good regime for all prisoners in the establishment, that such a prisoner was appropriately occupied with, for example, work, education or offending behaviour programmes

- keeping a closer watch over the material, such as films, to which such a prisoner had access, and exercising control over their suitability.

To that list one might add checking with the Security Department about the existence of any useful intelligence about the prisoner and what was known about their previous behaviour in prison. It is, of course, impossible to say whether any of these steps would have been taken if staff on Swallow had been told of Stewart's personality disorder. They would also have had to be informed of its severity, and that Stewart posed a danger to other prisoners, despite the relatively non-serious nature of his offending and his unproblematic behaviour during his recent spells in custody. And apart from putting Stewart in a cell on his own, it is a matter of speculation whether the taking of these steps would have resulted in a different outcome.

Chapter 51: Race relations at Feltham

The Butt report

51.1 Although I have treated it as established that Feltham was institutionally racist, it has still been necessary to identify how extensive racism was there. The prevalence of racism at the establishment has informed my views about whether shortcomings on the part of individual officers were attributable to the culture of indifference and insensitivity to black people and people from ethnic minorities which institutional racism breeds, and whether it was sufficiently recognised and tackled by Feltham's management and at Prison Service headquarters. It is here that the requirement in the Inquiry's terms of reference for it to take into account the investigations which have already taken place assumes particular importance. That is because racism at the establishment and within the Prison Service was the focus of the CRE's report, and because Part 2 of the Butt report was exclusively concerned with racism at Feltham.

51.2 The Prison Service's investigation into racism at Feltham was originally to be carried out by Judy Clements, who was then the Race Equality Adviser to the Prison Service. It was only when other commitments made that impossible that Mr Butt was asked to lead it. His team examined a variety of documents and relied on questionnaires modelled on those used at Brixton Prison in South London. About 10% of the staff and prisoners at Feltham were interviewed about their experiences. Fifty per cent of the staff who were interviewed were black or from ethnic minorities.* The ethnic origin of the prisoners who were interviewed reflected the ethnic breakdown of the inmates at the establishment as a whole.

51.3 Mr Butt and his team began this part of their work on 22 September 2000. Part 2 of his report which covers race and racism is dated 13 November 2000. It therefore addressed the state of race relations at Feltham a number of months after Zahid's death. Although Feltham as a whole was an even more worrying establishment by the time Part 2 of the Butt report was published – attributable, in part, to the changes of Governor during the year – there is no special reason to think that race relations had got any worse. However, Mr Butt's team did not get the full co-operation of the establishment. The Education Department, for instance, did not provide them with the information they asked for, and many staff did not meet Mr Butt's team at the appointed time or place. They claimed they had not been informed of their appointments, or had not been released from their duties to attend the interviews which had been arranged.

---

* Black prisoners and staff, and prisoners and staff from ethnic minorities, will be referred to as BME prisoners or BME staff.

51.4 Mr Butt found that "a small number of staff sustained and promoted overtly racist behaviour". But a wider dynamic was at work here. Not all the racism was overt. The report talked of "more subtle methods" of discriminating against BME prisoners. It was referring to discrimination which only became apparent when ethnic monitoring revealed worrying trends. Examples of that which the report identified were the disproportionate number of BME prisoners on whom force was used to restrain them, the disproportionate number of BME prisoners who were on the anti-bullying unit,* and the disproportionate number of BME prisoners who were sent to the segregation unit after fighting with a white prisoner, with the latter invariably remaining on the residential unit.

51.5 Nor was it just BME prisoners who were the target of racist attitudes. BME staff could only "be accepted as part of the team at Feltham… by enduring racist comments and racist banter/jokes". And the report also noted that "there are issues surrounding both staff and prisoners", which I have taken to mean that racially discriminatory attitudes or practices were not only the province of staff. Prisoners displayed them as well. Examples of that were racist language commonly used by prisoners, including BME ones, and the domination of the use of the gym by BME prisoners.

51.6 The report identified a number of possible reasons for these serious shortcomings. One of the principal ones was "a lack of awareness" on the part of staff "as to what [was] happening around them". Another was that staff had very little understanding of race relations or of RESPOND, the acronym for the initiative launched by the Prison Service to promote Racial Equality among Staff and Prisoners. That may well have been due to a lack of training on the topic. Less than 10% of Feltham's supervisory staff had complied with a recent Governor's Notice to make their staff available for race relations training, even though such training was mandatory, and the consequence was that less than 30% of staff had received such training. Indeed, the authenticity of the training records purporting to show which members of staff had received race relations training was itself questionable. As for RESPOND, awareness of the initiative at the time of Mr Butt's investigation was "virtually non-existent", even though at the time of its launch in November 1999 a notice had been issued about it, staff had attended a briefing on it, and cards and booklets explaining it had been circulated. More than 80% of staff had not even seen the video promoting it.

---

* Feltham's Board of Visitors noted that on the unit which mirrored the anti-bullying unit, namely the unit for vulnerable prisoners, there was a disproportionate number of white prisoners. The Board also noted disproportionate numbers of white prisoners serving meals.

51.7 The other principal reason for the shortcomings which the report identified was management's lack of commitment to the promotion of good race relations. The race relations management team was ineffective. The team met every two months, but when incidents were reported to it, they were not discussed in any depth. Ethnic monitoring data was collated effectively, and was discussed at team meetings where problems were highlighted, but there was little evidence of any solutions being identified and implemented. Not all team members had undergone the appropriate training, and of those who had not, none had applied to go on the relevant course. In short, the team was said to be re-active rather than pro-active, with no evidence of team members going about the establishment actively promoting good race relations.

51.8 Mr Butt's team were also concerned about the key post of Race Relations Liaison Officer, which was filled at the time by Mr Byrd. They thought the job description for the post was superficial and unclear, and that raised the question whether the holder of the post had been sufficiently briefed or given the time to carry out his job effectively. Some of his key duties had been wrongly delegated to the Equal Opportunities Officer, and that had resulted in the Race Relations Liaison Officer having a low profile, with many members of staff equating his role with that of the Equal Opportunities Officer. But with his other duties as a residential governor, the team thought that he did not have the time needed to carry out all the duties of the post. Something had to give, and what suffered most was the reporting, recording and investigating of racist incidents as perceived by staff or prisoners, and the investigation of formal complaints about alleged racist behaviour.

51.9 Very few racist incidents as witnessed by staff or inmates were reported and recorded. Staggeringly, only 11 such incidents were reported by staff and recorded in the race relations incident log over a five-year period up to July 2000. The report found that this extremely low number did not reflect the number of incidents recorded in the wing observation books for each of the residential units in the six months before the attack on Zahid. They revealed that 40 incidents had been recorded as racist incidents of some kind. Not one of them had been reported to the Race Relations Liaison Officer and recorded in the race relations incident log. Unsurprisingly, the report concluded that "the procedures in place for reporting and recording racist incidents are poor, inconsistent and not communicated to those who may need to know them". And of the very few incidents which the Race Relations Liaison Officer investigated, it was not possible for Mr Butt's team to identify with accuracy how well they were examined. The documents recording the investigative process were only retained if there was to be a subsequent disciplinary investigation. But that did not stop Mr Butt from concluding that "the procedures for investigating such incidents are haphazard, incomplete and again inconsistently applied". The report concluded that it was "no wonder that staff, prisoners and even prisoners' families have no confidence in those procedures".

51.10 In addition to the reporting and recording of perceived racist incidents, there were 17 formal complaints of racist behaviour brought by prisoners against members of staff recorded in the race relations incident log. The report did not discuss this extremely low number in any detail, but it suggests that prisoners had little confidence that any complaint of racism would be investigated properly. And on the question of prisoners' complaints generally, the report noted that the complaints system was not trusted by them. Prisoners did not know how to complain, they were afraid to do so and there was a total lack of confidentiality in the system. As for how the complaints were investigated on the few occasions they were made, the report noted that "due to the absence of any evidence of investigations having been carried out, many complaints cannot be assessed or investigated properly". It is unclear whether this was intended to mean that the complaints were not properly investigated at the time, or that Mr Butt's team was not able to assess whether the complaints had been properly investigated at the time because the paperwork was no longer available.

The CRE's report

51.11 Many of the themes identified by the Butt report were picked up, and elaborated upon, in the CRE's report. It is unnecessary to repeat them here. But the CRE made a number of additional comments about the state of race relations at Feltham. Staff used language reflecting inappropriate stereotypical views of national and ethnic minorities. Racist abuse on the part of prisoners was rife, but no effective measures were taken to deal with the problem. The same was true of racial harassment on the part of inmates. A disproportionate number of black prisoners were suspected of drug-dealing or drug-taking and were therefore subjected to drug tests. A disproportionate number of black and Asian prisoners were the subject of disciplinary charges. A disproportionate number of black prisoners were on the basic level of the incentives and earned privileges scheme. And there was disproportionate representation on work parties.

51.12 The CRE was particularly concerned about formal complaints by inmates of racist behaviour. Apart from the problems identified by the Butt report, the CRE criticised Feltham for the refusal of officers on occasions to give out the appropriate complaint forms when they were requested, and for the over-use of attempts to seek the informal resolution of such complaints. Prisoners were not only afraid of reprisals from other prisoners. They thought that if they proceeded with a complaint, they could be demoted to a lower level on the incentives and earned privileges scheme or moved to another wing or lose their job. And without identifying Feltham as a particular source of the problem – but without excluding it either – the CRE criticised the high standard of proof which those investigating complaints of racism required, thereby letting officers facing allegations of racial discrimination off the hook rather than objectively searching for the truth.

51.13 There was one episode the CRE referred to in some detail which highlighted a number of these problems. Two Asian prisoners claimed to have been assaulted on 23 January 2000 by two white prisoners as they were watching television in a room where they ought to have been, but were not being, supervised by prison officers, even though a full complement of staff was on duty. The injuries sustained by one of them, which included a broken jaw, were so serious that he had to spend 19 days in hospital. He said that he had been racially insulted during the attack, but asked for it not to be treated as a racist incident. While he was convalescing, he was told that Mr Clifford was dealing with the case. However, Mr Pascoe later claimed in a letter to Feltham's Imam that he was not aware that the case had ever been raised with Mr Clifford. Ultimately, no disciplinary proceedings were ever instigated, because, so staff claimed, there was no evidence to support disciplinary charges since no prison officer had witnessed the attack, thereby ignoring the evidence of the two Asian prisoners themselves. The incident only saw the light of day a year or so later when it was taken up by the Imam. The case was then referred to the police who expressed the opinion that there was sufficient evidence to justify charging the assailants with assault occasioning actual bodily harm.

51.14 But the CRE's overarching point was that Feltham's shortcomings in the field of race relations were there for all to see if anyone had chosen to look for them. There was a culture within the Prison Service, and maybe on the part of the independent watchdogs as well, to treat race relations as divorced from the basic operational requirements of prison work. There was a real tendency to ignore the holistic nature of race relations as something which affected every aspect of prison life. That was reflected in the Inspectorate's reports on Feltham. They were devastating in their condemnation of Feltham's many failings, but they did not mention the problems with race relations at all. That was why there was nothing in the surviving documents relating to the work of the task force about race relations, why Mr Atherton never discussed race relations with

Mr Clifford, and why race relations were hardly ever mentioned at the regular meetings of Feltham's senior management team. Mr Darken told the Inquiry that the majority of the POA's members at Feltham did not see Feltham in the way it had been portrayed by Mr Butt and the CRE. If that is the case, it explains why the majority of staff – except, of course, those officers who were overtly racist themselves – continued to be in denial about the appalling state of race relations there.

51.15 The CRE also thought that management at Feltham simply did not understand racial issues or how to deal with them. For instance, when white prisoners complained about having to use hair clippers used by black prisoners, the solution proposed was to get more hair clippers rather than to confront the white prisoners' prejudices. And when a Muslim complained among other things about being offered a pork chop, the complaint was rejected on the basis that the action complained of had not been "racially motivated" without appreciating that the failure to provide a proper Halal diet may amount to indirect racial discrimination. Nor did they have a sense of the wider picture. The example the CRE gave of that was the absence of any recognition of the dangers inherent in the combination of white racist prisoners with violent backgrounds and prisoners from different ethnic minorities displaying different coping strategies while in prison.

The Hounslow survey

51.16 Towards the end of 2000, the possibility of seeking the views of prisoners on the state of race relations at Feltham was discussed at a meeting of Feltham's race relations management team. Satvinder Buttar, a member of the team, and the Director of the Hounslow Racial Equality Council – Hounslow being the London borough in which Feltham is situated – offered his assistance. He helped to conduct a series of focus groups which were held between January and May 2001. A total of 54 BME prisoners participated in five sessions, and the Inquiry was provided by the CRE with a draft of the executive summary of the report written by Mr Buttar and completed in September 2001. The CRE has told the Inquiry that it got it from Hounslow Racial Equality Council. If a report in its final form was ever completed, the Inquiry was not provided with a copy of it. There is no reason to suppose that the findings in the draft of the executive summary did not apply to the period leading up to Zahid's death. Bearing in mind that staff knew that race relations at Feltham was under the spotlight after that, it is fair to assume that, if anything, the situation would have been worse prior to the murder.

51.17 The draft mirrored many of the findings in the Butt report and anticipated many of those which the CRE's report highlighted. It mentioned a number of instances of disproportionate treatment of BME prisoners. But the most worrying feature of the draft was the prevalence of explicit racism on the part of individual officers. Racist abuse of BME prisoners by some white officers was said to be "common practice". BME prisoners were called "monkeys" and "black bastards", and they were told that "they should be sent back to their own country". Following Zahid's murder, officers had "become more discreet in expressing racist attitudes", but that did not mean that they were any less racist than before. They had just become more subtle about it. It was felt that this was being done so that BME prisoners "would find it difficult to cope and might attempt suicide". Officers discouraged prisoners from complaining – by offering to "shake hands and make up" – but when prisoners did complain, their complaint forms would not be forwarded. BME prisoners were sometimes accused of racism themselves in order to divert attention from what some of the white prison officers were doing. Some BME officers were no better: they would turn a blind eye to what was going on, and sometimes even collude in what was happening, "in order to fit in with their white colleagues".

51.18 There may have been an element of settling old scores in the focus groups, but in view of Mr Butt's conclusion that there was "a small number of staff [who] sustained and promoted overtly racist behaviour", there is no reason to suppose that the participants in the focus groups were exaggerating things too much. I proceed on the basis that what they were saying represented their genuine perception of the state of race relations at Feltham at the time.

51.19 If the minutes of the meetings of the race relations management team are a fair reflection of what was discussed at them, the draft was never discussed at these meetings. That fact rather suggests that the draft was never sent to the race relations management team. That is consistent with the fact that the Inquiry was provided with the draft by the CRE, not by the Prison Service, and that it consists only of a draft of the executive summary. That explains why Mr Byrd told the Inquiry that he had not seen the document until a couple of weeks before he gave evidence to the Inquiry. I do not doubt that. But when the document was shown to him, Mr Byrd claimed not to have known what it was. He offered the suggestion that the CRE had carried out some focus groups in the course of its investigation into Zahid's murder. I am sceptical about Mr Byrd's claim not to have known what the draft was. I appreciate that almost four years had elapsed since the focus groups had taken place, but if it really had not occurred to Mr Byrd that the draft related to these focus groups, it is an indication of how unimportant he had regarded them. In fact, the focus groups were an important source of information about prejudiced staff, and although management must have known they were taking place, nothing was done to find out what they had revealed.

Minimising racial tensions

51.20 One of the features of the evidence produced to the Inquiry by staff at Feltham was that racial conflict between prisoners was extremely rare. Indeed, many of them were in denial about the prevalence of racist abuse. And even when staff were prepared to admit that racist abuse was common, they tended to regard it as a form of insult rather than as a manifestation of underlying racial tensions. It was only as one advanced up the management tree that there was a greater recognition of the significance of racist abuse.

51.21 Mr Clifford recognised the routine racist abuse which passed for normal at Feltham. It tended to occur when prisoners were not being supervised, or when it would be difficult to identify them, such as when it was being shouted through cell windows. He expected staff to report such abuse even if it was going on all the time. Some did and some did not, depending on how keen they were to do their job properly or how intent they were on having an easy life. But he was aware of instances of racist jibes which amounted to the sinister and deliberate targeting of some prisoners. He did not doubt that some prisoners were out-and-out racists, and he saw a racial subtext in the tribal loyalties which occur in prison, whether based on gang membership or support for particular football clubs or between prisoners who came from the same part of London or from the same part of the country.

51.22 Ms Clements saw things in the same way, though she talked about London prisons in general, rather than Feltham in particular. In her opinion, staff did not see the racist dimension in racial name-calling, and were slow to see deliberate or explicit racism on the part of prisoners. Without wishing to underestimate prisoner-on-prisoner racism, she saw the way prisoners were being discriminated against by staff as the bigger issue. Like Mr Clifford she was aware of very different standards in the way staff reacted to racist abuse. There were the dinosaurs – some of whom would have been out-and-out racists – who were not prepared in any way to embrace the culture of decency in the way prisoners were treated. On the other hand, there were members of staff who cared very deeply for the welfare of the prisoners in their charge.

All of this was very much in line with the thinking of the CRE, which saw racism going far beyond prisoner-on-prisoner racist abuse. It described racial harassment on the part of prisoners as one of the features of prison life.

51.23 So there was a disturbing readiness on the part of staff at Feltham to downplay racial tensions, and to regard racist abuse as a slight on a prisoner's character rather than a disparagement of his ethnic origin. Indeed, some staff might have been motivated to downplay racist abuse because of their own bigotry. I acknowledge that staff might have been painting a rosier picture in their evidence than they might have been prepared to acknowledge in other circumstances. And they might have been reluctant to label a prisoner a racist even though the circumstances clearly demanded it. An example of that was Deborah Hogg's initial reluctance to accept that Stewart's intercepted letter revealed him to be racist. But the tendency on the part of staff to minimise the significance of racist abuse cannot be doubted.

51.24 Mr Martindale's "softly softly" approach to Stewart's racist letter was an example of the readiness of staff to treat racist abuse otherwise than with the vigour it deserved. The failure to recognise racist abuse for what it is was the most obvious manifestation of an even more serious malaise – the lack of intuitive skills on the part of staff to see things against the background of their racial dimension. Of course, with staff who harboured deep prejudices, this lack of intuition would have been superseded by a lack of will. But the failure of staff to use such intuitive skills as they had – for whatever reason – explains why the possibility that Stewart might have been a racist who was hostile to Asians like Zahid, and the possibility that Zahid might have been uncomfortable about sharing a cell with someone who looked like Stewart, were issues which simply did not occur to them.

The reporting of racist incidents

51.25 Perhaps the most significant feature of Mr Martindale's handling of Stewart's racist letter was the fact that its interception was not reported to the Race Relations Liaison Officer. But he was not alone in failing to report racist incidents. Racist incidents had to be reported to the Race Relations Liaison Officer and recorded in the race relations incident log. When an officer witnessed a racist incident, or came across evidence of one, or was notified of one by a prisoner, he had to ensure that it was reported. The interception of Stewart's racist letter was an example of that. Both the Butt report and the CRE's report noted the remarkably low number of racist incidents reported to the Race Relations Liaison Officer. Bearing in mind that the Stephen Lawrence Inquiry defined a racist incident as "any incident which is perceived to be racist by the victim or any other person", and not just by the officer who witnessed it or was told about it, the comparative rarity of such incidents being reported after February 1999 when the report of the Inquiry was published is very significant.

51.26 There could, no doubt, have been many reasons for that. There could have been a failure or an unwillingness to recognise the incident as a racist one. That was how Mr Martindale attempted to justify his inaction over Stewart's intercepted letter. There could have been a reluctance to complete the necessary paperwork – whether because of apathy or pressure of work or both. There could have been hostility or indifference to action in the field of race relations or to the welfare of BME prisoners. If the incident amounted to a complaint against a member of staff, there could have been a deliberate attempt to obstruct any investigation into their behaviour. And it could simply have been because some staff did not know that racist incidents had to be reported. All of these factors could have been in play.

51.27 There is one other possible reason for inaction, and that was the desire on the part of staff not to be too inflexible in invoking formal procedures in the management of prisoners. That, too, was a reason given by Mr Martindale to explain his handling of Stewart's racist letter. It will be recalled that thinking of that kind was present in Mr MacGowan's evidence. There is much to be said for looking at an incident on its merits in most areas of prison life. The rigid enforcement of rules can be as counter-productive as too relaxed an approach. There is often room for flexibility. But none of that should apply to the reporting of racist incidents. As we saw in paragraph 21.21, staff had recently been reminded of that in a Governor's Order issued by Mr Clifford in July 1999. And it was not as if only racist incidents of some gravity had to be reported. Mr Clifford's Order had made it clear that all racist incidents – including minor ones which had been resolved informally – had to be reported.

51.28 Mr Byrd must bear some responsibility for not tackling the problem with greater vigour. He had not arranged for the introduction within Feltham of the dedicated form to be used to report racist incidents based on the model form attached to PSO 2800, the Prison Service Order on race relations. It was not until well after Zahid's murder that complaints of racism could be made by the use of confidential boxes. He admitted that he was aware of the under-reporting of racist incidents, but he claimed that the scale of the problem had come as a surprise to him when he read Mr Butt's report. If that claim is true, it shows that he must have been doing very little to keep abreast of events, since the derisory number of incidents being reported should have told him about the scale of the problem. I do not suggest that he was in a position to compel staff to do something which many of them may have been reluctant to do anyway. But if he had been aware of the level of the under-reporting of racist incidents, he should have been much more pro-active than he was in emphasising to staff on his rounds that racist incidents had to be reported. For example, he could have looked at prisoners' wing files or the wing observation books for entries about racist incidents, and if it transpired that they had not been reported to him, he could have asked why. His evidence was that he could not recall a single occasion when he had noticed something like that.

The managerial shortcomings

51.29 As I explained earlier, it is questionable whether the outcome would have been any different if Mr Byrd had been informed of Stewart's racist letter. But Stewart might well not have remained in a cell with Zahid if staff on Swallow had been more sensitive to the message of hostility towards BME prisoners which Stewart may have been sending about himself by his behaviour and appearance, and more aware of what an Asian teenager like Zahid might have thought about him. That lies at the very heart of what happened to Zahid. A collective oversight of that kind on the part of staff on Swallow is far more likely to happen in an establishment where racial tensions are consistently made light of and swept under the carpet as if they did not exist – and where institutional and individual racism are allowed to fester.

51.30 Much of that was down to the relatively few members of staff who had received training in race relations – a topic highlighted by both Mr Butt and the CRE. Mr Clifford claimed that staff could not be spared to go on training courses, but that argument has to be seen in the context of the greater effort which Feltham could have made to recruit and retain its staff. Having said that, training alone could not have been the panacea for Feltham's problems on race relations. Staff had to be given a lead from those responsible for the oversight of race relations, and they were not getting that at all.

51.31 Where did responsibility for that state of affairs at Feltham lie? It would be tempting to oversimplify things, and point the finger of blame at Mr Byrd. True, he must take his fair share of responsibility, but responsibility for the poor state of race relations at Feltham – which should have been apparent, at least to some extent, to anyone who worked there and thought about it – lies in many places. But I must start with Mr Byrd, who I think was a singularly ineffective Race Relations Liaison Officer. He most of all should have been alive to the poor state of race relations at Feltham. But he did not see race relations as a problematic area at all, and that may have been in part because of how he saw his role. Apart from complying with the mandatory requirements of PSO 2800, he regarded his role as a reactive one. His priorities were to compile statistics for the purpose of ethnic monitoring and to ensure that the bi-monthly meeting of the race relations management team took place. Even then, there was some slippage on both fronts. He acknowledged that assembling statistics was not the most productive use of his time, but the work had historically been done by the Race Relations Liaison Officer, and there was no-one else to do it.

51.32 Mr Byrd's description of what his priorities were mirrors the way he saw his role as residential governor. He was more comfortable in completing tasks which did not require pro-active management on his part. And when he analysed the results of ethnic monitoring or investigated a formal complaint of racism, his approach for the most part was to look for an outcome which avoided confrontation. For example, if ethnic monitoring showed that a disproportionate number of BME prisoners were being treated in a particular adverse way, he had a tendency to look for something other than racial prejudice which would have accounted for it. And when he had to investigate a formal complaint of racism, he would try to resolve the complaint informally so that the parties directly affected were satisfied – or at any rate professed to be satisfied – rather than consider whether there was a wider problem underlying the complaint. So when on one occasion a prisoner lodged a series of complaints, he did not investigate them sufficiently, citing pressure of work as one reason and the prisoner's transfer to another establishment as another. Mr Byrd should have prioritised his time in such a way so as to enable him to investigate these complaints properly. And he should not have allowed the prisoner's transfer to pre-empt the completion of the investigation. An extremely common complaint among BME prisoners was that if they made a formal complaint about racism they were "shipped out" to another establishment. As it was, the prisoner had alleged that his transfer was a result of his complaints. Even if Mr Byrd did not believe that to be the case, the complaints raised wider issues which should have been investigated anyway.

51.33 Mr Byrd took over the role of Race Relations Liaison Officer from Mr Greenslade shortly before Mr Welsh left Feltham. And he went on a two-week training course for race relations liaison officers in October

1999. But it would be wrong not to mention in his defence the pressures he was under. Poor race relations had probably been a feature of life at Feltham for many years, and Mr Byrd could not have been expected to change that overnight. Mr Welsh told him that Mr Greenslade had been struggling in the post. Perhaps that had been because Mr Greenslade had not had any training for the job at all. Mr Byrd had not had any experience of this kind of work before, and the briefing he got from Mr Greenslade was minimal. It had consisted of an explanation of the records which had to be maintained. He was in effect given a copy of PSO 2800 and told to get on with things. Moreover, he had to perform the role of Race Relations Liaison Officer in tandem with his duties as a residential governor – just as Mr Greenslade had performed it in tandem with his duties as a principal officer. The fact that the role should have been full-time was recognised after Zahid's death. Mr Byrd did not believe that prior to then he had had sufficient time to do the job properly, but he could not recall whether he had ever mentioned that to Mr Clifford.

51.34 Despite all this, it remains the case that Mr Byrd was not the man for the job. It called for skills, knowledge and experience he did not have. His strengths lay, I suspect, in dealing with prisoners face to face. A role which gave him responsibility across the whole of an establishment for an area which called for a measure of imaginative thinking was not for him. That was something both Mr Welsh and Mr Clifford should have realised – and in the case of Mr Clifford I think he did – though I acknowledge that there may not have been anyone else in a governor grade who was better suited to the role and could be spared from devoting all their time to their current post.

51.35 I turn to the race relations management team. To call this body a management team was a misnomer. The name suggests a group with managerial responsibility for considering issues of policy relating to race relations, with the Race Relations Liaison Officer acting as its executive arm implementing any decisions it made. In fact, the team had no independent existence apart from the meetings which members attended every couple of months. That is not to say that it did not serve a useful function. The minutes of the meetings show that they provided an opportunity for the Race Relations Liaison Officer to present the statistics he had assembled for the purpose of ethnic monitoring and to report on investigations which had been conducted. It was also the forum where the many operational issues relating to race relations could be debated. There was some discussion about disturbing trends behind such under-representation or over-representation of BME prisoners which the statistics revealed, but they rarely resulted in any definitive conclusion or a suggestion that action of a particular kind be taken.

There was no sense of the team having an appreciation of the poor state of race relations at Feltham, or of Mr Byrd's shortcomings as Race Relations Liaison Officer.

51.36 More significant was the surprising thinking about race relations issues on the part of some members of the team. Some of the following examples post-date Zahid's murder, but there is no reason to suppose that they do not reflect attitudes which were prevalent before then. The minutes of the team's meetings show that some members were concerned about permitting the Society of Black Lawyers to hold a series of seminars for black prisoners because it "would appear to be positive discrimination of black inmates". No member of the team challenged a governor's view that an attack by black prisoners on two white prisoners who were Irish travellers had not been racially motivated, because the attack was more likely to have been attributable to the fact that they were tall, and therefore might present a challenge to their assailants, and were softly spoken, and therefore might be easy targets. Some members of the team questioned whether a letter containing racist remarks should be regarded as racist if the person to whom it was sent would not have regarded it as racist – thereby overlooking the definition of a racist incident adopted by the Stephen Lawrence Inquiry, namely "any incident which is perceived to be racist by the victim *or any other person*". And the team seems to have attributed the disproportionate number of BME prisoners on whom force was used to restrain them to staff shortages and hot weather.

51.37 I hesitate to describe the race relations management team as wholly ineffective, because there was undoubtedly real value in the discussions generated on the operational issues brought to its attention. But it was not the forum for strategic thinking about race relations. It would have been more effective if staff shortages had not prevented the regular attendance of unit representatives, if prisoners had been properly represented on it, if its members had had the benefit of some training, and if Mr Clifford had taken a more active interest in its work.

51.38 That brings me to Mr Clifford's own responsibility for the deplorable state of race relations at Feltham. Mr Clifford had a sense that race relations were bad. He was aware that racist abuse was tolerated, that racial harassment of prisoners by prisoners was not uncommon, and that formal complaints of racism were not being investigated as they should have been, even though he thought the investigation of them had not become so bad that he needed to do something about it. Some of these things happened in other establishments, and I do not think that he realised just how bad things really were at Feltham. That explains why his approach was not to treat race relations as a separate workstream. Feltham was an establishment which was failing on so many fronts that it was necessary to get the place working properly again before it was possible to start tackling particular parts of it. The effect of this approach was that BME prisoners experienced a "double whammy" in that inaction on the race relations front compounded the adverse effects of the impoverished regime which all prisoners suffered from. But Mr Clifford was lulled into thinking that things were not all that bad by the absence of any real concern about race relations at Feltham on the part of those bodies from outside the establishment responsible for monitoring its performance. That is the topic to which I now turn.

Lack of external oversight

51.39 The remarkable feature of the branding of Feltham as institutionally racist by Mr Butt in November 2000 was that no-one from outside had seen it coming. As Ms Clements said, how could we have been so blind? There was nothing in the Inspectorate's reports following its inspection of Feltham in 1996 and 1998 to suggest that race relations were a significant area of concern – certainly not when you compare what was said about race relations with some of the devastating criticisms of other aspects of life at Feltham. Nor was there anything in the report of the team from the Prison Service's Standards Audit Unit following its visit to Feltham in 1999 which raised concerns about race relations.* The team found race relations at Feltham to be acceptable, though it concentrated more on whether the appropriate systems were in place rather than whether they were delivering what they were supposed to. Although the team commented on two areas of non-compliance with PSO 2800 – namely the reporting of racist incidents and staff training – it noted that implementation of PSO 2800 was well under way. The failure of the teams from the Inspectorate and the Standards Audit Unit to detect any signs of racial discord – which was a disservice to BME staff and inmates alike – suggests the possibility that, using the definition of institutional racism adopted by the Stephen Lawrence Inquiry, they were themselves guilty of institutional racism.

51.40 Feltham's Board of Visitors was not much different. The minutes of its meetings in the couple of years up to Zahid's murder show that when race relations were discussed, there was no real expression of concern about complaints of a racist nature not being investigated, or a disproportionate number of BME prisoners being treated in a

---

* The Inquiry was not provided with the report of the Standards Audit Unit on Feltham following its visit to Feltham in 1997.

particular way. And its annual reports referred to race relations in terms which tended to suggest that this was not a major area of concern. That perhaps reflected what the Board saw as the priority for Feltham, which was to improve the regime and get inmates out of their cells for much longer. However, Mrs Bogue said – and there is no reason to doubt it – that concerns about race relations began to emerge in the months leading up to Zahid's death. They related to the way in which complaints of a racist nature were being investigated, culminating in two incidents in the early part of 2000. She began to think that the Board had been too accepting of explanations which had been given to it in the past, and Zahid's death gave the Board the courage to challenge racial issues more robustly than it had done previously.

51.41 The lesson to be learned from all this is that racial discrimination can be missed if you are not specifically looking out for it. That is a consequence of race relations affecting all aspects of prison life. If you spend time in the Security Department, for example, looking at its systems and seeing whether they are working, you should be able to assess whether the systems are flawed, or whether they are delivering what you want, and whether staff have the necessary skills and enthusiasm for the job. But paradoxically something as all-embracing as race relations, which is not confined to a particular function within a prison, can easily be lost sight of if you look at the various individual sections of the prison – whether it be reception, or the healthcare centre, or the Security Department, or the residential units, or whatever – where the daily life of the prison goes on. It needed the recognition by the Stephen Lawrence Inquiry of the concept of institutional racism to bring home the need for the independent watchdogs to be on the specific lookout for racial discrimination.

51.42 Having said that, I do not believe that the Board of Visitors can be excused entirely for what Mrs Bogue accepted was an attitude which in the past had been too unquestioning. I acknowledge that if the professional watchdogs from outside the Prison Service (the Inspectorate) and within the Prison Service (the Standards Audit Unit) had not detected any particular problems in the field of race relations at Feltham, it may be expecting a little too much to get a greater insight into them from volunteers, who give up their time to ensure that prisoners are cared for decently and humanely, and whose training in the old days gave what Mrs Bogue described as only a limited awareness of race relations issues. It is to the Board's credit that it had begun to recognise the worrying signs. But problems with race relations had never come within the Board's field of vision, even though one of its members represented the Board at meetings of the race relations management team, and members of the Board spent time on the units whenever they visited

Feltham. Although they were dependent to a great extent on what they were told, one might have expected them to question whether they were acquiescing a little too readily to such explanations as they were being given for what might otherwise have been regarded as a concerning incident.

51.43 The consequence of all this was that concerns about race relations were not brought to the attention of those at Prison Service headquarters who were responsible for Feltham. Adrian Smith, the head of the task force, said that since race relations had not been flagged up as an issue in the Inspectorate or the Board of Visitors' reports, the issue had not appeared on his radar. Mr Atherton said much the same thing. He met representatives of the Hounslow Racial Equality Council, and had quarterly meetings with the chairs of the Boards of Visitors in his area. They had not said that this was a particularly problematic area for Feltham. He acknowledged that the absence of any concerns about race relations in an establishment where half the prisoners were BME prisoners and the staff were almost wholly white should itself perhaps have alerted him to question the state of race relations at Feltham. But he had enough on his plate looking at the problems which had been brought to his attention without looking for others.

51.44 Nevertheless, there was at least one occasion when worrying information about race relations at Feltham came into Prison Service headquarters and nothing was done about it. That information was contained in the annual checklist which had to be completed by the Race Relations Liaison Officer in consultation with the race relations management team and then sent to Prison Service headquarters. The checklist for the year ending 31 July 1999 contained a number of worrying entries – for example, that the Race Relations Liaison Officer thought that he did not have sufficient time to carry out his duties, and that a new or revised race relations action plan had not been produced in the last 12 months.* But most concerning of all was the statistic that only six racist incidents had been recorded in the race relations incident log that year, and that all of them had been resolved informally. Mr Atherton accepted that this should have set alarm bells ringing. Yet neither his own staff in the area office, nor the race relations team in the Prisoner Administration Group in the Directorate of Resettlement at Prison Service headquarters, ever drew his attention to any concerns about Feltham or any other establishment for which he was responsible on the basis of information contained in the annual checklist – or in the less comprehensive quarterly returns either for that matter. Indeed,

---

* The checklist for the previous year revealed that no such action plan had been produced in that year either.

Mr Atherton was not convinced that the information in the checklists had been looked at in any detail, and it may be that the only real role that the checklists played was as a source for the statistics to be included in the Prison Service's annual race relations report.

51.45 Although Mr Narey undoubtedly attached great weight to good race relations, and regarded it as an integral part of his decency agenda, he was prepared to acknowledge that race relations work had become marginalised at Prison Service headquarters. One of the reasons for that may have been the emphasis on security issues which had dominated much of the Prison Service's thinking in the mid-1990s. Another may have been that the Prisoner Administration Group had been a very small team, compared with the number of people who were eventually to work on the RESPOND initiative in the Directorate of Personnel under Ms Clements. Yet another may have been a sense of complacency after the issue of the Prison Service Order on race relations, and the creation of race relations liaison officers and race relations management teams. It was only when it was realised that these measures were not making sufficient headway in terms of changing the attitudes of staff that the Advisory Group on Race was established to revive the impetus which seemed to be flagging.

51.46 Ms Clements acknowledged that when she arrived her initial focus had been on the problems faced by BME staff. At that time their problems were seen as more pressing than those faced by BME prisoners in the light of a report by MaST International Organisation plc, commissioned in 1998, which contained disturbing findings about the blatant discrimination on the part of some white staff which many BME staff had to contend with. The MaST report – which was based on the findings of focus groups with BME staff and BME and non-BME managers – showed that many black and Asian staff were the victims of unashamed racist prejudice from some white colleagues, which left them feeling "isolated", "vulnerable", "unappreciated" and "undervalued". Inappropriate language and humour appeared to be "commonplace", harassment and discrimination were perceived to be "widespread", and membership of the National Front was thought to be "common".* Indeed, the level of individual racism faced by BME staff was so extreme that some of them claimed to have been the victims of racist violence. One revealed that he had had his tyres "punctured and slashed" within days of moving to a new prison. And it was not just the effect of all this on BME staff not being recognised – although that was

---

* The Prison Service was subsequently to take the commendable step of declaring that membership of the National Front and other extreme right wing groups was incompatible with working in the Prison Service.

one of the report's findings. The report found that managers were not challenging inappropriate behaviour when they encountered it. Some of them tolerated it, or even engaged in it themselves.

51.47 These findings about what BME staff thought were indeed worrying, but to concentrate on the problems of BME staff was itself a blinkered view because it had not occurred to anyone to find out what BME *prisoners* thought. No-one seems to have realised that if BME staff were on the receiving end of ignorance and bigotry from their white colleagues, it was even more likely that BME prisoners were. That was a powerful example of the tunnel vision about race relations within the Prison Service at the time. And it was not helped, following Ms Clements's arrival, by the organisational separation of staff issues, which were addressed by her team in the Directorate of Personnel, from prisoners' issues, which were addressed by the Prisoner Administration Group in the Directorate of Resettlement.

51.48 Ms Clements cannot be blamed for the poor state of race relations at Feltham at the time of Zahid's murder. She had only been in post for six months by then. During that time, she had been involved in investigations at two particular establishments, and there had not been enough time for her to have identified Feltham as requiring particular attention in terms of race relations. But the key point is that good race relations can always be expected to be a major casualty in failing establishments. Feltham was not alone in this respect. Although the evidence was impressionistic, it was not untypical of establishments with its sort of ethnic mix. That is what Ms Clements thought, and there is no reason to question the correctness of that view. And Mr Narey did not think that the establishment would have stood out in terms of a readiness to underestimate the extent of problematic race relations. But that only made matters worse. It cannot be said that Feltham was a wart on an otherwise healthy body. There were other establishments in the same boat, and they would have been under the spotlight as well had a similar tragedy occurred there.

Chapter 52: Monitoring Feltham's performance

Feltham's self-auditing procedures

52.1 The Prison Service issued standards relating to all aspects of prison life which establishments were expected to adhere to. Prisons had to monitor the extent to which these standards were being complied with. Graham Davies – who was the night orderly officer on the night Zahid was attacked – was appointed by Mr Clifford to be Feltham's first audit manager, responsible for ensuring that these standards were being properly monitored.

52.2 The system to be used was laid down by Prison Service headquarters. At least that was what Mr Davies said, and no-one contradicted him. The way it worked was that the head of the department for the function covered by the standard in question would arrange for a member of his or her staff to complete the relevant self-auditing documentation. That involved identifying the extent to which the requirements in the standard, known as the key audit baselines, were being adhered to. If the documentation showed that the key audit baselines were being met, Mr Davies would bring that to Mr Clifford's attention, and no further action would be taken. But if any of the key audit baselines were not being met, an action plan would be drawn up to address the deficiencies. The head of the department would then produce a document identifying what work would have to be done for the baselines to be met, who should do it and by when. A new audit of the baselines would be commissioned 28 days after the work should have been completed. That would be carried out by a member of staff who did not work in the department in question. The purpose of the new audit was to find out if the deficiencies identified in the department's own audit had been addressed. If they had, Mr Clifford would be informed of that. But if they had not, Mr Davies would arrange a meeting between Mr Clifford, the head of the department in question and himself to discuss why the baselines were still not being met.

52.3 This system was not conducive to the speedy confirmation that urgent deficiencies discovered during the first audit had been remedied. Take an urgent problem which had to be remedied within seven days. Suppose that problem was included in an action plan which also included a problem which had to be remedied in three months. You would not know for many months whether the urgent problem had been remedied. You would have to wait for three months for the other problem to be remedied, for the 28 days before the new audit would be done, and for whatever time it took for the new audit to be completed. Mr Davies said that he and Mr Clifford were aware of the problem, but the system which was operated was the one laid down by Prison Service headquarters.

He acknowledged that the system was labour intensive, and that it did not allow for problems to be resolved quickly.

52.4 Bearing in mind that establishments are supposed to be subjected regularly to external monitoring by the Prison Service's Standards Audit Unit, do these internal audits have any value? It has been suggested that they do not – at any rate not in an establishment which is not performing well where the problems should be readily apparent and where those which are unlikely to be immediately obvious should be picked up by external monitoring. I do not share that view. It may be that there is a duplication of effort here, but external monitoring takes place at irregular intervals, and it would not be sensible to rely on external monitoring alone to highlight deficiencies. In-house monitoring has the advantage of being able to pick up those deficiencies which have crept into the establishment since the previous visit of an audit team from the Standards Audit Unit, and which may not otherwise be spotted until the audit team's next visit. But if in-house monitoring is to retain its value, its procedures will have to be revised to ensure that checking that urgent deficiencies have been put right can be done quickly.

The action plans for Feltham

52.5 The conventional way of remedying deficiencies in an establishment's procedures which have been identified by the Standards Audit Unit or the Inspectorate has been to draw up an action plan for their solution. Feltham had many such plans: an action plan as a result of the report following the Inspectorate's inspection of Feltham in 1996, an action plan following the Standards Audit Unit's visit to Feltham in late 1997, and an action plan drawn up by the task force. It would have had an action plan as a result of the report following the Inspectorate's visit to Feltham in 1998 but for the fact that one from the task force was anticipated.

52.6 The disadvantages of a multiplicity of action plans are obvious. You lose sight of the things you have to do if they are duplicated in many places. And to the extent that they contain overlapping recommendations, it may be difficult to know exactly what you are being asked to do. Lord Woolf in his report on the prison disturbances in 1990 spoke of the "confetti of instructions descending from headquarters", and a similar comment could be made about the proliferation of action plans. So Mrs Clayton-Hoar was given the task of producing a document consolidating the outstanding points listed in the previous action plans.

The result was Feltham's Strategic Development Plan. It stated that it was updated on 20 October 1999, which probably meant that this was the final version, taking into account other plans which had not been incorporated into earlier drafts. But within a few months, Feltham had got two more action plans: the action plan following the Standards Audit Unit's visit to Feltham in November and December 1999, and an action plan comprising the recommendations made in the report following the Inspectorate's inspection of Feltham in September 1999.

52.7 But the real problem was not so much the fact that Feltham had too many action plans, but that an action plan itself – especially the detailed action plans the Prison Service has grown to expect – can result in an establishment's management team not looking at the bigger picture. They can become so concerned about addressing each of the many action points that they lose sight of the wider strategic approach which may be necessary to resolve the establishment's underlying problems. There is undoubtedly a place for action plans. They provide an extremely useful checklist of the problems which need to be addressed. And in a failing establishment like Feltham, that can be particularly important. But the danger is that compliance with the action plan may wrongly be regarded by management as the solution to a prison's problems.

52.8 That is graphically illustrated by Feltham's Strategic Development Plan. Everyone agrees that the regime for prisoners at the time was inadequate. Yet the plan did not deal with the regime, or indeed with the amount of association which prisoners should have. That may have been because none of the earlier action plans had expressly made recommendations for the improvement of the regime, even if the reports on which those plans had been based had been critical of it. It may have been because it was thought that the problem with the regime would be resolved if the individual points in the action plans were addressed. As it was, the regime only improved much later, after Feltham had benefited from increased funding, the number of prisoners had been reduced, and it had its full complement of staff.

Oversight from Prison Service headquarters

52.9 The final question here is whether the top brass in Prison Service headquarters gave Feltham the attention it needed. Mr Narey became Director General in March 1999, though since his appointment had been announced in the previous December, he had been preparing to take over for some time. Mr Wheatley became Deputy Director General in May 1999. Feltham's problems would have crossed Mr Narey's desk almost immediately since as Director General he was the *ex officio* chairman of the steering group. But the suggestion was made that with the disbanding of the task force Feltham stopped getting the centralised attention it deserved. In effect, it was left to a new and forceful Governor, with a proven track record, to put the recommendations which the task force had made into place. Mr Clifford thought that might be "a fair assessment". The result was that it was only after Feltham's *annus horribilis* that the Prison Service took the decisive action the situation demanded. Although Zahid's murder had been the most shocking event in 2000, there was also a riot in Quail that year, as well as the loss of two Governors – Mr Clifford and his successor through illness – in quick succession.

52.10 There are, I think, some points which might be regarded as superficial support for the suggestion that Mr Narey and Mr Wheatley took their eyes off Feltham. Mr Wheatley visited Feltham only once between their appointment and Zahid's murder, and Mr Narey did not visit it at all. Feltham was said not to have been discussed at meetings of the Prison Service Management Board during the period. Not just the task force but the steering group as well had been disbanded. And it was said that Mr Narey was underestimating the problems at Feltham in such a way as to suggest that he did not think that things were as bad as had been made out. The occasions when he was said to have done that were in his criticism of the preface to the Inspectorate's report following its visit to Feltham in 1998, and in his meetings with the Minister then responsible for prisons, Lord Williams of Mostyn.

52.11 I do not think that this criticism of Mr Narey and Mr Wheatley is justified. Mr Narey could legitimately take the view that visits by the Director General are not so much to inform the Director General about how an establishment is performing. After all, he can get that information from speaking to the Governor – and Mr Narey spoke at length to Mr Clifford shortly after his appointment – and from reports to him by the Area Manager. They are more to let the staff know that the establishment is being given high priority at Prison Service headquarters. But in Feltham's case the staff did not need visits from the Director General to tell them that. They had had members of the task force crawling all over the establishment for a good few weeks. Mr Wheatley had a slightly more "hands on" role. The time he visited Feltham within the period in question was just five weeks after he had become Deputy Director General. He did so because he was concerned about the establishment. He did not return until after Zahid's murder, not because he underestimated its problems, but because he believed that it was being effectively run by Mr Clifford. In any event, he was regularly briefed about Feltham by Mr

Atherton, who he met every month, and who he spoke to less formally when the need arose. For his part, Mr Atherton was regularly in touch with Mr Clifford, visiting Feltham on a number of occasions.

52.12 As for the winding down of the steering group, its function had been to decide whether the recommendations of the task force should be adopted in the light of whether those recommendations needed input from Prison Service headquarters for their implementation. Once those decisions had been made – and once it had been decided that the implementation of the recommendations at local level was to be carried out by the senior management team at Feltham – there was little left for the steering group to do. The oversight of Feltham from Prison Service headquarters would then be the same as for other establishments – from Mr Narey, through Mr Wheatley and Mr Atherton, all the way down to Mr Clifford, who would report key developments back up the chain.

52.13 In order to judge the significance of Feltham not having been discussed at the meetings of the Prison Service Management Board, I was provided on a confidential basis with copies of the minutes of the board for the period from 12 July 1999 to 25 April 2000. The only meeting for which a copy of the minutes was not apparently provided was that of 18 October 1999. Feltham was mentioned only twice. A few other establishments were mentioned more often, but establishments tended to be discussed only in the context of specific incidents which had occurred there. The board was plainly not the forum at which the performance of establishments which required closer managerial attention was discussed as a matter of course. How such establishments were getting on was discussed at the meetings Mr Wheatley regularly had with the area managers with line responsibility for those establishments. So the absence of any detailed discussions about Feltham was not significant.

52.14 I turn to the suggestion that what Mr Narey himself said about Feltham shows that he underestimated its problems. One of the grounds for this suggestion was Mr Narey's belief that the prefaces to the Inspectorate's reports on Feltham did not accurately reflect the body of the reports. That led him to compliment Feltham's Board of Visitors on one occasion for writing a more balanced and accurate report. But since he was telling the Board of Visitors at the same time that its report had not conveyed the urgency with which things needed to be attended to at Feltham, the suggestion was made that Mr Narey was trying to drive a wedge between the Board of Visitors and the Inspectorate for presentational purposes, thereby enabling him to criticise the Inspectorate for painting too gloomy a picture about Feltham, and to criticise the Board of Visitors for not speaking out about Feltham enough. I do not believe that Mr Narey resorted to such Machiavellian tactics. His quarrel with the Inspectorate was only over the prefaces to the reports. He thought that they were over the top – sometimes too critical, but at other times "ludicrously over-optimistic". Maybe that was a consequence of the prefaces having been written by the Chief Inspector himself. But Mr Narey did not think that the body of the reports – which were presumably written by the team which actually visited Feltham – overstated the extent of the problems at Feltham or the urgency with which they had to be addressed, or understated them either.

52.15 The other ground for the suggestion that Mr Narey's own words show that he underestimated Feltham's problems related to what the Minister then responsible for prisons, Lord Williams of Mostyn, told the House of Lords about Feltham in a parliamentary debate in June 1999. He said:

> "If Sir David [Ramsbotham] returns [to Feltham] and finds in a sensible period of time – perhaps 12 months or so – that the overwhelming bulk of his recommendations have not been put into effect, people will have to reconsider their position with some care."

The implication is said to be that the Minister had been advised – presumably by Mr Narey – that 12 months would be a sufficient time to turn the establishment round. If that is what Mr Narey had thought then, so the argument goes, he seriously under-estimated Feltham's problems. Mr Narey's response to this criticism is that 12 months or so would be a realistic estimate of the time it would take to achieve some of his objectives – the successful separation of Feltham A and Feltham B, the transfer of the healthcare centre to a refurbished unit, to name but two. But he never suggested to the Minister that putting Feltham B on the road to recovery so that it was an establishment which the Prison Service would no longer be ashamed of was not going to take some time. Everyone knew that. It takes time to turn an oil tanker round. I have no reason not to take Mr Narey's words at their face value.

Chapter 53: An overview of Feltham's underlying problems

53.1 Many problems contributed to Feltham's fall from grace. But the two which combined more than anything else to bring it to its knees were the high number of prisoners it held and the relatively low number of staff available to look after them. It is no coincidence that the establishment started to improve when the number of prisoners it took was reduced, and the size of its workforce began to increase.

53.2 The combined effect of the twin problems of overcrowding and staff shortages permeated every aspect of life at Feltham. Staff shortages put extra pressure on the existing staff. That affected the quality of their work and their enthusiasm for the job. Standards slipped, morale declined, and absence levels through sickness increased. Cross-deployment became a fact of life, staff could not get time off for training, and flexible tasks, namely those which did not have to be done every day, were marginalised. And senior officers had less time to supervise staff. Overcrowding resulted in increased pressure on such facilities as Feltham offered, and the ever-changing level of its population affected the flow of information about individual prisoners. All of these factors helped to reduce the time prisoners had out of their cells to a minimum, and that made prisoners more likely to take out their frustrations on their cellmates.

53.3 There were other problems as well. Feltham B was fast becoming the poor relation of Feltham A, with the loss of some of its better staff and its comparatively poor ratio of staff to prisoners. There was a worrying absence of procedures in some areas. There was, for example, no procedure for allocating prisoners to cells, no induction to speak of, and no sentence planning. There was a lack of clarity in many of the existing procedures. Examples of that related to the identification of those prisoners whose correspondence had to be monitored, and the flow and use of information about prisoners. Racist abuse was rife, complaints of racism were not investigated properly, staff were insensitive to racial issues and some officers were out-and-out racists themselves. The separation of Feltham A and Feltham B was beyond the control of Feltham's management, but procedural and systemic shortcomings were obvious symptoms of Feltham's decline, which was itself the product of staff shortages and overcrowding.

53.4 Ultimately, those problems were themselves attributable to a lack of funds. If Feltham had been given more money, it would have been better able to cope with the large number of prisoners it had to look after – if only because more staff could have been recruited. This lack of funds was not the fault of the Prison Service. It had to be prudent with such funds as it received from central government, bearing in mind the many calls on its resources. The real problem for the Prison Service was that it was having to cope with a budget which had been set at a level which did not give sufficient recognition to the dramatic increase in the size of the overall prison population. There was a mismatch between sentencing policy and the resources given to the Prison Service. If more people were being sent to prison, more resources had to be made available to the Prison Service if the decency agenda was not to be compromised.

53.5 The bottom line is that you are only going to get the prisons you are prepared to pay for. Either you keep the prison population down by changing sentencing policy. Or you accept that the prison population will increase, and you inject sufficient funds into the system to ensure that prisoners are treated decently and humanely. The trouble is that neither of these options is a vote-winner. Electoral success rarely comes to those who say that fewer people should be locked up, just as it rarely comes to those who argue that more money should be spent on prisons and the prisoners detained in them. It is almost too obvious to say it, but if you ask where prisons come in the pecking order for funds compared with hospitals and schools, prisons will always come last.

Part 5

The Way Forward

Chapter 54: The scope of the recommendations

54.1 The focus of the Inquiry was inevitably on Feltham where the tragedy which the Inquiry was investigating occurred. But although Feltham had problems of its own, so too did many other young offender institutions. Shortly after Zahid's murder, Mr Narey visited the establishment and said that his "early view was that the terrible tragedy could just as easily have occurred in any other young offender institution". Mr Narey may have been saying that because he did not want the staff at Feltham to become too dispirited by the murder. But the problems associated with young offender institutions had been highlighted by the Inspectorate's thematic review of the young offender estate in 1997. It described a group of establishments with a population which was rising, armed with resources which were inadequate to provide a decent regime for the youngsters in their care. And if the Inspectorate's reports on other young offender institutions are anything to go by, the problems which Feltham faced were present elsewhere.

54.2 The six years or so which have elapsed since Zahid's murder have given the Prison Service a real opportunity to address the systemic shortcomings which the attack on him has exposed. Everyone recognises that much has been done. As the current Chief Inspector, Anne Owers, said in her comments on the statement provided to the Inquiry by the Prison Service:

> "There have undoubtedly been improvements in, and a heightened focus on, the management of risk, race relations, and the achievement of decent and safe environments within prisons: from a time when security was the overriding priority."

The consequence is that many of the recommendations an inquiry of this kind would have made if it had been looking a few months after Zahid's death at what had happened to him have now been overtaken by events. Much of what would have been recommended is now in place – or at any rate plans are well advanced for them to be in place. Examples include a new system for information flow, the new cell-sharing risk assessment and the introduction of other risk assessment tools. Many of the systemic shortcomings this report has laid bare have been eliminated.

54.3 That is not to say that there is still not work to be done. There is no room for complacency. Prisons are extremely complex institutions, and the dynamics involved in housing in secure, decent and safe conditions extremely large numbers of volatile men and women who do not want to be there, and may want to be as disruptive as possible, call for carefully planned systems to be in place. Despite the good work over the last few years, there will inevitably still be room for real improvement. In this part of the report, I identify what can still be done to make prisoners less vulnerable to in-cell attacks by their cellmates, though there will always be some cases which slip through the net. No system can ensure that such attacks will be eliminated altogether.

54.4 This leads on to an important point. It is all very well having proper systems in place, but the critical question is whether they are working properly. They can only be really effective if they are. Take whistleblowing, for example. The Prison Service has well-documented and well-drafted policies in place to encourage staff to report other members of staff who treat prisoners inappropriately. Procedures exist for ensuring that the anonymity of those reporting bad practice, wherever possible, will be preserved, and for reducing the risk of them being subjected to unacceptable reprisals. But whistleblowing on your colleagues can be very difficult. The procedures which are in place will be meaningless if officers are unable to rise above their loyalty – albeit misplaced – to their colleagues. This disconnection between aspiration and reality has been likened by the Chief Inspector to "the 'virtual prison' – the one that exists in the governor's office, at headquarters, in the minister's red boxes – as compared with the 'actual prison' being operated on the ground". As the Chief Inspector said, that is because "insufficient management attention has been paid to outcomes rather than processes". The Prison Service must at all times be vigilant to ensure that its policies and procedures are matched by good practice on the landings and the wings. That is the challenge which it faces.

Chapter 55: Cell-sharing

Enforced cell-sharing

55.1 The most obvious and dramatic way of reducing prisoner-on-prisoner in-cell attacks is by eliminating cell-sharing. Such a step would not be inconsistent with current thinking about how prisoners should be accommodated. As we have seen, it has been regarded as desirable for many years that, if possible, prisoners should be accommodated in cells on their own. The reasons for that are obvious, although I do not recall having seen them spelt out anywhere. In short, there are countless things prisoners are comfortable about doing in private, but less comfortable about doing if someone else is there. There are some very intimate things, such as masturbating or using the lavatory, which many people would be extremely unhappy about doing in the presence of others, and equally unhappy about others doing in their presence. And apart from the lack of privacy, sharing a cell with someone has its own particular problems. You may not like your cellmate. They may have habits which in the normal course of things you would be able to put up with, but which you become much more aware of in the confines of a prison cell. They may get on your nerves. They may have the sort of habits, such as smoking, which you should not have to put up with. And sharing a confined space with someone will have its own tensions – for example, disagreements about what television channel to watch, what sort of music to listen to, and about the use being made of the other's possessions. These tensions may have contributed to Stewart's attack on Zahid. In the end, we all need our personal space. That goes particularly for prisoners who have to conform to a host of rules regulating their behaviour when they are out of their cells. It is not surprising that the Inquiry's focus groups revealed that inmates overwhelmingly expressed a strong preference to be in cells on their own.

55.2 For these reasons, the objective of the Prison Service to bring *enforced* cell-sharing to an end, save for those prisoners at risk of suicide or self-harm, is entirely understandable. Enforced cell-sharing is a serious impediment to the proper implementation of the decency agenda, and the principle which lies behind it – that offenders go to prison *as* punishment, and not *for* punishment. This objective cannot be achieved at present because the Prison Service has to give way to the practical expediency of accommodating all the offenders who are sent to prison by the courts. It has to make do with the cellular accommodation it currently has, and the architecture of many prisons, with only a limited number of single cells available, makes the elimination of enforced cell-sharing unattainable at present. And although there is a continuing programme for building more prisons, other calls on the resources available to the Prison Service are being given a higher priority than the elimination of enforced cell-sharing.

55.3 But the goal of eliminating enforced cell-sharing should remain the objective of the Prison Service, and its achievement should be regarded as a high priority. More than 15 years have elapsed since Lord Woolf added his voice to the call for single cells in the European Prison Rules, and there are still many prisons – for the most part local prisons – where few single cells exist. It is impossible for the Inquiry to make an informed judgement about the date by when this objective could be achieved. That would require a far-reaching review of the cost of converting existing cells, the current and planned rebuilding programme, and the resources available to the Prison Service. I know that the cost of realising this goal would be enormous. But the Prison Service should review whether the resources currently available to it might be better deployed towards achieving this goal, without compromising standards in other areas, and should set a date for realising this objective. And if the resources currently available to the Prison Service are simply insufficient to make any significant contribution towards the realisation of this objective, central government should allocate further funds to the Prison Service to enable more prisoners to be accommodated in cells on their own.

Recommendation 1

The elimination of enforced cell-sharing should remain the objective of the Prison Service, and the achievement of this goal should be regarded as a high priority.

Recommendation 2

The Prison Service should review whether the resources currently available to it might be better deployed towards achieving this goal, without compromising standards in other areas, and should set a date for realising this objective.

Recommendation 3

If the resources currently available to the Prison Service are insufficient to produce a significant decrease in enforced cell-sharing, central government should allocate further funds to the Prison Service to enable more prisoners to be accommodated in cells on their own.

Prisoners at risk of self-harm

55.4 While it remains not possible for all prisoners to be accommodated in single cells, hard choices have to be made about which inmates should not be allocated the valuable resource of a single cell. No prisoner should be allowed to be in a single cell if it is believed to be important that they do not remain on their own. The example which is always given is that of the inmate who appears to be at risk of suicide or self-harm. It was beyond the Inquiry's terms of reference to consider whether there is room for improvement in the identification and management of such prisoners, although the high number of inmates who continue to commit suicide every year remains a source of real concern. The relevance of such prisoners to the Inquiry's work lies in the fact that any instances of cell-sharing increase the risk of prisoner-on-prisoner in-cell attacks.

55.5 The current policy is set out in PSO 2700, the Prison Service Order on Suicide and Self-Harm Prevention:

> "At-risk prisoners should be routinely allocated to shared accommodation, unless the prisoner represents a risk to others, their behaviour is too disturbing to other prisoners or shared accommodation is not available."

The rationale for the policy is not spelt out, but the conventional wisdom is that such prisoners should share a cell with a "buddy" to whom they can talk when they feel depressed. They should not be left on their own, because that might increase their tendency to dwell on things. The more they do that without having the outlet of someone to confide in, the more likely they are to harm themselves.

55.6 There is a respectable argument for doubting the correctness of this line of thinking. A "buddy" does not have counselling skills – unlike a listener, who is selected by Samaritans and is trained to provide peer support – and any advice they give may cause harm rather than contribute to the desired outcome. In any event, it is not a task which should be delegated to prisoners. Moreover, if the inmate at risk confides in his "buddy", the "buddy" is likely to acquire a good deal of information about the prisoner, and maybe others. In prison, knowledge is power, and can be used in many ways – not necessarily ones which advance the interests of the prisoner at risk. And if an inmate is at risk because of their inability to cope with harassment from staff or other prisoners, a "buddy" might, for reasons of their own, persuade the inmate at risk not to pursue any complaint about them.

55.7 For the most part, prisoners who participated in the Inquiry's focus groups were reluctant to take on the role of "buddy". It is difficult enough looking after yourself in prison without having to worry about someone else. If the inmate at risk is on suicide watch, you are going to be woken at night by the night patrol officer switching the lights in your cell on. And should something happen to the prisoner at risk, it may be difficult coping with the almost inevitable sense of guilt you will experience. You will keep on asking yourself: "Did I do wrong? Could I have done something more?"

55.8 These are powerful arguments, but I am sure that the better view is that it is preferable for prisoners at risk of self-harm to have someone on hand they can turn to in times of crisis, rather than to brood on things. Prison can be a very frightening place when staff have gone off duty, and wings are on patrol state. The abuse shouted from one cell to another can be extremely intimidating. All prisoners say that prison is about survival. In that kind of environment, the vulnerable need all the help they can get. Leaving aside inmates who are on suicide watch, the only support a prisoner at risk can get after lock up is from their cellmate. That does not mean that "buddies" need to be trained. What you are trying to harness is their willingness to help a prisoner in distress. They are something more than a babysitter, but something far less than a counsellor. They are there because support from someone perceived to be a friend can be very helpful and because they are prepared to give it. And on a more mundane level, if the prisoner at risk tries to harm themselves, the "buddy" is on hand to stop them and to raise the alarm.

55.9 There are, of course, some inmates who are at such risk of suicide that they have to be watched all the time or placed in special cells which have been rendered safer by, for example, the removal of all obvious ligature points. But for those prisoners for whom such extreme measures are not necessary, the advantages of sharing a cell with a prisoner who is prepared to act as a "buddy" have been sufficiently demonstrated. So even though the "buddy" system means that some prisoners continue to share cells, thereby making prisoner-on-prisoner in-cell attacks possible, it is still a system which should continue while single cells are so rare a resource in some prisons, and even when single cells become the norm across the prison estate. It is more questionable whether the "buddy" system should apply to young offender institutions. Many young offenders will lack the maturity to take on the role of "buddy". But in some cases the mere presence of a "buddy" might inhibit vulnerable inmates from harming themselves, and provided that the "buddy" is willing to assume the responsibility which the role involves, the practice should continue in young offender institutions. As for women's prisons, the Inspectorate has found that in some of them cell-sharing is not permitted at all. That is wrong: women who are at risk of suicide or self-harm should not be in a cell on their own, unless they need to be on suicide watch at all times.

> Recommendation 4
>
> The Prison Service should retain its practice of placing prisoners who are at risk of suicide or self-harm, but who are not so vulnerable as to require being on suicide watch at all times or accommodated in a safer cell, in a cell with another prisoner who they can talk to in times of crisis. The practice should be extended to women's prisons to the extent that it is not already happening.

Prisoners who prefer to share cells

55.10 In paragraph 49.26, I made the point that although the majority of prisoners would prefer to be in a cell on their own given the choice, a few – those who particularly enjoy the company of others – may be happier sharing a cell. Having a cellmate helps to pass the time. You have someone to talk to and play cards with. It would be foolish to squander the valuable resource of a single cell on someone who does not want it. At present, there is no formal system in place when a prisoner arrives in prison for asking them what their preference would be. Should inmates therefore not routinely be asked – on reception, or while they are in the first night centre, or during their induction – whether they would prefer to share a cell or be on their own?

55.11 The problem of a valuable resource being squandered is more apparent than real. If a prisoner wants to share a cell, it will invariably be because they have a particular cellmate in mind. However gregarious a prisoner might be, they would prefer to be on their own rather than with someone they do not get on with. So the chances of a prisoner ever saying – while they do not know which wing they are going to be on or who might be on it – that they would prefer to share a cell rather than be on their own is very remote. The reality is that if an inmate who is given a single cell wants to move to a double cell, it will invariably be because they want to have a particular cellmate. And if that is what they want, they will say so.

55.12 Moreover, there is a significant disadvantage in prisoners routinely being asked when they arrive at a prison whether they would prefer to be in a single cell. Since they will inevitably say that they would prefer to be in a single cell, it is a preference which the prison frequently cannot meet in view of the limited number of single cells available in some prisons. By asking the inmate what their preference is, you give them an expectation that their preference is capable of being met. And when it is not, the prisoner will think that the Prison Service is only paying lip service to the desirability of finding out what prisoners' preferences are, and they will think that this is just another of the Prison Service's unfulfilled promises. Of course, there is less likelihood of the inmate thinking that if they are asked whether they would prefer to share a cell, rather than if they are asked whether they would prefer to be in a cell on their own. And I can see how finding out what a prisoner's preference is can be done in such a way as not to create a false expectation on their part. But what is the point of asking inmates what their preference is if they will inevitably say that they would prefer to be on their own while they do not know who they might be sharing with, and if it is a preference which may not be capable of being met?

55.13 So the best way of proceeding is by doing nothing to find out what a prisoner's preference is before they get to their wing. Once there, they should be put in a single cell if they are a risk to other inmates, or in a double cell if they are at risk of suicide or self-harm. But if they are neither, they can be put in a single or double cell until such time as they find their feet. If they are put in a single cell, but would prefer to share, they will not be slow in coming forward and saying so.

> Recommendation 5
>
> The Prison Service should retain the present practice of not asking new prisoners at reception or in the first night centre or during induction whether they would prefer to be in a cell on their own or to share a cell with another prisoner.

Allocating prisoners to double cells

55.14 If prisoners are to be asked to share cells, it is desirable that they should share cells, if possible, with people who it is appropriate for them to share with and who they are compatible with. Is it appropriate for unconvicted prisoners to share cells with convicted prisoners? Is it desirable for prisoners with different religious backgrounds or different ethnic origins to share cells? And should you try to accommodate a prisoner's wish to share a cell with a particular cellmate?

Convicted and unconvicted prisoners

55.15 As we have seen, it is unlawful for an unconvicted prisoner to be "required" to share a cell with a convicted prisoner – in other words, to be allocated to such a cell without their express consent. Yet that happens on every wing on a daily basis in some local prisons. I saw it for myself when I visited Pentonville Prison and Wormwood Scrubs.

55.16 The original reason for separating convicted and unconvicted prisoners was a practical one. They were subject to very different regimes within a prison. Unconvicted prisoners could not be required to work. They could wear their own clothes. They could have food brought in, and even alcohol! It would not have been right for convicted prisoners to be on the same wing, let alone in the same cell, as prisoners who enjoyed those privileges. But since time on remand counts towards one's sentence, unconvicted prisoners would try to string it out so that they continued to have their privileges. Eventually, many of the privileges were phased out, although the regime remains different for unconvicted prisoners in some respects. For example, unconvicted prisoners need ready access to their lawyers in a way that convicted prisoners do not.

55.17 So the current justification for the rule requiring convicted and unconvicted prisoners to be separated is more to do with the need to protect the unconvicted from the convicted. As a matter of principle, the innocent should not have to mix with the guilty. It is not simply that they would run the risk of being converted to a life of crime. Their right to increased visits might result in them being pressurised to smuggle things into prison or to pass messages in and out of the establishment, and even those who are not especially naïve can be manipulated or groomed to do what the more experienced inmate wants. Of course, that does not always happen. It would not happen, for example, to a convicted prisoner in prison for the first time sharing a cell with an unconvicted prisoner with many previous convictions. And the problem would not necessarily be avoided by accommodating unconvicted prisoners separately: what about the unconvicted prisoner with many previous convictions sharing a cell with an unconvicted prisoner in prison for the first time?

55.18 That is why many of those with experience of working within prisons say that cell-sharing should not be based on the status of the inmate. They argue that there is nothing wrong with convicted and unconvicted prisoners sharing a cell, provided that you do not put a prisoner in with one who will be a bad influence on them. Indeed, allocating cells on the basis of status would prevent an experienced and trusted inmate from introducing the novice to the ways of prison life in a way which could be extremely valuable. And preventing unconvicted prisoners from sharing a cell with convicted ones would prevent prisoners who ought to share cells with each other from doing so. Examples include a convicted prisoner who is a Samaritan-trained listener sharing with a vulnerable but unconvicted prisoner, or a wise convicted prisoner sharing with his unworldly and unconvicted nephew. And apart from anything else, mixing convicted and unconvicted prisoners would give allocating officers much-needed flexibility in busy local prisons which are close to their operational capacity. They would like to have separate wings for convicted and unconvicted prisoners, but inevitably there will be times when a prison has more inmates than can fit neatly into a particular wing, and they will spill over onto another wing.

55.19 I have not been persuaded by these arguments. It might be necessary to have wings which contain convicted and unconvicted prisoners – simply because at times the overall population of a prison will not neatly correspond to the number of places available on wings for convicted prisoners and those available on wings for unconvicted prisoners. But that does not mean that they have to be put in the same cell. Even on a mixed wing, it is possible for unconvicted prisoners only to share cells with other unconvicted ones.

55.20 I acknowledge, of course, that there will be some cases in which the unconvicted prisoner would gain, perhaps significantly, from sharing a cell with a particular convicted prisoner – a family member, for example, or a trained listener. But those cases can be catered for under the rules as they currently stand – which permit an unconvicted prisoner to share a cell with a convicted prisoner if the unconvicted prisoner consents. Moreover, identifying those convicted prisoners who will not be a bad influence on the unconvicted prisoner is far easier said than done. They may well have their own agenda for wanting to share with someone who is new to prison life, and who has greater links with the outside world by virtue of being on remand. Prisoners can be very convincing, and many of them would not find it difficult to convince staff that it would be appropriate for them to share a cell with an unconvicted prisoner.

55.21 I have some concerns about how an unconvicted prisoner's consent to sharing a cell with a convicted prisoner is obtained. There is a danger that an unconvicted prisoner will agree to share a cell with a convicted one because they do not want to appear to staff to be awkward. They may not want to share a cell with a convicted prisoner, but they may be apprehensive about saying that for fear of being regarded as someone who rocks the boat. And an unconvicted prisoner may well be willing to share a cell with a convicted prisoner they know, but not with one they do not. For that reason, rules 7(2)(a) and 7(2)(b) of the Prison Rules should be interpreted as permitting convicted and unconvicted prisoners to share a cell only if the unconvicted prisoner has consented to share a cell *with a particular prisoner*, rather than with convicted prisoners in general.

55.22 A prisoner's status from unconvicted to convicted will change as a result of an appearance at court. A change of status from convicted to unconvicted could also result from an appearance at court – for example, the quashing of a conviction by the Court of Appeal, but with the prisoner remaining in custody awaiting a retrial. But it could also result – as happened with Stewart – otherwise than from an appearance at court. Some of the establishments visited by the Inquiry did not have a system for ensuring that effect was immediately given to a prisoner's change of status, by making certain that they do not share a cell with a prisoner of a different status. That is something which needs to be remedied.

Recommendation 6
Subject to recommendation 7, the rule that an unconvicted prisoner should not be required to share a cell with a convicted prisoner should always be complied with.

Recommendation 7
The sole exception to that rule – namely when the unconvicted prisoner consents to share a cell with a convicted prisoner – should be regarded as applying only when the unconvicted prisoner consents to share a cell with a particular convicted prisoner, not with convicted prisoners in general.

Recommendation 8
All establishments should have a system for ensuring that immediate effect is given to a prisoner's change of status, by making certain that they do not share a cell with a prisoner of a different status.

Prisoners from different backgrounds

55.23 Sharing a cell can be difficult at the best of times. It involves being with a cellmate at moments of great intimacy and privacy. It would almost certainly be easier for the overwhelming majority of prisoners to cope with the invasion of their personal space which cell-sharing necessarily involves if they share a cell with someone they feel more comfortable with. You are more conscious of your lack of privacy if you have to share your quarters with someone who is different from you. So when it comes to allocating prisoners to double cells, some attempt should be made to match prisoners with cellmates they will be more at ease with.

55.24 Many prisoners will be more comfortable sharing with those who come from a background they find it easy to identify with. Conspicuous examples of this are the many black prisoners who feel more comfortable about sharing their cells with other black prisoners. Other prisoners – for example some Muslim prisoners – undoubtedly prefer to be with inmates of the same faith. Such preferences should not be misunderstood as being an expression of racism on their part. When two people are living cheek by jowl – sometimes quite literally on top of each other, bearing in mind the number of bunk beds still in some prisons – it is only natural for them to feel better able to handle the lack of privacy if they are sharing with someone who they are likely to have much in common with. At least there will not be another hurdle to overcome in addition to the invasion of their personal space. A preference for sharing with people from a similar background is understandable.

55.25 But sharing with a prisoner of a similar ethnic background or religion will not necessarily be what every prisoner wants. Prisoners who speak little or no English will want to share with a prisoner they can talk to in their own language. Elderly prisoners will often not want to share with young prisoners, whose musical tastes and interests may be completely different from theirs. Prisoners from one part of the country may not want to share with prisoners from another part of the country. And if football is the new tribalism, supporters of one football team may not want to share with supporters of another. And prisoners' habits are important as well. Few prisoners would want to share with a prisoner who is dirty and smelly, or has no sense of personal hygiene. Few prisoners would want to share with someone whose habits or practices are "in your face" and interfere with daily life in the cell – the fitness fanatic who spends his time doing exercises or someone who is devout and prays much of the time. And there are some prisoners who do not wish to share a cell with prisoners who have committed particular types of crime.

55.26 If one leaves aside requests by prisoners to have a particular cellmate, I have virtually no sense of considerations of this kind playing any part in decisions about who prisoners are required to share their cell with. Although attention is sometimes paid to prisoners who are obviously incompatible, the impression I have is that prisoners are allocated to cells on the basis of convenience. If any differences between prisoners are currently taken into account at all, they are limited to a tendency to avoid putting, say, too many black prisoners on the same wing, because of the alleged security imperative of not giving any particular group of prisoners a power base. Apart from the cell-sharing risk assessment scheme – which identifies which prisoners should be on their own, and what classes of prisoners may be at risk from such a prisoner – there are no national guidelines about cell-sharing. There is nothing to help allocating officers decide, in the case of prisoners who have to share a cell, who they should share a cell with. That is a serious gap in the Prison Service's procedures. But I have no doubt whatever that the despondency and the sense of alienation which a lack of privacy creates can be ameliorated if values and racial identities are judiciously taken into account. Stewart may not have felt as disaffected as he was at Feltham if his cellmate had been another white racist from the Manchester area. Zahid may not have felt as isolated as he probably did if, instead of sharing a cell with someone he thought was racist and kept staring at him, he had shared a cell with someone he felt more at home with. A shared sense of identity would be likely to remove at least some of the tensions which inevitably arise when people live so close to each other. That is why, if the decency agenda is to have any impact on the lack of privacy which sharing a cell entails, prisoners' ethnic and religious backgrounds should be taken into account in deciding who should share a cell with whom.

55.27 But a blanket policy of putting black prisoners together, or Muslim prisoners together, would be just as bad. Their shared common background should be regarded as indicative of their suitability to share a cell with each other, but it is then necessary to consider whether there may be particular reasons why in their case they should not share with each other. Each prisoner should be considered separately, and asked about their own personal preferences. That should be done while they are in the first night centre, or at any rate during their induction, and the information should be passed to the wing where cell allocation decisions are made. The allocation should, where possible, be made by a senior officer, but if that cannot be done, it should be reviewed by a senior officer at an early opportunity. The suitability of the two prisoners to continue to share with each other should be reviewed at regular intervals, with the prisoners' personal officers being consulted over the issue.

> Recommendation 9
>
> The Prison Service should publish guidelines to assist officers in allocating cells to those prisoners who have to share a cell.

> ### Recommendation 10
> The guidelines should proceed on the assumption that the lack of privacy which cell-sharing entails is more likely to be ameliorated if prisoners with a common ethnic and religious background share cells. But that should only be the starting point for the process. All prisoners should be interviewed on their arrival, either in the first night centre or during their induction, to enable them to explain their preferences for the type of prisoner they would prefer to share a cell with.
>
> ### Recommendation 11
> All decisions about who a prisoner should share a cell with should be made, if possible, by a senior officer. If that cannot be done, the decision should be reviewed by a senior officer at an early opportunity. The suitability of the two prisoners to continue to share with each other should be reviewed at regular intervals, with the prisoners' personal officers being consulted over the issue.

Accommodating prisoners' requests

55.28 Prisoners frequently ask to share a cell with a particular prisoner. They may have been friends on the outside. More usually they will have become friends in prison. The anecdotal evidence suggests that often such requests are not met. They are either ignored or promises to look into them are not kept. Certainly that is what the prisoners who participated in the Inquiry's focus groups thought. Their impressions chimed with the evidence of the officers on Swallow when Stewart and Zahid were there. It will be recalled that at least some officers thought that the practical obstacles were such that invariably those requests had to be refused. You would be spending all day moving people if every request by a prisoner to share a cell with a friend was met.

55.29 There are no national guidelines about how such requests should be handled. It is obvious that not every request should be met. It is necessary to check whether it is appropriate for two particular prisoners to share a cell with each other. There may be many reasons why it might not be appropriate. One of them may have been putting pressure on the other to share, and the other may have gone along with that for fear of causing offence. Or one of them may have an ulterior motive. For example, if they are co-defendants, one may want to put pressure on the other to take a particular line at their trial. Prison officers have to use what they know about the prisoners to make sensible decisions about whether it is appropriate for them to share. They must speak to the prisoners concerned and find out what they have to say about it. They may have to read the prisoners' wing files, and perhaps their security files and adjudication records as well. That may take some time, especially as there are many other calls on an officer's time in a busy local prison.

55.30 But prisoners should not be left with the impression that their requests to share a cell with a particular prisoner are being ignored. If it is taking time to consider them, they should be told that. And if the decision is that they should not share a cell with a particular prisoner, they should be told why, unless security considerations or issues of confidentiality make that inappropriate. Nor should practical problems be treated as an insuperable obstacle preventing an otherwise sensible move of a prisoner from one cell to another – not even in a busy local prison. I acknowledge that such a move is not entirely straightforward. You have to ensure that the prisoner's property is properly bagged up, and taken to their new cell. If that has to be supervised by an officer, that is an additional call on their time. But the time that takes can be exaggerated, and the long-term advantage of a prisoner being more settled because they are sharing a cell with a friend is something which should not be overlooked.

55.31 There are inconsistencies in practice about whether a prisoner should put their request in writing. Some officers require that to be done. Others do not. The better view is that there should be something in writing to confirm that the request has been made. Otherwise, it might be overlooked if the officer to whom it was made forgets about it or goes on leave. And if there is something in writing – assuming that it does not get "lost" – there will be a record of the request having been made in the event of any dispute. But the request does not need to be treated as a formal application under the requests and complaints procedure. A simple form which the prisoner is required to sign confirming that they have asked to share a cell with the prisoner named on the form is all that is necessary.

Recommendation 12

The Prison Service should publish guidelines to assist officers in handling requests by prisoners to share a cell with a particular prisoner. Practical problems should not be treated as an insuperable hurdle preventing an otherwise suitable move of a prisoner from one cell to another.

> **Recommendation 13**
>
> The guidelines should require officers to keep prisoners informed of the progress of their requests, and if the request is refused, to notify prisoners of the reason for the refusal, unless security considerations or issues of confidentiality make that inappropriate.
>
> **Recommendation 14**
>
> The guidelines should contain guidance on how such requests should be recorded, but there is no need for such requests to be treated as formal applications under the requests and complaints procedures.

Allocating prisoners to the same wing

55.32 The focus of the Inquiry was on prisoners of different status sharing cells. But if convicted and unconvicted prisoners are only exceptionally permitted to share cells, what about the wings? Should convicted and unconvicted prisoners be allowed on the same wing? And what about young offenders and adult prisoners? Should they be allowed on the same wing? These issues arose during the Inquiry's visits to various establishments, and although tangential to the Inquiry's work, I discuss them briefly here.

Convicted and unconvicted prisoners

55.33 Mixed wings are only permissible if the Governor does not think that it is reasonably possible to keep convicted and unconvicted prisoners apart. That is the effect of rule 7(2)(a) of the Prison Rules which requires unconvicted prisoners to "be kept out of contact with convicted prisoners as far as the Governor considers it can reasonably be done, unless and to the extent that they have consented to… participate in any activity with convicted prisoners". So mixed wings are permissible if the number of convicted and unconvicted prisoners within an establishment at any particular time does not correspond with the number of places available for them on dedicated wings.

55.34 But mixed wings are far from ideal. Convicted and unconvicted prisoners have very different needs. They will make different demands on the establishment. They will have different expectations of their time in custody. And they will differ in their willingness to co-operate with staff and in their propensity for disruption. Many convicted prisoners will just want to get on with their sentence. They will want to get into a routine which suits them, and get the benefit of such purposeful activity as is available for them. The unconvicted population will be much more volatile. Their future is uncertain, they need time off the wing to meet their lawyers, and their turnover is high. Not only will the atmosphere on the wing be very different, but the regime which is appropriate for them should be as well. And they are in prison for very different reasons. The unconvicted are there to secure their attendance at court or to prevent them from undermining the integrity of their trial by what they might do on the outside. The convicted – once they have been sentenced – are there as punishment and for their rehabilitation. So mixed wings should be kept to a minimum, and should only be used when there is no operational alternative.

> ### Recommendation 15
> Wings holding convicted and unconvicted prisoners together should be kept to a minimum, and should only be used when there is no operational alternative.

Young offenders and adult prisoners

55.35 Whether young offenders and adult prisoners should be on the same wing was not something which had occurred to the Inquiry to consider. I had assumed that they were never on the same wing, and neither Mr Papps nor Mr Cummines, my two advisers on issues relating to prisons, were aware of it happening. But we discovered that it was happening at Altcourse, and we were subsequently told that it happens at a handful of other places as well. Young offenders and adult prisoners never share a cell, but they are occasionally housed on the same wing.

55.36 The legality of the practice is highly questionable. The law as it stands requires young offenders to be held in a designated young offender institution. But if you designate a part of a prison as a young offender institution, there is no reason why adult prisoners should not be held in another part of it. And, so the argument goes, if you designate a particular cell as a young offender institution, there is no reason why adult prisoners should not be held on the wing. That is the device currently being used to legitimise the practice. If the practice is to continue, the law should be clarified to put its legality beyond doubt.

55.37 But should the practice continue? Young offenders are generally regarded as being much more disruptive than adult prisoners. They are noisier, they are more boisterous, and they fight more often. The justification for allowing them to mix with adult prisoners is that the maturity of the adults is likely to have a calming influence on their volatility. Officers at Altcourse stressed how different their young offenders were once they had been moved from a dedicated wing to a mixed wing. The other side of the coin is that many of the adult prisoners – particularly the older ones – did not welcome the arrival on the wing of a group of unruly teenagers. They wanted a calmer, more settled environment. But the real objections to mixing young offenders with adult prisoners were that they tended to regard the successful adult criminals as role models, and could be encouraged to emulate them by taking up crime as a way of life. It also gave the less scrupulous adult prisoners the opportunity to manipulate them into running errands for them, and to groom them into becoming their followers.

55.38 The opportunity I had to speak to an adult prisoner and a young offender about their experiences of life on a mixed wing at Altcourse was nowhere near enough to enable me to form a view whether this innovative initiative should be tried at other establishments, or whether its disadvantages outweigh its advantages. More research needs to be done on its viability, but it is not an initiative which should be rejected out of hand. There may well be room for extending its use.

> ### Recommendation 16
> The Prison Service should review whether the advantages of holding young offenders on the same wing as adult prisoners outweigh the disadvantages, and whether the practice should be extended to other establishments.
>
> ### Recommendation 17
> If the practice of holding young offenders on the same wing as adult prisoners is to continue, the law should be clarified to put its legality beyond doubt.

Chapter 56: Reducing risks in cells

Cell furniture

56.1 Stewart used part of the furniture in his cell to club Zahid to death with. That raises the question of whether cells should have furniture which can be dismantled or broken up to create weapons. It also raises the question of whether the current arrangements for searching cells are sufficient to reveal weapons which prisoners keep in their cells.

56.2 The comparative frequency of suicides in prison resulted in the introduction some years ago of safer cells. These are single cells intended for prisoners at risk of suicide or self-harm. They have had all obvious ligature points removed, and the furniture in the cell cannot be broken up to fashion ligatures because the furniture has been built into the fabric of the cell. There are about 4,200 such cells across the prison estate, but their cost is high. Converting a normal cell into a safer cell costs about £31,000 – although the cost comes down if you convert many at the same time – but including some safer cells in the design for a new establishment costs about £8,000 for each cell. It would be prohibitively expensive for all cells to be safer cells.

56.3 Prisoners who are not at risk of suicide or self-harm still have to be protected from attack by their cellmates, and that involves the elimination from cells of objects which can be used as weapons. That is why the issue briefly discussed earlier in this report – whether cells should have free-standing wooden furniture or bolted-down metal furniture – is an important one. The prisoners who participated in the Inquiry's focus groups were much keener to have cells which gave their lives a measure of normality than cells which were relatively safe but sterile. Their views were shaped by their awareness that if a prisoner wants to attack their cellmate, they will find ways of doing that even if they cannot use the furniture in the cell. Not only can they surreptitiously bring objects which can be used as weapons into the cell – snooker balls wrapped in a sock are not uncommon – but also the resourcefulness of prisoners to create weapons out of seemingly unpromising materials knows no bounds.

56.4 Bolted-down furniture came to be used in prisons in order to prevent prisoners from using their furniture as barricades. That became less necessary with the advent of reversible cell doors which open outwards as well as inwards, thereby making barricading a cell a far less successful means of keeping staff out. And prisoners may respect furniture all the more if it is not bolted down because it gives them a greater sense of homeliness. But bolted-down furniture is still regarded by the Prison Service as preferable to free-standing furniture – even apart from its inability to be broken up and used as weapons. Although it means that prisoners cannot move the furniture around – for example, to see their television from a different angle – bolted-down furniture has a much longer life than furniture which is free-standing.

56.5 At present, the Prison Service is trialling a compromise solution, which retains the security feature of having the furniture bolted down, but which avoids the sense of the clinical which metal furniture inspires. These new cells are being fitted with fixed furniture made from inexpensive white wood. To put this furniture into a cell costs about £1,800 a cell. It will be interesting to see how prisoners react to this furniture, and it would be premature for me to make any recommendations which assume that a particular approach is preferable. But it goes without saying that what is appropriate for a high security prison will be very different from what is appropriate for a category C or an open prison.

> Recommendation 18
>
> As soon as practicable, the Prison Service should assess the popularity of the bolted-down furniture made from white wood which is currently being trialled. It should then formulate a policy about the most appropriate form of furniture for use in cells, balancing the need to keep prisoners safe from their cellmates against the need for prisoners to live in cells which have a measure of homeliness, and taking into account prisoners' preferences and cost.

Searching for weapons

56.6 Cell-searching differs from establishment to establishment. They each have their own written strategy, but even so fabric checks always take place every day, and full cell searches at regular intervals. In addition, searches for weapons or contraband occur when intelligence suggests their presence in a particular cell. Such targeted searches can occur at any time.

56.7 Hidden weapons are unlikely to be found during a fabric check. It is not a search of the cell at all. As we have seen, its function is to detect any evidence of an attempt to break out of the cell. It is the fabric of the cell – window frames and bars, and walls, floors and ceilings – which have to be checked. It is done by wing staff, and does not take more than a minute or two to complete. Full cell searches take much longer. They take place in the presence of the prisoner who is strip-searched. In some establishments, the searches are done by security staff; in others, by wing staff. Hidden weapons are likely to be found during such searches, but however thorough the search, some weapons may not be found – if only because of the ingenuity of prisoners in discovering new ways to hide them. Most of the establishments the Inquiry visited require all cells to be fully searched once every three months, although at Feltham at the time of our visit all cells had to be searched once every six months. The effect of the Feltham approach can be that a cell which is searched at the beginning of one six-month cycle and towards the end of the next may go for almost a year without being searched. This is too long a lapse of time.

56.8 I raised with the Prison Service whether it had got the balance right between the frequency of the fabric checks and the infrequency of the full cell searches. I was told that it thought it had. You need fabric checks every day, I was informed, to check that prisoners have not tried to cut through their bars or burrow out of their cells overnight. And a full cell search takes a considerable amount of time if it is to be done properly. At current manning levels it is not possible to allow more time in an officer's working day to permit full cell searches to take place more frequently. There was not, so I was told, a halfway house between the two types of searches: a search exclusively devoted to finding weapons, which would obviously take longer than a fabric check but not as long as a full cell search. You cannot effectively search for weapons without a search as thorough as the full cell search. Moreover, both a search for weapons and a full cell search would involve going through a prisoner's possessions. So intrusive a search can upset prisoners' equilibrium quite significantly, and should be avoided unless it is absolutely necessary. Mr Papps agreed that there was no halfway house between an effective search for weapons and a full cell search, but he thought there may be some scope for reducing the frequency of fabric checks and increasing the frequency of full cell searches in certain prisons. He also thought that there may be some room for cell-searching to be conducted on a more random basis.

56.9 There is an alternative view. The importance of security should not be minimised. But keeping prisoners safe from their cellmates is no less important than keeping the public safe from escaping prisoners. And escapes these days are pretty rare. By 23 September 2005 when the seminar which addressed issues such as cell-searching took place, there had been only five escapes during 2005, and only one was from a prison. The other four had been while prisoners were in the custody of escorting contractors. The Prison Service says that daily fabric checks are one reason for the low incidence of successful escapes. That may be so, but it is possible that less frequent fabric checks – on random days and at random times – would be sufficient.

56.10 I acknowledge that an effective search for weapons will take some time, and I do not have a sufficient sense of the operational practicalities to contradict the Prison Service's view that it would take as long as a full cell search. But I believe that a regular search for weapons is important. And since the majority of prisoners do not want to have weapons themselves and feel threatened by those who do, I imagine they would be less likely to object to such searches. It may be that all prisoners regard searches of their cells as an unwelcome intrusion. But I suspect that the equilibrium of only those prisoners who really have something to hide is likely to be significantly disturbed by them. Could such searches not be done by wing staff at irregular intervals, thereby using the time which would otherwise have been used for the fabric checks? They could be done in the presence of the prisoners whose cell is being searched, so that they can see that the search is being done with sufficient sensitivity for their personal possessions, and to avoid allegations that any weapon which is found was "planted" by the officers. If there were to be regular searches for weapons – in addition to the fabric checks and the full cell searches – prisoners may be less likely to keep weapons, knowing that they are likely to be found.

56.11 I should like the Prison Service to take a fresh look at its cell-searching policy. It should try to increase the chances of finding concealed weapons in cells by exploring further the balance to be struck between less frequent fabric checks and more frequent full cell searches. It should also consider whether a search for weapons would really take as long as a full cell search. These are topics which classically come within the Prison Service's own operational experience, but there may be room for some refinement of its procedures. Different prisons may well require different strategies. For example, some prisons have reinforced concrete outer walls and specially strengthened cell bars which take much longer to cut through and require very special blades to do so. The interval between fabric checks could be calibrated against the speed the most effective blade would take to get through such bars.

Recommendation 19
The Prison Service should consider whether dedicated searches of cells for concealed weapons would be tantamount to a full cell search.

> **Recommendation 20**
>
> In any event, the Prison Service should assess the resource and security implications of less frequent but random fabric checks against more frequent and more random full cell searches, bearing in mind that different strategies may be required for different establishments.

56.12 It is necessary to refer to the individual and systemic failings which occurred at Feltham. The fabric checks were not being carried out properly. In order to check the wall behind Stewart's table, staff would have had to look under it. In order to check the wall at the head of Stewart's bed, staff would have had to look at the pipes behind it. The likelihood is that they did neither of those things. The fact that fabric checks were not being carried out properly should have been picked up by the senior officer on the unit. When what was left of the crossbar was found in the toilet, the officer who found it should have realised that it could have come from the tables in the cell, and he should have checked them. As for the full cell searches, they were not taking place on the unit at all. The senior officer on the unit should have done something about that, as should the principal officer and the residential governor when it was brought to their notice at the daily operational meetings of senior staff. Finally, a system which required a signed return to be submitted once every three months meant that if full cell searches were not taking place that could go unnoticed by the Security Department for some time.

56.13 It has not been possible to tell how widespread shortcomings of this kind currently are. But senior officers should ensure that their staff know how to carry out fabric checks. In particular, they should ensure that officers realise that in order to check the walls of the cell, it will be necessary to look behind or under the furniture next to them. If that can only be done by moving the furniture, the furniture should be moved. If in the course of doing so they discover that the furniture is broken, they should check whether any parts of it can be used as a weapon. Senior officers should ensure that full cell searches are taking place as regularly as their establishment's cell-searching strategy lays down. Returns showing which cells have been fully searched, and when, should be submitted monthly. The department – normally the Security Department – which is supposed to scrutinise the returns should do so speedily, and notify the senior officer of the unit and its principal officer if that is not happening.

> ### Recommendation 21
> Senior officers should ensure that their staff know how to carry out fabric checks. They should ensure that officers realise that in order to check the walls of a cell, it will be necessary to look behind or under the furniture next to them. If that can only be done by moving the furniture, the furniture should be moved. If in the course of doing so they discover that the furniture is broken, they should check whether any parts of it could be used as a weapon.
>
> ### Recommendation 22
> An establishment's written cell-searching strategy should require each cell to be fully searched at least once in every three months. Senior officers should ensure that full cell searches are taking place as regularly as the strategy requires. Returns showing which cells have been fully searched, and when, should be submitted monthly. The department which is supposed to scrutinise the returns should do so speedily, and notify the senior officer of the unit and its principal officer if that is not happening.

Violence reduction

56.14 The Prison Service has had anti-bullying policies in place since the 1990s. More recently, it has sought to tackle violence by prisoners in all its various forms. It has developed an overarching strategy for violence reduction. All establishments are required to have their own local strategy for combating violence.* This is an important initiative, but it concentrates on making all parts of the establishment safer places to be, not just cells, and deals with bullies and other violent prisoners once they have been identified, rather than detecting their dangerousness in the first place. In any event, the initiative is still in its infancy, and it is too early to tell whether real change has been effected by it. The Inspectorate's view is that in some establishments the initiative appears at present to be little more than a change of name from the previous anti-bullying and safer custody strategies. The Prison Service will, no doubt, be monitoring its performance closely in the years to come,

---

* Dr Kimmett Edgar, the Head of Prison Research at the Prison Reform Trust and an acknowledged authority on violence in prisons, told one of the Inquiry's seminars that this strategy was "a tremendous step forward because it focuses on the ways in which interaction and the sociology of a prison can either contribute to or reduce the chances of violence".

and seeing whether it is effective in tackling the culture of weapons in prison.

56.15 Reductions in the scale of prison violence, and therefore in in-cell prisoner-on-prisoner attacks, can also be achieved by encouraging prisoners to feel that they have a personal stake in making their prison safe. Making prisoners think that they have let other prisoners down if they resort to violence is one way of achieving that. Another is by letting prisoners have a say in the running of their prison through prisoner forums. A number of establishments have prisoner councils, and their replication across the prison estate should be encouraged. Enver Solomon's and Kimmett Edgar's report, *Having Their Say: The Work of Prisoner Councils*, published by the Prison Reform Trust in 2004, is an in-depth study of prisoner councils. Their core proposal – that every prison should be required to have a functioning prisoner council made up of elected representatives which meets at regular intervals – is one which I endorse.

> ### Recommendation 23
> The violence reduction strategy should be used as a vehicle to encourage prisoners to feel that they have a stake in making their prison safe – in particular, by encouraging prisoners to think that they have let other prisoners down if they resort to violence, and by letting prisoners have a say in the running of their prison through prisoner councils. Every prison should be required to have a functioning prisoner council made up of elected representatives which meets at regular intervals.

Chapter 57: The flow and use of information

NOMIS

57.1 For the six weeks that Stewart remained in a cell with Zahid, none of the staff on Swallow – with the exception of Mr Morse who had read the warnings about Stewart in his temporary wing file – knew anything about Stewart's racism, his possible involvement in a murder at another young offender institution, or his disruptive behaviour during his previous spells in custody. Nor did they know about his severe personality disorder which had robbed him of any conscience or sense of guilt over his actions. So they treated him no differently from any other inmate who was serving a short sentence for run-of-the-mill offences. Despite his unusual reserve and his strange appearance, it did not occur to them that he posed a risk to his cellmate.

57.2 The flow of information about a prisoner to residential wings, and the use which is made there of that information, was therefore a topic which the Inquiry addressed in some detail. Very many flaws were detected in the flow and use of information about Stewart, both at Feltham and at the other establishments he had been in. That was partly due to the over-reliance on paper systems. But it was also because practice relating to the passing on of information and documents about prisoners was inconsistent and haphazard. And it was also because of the tendency of officers to trust their judgement about prisoners rather than reading up on them.

57.3 To combat the problems associated with the flow and use of information about prisoners, the Prison Service decided to replace its paper-based Inmate Personal Record System and its computerised systems, including the Local Inmate Database System, with a new integrated information system to be known as PRIME – the Prisoner Records and Integrated Management Environment. But when it was decided to consolidate the functions of the Prison Service and the Probation Service under the aegis of the National Offender Management Service (NOMS), it was also decided to create a national database for all offenders who came into the custody of the Prison Service or who had dealings with the Probation Service. PRIME was therefore replaced by NOMIS – the National Offender Management Information System.

57.4 NOMIS will be implemented in stages. The first phase will be implemented in some establishments by July 2006, with all establishments having access to the system by November 2007. The second phase will address how the system can be expanded in other ways. It is not a bespoke system which has been developed from scratch. It is a commercial "off the shelf" product which has been used in criminal justice systems overseas and is being substantially modified to suit the requirements of NOMS. The experience of prison officers has been taken into account in its development. The success of the system elsewhere increases its chances of success here. The POA – and other trade unions – have been consulted over its introduction, as their members will be some of the principal users of the system, and they have been very positive about it.

57.5 NOMIS has a number of key features which will eliminate many of the problems associated with current procedures. At present, even if a prisoner has been to prison before, they get a new prison number if they are back in prison – whether on a new charge if unconvicted, or for a new offence if convicted but not sentenced, or serving a new sentence. That is why such prisoners are called "new numbers". But under NOMIS anyone who comes into the custody of the Prison Service, or has dealings with the Probation Service, will be given a NOMS number, and they will retain that number for the rest of their lives. So when information is retrieved from NOMIS about a particular prisoner, it will be possible to retrieve details about them relating to previous offences and sentences.*

57.6 Secondly, information about a prisoner can both be entered at, and retrieved from, any terminal within the system, wherever it might be. The system is completely networked, so that information entered by the Prison Service can be retrieved by the Probation Service, and vice versa, and information entered at one establishment can be retrieved at another.

57.7 Thirdly, NOMIS is a "real-time" system, so as soon as information is entered on it, all authorised users have immediate access to it. The information need only be entered onto it once. It cannot be removed, although it can be updated and corrections added. Outdated information can be archived. And it does not need a dedicated team of operators to enter information onto it. Information can be entered by anyone who is authorised to have access to any of its functions. But officers will not have access to all the information held on NOMIS. They will only have access to the information they need.

---

* Currently, that information would be in files in the dead records store of the establishment in which the prisoner was last held or in the Prison Service Records Registry, and would only go to the new establishment if a request was made for them.

The applications of NOMIS

Information from the Probation Service

57.8 Because NOMIS serves both the Prison Service and the Probation Service, the problems associated with the flow of information between the two services should be eliminated. Information on a prisoner held by the Probation Service will be available to the Prison Service once a probation officer has entered it onto NOMIS. Moreover, the documents generated by the Probation Service for the use of the courts, such as bail information reports and pre-sentence reports, will often contain information of considerable use to those having eventually to manage the prisoner in custody. Those reports will be accessible by prison officers on NOMIS.

Information from the police

57.9 The Police National Computer contains the details of an offender's convictions. When someone is given a NOMS number, the information relating to that person's convictions will automatically be transferred to NOMIS. NOMIS will also hold details of any outstanding charges the prisoner faces. In that way, wing staff will have ready access to the offending history of the prisoners in their care. But merely knowing the offences someone has committed or the charges they are facing tells only half the story – and possibly a misleading one at that. If someone has a conviction for robbery, for example, it would be helpful to know if that was for an armed robbery with shotguns in a crowded bank or for threatening to snatch a woman's handbag when disturbed in the course of pickpocketing. Stewart's case was a paradigm example of that. If the facts of the offences for which he was awaiting trial had been known, they would have shown that at least one of the letters he wrote contained racist abuse, even though the harassment he was charged with was not alleged to have been racially aggravated. So accompanying the list of someone's convictions and outstanding charges should be a short statement of the facts of each offence or charge. It need not be more than a sentence or two, but it should be sufficient to identify what the offender did or is alleged to have done.

> **Recommendation 24**
>
> Information about a prisoner's convictions and outstanding charges held on NOMIS should include a short statement of the facts of each offence or charge.

Information generated in prison

57.10 This is the application of NOMIS which is by far the most relevant to the Inquiry's work. The information in the documents which the Inmate Personal Record System generates will in future be entered directly onto NOMIS. That will include information which would now be entered on a prisoner's core record, or in their wing file, or on a self-harm at risk form, or in their adjudication records, or on the information of special importance form. The officer who makes the entry, together with the time and date, will be identified. These entries will be free-text entries, which means that whoever enters them will be able to choose what they wish to say. In this way, wing staff will have ready access to all the available information about the behaviour in prison of the prisoners in their care.

Risk assessments

57.11 In chapter 59, I deal with the risk assessments the Prison Service has introduced since Zahid's murder. An assessment under the Offender Assessment and Management System (OASys) is carried out online at present, but a cell-sharing risk assessment is not carried out online. When NOMIS is fully operational, the cell-sharing risk assessment will be online as well, and anyone needing to see the risk assessments of a particular prisoner will be able to view them through NOMIS.

Flags, alerts and responses

57.12 One of the features of NOMIS is its ability to flag up prisoners who come within certain categories – for example, prisoners at risk of self-harm, prisoners who pose risks to staff and other inmates, and prisoners with racist views. Anyone calling up the details of someone with a NOMS number would be alerted to the prisoner's inclusion in such a category, and there will be an explanation of what the prisoner has done to justify such an alert. A particular application of this is the facility to identify those prisoners who need to be separated from each other. The prisoner's cell number and wing is entered onto NOMIS as soon as the allocation takes place. So the moment an entry is made that another prisoner is to be allocated to a wing where there is already a prisoner who that inmate needs to be kept apart from, an alert will appear with a warning that the proposed allocation should not take place. The system will not produce an alert when, say, a prisoner with racist views is allocated to a wing with black or Asian prisoners already on it. But since the inmate's racism will be flagged up, an informed decision can be made whether the allocation is appropriate.

57.13 There are other related applications of NOMIS. One is its ability to require an acknowledgement when a particular piece of information is entered onto it. The facility is intended to ensure that information which requires some positive action to be taken has been read. Careful thought will have to be given to the many situations in which an acknowledgement should be required. Another related application is its ability to flag up something which needs to be done on or by a particular date. For example, if a prisoner's change of status from being a convicted to an unconvicted prisoner on a particular date was flagged up, that would be a sufficient prompt for the prisoner to be moved to a location more appropriate to their new status. It was the absence of such a prompt that resulted in Stewart continuing to share a cell with Zahid after he had completed his sentence and was being held as a remand prisoner. The discharge sheet was not a sufficient trigger for that to happen. It has yet to be decided whether that particular prompt should be factored into NOMIS. It should be.

> Recommendation 25
>
> If a convicted prisoner is not due to be released when they complete their sentence because they were remanded in custody awaiting trial on other charges, NOMIS should flag up the date on which their change of status is due to occur.

The limitations of NOMIS

Juveniles

57.14 Information about a juvenile under the age of 18 who has dealings with the Probation Service or who comes into the custody of the Prison Service will be entered onto NOMIS. But information held on such a prisoner by social services departments and youth offending teams will not. That is because their systems are integrated with that of the Probation Service, but not with NOMIS. The information may well be useful to their management at the secure training centres they are held at while they are still juveniles, and at the establishments they go on to. The Prison Service is alive to this gap in the centralised information function which NOMIS is intended to perform, and is working on ways to plug it.

Medical and psychiatric information

57.15 Information currently held in a prisoner's medical record will not be entered onto NOMIS. That is as it should be in view of patient confidentiality. But that does not mean that information held within the medical record can never be disclosed to non-medical staff, and I return to this issue later when I deal with prisoners with mental disorders.

Security information

57.16 By far the most important limitation of NOMIS is that it will not include security information – at any rate not in its first phase. The reason is that security information can be extremely sensitive, and people who provide such information will be less likely to do so in the future if they know that the information is likely to be readily accessible. The continued flow of intelligence about prisoners and prison life is very important, and nothing should be done which might interrupt it.

57.17 But much of the information coming in via a security information report is not information about security issues at all. It is invariably about controlling prisoners or groups of prisoners. That information ought to be shared with wing staff, as it affects how the prisoners may be managed. There is no reason at all why Security Departments should not be able to distinguish between information of that kind, which can be entered onto NOMIS when the first phase of NOMIS becomes operational, and that small amount of information which really is about intelligence and which may be too sensitive for wider dissemination.

Recommendation 26

Although there are no plans for security information to be entered onto NOMIS in its first phase, Security Departments should enter any information which can be shared with the majority of staff when the first phase of NOMIS becomes operational.

57.18 There may be information which is too sensitive for wider dissemination but which could affect the way a particular prisoner is managed. It is important that such information is provided to the wings subject to appropriate safeguards about its use. I do not suppose that there would be any problem about NOMIS containing an alert that such information is being held on that prisoner. An officer at the grade of senior officer or above could ask for that information, and the request could be considered by the governor with line management responsibility for the Security Department. The governor would be able to refuse the request, or grant it on condition that the senior officer does not reveal the information to anyone, or on condition that the senior officer can tell their wing staff about it on the understanding that it is not to go any further.

> Recommendation 27
>
> NOMIS should include a facility for an alert to appear if information is held by the Security Department on prisoners which could affect their management but which is too sensitive for wider dissemination. An officer at the grade of senior officer or above should be able to ask for that information, and the request should be considered by the governor with line management responsibility for the Security Department. The governor should be able to refuse the request, or grant it on condition that the senior officer does not reveal the information to anyone, or on condition that the senior officer can tell their wing staff about it on the understanding that it is not to go any further.

Training in and use of NOMIS

57.19 The Prison Service says that NOMIS is extremely user-friendly. It will not be difficult for staff to get the hang of it. That is probably right if the simulated screen the Inquiry was shown is anything to go by. It is relatively easy to read and contains less jargon than the Local Inmate Database System. But it is important that staff do not feel swamped by so much information that they become disinclined to use it. If information overload is to be avoided, staff must be able to get the information they need quickly and to bypass the information they do not. It is also important that the technology is up to date. The participants in the Inquiry's focus groups for prison staff said that the technology currently being used across the prison estate is behind the times, with the making of entries onto the present systems more time-consuming than making paper entries, and the systems often crash. They also complained that there are too few terminals at present, and that they are often unavailable because of the time people use them for. All these issues will have to be addressed, although I know there is an ongoing debate within the Prison Service on topics like touch-screen as opposed to mouse technology, and wireless terminals to provide flexibility for their location.

57.20 The Prison Service acknowledges how important training on NOMIS is going to be – especially for the older generation of prison officers who may not be so adept at using information technology. If staff are not given time off to go on suitable training courses, the Prison Service will not get the benefits which the system is designed to procure. The Prison Service has sensibly decided to make the training available locally at each establishment. That should make it easier to free up the time staff will need to become acquainted with the system. It should also make it easier for staff to receive far more individualised training – which proceeds at their own pace – than is possible if training is centralised, with large numbers of officers being trained at the same time. This is not an area in which time for training should be curtailed. That would only prove to be a false economy in the long run.

57.21 But training on how to enter and retrieve information is not enough. Staff must understand how important it is that information entered onto the system is accurate, comprehensive and unambiguous. When looking at Stewart's files, we saw too many examples of information which was inaccurate, skimpy and unclear. And staff must also understand how important it is to log on regularly, and to read the information NOMIS holds on the prisoners in their care. It is all very well having a sophisticated system for the flow of information, but it becomes a white elephant if it is not being used. The irony is that the information on Stewart which would have told staff about his racism, his disruptive behaviour in prison and his possible involvement in a murder was in the files if only staff had seen them. Many officers are still inclined to think that there is no need to find out how a prisoner has behaved in prison in the past if their current behaviour does not give cause for concern. And some officers still think that the less they know about the background and offending history of prisoners on their wing, the better – on the basis that they can then manage all the prisoners in their charge more consistently. These are outmoded views, as the Prison Service itself acknowledges. The fact is that logging onto the system and retrieving information from it – in addition to entering relevant information onto it – will require a real change of culture on the part of many staff. They must be up to the challenge.

57.22 In an ideal world, it would be useful if NOMIS could be interrogated to find out when a particular officer had logged on, and what information had been looked at. In that way, checks could be made to see if officers were using NOMIS properly and frequently enough. The Inquiry was told that this would not be possible. It would require a large increase in the system's capacity to provide that facility, and the increased cost would not justify the relatively modest gain. The Inquiry did not pursue that suggestion further.

> ### Recommendation 28
> Information overload should be avoided by enabling officers to get to the information they need quickly and to bypass the information they do not need. The technology should be up to date, and sufficient terminals should be provided to ensure that staff have ready access to NOMIS at all times.
>
> ### Recommendation 29
> The training which staff receive on NOMIS should not merely address how to log on, enter information and retrieve it. It should reinforce the need for any information which is to be entered to be accurate, comprehensive and unambiguous. It should also reinforce the need for all staff to be aware of the background and offending history of the prisoners in their charge, as well as their previous behaviour in prison. Staff should learn that the system will be useless if they do not use it properly.

Data migration

57.23 "Data migration" is the technical term for the transfer of information from one system to another. The transfer of information currently held on prisoners onto NOMIS is a huge task, and it will not be possible for all the information to be transferred. The Prison Service is therefore looking at which information should be prioritised. It has decided that it will not be going back to information held on files in dead records stores or in the Prison Service Records Registry. It will be concentrating on files which are currently active. Plainly the priority is for information relating to current prisoners, and to prisoners returning to prison who have been to prison before. And among these prisoners, the priority is for information relating to those prisoners who are serving longer sentences – although what Stewart did means that prisoners serving a short sentence for run-of-the-mill offences can be a real risk as well. This is an issue the Prison Service is currently working on, and there is little of substance I can add.

Transitional arrangements

57.24 Until NOMIS is operational, the current procedures for the transfer of information to establishments, between establishments and within establishments will continue. In the rest of this chapter, I discuss the way in which those procedures can be improved, although I recognise that root and branch reform would be inappropriate. By the time any radical recommendations were implemented and had had time to bed down, they would have been superseded by the introduction of NOMIS.

Documents from the Probation Service

57.25 The documents generated by the Probation Service which contain useful information about prisoners are the bail information report and the pre-sentence report. They will have been considered by the court which sentenced the prisoner to a custodial sentence or remanded them in custody. They are supposed to accompany the prisoner from court to prison, and to be handed to prison staff at reception by the escort contractors along with such other documents as accompany the prisoner, including the warrant authorising the prisoner's detention. That does not happen very often. Sometimes the reports do not get to the officer guarding the prisoner in the dock. And when they do, the van may already have left court. There is pressure on escort contractors to get prisoners to prison quickly in order to avoid incurring financial penalties for late arrivals.

57.26 The reason reports do not get to the dock officer is because there is no formalised system in place for that to happen. Such a system should be devised. It is not rocket science. The probation officer should make sure that a copy of their report is available for the escort contractor, and there should be someone in court whose responsibility it is to ensure that the dock officer gets it. Escort contractors should have a list of the documents which should accompany prisoners when they leave court, but if a prisoner leaves court without all the documents, the court should ensure that they are sent on to the prison without delay.

> **Recommendation 30**
>
> To avoid prisoners leaving court without being accompanied by bail information reports or pre-sentence reports, the probation officer should ensure that a copy of the report is available for the escort contractor, and there should be someone in court whose responsibility it is to ensure that the dock officer gets it. Escort contractors should have a list of the documents which should accompany prisoners when they leave court, but if a prisoner leaves court without all the documents, the court should ensure that they are sent on to the prison without delay.

Documents from the courts

57.27 Apart from the bail information report and the pre-sentence report, the documents which the courts are supposed to provide the escort contractor with are copies of the warrant authorising the prisoner's detention, a list of the prisoner's convictions, and the indictment – or the charge sheet if the prisoner is being tried in a magistrates' court. Apart from the list of convictions, which is generated by the police, these documents will have been generated by the court. A copy of the warrant always goes to the prison. If it does not, the establishment will not accept the prisoner. But practice relating to copies of the indictment or the charge sheet and the list of convictions is haphazard. The arrangements for copies of these documents to accompany the prisoner to prison should be tightened to ensure that they always go with the prisoner. There should be someone in court whose responsibility it is to ensure that the dock officer gets copies of them.

57.28 There was a time when the prison received a note of the judge's sentencing remarks. The note would have been made by the dock officer. That does not happen nowadays, and if it did it would be better if the prison received a verbatim transcript of what the judge had said. But in the overwhelming majority of cases, I do not believe for one moment that what the judge says is likely to affect the management of the prisoner in custody at all. The only time it might is when the judge asks for their remarks to be brought to the attention of the Prison Service. When that happens, the court should assume responsibility for commissioning a transcript of what the judge said, and sending a copy to the prison.

57.29 Sometimes the court requests that a medical or psychiatric report be prepared on the prisoner. It may contain information which is useful to their subsequent management in prison. The Courts Service has sought legal advice on whether it is lawful to disclose such reports to prisons. The advice was that such disclosure was unlikely to be regarded as unlawful. Different considerations were said to apply to medical or psychiatric reports submitted to the court but on the instructions of both the prosecution and the defence. The advice which the Courts Service has received is that if the reports differ, the legality of the disclosure will depend on weighing conflicting interests. Prisoners have an interest in being properly looked after in prison. Other prisoners have an interest in being protected from them. And the public has an interest in order being maintained in prisons. The question is whether those interests outweigh any conflicting interest of the prisoner to have the reports kept back from the Prison Service. I do not understand why the outcome might be different if the reports do not differ, and in any event the Inquiry has not been told what advice, if any, has been received about a case when a report has been prepared on the instructions of the prosecution *or* the defence. The Courts Service must come to its own view about the legality of disclosing such reports, but plainly a policy decision is needed in the light of such further legal advice as it may receive.

Recommendation 31

There should be someone in court whose responsibility it is to ensure that the dock officer gets copies of the warrant authorising the prisoner's detention, the list of their convictions, and the indictment or charge sheet.

Recommendation 32

When a judge asks for any remarks which they make to be brought to the attention of the Prison Service, the court should assume responsibility for commissioning a transcript of what has been said and sending a copy to the prison.

Recommendation 33

In the light of such legal advice as the Courts Service receives, it should publish a policy on the disclosure to the prison of medical or psychiatric reports on a prisoner submitted to the court.

Documents from the police

57.30 The only document generated by the police which gets to prisons is the list of the prisoner's convictions, which goes to the prison via the court. This list is a print-out of information held on the Police National

Computer. For the reasons given in paragraph 57.9, the list should include a short statement of the facts of each offence and of the facts of the charges the prisoner is facing. Some prisons have direct access to the Police National Computer. But prisoners have been known to give false details about themselves when they arrive in prison, which may result in prisons getting a nil return when they access it. So it is better for prisons to use that access only as back-up rather than as a substitute for the list of convictions which is supposed to come from the court.

57.31 There is nevertheless a powerful argument for extending access to the Police National Computer to all establishments. There are two reasons for that. First, the Police National Computer may sometimes have useful intelligence about a prisoner which may affect their management in prison. Secondly, the police have been prepared in principle to let the Prison Service flag up on the Police National Computer those offenders who the Prison Service regards as a risk to themselves or to others. So if an establishment has access to the Police National Computer, an arriving prisoner who had been made the subject of such an alert could be identified as soon as an attempt is made to access the information held on them. There are security and training issues which will have to be resolved before the link to the Police National Computer can be established across the whole of the prison estate, but the need for it is undeniable.

57.32 In the meantime, any intelligence about a serving prisoner the police have which might affect their management in prison should be sent to the police liaison officer for the establishment at which the prisoner is being held. The police liaison officer can then decide, with the officer who provided the intelligence, how sensitive it is, and whether it can be widely disseminated within the prison, or whether it should be given to a governor for their eyes only, to enable them to give instructions for the management of the prisoner without disclosing either the existence or the nature of the intelligence.

Recommendation 34
The list of a prisoner's convictions sent to the prison should include a short statement of the facts of each offence and the charges the prisoner is facing.

> ### Recommendation 35
> The Police National Computer should be linked to the whole of the prison estate. In the meantime, any intelligence the police may have about prisoners which could affect their management in prison should be sent to the police liaison officers for the establishments at which the prisoners are being held. A decision can then be made whether the intelligence can be disseminated widely within the prison or given to a governor for their eyes only.

Transfers between establishments

57.33 Two simple lessons can be learned from the history of Stewart's time in custody. The first is that whenever a prisoner is transferred from one establishment to another, the receiving establishment should be told what the reason for the transfer is. The second is that if the prisoner to be transferred is a particularly problematic one, the receiving prison should be warned about the sort of prisoner it can expect. These things may be apparent from the documents accompanying the prisoner, but it is just as well to draw the receiving prison's attention to them specifically. In that way, there is no danger that the information will be missed. Both of these things should continue to be done after NOMIS becomes operational. The Inquiry saw no sign that either of these steps were being taken any more frequently than when Stewart was at Hindley and at Feltham.

57.34 When a prisoner is transferred to another establishment, it is critical that their files accompany them. That includes their wing files, their adjudication records, any self-harm at risk forms, any information of special importance forms, their medical record and their security file, as well as their core record and their main prison file. There are other important documents which should accompany them but which have not featured much so far in this report – their custodial documents file and their sentence planning file. So, too, should documents of the kind discussed in chapter 59 which have been introduced since Zahid's murder – the cell-sharing risk assessment form and the prisoner's OASys assessment. The strong impression the Inquiry got on its visits to various establishments was that the transfer of prisoners' files when they moved from one establishment to another was better than it was, although there was still room for improvement.

57.35 Responsibility for ensuring that transferring prisoners leave with their files lies with the staff on reception at the sending establishment. One way of making sure that they check whether all the files are accompanying the prisoner is by ticking them off against a checklist. If a particular file is not with the documentation being handed over to the escort contractor, the officer on reception should get in touch with the part of the prison where the missing file should be – whether the wing, the Security Department, the healthcare centre or the administrative section. Officers should not allow prisoners to leave unless all their files have been ticked as being present. In exceptional cases, prisoners may be allowed to leave without all their files, but that should only happen with the permission of a governor.

57.36 If prisoners arrive at the receiving establishment without all their files, it is the responsibility of the staff on reception at the receiving establishment to "notify the appropriate department" which should then chase them up. One way of making sure this is done is for a "missing file book" to be kept on reception. If a file was supposed to arrive with a prisoner but did not, an entry to that effect should be made in the book, identifying what file is missing, the action which has been taken to notify the appropriate department, the name of the officer making the entry and the date. The action taken to chase up the missing file should be noted in the book by whoever takes the action, and its eventual receipt should be recorded in the book as well.

> ### Recommendation 36
> Whenever a prisoner is transferred to another establishment, the receiving establishment should be told what the reason for the transfer is. If the transferring prisoner is a particularly problematic one, the receiving establishment should be warned beforehand.
>
> ### Recommendation 37
> To ensure that all files accompany prisoners on their transfer to another establishment, they should be ticked off at the reception of the sending establishment against a checklist. Prisoners should not be allowed to leave unless all their files have been ticked as present, except with the permission of a governor. Staff on reception at the receiving establishment should notify the department responsible for chasing up files which do not arrive with a prisoner, entering the action they have taken in a "missing file book". Consequential action and the eventual receipt of the files should also be entered in the book.

Information flow within establishments: documents held on the wing

57.37 Information flow within an establishment is all about getting information which might affect the management of prisoners to the wings on which they are held. Other than documents generated on the wing – such as those relating to the prisoner's level on the incentives and earned privileges scheme – the documents on a prisoner which the wing should always be provided with are their current wing file, a copy of the cell-sharing risk assessment form and a copy of the form notifying the wing if the prisoner has been charged with, or convicted of, an offence under the Protection from Harassment Act 1997. It is critical that these documents are always sent to the wing on which the prisoner is held.

57.38 The importance of the wing file cannot be exaggerated. That is where information about prisoners' current behaviour within the prison will primarily be found. The current wing file should have arrived with them if they had been transferred from another establishment. Alternatively, it should have been opened at reception on their arrival as a "new number", or opened on the wing or a previous wing if all the pages in the previous wing file had been used up or the previous wing file had been mislaid. There are still no guidelines about what should be done when prisoners arrive on a wing without their wing files. As far as the Inquiry could tell, that rarely happens now. But if it does happen, the practice should be that the prisoner should not be admitted to the wing without the permission of a governor. If the wing is on patrol state at the time, the prisoner should only be admitted to the wing with the permission of the night orderly officer. There is no systematic way of highlighting an important entry in a wing file, but Feltham's practice of entering it in red ink was a good idea, and should be followed elsewhere.

57.39 We never came across an example of a copy of the cell-sharing risk assessment form not arriving with the prisoner. But should it happen, the prisoner may still be admitted onto the wing, but they should only be put in a single cell. In that event, the prisoner will have to remain in a single cell until the cell-sharing risk assessment form turns up or a new one is completed.

57.40 Most of the establishments we visited had a system in place for ensuring that wings were informed of those prisoners who were charged with, or had been convicted of, offences under the Protection from Harassment Act 1997. Procedures differed from establishment to establishment, depending on whether it was reception, the Security Department or the administrative section which was supposed to give that information to the wing. Those establishments which do not have a set procedure should adopt one, ensuring that whoever is responsible for notifying the wing does so in writing.

> ### Recommendation 38
> Prisoners should not be admitted to a wing without their current wing file, save with the permission of a governor or the approval of the night orderly officer. Important entries in it should be made in red.
>
> ### Recommendation 39
> If prisoners arrive on a wing without a copy of the cell-sharing risk assessment form, they should be placed in a single cell until the form is found or a new one completed.
>
> ### Recommendation 40
> All establishments should have a procedure for notifying wings in writing that a prisoner is currently charged with, or has been convicted of, an offence under the Protection from Harassment Act 1997.

Information flow within establishments: documents held elsewhere in the establishment

57.41 In addition to the documents which should always be provided to the wings, important information about prisoners which may well affect their management may be contained in documents held elsewhere in the establishment – for example, the prisoner's security file and documents held in the establishment's administrative section. Particular problems arise about information held on prisoners in their medical record in view of patient confidentiality, and I return to that topic later.

57.42 After the wing file, the security file is the file which should contain the most information likely to affect the management of a prisoner on the wing. It is therefore very important that its contents are brought to the attention of the wing. And since security information is not to be included in NOMIS – at any rate not in its first phase – it is all the more important that procedures are in place for relaying information held in a prisoner's security file to the wing. This is another area where practice is haphazard. However, the Security Department of each establishment should have a system for reading the security files by the end of the working day following their arrival, for assessing whether they contain any information which should be relayed to wings, and for reviewing the file when new information about the prisoner is received via a security information report. Any information to be relayed to the wing should be in writing. In that way, there should be no subsequent dispute about whether the information was relayed to the wing and what that information was. And a written note should be made – either in the security file itself or on a dedicated form – giving the date and time when the file was read or reviewed, and stating by whom.

57.43 Information held in security files is entered onto the Security Intelligence System. I described how that worked in paragraphs 7.17–7.18. The system is now known in some establishments as the 5x5 system, because a revised form of the security information report requires two sets of five options to be ticked. Not every establishment has had its 4x4 system revised to reflect that. But the real problem is that the 4x4 or 5x5 systems have the drawback today which they had in 2000 – they are not networked systems, and they can only be accessed by members of the Security Department at the establishment where the system was set up. The recommendation of the Learmont report on prison security in 1995 that there should be a national database for security information has still not been implemented. Accordingly, the information on an inmate intelligence card is still treated as a sufficient summary of the contents of the security file at the time it was printed. And when a prisoner arrives with their security file at another establishment, the task of laboriously entering the contents of the inmate intelligence card onto the 4x4 or 5x5 system has to be completed – and without any further consideration being given to whether the contents of it are an accurate and sufficiently comprehensive summary of the security information reports on which the inmate intelligence card was based.

57.44 I repeat the call for a national database for security information. That does not mean that the present system needs to be dismantled. What is required is for those establishments which are still working on the 4x4 system to have their system converted to the 5x5 system, and for the systems to be integrated with each other and Prison Service headquarters.

57.45 A worrying feature about the transfer of security information relates to the security files of prisoners which were opened while they were serving previous sentences. They will have been kept in the Security Department or the dead records store of the establishment where the prisoners completed their sentence. If a prisoner returns to custody and is held at another establishment, it will be for the Security Department of the new establishment to ask for the old security file. As we have seen, this was not being done at Feltham or elsewhere in 2000. Little has changed since then. We only discovered one establishment which currently does it. Sometimes it is not done because the Security

Department in the new establishment does not know that a security file was opened on the prisoner during their previous sentence. Sometimes they may not know where they completed their last sentence. But by not getting the security file, the new establishment will be denying itself important information about the risks the prisoner might pose. Security files are automatically sent to the new establishment when a prisoner is transferred. But security files should be sought as a matter of course from the previous establishment when the prisoner comes back into custody.

57.46 I turn to the documents held in an establishment's administrative section. They may contain a wealth of information about a prisoner which could help shape their management on the wing. The most obvious ones are the adjudication records, any information of special importance forms, and the main prison file, which could contain much of value including previous wing files. But no-one looks at these documents to see whether any of the information in them should be relayed to the wing. One reason for that may be that a prisoner's main prison file can become so bulky, and the documents within it can be filed so haphazardly, that the prospect of going through it is extremely daunting. But it is also the case that the possibility that there may be information in those files which the wing should get has never really occurred to anyone. At Feltham at the time of Zahid's murder, a member of the Security Department was supposed to look at a prisoner's core record and their custodial documents file. But no-one looked at their main prison file. The same is true today, and not just at Feltham.

57.47 If NOMIS were not so imminent, I would have been recommending that the prison files of all serving prisoners should be tidied up. Documents in them which can have no conceivable value or which have been duplicated should be discarded. The documents which are left should be sorted out, so that, for example, the prisoner's previous wing files and adjudication records can be found easily and important information highlighted. That work would take a lot of time, and it would not be justified in the short time between the publication of this report and the gradual implementation of the first phase of NOMIS across the prison estate. But what can and should be done now is for establishments to have a system in place for the checking of those files relating to incoming prisoners which are kept in the establishment's administrative section. An officer from the Security Department is the obvious person to check those files, and the system can be along the lines of the system for the vetting of security files.

Recommendation 41

Each Security Department should establish a proper system for vetting security files to ensure that they are read by the end of the working day following their arrival, that any relevant information is relayed in writing to the wings, and that a record is kept of who vetted them, with the date and time.

Recommendation 42

Since security information is not to be included in the first phase of NOMIS, there remains a need for a national database for security information. Establishments should have the 4x4 system converted to the 5x5 system if that has not already been done, and the systems should be networked across the prison estate.

Recommendation 43

Where prisoners have served a sentence before, the Security Department should always obtain their security files from the establishment from which they were discharged.

Recommendation 44

Documents held in an establishment's administrative section should be vetted by staff from the Security Department, and each establishment should have a protocol for that work along the lines of the system for vetting security files.

Information flow within wings

57.48 Information about prisoners which comes to the wings has to be brought to the attention of individual members of staff. The senior officer on a wing should be responsible for ensuring that this is done. It would be unwise to rely on word of mouth, as the senior officer would only be able to speak to those officers who are on duty, and even then may not get round to speaking to all of them. The obvious place for the information to be recorded is in the wing observation book. The senior officer should record the information there accurately and succinctly. Particularly important information should be in red. If the senior officer is not there to do it, it should be done by the desk officer or the most experienced of the officers who are there. Principal officers should check that this is being done regularly. Staff will have to get into the habit of looking at the wing observation book when they come on duty, and reading all the entries in it since they were last on duty on the wing. Officers who are new to the wing should be briefed about any problematic prisoners by the senior officer. They will then be able to update that information by reading recent entries in the wing observation book just like the other officers.

> ### Recommendation 45
> The senior officer on a wing should ensure that information arriving on the wing about a prisoner is recorded in the wing observation book. Particularly important information should be in red. When coming on duty, staff should read any entries in the wing observation book made since they were last on duty.

Information flow on discharge

57.49 It will be recalled that shortly before Stewart was discharged from Lancaster Farms in December 1997, a discharge report was prepared on him by a prison officer. It was the only discharge report for Stewart which the Inquiry was provided with. Perhaps it is something which has fallen into disuse. But it is a convenient way of summarising prisoners' behaviour while they have been in prison for those who are to be responsible for supervising them in the future. It will be particularly useful with the advent of Custody Plus, a novel initiative in the Criminal Justice Act 2003 for making offenders sentenced to short terms of imprisonment serve part of their sentence in the community. And it can also be a valuable point of reference in the case of prisoners returning to prison: you will be able to see at a glance how they behaved during their previous sentence. The discharge report should be revived, completed as a matter of course, and a copy included in the prisoner's main prison file. It should be capable of being held on NOMIS when NOMIS becomes operational.

> ### Recommendation 46
> The discharge report which used to be prepared on prisoners on their discharge should be completed as a matter of course, and a copy included in their main prison file. It should be accessible on NOMIS when NOMIS becomes operational.

Other information

Prison Service Orders and other instructions

57.50 In addition to information about particular prisoners, staff need to know about Prison Service Orders and other instructions, whether national or local, which affect the management of the prisoners in their care. They are available on the Prison Service's own internal internet, the intranet, although access to the intranet is very limited on residential wings. Some of them should be read by staff, but some of them are too long to be read in their entirety, and may contain much information which staff do not need to know. In such cases, the gist of the instruction should be brought to their attention. The Prison Service leaves it to individual establishments to have sufficient arrangements in place to ensure that information about relevant instructions get to the right people. Such arrangements include briefings by management – but that means that staff who are not there may not know what the instructions require of them – the posting of notices and the issue of summaries. But some establishments do not have a standardised procedure in place. To make sure this happens, the Prison Service should publish a model procedure to be regarded as the procedure to be adopted by any establishment which does not produce one of its own.

Comments and recommendations in external reports

57.51 Staff as well as management should be informed of any relevant comments, whether critical or praiseworthy, or relevant recommendations in external reports, such as the reports of the Inspectorate or the annual report of the local Independent Monitoring Board. They will invariably contain a wealth of information which could have implications for the safety of prisoners. These reports are available on the intranet, but it would be expecting too much of staff to read them in their entirety. Staff tend to know whether their establishments are thought to be performing well or badly, but not much more than that. This is not an area where standardised procedures are necessary, but Governors should be alive to the need to bring the gist of relevant comments or recommendations to the attention of staff, and to ensure that this is done in a way in which the whole of the establishment's workforce is made aware of them.

> ### Recommendation 47
>
> The Prison Service should publish a model procedure dealing with how establishments should bring Prison Service Orders and other instructions, whether national or local, which affect the management of prisoners to the attention of staff. The model procedure should be regarded as having been adopted by any establishment which does not produce one of its own.
>
> ### Recommendation 48
>
> Governors should ensure that any relevant comments or recommendations in external reports about their establishments which have implications for the safety of prisoners be brought to the attention of the workforce.

Monitoring information flow

57.52 It will be recalled that one of the recommendations made in the report of the Coonan Inquiry following the death of Christopher Edwards was that "the Governor, the Senior Medical Officer and the Senior Probation Officer should review periodically the arrangements which govern the receipt and transfer of information which has been received from outside the prison". That recommendation was made in the context of Christopher Edwards's death, which arose as a result of the prison not getting information about Christopher Edwards's killer from outside agencies. But as I said in paragraph 30.29, this recommendation could apply just as sensibly to the transfer of information between establishments and within establishments. This recommendation has not been implemented, in part because Mr Wheatley thought that it did not fit easily into the respective functions of the Governor, the Senior Medical Officer and the Senior Probation Officer. But the spirit, if not the letter, of the recommendation should be followed. There is a compelling argument for saying that every establishment should appoint an officer not below the grade of governor to be responsible for the oversight of the flow of information. Such an officer should ensure that systems are in place for the transfer of information within an establishment. They should check that the systems are being followed. They should take action when they find that they are not. And they should review the arrangements periodically to ensure that best practice is being maintained.

> **Recommendation 49**
>
> Every establishment should appoint an officer not below the grade of governor to be responsible for overseeing the flow of information. Such an officer should ensure that systems are in place for the transfer of information within an establishment and that the systems are being followed. They should take action when they find that they are not, and should review the arrangements periodically to ensure that best practice is being maintained.

Chapter 58: The prisoner escort record

58.1 There is currently a debate within the Prison Service about whether the prisoner escort record should survive the introduction of NOMIS. Its future is currently the subject of a comprehensive review. I touched upon its functions in paragraph 19.2, but I now look at it in more detail, especially as there have been changes to the form since Zahid's murder.

58.2 The form which is currently used was revised in the latter part of 2000. It is in two parts. Part A identifies whether the prisoner is known to be a risk to themselves, or a risk to others, or an escape risk. This part is completed by the police for a prisoner who is taken from police custody to court, or by the escort contractor if it was only at court that the prisoner was remanded in custody, or by prison staff for a prisoner who is taken from a penal establishment to court or to another establishment. When it is completed by prison staff, it is completed by staff in the healthcare centre, in the Security Department and on reception, relying respectively on the prisoner's medical record, their security file and other documents. This part serves two functions. It lets the escorting staff know whether the prisoner comes within any of the categories of risk, so that they can take appropriate measures while the prisoner is in their custody. It also lets the receiving establishment know whether the prisoner is at risk of harm to themselves or others, so that they are managed appropriately when they get there.

58.3 Part B of the form is a record of the time during which the prisoner is in the custody of the escort contractor. This part is completed by the officers who escort the prisoner. It too serves two functions. It provides an auditable record of the prisoner's movements should that prove necessary. It also informs the receiving establishment of any incident which may have occurred while the prisoner was at court or in the custody of the escort contractor which may affect their management there.

58.4 The most important of these functions is the giving of relevant information about a prisoner to enable them to be appropriately managed at the receiving establishment. Certainly that is the function which is the most relevant to the Inquiry's work. But the value of that information has a very short lifespan. If the prisoner is returning to the establishment they have been in, they will be known there, and the information will not be new. If they are going to the establishment for the first time, their security file (if they have one), their medical record and their other documents will be reviewed within a day or two, and staff can then be informed of anything relevant in them.* So the form is only going to be useful if the prisoner is going to an establishment they have not been to before, and even then only for a couple of days or so. To be fair, Part A was probably not intended to have a wider use than that in the establishment which receives the prisoner.

58.5 There will still be a need for information of the kind which the form contains to accompany the prisoner even after NOMIS is implemented. That is because the receiving establishment will still need to be made aware, until the prisoner's security file, medical record and other documents can be checked, whether they are a risk to themselves or to others. NOMIS cannot be regarded as having all the information relevant to the identification of that risk since medical and psychiatric information, and for the time being security information, are not to be included in it. So even if a prisoner has a NOMS number, the fact that no alert that they are a risk to themselves or to others appears when information about them is accessed on NOMIS will by no means be decisive. There may be medical or psychiatric information which shows that they are a risk to themselves, or security information showing that they may be a risk to others. But if only NOMIS is accessed by staff, they will not be any the wiser.

58.6 So there is still a need for receiving establishments to be provided with information which serves the same function as Part A of the form. The prisoner escort record is as good a way of doing that as any. That, no doubt, was why the phasing out of the form was not recommended in a report on bureaucracy in the Prison and Probation Services by the Public Sector Team of the Regulatory Impact Unit of the Cabinet Office, which considered the efficacy of the form in 2004. The unit had been expected to recommend that the form be dispensed with. However, for the form to be effective, it must convey accurate information which is capable of being assimilated easily by staff on reception so that the prisoner's wing – invariably the first night centre or the induction wing – can be informed of any risk they pose.

58.7 The prisoner escort record is one of a number of forms which have to be completed by staff ticking certain boxes. The advantage of forms of this type is that the attention of staff is focused on particular options. The form itself includes a kind of checklist. Without that, a particular option might not have occurred to staff. But the disadvantage with forms like this is that they produce a "tick-box" mentality: less than complete thought may be given to whether a particular box should be

---

* If they are a "new number", the only information which Part A will contain will be that entered by the police or the escort contractor.

ticked or what the appropriate response should be. The cell-sharing risk assessment form is another document of that kind. It would be preferable if the prisoner escort record allowed officers to express themselves in their own words – thereby making the form much more accurate – while at the same time informing officers of the topics they have to address. That may have been appropriate if officers had much more time to complete the form, and had the luxury of being able to sit back and give real thought to it. But they have neither the time nor in some cases probably the skills to do that.

58.8 Apart from that, there is little wrong with the form itself. The problems which have arisen relate to the way the form has been completed. The team from the Cabinet Office found that the form was "not always" completed accurately, and that important information was often missing or incomplete. That was said to be particularly evident in busy local prisons where the turnover of prisoners is high. That was what the Inquiry found as well. The problems which were apparent to the Inquiry included the following:

- The form consists of a series of warning boxes which have to be ticked if any of them apply to the prisoner in question. If any of the boxes are ticked, information about the reason for this has to be included in another section headed "Further information about risk", unless an additional report is attached. An additional report is attached only occasionally. More often, it is not, and an entry has to be written in the section. That does not happen often, and when it does it is usually too abbreviated to be of any help.

- Although some of the warning boxes have to be ticked by staff in the Security Department, one establishment uses administrative staff who do not have access to prisoners' security files to tick the boxes. They rely on information in the Local Inmate Database System.

- Although the Prison Service has published a handbook giving guidance on how the form is to be completed, staff at some establishments had never seen it. Some did not even know of its existence. They learned how to complete the form by watching other staff do it, thereby perpetuating any bad practices which had crept in.

58.9 Moreover, there is a lack of consistency as to when some of the boxes have to be ticked. For example, the section in the form to be completed by staff in the Security Department includes a box marked "Violence". The handbook tells staff to tick it if the prisoner poses a risk of violence to staff or others "during this escort" – even though the form is also intended to be used to inform the management of the prisoner once the escort is over. And the only examples given in the handbook for when a prisoner might pose such a risk are where the prisoner has a history of violent behaviour or has recently assaulted a member of staff or another prisoner. The lack of clear guidance has resulted in wide inconsistencies in practice. Some staff only look at whether the prisoner has convictions for offences of violence. Some of the staff who do that regard rape as such an offence. Others do not. Others ignore the prisoner's convictions, and look at their behaviour in prison. And yet others look at both. The result is that, as in 1999 and 2000 when the Security Department at Hindley completed many prisoner escort records on Stewart, the violence box is ticked so often that its value as a true indicator of a risk to staff or other prisoners is substantially diminished.

58.10 Another example is the box marked "Conceals weapons". The handbook says that this must be ticked if the prisoner has a history of concealing weapons or is considered to be likely to do so during the transfer. Again, there is a concentration on what is likely to happen while the prisoner is in transit. Practice is haphazard here as well. Some staff tick the box if the prisoner has a conviction for an offence of possessing an offensive weapon. Others tick it if the prisoner has used a weapon in the course of committing an offence. Many staff do not consider whether the prisoner is likely to *conceal* weapons at all. Some officers even cross out the word "conceals" but then tick the box where a prisoner has convictions for offences involving the use of weapons.

58.11 The upshot of all this is that staff at the receiving establishment tend to regard the prisoner escort record as of little value. It was described to the Inquiry as little more than a "body receipt" or a "bus ticket". I entirely understand why staff are so sceptical of it. Without clear reasons why a particular box has been ticked, the form is of little practical use. Clearly, radical steps have to be taken to improve the way in which it is completed. The handbook should be revised to make it clear that the form does not cover prisoners just while they are in transit, but it is also intended to inform prisoners' management in the receiving establishment. It should give clear guidance to staff as to when a box should be ticked. Staff who are tasked with completing the form should be instructed on how to complete it by senior officers in their department. They should each be provided with a copy of the handbook, and most important of all they should be reminded of the need to spell out the reasons why a particular box has been ticked.

> ### Recommendation 50
> The handbook giving guidance on how to complete the prisoner escort record should be revised to make it clear that it is not merely of use while a prisoner is in transit, but it is also intended to inform the prisoner's management in the receiving establishment. It should give clear guidance to staff as to when a box should be ticked. Staff who are tasked with completing the form should be instructed on how to complete it by senior officers in their department. They should each be provided with a copy of the handbook, and they should be reminded of the need to spell out the reasons for a particular box being ticked.

Chapter 59: Assessing risk

The cell-sharing risk assessment

59.1 Assessing the risk a prisoner posed to staff and other inmates was not part of the culture of the Prison Service at the time of Zahid's murder. Steps were taken to manage those prisoners who were *known* to be dangerous: the scheme at Hindley for referring such prisoners to the Potentially Dangerous Offenders' Panel was an example of that. But no specific tools were available to identify those prisoners from whom others in the establishment needed to be protected. That changed after Zahid's murder. Cell-sharing risk assessments became a standard feature across the prison estate. Just as the prisoner escort record became the Prison Service's most visible response to the death of Christopher Edwards, the cell-sharing risk assessment form was its most obvious reaction to Zahid's murder.

59.2 The idea was that of Mr Clifford. In the immediate aftermath of the attack, he asked for a cell-sharing risk assessment tool to be devised at Feltham. A form called "the cell occupancy risk assessment" was introduced at the establishment within a week or so, and a revised form – known as "the first night cell occupancy risk assessment" – was brought in a few months later. It came in two versions – one for "new numbers" and one for transferees, recognising that only the latter would arrive at Feltham with information about their recent behaviour in custody. These forms were to be the model for the national cell-sharing risk assessment forms introduced in 2002. The forms were evaluated by the Research, Development and Statistics Directorate of the Home Office in 2003, and reviewed by a working group from the Prison Service following the death of a prisoner in Manchester Prison later that year. The forms have now been revised, and they have been in use in their current state since August 2005. When NOMIS is implemented, it will be possible to complete the forms online, and information on them can be retrieved when the prisoner's NOMS number is entered. The Prisons and Probation Ombudsman has considered the efficacy of the forms – both in their original and revised versions – in reports on the death of the prisoner in Manchester Prison and of a prisoner in Leeds Prison in 2004.

59.3 The cell-sharing risk assessment form originally consisted of two forms: XF001 and XF002. Form XF001 was unaffected by the recent review. It is the initial assessment of risk. It is to be completed for "new numbers" and transferees, even those transferees who are at the establishment for no more than a night or two. It is completed as part of the reception process or in the first night centre before prisoners spend their first night at the establishment. That is itself an improvement on what used to happen. When it was first introduced, it could be completed the following morning if it was not feasible to complete it before then, the safeguard being that staff on duty in the first night centre or the induction wing had to be informed that the assessment had not been carried out, and that vigilance was needed.

59.4 Form XF001 contains sections to be completed by an officer on reception or in the first night centre, and by a healthcare worker. The section to be completed by the officer on reception requires them to identify the documents on which the assessment is based and the prisoner's offending history. It requires them to state how the prisoner has behaved in prison before, whether they abuse alcohol or drugs, and whether a self-harm at risk form has ever been opened on them. The prisoner is asked whether they have any concerns about sharing a cell, and whether they would describe themselves as someone who gets angry or frustrated quickly. The officer completing the form is then required to tick one of three boxes to indicate the extent to which the prisoner poses a risk of harm to others – high, medium or low. The section to be completed by the healthcare worker requires them to state whether the prisoner is displaying symptoms which might make them a risk to others. Again, they are required to tick one of three boxes – high, medium or low – to indicate the extent of that risk. If neither section has the high risk box ticked, the prisoner is allowed to share a cell. However, in a marginal case – such as where there are indications that the prisoner might be a risk to others but there is insufficient information to be sure – advice can be sought from the duty governor. If either of the high risk boxes is ticked, the prisoner's allocation has to be decided by the duty governor. They can allocate the prisoner to a single or double cell. If they allocate the prisoner to a double cell, they can limit the kinds of inmates the prisoner can share with, and warn staff on the wing to watch the prisoner carefully.

59.5 The Inquiry found considerable variations in practice. Instructions issued by the Prison Service's Safer Custody Group for completing form XF001 stress that neither staff on reception or in the first night centre nor healthcare staff are responsible for deciding whether a prisoner can or cannot share a cell. That decision is made by the allocating officer for prisoners not assessed as a high risk or by the duty governor for prisoners who are, relying on the judgement of both reception or first night centre staff and healthcare staff together as to the level of risk which the prisoner poses. Nevertheless, at one establishment visited by the Inquiry, a recommendation by a doctor that a prisoner be allocated to a single cell is regarded as determining the issue. At another establishment, the trigger for considering whether the prisoner should be in a single cell is if either of the medium risk boxes is ticked, rather than either of the high risk boxes. At the same establishment, that decision is not made by the duty governor, but by the principal officer in reception. And the practice of some establishments is to complete form XF001 only for those transferees who arrive without a copy of the form completed when they were "new numbers".

59.6 It is questionable whether officers are correctly assessing the level of the risk. At some of the establishments the Inquiry visited, officers assessed prisoners as a high risk because they claimed to be prone to lose their temper, even though the officers thought they were only saying that in order to get a cell on their own. At some establishments, officers thought that they were assessing not merely the risk of harm *to* other prisoners, but also the risk of self-harm or the risk of harm *from* other prisoners. They might therefore tick the high risk box, even though the risk of harm to others was negligible, and the result might be that vulnerable prisoners at risk of self-harm might end up in a cell on their own. At some establishments, prisoners were being assessed as a high risk because of the temptation to be cautious. This over-defensive attitude was particularly apparent at Feltham. Staff were presumably unaware of the following guidance in the instructions:

> "As long as staff can show by filling in the form correctly that they have considered all the information available to them and made the best decision they could on that basis, they will *not* be blamed if the prisoner does go on to behave violently. On the contrary, filling in the form correctly is their best protection against blame. It will demonstrate that everything that could be done was done."

These problems stemmed from the absence of any training in the completion of the form. As with the prisoner escort record, officers learned how to complete the form by watching others do it, thereby perpetuating any bad practices which had crept in. Staff who are tasked with completing the form should be instructed on how to complete it by a senior officer.

Recommendation 51

Staff who are tasked with completing form XF001 should be instructed on how to complete it by a senior officer. In particular, they should be reminded that they are only assessing the risk prisoners pose to other inmates. They should not automatically assess prisoners as a high risk simply because they claim, for example, to be prone to lose their temper, but should ignore such claims if they believe them to be untrue, and they should guard against being over-defensive.

59.7 Leaving these problems aside, it is questionable whether this initial assessment results in an accurate predictor of risk in view of the limited information available on "new numbers", even those who have been in prison before. Things will be better when NOMIS is operational, but the only documents which an establishment always gets at present for a "new number" is the warrant authorising the prisoner's detention and the prisoner escort record. The former does not always identify the offence which the prisoner is charged with or has been convicted of. And the latter will contain very little information about "new numbers". Sometimes prisoners arrive with a list of previous convictions and a copy of the pre-sentence report on them, but whether they do or not is very much a hit-and-miss affair. As for transferees, they should arrive with their current wing file and their adjudication record, which will help the new establishment know how they have been behaving in custody.* The prisoner escort record will be fuller, but it will still not convey much information of value in the light of the way it is currently completed. So very often the assessment is based on what the prisoner says when questioned by the officer completing form XF001.

59.8 Invariably what the prisoner says is not reliable. The 2003 evaluation revealed that in only 43% of those cases where the prisoner had relevant previous convictions were those convictions identified. There is no reason to suppose that prisoners always tell the truth when asked, for example, whether they have been engaged in bullying, or racist behaviour, or assaults on staff or other inmates. If prisoners know that they have a better chance of being in a cell on their own if they claim to be racist or prone to lose their temper, they may well say so even if it is untrue. All this assumes that prisoners are capable of articulating sensible answers to the questions they are asked. That may not be the case. An increasing number of foreign nationals in our prisons mean that some arrivals may not speak or understand English well enough. And many prisoners may be coming off drugs.

59.9 The Inquiry noticed another problem. In a few cases, there is a tension between the prisoner's need to share a cell because they are at risk of self-harm and their need to be on their own because of the risks they pose to a cellmate. Few duty governors satisfactorily resolved that tension. The instructions state what the duty governor's options are,

---

* Ironically, neither the wing file nor the adjudication record are included in the documents listed in form XF001 which officers in reception or in the first night centre are supposed to base their assessment on – perhaps because form XF001 was drafted when it was thought there would be no need to complete it for transferees who arrived with a copy of the one completed when they were a "new number".

but they give no guidance on when one option is preferable to another. They should do so.

> ### Recommendation 52
> The instructions for completing the form should give duty governors guidance on how to exercise the options available to them when dealing with prisoners who are both at risk of self-harm and a risk to their cellmate.

59.10 All of this means that the initial assessment before prisoners spend their first night at the establishment is a rough and ready one. That makes an early review of the initial assessment when all the relevant documents are to hand so important. What used to happen was that the assessment would be reviewed in the course of the induction process and before the prisoner went on ordinary location. By then the relevant documents would have been available. After that, those prisoners who were assessed on that review to be a high risk had to be reviewed by the wing manager one month later, and then every three months while they continued to be regarded as a high risk. Those prisoners who were not assessed as a high risk following the review in the course of their induction did not have to be reviewed again, except when they were transferred to another establishment or some special event, such as an assault on a member of staff or another inmate, triggered the need for such a review. Form XF002 was used to record the results of those reviews. Practice varied here as well. Feltham reviewed all prisoners every seven days, whereas another establishment did not review transferees at all if they had been assessed in the last four weeks, unless their circumstances had changed since then.

59.11 Three significant changes have occurred as a result of the recent review by the working group from the Prison Service. First, form XF002 has been replaced. Reviews of the initial assessment now take place more frequently. That is partly because prisoners who have been assessed as a medium risk, as well as those assessed as a high risk, have to be reviewed regularly, and partly because the events which can trigger the need for a review have increased. They now include repeated or escalated threats of violence particularly towards cellmates, a prisoner's discharge from the segregation unit following violent or threatening behaviour, an unexpected conviction or a harsh sentence which might result in the prisoner being distressed on their return from court, and any evidence that the prisoner has armed themselves with a weapon. The form which has replaced form XF002 must now be completed by the prisoner's personal officer or another officer on the wing, and it has to be signed off by either the duty manager or the duty governor. And it focuses the mind of the officer completing it by asking a series of questions about the prisoner which the previous version did not.

59.12 Secondly, within seven days of the review, a plan has to be drawn up for those prisoners assessed as a high or medium risk, outlining the measures which have to be taken to minimise the risks which the prisoner poses. The processes for the implementation of these measures are monitored by a designated officer as part of the establishment's violence reduction strategy. Those contributing to the plan need not only be officers on the wing. The prisoners themselves take an active part in the process as attempts are made to find out what they think might trigger violence on their part, and how they think they might learn to control their behaviour. At the same time a decision about when the next review should take place is made in the absence of a specified event triggering it, thereby ensuring that reviews take place when they are needed.

59.13 This is a crucial step forward. Identifying the prisoners who pose a risk to other inmates is one thing. Managing them properly is another. That is what the risk minimisation plan is supposed to achieve. Problem prisoners in the past were not managed pro-actively. They would be shuttled between the wing, the healthcare centre and the segregation unit – or perhaps transferred to another establishment altogether when all else had failed – in order to ring the changes in the hope that this might make the prisoner change their ways. A focused risk minimisation plan is plainly the way forward.

59.14 Thirdly, establishments are now required to keep a register of prisoners assessed as high or medium risk. Staff will therefore be able to tell at a glance those prisoners who pose a risk to other prisoners, and what the level of that risk is. The Inquiry saw a system of this kind in operation at Wayland Prison. It was called Racist Assessment and Concerns Evaluation or RACE. The deputy governor is to be credited for this initiative, which was prompted by the Inquiry's impending visit.

59.15 Since the first review of the initial assessment is so critical, it should take place in every case, not just for prisoners assessed initially as a high or medium risk. And it is important to get the first review of the initial assessment right. I make three suggestions about how that might be achieved. First, all the relevant information about the prisoner must be obtained. That will include a list of their convictions and current charges, with a short statement of the facts of each, the bail information report or pre-sentence report, the OASys assessment – as to which see paragraphs 59.22–59.27 – if one has been prepared on them, and the prisoner escort record (for what it is worth). If the prisoner has been in prison before, it should also include previous wing files and the adjudication record, together with any discharge report. And most important of all, if a security file was opened on the prisoner, the officers reviewing the initial assessment should be briefed on what it contains.

59.16 Secondly, the first review of the initial assessment should be a multi-disciplinary exercise. A wing officer should be included in it, but so too should a healthcare worker who has reviewed the prisoner's medical record and an officer with responsibility for implementing the establishment's violence reduction strategy. Thirdly, the review must take place quickly if the limitations of the initial assessment are not to be perpetuated for longer than is necessary. It should take place no more than a week after the initial assessment. By then all the relevant documents should be available.

> ### Recommendation 53
> The first review of the initial assessment should take place within one week of the initial assessment, and should take place in every case. It should be a multi-disciplinary review, with representatives from the prisoner's wing, healthcare and the team responsible for implementing the establishment's violence reduction strategy all contributing to it. The documents set out in paragraph 59.15 should be considered, and the participants should have been briefed on the contents of the prisoner's security file if there is one.

59.17 There is a lack of clarity in the role of the duty manager or duty governor who signs off the review. Are they signing it off merely to confirm that the review has been completed? Or are they acknowledging that they agree with the assessment of the risk the prisoner poses? There is little point in the former because the form itself will show that the review has been completed. And there is little point in the latter unless the duty manager or duty governor themselves consider the material available to those who reviewed the assessment. I do not suppose that they would have the time to do that.

> ### Recommendation 54
> The role of the duty manager or duty governor in the review process should be clarified.

59.18 An unexpected conviction or a harsh sentence are not the only times when a prisoner might return distressed from court. They might have received pessimistic advice about the outcome of their trial, or a particular application which they were pinning their hopes on might have been refused. And even if their conviction is not unexpected, or their sentence not particularly harsh, the reality of being convicted and sentenced can hit a prisoner quite profoundly. This applies not just to returnees. Many things can trigger the need to review an assessment – bad news from home is an obvious example. Wing officers should be alive to things like that, and should not hesitate to call for a review of the assessment in such circumstances.

> ### Recommendation 55
> Wing officers should be reminded of the need to call for a review of an assessment when the necessity for one is triggered by some occurrence which might affect the prisoner's emotional well-being.

59.19 Much of this is what is envisaged by the Prison Service Instruction which introduced these changes. I have merely spelt out what needs to be done on the first review of the initial assessment if it is to be as effective as intended. I acknowledge that this review will take place for the most part at busy local prisons which are already overstretched, because that is where "new numbers" invariably go. But if the risk which a prisoner poses to their cellmate is to be considered properly before it is too late, an early and informed assessment of the risk is essential.

59.20 An early and informed assessment of the risk has another advantage. Experience has shown that when the assessment is made on too little information, officers tend to err on the side of caution. Prisoners might therefore be assessed as a risk to other inmates when they are not. That might delay their transfer to a training prison, and they may remain in a local prison where there are fewer opportunities for purposeful activity and fewer programmes which address their offending behaviour. So they remain in the very establishment which is more likely to perpetuate their problems.

59.21 I have two other suggestions. First, at present, a designated officer from the team responsible for implementing the establishment's violence reduction strategy is responsible for monitoring only *the processes* for the implementation of any measures to be taken to minimise the risks a prisoner poses. This officer should also be responsible for monitoring their actual implementation. Secondly, there is a need to identify those establishments which appear to be assessing more or fewer prisoners as high or medium risks than the norm. Once identified, their procedures can be looked at to see why they are out of kilter, and any bad practices can then be addressed. That can be achieved by the register of prisoners assessed as high or medium risk identifying what proportion of the establishment's population those prisoners represent.

> ### Recommendation 56
> The officer responsible for monitoring the processes for implementing measures outlined in risk minimisation plans should also be responsible for monitoring their actual implementation.
>
> ### Recommendation 57
> The register of prisoners assessed as high or medium risk should identify what proportion of the establishment's population those prisoners represent.

The OASys assessment

59.22 In the light of its terms of reference, the Inquiry was naturally concentrating on the risks a prisoner poses to other inmates. But prisoners pose other risks. They pose risks to members of staff. They pose risks to themselves by self-harm or suicide. They pose risks to the community by re-offending on their release. And they are at risk themselves from attack by other prisoners if they are especially vulnerable. Received wisdom is that a joined-up approach to risk assessment is likely to produce better results than assessments of particular kinds of risk. That is what the OASys assessments are intended to achieve.

59.23 OASys was introduced in 2003. Its implementation across the whole of the prison estate was expected to be completed by the end of 2004. However, OASys had to reflect the new sentencing regime introduced by the Criminal Justice Act 2003, and its implementation was not completed until the end of 2005. It does not apply to all prisoners. It applies to all young offenders, but it only applies to those adult prisoners who receive sentences of 12 months' imprisonment or more – although some prisoners sentenced to a term of less than 12 months may have been the subject of an OASys "assessment" for the purpose of the preparation of a pre-sentence report. And it does not apply to juveniles at all. Their needs are met by a separate tool, ASSET, which we were told is short for "assessment". An OASys assessment must be carried out within eight weeks of the prisoner being sentenced, but if the prisoner is a young offender who has less than eight weeks to serve, the assessment must be carried out as part of the induction process.

59.24 OASys's core function is to identify how prisoners can best be managed in order to protect the community from them when they are discharged and to reduce the risk of their re-offending. It replaces sentence planning. It identifies the programmes prisoners should undergo to reduce their offending behaviour, and it highlights the help they will need when they are back in the community. If, for example, their crimes are acquisitive crimes, it will identify what help they should be given to find accommodation and a job so as to reduce their need to steal. The assessment is carried out by assessors trained for the purpose. They interview the prisoners at some length, and have access to information held on them. A full OASys assessment will take about five hours. Detailed pictures of the prisoners emerge, with comprehensive sections not merely on their offending behaviour and their lifestyle, but also on their emotional well-being, their thinking and behaviour and their attitudes.

59.25 In addition to its core function, OASys has a number of other applications. One of them is the identification of the risk of harm which prisoners pose to others, including staff and other inmates. This function is regarded by the Prison Service as the principal tool, outside the specific context of cell-sharing, for identifying those prisoners posing such a risk – though the experience of the Inspectorate is that few establishments are using OASys for this purpose, and when they are the risks which have been identified are often not fed back to the wings. Time alone will tell us how accurate a predictor of this risk OASys is, but there are two significant areas on which information is not currently sought by OASys assessors. The first is information about the way the prisoner has behaved while serving previous sentences. They look at current records held on the wing, but not adjudication records or previous wing files. But by far the more important information not currently sought by OASys assessors is security information. They do not see information held in the security files of those prisoners who have them. Maybe the reason for that is that the document produced by the OASys assessment is an open document which the prisoner is entitled to see. But there is a part of the document which is set aside for information which may be withheld from prisoners, and some of the information held in security files may come into this category. Security information should be available to OASys assessors. Otherwise, I fear that an OASys assessment will be incomplete, and therefore an inaccurate predictor of the risk of harm which prisoners pose to staff and other inmates.

CHAPTER 59: ASSESSING RISK

> **Recommendation 58**
>
> OASys should be used by all establishments to identify the risks posed by prisoners to staff and other inmates, and the risks which are identified should be fed back to the wings.
>
> **Recommendation 59**
>
> OASys assessors should have access to information relating to prisoners' behaviour while serving previous sentences and to information held in security files.

59.26 Adult prisoners serving sentences of less than 12 months' imprisonment will not have an OASys assessment carried out in prison. But since the overwhelming majority of prisoners serving short sentences will have had a pre-sentence report prepared on them, there will have been an OASys assessment carried out on them prior to sentence. That is unlikely to have addressed the risk which these prisoners would pose to staff and other inmates if they were sent to prison, and that risk will have to be assessed once they get to prison. Their OASys assessment should be reviewed during the induction process, but the review need only address the risk which they pose to staff and other inmates.

59.27 That leaves those very few adult prisoners serving sentences of less than 12 months' imprisonment who will not have had an OASys assessment carried out before they were sentenced. Since they will be serving most of their sentence in the community when Custody Plus comes into effect later this year, it is the risk of them re-offending when they are released, rather than the risk of harm to staff and other inmates, which is the more relevant risk to assess. If resources permit, they should have an OASys assessment during their induction process.

> **Recommendation 60**
>
> All adult prisoners serving sentences of less than 12 months' imprisonment who had an OASys assessment before being sentenced should have that assessment reviewed during the induction process. The review need only address the risk of harm which the prisoner poses to staff and other inmates. If resources permit, adult prisoners serving sentences of less than 12 months' imprisonment who did not have an OASys assessment before being sentenced should have one during the induction process.

MAPPA

59.28 Multi-Agency Public Protection Arrangements, or MAPPA, were created by the Criminal Justice and Court Services Act 2000. They required police forces and the Probation Service to work together to manage the risks posed by dangerous offenders when they are released into the community. The Prison Service now participates in these arrangements as a result of the Criminal Justice Act 2003. The arrangements apply to offenders convicted of murder, offenders sentenced to imprisonment or detention of 12 months or more for a serious violent or sexual offence, and offenders who might cause serious harm to the public. The focus is on the protection of the public on their release, not the risk the offenders may pose to staff or other inmates while serving their sentence.

59.29 The tool MAPPA uses to identify the level of risk which such a prisoner poses is the OASys assessment. But the Prison Service has introduced a risk management model for establishments to adopt for the management of those prisoners to whom MAPPA applies and who have been identified as posing the greatest risk to the public. The model envisages the creation of an inter-departmental risk management team responsible for providing regular assessments of such prisoners. There is no reason why this model cannot be used to manage all prisoners who have been identified as posing a risk to staff and other inmates. It would then serve the same function as the Potentially Dangerous Offenders' Panel at Hindley. It would be a convenient forum for considering what measures are appropriate for managing that risk. This model should be adopted by all establishments, and prisoners who have been identified as being a high risk to their cellmate on any review of the cell-sharing risk assessment, or as posing a very high or high risk to staff or other inmates on the OASys assessment, should be referred to this team.

> ### Recommendation 61
> The risk management model for the management of prisoners to whom MAPPA applies and who have been identified as posing the greatest risk to the public should be adopted by all establishments. Prisoners who have been identified as being a high risk to their cellmate on any review of the cell-sharing risk assessment, or posing a very high or high risk to staff and other inmates on the OASys assessment, should be referred to the inter-departmental risk management team envisaged by the model.

A risk classification?

59.30 All prisoners are assigned a security classification. This identifies the category of prison to which they should be sent. Such risk assessments as are carried out when determining what a prisoner's security classification should be are relatively rudimentary, and only address the risk of the prisoner attempting to escape and the risk of harm to the public in the event of an escape. Those risk assessments do not address the risk which prisoners pose to staff and other inmates.

59.31 The existence of a system for classifying prisoners according to the security risk they pose to the public led the Inquiry to consider whether there should be a system for classifying prisoners according to the risk of harm they pose to staff and other inmates. The benefit of such a classification would be that staff would know which prisoners to keep a special watch over. However, staff should know that anyway. They are expected to know which prisoners on their wing have been assessed as posing a high risk to their cellmates under the cell-sharing risk assessment or a high or very high risk to staff and other inmates under OASys. So there should not be a need for a risk classification. Moreover, it would be difficult to keep from other prisoners the risk classification which a prisoner has got, and certainly not from the prisoner concerned. These things have a habit of getting out. In addition, prisoners who know that they have been given a high risk classification may want to live up to the label. Of course, that can apply just as much to the cell-sharing risk assessment and the OASys assessment, but there is something about a bare risk classification which might make prisoners react adversely to it. I have concluded that its introduction is neither necessary nor desirable.

> ### Recommendation 62
> It is neither necessary nor desirable to introduce a risk classification, similar to the security classification, which identifies the degree of risk which a prisoner poses to staff and other inmates.

Chapter 60: Dealing with prisoners

The key attributes

60.1 People unfamiliar with the Prison Service often refer to prison officers as "guards" or "warders". This language reflects the popular belief that the prison officer's role is concerned with security and control. There is a widespread notion that the nuts and bolts of an officer's work – the locking and the unlocking, the escorting and the supervising – is what the job is all about. And similar thinking informs typical perceptions of what prison officers are actually like. They are seen either as the unbending and unsympathetic Mr Mackay, not prepared to give old lags like Fletcher an inch, or the unworldly and trusting Mr Barraclough, capable of being manipulated even by a relatively unsophisticated and likeable youngster like Godber.*

60.2 The truth, of course, is more complex. Prison officers have much more to do than maintaining security and control and performing basic routine tasks. They spend so much time with prisoners that the relationships which are built up are central to their role:

> "At every point of the day, the relationships an officer has established with prisoners are called upon: to unlock prisoners successfully without rancour, to cajole stragglers along to work, to make sure that the visits policy is explained clearly to dispel anxiety in a prisoner who is missing his or her family. Even in seemingly 'technical' matters – for example, censoring letters (an officer can draw upon their knowledge of a wing and the prisoner in reading letters) or in completing the locks, bolts and bars (checking around a prisoner's cell – their home – in a way that does not disturb or upset them) – relationships matter."**

So it is not surprising that "it is the relationships an officer establishes with prisoners that hold the key to being a successful prison officer" and are at "the heart of prison work". Getting the balance right is difficult to achieve at the best of times – given the potential for conflict inherent in maintaining good order and discipline while at the same time interacting with prisoners in a positive, caring and humane way. It is even more difficult to get to know inmates well in a busy prison, with a large number of inmates and a high turnover of prisoners, and with limited numbers of staff, while maintaining the appropriate boundaries and not allowing prisoners to exploit any weaknesses which staff may have. Empathising with inmates is a good thing, but prison officers have to keep their distance as well. Too thick a skin is dangerous because an officer can

---

* Characters in *Porridge*, the long-running BBC comedy series about prison life.
**Liebling and Price, *The Prison Officer*, 2001, p.44

lose touch with a prisoner, but there has to be a measure of resilience if they are not to take on the prisoner's problems themselves.

60.3 Two of the key attributes required of a prison officer are at the heart of the Inquiry's work. The first is the officer's ability to notice what is happening on the wing. Their antennae must be sufficiently attuned to pick up the complex rhythms of prison life. They must be able to put themselves into the prisoners' shoes and see things from their perspective. Had the officers on Swallow been more alive to the dynamics of life on the wing, there would have been a far greater chance that they would all have realised that Stewart needed to be watched, that he was a racist who might be hostile to Zahid, that Zahid might well have been uncomfortable about sharing a cell with him, and that Zahid might not have shared his concerns with them for fear of it getting back to Stewart.

60.4 The second key attribute is the officer's ability to earn the respect of the prisoners on the wing. It is not simply enough, for example, for inmates to trust an officer to put them on report only as a last resort, not to be too rigid in their enforcement of rules, and to use their discretion fairly and humanely. They must also realise that they can confide in officers if they want to, knowing that they will get sound and impartial advice and that their confidentiality will not be compromised. If Zahid had thought that, maybe he would have been prepared to tell officers about his discomfort at being in a cell with Stewart, and maybe action would have been taken to move one of them.

60.5 These are attributes which *all* prison officers should have. Prisoners have to be treated consistently so that they know where they stand. There is nothing worse than one member of staff saying and doing one thing, and another saying or doing something else. But there is no obvious way of ensuring that all prison officers possess these attributes. Prison officers, like everyone else, have different strengths. Some will instinctively have a feel for the work. Others less so. And ironically those who naturally have these attributes will be the high achievers who are likely to enjoy rapid promotion and will only be working on the front line with prisoners for a short time. What the Prison Service can do, though, is ensure that the training prison officers receive makes them aware of the need to develop their skills so that they have a keen sense of the nuances of life on the wing, and are regarded by prisoners as approachable and sympathetic.

Training in inter-personal skills

60.6 Prison officers undergo an eight-week basic training course. The first week is spent at the establishment they will be working at – as will the fifth week during which they get to know the establishment and see some of the things they have already learned being put into practice. The other six weeks are spent at the Prison Service Training College at Newbold Revel near Rugby in Warwickshire or at a local training centre. The training now concentrates much more than it did on helping officers to develop their inter-personal skills, and to look after the prisoners in their care decently and humanely. For example, they are told to treat prisoners as they would want their sons or daughters to be treated if they were in prison. But I do not believe that it is as focused as it might be on some of the key attributes which officers need. For example, the circumstances of Zahid's murder are used in one of the sessions to get trainees to think how the tragedy might have been averted if staff had acted differently. One of the themes explored is "the importance of using inter-personal skills and interacting with prisoners". That includes looking out for signs that individual prisoners may be a risk to others. But trainees are not at the same time being told that two of the critical lessons to be learned *from what happened to Zahid* are the need to put themselves into the shoes of those prisoners who might be at risk and to see things from their point of view, and the need to give prisoners confidence, so that they know that officers are there to advise them if need be. It may be that the lessons to be learned from Zahid's murder will be clearer now that this report is being published. But I do not believe that it should have required this report for the desirability of officers to develop these particular skills to be emphasised.

60.7 One way of getting an insight into the ways prisoners think is by ex-offenders having an input into prison officers' basic training. Indeed, anything which tells trainees about real life on the wings before they experience it themselves is a good thing – and prison life from the vantage point of the prisoner is a critical part of the equation. I know how much I was helped in this Inquiry by having two advisers who could tell me about the real world of prisons. And the Inspectorate has used ex-offenders as members of its inspection teams. There may be logistical difficulties about getting people from outside the Prison Service to commit themselves sufficiently in advance to take part in training sessions, but these problems should be capable of being resolved. It goes without saying that very many ex-offenders would be wholly unsuitable for a role of this kind, but Mr Wheatley said that he could think of some ex-offenders he could use.

> ### Recommendation 63
> That part of the basic training course for new prison officers which focuses on the development of their inter-personal skills should be reviewed in the light of this report and the lessons to be learned from Zahid's murder. In particular, two of the key attributes required of the prison officer should be stressed. They are the ability to pick up on what is happening on the wing, which prisoners pose a risk to other inmates, and what prisoners might be worried about, and the ability to earn the respect of the prisoners on the wing so that they are prepared to confide in them without fear of it getting out.
>
> ### Recommendation 64
> Ex-offenders should be used to give trainees an insight into prison life from the perspective of prisoners.

60.8 The length of the basic training course was discussed at one of the seminars the Inquiry held. The length of the course is driven by the resources available to fund it, not by the need to get officers into overcrowded prisons quickly to relieve the pressure on existing staff. But is eight weeks sufficiently long to arm the new recruit with the necessary skills to be able to operate effectively on the wings?* This is one of the topics referred to earlier which cannot be properly addressed without the Inquiry becoming an investigation into a root and branch reform of the Prison Service, and going far beyond its limited terms of reference. But my instincts are that although the course might benefit from being a week or two longer – indeed one of the trainers who gave the Inquiry a presentation about what the course involves thought that it could do with another week – a course in excess of 10 weeks is likely to be counter-productive. I have touched on this issue before. There is a limit to what trainee prison officers can be expected to absorb in a training course which concentrates on the practical application of basic skills. After 8–10 weeks trainees will be itching to put what they have learned into practice. And the longer the basic training course is, the more theoretical it is likely to become. That could make new recruits vulnerable to manipulation by some of the dinosaurs still in the Prison Service – the "conscientious objectors" to the decency agenda who have not been able to adapt to the changing culture within the Prison Service – who will tell new recruits things like: "Forget what you've learned in basic training. This is the real world. This is how

---

* The point was also made that very few officers fail the course. The Prison Service says that this is because those who are unsuitable to be prison officers will have been weeded out at job simulation assessment centres.

things are done." That is not to say that their learning should end when they complete basic training. Going on to the wing is itself a steep learning curve, and new recruits must appreciate that learning by on-the-job experience is just as important – maybe even more so – as going through basic training. No doubt that is drummed into them.

60.9 The job prison officers do is not one which requires them to be particularly gifted academically. The skills which make a good prison officer are an ability to get on with people, an ability to be decisive, an ability to think quickly and keep your cool when confronted by something unexpected, a sense of when to be robust and when to be tolerant, a sense of when to be firm and when to make light of things, and an ability to defuse a situation by humour or reasonableness before things get confrontational and ugly. Ultimately they cannot be taught, but trainees can be told what is expected of them so that they can build on the training they receive to develop their own "jailcraft".

Personal officers

60.10 The context in which the most effective work with prisoners can be done on a daily basis is the personal officer scheme. There is no mandatory requirement for an establishment to have such a scheme, though most of the prisons the Inquiry visited had one. If an establishment does not have one, it must have what the relevant Prison Service Order called "a group officer scheme" or "a shared working arrangement". No description of how they were supposed to work was given.

60.11 The two establishments visited by the Inquiry which did not have a personal officer scheme were the two local prisons. That reflected their view that their high turnover of prisoners made a proper personal officer scheme unworkable. One of these prisons, Pentonville, had a scheme nominally in place, but the way it was supposed to work was never put in writing, and it did not operate in practice. Lack of resources and competing priorities were cited as the reasons for that in addition to the high turnover of prisoners. Instead, the landing officer was the personal officer for all prisoners on the landing, but there were far too many of them for one officer to be their personal officer. In any event, since officers took turns to be the landing officer, there was no continuity in who a particular inmate's personal officer might be. The other local prison, Wormwood Scrubs, was not dissimilar. Each wing had what the establishment called "support officers". Since Wormwood Scrubs did not have a dedicated unit for vulnerable prisoners, their principal role was to ensure that such inmates were not exposed to undue risks. But they were not matched to particular prisoners. So again there was no continuity in who a particular prisoner's support officer might be.

60.12 I remain unpersuaded that it is not possible to operate a simple personal officer scheme even in a busy local prison. The high turnover of prisoners means that the time for personal officers to get to know the people they are responsible for will often be quite short. Inmates could be released or moved on elsewhere before they have been able to build up a relationship with their personal officer. But that should not prevent members of staff getting to know them while they are there. And anything is better than officers not being matched to particular prisoners. If an inmate has a particular officer as their personal officer, at the very least that officer can be the prisoner's point of contact with members of staff.

60.13 The other problem in busy local prisons is said to be that officers have so much else to do that finding the time for personal officer work is a luxury they cannot afford. Without wishing to minimise the many calls on a prison officer's time in a local prison, I do not believe that no time can be devoted to personal officer work. A couple of minutes with a prisoner – perhaps a couple of times a week – to find out how things are going is all that is needed to let the prisoner know that there is someone there looking out for them. It is different, of course, if the prisoner has a particular problem. The personal officer will have to devote the time necessary to help them sort it out. But that aside, the work of the personal officer is not so burdensome that profiled time needs to be set aside for it. So although I accept that the realities of a busy local prison make personal officer schemes less effective than elsewhere, there is still a place for them.

60.14 Effective personal officer work involves quality interaction with prisoners. That is less achievable if the regime is such that prisoners spend unduly long periods in their cell and correspondingly less time on association. The opportunity for quality time for prisoners can also be limited if officers are worked off their feet. It is important in these circumstances for officers not to spread their time too thinly with the result that they do not have the time to do anything really constructive with anyone. That may result in prisoners having to take turns in getting access to their personal officers, but that is better than time being squandered by personal officers devoting what little time they have to too many prisoners.

> **Recommendation 65**
> It should be mandatory for all establishments to have a personal officer scheme. That includes busy local prisons, although if time for personal officer work is limited, it should be used constructively.

60.15 Even in those establishments which operate a personal officer scheme, there are wide variations in practice. Feltham's approach of assigning a personal officer to a group of cells rather than matching the officer to individual prisoners is not uncommon, although some of the establishments the Inquiry visited assigned personal officers to particular prisoners. Feltham's practice is not a good one. If the inmate changes cell, they will have a new personal officer, and continuity of advice and support will be broken. And if a prisoner knows that their cellmate has the same personal officer, they might be less forthcoming about any concerns they have about their cellmate. These problems are less likely to arise in training prisons, since many prisoners there have single cells and they tend to remain in the same cell for a long time. But it is better practice for personal officers to be assigned to particular prisoners rather than to a group of cells, and that should be the case across the prison estate.

60.16 It is necessary for establishments to cater for times when the personal officer is not at work. Feltham's practice is to assign two officers to each cell to provide continuity in the absence of one of them. But unless their shift patterns and leave are co-ordinated, there are times when neither of them are on duty. A better practice is the one adopted at Lancaster Farms. There, each wing has three or four teams of personal officers. A prisoner is assigned to a particular personal officer, but if that officer is not on duty, the prisoner is advised to speak to any of the other officers in the team if they have a problem or want to raise something. There are three or four officers in each team, and inmates know which officers are in which team because the teams are colour-coded, and prisoners are provided with a cell card matching the appropriate colour.

60.17 There are different views about the role of the personal officer. The Inquiry was told that at Feltham their role was "to gain a one-to-one relationship with the lad… you're the first point of contact for them… they expect us to give them advice and support". Elsewhere, the role was variously described as "assisting with any problems they may have", "a focal point for prisoners to turn to with any problems", and "midway between being the first port of call for prisoners and being a more pro-active confidant or friend". And at Hindley, in addition to being "a reference point for any problems", personal officers are "encouraged to take on a pastoral role", although a balance has to be struck between approachability and security.

60.18 The role of the personal officer needs to be spelt out so that everyone has a clear idea of what is expected of them. It is much more than a prisoner's first point of contact if they have a problem or want to raise something, though it is that as well. The role is a pastoral one, checking up on the prisoners in their care to see whether anything is troubling them, getting to know them so that they can sense when they are dispirited and need cheering up, and providing them with an outlet for getting things off their chest. In short, the role is to build up the sort of relationship which will enable prisoners in their charge to confide in them when need be, while at the same time maintaining appropriate boundaries with them. All of this should be recorded in each establishment's personal officer scheme. The Prison Service should publish a model scheme, which should be regarded as having been adopted by any establishment which does not produce one of its own.

60.19 Before taking on the role of personal officer, prison officers should receive some training to prepare them for the task. The Prison Service says that the skills required for personal officer work are now "threaded through" an officer's basic training. That has only recently been introduced, but from the Prison Service's description of it, I doubt whether it is sufficient to prepare staff for personal officer work itself. Dedicated personal officer training is needed. Since the abolition of mandatory training in 2003, and the introduction in 2004 of programmes of continuing training to be delivered locally, the officer's establishment is the obvious place for training in personal officer work to be given.

Recommendation 66

Personal officers should be assigned to individual prisoners, not to a group of cells. They should be members of a small team, so that when a prisoner's personal officer is not on duty, the prisoner can approach another member of the team.

Recommendation 67

The role of the personal officer should be clearly defined in each establishment's personal officer scheme. The Prison Service should publish a model scheme, which should be regarded as having been adopted by every establishment which does not produce one of its own.

> **Recommendation 68**
> Before officers begin personal officer work, they should receive training locally on what the work involves.

60.20 There is one other point which should be made. A closed environment like a prison wing is paradoxically a very public place. Because so many people work and live in close proximity to each other, it is difficult to keep things under wraps. The impression I got when I spent time on a wing was that there was little sense of the need to be discreet. Staff as well as prisoners shouted things across the wing. Everything was for public consumption. That may mean it is difficult for an officer to have a really private conversation with a prisoner, at which the prisoner can truly open up. But if personal officer work is to be really effective, inmates have to be absolutely confident that what they say is not going to get out. That does not mean that officers cannot share with other staff information they are given by prisoners for whom they are responsible. But it does mean that inmates have to be reassured that what they are saying will not go beyond those members of staff who need to be told about it.

Whistleblowing

60.21 I have said elsewhere in this report that there will occasionally be times when prison officers treat prisoners inappropriately. That is inevitable in an organisation the size of the Prison Service. Instances of brutality and serious mistreatment of inmates on the part of prison officers occur from time to time. It is important that when they do, they are reported so that the perpetrators can be dealt with. If officers know that any mistreatment of prisoners is likely to be reported, they will be less likely to mistreat them.

60.22 But breaking ranks is very difficult. The bond between prison officers is a strong one. One commentator said that prison officers were

> "… a close-knit group of mainly family men – looking to each other for social life and support, feeling misunderstood, unappreciated and looking at life with a semi-humorous, semi-bitter cynical pessimism – a group where breaking ranks in any way is very difficult, because the bonds are strong, professionally, socially and culturally."[*]

---

* Stern, *Bricks of Shame*, 1989, p.67

That was written at about the time prison officers ceased to live in small communities in quarters provided by the Prison Service close to the prison where they worked. Their social lives now are less dominated by their colleagues. But prison officers and their families still mix with each other, and the overwhelming pressure not to "shop" someone you know well cannot be underestimated.

60.23 There are a host of other reasons which might make officers reluctant to "grass" on their colleagues. No-one likes to be seen as someone who rocks the boat or as someone who is prepared to let his colleagues down. Would-be whistleblowers* tend to rally round a colleague in trouble. There may well be pressures to ostracise the person who has put a fellow officer in that position, and to leave the person in no doubt where their loyalties should have been.** And if the officer thinks nothing is likely to come of their reporting another officer's wrongdoing, they may well decide to do nothing about it. That feeling of impotence will only increase their own sense of alienation.

60.24 How to combat these problems was considered at some length in the report of the Shipman Inquiry. It was noted that devising a system to encourage whistleblowing was relatively easy. The real challenge was to develop a culture where every member of every team felt a sense of responsibility for the actions of the others. The aim was to create a climate in which the person responsible for the wrongdoing would be regarded as letting the team down and not the whistleblower. The report stated that it was generally acknowledged that raising concerns within an organisation was preferable to disclosure, normally on an anonymous basis, to outside regulators or the media. And it applauded the passing of the Public Interest Disclosure Act in 1998, which was designed to give employees sufficient confidence to raise their concerns internally, and to encourage external disclosure only when internal disclosure was inappropriate or unlikely to be fruitful. The report suggested a number of amendments which could be made to the Act to encourage whistleblowing even further.

60.25 The Prison Service has responded to this important statutory initiative in a positive way. A Prison Service Order issued in February 2003 on Professional Standards included a chapter on reporting wrongdoing.

---

* A whistleblower used to be regarded as someone who brought to the attention of the public some reprehensible behaviour within the organisation in which they worked or with which they were connected in some way. It is now used to describe someone who brings the wrongdoing to the attention of the organisation itself. That is the sense in which I have used the term in this report.

**There are recorded instances of officers being sent grass in the post as a sign of what other people think of them.

Staff are required to report wrongdoing by others in the Prison Service which they either witness or become aware of. A reporting wrongdoing hotline was established, and those who call it are assured that any requests for confidentiality will be honoured, except when it conflicts with a countervailing public interest, such as the prevention or prosecution of serious crime or if disclosure is required by statute or ordered by a court. It emphasised that the victimisation and bullying of those who report wrongdoing are disciplinary offences, and it underlined the support which whistleblowers can expect from the Prison Service, and the protection they will receive against any form of victimisation, provided that the report is made "in good faith" and there is "a reasonable belief" on the part of the member of staff making the report that the information is true. This proviso mirrored the language of the 1998 Act.

60.26 These measures were supplemented by a further Prison Service Order issued in June 2005, which reinforced the message of the previous order, and outlined the procedures for members of staff to report instances of wrongdoing, including confidential access to appropriate levels of management outside the normal management line, where the suspected wrongdoing involves senior members of staff. The Prison Service has also recognised the need to promote a culture which values integrity above everything else, and which rejects corruption, dishonesty and inappropriate behaviour wherever it may be. To that end, it has created the Professional Standards Unit to detect and prevent corruption, including inappropriate behaviour on the part of members of staff. Members of the unit are available to deal with any information it receives, whether in confidence or not.

60.27 For the most part, these measures meet the key elements of an effective whistleblowing policy as recommended by Public Concern at Work, a small but influential pressure group described in the report of the Shipman Inquiry as having done a great deal of work to promote the legal and cultural climate in which people feel confident about raising their concerns, and endorsed by the Nolan Committee on Standards in Public Life. But to be even more effective, the Prison Service's policy should identify the most appropriate way for staff, in an exceptional case, to get confidential advice from an independent outsider and to raise their concerns outside the Prison Service. It should also ensure that the members of staff of companies who contract with the Prison Service, such as escort contractors and those responsible for the running of the contracted-out establishments, have access to the Prison Service's whistleblowing policy. And to ensure that the whistleblowing policy is not abused, it should be made clear that making a false and malicious allegation is a disciplinary offence for which dismissal from the Prison Service may be an appropriate sanction.

> ### Recommendation 69
> The Prison Service's policy on whistleblowing should identify the most appropriate way for staff, in an exceptional case, to get confidential advice from an independent outsider and to raise their concerns outside the Prison Service. It should also ensure that the members of staff of companies who contract with the Prison Service, such as escort contractors and those responsible for the running of the contracted-out establishments, have access to the Prison Service's whistleblowing policy.
>
> ### Recommendation 70
> Making a false and malicious allegation that wrongdoing has taken place should be expressly stated to be a disciplinary offence, for which dismissal from the Prison Service may be an appropriate sanction.

60.28 Ultimately, requiring staff to report wrongdoing would be ineffective in the absence of any sanctions for the failure to report wrongdoing. So it is encouraging that in the Prison Service Order on Conduct and Discipline issued at about the same time as the Prison Service Order on Professional Standards, the wilful failure to report acts of serious misconduct by other members of staff was identified as misconduct which might attract disciplinary action. The obligation to report wrongdoing and the designation of a failure to do so as a disciplinary offence have now been in existence for long enough for research to be conducted on how effective these measures have been, by comparing the number of instances of reported wrongdoing before and after these measures were implemented. If the research shows that they have not resulted in a significant increase in wrongdoing being reported, further thought will have to be given to the problem.

> ### Recommendation 71
> Research should be conducted on how effective the obligation to report wrongdoing – and the designation of a failure to do so as a disciplinary offence – has been. This should be done by comparing the number of instances of reported wrongdoing before and after these measures were implemented.

60.29 I return to the need to develop a culture where every member of the Prison Service feels a sense of responsibility for the actions of their colleagues. It has to be acknowledged that wrongdoing is less likely to be reported at establishments where staff have little pride in their work and lack respect for senior managers. If, for example, staff think that their managers are full of "woolly, liberal ideas" and are out of touch with "the real world", or if they think that senior management has lost a sense of what front-line prison officers have to face on the wings every day, they will tend to side with their colleagues and be less inclined to report any wrongdoing on their part. Conversely, if staff take a pride in their work, they will be more inclined to report bad behaviour because they would be more likely to regard it as undermining the goals they are striving to achieve. So ultimately the key to reducing the reluctance to report recalcitrant colleagues is by encouraging officers to take pride in their work, by showing them that management is alive to their problems and their needs, and by instilling in them a sense that they and senior management are working together towards common goals.

60.30 It was accepted at the Inquiry's seminar at which whistleblowing was discussed – even by those critical of the Prison Service – that much had been done by the Prison Service to encourage the reporting of wrongdoing. But it would be naïve to suppose that responsible officers always get the support and protection they need. There is the well-known recent case of the officer at Wakefield Prison who was awarded a very substantial sum by an employment tribunal following her enforced resignation after she had reported wholly inappropriate behaviour on the part of a principal officer. This is an area in which there is no room for complacency. Although plainly less common than in the past, it is impossible to say how prevalent the non-reporting of wrongdoing now is. All that can be said is that the gulf between policy and practice could still be considerable.

Chapter 61: Mentally disordered prisoners

The issues the Inquiry addressed

61.1 Prisons have a very large number of inmates with mental disorders. The survey carried out by the Office for National Statistics showed that as many as nine prisoners in 10 arrive at establishments with mental health problems of some kind. Those suffering from acute mental illness can be transferred to secure hospitals, and prisoners with severe personality disorders which make them particularly dangerous can be held in secure hospitals and dedicated units under the Dangerous and Severe Personality Disorder Programme. But the overwhelming majority of prisoners with mental disorders are held on ordinary location, and the risk they pose to staff and other inmates depends on the nature of their condition and how they are managed in the light of it.

61.2 The care and treatment in prison of mentally disordered offenders is a huge subject. The Inquiry was alive to the many issues which it raises. One was highlighted by Stewart's personality disorder. We have seen that a prisoner's condition needs to be treatable if they are to be transferred to a secure hospital. The conventional wisdom is that, although you can work on the manifestations of the disorder, personality disorders themselves are not treatable. The result has been that classifying a prisoner as suffering from a personality disorder has been regarded as a "diagnosis of exclusion" from NHS services. That raises the question whether the requirement of treatability in sections 47 and 48 of the Mental Health Act 1983 should be removed, and whether the definition of mental disorder should be widened. Another issue relates to the number of places in dedicated units or secure hospitals for such offenders. If it is accepted that more places should be found for them, how can that be funded in such a way as to minimise the effect on existing services? And what practical steps can be taken to speed up the transfer to secure hospitals of those prisoners who it has been decided should go there?

61.3 But it was important that the Inquiry did not bite off more than it could chew, and that it remained focused on its terms of reference. These issues could not be tackled by an Inquiry concentrating on prisoner-on-prisoner in-cell attacks. Just as the Inquiry was not addressing how offenders came into prison in the first place, so too it was not addressing why many of them came to remain there rather than be transferred elsewhere. The Inquiry's focus was on how prisoners with mental disorders can be identified, how the risks they pose can be assessed, and how they can best be managed on the wings so that the threat they pose to their cellmates is minimised. These are the issues addressed in this chapter, although some preliminary comment about the current state of mental healthcare in prisons is called for.

The need for change

61.4 The care of prisoners with mental health problems was unacceptably poor at the time of Zahid's murder. They were shuffled between the segregation unit if they misbehaved and the healthcare centre where they were dumped if they were difficult to manage. There they were housed alongside other prisoners who had been classed as vulnerable, often in banks of cells with little or no recreation or association. The emphasis was on the provision of cellular accommodation separate from the rest of the establishment, with little recognition of the need for a therapeutic service. There were many dedicated staff committed to doing what they could for the mentally disordered prisoners in their care, but it was not uncommon for others to adopt an uncaring, aloof and disconnected approach as a coping mechanism for the circumstances in which they found themselves.

61.5 Two factors contributed to this shocking state of affairs. The first was the high level of psychiatric morbidity in the prison population. The second was that mentally disordered prisoners did not represent a static group. Very many of them were serving relatively short sentences, and those serving longer sentences were often moved from one establishment to another – in the hope that a change of scene might calm them down. This made it exceptionally difficult for staff – often working in cramped and difficult conditions and under considerable pressures of time – to determine in a structured way the particular needs of the prisoners coming into their care.

61.6 This assessment of the problems which mentally disordered prisoners faced is not mine. It is based on what John Boyington said he found when he joined the Prison Service as Head of the Prison Health Task Force in March 2000. It mirrored the findings in the report of a working group from the Prison Service and the NHS Executive published in March 1999, and in *Changing the Outlook*, a document published by the Department of Health and the Prison Service in December 1999.

61.7 But structural change was already in the air. In 1996, the Inspectorate noted that healthcare in prisons did not match up to NHS standards. They said that prisoners requiring healthcare should be seen as patients, and should be given the same level of healthcare as that provided in the community. That led to the creation in April 2000 of a formal partnership between the Prison Service and the NHS for the provision of healthcare across the prison estate. In April 2003, budgetary responsibility for healthcare in publicly run prisons was transferred to the Department of Health, and from April 2004 Primary Care Trusts began to assume responsibility for commissioning public healthcare services in prisons in their localities. Responsibility for commissioning these services was due to have been completed by April 2006.

61.8 These structural changes were accompanied by initiatives in the field of mental health. *Changing the Outlook* required all establishments and their local NHS partners to have completed a detailed review of their mental health needs by September 2002. They were to identify any gaps between the mental health services available at the establishment and the kind of service contemplated by *Changing the Outlook*, and to develop action plans to implement the changes needed to fill those gaps. The principal means by which this objective was to be achieved was the introduction into prisons of multi-disciplinary mental health in-reach teams. These were designed to provide mental health services for prisoners along the lines of the community mental health outreach teams, which provide services in the community at large. These in-reach teams were due to have been progressively introduced into all the establishments in the prison estate by the end of the 2005/06 financial year, and NHS investment into the project is now in the region of £20m a year. The National Institute for Mental Health in England is working on a comprehensive national prison mental health programme. In the meantime, it published in July 2005 a document which laid down best practice templates to guide those who provide and commission mental health services for prisoners.

61.9 Prison may provide some offenders with a structure which enables them to cope better with the pressures of life, because the need to make everyday decisions is removed for the most part. But for the overwhelming majority of inmates, prison is a very stressful place, and will exacerbate any underlying mental health problems. It is doubtful whether the important initiatives taken in recent years will effectively meet prisoners' mental health needs. Mr Boyington accepted at one of the Inquiry's seminars that "we are scratching the surface of the real limits of need within the prison environment and a lot more needs to be done and that will require additional resources". And concerns have been expressed in some quarters – notably by the POA – that the assumption of responsibility by Primary Care Trusts for commissioning primary healthcare services in prisons will militate against a satisfactory working partnership between custodial and healthcare staff. But the presence in every establishment of multi-disciplinary mental health in-reach teams, along the lines of similar outreach teams in the community, is obviously a very significant development. Their composition depends on the funding allocated to each prison, which is itself based on the profile of each prison's population. A comprehensive review of the quality of care provided to inmates with mental health problems and its effectiveness – including those with personality disorders – should be conducted once these initiatives have had a chance to bed down.* It would not be appropriate for me to say when that review should take place. The Prison Service, the Department of Health and the Inspectorate are all in a better position to make that judgement than me, but the undoubted changes which have taken place should be evaluated to assess whether the benefits they were designed to usher in have indeed been brought about.

> **Recommendation 72**
>
> A comprehensive review of the quality of care provided to prisoners with mental health problems and its effectiveness should be conducted once the changes introduced since Zahid's murder have had a chance to work.

Identifying mentally disordered prisoners

61.10 The initial opportunity to identify prisoners with mental health problems is the first reception health screen. Since Zahid's murder, the first reception health screen questionnaire has been revised. In addition to those charged with murder or manslaughter, prisoners who give certain answers to particular questions must be referred to a mental health professional on the healthcare team – who can be a nurse, doctor, occupational therapist, psychologist or social worker. These questions relate to whether the inmate has ever received treatment from a psychiatrist outside prison, or ever received medication for any mental health problems, or ever tried to harm themselves outside prison. The professional to whom the prisoner is referred will then decide whether a mental health assessment needs to be made. If it does, the inmate will be referred to the in-reach team for that assessment to be carried out. Just like a GP in the community, the in-reach team can refer a prisoner to a psychiatrist, whether a general or a forensic one, where the team has particular concerns about the prisoner.

---

* Important work on this topic has recently been done by the Prison Reform Trust in its *Troubled Inside* series of reports on responding to the mental health needs of prisoners.

61.11 I am uneasy that a prisoner with a history of harming themselves in prison, but not on the outside, is not automatically referred to a mental health professional on the healthcare team. I appreciate that the pressures to which vulnerable prisoners may be subjected in prison may make them more prone to harm themselves, but instances of self-harm, wherever they take place, could be suggestive of mental health problems. I was not told of any particular reason why a history of self-harm merely in prison did not trigger an automatic referral to a mental health professional, and unless there are particular reasons which have not been disclosed to me, the questionnaire should be further revised to cater for such a referral.

61.12 Prisoners with a personality disorder may well not have had a history of self-harm or psychiatric treatment or medication for mental health problems. So they will not be referred to a mental health professional on first reception. But the possibility that they have a personality disorder may well emerge when they are first seen by healthcare staff. From the things they say and their body language, they may well present with the outward manifestations of a personality disorder. That is one of the things healthcare staff in reception should be looking out for. So if the member of staff completing the questionnaire senses that there is something not quite right about the prisoner and suspects that they may have a personality disorder – or mental illness which has not been picked up before – the questionnaire should require the member of staff to refer the inmate to a mental health professional.

> ### Recommendation 73
> The first reception health screen questionnaire should be revised so as to trigger a referral to a mental health professional on the healthcare team even if the prisoner has only self-harmed in prison. A referral should also be triggered where the prisoner's behaviour is such that the healthcare officer completing the questionnaire considers it desirable.

Identifying the risk

61.13 The primary function of mental health professionals is to diagnose the condition of the patient who is referred to them, and to consider how the patient's mental health needs should be addressed. But in a penal setting, they should also assess the risk the prisoner poses – whether to themselves, or to staff and other inmates. As we have seen, both

Professor Gunn and Professor Maden agree on the important role mental health professionals have in the assessment of risk, even though Professor Maden thought that this role was limited to people suffering from mental illness, and that they had little to offer in the assessment of risk of people suffering from a personality disorder. So if a prisoner is referred to a mental health professional on the healthcare team – or if they are then referred to the in-reach team for a mental health assessment – it is important that the question of whether they pose a risk to staff or other inmates is carefully considered.

> ### Recommendation 74
> When prisoners are referred for a mental health assessment, the assessment should address the risk which they pose to staff and other inmates.

Mental health awareness training

61.14 If a prisoner is not identified following the first reception health screen as having mental health problems, the chances are that if the possibility is to become apparent at all, it will only happen while they are on ordinary location. That makes it all the more important for all prison officers to have some awareness about mental health – not just to enable them to spot the prisoner who might have mental health problems, but also to be able to manage them more effectively on the wing.

61.15 Since Zahid's murder – although not as a result of it – the Prison Service commissioned the Institute of Health and Community Studies at the University of Bournemouth to develop a mental health awareness training programme. The course lasts for two days – three days if officers are also training to become ACCT (Assessment, Care in Custody and Teamwork) assessors, which is a new programme for the care of vulnerable prisoners. Ideally, all front-line staff will go on this course, but at the time of writing it is only being provided to staff at those establishments with in-reach teams in place – and even then only to officers training to become ACCT assessors. The trainer's manual and the manual for those attending the course are impressive. Participants are told what the symptoms of various disorders are, what behavioural traits are associated with them, and how prisoners who are suffering from them are likely to present. They are given guidance on how to respond to such inmates so as not to exacerbate their condition or provoke harmful or disruptive episodes. Above all, they are told about the practical and suitable interventions which can be made to integrate the prisoner into life on the wing. For the many front-line officers who currently are not going on this course, a booklet has been produced, which explains the principal components of the course.

61.16 It was anticipated that by the end of 2005, 765 members of staff would have been on the course. That is a sufficient number to begin to assess how effective the course is. As is usual with occupational training, participants are no doubt asked to complete a questionnaire identifying what parts of the course they found helpful, and in what ways it could be improved. This data should now be analysed, and consideration given to improving the effectiveness of the course in the light of that data. Resources and staff deployment permitting, the availability of the course to other full-time officers should be increased.

> Recommendation 75
>
> The responses of those members of staff who have attended the mental health awareness training course should be analysed to determine whether the course can be improved. The number of front-line staff attending the course should be increased, resources and staff deployment permitting.

61.17 Although personality disorders are addressed on this course, a dedicated training course on personality disorders is currently being developed. The course will be based on the National Institute of Mental Health's Personality Disorder Capabilities Framework, *Breaking the Cycle of Rejection*. But until course materials are available, the effectiveness of the course cannot be assessed.

Management on the wings

61.18 How prisoners with mental health problems should be managed on the wings depends on the nature of their disorder. Those who suffer from an anxiety state should be encouraged to take exercise and engage in purposeful activity – both to distract them from what is causing their anxiety and to help them build up confidence. Staff should discuss their anxieties with them, so that if they stem from, say, a fear of being bullied, steps can be taken to reduce that fear. On the other hand, prisoners suffering from a psychotic illness should have a named member of the healthcare team responsible for liaising with and advising the officer in charge of the wing on the prisoner's care. A multi-disciplinary plan for action should be agreed, which includes:

- locating the prisoner with a carefully selected cellmate

- identifying how the prisoner should spend their day

- ensuring that they have regular access to their medication, and having contingency arrangements in place in case they have not taken it

- advising staff on how to deal with them, including avoiding confronting or criticising them unless that is necessary to prevent harmful or disruptive behaviour, responding to them gently and with reassurance, giving them concise instructions, and making sure that the body language of staff is clear and thoughtful.

61.19 These examples are not mine. They come from the manual for the participants in the mental health awareness training course. There are many other examples given in the manual, and they cover the various disorders from which prisoners will be suffering. Taken together, they represent a template of best practice, worked out by professionals in the field, for managing such prisoners on the wing in terms of their mental health needs and integrating them into the life of the wing. These are precisely the things which all staff on the wing need to know about, and yet they are not published anywhere. So staff who have not gone on the course will not be aware of them, unless they have read and absorbed the contents of the booklet summarising the principal components of the course – provided, of course, that the summary includes advice on how prisoners should be managed on the wing. Reading the booklet is therefore critical, and profiled time should be set aside for officers to do that.

> **Recommendation 76**
>
> Profiled time should be set aside for staff to read the booklet explaining the main components of the mental health awareness training course. The booklet should include advice given on the course about how prisoners with particular disorders should be managed on the wing. That advice should be published and made freely available.

61.20 But the Inquiry's focus was not on how such prisoners have to be managed to meet their mental health needs – important though that is – but on how they have to be managed so that the threat they pose to staff and other inmates can be minimised. That will vary from prisoner to prisoner, but the measures identified earlier which could have been taken for the management on ordinary location of Stewart will apply to many prisoners with mental disorders. They are:

- not placing such a prisoner in a shared cell

- if the prisoner is to share a cell, carefully selecting their cellmate

- ensuring that, whatever difficulties there may be in operating a proper personal officer scheme, such a prisoner has a personal officer who is fully aware of their background and who makes a particular effort to get to know them and keeps an eye on their state of mind

- checking the correspondence and searching the cell of such a prisoner more frequently and carefully than would otherwise have been the case

- ensuring, again regardless of the difficulties which might be faced in providing a good regime for all prisoners in the establishment, that such a prisoner is appropriately occupied with, for example, work, education or offending behaviour programmes

- keeping a closer watch over material such as films, to which such a prisoner has access, and exercising control over their suitability

- checking on NOMIS or with the Security Department about the existence of any useful intelligence about such a prisoner and what is known about their previous behaviour in prison.

Recommendation 77

The measures which should be taken to minimise the risk which a mentally disordered prisoner on ordinary location poses to staff and other inmates includes:

- not placing such a prisoner in a shared cell

- if such a prisoner is to share a cell, carefully selecting their cellmate

- ensuring that, whatever difficulties there may be in operating a proper personal officer scheme, such a prisoner has a personal officer who is fully aware of their background and who makes a particular effort to get to know them and keeps an eye on their state of mind

- checking the correspondence and searching the cell of such a prisoner more frequently and carefully than would otherwise have been the case

- ensuring, again regardless of the difficulties which might be faced in providing a good regime for all prisoners in the establishment, that such a prisoner is appropriately occupied with, for example, work, education or offending behaviour programmes

- keeping a closer watch over material such as films, to which such a prisoner has access, and exercising control over their suitability

- checking on NOMIS or with the Security Department about the existence of any useful intelligence about such a prisoner and what is known about their previous behaviour in prison.

Sharing information

61.21 How prisoners with mental disorders are managed on the wing will also depend – at least in part – on what officers are told by healthcare staff about their condition. If officers are told that a prisoner has a condition which makes them, say, unpredictable, or liable to lose their temper, or a risk to staff or other inmates, they will manage the prisoner with that in mind.

61.22 In the past healthcare workers in prison have been very reluctant to pass on information about prisoners to operational staff for fear of breaking the rule that personal information about a prisoner acquired in the course of a professional relationship should be kept confidential unless the prisoner consents to its disclosure. The problem has arisen where the consent for the release of such information has been withheld, or in those exceptional circumstances where the prisoner has not been competent to give their consent. That does not mean that the information can never be disclosed. It can be disclosed if the public interest – and that of the prisoner – in keeping such information about them confidential is outweighed by some other public interest which favours disclosure.

61.23 The difficulty is in identifying the particular circumstances when a countervailing public interest justifies disclosure of such information without the prisoner's consent. The only guidance given by the relevant

Prison Service Instruction, which was issued in May 2002, is that disclosure is justified

> "... when the information is required by statute or court order, where disclosure is essential to protect the [prisoner], or someone else from risk of death or serious harm, or for the prevention, detection or prosecution of serious crime."

This is fine so far as it goes, but healthcare staff need additional guidance to help them apply that principle effectively in the course of their work. No additional guidance is given in the current information pack, *SECURE*, about information rights in the context of prison healthcare.*

61.24 Some additional advice is to be found in one of the guides to good practice published in 2004 by Nacro, *Information sharing: challenges and opportunities*. A list of the "criteria for sharing information when consent has not been given" includes situations where there is:

- a history of suicide attempts or serious self-harm

- a current risk of suicide attempts or serious self-harm

- a history of violence or an earlier assessment that the prisoner is prone to violence

- a significant and relevant medical history which may influence the current assessment of risk or decisions about the prisoner's management.

These are not really criteria for determining whether personal information should be disclosed. They are examples of when the circumstances outlined in the Prison Service Instruction might be triggered. So if a member of the healthcare staff believes that a prisoner poses a risk of serious harm to other prisoners, it would be open to the member of staff to conclude that disclosure of that fact was "essential to protect... someone else from... serious harm, or for the prevention... of serious crime". That would apply whether that belief was based on the prisoner's previous history of violence, or on their current behaviour, or on what they disclosed about themselves or their feelings to the member of staff.

61.25 An exercise of this kind calls for difficult judgements to be made by healthcare staff. But their task is not assisted by the lack of guidance on, for example, the degree of risk of serious harm which needs to be

---

* A similar information pack, *FOCUS*, concentrates on the juvenile estate.

present, or the kinds of harm which can be properly described as serious, or those crimes which can properly be classified as serious.* And even if it is necessary to disclose personal information about a prisoner in order to protect other prisoners who are at risk of harm from them, there is no guidance about the nature of the information which can be disclosed. Only the minimum information required to protect other prisoners from them can be disclosed. But does that mean that only the risk itself can be disclosed, or can the reasons which the member of the healthcare staff has for believing in the existence of the risk be disclosed as well? And if the reasons for believing that the prisoner poses a risk to other inmates can be disclosed, do those reasons only include those which may be discoverable from other sources, such as the prisoner's history of violence, or can they include those things which emerge as a result of the prisoner seeing the member of the healthcare staff, such as their behaviour and what they disclose about themselves or their feelings?

61.26 The fact is that in many cases it would be entirely appropriate for healthcare staff to inform officers on the wings that a prisoner poses a risk to other inmates, without saying why or disclosing the material on which that assessment was based. That needs to be clearly spelt out. I acknowledge that it is impossible to give such detailed guidance as will provide healthcare staff with the right answer in every case they encounter. Apart from anything else, much will depend on their personal judgement. But they have to be provided with a more comprehensive framework within which to work than currently exists, to enable them the better to decide when patient confidentiality can and should be overridden. The Prison Service should therefore prepare a readable guide, uncluttered by detailed explanations of statutory materials such as the Data Protection Act 1998 which the current information packs contain, and which clearly explains the circumstances in which personal information about a prisoner should be disclosed by healthcare staff to officers on the wings. A series of practical examples should be included, illustrating specific instances when disclosure should or should not be made.

Recommendation 78

The Prison Service should prepare a readable guide, which explains the circumstances in which personal information about a prisoner should be disclosed by healthcare staff to officers on the wing. The guide should contain practical examples of situations where disclosure should or should not be made.

---

* Buried in the information pack is a short list of examples of crimes which are regarded as serious, but the list contains only six offences, is illustrative only, and does not include many other offences to the person which are obviously serious, such as serious assault.

Chapter 62: Racism and religious intolerance

The Inquiry's focus

62.1 Racism in prisons is now high on the agenda – not simply because Zahid was the victim of a horrific murder in which his killer's virulent racism may have played a significant part, but also because the recognition of the Prison Service as institutionally racist has required it to address the problem urgently. Eradicating racism should be the Prison Service's priority. Religious intolerance, in particular the position of Muslims in prison, is another issue which has to be addressed – not merely because Zahid was a Muslim, but also because of the significant increase in Muslim prisoners in recent years, and the increased levels of Islamophobia in the wake of the attacks in the United States in September 2001, the "war on terrorism" and the London bombings of July 2005.

62.2 The Inquiry's focus on racism and religious intolerance has been on Feltham. As we have seen, I regarded my terms of reference as sufficiently wide to require me to investigate:

- whether the series of events which resulted in Stewart sharing a cell with Zahid, despite what was known about him, was in any way attributable to a collective organisational failure which was itself informed and shaped by the institutional racism with which Feltham was infected

- to the extent that there were shortcomings on the part of officers who had dealings with Stewart and Zahid, whether those shortcomings were acts of personal racism or attributable in any way to the culture of indifference and insensitivity which institutional racism breeds

- to the extent that those shortcomings were attributable to systemic failings, where responsibility for those systemic failings lay.

I have addressed those issues in earlier parts of the report.

62.3 But there was a limit to what an inquiry of this kind could do. It operated under two constraints. First, it was not equipped to investigate the present state of race relations in our prisons. It took three years for the CRE to produce its report, and that was based on just three prisons.* If the Inquiry had embarked on such an investigation itself, the publication of this report would have been put back for an unacceptably long time. In any event, an investigation as comprehensive as would have been

---

* Feltham, Brixton Prison in South London and Parc Prison in Cardiff.

necessary is far best left to professionals in the field. Secondly, there are many factors which contribute to a prison's poor performance, and which create the setting for violence on the part of prisoners to be more prevalent. Racism and religious intolerance are just two of them. If the Inquiry had investigated in its second phase where the Prison Service now is on these topics, and had considered what recommendations could be made for improvements in these areas, it would have had to address the many other things which make a prison unhealthy – however indirect their connection with prisoner-on-prisoner in-cell attacks may be. So the implications which racism and religious intolerance have for the safety of prisoners were never going to be the subject of detailed investigation in the second phase of the Inquiry.

62.4 It is not as if there has been no scrutiny of the Prison Service in this area. The performance of the Prison Service in the field of race relations is currently being monitored by the CRE. The action plan, *Implementing Race Equality: A Shared Strategy for Change*, which the Prison Service produced in partnership with the CRE, is the blueprint for the progress which the Prison Service is working towards. At the same time, the Inspectorate is watching developments closely. In December 2005, it published a review of race relations in prisons, in which it highlighted what it saw as the key areas which needed to be developed to implement the action plan effectively. Mr Ali, my adviser on race and diversity, has some interesting ideas of his own which have occurred to him in the course of the Inquiry, and he will be discussing these with the Prison Service and the CRE.

62.5 Having said all that, it has been possible for me to identify a number of issues which, while not specifically relating to the safety of prisoners so as to bring them directly within the Inquiry's terms of reference, are sufficiently connected with the Inquiry's work to justify some comment. But first it is necessary to summarise the latest work in this area.

Parallel Worlds

62.6 The Inspectorate's recent review of race relations in prison is called *Parallel Worlds*. The title was chosen to reflect the Inspectorate's conclusion that there is a profound disconnection between staff and prisoners, and within different groups of staff and prisoners, about race issues within prisons. Governors and non-BME race relations liaison officers believe that the regime operates fairly for the most part, although they recognise that more needs to be done. Non-BME staff tend to think that the needs of BME prisoners are being met, and they see racism as principally an issue between inmates. On the other hand, few BME staff think that their prison is tackling race effectively, although most believe that some progress has been made. A few speak of overt racism, and many talk of subtle racism on the part of non-BME colleagues, about which they are reluctant to complain. In some establishments, they do not feel they are sufficiently supported when they apply for promotion, and overwhelmingly they are looking for visible and robust support from senior managers.

62.7 The experience of BME prisoners mirrors the perceptions of BME staff. Most BME prisoners believe that racism is present in their establishments, manifesting itself in the different way they are treated by staff and the extent to which they have access to the facilities the prison has to offer compared with non-BME inmates. The examples noted by the Inspectorate in its summary of its findings were the way prisoners are spoken to, searched and have their requests dealt with, or the length of time they have to wait for the things they want or need. Overall, they report poorer experiences than non-BME prisoners across all of the Inspectorate's four tests of a healthy prison – safety, respect, purposeful activity and resettlement. And the predominant concerns of BME inmates differ from each other. Fewer black prisoners than Asian prisoners think that staff treat them with respect, but more black prisoners than Asian prisoners feel safe in prison. For Asian prisoners, the reverse is the case, with more of them thinking that they are treated with respect, but with fewer of them feeling safe.

62.8 Beyond noting that its surveys of prisoners regularly and routinely show that BME prisoners have worse perceptions of their treatment than non-BME prisoners across many key areas of prison life, the Inspectorate did not express any view about whether these perceptions accurately reflected real differences of treatment between BME and non-BME prisoners. But it was concerned about the lack of information generated by the tools which could be expected to provide data about whether BME prisoners were getting a raw deal. One of those tools – the survey of prisoners measuring the quality of prison life – was found by the Inspectorate to be of very little value in determining the state of race relations in an establishment, as it is partly made up of non-BME prisoners' views about what BME prisoners are experiencing and how they are being treated. It could therefore create a false sense of confidence among prison governors.

62.9 The other tool is ethnic monitoring. But this too was found by the Inspectorate to have its limitations. It can only address outcomes rather than the way things are done, and can therefore miss areas where BME prisoners say they often experience racism or intolerance. In addition, there are many areas capable of being monitored but are not. For example, there is very little monitoring of access to offending behaviour or educational programmes, applications for transfers, release on temporary licence and resettlement opportunities. Moreover, some areas where ethnic monitoring takes place involve too few inmates for the results to be meaningful. Examples the report gives are those prisoners who are put on report or sent to segregation, and those who are released on home detention curfew or temporary licence, unless the establishment is carrying out these activities on a large scale. Finally, the Inspectorate referred to the "danger that ethnic monitoring is treated as a process to be satisfied rather than a means whereby managers inform themselves about the outcomes of decisions, policies and practices". No view was expressed whether that was actually happening or not, but it was another factor which contributed to ethnic monitoring being regarded of little value.

62.10 The two other areas specifically looked at by the Inspectorate were race relations management teams and formal complaints of racism. Meetings of race relations management teams were often irregular, and the breadth of representation and levels of attendance at them were poor. That suggested that race relations was not a management priority. Most worrying of all, action was clearly identified at such meetings and reliably followed up in only two of the 18 establishments visited, which suggests that meetings of race relations management teams are little more than the forum at which trends revealed by ethnic monitoring and the race relations incident log are discussed, along with operational issues relating to race relations. As for formal complaints of racism, the greatest number were complaints by prisoners about other prisoners, followed by complaints by prisoners that decisions made by staff about the regime were discriminatory. There were fewer numbers of complaints by prisoners about racist language used by staff, and by staff about racist language used by prisoners. But formal complaints of racism do not accurately reflect the level of such incidents. In almost three-quarters of the focus groups which the Inspectorate conducted, prisoners said that they would use the racist incident complaints system, but of those two-thirds said that they would only do so as a last resort. Some said this was because forms were not available, some expressed doubts about whether anyone would look at them, and others feared a backlash.* The report noted that some prisoners said that the process was too long-winded, but whether that was cited by them as a reason for not invoking it is unclear. The Inspectorate did not itself express a view about the quality of the investigation of complaints, but BME prisoners were found to be less likely than non-BME prisoners to believe that complaints are investigated fairly, with black prisoners being less happy than any other racial group. Complaints of racism can range, of course, from blatant examples of overt racism, through to discriminatory treatment, and at the lower end of the scale to favouritism based – maybe unconsciously – on ethnic origin. But the report did not identify which sort of complaints were perceived as being the least likely to be investigated fairly.

62.11 *Parallel Worlds* shows that although there has been some progress in recent years, there remains much work to be done. The existence of an action plan agreed with the CRE made it inappropriate, so the Inspectorate thought, for it to make recommendations of its own. Instead, it highlighted the key areas which in its view needed to be developed to implement the action plan effectively. I endorse those areas for development, and I turn to those topics on which I propose to add some comments of my own.

> Recommendation 79
>
> The Prison Service and the CRE should address the key areas for development identified by the Inspectorate in *Parallel Worlds* in managing the action plan, *Implementing Race Equality: A Shared Agenda for Change.*

Training on BME perspectives

62.12 *Parallel Worlds* reported "a remarkable lack of insight on the part of some white staff" into the perspectives of BME staff and prisoners about prison life. That mirrored the lack of awareness at Feltham at the time about how an Asian teenager like Zahid, in custody for the first

---

* These findings were not dissimilar to research conducted by Kimmett Edgar for the Prison Reform Trust in 2000. Experience also shows that young offenders are even less likely to make formal complaints than adult prisoners. Findings based on research undertaken in 2003 by Professor David Wilson of the University of Central England into the attitudes of 45 black prisoners in three young offender institutions revealed a widespread ignorance of the procedure for making complaints of racism, and a total lack of faith in the system on the part of the few who knew how to use it.

time, might have felt about sharing a cell with someone who looked like Stewart with his offending history, and about whether there might have been reasons arising from his ethnicity and religion which inhibited Zahid from mentioning to officers any concerns he had about Stewart. That highlights the need for officers to be able to stand in the shoes of BME prisoners, and have some understanding about the way they feel about things. That is something which the diversity training which officers get as part of the basic training course should stress, and they should be told about the techniques they can use to develop that skill.

62.13 But that does not happen. Two half-day sessions are devoted to what is called diversity training but which in reality concentrates on race. The focus of that training is on other things: the myths which generate racial prejudice and ethnic stereotyping, political correctness, institutional racism, racist language, and a number of others. All these are topics which are rightly addressed, but I regard the need for officers to have some awareness of how BME prisoners see things as critical. The discussion in one of the sessions on diversity training about the circumstances of Zahid's murder could have been the opportunity to get across to trainees the need to put themselves in the position of BME prisoners and see things from their point of view. That did not happen, either then or throughout the course.

> Recommendation 80
>
> The diversity training which prison officers receive as part of their basic training should stress the need for them to put themselves in the position of BME prisoners and see things from their point of view. They should be told about the techniques they can use to develop that skill.

62.14 At my request, Mr Ali visited the Prison Service Training College at Newbold Revel, and attended both sessions of the diversity training. Recommendation 80 is based in part on his advice to me about what the training includes, and what the Prison Service has told me about how the circumstances of Zahid's murder are used in one of these sessions. The recommendation mirrors one of the areas for development highlighted in *Parallel Worlds*, namely that there should be "training in cultural awareness for staff, which builds awareness of the different perceptions and experiences of different visible minority groups". Mr Ali had some valuable insights on the topic, and he will be bringing them to the attention of the Prison Service and the CRE.

The investigation of complaints

62.15 One of the keys to the improvement of race relations in prison, I believe, is in the way complaints of racism are investigated. The better investigated they are, the more their outcome is likely to be accepted by prisoners and staff alike. That would result in fewer prisoners and staff being reluctant to pursue such complaints, and the increase in the number of complaints being made would cause recalcitrant officers to think about modifying their behaviour for fear of being disciplined following an investigation which was sufficiently open and thorough to result in a finding of guilt.

62.16 But complaints will not be investigated, let alone investigated fairly, if they are not made in the first place. Prisoners may not bother to do that if they are serving a short sentence or nearing the end of a longer one. There is anecdotal evidence suggesting that the anonymity which is supposed to be given to those who want complaint forms is not being accorded universally. A representative from the Inspectorate told one of the Inquiry's seminars that only six weeks earlier his team had visited an establishment where a prisoner had to go into the staff office which was busy at the time to request a complaint form – which admittedly may or may not have been about racism – and had to return it to a member of staff once it had been completed. What should have happened was that the forms should have been available in an unobtrusive leaflet holder, and there should have been a box for the completed form to be posted in. And if prisoners distrust the fairness of the investigation, they will not be inclined to use the system at all.

62.17 The authors of *Parallel Worlds* took the view that the investigation of complaints of racism was "generally undertaken conscientiously". That may be so, but after speaking to a number of race relations liaison officers and their deputies, I was by no means convinced that investigations were effective or that their outcomes were justified. Take a complaint that a member of staff has used racist language to a prisoner. Invariably the officer will deny that they said what the prisoner attributes to them. The investigating officer will have to decide who is telling the truth, in circumstances in which there may have been no-one else around at the time. So it will often be the prisoner's word against that of the officer. Frequently I was told that the complaint could not be taken further for lack of evidence. But there *was* evidence: there was the prisoner's account of what was said. What I was really being told was that there was no evidence to corroborate what the prisoner was saying. I can well understand why an investigating officer would be reluctant to put an officer's career in jeopardy on the word of a prisoner who may have motives of their own. But although corroborative evidence is undoubtedly desirable, it is not essential, and investigating officers will sometimes have to make hard decisions based on the evidence which is available.

62.18 Again, take complaints by prisoners that decisions made by staff about the regime were discriminatory. An example might be that the prisoner was demoted to the basic level of the establishment's incentives and earned privileges scheme because they are black. The question for the investigating officer to decide is not who is telling the truth – the fact of the demotion is unlikely to be denied – but what the officer's reason for demoting the prisoner was. No doubt the officer will say that the prisoner's behaviour justified their demotion, and that their colour had nothing to do with it. But the impression I got was that an explanation of that kind would invariably be accepted. In other words, if there could have been a racially neutral reason for the treatment of the prisoner, there would be an almost automatic acceptance – perhaps unconsciously – that the treatment had been for that reason.

62.19 These sentiments are impressionistic only, and are based on very little data. The Inquiry did not commission any research on the topic, because the investigation of complaints of racism – though a hugely important topic – is at the periphery of an inquiry into prisoner-on-prisoner in-cell attacks. But I have concluded that it would have been wrong not to alert the Prison Service and the CRE to my concerns, so that they can be factored into their action plan on the way such complaints are investigated. The training of any officer responsible for investigating complaints of racism should stress that corroborative evidence of a complaint, though desirable, is not essential, and that officers need to guard against falling into the trap of seeing as decisive the existence of a possible racially neutral reason for treatment which would otherwise be discriminatory.

> ### Recommendation 81
> The training of any officer responsible for investigating complaints of racism should stress that corroborative evidence of a complaint, though desirable, is not essential. Officers should be reminded of the need to guard against falling into the trap of seeing as decisive the existence of a possible racially neutral reason for treatment which would otherwise be discriminatory.

62.20 There is one other trend in the investigation of complaints of racism which causes me particular concern. That relates to the use in some prisons – including one visited by the Inquiry, Wayland Prison – of BME prisoners by race relations liaison officers to assist in investigations. The function of such prisoners was to speak to the complainant to find out what their complaint was, to refer it on to the Race Relations Liaison Officer if it could properly be classified as a complaint of racism, but to discourage the complainant from pursuing it – at least with the Race Relations Liaison Officer – if it was not. This system has the advantage that the prisoner's attention is focused on whether their complaint really is one of racism before bringing it to the Race Relations Liaison Officer. But there is a real possibility that prisoners will be discouraged by this process from pursuing their complaints – not because they are not complaints of racism, but because the BME prisoners assisting the Race Relations Liaison Officer think that the complaint is unfounded or that the prisoner will not be believed or that for some other reason the complaint should not be pursued. The risk that this initiative might result in genuine complaints not being investigated is quite significant. I have concluded that prisoners should not be used under any circumstances to assist in the investigation of complaints of racism, or to act as an intermediary between the complainant and the investigating officer.

Recommendation 82

Prisoners should not be used under any circumstances to assist in the investigation of complaints of racism, or to act as an intermediary between the complainant and the investigating officer.

62.21 These last two recommendations relate to complaints of racism. What is a complaint of racism? In view of the Stephen Lawrence Inquiry's definition of a "racist incident", a complaint of racism is one where the action complained of is perceived to be racist by the victim or any other person. Some concern has been expressed to the Inquiry about this definition in the context of prisons. The definition is said to create false expectations for prisoners, who are being told that if they think that the treatment they are complaining about was racist, their complaint is going to be taken seriously – only for that expectation to be dashed when a non-BME officer decides that the treatment was not racist. And the definition is said to cause undue concern for non-BME officers, who know that all it takes for them to be accused of racism is the belief by the prisoner concerned that they were treated in a racist way.

62.22 I do not think that these concerns arise out of the definition of what constitutes a complaint of racism. The definition focuses on what is needed to trigger an investigation into conduct which is alleged to be racist. It is a wide one to ensure that conduct alleged to be racist *by anyone* results in an investigation. There is no rational basis for a prisoner to think that the definition means that, simply because *they* think that the conduct was racist, the outcome of the investigation has to confirm that belief. Similarly, there is no rational basis for a member of staff to think that the mere description of the complaint as racist makes it look as if a judgement about their conduct has already been made. Nor am I troubled by the fact that all it takes to mount an investigation into racism is an allegation of racism. If the allegation is patently absurd, the investigation will reveal that. But if the allegation is one which has apparent substance, it is only right that a proper investigation should take place.

> Recommendation 83
>
> The definition of a racist incident adopted by the Stephen Lawrence Inquiry should be used to identify what constitutes a complaint of racism, so that a complaint of racism is one where the action complained of is perceived to be racist by the victim or any other person.

62.23 The distrust which prisoners have about investigations of complaints of racism is disturbing. Much of that distrust is based on the belief that it is difficult for prison officers to be judged impartially by their own. So it has been said that the investigation of such complaints – indeed, the investigation of all serious complaints, not just those of racism – would be seen to be infinitely more effective if they were carried out by an independent body, or at least if there was a strong independent element built into the process. It goes without saying that run-of-the-mill everyday complaints which are part and parcel of prison life would be completely inappropriate for scrutiny from outside. But what about complaints of a serious nature, such as brutality, corruption or racism?

62.24 The Prison Service says that complaints of a serious nature *are* subjected to outside scrutiny. Any complaint which amounts to an allegation of a criminal offence is investigated by the police. But what about those complaints which the police decide not to proceed with – perhaps because the chances of conviction are not sufficiently high to warrant a prosecution – or serious cases of racism which do not amount to a criminal offence?

62.25 With the work currently being done to improve the investigation of complaints of racism in the context of the action plan agreed between the Prison Service and the CRE, it would be premature for the Inquiry to consider whether the investigation of complaints of racism – or other serious complaints for that matter – should have a strong independent element built into the process. Indeed, such an issue only comes within the Inquiry's terms of reference in an indirect way. But it is a topic for consideration by the Prison Service, the Inspectorate and the CRE, when future research along the lines of *Parallel Worlds* has shown whether the investigation of complaints has improved so as to reduce much of the current distrust in the way complaints are investigated now.

Recommendation 84

The Prison Service, the Inspectorate and the CRE should consider whether there is a need for the investigation of complaints of racism and other serious complaints to be carried out by an independent body, or at least to be carried out with a strong independent element built into the process.

The role of race relations liaison officers

62.26 There is one other topic which should be addressed by the CRE in the course of its scrutiny of race relations in prisons, and that relates to the role of the race relations liaison officer. Race relations liaison officers have a key function in the management of race relations in their prisons. They set the tone for the establishment by putting proper monitoring systems in place, by taking steps to rectify disturbing trends, by investigating complaints of racism properly, and by adjudicating them fairly. They are drawn from the ranks of prison officers working in the prison. The question is whether the role – which should cover equality and diversity functions not limited to race relations – requires such a degree of professionalism in the field of race relations and other equality and diversity issues that they should be recruited from outside the Prison Service. The Prison Service and the CRE should investigate the desirability and feasibility of taking that course.

Recommendation 85

The Prison Service and the CRE should investigate the desirability and feasibility of race relations liaison officers being recruited from outside the Prison Service.

The position of Muslim prisoners

62.27 Although the religious needs of Muslim prisoners are, generally speaking, better catered for now than they were some years ago, unpublished research conducted on behalf of the Prison Reform Trust suggests that Muslim prisoners are experiencing the backlash of what many observers believe to be an increased level of Islamophobia in society. Maqsood Ahmed, the Muslim Adviser to the Prison Service, was inclined to think that such backlash as there might be is muted and low-key. In any event, any impressions are likely to be affected by the larger number of Muslims being sent to prison, and the fact that many of them are devout.* The Inquiry's terms of reference did not, of course, permit it to investigate generally how Muslim prisoners are treated in prison. It is an important topic which should be properly investigated by professionals in the field. But the perception that Islamophobia is on the rise highlights the fact that the definition of institutional racism adopted by the Stephen Lawrence Inquiry focused on discrimination and prejudice because of a person's colour, culture or ethnic origin. It did not refer to the person's religion. There is no reason why institutional prejudice should be limited to race, and thought should be given by the Home Office to recognising the concept of institutional religious intolerance. Since the Stephen Lawrence Inquiry's definition of institutional racism was accepted by the Government, there is no reason why it should not be adapted to define institutional religious intolerance as follows:

> "The collective failure of an organisation to provide an appropriate and professional service to people because of their religion. It can be seen or detected in processes, attitudes and behaviour which amount to discrimination through unwitting prejudice, ignorance, thoughtlessness and stereotyping which disadvantage people of a particular religion."

62.28 I am very far from suggesting that the Prison Service should be regarded as infected with institutional religious intolerance. Not because I am sure that institutional religious intolerance does not exist, but because it is not a topic which the Inquiry has investigated. The Inquiry has simply been the catalyst for concerns about the treatment of Muslim prisoners to receive a wider currency, and that has drawn attention to the fact that religion was not included in the concept of institutional racism.

---

* There have been suggestions that some Muslim prisoners say they are devout – and that some prisoners even become Muslims – to get better food. There is also a suspicion that some young prisoners are being coerced to become Muslims to give the Muslim population in prison greater authority among other prisoners.

CHAPTER 62: RACISM AND RELIGIOUS INTOLERANCE

> Recommendation 86
>
> Without suggesting in any way that the Prison Service should be regarded as institutionally infected with religious intolerance, thought should be given by the Home Office to recognising the concept of institutional religious intolerance, along the lines of the definition of institutional racism adopted by the Stephen Lawrence Inquiry.

62.29 The Prison Service is already actively engaged in trying to recruit more Muslim staff, and it recognises the necessity for an increased awareness on the part of non-Muslim staff of the needs of Muslim prisoners. But there is one aspect of prison life for Muslim prisoners which Zahid's time at Feltham has put under the spotlight, and that is the position of the Imam. There are full- or part-time Imams at all establishments, and they provide for the religious needs of Muslim prisoners – leading Friday prayers, checking that Halal dietary rules are complied with, ensuring that Muslim prisoners are provided with the artefacts of their religion, such as prayer mats, copies of the Quran and the like. However, unlike their Christian counterparts, it does not look as if all of them see themselves as having a pastoral role. For example, the only recollection which the then Imam at Feltham, Abdul Qureshi, has of Zahid relates to the occasion when he tried to get Zahid to go to Friday prayers.

62.30 I make it absolutely clear that I do not criticise the Imam in any way. But the fact remains that if Imams have a pastoral role, a Muslim prisoner who, say, is concerned about his cellmate but does not want to raise the matter with staff may find it easier to confide in the Imam. It might then be possible for the Imam to bring the prisoner's concern to the attention of staff, provided that he has the prisoner's permission to do so. Undertaking pastoral duties may not be something which some Imams are familiar or even comfortable with, but the Muslim Adviser to the Prison Service should consider how their role could be expanded – without in any way compromising their religious role – so as to make them readier to assist with the non-religious needs of Muslim prisoners.

> Recommendation 87
>
> The Muslim Adviser to the Prison Service should consider how the role of prison Imams can be expanded – without in any way compromising their religious role – so as to make them readier to assist with the non-religious needs of Muslim prisoners.

External scrutiny

62.31 It will be recalled that the Inspectorate did not identify race relations as a significant area of concern in the course of its visits to Feltham in 1996 and 1998. And it was only in the months leading up to Zahid's murder that concerns about race relations began to emerge in the thinking of Feltham's Board of Visitors. So if Feltham's institutional racism was so obvious to Mr Butt and the CRE, why was that not noticed earlier? Why did it take Zahid's death to be the catalyst for the recognition of how bad race relations at Feltham had become? As I have said elsewhere, the answer – in part at least – is that race relations is an area in which shortcomings can be missed if you are not specifically looking out for them. And even if you are, you are still liable to miss them if you do not have the expertise to know what you are looking for. The Inspectorate has assured me that it has learned from the past. The Inspectorate now has a specialist race adviser, and inspection teams now include specialists in race relations, they speak to BME and non-BME prisoners separately, and they conduct their own ethnic monitoring before any inspection takes place. I have no reason to think that Independent Monitoring Boards have not learned a similar lesson. Although there is no room for complacency, I have little doubt that the focus on race relations by the independent watchdogs is now far more intense than it was. Indeed, since the enactment of the Race Relations (Amendment) Act 2000, the agencies responsible for auditing or inspecting public authorities, such as the Inspectorate, have themselves been subject to the general duty to eliminate unlawful discrimination, and to promote equality of opportunity and good relations between people of different racial groups. They should therefore have built race equality measures into their audit or inspection procedures by now.

Race equality schemes

62.32 All government departments – of which the Prison Service is one – have to publish a race equality scheme showing how they intend to fulfil their duty to carry out their functions with due regard to the need to eliminate unlawful discrimination. Individual prisons do not have to do that. They only have to conform to the scheme published by the Prison Service, and to assess and monitor the result of the scheme on seven specified areas affecting the lives of prisoners. This is to be contrasted with schools and hospitals. School managers and NHS Trusts have to publish race equality policies and race equality schemes for them respectively. Every prison should do the same. It would focus the attention of each establishment on the need to have its own race equality policy in place, and would enable each of them to be subject to scrutiny by the CRE.

Recommendation 88

The Home Office should promote legislation to add each prison to the list of bodies required to publish race equality policies or race equality schemes under the Race Relations Act 1976.

Chapter 63: Final observations

Acknowledgements

63.1 Many people contributed to the work of the Inquiry. My first thanks must go to those who provided statements to the Inquiry and who gave oral evidence for co-operating with the Inquiry in its work. But there are many others to whom I owe a considerable debt. The Inquiry team has worked throughout with the utmost professionalism. The administration of the Inquiry, under the sure hand of Bruce Gill and his deputy Ian Short, was superbly organised. Katie Twomey was responsible, among other things, for the collation of the documents. Her mastery of the technology, her willingness to work all hours and her great ability to work under pressure made her absolutely indispensable. Paul Rees, the Inquiry's head of communications, and Gemma Wilkie, the Inquiry's press officer, edited the Inquiry's website and were responsible for the good relations which the Inquiry enjoyed with the press. My thanks are also due in no small measure to Angela Larbie, our administrative assistant, to the staff of KrollOntrack for scanning the documents and ensuring they were displayed on our monitors at the hearing so quickly, and to the staff of Wordwave Ltd for their steady stream of highly efficient stenographers and for producing the running transcripts so efficiently.

63.2 The Inquiry's legal team could not have applied themselves to their task with greater diligence. Nigel Giffin and Neil Sheldon know how much I am indebted to them. They had a consummate mastery of the documents, their questioning of the witnesses was focused and comprehensive with the appropriate degree of tact and discretion, and the advice they gave me – and the submissions they prepared – were exceptionally thorough and well-argued. None of that could have been done without a great deal of hard work. The contribution of Duncan Henderson and his team – Joyti Manjdadria, his deputy, Jason La Corbiniere and Bela Buchanan, the paralegals, and Hannah Fitzgerald, the legal support assistant – was no less significant. They worked the long hours which the Inquiry demanded of them, and did so with dedication and good cheer. My thanks are also due to the legal teams of the Interested Parties. They too worked exceptionally hard to represent their clients' interests, and it was plain that they worked with members of the Inquiry team in a spirit of harmony and co-operation.

63.3 I should also mention the debt I owe to the Prison Service. Unsurprisingly, there was much information which the Inquiry wanted from the Prison Service – before, during and after the public hearings. The Inquiry also needed the co-operation of the Prison Service for the prison visits and the focus groups, and to make the seminars a success. There was never an occasion when I sensed any resistance to our requests for help. It is invidious to single out individuals, but I know that the Inquiry's secretariat was given a great deal of valuable help by Elizabeth Allen, the Prison Service's Inquiry Liaison Officer. My thanks are also due to the many institutions and organisations which provided comments and suggestions to the Inquiry, and to those people who gave up their valuable time and participated in the Inquiry's seminars.

Concluding remarks

63.4 The death of Zahid Mubarek was just one of the many deaths in custody which occur every year. In the overwhelming majority of them, the prisoner commits suicide. But there are lessons to be learned from every death in prison. That is why bodies such as INQUEST, which provides legal advice and support to the friends and families of those who die in custody, have been pressing for a standing commission on deaths in custody. Indeed, in December 2004 the Joint Committee on Human Rights recommended that the Home Office and the Department of Health should establish a cross-government expert task force on deaths in custody. For its part, the Government acknowledges that there is a need for experiences to be shared and for responses to be co-ordinated. It believes that this can be achieved by building on existing working groups, such as the Suicide Prevention Strategy Advisory Group, to create a multi-agency grouping, which brings together, among others, the police, the Prison Service, the Inspectorate and the Prisons and Probation Ombudsman. This is an important initiative, because I have become convinced that only a multi-disciplinary approach will have any chance of reducing deaths in custody. The Government has promised to keep the initiative under review, and I trust that it will do so.

63.5 It has not been practicable to identify a date by when each of the recommendations which this report contains should be implemented. But if they are accepted, I expect them to be implemented quickly, and their implementation kept under review. The report must not be allowed to gather dust. One recent inquiry – the Bichard Inquiry – reconvened six months after the presentation of its report to assess progress on those of its recommendations which the Government had chosen to accept. That was possible because of the limited scope of the Inquiry and its recommendations, and the short time which it was anticipated it would take to put the recommendations into effect. It is just not practicable for this Inquiry to take that course, but I am confident that the independent watchdogs – the Inspectorate, the Independent Monitoring Boards and the CRE or the Commission for Equality and Human Rights into which the CRE is soon to be absorbed – will monitor the progress of their implementation.

63.6 I conclude this report with one final comment. The focus of the Inquiry has been on violence in prisons, specifically on prisoner-on-prisoner in-cell attacks. In this part of the report, I have concentrated on those particular areas where things can be done to make prisoners less vulnerable to such attacks. But on a wider front, one of the recurring themes throughout the report has been that such attacks are more likely to occur in prisons which are performing badly. Many factors contribute to a prison's poor performance, and it was, of course, not possible for an inquiry of this kind to investigate them all without the Inquiry becoming an investigation into all aspects of the Prison Service, going far beyond its limited terms of reference.

63.7 Having said that, in Part 4 of the report I considered the factors which had contributed to Feltham's degeneration into an establishment which was performing badly and in which prisoners were therefore more likely to be exposed to attacks by their cellmates. There are many lessons to be learned from Feltham's decline, but the most important is that population pressures and understaffing can combine to undermine the decency agenda and compromise the Prison Service's ability to run prisons efficiently. When that happens, it is important for the Prison Service to tell ministers that, and they should listen very carefully to what the Prison Service has to say. The Prison Service will no doubt continue to strive to do the best it can with the resources it has. But if those resources are simply not enough, and the prison population continues to increase, ministers must find the extra money to enable the Prison Service to deliver a proper regime for the prisoners it is required to hold. If more resources are needed to ensure that our prisons are truly representative of the civilised society which we aspire to be, nothing less will do.